# DICTIONARY OF AMERICAN LITERARY CHARACTERS

## SECOND EDITION

# DICTIONARY OF AMERICAN LITERARY CHARACTERS

## SECOND EDITION

❦

## VOLUME II
## 1961–2000

*Edited by Benjamin Franklin V*

Revised by American BookWorks Corporation

☑®
Facts On File, Inc.

Dictionary of American
literary characters

**Dictionary of American Literary Characters, Second Edition**

Copyright © 2002 by American BookWorks Corporation

An American BookWorks Corporation Project

Original Edition Copyright © 1990 by Bruccoli Clark Layman, Inc., and Facts On File, Inc.

Facts On File, Inc.
132 West 31st Street
New York NY 10001

**Library of Congress Cataloging-in-Publication Data**

Dictionary of American literary characters / edited by Benjamin Franklin, V; revised by American BookWorks Corporation.—2nd ed.
   p. cm.
  Includes indexes.
  Contents: v. 1. 1789–1960—v. 2. 1961–2000.
  ISBN 0-8160-4262-4 (set) (acid-free paper)
   1. American fiction—Dictionaries. 2. Characters and characteristics in literature—Dictionaries.
I. Franklin, Benjamin, 1939– II. American BookWorks Corporation.

PS374.C43 D5 2001
813.009'27'03—dc21                                                        2001033270

Facts On File books are available at special discounts when purchased in bulk quantities for businesses, associations, institutions or sales promotions. Please call our Special Sales Department in New York at (212) 967-8800 or (800) 322-8755.

You can find Facts On File on the World Wide Web at http://www.factsonfile.com

Text design and layout by Rachel L. Berlin
Cover illustration by Smart Graphics
Cover design by Cathy Rincon

Printed in the United States of America

VB FOF 10 9 8 7 6 5 4 3 2 1

This book is printed on acid-free paper.

# CONTENTS

# ACKNOWLEDGMENTS

❧

I would like to thank several people for their contributions beyond the call of duty. Rebecca Feind researched and provided the publication dates for the hundreds of novels in these volumes. Elaine Bender and Robert Geary helped to select and review the lists of books. My wife, Valerie Grayson, provided endless research assistance and editorial suggestions, as well as continued support during this project.

Fred N. Grayson, President
American BookWorks Corporation

# PREFACE

This second edition of the *Dictionary of American Literary Characters* describes the major characters in significant American novels—in addition to those in some uncelebrated novels and in a sampling of best-sellers—from 1789 through 2000. By *novels* we mean long works of fiction, or what is presented as fiction. A few of the books are often referred to as novellas, and some others as nonfiction novels.

We have added hundreds of new works and thousands of new characters, primarily from novels published between 1979, where the first edition stopped, to 2000. We have tried to include a wider sampling of literary, popular, and genre fiction. The books that have been added to this edition were selected by various methods. We chose novels that won or were short-listed for major book awards: the Pulitzer Prize, National Book Award, PEN/Faulkner, Edgar Allan Poe, and others. We also selected novels that were in the top five of major national and regional best-seller lists, and were on those lists for at least three months, since the mid-1970s. Finally, we received valuable suggestions from our contributors and relied on several literature professors to oversee the list, suggest new titles, eliminate others, and generally review the submissions. Because a novelist is included does not mean that characters from all of his or her novels are described.

Users of this book who cannot recall the name of a character in a novel, and therefore cannot turn directly to the desired character's entry, should consult the author index, which lists characters alphabetically by novel. The title index is a new feature for readers who know the title of the novel but not the author.

The two volumes of this edition are divided chronologically. Volume I covers novels published from 1789 through 1960; Volume II covers novels published from 1961 through 2000. Some novelists appear in both volumes, as noted in the author index. Each character has one entry, whether the character appears in one novel or in several; cross-references direct readers to the appropriate volume if the same character appears in novels published before and after 1960.

The entries are factual; they contain little interpretation. Although some characters, such as Babe Ruth and George Washington, are historical figures, they are treated in the same manner as obviously fictional characters.

**Captain (Aarfy) Aardvaark**   Fraternity man and navigator in Yossarian's squadron; rapes an Italian chambermaid and throws her out a window to her death to avoid a blot on his reputation in Joseph Heller's *Catch-22*.

**Jimmy Aaron**   Young black man who is murdered when he returns to the plantation to organize and lead his people during the civil rights movement in Ernest J. Gaines's *The Autobiography of Miss Jane Pittman*.

**Mother Abagail**   See Abagail Freemantle.

**Elizabeth (Liz, Gillespie Emerson) Abbott**   Woodcarver and clock winder who reconstitutes the Emerson family and salvages their neglected Baltimore home; as Gillespie, becomes the wife of Matthew Emerson and the mother of two children in Anne Tyler's *The Clock Winder*.

**Horace Abbott**   Gentle husband of Sally Page Abbott; dies of a heart attack as a result of a Halloween prank in John Gardner's *October Light*.

**John Abbott**   Pastor of Faith Baptist Church in Ellington, North Carolina, and father of Elizabeth Abbott in Anne Tyler's *The Clock Winder*.

**Julia Abbott**   Wife of John Abbott and mother of Elizabeth Abbott in Anne Tyler's *The Clock Winder*.

**Sally Page Abbott**   Eighty-year-old liberal who in self-defense plans the injury or death of her brother, James Page, until she nearly kills her niece, Ginny Hicks; widow of Horace Abbott in John Gardner's *October Light*.

**Abby**   See Abagail Freemantle.

**Abe**   Elderly government lawyer running away from corrupt politics and grief over the death of his wife and son; befriended by Anne and Phil Sorenson before plunging off a cliff to his death in Frederick Busch's *Manual Labor*.

**Abel (Abelito)**   American Indian and World War II veteran who is imprisoned for murder in N. Scott Momaday's *House Made of Dawn*.

**Francis (Frankie) Abel**   Jill's older brother; son of Max, Pearl's second husband; twenty-seven-year-old gambler who spends time in jail in Marge Piercy's *Braided Lives*.

**Leo Abel**   Jill's oldest brother; son of Max, Pearl's second husband; thirty-year-old who lives with his mother and stepfather when escaping the law in Marge Piercy's *Braided Lives*.

**Carol Abernathy**   Wife of Hunt Abernathy and mistress of Ron Grant; head of Hunt Hills Little Theatre and occultist in James Jones's *Go to the Widow-Maker*.

**Hunt Abernathy**   Husband of Carol Abernathy and friend of Ron Grant; general manager of a brick-making and lumberyard establishment in Indianapolis in James Jones's *Go to the Widow-Maker*.

**Abilene**   Pool shark, oil-well driller, and richest man (in cash) in Thalia, Texas, in Larry McMurtry's *The Last Picture Show*.

**Mr. Abraham**   Young Indian Christian man who serves as a guide for Being of the Fort St. Sebastian ruins in Madras; assiduously elegant and recently the recipient of a master's degree in commerce from the University of Madras; listens to test-match cricket from New Zealand on a transistor radio; his deportment has a protective haughtiness in Bharati Mukherjee's *The Holder of the World*.

**Eliot Abrams**   Raised by two gay men after parents' death; lover of Philip Benjamin; roommate of Jerene Parks; sophisticated and selfish; leaves Philip and goes to Europe in David Leavitt's *The Lost Language of Cranes*.

**Mike Abrams**   Lawyer; early romantic interest and later good friend of Salley Gardens in Susan Cheever's *Looking for Work*.

**Dr. Abe Abramson**   Physician; older cousin and surrogate father of Zeke Gurevich; patron of freethinkers in Greenwich Village in William Herrick's *The Itinerant*.

**Abyssinia (Sister 'ssinia)**   Dressmaker who travels with Arista Prolo as a costume designer; confides the story of Arista's life and death to Black Will in Carlene Hatcher Polite's *Sister X and the Victims of Foul Play*.

**Josh Ace**   Son of a team of Hollywood screenwriters from the 1930s and lover of Isadora Wing in Erica Jong's *How to Save Your Own Life*.

**Achilles**   Greek hero and lover of Helen; joins her in Egypt in H. D.'s *Helen in Egypt*.

**Charlie Achorn**   Cracker-barrel philosopher, temporary farmhand, and resident of Pretty Pass in Peter De Vries's *I Hear America Swinging*.

**Acoraci**   Guard at the exit from NESTER in Scott Spencer's *Last Night at the Brain Thieves' Ball*.

**Remedios Acosta**   Village gossip who relays information about Americans Richard and Sara Everton to inhabitants of Ibarra, Mexico, in Harriet Doerr's *Stones for Ibarra*.

**Ace Adair**   Husband of Jewel Adair; killed by a train in William Goyen's *Come, The Restorer*.

**Addis Adair**   Adopted son of Ace and Jewel Adair; searches for his biological father and becomes a saintlike figure in the wilderness in William Goyen's *Come, The Restorer*.

**Jewel Adair**   Wife of Ace Adair; seeks to fulfill her lustful desires in William Goyen's *Come, The Restorer*.

**Captain Jacob R. Adam**   Owner of the S.S. *Thespian,* home of Adam's Original and Unparalleled Floating Opera, and master of ceremonies of the minstrel show in John Barth's *The Floating Opera*.

**Carter Adams**   American acquaintance who introduces Charlie Stark to the beauty of the Hawaiian Islands in Peter Matthiessen's *Raditzer*.

**Mrs. Charles Fine Adams**   Elderly woman who brings to the narrator's library a book on growing flowers in hotel rooms by candlelight in Richard Brautigan's *The Abortion*.

**Darryl Adams**   Sells cocaine for Rodney Little at Ahab's, a fish restaurant; is cheating Rodney by selling only half of what he is supposed to; is shot and killed by Victor Dunham in Richard Price's *Clockers*.

**Elizabeth Adams**   Daughter of wealthy businessman; meets Calvin Marshall while an exchange student at Fisk University; becomes his lover and executive assistant; tells Andrea Marshall Calvin's last words were to tell Andrea he loved her; marries Gregory Townley after Calvin Marshall's death in Julius Lester's *And All Our Wounds Forgiven*.

**Grandfather Adams**   Grandfather of Pookie Adams; supplies Pookie with Casey Ruggles comic strips in John Nichols's *The Sterile Cuckoo*.

**Jane Adams**   Striking and talented actress who escapes an abusive marriage to find success on the hit television series *Manhattan* in Danielle Steel's *Secrets*.

**Kay Adams**   College girlfriend and later the second wife of Michael Corleone in Mario Puzo's *The Godfather*.

**Marian and Bob Adams**   Aunt and uncle of Pookie Adams; their Los Angeles home is a haven for Pookie in John Nichols's *The Sterile Cuckoo*.

**Pookie (Pooks) Adams**   Girlfriend of Jerry Payne; whimsical storyteller who falls in and out of love and finally commits suicide in John Nichols's *The Sterile Cuckoo*.

**Gerard (Gerry) Adamson**   Chairman of the English department at Quirn College, philosopher-poet, and husband of Louise Adamson, who leaves him for Vadim Vadimovich in Vladimir Nabokov's *Look at the Harlequins!*

**Louise Adamson**   Young wife of Gerry Adamson, whom she leaves for a less than felicitous marriage to Vadim Vadimovich, whose third wife she becomes in Vladimir Nabokov's *Look at the Harlequins!*

**Adelaide Adare**   Red-haired Polish woman who deserts her three children during the depression by flying off with stunt pilot The Great Omar; mother of Karl Adare, Mary Adare, and Jude Miller in Louise Erdrich's *The Beet Queen*.

**Dot (Wallacette) Adare**   Stocky, willful, aggressive part-Chippewa girl who at age eighteen becomes the Beet Queen in Argus, North Dakota; daughter of Celestine James and Karl Adare in Louise Erdrich's *The Beet Queen*.

**Karl Adare**   German-Polish boy deserted by his mother, Adelaide Adare, at age fourteen; glib salesman whose life is marked by an absence of meaningful relationships; lover of Wallace Pfef and Celestine James; father of Dot Adare in Louise Erdrich's *The Beet Queen*.

**Mary Adare**   German-Polish girl deserted by her mother, Adelaide Adare, at age eleven; foster child of Pete and Fritzie Kozka, who takes over operation of the Kozkas' butcher shop in Louise Erdrich's *The Beet Queen*.

**Adelina**   Mexican wife of Harrison; asphyxiated in Nicholas Delbanco's *News*.

**Boris (B., King B.) Adrian**   Critically respected film director who directs a pornographic movie in Terry Southern's *Blue Movie*.

**Aeore (Child-Star, Riri'an)**   Niaruna Indian warrior who becomes a jaguar-shaman and chief rival of Lewis Moon in Peter Matthiessen's *At Play in the Fields of the Lord*.

**Vladimir Afanasi**   Eskimo leader of Desolation, Alaska; builds successful community by integrating modern civilization and native practices in James Michener's *Alaska*.

**African Flower**   See Angela Williams Lavoisier.

**Robert Agar**   Specialist in keys and safecracking and an accomplice of Edward Pierce, whom Agar turns in to the police in Michael Crichton's *The Great Train Robbery*.

**Agnes**   Gilbert Imlay's lover; a childlike street minstrel; she laughs often and over very little in Frances Sherwood's *Vindication*.

**Roland (Rollie) Agni**   Talented rookie outfielder forced to play on the worst team in the Patriot League and bat eighth all year; reminds Angela Whittling Trust of her only true love, Luke Gofarmon, in Philip Roth's *The Great American Novel*.

**Agravaine**   Brother of Gawaine in Thomas Berger's *Arthur Rex*.

**Forney Aiken**   Alcoholic photographer who darkens his skin while researching his latest book on black life in the South in Walker Percy's *The Last Gentleman*.

**A. J. (Merchant of Sex)**   See Volume I.

**Ajax**   See Albert Jacks.

**Rosario "Baby" Alacran**   Homely, sickly daughter of the wealthy, well-connected Alacran family who is considered a burden by her parents; lonely, unloved, apolitical teenager who quits high school and elopes with Pepe Carreon in Jessica Hagedorn's *Dogeaters*.

**Severo Alacran**   Wealthy head of the leading business conglomerate in the Philippines; charismatic womanizer who frequently argues with his wife; neglectful husband and father; father of Baby Alacran in Jessica Hagedorn's *Dogeaters*.

**Arthur Alarcon**   Los Angeles Superior Court judge who replaces Alfred Peracca in the second trial of Gregory Powell and Jimmy Smith in Joseph Wambaugh's *The Onion Field*.

**Albert**   Husband of Celie; marries her to provide a housekeeper for his children when his wife dies; beats her; hides letters sent to her by Nettie; lover of Shug Avery; comes to understand himself and modifies his behavior as a result of Celie's growing independence in Alice Walker's *The Color Purple*.

**Albert**   Friend of Cecil Braithwaite in John Edgar Wideman's *Hurry Home*.

**Dewitt Albright**   Lawyer turned underworld handyman who hires private investigator Easy Rawlins to locate a missing woman, Daphne Monet; unpredictable, dangerous, and lacking morals or scruples, he attempts to ambush Rawlins, but is shot by Raymond "Mouse" Alexander in Walter Mosley's *Devil in a Blue Dress*.

**Mavis Albright**   Fugitive mother who abandons her family after the accidental death of her two youngest children; is one of the Convent women, a group of women with sullied pasts who now live together on the outskirts of Ruby, Oklahoma, an all-black town; is haunted by the ghosts of her two dead children in Toni Morrison's *Paradise*.

**Maria Katerina Lorca Guerrera (Kat) Alcazar**   American lesbian of Cuban descent; hired by Angel Stone as companion, secretary, bodyguard, and detective; narrator of M. F. Beal's *Angel Dance*.

**Sir John Alderston**   An owner of South Eastern Railway in Michael Crichton's *The Great Train Robbery*.

**Karen Susan Aldrich**   Former mental patient who finally succeeds in committing suicide in Judith Guest's *Ordinary People*.

**Grace Aldridge**   Wrote the autobiography Jean is typing; has had many husbands and is engaged to Edward Quill when she dies from falling down stairs in Ann Beattie's *My Life, Starring Dara Falcon*.

**Alejandra**   Young Mexican girl who lives on the La Purisima Ranch while not attending boarding school, and with whom John Grady Cole falls in love; she is forbidden to see him again after her grandaunt, Duena Alfonsa, pays Cole's ransom to secure his release from prison in Cormac McCarthy's *All the Pretty Horses*.

**Pavel Leonidovich (Pasha) Alekseyev**   Deputy commander of the Southwestern Theater for the Soviet Army who, with Marshal Rozhkov and Admiral Mazlov, plans Operation Polar Glory (invasion of Iceland) and seizure of Arabian oil fields; personally commands forward troops in action against NATO forces around Alfeld; engineers the coup that puts Sergetov in power and ends the nuclear threat; negotiates cease-fire with General Robinson (SACEUR) in Tom Clancy's *Red Storm Rising*.

**Fred Aleman**   Sober businessman to whom Joan Mitchell is engaged in Shirley Ann Grau's *The House on Coliseum Street*.

**Raymond "Mouse" Alexander**   Friend and partner to private investigator Easy Rawlins; kills stepfather in inheritance dispute; violent and unpredictable, he values loyalty; saves Rawlins's life on several occasions in Walter Mosley's *Devil in a Blue Dress*.

**Roland Alexander**    Four-year-old boy who dies after accidentally swallowing rat poison left in his bedroom; as a result of this tragedy, his father almost beats his mother to death before being locked up by police in Alexis Deveaux's *Spirits in the Street*.

**Rose Alexander**    Militant feminist dedicated to the subversion and destruction of patriarchal society; takes part in a bank robbery, during which an elderly male guard is killed; goes into hiding; is eventually arrested after being tricked by Spenser, a private detective hired by Harvey Shepard in Robert B. Parker's *Promised Land*.

**Suicide Alexander**    Manager of the California baseball team that signs Henry Wiggen when Wiggen is released from the New York Mammoths in Mark Harris's *It Looked Like For Ever*.

**Leonid Andreich Alexandrov**    Self-effacing Russian professor of engineering blinded by Peter Greene in John Barth's *Giles Goat-Boy*.

**Alexis**    See James Potts.

**Alexis**    Budding playwright and narrator who records the thwarted lives of young people living in her Harlem neighborhood in Alexis Deveaux's *Spirits in the Street*.

**Duena Alfonsa**    Matriarchal figure in charge of the La Purisima Ranch, where John Grady Cole and Lacey Rawlins work in Mexico; grandaunt and godmother of Alejandra; pays for the release of both John and Lacey on the condition that John never see Alejandra ever again in Cormac McCarthy's *All the Pretty Horses*.

**Alfonso (Fonso)**    Wife-beater and cousin of Eva Medina Canada in Gayl Jones's *Eva's Man*.

**Alfonso**    Male canary Birdy buys from Mr. Lincoln to mate with Birdie in William Wharton's *Birdy*.

**Algernon**    White mouse used for experiments involving increased intelligence who is treated by Charlie Gordon, another experimental subject, as Gordon's only peer in Daniel Keyes's *Flowers for Algernon*.

**Ali (Eli)**    Divorced Jewish father; first man Theresa Dunn allows to pick her up in a bar in Judith Rossner's *Looking for Mr. Goodbar*.

**Dubash (Oliver, Ortencio) Ali**    Handsome but consumptive man of thirty who works as the factory's dubash, or translator; stoned to death when explosives he plants to destroy Gabriel Legge's shipment instead blow up an alley in Bharati Mukherjee's *The Holder of the World*.

**Alice**    Wife of an unnamed sailor stationed in Newport; wants a baby so badly that she urges Theophilus North to impregnate her in Thornton Wilder's *Theophilus North*.

**Vasilia Aliena**    See Vasilia Fastolfe.

**Alison**    Gerald's married lover; disappears from the party for a while, but reappears dirty and beaten in Robert Coover's *Gerald's Party*.

**Alix**    Soon-to-be second wife of Ted in Reynolds Price's *Love and Work*.

**John F. Alkahest**    Bizarre paraplegic in violent pursuit of drug dealers in *The Smugglers of Lost Souls' Rock*, the interior novel within John Gardner's *October Light*.

**Tad Allagash**    Drug abuser and womanizing best friend of Jamie Conway who always falls prey to Tad's ploys to party hard and work less in Jay McInerney's *Bright Lights, Big City*.

**Allan**    Wealthy white radical, now a recluse in Vermont in Nicholas Delbanco's *News*.

**Karl Allberg**    Canadian police detective; divorced, middle-aged father of two female college students; investigates murder and finds romance with the town librarian in L. W. Wright's *The Suspect*.

**Clara Allen**    Former sweetheart of Augustus McRae; strong woman, talkative, kind; good horse trainer; has two daughters and had three sons, each of whom died; husband is an invalid; takes in Lorena Woods and July Johnson in Larry McMurtry's *Lonesome Dove*.

**Jim Allen**    Fellow employee of Falton Harron at Watkins & Company, manufacturer of microscopes in Susan Sontag's *Death Kit*.

**Risa Allen**    Woman with whom Edwin Locke becomes romantically obsessed in Joyce Carol Oates's *Cybele*.

**Landon Allgood**    Uncle of Mildred Sutton; sleeps in a church pew, waiting for his niece's funeral in Reynolds Price's *A Long and Happy Life*.

**Svetlana Alliluyeva**    Daughter of Joseph Stalin; neighbor of George Levanter in Princeton in Jerzy Kosinski's *Blind Date*.

**Dick Allison**    Chief of Haven, Maine, volunteer fire department in Stephen King's *The Tommyknockers*.

**Joseph (Joe) Allston**    Retired literary agent burdened by depression; husband of Ruth Allston and father of a dead son who haunts his thoughts; goes to Denmark to learn about his mother; his journal entries provide much of the first-person narrative for Wallace Stegner's *All the Little Live Things* and *The Spectator Bird*.

**Ruth Allston**    Loving wife of Joe Allston and mother of a dead son; serves as her husband's confidante and sounding board in Wallace Stegner's *All the Little Live Things* and *The Spectator Bird*.

**The Greek Almas**    Partner in the Regents Sportsmen's Club, Inc., and loan shark to whom Jerry Doherty owes $18,000;

kills Croce Torre in a gun battle in George V. Higgins's *The Digger's Game.*

**Almost Soup**   Humanlike white dog who is rescued as a puppy by Cally Roy and later protects Cally's spirit when she is ill; narrates two chapters in Louise Erdrich's *The Antelope Wife.*

**Isaac Alston**   Elderly town patriarch disabled by a stroke in Reynolds Price's *A Long and Happy Life.*

**Marina (Miss Marina) Alston**   Elderly and eccentric sister of Isaac Alston in Reynolds Price's *A Long and Happy Life.*

**Francisco Alvarado**   Twice widowed father and grandfather of two families; resort analyst for Mexican government; philandering lover of Frances Bowles; leaves her after he reads her badly written travel book about Mexico in Harriett Doerr's *Consider This, Senora.*

**Manuel (Manny) Alvarez**   Friend of Ruben Fontanez and Marty; dances in the subway for money in Jay Neugeboren's *Listen Ruben Fontanez.*

**Maria Alvarez**   Child patient at Sacred Heart Hospital, where she is a victim of attempted rape; dies of pneumonia in Edward Lewis Wallant's *The Children at the Gate.*

**Kelden Amadiro**   Prominent theoretical roboticist on the planet Aurora who secretly interrogates Gladia Delmarre's humaniform robot lover to discover its design and who later attempts to kidnap R. Daneel Olivaw for the same purpose; leader of faction opposing space exploration by any world but Aurora; chief political enemy and accuser of Dr. Han Fastolfe in Isaac Asimov's *The Robots of Dawn.*

**Lady Amalthea**   Unicorn who leaves the forest to discover if she is the last of her kind; turned into Lady Amalthea by Schmendrick in order to save her from Red Bull in Peter S. Beagle's *The Last Unicorn.*

**John (Johnny, Squirrel) Amato**   Compulsive gambler who plans the robbery of a mob-run card game with Frankie and Russell; killed by Jackie Cogan in George V. Higgins's *Cogan's Trade.*

**Amber**   Female healer who befriends Teray in Octavia E. Butler's *Patternmaster.*

**Darlene American Horse**   Attractive Native American woman and girlfriend of Cletus Purcel; lover of Dave Robicheaux; killed by Las Vegas hit man hired by Sally Dio; guides Robicheaux in a dream to half-buried bodies of two Native Americans killed by Dio's men in James Lee Burke's *Black Cherry Blues.*

**Charlotte Ames**   See Charlotte Ames Emory.

**Charlotte Ames**   Wife of Harry Ames and, on one occasion, sexual partner of Max Reddick in John A. Williams's *The Man Who Cried I Am.*

**Harry Ames**   Leading African-American novelist of his time; murdered by the CIA in order to suppress publication of a contingency plan, code-named King Alfred, for removing the minority population of the United States to concentration camps in John A. Williams's *The Man Who Cried I Am.*

**Lacey Debney Ames**   Obese mother of Charlotte Emory and wife of Murray Ames in Anne Tyler's *Earthly Possessions.*

**Murray Ames**   Dour photographer father of Charlotte Emory and husband of Lacey Debney Ames in Anne Tyler's *Earthly Possessions.*

**Susan Ames**   Divorced from Tim Ames; painter and artist; builds a home in Amapolas, Mexico; leaves Mexico but never sells her house there after Tim returns to remarry her in Harriett Doerr's *Consider This, Senora.*

**Tim Ames**   Former husband of Susan Ames; unsuccessful at various businesses; becomes a successful mountain climber; returns to Sue to remarry her in Harriett Doerr's *Consider This, Senora.*

**Amos**   Minister who attempted to burn down his own church; golf partner of Thomas Marshfield at the retreat in John Updike's *A Month of Sundays.*

**Amos**   Television character who turns in moochers Kingfish Stevens and Andy Brown to the police for robbing his place in Ishmael Reed's *The Last Days of Louisiana Red.*

**Harriet Shippen Amron**   Philadelphia blue blood married to Saul Amron in Paule Marshall's *The Chosen Place, the Timeless People.*

**Saul Amron**   American anthropologist who goes to the Caribbean as the leader of a research project designed to improve life for the poor people of Bourne Island; husband of Harriet Shippen Amron in Paule Marshall's *The Chosen Place, the Timeless People.*

**Jack Amsterdam**   Corrupt construction contractor for the Catholic Church and business and golf partner of Desmond Spellacy; arrested for the murder of Lois Fazenda in John Gregory Dunne's *True Confessions.*

**Anatole**   Twenty-four-year-old intellectual Congolese schoolteacher in the village of Kilanga; has scarified face; translates Nathan Price's sermons to his congregation; marries Leah Price, fathers four children; imprisoned by the corrupt Mobutu regime; moves with his family to an agricultural station in Angola in Barbara Kingsolver's *The Poisonwood Bible.*

**Lars Andemening**   Reclusive and overly literary book reviewer orphaned in Poland during World War II, now living in Stockholm; obsessed with and convinced he is the son of a famous Polish author who was murdered by the Nazis in Cynthia Ozick's *The Messiah of Stockholm.*

**Frau Anders**　Mistress of Hippolyte; sells her into slavery in Susan Sontag's *The Benefactor.*

**John Anders**　Police captain who investigates the murder of Angela Black in Michael Crichton's *The Terminal Man.*

**Anne (Sissy) Anderson**　Domineering older sister of Roberta (Bobbi) Anderson; travels to Haven to inform her sister of their father's death and is abducted for use in a macabre experiment in her sister's shed in Stephen King's *The Tommyknockers.*

**Argustus (Mr. Andy) Anderson**　Father of Mae Douglas; musician and supporter of his grandson, Raymond Douglas, in Herbert Simmons's *Man Walking on Eggshells.*

**Dolly Anderson**　Self-loathing teenage daughter of Viola Anderson; given to flights of fantasy that are a pretext for her murder in Hal Bennett's *The Black Wine.*

**Heaven Anderson**　Neglected daughter of television star Silver Anderson who goes on to have a prosperous career as a singer in Jackie Collins's *Hollywood Husbands.*

**Jan Anderson**　Strong-willed young protagonist who shoots Uncle Hake Nolan to protect his sister, Timmie Anderson, in Fred Chappell's *The Inkling.*

**Jenny Nolan Anderson**　Widowed mother of Jan and Timmie Anderson and sister of Hezekiah (Hake) Nolan; gradually loses control of her household and eventually dies of cancer in Fred Chappell's *The Inkling.*

**Leon Anderson**　Communications expert at NESTER in Scott Spencer's *Last Night at the Brain Thieves' Ball.*

**Roberta (Bobbi) Anderson**　Single, fortyish writer of western novels who uncovers an extraterrestrial power source on her property in Haven, Maine; friend and lover of Jim Gardener in Stephen King's *The Tommyknockers.*

**Silver Anderson**　Famous and vain television soap opera star and neglectful mother of Heaven Anderson; wife of Wes Money in Jackie Collins's *Hollywood Husbands.*

**Timmie Anderson**　Violently insane sister of Jan Anderson; tries to deflect Jan's penetrating gaze by persuading him to wear glasses and hopes to give him insight by cutting eyelike gashes in his hands and feet in Fred Chappell's *The Inkling.*

**Viola Anderson**　Friend of Eloise McLindon; cynical political activist, whorehouse madam, and mother of Dolly Anderson in Hal Bennett's *The Black Wine* and *Seventh Heaven.*

**Wilbur Anderson**　Son of Argustus Anderson and uncle of Raymond Douglas; trumpet player who buys Douglas his first trumpet and influences his musical style in Herbert Simmons's *Man Walking on Eggshells.*

**Andrew**　Beigh Master's first lover; a self-described untouchable from a Boston Brahmin family who leased a summer home next to the Masters in Bharati Mukherjee's *The Holder of the World.*

**Mr. Andrews**　Friend of Henry Fuseli's; a scientist with a haughty and exhausted manner; keeps a skeleton in his closet in Frances Sherwood's *Vindication.*

**Elizabeth (Polly) Andrews**　Medical technician and first employer of Libby MacAusland; member of the Group in Mary McCarthy's *The Group.*

**Thomas T. (Dad) Andrews**　Father of Todd Andrews; commits suicide after the collapse of his personal finances in the stock market crash of 1929; cofounder of the law firm Andrews and Bishop in John Barth's *The Floating Opera.*

**Todd Andrews**　Fifty-four-year-old lawyer who attempts suicide; narrator and central figure in John Barth's *The Floating Opera.*

**(General) Andreyev**　Commander of Soviet 234th Guards Air Assault Regiment; negotiates cease-fire in Iceland when Soviet air support is crippled and the ground situation untenable in Tom Clancy's *Red Storm Rising.*

**Nick Andros**　Deaf-mute chosen to lead The Stand, but who is killed unexpectedly in Stephen King's *The Stand.*

**Miss Ange**　Drag queen in New Orleans who dresses as Scarlett O'Hara, Desdemona, and Drusilla Duncan in John Rechy's *City of Night.*

**Stella Bast Angel (Engels)**　Cousin of Edward Bast; schemes to gain control of her family's General Roll Corporation in William Gaddis's *JR.*

**Max Angelo**　Sculptor; sometime lover of Salley Gardens in Susan Cheever's *Looking for Work.*

**Angel of Death**　See John Sallow.

**Angie (Ange)**　Married woman who claims she is pregnant by her lover, Billy Phelan, in order to test Phelan's love for her in William Kennedy's *Billy Phelan's Greatest Game.*

**Bertie Angstom**　English teacher of Carter Fisher; complains about his work in Sandra Scofield's *Beyond Deserving.*

**Harry "Rabbit" Angstrom**　Protagonist of John Updike's Rabbit tetralogy about middle-class suburban life from the 1950s through the 1980s, introduced in *Rabbit, Run.* In *Rabbit Is Rich* he is forty-six years old, the successful owner of an automobile dealership in Brewer, Pennsylvania, and caught up in the rampant consumerism of the late 1970s. He reunites with his wife, Janice, from whom he was separated in *Rabbit Redux,* and still as sexually charged as when he was young but increasingly aware of his aging body and his lost youth. Father of Nelson; the birth of his granddaughter drives home Harry's realization that he is now another generation closer to death—which he must confront in *Rabbit at Rest.*

**Janice (Jan) Springer Angstrom**   Wife of Harry "Rabbit" Angstrom in John Updike's Rabbit tetralogy; first introduced in *Rabbit, Run* as the frustrated housewife who turns to drink and accidentally drowns her infant daughter. In *Rabbit Redux,* has an affair with Charlie Stavros. Reunited with her husband in *Rabbit Is Rich,* she receives an inheritance that makes possible Harry's ability to own the auto dealership; mother of Nelson and grandmother of granddaughter born at end of the novel. Also appears in *Rabbit at Rest.*

**Judy Angstrom**   Daughter of Nelson and Pru Angstrom, sister of Roy, and granddaughter of Harry "Rabbit" and Janice Angstrom; born at the end of the third novel in John Updike's Rabbit tetralogy, *Rabbit Is Rich;* saved from drowning by her grandfather in *Rabbit at Rest.*

**Nelson Angstrom**   Son of Harry "Rabbit" and Janice Angstrom; first introduced as a young child in the first novel in John Updike's Rabbit tetralogy, *Rabbit, Run;* in later novels, husband of Pru and father of Judy and Roy. In *Rabbit at Rest,* he runs and ruins his parents' Pennsylvania auto dealership by embezzling assets to finance his cocaine habit; caught between bitter resentment of and love for his dying father.

**Teresa "Pru" Lubell Angstrom**   Wife of Nelson Angstrom; first introduced in *Rabbit Is Rich,* the third novel in John Updike's Rabbit tetralogy; mother of Judy and Roy; attempts to maintain order and stability as her husband's life is falling apart; has a sexual encounter with her father-in-law in *Rabbit at Rest.*

**Miss Ann (Our Lady of the Limitless Bladder)**   Client of C. Card and an accomplished beer drinker; kills the prostitute whose body she hires Card to steal from the morgue in Richard Brautigan's *Dreaming of Babylon.*

**Anna**   Traumatized victim of sexual assault who may be the saving love of Lancelot Lamar's new world in Walker Percy's *Lancelot.*

**Annabel**   Girlfriend of Carter Fisher; opens a pizza parlor with him; an heiress in Sandra Scofield's *Beyond Deserving.*

**Anne**   Sister of Katie, daughter of Grace and Neil, niece of Dan and Libby, Elinor, May, and Rachel, cousin of Jennie, Celia, Rossie, and Valerie; forever excited or ashamed; develops earlier than her cousins in Joan Chase's *During the Reign of the Queen of Persia.*

**Anne-Marie**   Student who serves on the Cinema Committee with Hill Gallagher during the student rebellion in James Jones's *The Merry Month of May.*

**Annette**   See Anna Ivanovna Blagovo.

**Annie**   Maid of the Wollstonecraft household; sexually abuses Mary in Frances Sherwood's *Vindication.*

**Billy Ansel**   Vietnam veteran who owns the town gas station; widower and father of nine-year-old twins who die in the bus wreck; has an affair with Risa Walker; refuses to join in the lawsuit Mitchell Stephens has filed against the city and the state; becomes an alcoholic in Russell Banks's *The Sweet Hereafter.*

**Karen Anson**   Assistant to Mark Hall in Project Wildfire in Michael Crichton's *The Andromeda Strain.*

**Anterrabae**   Forceful god in Yr, the mental world of Deborah Blau in Hannah Green's *I Never Promised You a Rose Garden.*

**Antheil**   Regulatory agent who forces John Converse to locate Marge Converse, who he believes has the smuggled heroin in Robert Stone's *Dog Soldiers.*

**Mel Anthis**   Art gallery administrator and secretly a writer; marries Jody; cares for and raises her son as she pursues her career in Ann Beattie's *Picturing Will.*

**Anthony**   Hospital orderly whom Willie Hall tries to indoctrinate politically in John Edgar Wideman's *The Lynchers.*

**Peggy Anthony**   Student at Haddan School who refuses all solid food, supplementing her milk diet with candy bars hidden in a suitcase under her bed in Alice Hoffman's *The River King.*

**Anton (the Quail)**   Son of Makar and lover of his sister, Ewka, in Jerzy Kosinski's *The Painted Bird.*

**Anulka**   Local witch who cures the narrator of a kick in the stomach by applying a dead mole to his abdomen in Jerzy Kosinski's *The Painted Bird.*

**Milton Appel**   Professor and editor of Jewish cultural monthly, *Inquiry;* Nathan Zuckerman's loudest critic and oldest nemesis; critical of Zuckerman's portrayal of Jewish people; once admired by a college-age Zuckerman for his portrayal of generational strife in Jewish families in Philip Roth's *The Anatomy Lesson.*

**Aharon Appelfeld**   Real-life Israeli novelist, whose works deal with his childhood experience as a Holocaust survivor; interviewed by his friend, American novelist Philip Roth, in Israel in 1988; advises Roth following his initial encounters with Moishe Pipik, an imposter using Roth's name for possibly nefarious purposes in Philip Roth's *Operation Shylock: A Confession.*

**Appleby**   Fellow squadron member who reports Yossarian for refusing to take atabrine tablets in Joseph Heller's *Catch-22.*

**Frank Appleby**   Bank trust officer married to Janet Appleby in John Updike's *Couples.*

**Janet Appleby**   Seductive wife of Frank Appleby; they couple swap with Marcia and Harold Smith in John Updike's *Couples.*

**Corinna Appleton**   Mother of Skippy Appleton, possibly by Louis Zimmerman instead of by Harry Appleton, the husband she abandons in John Updike's *The Centaur.*

**Harry (Doc) Appleton**   Physician who treats the Caldwell family; belongs to no church and subscribes to no belief system; twin brother of Hester Appleton; abandoned by his wife, Corinna; his son, Skippy, actually may be Louis Zimmerman's in John Updike's *The Centaur*.

**Hester Appleton**   Spinster sister of Doc Appleton; teacher of Latin and French; harbors longtime fantasies about her colleague George Caldwell in John Updike's *The Centaur*.

**Skippy Appleton**   Son of Corinna Appleton and possibly of Louis Zimmerman in John Updike's *The Centaur*.

**Arabella**   Lesbian movie star who acts in Boris Adrian's pornographic movie in Terry Southern's *Blue Movie*.

**Victory Wanda (Vicki) Arcenault**   Thirty-year-old nurse who has moved to New Jersey in the wake of a divorce from an abusive husband; romantically involved with Frank Bascombe; increasingly troubled by Frank's essential lack of deeply felt emotion; finally breaks up with him in Richard Ford's *The Sportswriter*.

**Archbishop of Chicago**   Religious leader who invites Roger Ashley to dinner at the height of Roger's journalistic fame and tells him the parable of the walls in Thornton Wilder's *The Eighth Day*.

**Archer**   Afghan mujaheddin guerrilla who engages in several attacks on Russian convoys and airfields and launches a major assault (repelled by Bondarenko) on the Bright Star facility in Tom Clancy's *The Cardinal of the Kremlin*.

**Helen Archer**   Friend and lover of Francis Phelan; homeless ex-singer who studied music at Vassar and now spends her days at the public library; is nostalgic and sentimental about Francis and about her life before she became homeless; has a stomach tumor that causes her not to eat in William Kennedy's *Ironweed*.

**Trudy Archer**   New to Runnymeade; opens a dance studio; has an affair with Chester; marries the town jeweler, but always believes that Chester loves her in Rita Mae Brown's *Loose Lips*.

**Harry Argent**   Generous, energetic lover of Eliza Quarles; movie producer in Alice Adams's *Listening to Billie*.

**Ariane**   Young woman of twenty-six who is the shipboard lover of both Allert Vanderveenan and Olaf; disappears mysteriously from the cruise ship in John Hawkes's *Death, Sleep & the Traveler*.

**Benny Aricia**   Executive who heads up a division of a company that has received a multibillion-dollar Navy contract; he purposely frames his company and then shows that it overbilled the government $600 million; his role in the fraudulent claim is revealed to the FBI in John Grisham's *The Partner*.

**Robert Ariyoshi**   Japanese fisherman who takes Charlie Stark fishing in Peter Matthiessen's *Raditzer*.

**Miss Arkaday**   Takes care of the rectory in Mary McGarry Morris's *Songs in Ordinary Time*.

**Arkie**   See James Parker McClellan.

**Margotte Arkin**   Widowed niece of Artur Sammler's dead wife; earnest and good-hearted but clumsy and verbose woman in whose apartment Sammler is provided a room in Saul Bellow's *Mr. Sammler's Planet*.

**Aunt Arlette**   Theodora Waite's mother's cousin; jewelry marks the divisions in her life; Theodora stays with her for a while after her mother dies; gives Abner $2,000 to take Theodora off her hands in Bette Pesetsky's *Midnight Sweets*.

**Armand**   Oldest living vampire who introduces Louis and Claudia to the Théâtre des Vampires in Anne Rice's *Interview with the Vampire*.

**Richie Armbriste**   Young pornography magnate in search of a movie erroneously thought to include footage of Hitler at an orgy in Don DeLillo's *Running Dog*.

**Elizabeth Armholtz**   Eighteen-year-old daughter of Inman Armholtz; alleges she was raped by Fareek Fanon in Tom Wolfe's *A Man In Full*.

**Inman Armholtz**   Chairman of large chemicals firm; father of Elizabeth in Tom Wolfe's *A Man In Full*.

**Lewis (Lew, Lo) Armistead**   Seasoned Confederate general in charge of one of George Pickett's brigades in Michael Shaara's *The Killer Angels*.

**William (Bill) Armiston**   Activist who betrays the group, brings a bomb into their home, and murders three of the men; murdered by Kam Wright in M. F. Beal's *Amazon One*.

**Claudine Arnaud**   Wife of Michel Arnaud; neglected and abused by her husband; suffers from alcoholism and eventual insanity; murders Mouche, her maid, during the slave uprising in 1791; saves herself and several other female refugees from marauding slaves by cutting off her own finger in order to surrender her wedding ring in Madison Smartt Bell's *All Souls' Rising*.

**Michel Arnaud**   Brutal master of plantation Habitation Arnaud in the French colony Saint Domingue; uses crucifixions and mutilations as routine punishments for disobedience among his slaves; fathers many children by his slaves but none by his wife, Claudine Arnaud, who is driven to alcoholism by his neglect; in fear of his life during a slave rebellion, he spends several months hiding in the wilderness in Madison Smartt Bell's *All Souls' Rising*.

**Desi Arnaz**   Bandleader from the same part of Cuba as the Castillo brothers; listens to and likes the Mambo Kings; puts Cesar and Nestor on an *I Love Lucy* episode; married to Lucille Ball; buys the rights to "Beautiful Maria of my Soul"; sends a letter of condolence to Cesar after Nestor dies in Oscar Hijuelos's *The Mambo Kings Play Songs of Love*.

**Mr. Erroll Arnold**   Another inmate of the home who knows how to build log cabins; Will Barrett will use his skills as he plans his own utopian community with Allie Huger in Walker Percy's *The Second Coming*.

**Carmen Arrellano**   Girlfriend of Gerardo Strasser Mendana and later of Antonio Strasser-Mendana in Joan Didion's *A Book of Common Prayer*.

**Lady Susannah Arrow**   Wealthy anarchist and bisexual lover in Paul Theroux's *The Family Arsenal*.

**Eleanor Arroway**   Radio astronomer who first discovers alien palimpsest; believes strongly in the existence of intelligent extraterrestrial life; uses direct and persistent approach to both personal and professional concerns; member of The World Message Consortium, and replaces Drumlin as a member of The Five in Carl Sagan's *Contact*.

**Art**   Lillian's husband and father of Adele and Carol; worked for Lillian's father; raises mink in Mona Simpson's *Anywhere but Here*.

**Art**   Friend of a friend of the narrator; lives in hotel with a prostitute and a cat in Richard Brautigan's *Trout Fishing in America*.

**Arthur**   Car captain of the Neighborhood Organization; leads a vigilante group and is shot; member of the American Legion in Bette Pesetsky's *Midnight Sweets*.

**Arthur**   Lifelong naif compromised by his vulnerability but sustained by his idealism; eponymous character in Thomas Berger's *Arthur Rex*.

**Curt Arvey**   Head of Arvey Film Studio; lends Vito Orsini money to produce a film and then attempts to take control of it in the middle of production in Judith Krantz's *Scruples*.

**Henry Arvis**   Sixty-year-old manager of the Brooklyn bakery The Cookie Lady in Bette Pesetsky's *Midnight Sweets*.

**Kane Bagley Asche**   Unemployed paper company manager; married; likes gardening; is fatally shot by Burke Devore in Donald E. Westlake's *The Ax*.

**Jacob (Jake) Ascher**   Lawyer and friend of the Isaacsons, whom he defends during their espionage trial; his defense is partially responsible for the Isaacsons being convicted and executed in E. L. Doctorow's *The Book of Daniel*.

**Edward Ashe**   Illegitimate son of Elias McCutcheon and Ellen Poe Ashe; falls in love with Betsy, fathers a child by her, and flees with them to Canada in Jesse Hill Ford's *The Raider*.

**Ellen Poe Ashe**   Woman abandoned by her husband; falls in love with Elias McCutcheon and bears their son, Edward Ashe; later marries Colonel Ennis Dalton in Jesse Hill Ford's *The Raider*.

**Brewster (Brew) Ashenden**   Millionaire playboy and eligible bachelor who copulates with a bear to save his life; narrator of *The Making of Ashenden*, a novella in Stanley Elkin's *Searches and Seizures*.

**Luann Asher**   Half-white, pill-addicted orphan adopted by Simon Asher; rejected by persons of both races in Hal Bennett's *A Wilderness of Vines*.

**Reed Ashford**   Lover of Daria Worthington and Eliza Quarles and love object of Evan Quarles; morose about his affair with Daria; takes an overdose of pills and dies in Alice Adams's *Listening to Billie*.

**Baron Ashkenazy**   See Tateh.

**Beata Kellerman Ashley**   See Beata Kellerman-Ashley.

**Constance (Constance Ashley-Nishimura) Ashley**   Youngest of the Ashley children; develops sympathy for the downtrodden and becomes internationally acclaimed as a social activist in Thornton Wilder's *The Eighth Day*.

**John Barrington Ashley**   Wrongly convicted as the murderer of Breckenridge Lansing; stolen from a train by unknown men; flees to Chile and later drowns at sea in Thornton Wilder's *The Eighth Day*.

**Lily Scolastica Ashley**   Oldest of the Ashley children; leaves Coaltown to become a world-famous concert singer in Thornton Wilder's *The Eighth Day*.

**Marie-Louise Scolastique Dubois Ashley**   Grandmother of John Ashley; she is the only member of his early family whose influence he consciously feels; he remembers her prayer to be used in the unfolding of God's plan in Thornton Wilder's *The Eighth Day*.

**Roger Berwyn (Trent Frazier) Ashley**   Only son of John and Beata Ashley and the first Ashley child to flee Coaltown; becomes a famous journalist in Chicago under the name of Trent Frazier and later as Berwyn Ashley; marries Félicité Lansing in Thornton Wilder's *The Eighth Day*.

**Sophia Ashley**   Daughter of John and Beata Ashley; after her father's disappearance, she takes control of the family's fortune in such enterprises as selling lemonade and books to travelers; insists on turning the family home into a boardinghouse; her hard work leads to a mental breakdown from which she never recovers in Thornton Wilder's *The Eighth Day*.

**Constance Ashley-Nishimura**   See Constance Ashley.

**Lucas (Luke) Asphalter**   Zoologist at the University of Chicago who tells Moses Herzog, his dearest friend, that Madeleine Herzog has cuckolded him with Val Gersbach; stands by Herzog in his time of emotional turmoil in Saul Bellow's *Herzog*.

**Brian Aspinwall**   Young teacher at Justin Martyr School and confidant of headmaster Francis Prescott; principal narrator who keeps a journal of various accounts of Prescott's life in Louis Auchincloss's *The Rector of Justin*.

**Carter Aster**   Byron Henry's first submarine commander; brave to the point of recklessness; has a clandestine affair with Byron's sister-in-law after her husband dies; turns command over to Byron and dies heroically when their ship is hit in Herman Wouk's *War and Remembrance*.

**Lieutenant Aster**   Nineteen-year-old female psychiatrist who attempts a therapeutic reprise on Georgie Cornell in Thomas Berger's *Regiment of Women*.

**Astrid**   Twenty-six-year-old estranged wife of the nameless narrator of Nicholas Delbanco's *In the Middle Distance*.

**Cora Atkins**   Implacable wife of Emerson Atkins; mother of Beulah Madge; devoted to the unending hard work of a depression-era Nebraska farm; dies of a stroke in Wright Morris's *Plains Song for Female Voices*.

**Emerson Atkins**   Taciturn and stoic Nebraska farmer; husband of Cora; father of Beulah Madge; labors over his farm through the depression and drought in Wright Morris's *Plains Song for Female Voices*.

**Fayrene Dee Atkins**   Third daughter of Belle and Orion, sister of Sharon Rose; plagued by disfiguring acne; marries Avery Dickel, who becomes a successful veterinarian in Wright Morris's *Plains Song for Female Voices*.

**(Beulah) Madge Atkins (Kibbee)**   Daughter of Cora and Emerson, Nebraska farmers; plump and placid as a child; dominated by but closely bonded to her cousin Sharon Rose; marries carpenter Ned Kibbee; cares for her three daughters as well as her husband and aging parents in Wright Morris's *Plains Song for Female Voices*.

**Orion Atkins**   Outgoing and impetuous brother of Emerson, husband of Belle Rooney, father of Sharon Rose; Nebraska farmer, but more interested in hunting; wife dies during the birth of their third daughter; returns mentally and physically disabled from World War I; dies of a stroke in Wright Morris's *Plains Song for Female Voices*.

**Sharon Rose Atkins**   Oldest daughter of Belle Rooney and Orion Atkins; dominates but is devoted to her older cousin Madge; attends the university in Chicago; never marries and has series of strong attachments to women in Wright Morris's *Plains Song for Female Voices*.

**Leto Atreides II**   Son of Paul Muad'Dib; rules the known universe by doling out rations of melange spice he stockpiled when he learned spice would no longer be readily available; his political goal through his tyrannical reign is called the Golden Path, in which the universe avoids a catastrophic war that would eliminate humankind; is assassinated on the day he will marry Hwi Noree in Frank Herbert's *God Emperor of Dune*.

**Moneo Atreides**   Serves as Leto II's majordomo and fathers Siona Atreides; originally a rebel against Leto II's reign; dies in the bridge collapse along with Leto II during the assassination by Duncan Idaho in Frank Herbert's *God Emperor of Dune*.

**Siona Atreides**   Daughter of Moneo; beautiful, headstrong girl who is part of a rebel group that works to overthrow the rule of Leto II; grudgingly agrees to work with the Emperor of Dune; with Duncan Idaho, assassinates Leto II in Frank Herbert's *God Emperor of Dune*.

**Attaroa**   Leader of a fierce tribe of man-hating woman warriors. Strong and cruel, Attaroa plans to kill a wounded Jondalar, and poses the biggest threat to the intertwined destinies of Ayla and Jondalar in Jean Auel's *The Plains of Passage*.

**Louise Attwater**   See Louise Attwater Eborn.

**Audrey**   Narrates memoir of her childhood; accident at birth causes defect in one eye, which is disfigured and technically blind; at fifteen, seduced by ophthalmologist; wants to be an actress, but becomes writer who fabricates self she might have been as she writes memoir in Lynne Sharon Schwartz's *Leaving Brooklyn*.

**Ann August**   Daughter of Adele Diamond and Hishan; moves from Bay City, Wisconsin, to Los Angeles at age twelve with her mother; likes to be alone, but rarely is apart from her mother, with whom she fights violently; goes to college in the East, and afterward, rarely visits her mother in Mona Simpson's *Anywhere but Here*.

**Botho August**   Lighthouse keeper; reclusive and rude; has slept with Margaret Handle and has an affair with Alaric; is murdered by Fabian Vas in Howard Norman's *The Bird Artist*.

**Constantius Augustus (Constans)**   Roman emperor who methodically exterminates all other surviving male members of his family with the exception of his cousins Gallus and Julian in Gore Vidal's *Julian*.

**Julian Augustus**   Roman emperor who struggles unsuccessfully to discredit Christianity and restore worship of the Greek gods; assassinated by Callistus in Gore Vidal's *Julian*.

**Mughal Emperor Aurangzeb**   Defender of Islam; a frail ascetic, he takes Hannah Legge prisoner and gives her a pearl necklace; his battle against Jadav Singh is his last great victory in Bharati Mukherjee's *The Holder of the World*.

**Benny Austin**   Best friend and business partner of Harry Wyeth in Joan Didion's *Play It As It Lays*.

**Ava (Delilah Lee)**   Aspiring dancer and lover of Isolde; names herself after Ava Gardner in Marilyn French's *The Women's Room*.

**Captain Andrew Avers**   Father of Raib Avers and Desmond Eden; dies aboard the *Lillias Eden* in Peter Matthiessen's *Far Tortuga*.

**Jim Eden (Buddy) Avers**   Quiet and frightened seventeen-year-old son of Raib Avers; determined to be a turtler even though he gets seasick and lacks ability; dies following the wreck of the *Lillias Eden* in Peter Matthiessen's *Far Tortuga.*

**Captain Raib Avers**   Skilled turtler and captain of the *Lillias Eden;* embittered by changes he has witnessed in the fishery business; attempts to take his crew over Misteriosa Reef at night, but wrecks his boat and dies with all but one of his crew in Peter Matthiessen's *Far Tortuga.*

**Megan Avery**   Caring coworker of Jamie Conway's at a prominent New York magazine who always tries to do her best for him even though she is repeatedly taken advantage of in Jay McInerney's *Bright Lights, Big City.*

**Shug Avery**   Singer; loves Celie and teaches her about sex; takes her from her husband to Memphis, Tennessee; leaves to go on singing tour with nineteen-year-old lover; later returns to Celie in Alice Walker's *The Color Purple.*

**Daisy Avila**   Daughter of opposition senator Domingo Avila; wins a government-sponsored beauty contest in the Philippines, then denounces the government in a media interview; falls in love with a rebel leader and joins his guerrilla forces; arrested after coming to her assassinated father's funeral; is tortured, gang-raped, and banished from the country, but returns to become a guerrilla fighter in Jessica Hagedorn's *Dogeaters.*

**Domingo Avila**   Philippine senator who is critical of the ruling regime's abuses and excesses; champion of human rights who is assassinated by the government; father of Daisy Avila in Jessica Hagedorn's *Dogeaters.*

**Arthur Axelrod**   Father of David Axelrod and a lawyer in Scott Spencer's *Endless Love.*

**David (Dave) Axelrod**   Obsessive lover of Jade Butterfield; narrator of Scott Spencer's *Endless Love.*

**Rose Axelrod**   Wife of Arthur Axelrod and mother of David Axelrod in Scott Spencer's *Endless Love.*

**Eeben Axelroot**   Disreputable pilot who frequently stays in Kilanga; involved in diamond smuggling and covert CIA operations, apparently has some involvement in the assassination of the prime minister of the Republic of Congo, Patrice Lumumba; takes Rachel to Johannesburg and becomes her lover in Barbara Kingsolver's *The Poisonwood Bible.*

**Willie Duke Aycock**   Sexual rival of Rosacoke Mustian for the affections of Wesley Beavers in Reynolds Price's *A Long and Happy Life.*

**Ayla**   Strong, resourceful, beautiful Cro-Magnon woman; lives in isolation after her unjust banishment from the Neanderthal Clan that raised her; discoverer of flint and iron pyrite as tools to make fire; expert hunter; skilled healer, eventual lover of Jondular; protagonist of Jean Auel's *The Valley of Horses, The Clan of the Cave Bear, The Plains of Passage,* and *The Mammoth Hunters.*

**Azarian**   Rock musician who becomes leader of a band when singer Bucky Wunderlick drops out; ultimately murdered in Don DeLillo's *Great Jones Street.*

**Azazruk**   Young shaman of Eskimo descent in 12,000 BPE; leads his tribe to start one of the earliest Aleut settlements on island of Lapak in James Michener's *Alaska.*

**Azusa**   Common-law wife of Wolfie, who yearns to return to her in Peter Matthiessen's *At Play in the Fields of the Lord.*

**Throat-Cut de Azvedo**   Pirate who had been a rabbi's son and a physician in Bharati Mukherjee's *The Holder of the World.*

**Babe**   Dayton Nickles's wild mare that Rayona Taylor tries to ride in the Havre rodeo in Michael Dorris's *A Yellow Raft in Blue Water.*

**Babe**   See Beatrice Greene.

**Baby Igor**   See Metzger.

**Baby Thor**   Son of Amanda Ziller conceived during an electrical storm in Tom Robbins's *Another Roadside Attraction.*

**Richard Bach**   Biplane-flying narrator of *Illusions: The Adventures of a Reluctant Messiah,* whose brief summer encounter with enigmatic Donald Shimoda sparks Bach's rocky journey to spiritual self-discovery.

**Octave Bacheron**   White pharmacist who supports the civil rights efforts of the Reverend Phillip Martin in Ernest J. Gaines's *In My Father's House.*

**Reginald Bacon**   Reverend who heads many political, social, and religious organizations in the Bronx; behind-the-scenes orchestrator of the case against Sherman McCoy in Tom Wolfe's *The Bonfire of the Vanities.*

**Sir Francis Bacon**   Writer and courtier in George Garrett's *Death of the Fox.*

**Miriam Bader**   Wife of Shmuel Bader; helps David Lurie with his German studies in Chaim Potok's *In the Beginning.*

**Shmuel Bader**   Torah teacher of David Lurie and European field director of an organization that brings Polish Jews to the United States in Chaim Potok's *In the Beginning.*

**The Bad Priest**   See V.

**Dr. Bagley**   President of Polycarp College in Peter De Vries's *Let Me Count the Ways.*

**Father Battista Baglione**   Catholic priest and member of the Common Sense Committee in Robert Coover's *The Origin of the Brunists.*

**Isadora Bailey**   Prim schoolteacher from Boston who attempts to blackmail Rutherford Calhoun into marriage; is about to marry Papa Zeringue when Rutherford disrupts the ceremony; accepts Rutherford's proposal of marriage and the responsibility of raising Baleka in Charles Johnson's *Middle Passage.*

**Kenneth Bailey**   Private detective that helps main character Jennifer Parker in her struggle as a young lawyer in Sidney Sheldon's *Rage of Angels.*

**Raymond Baillet**   Obliging Parisian taxi driver; may have inspired Jean-Louis Lebris de Kérouac's satori, or sudden illumination, in Jack Kerouac's *Satori in Paris.*

**Eva Baily**   Sister of Minna Baily; lives with Minna and their nephew in a 70th Street apartment building managed by Norman Moonbloom in Edward Lewis Wallant's *The Tenants of Moonbloom.*

**Minna Baily**   Sister of Eva Baily; lives with Eva and their nephew in a 70th Street apartment building managed by Norman Moonbloom in Edward Lewis Wallant's *The Tenants of Moonbloom.*

**Blair Bainbridge**   Wealthy male model, he has an affair with Sarah Vane-Tempest in Rita Mae Brown's *Cat on the Scent.*

**Guitar Bains**   Best friend of Macon (Milkman) Dead III and member of a racial revenge group called the Seven Days in Toni Morrison's *Song of Solomon.*

**Marie Baird**   Wife of Vincent Baird; a member of Margaret's church; owns a gift shop, The Gilded Peacock, in Gail Godwin's *Evensong*.

**Vincent Baird**   Husband of Marie Baird; has a styling shop above his wife's shop; cuts Margaret's and what is left of Adrian's hair in Gail Godwin's *Evensong*.

**Baker**   Friend who visits Anne and Phil Sorenson to recover from a divorce and clumsily seduces Anne in Frederick Busch's *Manual Labor*.

**Antoinette (Tony) Baker**   Pretty and flirtatious neighbor of the Eberhardts; has an affair with David Eberhardt and eventually marries him many years later in Sue Miller's *Family Pictures*.

**April Baker**   Spaced-out teenage sister of Nicole Baker Barrett; innocent companion of Gary Gilmore during his first murderous spree in Norman Mailer's *Executioner's Song*.

**Colonel Baker**   Orthopedic surgeon at Kilrainey Army Hospital who wants to amputate the right leg of Bobby Prell in James Jones's *Whistle*.

**Dorris Baker**   Father of a boy who accidentally drowns on the day Glen Davis returns from prison in Larry Brown's *Father and Son*.

**Mr. Baker**   President of the First National Bank in New Baytown who tries to use Ethan Allen Hawley to gain additional wealth and power for himself in John Steinbeck's *The Winter of Our Discontent*.

**Nancy May Baker**   Lover of Marshall Pearl; ornithologist studying eagles in New Mexico for the University of Chicago in Mark Helprin's *Refiner's Fire*.

**Nicole Baker**   See Nicole Kathryne Baker Barrett.

**Rena Baker**   Dying sanitorium patient beloved and mourned by Don Wanderhope in Peter De Vries's *The Blood of the Lamb*.

**Sue Baker**   Mother of a boy who accidentally drowns on the day Glen Davis returns from prison in Larry Brown's *Father and Son*.

**Gus Bakewell**   Thug and associate of Donald Washburn in Thomas Berger's *Who Is Teddy Villanova?*

**Daniel Balaban**   Cryptanalyst working for the United States during World War II; he is Louise Kahan's lover during the war; marries Abra Scott after the war, and they travel together to Japan in Marge Piercy's *Gone to Soldiers*.

**Simon Bale**   Religious fanatic whose wife dies in their burning house; accidentally killed by Henry Soames in John Gardner's *Nickel Mountain*.

**Baleka**   Eight-year-old Allmuseri slave on the *Republic*; is rescued along with Squibb and Rutherford and taken aboard the *Juno*, where she nurses Rutherford back to health; is "adopted" by Rutherford and Isadora and raised by them once they are married in Charles Johnson's *Middle Passage*.

**Elijah (Lije) Baley**   Agoraphobic Earth detective assigned to solve a politically sensitive case of roboticide and clear Dr. Han Fastolfe's name on the planet Aurora; founder of Earth's fledging movement to colonize unsettled worlds; investigative partner of R. Daneel Olivaw in Isaac Asimov's *The Robots of Dawn*.

**Drenka Balich**   Wife of Matija Balich and hostess at inn he owns; adulterous lover of Mickey Sabbath; dies of cancer in Philip Roth's *Sabbath's Theater*.

**Eliza Ballard**   Daughter of Judge and Mary Ballard; worked as a professional secretary for Rausch Cordage Company; local gossip in Helen Hooven Santmyer's "*. . . And Ladies of the Club.*"

**Gregory (Greg) Ballard**   Black fisherman from Cape Cod who fights for the loyalists in the Spanish civil war and against the racial hatred of Hitler; friend of Jake Starr in William Herrick's *Hermanos!*

**Mary Ballard**   Married to a judge in Waynesboro, Ohio; crusader for progressive causes such as temperance and women's suffrage in Helen Hooven Santmyer's "*. . . And Ladies of the Club.*"

**Drew Ballinger**   Sales supervisor for a large soft-drink company; spokesman for the laws of civilization who is killed during the three-day canoe trip on the Cahulawassee River in James Dickey's *Deliverance*.

**Old Bull (Old Bull Lewis, Smiley Bull Balloon) Balloon (Baloon)**   Alcoholic gambler who sells flyswatters door-to-door with Cody Pomeray, Sr., in Jack Kerouac's *Visions of Cody*; plays pool with Doctor Sax in *Doctor Sax*; appears as W. C. Fields in *Book of Dreams*; drinks with Emil Duluoz in *Visions of Gerard*.

**Mick Ballou**   Unofficial owner of "Grogan's" bar and much else; career criminal, soulmate, and former drinking partner of Matt Scudder in Lawrence Block's *A Dance at the Slaughterhouse*.

**Rocco (Bullets) Bambarella**   Macho gambler and police detective in Joseph Wambaugh's *The Black Marble*.

**Joseppi Banascalco**   Captain of the Europe-bound *Castel Felice*, on which most of the action centers in Calvin Hernton's *Scarecrow*.

**George R. (Brass Band, Tall George) Band**   First lieutenant in C-for-Charlie Company who replaces James Stein as company commander; his lust for heroism earns him the hatred of his men, and he is eventually relieved of command for failing to communicate with headquarters in James Jones's *The Thin Red Line*.

**Joe Banion**   Black hired hand on Mat Feltner's Kentucky tobacco farm; husband of Nettie Banion in Wendell Berry's *A Place on Earth* and *The Memory of Old Jack*.

**Nettie Banion**   Black housekeeper and cook on Mat Feltner's Kentucky tobacco farm; wife of Joe Banion in Wendell Berry's *A Place on Earth* and *The Memory of Old Jack*.

**Alonzo (Lonnie) Banks**   Younger brother of the black councilman Randolph Banks; dedicated Communist expelled from the party for opposing its stand on domestic issues in Julian Mayfield's *The Grand Parade*.

**Billy Banks**   School friend of Terry Wilson, whom he tries to help get off drugs in Donald Goines's *Dopefiend*.

**Margaret Banks**   Wife of Michael Banks; kidnapped and beaten by a group of killers and thieves who want to benefit from her husband's theft of a horse, Rock Castle, which they expect to win one race in John Hawkes's *The Lime Twig*.

**Michael Banks**   Husband of Margaret Banks, who is convinced by his lodger, William Hencher, to steal a horse, Rock Castle, to win one race, but becomes entangled in a group of killers and thieves who want to benefit from his theft in John Hawkes's *The Lime Twig*.

**Randolph (Randy) Banks**   Black city councilman and Harvard Law School graduate; brother of Lonnie Banks and lover of Patty Speed in Julian Mayfield's *The Grand Parade*.

**Ethel Banning**   Instructor of Spanish and French and one of Jacob Horner's interviewers at Wicomico State Teachers College in John Barth's *The End of the Road*.

**Thomas Bannister**   Barrister who represents Abe Cady in Leon Uris's *QB VII*.

**Homer Lisle (Granddad) Bannon**   Second husband of Jewel Bannon and grandfather of Lonnie Bannon; ranch owner with a diseased cattle herd; killed by his stepson Hud in Larry McMurtry's *Horseman, Pass By*.

**Jewel Bannon**   Second wife of Homer Bannon, mother of Hud, and stepgrandmother of Lonnie Bannon in Larry McMurtry's *Horseman, Pass By*.

**Lonnie Bannon**   Stepnephew of Hud; leaves the ranch after the death of his grandfather, Homer Bannon; narrator of Larry McMurtry's *Horseman, Pass By*.

**Scott (Hud, Huddie) Bannon**   See Hud.

**Aleksandr Baranov**   Visionary, steadfast Russian merchant sent to found and manage fur company affairs in Kodiak, Alaska; creates ordered settlement and establishes capital at Sitka; ultimately dishonored through bureaucratic harassment in James Michener's *Alaska*.

**Joseph Barbanel**   Former lumber dealer; member of Kovno ghetto council; keeps secret record of all actions and regulations by Gestapo; lists names of members; records fate of Jews killed or transported; lover of Greta Margolin; uses Yehoshua Mendelssohn to smuggle manuscript in E.L. Doctorow's *City of God*.

**Barbara**   Runs the pressers at Kolditis Cleaners in Mary McGarry Morris's *A Dangerous Woman*.

**Barbara**   Attorney and agent of Henry Wiggen in Mark Harris's *It Looked Like For Ever*.

**Barbara**   Sexual conquest of Carol Severin Swanson in Jim Harrison's *Wolf*.

**Captain Barbatov**   Russian military martinet outsmarted by George Levanter in Jerzy Kosinski's *Blind Date*.

**Helen Van Vleck Barber**   First love of Nelson Dewey; marries Joel Barber and dies in childbirth in August Derleth's *The Shadow in the Glass*.

**Joel Barber**   Law partner of Nelson Dewey; successfully competes with Dewey for Helen Van Vleck in August Derleth's *The Shadow in the Glass*.

**Stephanie Barboulis**   Jill's roommate her senior year; Greek girl who likes Howie and later marries him in Marge Piercy's *Braided Lives*.

**Juanita Collins Harmeyer (Mother Goddam) Barefoot**   Madam and friend of Perry in James Leo Herlihy's *Midnight Cowboy*.

**Tombaby (Princess) Barefoot**   Son of Juanita Barefoot in James Leo Herlihy's *Midnight Cowboy*.

**Bargetta**   Described as the only black friend the unnamed male narrator had in college; a tall, striking young woman from Memphis who remains aloof to the social and racial politics among other young blacks in the college set; dates only white men; follows a French artist to Paris, where she is eventually abandoned by him and expelled from his apartment by his disapproving mother in Darryl Pinckney's *High Cotton*.

**Penny Barker**   Former girlfriend of Clyde Stout, whose grammar she corrects in Jack Matthews's *Hanger Stout, Awake!*

**Rolfe Barker**   Boy who takes Anne into a back room and puts his hands on her in Joan Chase's *During the Reign of the Queen of Persia*.

**Barlow**   Mugger turned cabdriver who works for Edward Pierce in Michael Crichton's *The Great Train Robbery*.

**Barlow**   Vampire and owner, with his partner Richard Straker, of Marsten House in Stephen King's *'Salem's Lot*.

**Frankie Barlow**   Roadhouse owner ruthlessly murdered by Glen Davis after his release from prison in Larry Brown's *Father and Son*.

**Frank X. Barlow**   See Dr. Robert Fender.

**Djuna Barnes**   Literary figure, portrayed here in advanced age in her apartment at Patchin Place in New York's Greenwich Village; asks the narrator to hand-wash a blouse, followed by an observation about the "touchiness" of blacks, which causes a fatal rupture in their friendship in Darryl Pinckney's *High Cotton.*

**Osella Barnes**   Childhood nurse of Gavin Hexam and later a maid for Gavin and N. Hexam; quits her job as maid because she believes N. Hexam is a witch in Diane Johnson's *The Shadow Knows.*

**Edith Dewar Barnstorff**   Grandmother of Jane Clifford in Gail Godwin's *The Odd Woman.*

**Arthur (Art) Baron**   Company division head responsible for replacing Andy Kagle with Bob Slocum in Joseph Heller's *Something Happened.*

**Ed Barrett**   Father of Will Barrett; his suicide haunts Will in Walker Percy's *The Last Gentleman.*

**Jennifer Cavilleri (Jenny) Barrett**   Daughter of Philip Cavilleri; working-class Radcliffe graduate who marries Oliver Barrett IV against his family's wishes; dies of leukemia in Erich Segal's *Love Story.*

**Joshua Barrett**   Little bully who sustains a head injury after Martha Horgan hits him with an iron ladle in Mary McGarry Morris's *A Dangerous Woman.*

**Marion Peabody Barrett**   Homely northern woman of wealth whom Will Barrett marries because he likes to see her happy; a fervent "social Christian" who eats herself to death in Walker Percy's *The Second Coming.*

**Nicole Kathryne Baker (Nicole Kathryne Gilmore, Nucoa Butterball) Barrett**   Girlfriend of Gary Gilmore in Norman Mailer's The *Executioner's Song.*

**Oliver (Old Stonyface) Barrett III**   Olympic rower, textile mill owner, and father of Oliver Barrett IV; disapproves of his son's wife in Erich Segal's *Love Story;* brings his son into the family firm in *Oliver's Story.*

**Oliver (Ollie) Barrett IV**   Wealthy Harvard graduate who marries Jennifer Cavilleri, a working-class woman, against his family's wishes in Erich Segal's *Love Story;* falls in love with Marcie Binnendale Nash but finds that she is shallow and unethical in *Oliver's Story.*

**Pamela (Pam) Barrett**   Television reporter in William Bayer's *Peregrine;* witnesses a fatal Peregrine falcon attack on a girl; becomes the object of the falconer's obsession.

**Sylvia (Syl) Barrett**   First-year teacher who learns the intricacies of life at Calvin Coolidge High School; finds herself buried in meaningless paperwork with little time or support to teach in Bel Kaufman's *Up the Down Staircase.*

**Will Barrett**   Seeker of love and divine truth; a successful lawyer, Will is less good as a husband and father; he must com-prehend his history with his own father before he can begin to live a genuine life in Walker Percy's *The Second Coming.*

**Willston Bibb (Billy, Will) Barrett**   Humidification engineer who crosses America, trying to live as the epitome of southern honor in Walker Percy's *The Last Gentleman.*

**Paul Barringer**   Glamour boy of the Calvin Coolidge High School English faculty; unpublished writer who composes a poem for every occasion; pursues Sylvia Barrett; responds to a love letter from a student by correcting it grammatically in Bel Kaufman's *Up the Down Staircase.*

**Fred T. Barry**   Wealthy businessman and arts patron in Kurt Vonnegut's *Breakfast of Champions.*

**Bart**   Son of Utch Thalhammer and the unnamed narrator, brother of Jack, and playmate and friend of Fiordiligi and Dorabella Winter; favored by Severin Winter, who thinks that Bart will be an excellent 177-pound wrestler in John Irving's *The 158-Pound Marriage.*

**Arlene Bartlett**   Mother of Laney Bartlett; poor but vital widow who takes several lovers and is frequently pregnant in Joyce Carol Oates's *Childwold.*

**Dickie Bartlett**   Teenage helper of Clem Streeter; held prisoner and then released by Legs Diamond in William Kennedy's *Legs.*

**Edward Bartlett**   Artist from Los Angeles hired to draw Nicole for a Stephanie Sykes doll; is caught naked with Nicole in the woods and is sent back to California in Ann Beattie's *Love Always.*

**Evangeline Ann (Laney) Bartlett**   Teenager from an impoverished rural area who becomes the focus of the eccentric Fitz John Kasch's obsession; daughter of Arlene Bartlett in Joyce Carol Oates's *Childwold.*

**Vale Bartlett**   Embittered Vietnam veteran and son of Arlene Bartlett in Joyce Carol Oates's *Childwold.*

**Birchie Bartley**   Insane twelve-year-old daughter of Lizzie Bartley and Blessed Belshazzar; her trial for murder is used by the state of Virginia to punish blacks for the crime of pretending to be white in Hal Bennett's *A Wilderness of Vines.*

**Calvin LeRoy Bartley**   Youngest son of Lizzie Bartley; rejected by Darlene Mosby, he commits suicide by covering himself with pitchlime in Hal Bennett's *A Wilderness of Vines.*

**Lizzie Bartley**   Matriarch of the Bartley clan noted for dark-skin good looks and virility; also mother by Blessed Belshazzar of Birchie Bartley in Hal Bennett's *A Wilderness of Vines* and *The Black Wine.*

**Robert Bartley**   Father of thirteen children and lover of Neva Stapleton and Eloise McLindon; responsible for the death of Otha Manning during World War I in Hal Bennett's *A Wilderness of Vines* and *The Black Wine.*

**Count Bartolomé**   Attractive, courtly man who allows the difficult child Robin Empson to ride on his palomino mare in Gail Godwin's *The Perfectionists*.

**Miss Lavinia Barton**   Mother of Odessa Barton Market and disapproving mother-in-law of Joe Market in Hal Bennett's *Lord of Dark Places*.

**Odessa Barton**   See Odessa Barton Market.

**Clarissa Bascombe**   Twelve-year-old daughter of Frank Bascombe, who is as grounded as her older brother, Paul, is troubled; lives with her mother and stepfather in upscale Deep River, Connecticut; is fiercely loyal to her brother and surreptitiously refuses to offer her parents any insight to his problems or their solutions; describes herself as "thirty-twelve" in Richard Ford's *Independence Day*.

**Frank Bascombe**   Divorced forty-four-year-old writer turned real estate agent in Haddam, New Jersey, first introduced in Richard Ford's *The Sportswriter*. Offers detached yet detailed descriptions of the ordinary concerns that make up his life while he takes his troubled teenage son on a July 4th weekend trip to the basketball and baseball halls of fame; faced with a serious accident that will potentially cause him to become reengaged in his own life in *Independence Day*.

**Lena Bascombe**   Actress playing the mother in the film version of Osgood Wallop's *The Duchess of Obloquy* in Peter De Vries's *Mrs. Wallop*.

**Paul Bascombe**   Troubled fifteen-year-old-son of Frank Bascombe, who is awaiting trial for shoplifting three boxes of condoms; accompanies his father on a July 4th trip to visit the basketball and baseball halls of fame and has an encounter with a seventy-five-mile-per-hour baseball in Richard Ford's *Independence Day*.

**"X" Dykstra-Bascombe**   Former wife of Frank Bascombe; their marriage produced three children, one of whom, Ralph, died at age nine; once a model, has begun a new career as a golf pro at the local country club; attempts to help her ex-husband weather a personal crisis in Richard Ford's *The Sportswriter*.

**Basellecci**   Elderly teacher of Italian; afflicted with cancer of the bowel; lives in the Mott Street building managed by Norman Moonbloom in Edward Lewis Wallant's *The Tenants of Moonbloom*.

**Bashele**   Wife of Zelig, mother of Shosha, and mother-in-law of Aaron Greidinger in Isaac Bashevis Singer's *Shosha*.

**Harold Basie**   Lawyer hired to represent Oscar Crease in his suit against Erebus Entertainment who provides competent representation but is found to have lied about his credentials and must flee the law before the case is won in William Gaddis's *A Frolic of His Own*.

**Herman Baskerville**   Homosexual mentor of Bill Kelsey and student of racial mythology and revolution in Hal Bennett's *Seventh Heaven*.

**George Baso**   Japanese Zen master suffering from tuberculosis; friend visited by Jack Duluoz and Dave Wain in Jack Kerouac's *Big Sur*.

**Jonathan Staunch Bass**   Son of Pourty F. Bloodworth; half brother of Amos-Otis Thigpen, LaDonna Scales, Regal Pettibone, and Noah Grandberry; minister who counsels Thigpen and Abraham Dolphin in Leon Forrest's *The Bloodworth Orphans*.

**Lucy Nelson Bassart**   Granddaughter of Willard Carroll and daughter of Myra and Duane Nelson; her dreams of independence are thwarted by premarital pregnancy; marriage to Roy Bassart and motherhood bring her no happiness in Philip Roth's *When She Was Good*.

**Roy Bassart**   Dreamy World War II veteran who becomes a photographer and marries his pregnant girlfriend Lucy Nelson in Philip Roth's *When She Was Good*.

**Edward Bast**   Young composer who reluctantly becomes JR's business representative in William Gaddis's *JR*.

**Jay Basu**   Partner of Venn at the Massachusettes Institute of Technology; works on constructing virtual reality; a fan of *Murder, She Wrote* in Bharati Mukherjee's *The Holder of the World*.

**Carole (C. B.) Batelle**   Single mother of Dawn Batelle; activist and only member of the group to be captured; serving an indeterminate prison sentence at the end of M. F. Beal's *Amazon One*.

**Dawn Melody (Dawn Melody Topp) Batelle**   Illegitimate daughter of Carole Batelle; reared to age seven by Topper; after her mother's arrest, sent to live with foster parents in M. F. Beal's *Amazon One*.

**Glen Bateman**   Sociology professor and fourth lead in The Stand in Stephen King's *The Stand*.

**Patrick Bateman**   Handsome, well-educated twenty-six-year-old; works by day on Wall Street earning a fortune to add to the money that he was born with; spends his nights committing acts of violence against women as a psychopathic serial killer in Bret Easton Ellis's *American Psycho*.

**Digby Bates**   Deputy chief of the Los Angeles Police Department; publicity hound in Joseph Wambaugh's *The Black Marble*.

**Paulette Bath**   Librarian; raised in London; helps Fabian by paying for his art supplies in Howard Norman's *The Bird Artist*.

**Billy Bathgate**   Young man, once known as Billy Behan, from the Bronx (Bathgate Avenue) who impresses the mobster Dutch

Schultz enough to join his gang though Dutch's influence is waning; Bathgate survives Dutch's demise in E. L. Doctorow's *Billy Bathgate*.

**Bathsheba**   Beautiful woman with whom King David falls passionately and permanently in love; eighth wife of David's harem who insists on being made his queen; doting mother who continually attempts to advance their son Solomon by asking David to name him as heir to the throne in Joseph Heller's *God Knows*.

**Billy Batson**   Leader of the warrior faction of the Indians; committed to fighting government troops head-on and dying rather than dispersing peacefully throughout the United States in Marge Piercy's *Dance the Eagle to Sleep*.

**Santa Battaglia**   Native New Orleanian and aunt of patrolman Angelo Mancuso; a widow who dotes on the memory of her departed mother; meets Mrs. Reilly through her nephew; helps Mrs. Reilly leave her abusive son and find a new love in John Kennedy Toole's *A Confederacy of Dunces*.

**Vance Battle**   The town doctor and Will Barrett's golf partner who takes great pride in curing his patients' physical ills in Walker Percy's *The Second Coming*.

**Karl Baumgartner**   Alcoholic lawyer from Mexico City traveling with his abused wife and fearful son in Katherine Anne Porter's *Ship of Fools*.

**Baxter**   Puritan preacher whose attempts to eliminate heresy and anarchic distemper in Cromwell's army force the soldiers to begin meeting secretly in order to obtain privacy in Mary Lee Settle's *Prisons*.

**Abner Baxter**   Violent coal miner who succeeds Ely Collins as the pastor of the Nazarene church in Robert Coover's *The Origin of the Brunists*.

**Charlie Ryan Baxter**   Writer of experimental novels in Alison Lurie's *Real People*.

**Frances (Black Piggy, Franny) Baxter**   Daughter of Abner and Sarah Baxter in Robert Coover's *The Origin of the Brunists*.

**Nathan (Black Hand, Nat) Baxter**   Son of Abner and Sarah Baxter in Robert Coover's *The Origin of the Brunists*.

**Paul (Black Peter, Paulie) Baxter**   Son of Abner and Sarah Baxter in Robert Coover's *The Origin of the Brunists*.

**Sarah Baxter**   Intimidated wife of Abner Baxter in Robert Coover's *The Origin of the Brunists*.

**Pelly Bay**   Teenage portrait artist who lives in Quill, a small Canadian village, with his aunt Hettie and uncle Sam; dies when his unicycle falls through the ice as he performs stunts for the village in Howard Norman's *Northern Lights*.

**Turget Bay**   A businessman from Istanbul; known for running guns to the Middle East; his beautiful daughter, Lale, drowns with the other students; his tragedy is very graphically described in Mary Lee Settle's *Blood Tie*.

**Bay Boy**   Boy Claudia MacTeer challenges to defend Frieda MacTeer in school playground fight in Toni Morrison's *The Bluest Eye*.

**Walter Bayles**   Danny's partner of eight years; lawyer who lives in the suburbs; is addicted to pornography and is thinking of leaving Danny in David Leavitt's *Equal Affections*.

**Arthur Bayson**   Ineffectual husband of Betty Starr Bayson in Thomas Berger's *Killing Time*.

**Betty Starr Bayson**   Venal woman whose mother and sister were murdered by Joseph Detweiler in Thomas Berger's *Killing Time*.

**Bea**   Operator and mistress of ceremonies in the Hippodrome; mother of Iris; dies of a heart attack in Cyrus Colter's *The Hippodrome*.

**Deanna Whiteheart Beads**   Mostly Ojibwa girl; daughter of Rozina Roy and Richard Whiteheart Beads and twin sister of Cally Roy; dies as a result of her father's suicide attempt in Louise Erdrich's *The Antelope Wife*.

**Richard Whiteheart Beads**   Urban, mostly Ojibwa trash contractor whose obsessive love for his wife, Rozina Roy, alienates her and whose suicide attempt results in the death of his daughter Deanna in Louise Erdrich's *The Antelope Wife*.

**Elizabeth (Lizzie) Bean**   Psychological counselor at a college in upstate New York; pregnant by Horace L'Ordinet, she gives birth to the baby boy later adopted by Annie and Phil Sorenson; lover of Eli Silver in Frederick Busch's *Rounds*.

**Titus Bean**   Journalist and friend of Mabry Jenkins; writes scripts for pornographic movies in addition to writing stories about a chemical company's illicit activities in Peter Gent's *Texas Celebrity Turkey Trot*.

**Petal Bear**   First wife of Quoyle; killed in car accident after selling their two daughters, who are later recovered, to a maker of pornographic videos in E. Annie Proulx's *The Shipping News*.

**Mr. Beaton**   Secretary and general counsel for Typon International, whose admiration for Amy Joubert leads him to plot for her control of the company in William Gaddis's *JR*.

**Bobo Beauchamp**   Groom in William Faulkner's *The Reivers*.

**James Thucydides (Tennie's Jim, Thucydus) Beauchamp**   See Volume I.

**Lucas Quintus Carothers McCaslin Beauchamp**   See Volume I.

**Tennie Beauchamp**   See Volume I.

**Bob Beaudreau**   Football fanatic and financier who loses his girlfriend to Phil Elliott in Peter Gent's *North Dallas Forty*.

**Clair Beaudry**   Abusive, wife-beating landlord who rents an apartment to Yolanda Garcia in Julia Alvarez's *Yo!*

**Marie Beaudry**   Abused wife of Clair Beaudry; rents an apartment to Yolanda Garcia; encouraged by Yo to permanently separate from Clair in Julia Alvarez's *Yo!*

**Justin Beaufils**   Childhood friend of Ursa Mackenzie; defeats Primus Mackenzie in election in Paule Marshall's *Daughters*.

**Maria McInnis Beaufort**   Banker's daughter who marries a university professor-psychiatrist after an affair with Jed Tewksbury in Robert Penn Warren's *A Place to Come To*.

**Pussy (Mrs. Beau) Beauseigneur**   Example of encroaching commuters in Woodsmoke, Connecticut; employs Frank Spofford as a handyman in Peter De Vries's *Reuben, Reuben*.

**Ollie Totem Head Water Beaver**   Guide on the Alaskan hunting expedition in Norman Mailer's *Why Are We in Vietnam?*

**Myrlene Beavers**   Elderly resident of the solidly black, working-class neighborhood of Wallace Hill in Haddam, New Jersey; in a moment of forgetfulness, calls the police on her old acquaintance, Frank Bascombe, as he tries to collect rent from her neighbors in Richard Ford's *Independence Day*.

**Wesley Beavers**   Sexually magnetic protagonist in Reynolds Price's *A Long and Happy Life*.

**Hannah Bech**   Mother of Henry Bech; dies in a Riverdale nursing home in John Updike's *Bech: A Book*.

**Henry Bech**   Middle-aged Jewish writer from New York; experiences writer's block after publishing two novels, *Travel Light* and *The Chosen*, the novella *Brother Pig*, and two collections, *When the Saints* and *The Best of Bech*; his travels take him to Russia, Romania, Bulgaria, London, Martha's Vineyard, and Virginia in John Updike's *Bech: A Book*.

**Craig Beckerman**   Electrode implantation volunteer at Neuropsychiatric Research Unit in Michael Crichton's *The Terminal Man*.

**William Beckford**   Second cousin of the Cavaliere, twenty years old, stupendously rich, the author of a slim ironic book of imaginary biographies; homosexual; becomes a misanthropic recluse in his forties in Susan Sontag's *The Volcano Lover*.

**Bee Bedloe**   Mother of Claudia, Danny, and Ian and wife of Doug; unkempt, but believes every part of her life is wonderful; becomes disabled from arthritis in Anne Tyler's *Saint Maybe*.

**Danny Bedloe**   Middle child of Bee and Doug Bedloe and brother of Claudia and Ian; husband of Lucy Dean and father of Daphne; works at the post office; commits suicide after he hears that Lucy may be having an affair in Anne Tyler's *Saint Maybe*.

**Daphne Bedloe**   Daughter of Lucy Dean and Danny Bedloe; after her mother's death, is raised by her uncle, Ian; does not want to move out of the home that she occupies with Ian and her grandparents Dee and Doug in Anne Tyler's *Saint Maybe*.

**Doug Bedloe**   Father of Claudia, Danny, and Ian and husband of Bee; quiet high school baseball coach who retires and assists the neighbors with home repairs; helps take care of Agatha, Thomas, and Daphne in Anne Tyler's *Saint Maybe*.

**Ian Bedloe**   Youngest child of Bee and Doug Bedloe and brother of Claudia and Danny; feels responsible for Danny's suicide; finds guidance through The Church of the Second Chance, where he feels welcome; drops out of college at nineteen and becomes a carpenter; marries Rita DiCarlo in Anne Tyler's *Saint Maybe*.

**Claudia Bedloe-Daley**   Oldest child of Bee and Doug Bedloe and sister of Danny and Ian; wife of Macy Daley and mother of Abbie, Barney, Cindy, Davey, and Francis; dropped out of college her senior year to get married in Anne Tyler's *Saint Maybe*.

**Beulah Beecham**   See Beulah Beecham Renfro.

**Frances Beecham**   Forty-eight-year-old aunt of Martha Horgan; sister of Floyd Horgan; widow of Horace Beecham, at one time the wealthiest man in southern Vermont, whom she married when she was twenty-one and he was sixty-one; longtime lover of Steve Bell in Mary McGarry Morris's *A Dangerous Woman*.

**John Beecham**   Former enlisted Army trooper with history of violent acts; also known as Japheth Dury; suspected by Dr. Lazlo Kriezler of committing grisly New York City serial murders in Caleb Carr's *The Alienist*.

**Clara Beechum**   See Clara Beechum Pettit.

**Jack (Old Jack) Beechum**   Subsistence farmer and representative patriarch of Port William, Kentucky; overextending his farm to please his wife, Ruth Lightwood, he becomes estranged from her and has an affair with Rose McInnis; central presence whose thoughts organize Wendell Berry's *The Memory of Old Jack*; also appears in *Nathan Coulter* and *A Place on Earth*.

**Nancy Beechum**   See Nancy Beechum Feltner.

**Ruth Beechum**   See Ruth Lightwood.

**Old Man Beeler**   Retired pharmacist living with his daughter Sheryl Beeler in a Mott Street apartment managed by Norman Moonbloom in Edward Lewis Wallant's *The Tenants of Moonbloom*.

**Sheryl Beeler**   Daughter of Old Man Beeler; exchanges sexual favors with Norman Moonbloom for rent cuts in Edward Lewis Wallant's *The Tenants of Moonbloom*.

**Maria Befies**   Daughter of the designer of a black housing development and married lover of Bill Kelsey; dispatching black rivals, she proves the strength of white Juju in Hal Bennett's *Seventh Heaven*.

**Nawab Haider Beg**   The underling of the Mughal emperor Aurangzeb in Bharati Mukherjee's *The Holder of the World*.

**Edmond (Sordino) Behr-Bleibtreau**   Psychologist and hypnotist who disrupts a radio talk show hosted by Dick Gibson in Stanley Elkin's *The Dick Gibson Show*.

**Dr. Beineke**   Fantasy leader of an expedition with which Margaret Reynolds travels to the interior of the Amazon to study the primitive Itwo tribe in Anne Richardson Roiphe's *Up the Sandbox!*

**Bel**   See Isabel.

**Judy Belden**   See Jennie Denton.

**Angelica Bell**   Pretty five-year-old daughter of Vanessa Bell in Michael Cunningham's *The Hours*.

**Anita Bell**   Alcoholic wife of Steve Bell in Mary McGarry Morris's *A Dangerous Woman*.

**Clinton Harkavy Bell**   Advertising executive and father of David Bell; figures prominently in his son's extended flashback in Don DeLillo's *Americana*.

**David Bell**   New York television producer who travels west with friends to make a documentary about the Navaho but becomes obsessed with a zany film of his own creation; narrator of Don DeLillo's *Americana*.

**Diana Bell**   Older daughter of a prominent Newport family who is about to elope with Hilary Jones, a married man, until Theophilus North manages to halt them in Thornton Wilder's *Theophilus North*.

**Irene Bell**   Actress who leaves Willie Spearmint for Harry Lesser in Bernard Malamud's *The Tenants*.

**Jan Bell**   Oldest daughter of Steve Bell; recently divorced and moved back in with her parents in Mary McGarry Morris's *A Dangerous Woman*.

**John Bell**   Private, then sergeant, stationed in the Pacific; haunted by memories of his wife; receives news of his promotion to lieutenant the same day he learns of his wife's intention to leave him for another man in James Jones's *The Thin Red Line*.

**Julian Bell**   Grave, handsome fifteen-year-old son of Vanessa Bell; bluff, sturdy, and gracefully muscular in Michael Cunningham's *The Hours*.

**Margaret Bell**   Full professor of English at Moo University, the youngest full professor and most heavily recruited; African American; friends with Helen Levy and Timothy Monahan in Jane Smiley's *Moo*.

**Patsy Bell**   Youngest daughter of Steve Bell; recently divorced; a high-school French teacher in Hanover, New Hampshire, who has sublet her apartment and moved back in with her parents in Mary McGarry Morris's *A Dangerous Woman*.

**Quentin Bell**   Ruddy young son of Vanessa Bell in Michael Cunningham's *The Hours*.

**Steve Bell**   Husband of Anita Bell, longtime attorney and lover of Frances Beecham; always eager to smooth out any discord in Mary McGarry Morris's *A Dangerous Woman*.

**Vanessa Bell**   Loving sister of Virginia Woolf; voluptuous and spirited in Michael Cunningham's *The Hours*.

**Bella**   Dark-haired lesbian prostitute who enthusiastically tattoos and tortures Peter Leland in Fred Chappell's *Dagon*.

**Alice Bellantoni**   Daughter of Polina Bellantoni in Rita Mae Brown's *Rubyfruit Jungle*.

**Polina Bellantoni**   Columbia University professor, mother of Alice Bellantoni, and lover of Paul Digita and Molly Bolt in Rita Mae Brown's *Rubyfruit Jungle*.

**Celestine Bellegarde**   Raised politician Primus Mackenzie; has little regard for his wife in Paule Marshall's *Daughters*.

**La Belle Isold**   Lover of Tristram; dies when his body is found in Thomas Berger's *Arthur Rex*.

**Bellerophon**   King of Lycia and slayer of the Chimera; must leave his city and assume an artificial identity in the *Bellerophoniad*, a novella in John Barth's *Chimera*.

**Amy (Anne Frank) Bellette**   Librarian and former student of E. I. Lonoff; wants Lonoff to leave his wife and live with her in Italy; imagined by Nathan Zuckerman to be Anne Frank in Philip Roth's *The Ghost Writer*.

**Mildred Belloussovsky-Dommergues**   Often-married writer seated next to Henry Bech at his induction ceremony in John Updike's *Bech: A Book*.

**Esther Leonie Beloff**   Sensual daughter of the Reverend Marian Miles Beloff and the object of religious leader Nathan Vickery's tormented sexual attraction in Joyce Carol Oates's *Son of the Morning*.

**Reverend Marian Miles Beloff**   Exploitative, materialistic religious leader who employs the young Nathan Vickery in his ministry; father of Leonie Beloff in Joyce Carol Oates's *Son of the Morning*.

**Beloved**   Sethe's dead baby; returns eighteen years after her death and exhibits characteristics of a young child; occupies all of Sethe's time and energy; forces Paul D out of the house and seduces him; is exorcised by the women in the community in Toni Morrison's *Beloved*.

**Blessed Belshazzar**    Escaped rapist, leader of the sect of the Blessed Belshazzar, and father of Birchie Bartley in Hal Bennett's *A Wilderness of Vines*.

**Belt (Alonzo Fiber)**    Master of the dojo at the Sun N Fun motel in Florida in Harry Crews's *Karate Is a Thing of the Spirit*.

**Bill Belton**    Local pilot and neighbor to Spence and Lila Culpepper; expands Spence's horizons by planting marijuana in his cornfields and by taking Spence into his plane to fly over Spence's farm in Bobbie Ann Mason's *Spence and Lila*.

**Lina Beltrán**    Mother of Rafael; is sick and self-centered; monopolizes her son's time and does not like his teaching her cook how to read; enjoys being doted on in Sandra Benítez's *A Place Where the Sea Remembers*.

**Rafael Beltrán**    Forty-one-year-old schoolteacher; son of Lina, with whom he has lunch every day; teaches his mother's cook how to read; falls in love with and marries Esperanza Clemente in Sandra Benítez's *A Place Where the Sea Remembers*.

**Luther (Lute) Bemis**    Former partner of Jud Clasby; convicted and hanged for his part in the Indian massacre in Jessamyn West's *The Massacre at Fall Creek*.

**Ora (Ory) Bemis**    Wife of Luther Bemis in Jessamyn West's *The Massacre at Fall Creek*.

**Karl Bemish**    Amiable sixty-five-year-old operator of Franks, a birch beer stand outside of Haddam, New Jersey; runs a tight ship and enjoys offering advice to Frank Bascombe in Richard Ford's *Independence Day*.

**Ben**    First husband of Deirdre in Bette Pesetky's *Midnight Sweets*.

**Ben**    Financier; European Jewish immigrant to the United States; Harvard educated; formerly married to Rachel, who divorced him; falls in love with Veronique Decaze, a married French woman who is the cousin of his best friend Jack; communicates his ambiguity about marrying her to Veronique; rejected by her, he commits suicide in Louis Begley's *The Man Who Was Late*.

**Ben Benally**    Friend and roommate of Abel in N. Scott Momaday's *House Made of Dawn*.

**Cassie Bender**    Much married and divorced art dealer; has affairs with painters in her shows; once lover of Major Wedburn in Dawn Powell's *The Golden Spur*.

**George James Bender**    Excellent wrestler who injures his knee as a sophomore at Iowa State and fails to win the Big Eight championship; beaten by Willard Buzzard because Edith Winter tries to seduce and humble Bender in John Irving's *The 158-Pound Marriage*.

**Alan Benedict**    Doctor in Piedmont, Arizona, who opens the Scoop VII satellite and unleashes the Andromeda Strain in Michael Crichton's *The Andromeda Strain*.

**Benjamin**    See Benjamin Eliezer.

**Owen Benjamin**    Married to Rose; father of Philip; director of admissions at private boys' school; hidden homosexual whose only outlet is pornographic movies; eventually reveals self to wife and gay son in David Leavitt's *The Lost Language of Cranes*.

**Philip Benjamin**    Son of Rose and Owen; edits romance novels; unsophisticated homosexual; falls in love with Eliot Abrams; later becomes lover of former college friend Brad Robinson; sympathetic when father reveals hidden homosexuality; becomes Brad's lover in David Leavitt's *The Lost Language of Cranes*.

**Rose Benjamin**    Married to Owen; mother of Philip; copy editor; comfortable marriage without passion leads to five-year affair with coworker; shocked by son's revelation of homosexuality; realizes before husband tells her he is hidden homosexual in David Leavitt's *The Lost Language of Cranes*.

**Martin Benn**    Retired journalist; friend of Carlos Rueda; skeptic and realist; finds it difficult to believe in Carlos's gift of vision; narrates Carlos's story in Lawrence Thornton's *Imagining Argentina*.

**Peaches Benner (or Benez)**    Young neglected daughter of a prostitute in Maureen Howard's *Natural History*.

**Cuthbert (Couth) Bennett**    Friend of Fred Trumper; catches a venereal disease from Elsbeth Malkas; caretaker at the Pillsbury Estate, who eventually marries Sue Kunft Trumper and cares for Colm Trumper in John Irving's *The Water-Method Man*.

**F. W. Bennett**    Industrialist and a patron to Warren Penfield whose house on Loon Lake brings Warren, Joe Patterson, and Clara Lukaks together and who remains an ambiguous symbol of glory and greed in E. L. Doctorow's *Loon Lake*.

**George Bennett**    Former army buddy of Jack Sellars; persuades Jack and Bebe Sellars to manage his property at Pickerel Beach in Doris Betts's *The River to Pickle Beach*.

**Lucinda Bailey Bennett**    Wife of F. W. Bennett and lover of Warren Penfield; she is a celebrated aviatrix but crashes into the ocean with Penfield after they have planned to fly away together in E. L. Doctorow's *Loon Lake*.

**Sue Kunft Trumper (Biggie) Bennett**    Mother, by her husband Fred Trumper, of Colin Trumper; divorces Trumper and marries Cuthbert Bennett in John Irving's *The Water-Method Man*.

**George Benson** Murderer of Folded Leaf; convicted and hanged in Jessamyn West's *The Massacre at Fall Creek*.

**Harold Franklin (Harry) Benson** Computer scientist upon whom the stage-three operation is performed in Michael Crichton's *The Terminal Man*.

**Steven (Chuckie, Dandy, Steve, Stevie) Benson** Narrator and central character in Ed Bullins's *The Reluctant Rapist*.

**Walter Arlis Benson** See Walter Boyle.

**Elkanah Bent** Officer in the Union Army; has a grudge against Orry Main and George Hazard that reaches back to their days together at West Point and will do anything to exact his revenge in John Jakes's *Love and War*.

**R. B. "Arby" Benton** Short, eleven-year-old African-American seventh-grader and computer genius; best friend of Kelly Curtis; student assistant of Richard Levine; stowaway onboard RV laboratory trailer destined for dinosaur-infested Costa Rican jungle in Michael Crichton's *The Lost World*.

**Sheila Benton** Health and beauty editor for *Vogue* magazine who is obsessed by her passion for Ambrose Clay in Gail Godwin's *Violet Clay*.

**Billy Bentson** Small-time Dallas gambler and friend of Mabry Jenkins; reaches the big time by taking Junior Everett for several hundred thousand dollars in Peter Gent's *Texas Celebrity Turkey Trot*.

**Dr. (Doc) Benway** See Volume I.

**Berbelang** Leader of the Third World group that returns art from Western museums to its true owners; killed by Biff Musclewhite in Ishmael Reed's *Mumbo Jumbo*.

**Mack Berg** Volunteer in an American battalion in the Spanish civil war; killed and mutilated in the loyalists' efforts to raise the siege of Madrid in William Herrick's *Hermanos!*

**Miriam Berg** See Miriam Berg Stone.

**Theodore (Teddy) Berg** Famous American composer in Alison Lurie's *Real People*.

**P. O. Bergdahl** Mysterious character; possibly the father of O. P. Dahlberg or possibly Dahlberg himself in Wright Morris's *The Fork River Space Project*.

**Tyrone C. Berger** Psychiatrist who counsels Conrad Jarrett after Conrad's suicide attempt in Judith Guest's *Ordinary People*.

**Hogo (Roy) de Bergerac** Loathsome troublemaker and antiprince in Donald Barthelme's *Snow White*.

**Vinny Bergerac** See Volume I.

**Vitus Bering** Unassuming but decisive Danish sea captain of several expeditions commissioned by Tsar Peter Romanoff in the waters east of Siberia; one of the first Russian explorers to reach Alaska in James Michener's *Alaska*.

**Lightning Berlew** Hired hand of Mat Feltner and husband of Sylvania Berlew; alienated from the land in Wendell Berry's *The Memory of Old Jack*.

**Sylvania (Smoothbore) Berlew** Wife of Lightning Berlew in Wendell Berry's *The Memory of Old Jack*.

**Paul Berlin** Army infantry specialist stationed in Vietnam; compelled to imagine the diverse realities of the war in Tim O'Brien's *Going After Cacciato*.

**Benjamin Samson (Ben) Berman** Jewish father of Samuel Paul Berman; retired cabdriver and former radio actor in Jay Neugeboren's *Sam's Legacy*.

**Morrie Berman** Former pimp, gambler, and backer of Billy Phelan's bowling and pool games; involved in Charlie Boy McCall's kidnapping in William Kennedy's *Billy Phelan's Greatest Game*.

**Otto "Abbadabba" Berman** Right-hand man and accountant to Dutch Schultz who shows particular favor to Billy Bathgate in E. L. Doctorow's *Billy Bathgate*.

**Samuel Paul (Sam) Berman** Son of Benjamin Samson Berman, professional gambler, and lover of Stella; moves to California to escape paying gambling debts in Jay Neugeboren's *Sam's Legacy*.

**Bernard** Student who serves on the Cinema Committee with Hill Gallagher during the student rebellion in James Jones's *The Merry Month of May*.

**Jesse (Jess) Bernarr** Active telepath who joins the Pattern, a vast network of mental links in Octavia E. Butler's *Mind of My Mind*.

**Mark Berquist** Former senior foreign policy aide; becomes a senator unwilling to admit any knowledge of the cold war intrigue that led to the death of Elena McMahon in Joan Didion's *The Last Thing He Wanted*.

**Bob Berry** Grandfather of the Berry children; an aging wrestling coach and confidante to his grandson, John Berry in John Irving's *The Hotel New Hampshire*.

**Egg Berry** Youngest child in the Berry family; dies in a plane accident when the Berry family flies from the United States to Vienna in John Irving's *The Hotel New Hampshire*.

**Frank Berry** Oldest child of the Berry family; a closeted homosexual who leads his siblings with a quiet authority in John Irving's *The Hotel New Hampshire*.

**Franny Berry**   Oldest daughter in the Berry family; devoted sister and best friend of John Berry in John Irving's *The Hotel New Hampshire.*

**John Berry**   Pathologist and narrator; former law student and military policeman (MP); husband of Judith and good friend of Dr. Arthur Lee; investigates the murder charges against Dr. Lee in Jeffery Hudson's *A Case of Need.*

**John Berry**   Narrator who details the wild experiences of his family as they live in the United States and abroad in John Irving's *The Hotel New Hampshire.*

**Lilly Berry**   Youngest daughter in the Berry family; possesses a talent for writing and publishes a best-seller before her suicide in John Irving's *The Hotel New Hampshire.*

**Mary Berry**   Matriarch of the Berry family; is killed with her youngest son, Egg, in a plane accident that occurs while the family is flying from the United States to Vienna in John Irving's *The Hotel New Hampshire.*

**Win Berry**   Patriarch of the Berry family; rears his children in Vienna after his wife and son's deaths in John Irving's *The Hotel New Hampshire.*

**Big Bertha**   Black cook on the wandering island in John Hawkes's *Second Skin.*

**Bertilia (Bert)**   Daughter of Suzanne Winograd, who behaves more maturely than her mother in Mark Harris's *It Looked Like For Ever.*

**Solange Bertrand (Walker)**   Beautiful Frenchwoman living in France during the German occupation of World War II; loving mother of three children; wife of Sam Walker in Danielle Steel's *Kaleidoscope.*

**Aunt Bess (Bessie)**   Wife of Uncle Clyde; boards Dandy Benson at her Maryland farm during summers in his boyhood in Ed Bullins's *The Reluctant Rapist.*

**Bessy Mae**   Sister of Teddy, who steals Bessy Mae's ADC check to support his heroin addiction in Donald Goines's *Dopefiend.*

**Jack Best**   Publicist who attempts to blackmail Gordon Walker and Lee (LuAnne) Verger with a compromising photo in Robert Stone's *Children of Light.*

**Samuel Bester**   Chairman of the language arts department at Calvin Coolidge High School; observes teachers and leaves extensive memos; believes all students should read Charles Dickens and Shakespeare in Bel Kaufman's *Up the Down Staircase.*

**Wilfrid (Wilf) Bestudik**   Dimwitted priest, rector of St. Clement's Hill Retreat House, and superior of Father Urban in J. F. Powers's *Morte D'Urban.*

**Brother Bethune**   Baptist minister at the Beecham family reunion in Eudora Welty's *Losing Battles.*

**Betonie**   The old Dine (Navajo) medicine man who guides Tayo through the ceremony that sets into motion his quest for the cattle and healing in Leslie Marmon Silko's *Ceremony.*

**Betsy**   Slave owned by Ellen Ashe and sold after Edward Ashe falls in love with her; Edward finds Betsy and their child and moves with them to Canada in Jesse Hill Ford's *The Raider.*

**Betsy**   Wholesome friend of Esther Greenwood and her fellow guest editor at a New York fashion magazine; she and Esther suffer ptomaine poisoning at a *Ladies' Day* magazine banquet in Sylvia Plath's *The Bell Jar.*

**Betty**   Window designer for Saks who does layouts for Renate's planned magazine in Anaïs Nin's *Collages.*

**Betty**   Owner and operator of a dive called The Melody Coast, where the unnamed male narrator becomes a regular in Darryl Pinckney's *High Cotton.*

**Lillian Beye**   See Volume I.

**Bhagmati**   Born with the name of Bindu Bashini into a Hindu merchant family; works for Henry Hedges, and he falls in love with her; after he dies, she becomes a serving girl for Hannah in Fort St. Sebastian; accompanies Hannah on her journeys and dies in the battle between Emperor Aurangdev and Jadav Singh; is buried under the name Hester Hedges in Bharati Mukherjee's *The Holder of the World.*

**Bella Biaggi**   See Bella Biaggi Dehn.

**William (Billy, Club) Bibbit**   Stuttering, mother-dominated mental patient who slits his throat in response to the domination of Big Nurse in Ken Kesey's *One Flew Over the Cuckoo's Nest.*

**Lila Chand Bibi**   Name assumed by Arista Prolo on tour in Tokyo in Carlene Hatcher Polite's *Sister X and the Victims of Foul Play.*

**B. A. Bibokov**   Investigating magistrate for Cases of Extraordinary Importance; tries to help clear Yakov Bok of murder charges in Bernard Malamud's *The Fixer.*

**Fanny Bick**   Young woman who has an intense affair with the much older William Dubin in Bernard Malamud's *Dubin's Lives.*

**Harry Bidwell**   Grandfather of Pinky; stalks a Fifth Avenue apartment dressed for business when there is no business to go to in the 1930s; reads British murder mysteries in Maureen Howard's *Expensive Habits.*

**Mrs. Bidwell**   Grandmother of Pinky; of missionary descent; as sweet and cold as the Schrafft's lemon sherbet she invariably serves with one cream wafer for dessert in Maureen Howard's *Expensive Habits*.

**Dr. Zbigniew (Papa) Bieganska**   Polish professor, author of an anti-Semitic pamphlet, and father of Sophie Zawistowska; executed by the Nazis in William Styron's *Sophie's Choice*.

**Daddy Big**   Cousin of Bindy McCall; former gambler and pool hustler; jailed for two years for a crime he did not commit; assisted by Billy Phelan in William Kennedy's *Billy Phelan's Greatest Game*.

**Big Laura**   Leader of a group of ex-slaves heading north after the Civil War; killed while defending them from vengeful whites in Ernest J. Gaines's *The Autobiography of Miss Jane Pittman*.

**Big Lot**   Young man who spends the night with Charlie and causes the breakup in the relationship between Charlie and the male narrator of Tennessee Williams's *Moise and the World of Reason*.

**Big Nurse**   See Nurse Ratched.

**Big Sally**   Black woman who drives a Mercedes and talks of her oppression in Ishmael Reed's *The Last Days of Louisiana Red*.

**Big Tub**   Leader of the Rastas in Mark Helprin's *Refiner's Fire*.

**Nancy Bigears**   Native Tlingit Indian; daughter of Sam Bigears; has brief affair with Tom Venn; after a few weeks at the university in Seattle returns to Alaska to defend native rights; marries Chinese immigrant Ah Ting; has daughter Tammy Bigears Ting in James Michener's *Alaska*.

**Sam Bigears**   Native Tlingit; loses land and fishing rights to cannery near Juneau; passionate defender of native rights; father of Nancy Bigears in James Michener's *Alaska*.

**Chester Biggs**   Trainer and handler of Victoria Regina, a miniature schnauzer stolen in Joseph Wambaugh's *The Black Marble*.

**Theresa (Theresa Haug) Bigoness**   Coworker of Martha Reganhart; becomes pregnant by a man other than her husband, passes herself off as single, bears a daughter, gives the child up for adoption, and returns to her harsh marriage in Philip Roth's *Letting Go*.

**Bill**   Reporter for *Field and Stream* and lover of Lisa in Anaïs Nin's *Collages*.

**Bill**   Leader of the seven impotent capitalists who live with Snow White, wash windows, and make Chinese baby food; hanged for throwing two six-packs of beer through a windshield in Donald Barthelme's *Snow White*.

**M. A. (Medium Asshole) Bill**   Personnel director for Pure Pores Filters Company; goes on the Alaskan hunting expedition in Norman Mailer's *Why Are We in Vietnam?*

**Miss Billie**   Friend of Marie Canada and mother of Charlotte; gives a wooden bracelet to Eva Medina Canada in Gayl Jones's *Eva's Man*.

**George Billings**   Former astronaut who serves as Jace Everett's troubleshooter; hires Mabry Jenkins to work for Everett's radio station but fires him when the ratings slip in Peter Gent's *Texas Celebrity Turkey Trot*.

**Roe Billins**   College roommate of Jerry Payne; spring house-party date of Nancy Putnam in John Nichols's *The Sterile Cuckoo*.

**Billy**   Vietnam veteran who is impatient with passive Civil Rights–era methods of the Reverend Phillip Martin in Ernest J. Gaines's *In My Father's House*.

**Billy**   Retarded and abandoned sweeper of a pool hall who is employed and protected by Sam the Lion; butt of practical jokes; killed by a truck while sweeping the streets in Larry McMurtry's *The Last Picture Show*.

**Uncle Billy**   Belly-bumping champion whom Skipper defeats and from whom Skipper receives the crucifix he later gives to Catalina Kate in John Hawkes's *Second Skin*.

**Lucius Binford**   See Volume I.

**Craig Binky**   Unintelligent and unintelligible but extremely rich owner of *The Ghost* newspaper, competitor of Harry Penn's *The Sun* in Mark Helprin's *Winter's Tale*.

**Marcie Binnendale**   See Marcie Birmendale Nash.

**Beansy Binz**   Young left-handed pitcher who replaces Henry Wiggen on the New York Mammoths in Mark Harris's *It Looked Like For Ever*.

**Jimmy Biondo**   Gangster who threatens to kill Legs Diamond in William Kennedy's *Legs*.

**Constance Birch**   Moves from Ohio to Greenwich Village in 1927; secretary and typist for artists and writers; becomes pregnant; returns to Ohio and marries Johnathan Jaimison in Dawn Powell's *The Golden Spur*.

**Marilyn Birchfield**   Kindhearted social worker who tries to befriend Sol Nazerman in Edward Lewis Wallant's *The Pawnbroker*.

**Birdie**   Birdy's canary persona in his fantasy bird life in William Wharton's *Birdy*.

**Bisch**   Prison cellmate of Leo Feldman; tailor who creates Feldman's fool suit in Stanley Elkin's *A Bad Man*.

**Mary Frances Bishop**   Daughter of Eliza and Mr. Bishop; she dies of dysentery after Eliza flees her abusive husband and leaves her, with the idea that she will go back to get her in the care of others in Frances Sherwood's *Vindication*.

**Mr. Bishop**   Husband of Eliza Bishop and father of Mary Frances Bishop; beats Eliza until she leaves him in Frances Sherwood's *Vindication*.

**Leota B. Bisland**   Sixth-grade classmate and first lover of Molly Bolt in Rita Mae Brown's *Rubyfruit Jungle*.

**(Extra) Billy Bitters**   Mary's beau and later husband; has a bad reputation in Runnymeade and is thought of as "white trash"; handsome; fights in World War II in Rita Mae Brown's *Six of One* and *Loose Lips*.

**Jimmy Bivens**   White grocer beaten by Sonny Boy Mosby; his death convinces the town of Somerton that blacks have set out to kill all the white people in Jesse Hill Ford's *The Liberation of Lord Byron Jones*.

**B. J.**   Character addressed by William Lee in William S. Burroughs's *The Ticket That Exploded;* consultant to the CIA on the fate of the British monarchy in *Exterminator!*

**Angela (Doris Blankfurt) Black**   Stripper killed by Harold Benson in Michael Crichton's *The Terminal Man*.

**Captain Black**   Squadron intelligence officer who spearheads the Glorious Loyalty Oath Campaign in Joseph Heller's *Catch-22*.

**Harry Black**   Machinist, union shop steward, and strike leader who resents the sexual demands of his wife and who, despite his apparent total masculinity, becomes intrigued by, then infatuated with, and later scorned by a series of male homosexuals and transvestites; ultimately sexually molests a ten-year-old boy and is beaten by a mob in Hubert Selby, Jr.,'s *Last Exit to Brooklyn*.

**Iris Black**   Beautiful sister of Ivor Black and first wife of Vadim Vadimovich; killed by a crazed lover in front of her brother and husband, who claims that Iris and his unnamed fourth wife were the only women he truly loved in Vladimir Nabokov's *Look at the Harlequins!*

**Ivor Black**   Brother of Iris Black and Cambridge friend of Vadim Vadimovich, whom he offhandedly invites to his Riviera villa, where Vadim meets Iris in Vladimir Nabokov's *Look at the Harlequins!*

**James (J. B.) Black**   Community storyteller who takes pride in his African roots in George Cain's *Blueschild Baby*.

**Willis B. Black**   See Black Will.

**Black Antler**   Seneca Indian and follower of a Seneca prophet in Jessamyn West's *The Massacre at Fall Creek*.

**Black Cat**   Guitar player who plays while Ideal, as a little girl, is implored to dance on a big brass bed in Carlene Hatcher Polite's *The Flagellants*.

**Black Herman**   Noted occultist in Ishmael Reed's *Mumbo Jumbo*.

**Captain Abraham Blackman**   Black career soldier cut down by snipers in Vietnam; in delirium, imagines he participates in outstanding moments of black military history, from the Battle of Bunker Hill in the American Revolution to the Abraham Lincoln Brigade in the Spanish Civil War, in John A. Williams's *Captain Blackman*.

**Black One**   Six-year-old narrator who, beginning in 1939, wanders throughout eastern Europe and experiences the cruelty and barbarity of those who shun him in Jerzy Kosinski's *The Painted Bird*.

**Garrett Roger Blackstone**   Unemployed man with twenty-six years' experience in the paper industry; has a wife and four sons; Burke Devore decides not to kill him when he finds out that Garrett has already been hired at a paper company in Donald E. Westlake's *The Ax*.

**Alexandra Blackwell**   Very attractive, pleasant woman who half-heartedly inherits a family fortune and business; people pleaser; twin sister of Eve Blackwell in Sidney Sheldon's *Master of the Game*.

**David Blackwell**   American from Oregon who works his way up to the head of an international conglomerate in South Africa and marries into it; husband of Kate Blackwell in Sidney Sheldon's *Master of the Game*.

**Eve Blackwell**   Very attractive, conniving woman who spends her life trying to make the world hers and finds only suffering; twin sister of Alexandra Blackwell in Sidney Sheldon's *Master of the Game*.

**Kate Blackwell**   Strong, successful, beautiful woman who parlays her inheritance into an international conglomerate; grateful daughter, manipulative wife, mother, grandmother and great-grandmother; daughter of Jamie McGregor in Sidney Sheldon's *Master of the Game*.

**Tony Blackwell**   Artistic dreamer who goes insane after not being aloud to follow his lifelong dream of being a painter; son of Kate Blackwell in Sidney Sheldon's *Master of the Game*.

**Black Will (Willis B. Black)**   Well traveled African American and confidant of Abyssinia in Carlene Hatcher Polite's *Sister X and the Victims of Foul Play*.

**Charles Blackwood**   Brother of Julian Blackwood and cousin of Constance and Mary Katherine Blackwood; enters the Blackwood home to secure the family fortune for himself and brings about the destruction of house and family in Shirley Jackson's *We Have Always Lived in the Castle*.

**Constance Blackwood**   Older sister of Mary Katherine Blackwood and nominal head of the household; accused but acquitted of the Blackwood family poisoning; never leaves the house and grounds because she is feared and hated in the village in Shirley Jackson's *We Have Always Lived in the Castle*.

**Julian Blackwood**   Elderly invalid uncle of Constance and Mary Katherine Blackwood; sole survivor of the Blackwood family poisoning, about which he is writing a book in Shirley Jackson's *We Have Always Lived in the Castle.*

**Mary Katherine (Merricat) Blackwood**   Reclusive, psychotic eighteen-year-old who lives in the family manse with her older sister, Constance Blackwood, and her uncle, Julian Blackwood; as a child, poisoned most of her family in Shirley Jackson's *We Have Always Lived in the Castle.*

**Harlow Blade, Jr.**   Teenage author of a book on masturbation, which he delivers to the narrator's library in Richard Brautigan's *The Abortion.*

**Anna Ivanovna (Annette) Blagovo**   Typist for Vadim Vadimovich; becomes his second wife and the mother of their daughter, Isabel; leaves Vadim under the influence of Ninel Langley, with whom she drowns in floods resulting from a hurricane in Vladimir Nabokov's *Look at the Harlequins!*

**Blair**   High school girlfriend of Clay who enjoys life in Los Angeles and wants Clay to remain on the West Coast, though he intends to attend college in New Hampshire in Bret Easton Ellis's *Less Than Zero.*

**Blake**   Beigh Masters's lover during her freshman year in Bharati Mukherjee's *The Holder of the World.*

**Alice Blake**   Student at Calvin Coolidge High School who throws herself out of a window because of her unreturned love for English teacher Paul Barringer, whose response to her love letter was to correct it grammatically in Bel Kaufman's *Up the Down Staircase.*

**Blacky Blake**   Forest ranger who supervises and befriends Glacier District lookouts Jarry Wagner and Jack Duluoz in Jack Kerouac's *Desolation Angels.*

**Catherine Blake**   Wife of William Blake; has a ménage à trois with William and Mary in Frances Sherwood's *Vindication.*

**Hagar Weylin Blake**   Great-grandmother of Dana Franklin in Octavia E. Butler's *Kindred.*

**Ron Blake**   Teenage beatnik and singer; admirer of Evelyn Pomeray and companion of Jack Duluoz during a retreat to a remote cabin in Jack Kerouac's *Big Sur.*

**William Blake**   Thursday-night dinner guest of Joseph Johnson; has a ménage à trois with Catherine and Mary in Frances Sherwood's *Vindication.*

**Bobby Blanchard**   Mary and Virgil's son; the county sheriff and a sensitive and caring man who falls in love with Jewell Coleman in Larry Brown's *Father and Son.*

**Mary Blanchard**   Virgil's lover before he goes off to fight in World War II; she marries another man while pregnant with

Virgil's child; later she becomes a teacher and successfully raises her son in Larry Brown's *Father and Son.*

**Rita Blanchard**   Paramour of Walter Knight and onetime owner of a ranch coveted by Joe Templeton in Joan Didion's *Run River.*

**Blanche**   Prostitute with Jake Jackson when he is robbed by a pickpocket in Richard Wright's *Lawd Today.*

**Alexander Blaney**   Homosexual man killed accidentally by Los Angeles policeman Sam Niles in Joseph Wambaugh's *The Choirboys.*

**Mrs. Blankenship**   Wife of the mill owner in Hopewell, Kentucky; after James and Christianna Wheeler's quintuplets die, Mrs. Blankenship helps arrange for the Wheelers' to tour with the remains of the quints in Bobbie Ann Mason's *Feather Crowns.*

**Doris Blankfurt**   See Angela Black.

**Bernice Blau**   Museum curator Jack Flood consults about the fan Yin-Li sends him; a virginal thirty-five; not noticeably pretty except when she is aroused by the fan in Maureen Howard's *Expensive Habits.*

**Deborah (Deb) Blau**   Mentally ill teenage Jewish heroine committed to a mental hospital in Hannah Green's *I Never Promised You a Rose Garden.*

**Esther Blau**   Distraught, yet strong mother of Deborah Blau; has to fight herself and her family to help her daughter by committing her to a mental hospital in Hannah Green's *I Never Promised You a Rose Garden.*

**Jacob Blau**   Accountant whose family emigrated from Poland; father of Deborah Blau; feels the pressures of guilt, failure, and love in Hannah Green's *I Never Promised You a Rose Garden.*

**Susan (Suzy) Blau**   Younger sister of Deborah Blau; has to live in the shadow of a sister who is not present in Hannah Green's *I Never Promised You a Rose Garden.*

**Jerry Bledsoe**   Sawyer's and Sloat's electrician and handyman; electrocuted in Stephen King's and Peter Straub's *The Talisman.*

**Queen Blenda**   Mother of Charles Xavier, the last king of Zembla; erects a tasteless monument on the site of her husband's death in Vladimir Nabokov's *Pale Fire.*

**Shenandoah Blessing**   Army lieutenant and friend of Sean O'Sullivan; heads police services in Rombaden in post–World War II Germany in Leon Uris's *Armageddon.*

**Deni Bleu**   Seaman and friend of Jack Duluoz in New York in Jack Kerouac's *Visions of Cody;* also appears in *Book of Dreams* and *Desolation Angels.*

**Jimmy Blevins**   Young boy whom John Grady Cole and Lacey Rawlins encounter while traveling to Mexico. He fears God will take his life during a rain storm, and during one such storm he loses his horse, which he steals from the person who recovered it. Blevins is eventually killed after being tortured by the police captain in Cormac McCarthy's *All the Pretty Horses*.

**Captain Dominus Blicero**   See Lieutenant Weissmann.

**Bliss**   Native of Gaia who joins Golan Trevize and Janov Pelorat in order to teach them about Gaia, is suspected by Trevize of being a robot; paramour of Pelorat in Isaac Asimov's *Foundation's Edge*.

**Bliss**   Boyhood name of Senator Adam Sunraider in Ralph Ellison's *Juneteenth*.

**Dorothy Bliss**   Elderly Jewish widow who lives in the Towers condominium complex in Miami, Florida; mother of Ellen, Marvin, and Frank in *Mrs. Ted Bliss*, by Stanley Elkin.

**Ellen Bliss**   Dorothy Bliss's daughter-in-law; widow of Marvin Bliss; health food fanatic and shoe salesperson; marries Milton Yellin in *Mrs. Ted Bliss*, by Stanley Elkin.

**Frank Bliss**   Dorothy Bliss's son; sociology professor; doesn't like Manny Tressler helping Mrs. Bliss; lives in Pittsburgh, and later in Providence in *Mrs. Ted Bliss*, by Stanley Elkin.

**Marvin Bliss**   Dorothy Bliss's deceased son; dies in his thirties of leukemia in *Mrs. Ted Bliss*, by Stanley Elkin.

**Maxine Bliss**   Dorothy Bliss's daughter; lives in Cincinnati in *Mrs. Ted Bliss*, by Stanley Elkin.

**Ted Bliss**   Deceased husband of Dorothy; dies in his early seventies of cancer and is returned to Chicago to be buried; was a butcher and sold meat on the black market during World War II in *Mrs. Ted Bliss*, by Stanley Elkin.

**Karen Blixen**   Famous writer whom the Allstons meet on their journey to Denmark; introduces the possibility that Joe Allston's peasant mother may have immigrated to America to escape the sexual advances of Astrid's father, an experimenter in genetic purity in Wallace Stegner's *The Spectator Bird*.

**Shifrah Puah Bloch**   Polish concentration camp survivor and mother of Masha Tortshiner in Isaac Bashevis Singer's *Enemies, A Love Story*.

**Dr. Jules Blomburg**   First of John Wilder's psychiatrists; Wilder calls him a dead-silent bullshit artist in Richard Yates's *Disturbing the Peace*.

**Fanny Blood**   Friend of Mary Wollstonecraft since childhood; quick with numbers; marries Hugh Skeys and moves to Portugal; dies a few months after she miscarries in Frances Sherwood's *Vindication*.

**Jewell Blood**   Mother of Loyal, Marvin (Dub), and Mernelle Blood and wife of Mink Blood; sells the farm after Mink's death;

learns how to drive; makes money by working for a vegetable canning company and knitting for a ski shop; while on a drive, dies of an aneurysm, although her body is never found; wedding ring is buried in her place in E. Annie Proulx's *Postcards*.

**Loyal Blood**   Oldest child of Mink and Jewell Blood and brother of Marvin (Dub) and Mernelle Blood; kills his girlfriend, Billy Handy, then tries to cover up his murder by moving away; keeps a journal and sends postcards to his family; becomes a uranium prospector; is almost blinded in one eye by a splinter, and in the hospital meets Bullet Wulff; becomes a fossil hunter with Wulff; buys a farm in North Dakota and raises beans, but the farm burns down; traps coyotes for their pelts; as an old man, reflects on his itinerant life and collects hats in E. Annie Proulx's *Postcards*.

**Marvin (Dub) Blood**   Son of Mink and Jewell Blood and brother of Loyal and Mernelle Blood; lost an arm in a train accident; dates Myrtle, who leaves him; burns his father's barn at his father's request and goes to jail for a year; moves to Miami and initially makes his money by swindling people through a bogus letter written from a Mexican jail; becomes a realtor, then meets and marries Pala Suarez in E. Annie Proulx's *Postcards*.

**Mernelle Blood**   Daughter of Mink and Jewell Blood and sister of Loyal and Marvin (Dub) Blood; as a child, has pen pals and enjoys receiving mail; answers an advertisement in the newspaper for a wife from Ray MacWay; marries Ray; visits her mother often and takes care of her in E. Annie Proulx's *Postcards*.

**Minkton (Mink) Blood**   Father of Loyal, Marvin (Dub), and Mernelle and husband of Jewell Blood; has arthritis, but works hard on the dairy farm; asks Dub to burn their barn for the insurance money; the arson is found out and he goes to jail for two years; hangs himself in his cell in E. Annie Proulx's *Postcards*.

**Arlington Bloodworth, Sr.**   Plantation and slave owner who adopts and rears Pourty Bloodworth in Leon Forrest's *The Bloodworth Orphans*.

**Arlington Bloodworth III**   Father, by Rachel Rebecca Carpenter Flowers, of Industrious Bowman and Carl-Rae Bowman in Leon Forrest's *The Bloodworth Orphans*.

**Pourty Ford Worthy Bloodworth y Bloodworth**   Foundling reared by Arlington Bloodworth, Sr.; father of LaDonna Scales, Regal Pettibone, Amos Otis Thigpen, Noah Grandberry, and Jonathan Bass; kills his foster father in Leon Forrest's *The Bloodworth Orphans*.

**Anatole Bloomberg**   Tackle for the Logos College football team and philosophizing roommate of Gary Harkness in Don DeLillo's *End Zone*.

**Harold Bloomguard**   Los Angeles policeman and organizer of off-duty meetings in MacArthur Park; one of ten protagonists in Joseph Wambaugh's *The Choirboys*.

**Billy Blue**   Gangster who attempts to assassinate Legs Diamond and is eventually killed by Diamond in William Kennedy's *Legs*.

**Blue Fairy Godmother**   See Frank Wirtanen.

**Mr. Blue**   Short, aging aluminum siding salesman who befriends Frederick Exley in the apartment of the Counselor and recruits him to work as his canvasser; talks incessantly about oral sex; dominated by his common-law wife, Deborah, he is a pathetic figure of frustration and missed opportunities in Frederick Exley's *A Fan's Notes.*

**Blue Jack**   Only supportive figure in Cholly's life; taught him about history, life, and family in Toni Morrison's *The Bluest Eye.*

**Blue Juice**   Pimp who assaults Jake Jackson after Jackson accuses the prostitute Blanche of picking his pocket in Richard Wright's *Lawd Today.*

**Blue Prairie Woman**   Nineteenth-century Ojibway woman whose infant daughter is carried away on the back of a dog during a U.S. Cavalry raid; grandmother of Zosie and Mary Shawano in Louise Erdrich's *The Antelope Wife.*

**Freddy Blum**   Randy resident of Emma Lazarus Retirement Home; believed by Mandy Dattner to be the father of her unborn child in Alan Isler's *The Prince of West End Avenue.*

**Monroe Blumenfeld**   First child to have his bar mitzvah in the temple David Dehn builds; announces at his bar mitzvah that as an adult he will live in Israel in Jerome Weidman's *The Temple.*

**Sarah Blumenthal**   Rabbi at Synagogue of Evolutionary Judaism; married to Rabbi Joshua Gruen; daughter of man known as Yehoshua Mendelssohn; continues to run synagogue after husband's death; falls in love with and marries Thomas Pemberton in E. L. Doctorow's *City of God.*

**Terrence (Terry) Bluvard**   Writer and wealthy white lesbian lover of Renay Davis in Ann Allen Shockley's *Loving Her.*

**Alma Boatwright**   Sister of Anney and aunt of Bone and Reese; wife of Wade; leaves Wade after discovering his affairs; has nervous breakdown when her husband claims not to love her; eventually reconciles with Wade in Dorothy Allison's *Bastard Out of Carolina.*

**Anney Boatwright**   See Anney Boatwright Parson Waddell.

**Carr Boatwright**   Only woman in her family to marry an outsider and leave South Carolina; rumored to have been in love with Wade and jealous of her sisters' good looks as a teenager in Dorothy Allison's *Bastard Out of Carolina.*

**Earl (Black) Boatwright**   Brother of Anney and favorite uncle of Bone and Reese; fighting and infidelities cost him his happiness; tries to kill Glen Waddell for beating Bone in Dorothy Allison's *Bastard Out of Carolina.*

**Fay Boatwright**   Wife of Nevil; reported to be the fattest as well as most quiet woman in Greenville County in Dorothy Allison's *Bastard Out of Carolina.*

**Granny Boatwright**   Granddaughter of a Cherokee; matriarch of the Boatwright family; the family storyteller; first in the family to express her distrust of Glen Waddell in Dorothy Allison's *Bastard Out of Carolina.*

**Moses Lincoln Boatwright**   Black, Harvard-educated philosopher who murdered and cannibalized his victim; interviewed in prison by Max Reddick in John A. Williams's *The Man Who Cried I Am.*

**Nevil Boatwright**   Husband of Fay; heavy drinker; overhears his mother compare him and his wife to furniture (taking up space and shedding dust); vows to kill Glen Waddell after discovering the rape in Dorothy Allison's *Bastard Out of Carolina.*

**Raylene Boatwright**   Sister of Anney and aunt of Bone and Reese; discovers bruises and belt welts on Bone; asks her brother Earle to kill Glen Waddell; Bone moves in with her after Anney leaves; she is a lesbian and the most stable member of the family in Dorothy Allison's *Bastard Out of Carolina.*

**Ruth Boatwright**   Sister to Anney and aunt to Bone and Reese; married to Travis; mother of eight children; works in a factory; when she becomes ill with cancer, Bone moves in to help care for her; on her deathbed Ruth is the first adult to discuss Bone's abuse, which validates the problem for her niece in Dorothy Allison's *Bastard Out of Carolina.*

**Ruth Anne (Bone) Boatwright**   Thirteen-year-old daughter of Anney Boatwright; rejects religion as a salvation from the violence of her stepfather, Glen Waddell; moves in with her aunt to escape her stepfather, who rapes and beats her; rejected by her mother, who chooses Glen over her in Dorothy Allison's *Bastard Out of Carolina.*

**Bob**   Husband of Constance Marlow; the Logan brothers mistake Bob and Constance for bowling trophy thieves and shoot them in Richard Brautigan's *Willard and His Bowling Trophies.*

**Bobochka**   Soviet Writers' Union official in charge of Henry Bech's itinerary in Russia in John Updike's *Bech: A Book.*

**Billy Bocksfuss**   See George Giles.

**Junior (Speedy, Speedy-Boy) Bodden**   Tough and determined crew member of the *Lillias Eden* and only survivor of its wreck in Peter Matthiessen's *Far Tortuga.*

**Bodger**   Dean of students at Steering School and friend of Jennie Fields and Garp in John Irving's *The World According to Garp.*

**Bodien**   Disbarred plumber employed by Norman Moonbloom in Edward Lewis Wallant's *The Tenants of Moonbloom.*

**Pig Bodine**   Former shipmate of Benny Profane; involved with the Whole Sick Crew in Thomas Pynchon's *V.;* possibly Seaman Bodine in *Gravity's Rainbow.*

**Seaman Bodine**   AWOL seaman who befriends Tyrone Slothrop and Roger Mexico in Thomas Pynchon's *Gravity's Rainbow*; possibly Pig Bodine in *V*.

**William S. (Willie) Body (Bloodworth)**   Lover of Lavinia Masterson and father, by his half sister Carrie Trout, of Abraham Dolphin in Leon Forrest's *The Bloodworth Orphans*.

**Charles Bogan**   Senior partner at Bogan, Rapley, Vitrano, and Havarac; cousin to the Senator who assists Aricia in obtaining his reward for being a whistle blower; his role in the conspiracy against the government is revealed by Patrick Lanigan, and he is indicted by the federal government in John Grisham's *The Partner*.

**Jack (Jackie, Jacques) Bogardes**   Wealthy but neurotic journalist who lives with his mother on Park Avenue; friend of Eric Eisner and lover of Marie Curtin in Phillip Lopate's *Confessions of Summer*.

**Peter Bogardus**   Orderly in a Chicago hospital where Roger Ashley works briefly; the first to expose Ashley to the concept of reincarnation in Thornton Wilder's *The Eighth Day*.

**Dr. Dominie Bogart**   Clergyman and longtime friend of Aaron Burr; officiates at Burr's marriage to Eliza Bowen Jumel in Gore Vidal's *Burr*.

**Marin Bogart**   Daughter of Charlotte Douglas and Warren Bogart; runs off with leftist revolutionaries in Joan Didion's *A Book of Common Prayer*.

**Warren Bogart**   Wandering ne'er-do-well; first husband of Charlotte Douglas and later her lover; father of Marin Bogart in Joan Didion's *A Book of Common Prayer*.

**George Bogger**   Epileptic who lives with his parents and works as a roadman with the highway department; dies of a seizure while hunting frogs in Mark Steadman's *A Lion's Share*.

**Bohack**   Leader of Happy Valley Commune in Don DeLillo's *Great Jones Street*.

**Jimmy Bohl**   Argus, North Dakota, steakhouse owner briefly married to Sita Kozka in Louise Erdrich's *The Beet Queen*.

**Lotte Böhm**   Lover of Igor Karlovy in Leon Uris's *Armageddon*.

**Boise (Boy)**   Cat that is Thomas Hudson's companion in Ernest Hemingway's *Islands in the Stream*.

**Yakov Shepsovitch (Yakov Ivanovitch Dologushev) Bok**   Jewish handyman arrested for the murder of a young boy and sent to prison in Bernard Malamud's *The Fixer*.

**Bokonon**   See Lionel Boyd Johnson.

**Paul (Kid Faro, Scot, Scotch, Scotcho, Scotty) Boldieu**   See Volume I.

**Lester Bolin**   Scientist who assists Robert Softly in developing a cosmic language based on mathematical principles in Don DeLillo's *Ratner's Star*.

**Dr. Bolling**   Romantic and restless father of Binx Bolling; joins the R.C.A.F. and dies during World War II in Walker Percy's *The Moviegoer*.

**Emily Bolling**   See Emily Bolling Cutrer.

**John Bickerson (Binx, Jack) Bolling**   New Orleans stockbroker and film buff who pursues money, women, and God; narrator of Walker Percy's *The Moviegoer*.

**Kate Cutrer Bolling**   See Kate Cutrer.

**Cameron Bolt**   Husband of Francesca Fox Bolt; district attorney seeking election as attorney general of California in Gail Godwin's *Glass People*.

**Carl Bolt**   Adoptive father of Molly Bolt in Rita Mae Brown's *Rubyfruit Jungle*.

**Carrie Bolt**   Adoptive mother of Molly Bolt in Rita Mae Brown's *Rubyfruit Jungle*.

**Francesca Fox Bolt**   Wife of Cameron Bolt and, briefly, seeker of her own identity in Gail Godwin's *Glass People*.

**Molly (Moll) Bolt**   Illegitimate child, adopted daughter of Carl and Carrie Bolt, lesbian heroine, and narrator of Rita Mae Brown's *Rubyfruit Jungle*.

**Chick Bolton**   Black racketeer obsessed with hatred for all whites; counterpart of Hank Dean in Julian Mayfield's *The Grand Parade*.

**Bella-Lenore Boltwood**   Associate of Nathaniel Turner Witherspoon and lover of fairy tales in Leon Forrest's *The Bloodworth Orphans*.

**Angela (Angie) Bonali**   Daughter of Vince Bonali; necks in a car during a high school basketball game while the mine accident occurs in Robert Coover's *The Origin of the Brunists*.

**Charlie Bonali**   Disaffected wastrel son of Vince Bonali; goes AWOL from the marines in Robert Coover's *The Origin of the Brunists*.

**Etta Bonali**   Fat, long-suffering wife of Vince Bonali in Robert Coover's *The Origin of the Brunists*.

**Vince Bonali**   Supervisor at the Deepwater Mine who becomes involved in efforts to stop the Brunist cult in Robert Coover's *The Origin of the Brunists*.

**Louise Bonbon**   Childish wife of Sidney Bonbon; ignored by her husband, she becomes romantically involved with Marcus Payne in Ernest J. Gaines's *Of Love and Dust*.

**Sidney Bonbon**   Cajun plantation overseer who kills Marcus Payne in Ernest J. Gaines's *Of Love and Dust.*

**Gennady Iosifovich Bondarenko**   Soviet colonel assigned to evaluate Bright Star, an antiballistic-missile defense laser; takes command of the security forces to defend the project from an Afghan assault; is eventually given command of the facility in Tom Clancy's *The Cardinal of the Kremlin.*

**Al Bonham**   Expert skin diver and small businessman in Ganado Bay, Jamaica; teaches Ron Grant to skin-dive in James Jones's *Go to the Widow-Maker.*

**Letta Bonham**   Jamaican schoolteacher and wife of Al Bonham; divorces Bonham and moves to Kingston in James Jones's *Go to the Widow-Maker.*

**Eunice Bonifante**   Aunt of Lester Stoner; widow of Al Bonifante, who committed suicide; lover of Sonny, her sister-in-law's husband; finds a new boyfriend; owns a restaurant in Mary McGarry Morris's *Songs in Ordinary Time.*

**Bonkers (Bonkie)**   Newfoundland retriever who bites off part of Garp's left ear; Garp bites off one of Bonkers's ears in John Irving's *The World According to Garp.*

**Père Bonne-chance**   Good-hearted priest of a country parish in the French colony Saint Domingue; lives with a mistress, Fontelle, by whom he has many children; is executed after a slave rebellion for crimes he did not commit in Madison Smartt Bell's *All Souls' Rising.*

**Adrian Bonner**   Husband of Margaret; chaplain and headmaster at Fair Haven School; dies of lung problems in Gail Godwin's *Evensong.*

**Benny Bonner**   Psychology student and older maternal cousin who practices analysis on Joe Sandwich in Peter De Vries's *The Vale of Laughter.*

**Carl Bonner**   Attorney who represents Hanna Trout in her divorce from Paris; married to Leslie Morgan Bonner; was the youngest Eagle Scout in the history of Georgia and feels he has to live up to his "Eagle Scout" image; is shot and killed by Paris Trout in Pete Dexter's *Paris Trout.*

**Evette Bonner**   Mother of Adrian, wife of Joseph; deserts Adrian at an orphanage when he is six; dies eight months later of cancer in Gail Godwin's *Evensong.*

**Joseph Anthony (Tony) Bonner**   Father of Adrian, husband of Evette; leaves Adrian at an orphanage when he is six; later confesses to Margaret that he is Adrian's father and has served time in prison; lives in a house near Margaret and Adrian; outlives his son Adrian and dies at ninety-six in Gail Godwin's *Evensong.*

**Margaret Bonner**   Thirty-three-year-old wife of Adrian, an Anglican pastor at the parish of All Saints High Balsam; her church burns down; she has a daughter; moves to New York after Adrian's death in Gail Godwin's *Evensong.*

**Craig Booker**   Nine-year-old twin of Scott and brother of Joe; son of Frank and Diane Booker; grandson of Daniel and Ellen Booker; pestiferous source of comic relief in Nicholas Evans's *The Horse Whisperer.*

**Diane Booker**   Wife of Frank Booker; mother of Joe, Scott, and Craig Booker; daughter-in-law of Ellen Booker; sister-in-law and possessive caretaker of Tom Booker; jealous observer of Annie Graves Maclean's relationship with Tom; alerts Grace Maclean to her mother's affair in Nicholas Evans's *The Horse Whisperer.*

**Ellen Booker**   Quiet but strong widow of rancher Daniel Booker; mother of Tom, Rosie, and Frank Booker and grandmother of Joe, Craig, and Scott Booker in Nicholas Evans's *The Horse Whisperer.*

**Frank Booker**   Brother, partner, and friend of Tom Booker; co-owner of the Booker ranch; father of Joe, Scott, and Craig Booker; son of Ellen Booker; brother of Rosie Booker; arranges Grace's celebration and going-home party at the ranch in Nicholas Evans's *The Horse Whisperer.*

**Joe Booker**   Twelve-year-old son of Frank and Diane Booker; nephew of Tom Booker; helps Grace Maclean to ride again following her amputation; heir apparent to Tom Booker's talent as a trainer and friend of horses in Nicholas Evans's *The Horse Whisperer.*

**Knobby Booker**   Informer for Bumper Morgan against Timothy Landry in Joseph Wambaugh's *The Blue Knight.*

**Rose Booker**   Mother of two young daughters; daughter of Daniel and Ellen Booker, the latter of whom lives with her; sister of Frank and Tom Booker; assistant at the ranch in Nicholas Evans's *The Horse Whisperer.*

**Scott Booker**   Nine-year-old twin of Craig and brother of Joe; son of Frank and Diane Booker; source of comic relief in Nicholas Evans's *The Horse Whisperer.*

**Tom Booker**   Son of Daniel and Ellen Booker; brother of Rosie and Frank Booker; uncle to Joe, Scott, and Craig Booker; partner in the Booker ranch, where he manages the horses; ex-husband of cellist Rachel Feinerman Booker and father of Hal Booker; lover of Annie Graves Maclean; sacrifices himself to protect the Maclean family in Nicholas Evans's *The Horse Whisperer.*

**Calvin (Uncle Cal) Bookwright**   See Volume I.

**Father Boomer**   Nondescript priest who baptizes the dying Jamie Vaught in Walker Percy's *The Last Gentleman.*

**Avery Boone**   He runs a successful fishing business in Moray Key; hires Bob Dubois as his assistant; smuggles drugs in Russell Banks's *Continental Drift.*

**Elizabeth Booth**   With William and Adolph, a beneficiary of the Vorakers' fortune who is loyal to her husband, Paul Booth, though he is absorbed by his attempts to earn capital in William Gaddis's *Carpenter's Gothic*.

**Paul Booth**   Conniving businessman who schemes to take advantage of the wealth of Elizabeth Booth, his wife in William Gaddis's *Carpenter's Gothic*.

**Dolly von Borg**   Granddaughter of Russian friends of Vadim Vadimovich, the object of a childhood crush and later her lover in Vladimir Nabokov's *Look at the Harlequins!*

**Paul R. Borg**   Self-satisfied lawyer and friend of John and Janice Wilder in Richard Yates's *Disturbing the Peace*.

**Katje (Domina Nocturna) Borgesius**   Agent of Dutch descent with no fixed allegiance; involved in various sexual liaisons with Lieutenant Weissmann, Tyrone Slothrop, Gottfried, Pirate Prentice, and Brigadier Ernest Pudding in Thomas Pynchon's *Gravity's Rainbow*.

**Thaddeus (Ned) Bork**   Effeminate assistant minister to Thomas Marshfield; sleeps with Alicia Crick; professes liberal political and social ideas in John Updike's *A Month of Sundays*.

**Boronai**   Leader of the tribe of Niaruna Indians into which Lewis Moon comes as a spirit leader in Peter Matthiessen's *At Play in the Fields of the Lord*.

**Emory Bortz**   Professor of English and editor of the Lectern Press edition of Richard Wharfinger's *The Courier's Tragedy* in Thomas Pynchon's *The Crying of Lot 49*.

**Dr. Bosco**   Boston surgeon who becomes so fascinated with the hints that Theophilus North effects cures with his hands that he urges North to become associated with Bosco's medical practice in Thornton Wilder's *Theophilus North*.

**Sugar Boss (Hornbuckle)**   Second cousin of Alice; married a Cherokee; her picture appears in *Life* magazine with the sign "Welcome to Heaven"; serves as the connection between Turtle's white foster family and her Cherokee tribe in Barbara Kingsolver's *Pigs in Heaven*.

**James Boswell**   Professional strongman and collector of great men; yearns for immortality and authors a diary in Stanley Elkin's *Boswell*.

**Margaret Boswell**   See Principessa Margaret dei Medici.

**Bosworth ("Boz")**   Went to law school with Lexi and lived with her in Elizabeth Benedict's *Slow Dancing*.

**Dr. James McHenry Bosworth**   Former diplomat and author of several books on American architecture; elderly resident of Newport who is a virtual captive in his home because of incontinence, a problem Theophilus North helps alleviate in Thornton Wilder's *Theophilus North*.

**Sarah Bosworth**   Daughter of Dr. James Bosworth; because she dislikes Theophilus North, she seeks to hinder his efforts to aid her father in Thornton Wilder's *Theophilus North*.

**Loretta Botsford**   See Loretta Botsford Wendall.

**Happy Bottom**   Buxom nurse, letter writer extraordinaire, and bedmate of Justin Miller in Robert Coover's *The Origin of the Brunists*.

**Sulie Boudrault**   Longtime servant in the Peck household; widow of a ragtime pianist in Anne Tyler's *Searching for Caleb*.

**Hal Boudreau**   Hired hand and tenant on the Sherbrooke estate; drunkard and possible lover of Maggie Sherbrooke in Nicholas Delbanco's *Sherbrookes*.

**Angelina (Nanane) Bouie**   Aged godmother of the Reverend Phillip Martin in Ernest J. Gaines's *In My Father's House*.

**Michelle Bouilloux**   Longtime secret lover of Harry Ames entrusted to deliver his message from beyond the grave to Max Reddick in John A. Williams's *The Man Who Cried I Am*.

**Catherine Bourne**   Young wife of David Bourne; jealous of husband's writing life; introduces David to unusual sexual practices; falls in love with Marita; burns David's manuscripts, press clippings, and reviews; grows progressively more psychotic; leaves David in Ernest Hemingway's *The Garden of Eden*.

**David Bourne**   American writer of two successful novels; living in Europe with wife, Catherine; acquiesces to wife's sexual experiments; falls in love with Marita; loses ability to write as a result of emotional and sexual relationships with Catherine and Marita; regains it when wife leaves and he stays with Marita in Ernest Hemingway's *The Garden of Eden*.

**Jack Bowen**   Brother of Marie Ann Bowen and friend of Steve Benson from summers in Maryland in Ed Bullins's *The Reluctant Rapist*.

**Lora Bowen**   See Lora Bowen Nolan.

**Marie Ann Bowen**   Sister of Jack Bowen and girlfriend of Dandy Benson in Ed Bullins's *The Reluctant Rapist*.

**George Bowlegs**   Fourteen-year-old Navajo Indian who lives on the Zuni reservation in New Mexico; steals artifacts from Chester Reynolds's anthropological dig site; believes he must make reparation to the Zuni spirits for his attempt to learn secrets of Zuni religion; killed by Reynolds in Tony Hillerman's *Dance Hall of the Dead*.

**Frances Bowles**   Twice-divorced travel writer; builds a house in Mexican town of Amapolas; left by boyfriend Francisco Alvarado; meets an archaeologist in Yucatán while researching a book; sells her home in Amapolas and leaves permanently in Harriet Doerr's *Consider This, Senora*.

**Ursula Bowles**   Widowed mother of Frances Bowles; revisits childhood home in Mexico before her death in Harriett Doerr's *Consider This, Senora.*

**Florence Cochran (Mrs. Ralph) Bowlsby**   Divorcée and friend of Garp; teaches English at a university where she has affairs with senior faculty members in John Irving's *The World According to Garp.*

**Carl-Rae Bowman**   Son of Arlington Bloodworth III and Rachel Rebecca Carpenter Flowers; brother of Industrious Bowman in Leon Forrest's *The Bloodworth Orphans.*

**Industrious Bowman**   Son of Arlington Bloodworth III and Rachel Rebecca Carpenter Flowers; brother of Carl-Rae Bowman; associate of Nathaniel Turner Witherspoon in Leon Forrest's *The Bloodworth Orphans.*

**Ramelle Bowman**   Celeste and Curtis Chalfonte's lover; has a daughter by Curtis; moves in with Celeste at twenty-one; plays bridge with Celeste, Fairy, and Fannie; dies of lung cancer at seventy-four in Rita Mae Brown's *Six of One.* Also appears in *Loose Lips.*

**Nelly Boxall**   Ever-indignant servant of the Woolfs; competent and precise, treats Virginia with exasperation in Michael Cunningham's *The Hours.*

**Henry Ray Boxer**   Mary McNutt's oldest son (twenty-one); is short-tempered; works as a cleaner at the state asylum; buys a 1949 Chevrolet and car insurance from Paris Trout, but wrecks the car immediately; leaves the car at Trout's store when Trout refuses to honor the insurance in Pete Dexter's *Paris Trout.*

**Miss Tee (Auntee) Boykin**   Loving presence and mother of Scooter in Albert Murray's *Train Whistle Guitar.*

**Mary Rose Boyle ("Mizz Bee")**   Roommate of Catherine Bray; union official's daughter in her early forties; former nun, now a social worker; has a brief affair with James Bray in Maureen Howard's *Natural History.*

**Walter (Walter Arlis Benson) Boyle**   Salesman, sometimes sanctimonious, sometimes involved in petty crimes; lives separate lives under different names in John Gardner's *The Sunlight Dialogues.*

**Jim Boynton**   Friend who encourages Clyde Stout to stop letting people take advantage of him; owns a 1963 Corvette in Jack Matthews's *Hanger Stout, Awake!*

**Sarah Bracknell**   See Sarah Bracknell Hazlett.

**Nelson Goodfellow (Big Nellie) Bradbury**   American journalist who first reports the Berlin airlift in Leon Uris's *Armageddon.*

**Jellie Braden**   Wife of James Lee Braden III; married twenty years earlier in India to Dhiren Velayudum, a revolutionary separatist and poet killed in an ambush, with whom she had a daughter, Jaya; while married to Braden and living in Cedar Bend, has an affair with Michael Tillman; then flees to India in Robert James Waller's *Slow Waltz In Cedar Bend.*

**Ardis Bradley**   Wife of Tuck Bradley in Joan Didion's *A Book of Common Prayer.*

**Austin Bradley**   Owner of Happy's Café, following Tadpole McCormick's ownership of it in Gayl Jones's *Corregidora.*

**Thorne Bradley**   Friend of Forrest Mayfield; refuses to continue their friendship after Forrest elopes in Reynolds Price's *The Surface of Earth.*

**Tuck Bradley**   American ambassador to Boca Grande in Joan Didion's *A Book of Common Prayer.*

**Colonel Bradly**   Member of the expedition against the wild boys; later joins them and shoots a movie of them in William S. Burroughs's *The Wild Boys.*

**Cecil Otis Braithwaite**   Black lawyer, janitor, and hairdresser who travels to Europe and Africa before returning to his wife in John Edgar Wideman's *Hurry Home.*

**Esther Brown Braithwaite**   Wife of Cecil Braithwaite, whom she supports through law school, only to have him desert her in John Edgar Wideman's *Hurry Home.*

**Simon Braithwaite**   Stillborn son of Esther Brown and Cecil Braithwaite in John Edgar Wideman's *Hurry Home.*

**Linda Braller**   A student in Benjamin Fermoyle's class in Mary McGarry Morris's *Songs in Ordinary Time.*

**Della Brame**   Young black woman whose several sexual encounters with Buck Russell may have produced her son in Reynolds Price's *A Generous Man.*

**Miriam Brancher**   Body model for art students; short-term lover/fiancée of Warren in Joyce Carol Oates's *You Must Remember This.*

**Bobby Brand**   Vietnam veteran and former junkie who accompanies David Bell and friends on a trip west to make a documentary film in Don DeLillo's *Americana.*

**Mark Brandler**   California Superior Court judge who presides at the first trial of Gregory Powell and Jimmy Smith in Joseph Wambaugh's *The Onion Field.*

**Gregory Brandon**   Sir Walter Ralegh's executioner in George Garrett's *Death of the Fox.*

**Mrs. Brandon**   Owns the variety store and phones mothers if kids take a pack of gum in Alice Hoffman's *Local Girls.*

**Oliver Brandon**   Black companion and employee of William Howland; helps Abigail Tolliver fight a mob and save the Howland home in Shirley Ann Grau's *The Keepers of the House.*

**Hannah Brandt**   Historical character Margaret is writing about; once active in the American Communist Party and the National Woman's Party; is senile and bitter in her old age when Margaret interviews her in Maureen Howard's *Expensive Habits*.

**Jimmy Branley**   Architect who lives with Ellen Proctorr; a cheerful, amiable man; nearly fifty, with two grown kids in Donald E. Westlake's *The Hook*.

**Harla Branno**   Ambitious Mayor of Terminus who exiles Councilman Golan Trevize from Terminus and sends him to search for the rival Second Foundation in order to destroy it and found a second Galactic Empire during her administration in Isaac Asimov's *Foundation's Edge*.

**Luca Brasi**   Close friend of Don Corleone; killed by rival gangsters in Mario Puzo's *The Godfather*.

**Carlton Braun**   See Carl Brown.

**Thalia Braunbeck-Corcoran**   Corky's stepdaughter from Charlotte's first marriage; wild, neurotic, and a hippy; friend of Mailee Plummer in Joyce Carol Oates's *What I Lived For*.

**Inez Braverman**   Widow of Leslie Braverman in Wallace Markfield's *To an Early Grave*.

**Leslie Braverman**   Deceased writer who is the subject of recollections by several of his friends in Wallace Markfield's *To an Early Grave*.

**Catherine "Cath" Bray**   Daughter of Nell Bray and sister of James Bray; in adulthood works as a copy editor in New York, has affairs with married men, attempts suicide twice; returns to Bridgeport, becomes a spinner and weaver; keeps the secret that her father had an affair with Isabelle Poole in Maureen Howard's *Natural History*.

**Eamonn Bray**   James Bray's son by his first marriage, becomes a banker in London in Maureen Howard's *Natural History*.

**Harold (Harry) Bray**   Protean figure; the false Grand Tutor whom George Giles drives out of the college in John Barth's *Giles Goat-Boy*.

**James Bray**   Son of Nell Bray and brother of Cath Bray; becomes an actor in Los Angeles and New York; married twice, the second time to Lilah Lee Hulburt; father of two, his second child is Jen Bray in Maureen Howard's *Natural History*.

**Jen Bray**   Daughter of James and Lilah Lee Bray in Maureen Howard's *Natural History*.

**Lilah Lee Bray**   Second wife of James Bray and mother of Jen Bray; the only beautiful one of seven children; has affair with Morty Ziff; loves her Arabian horse, Falada, in Maureen Howard's *Natural History*.

**Nell Bray**   Mother of Catherine and James Bray; former teacher; dreamy and distant; naturally grand though unaffected in Maureen Howard's *Natural History*.

**William Aloysius "Bill" or "Billy" Bray**   Husband of Nell Bray and father of Catherine and James Bray; county detective in the state's attorney's office; former soldier in Normandy; dies in 1955 in Maureen Howard's *Natural History*.

**Myra (Myron) Breckinridge**   Female transsexual, born Myron Breckinridge, seeking to destroy traditional sex roles; rapes Rusty Godowsky and tries to seduce Mary-Ann Pringle; reverts to her original sex and marries Mary-Ann in Gore Vidal's *Myra Breckinridge*.

**Baroness Bredow (née Tolstoy)**   Extraordinary aunt of Vadim Vadimovich, who exhorted him as a child to quit moping and use his imagination to invent reality by looking at the harlequins in Vladimir Nabokov's *Look at the Harlequins!*

**Cholly Breedlove**   Husband of Pauline; father of Sammy and Pecola; unemployed alcoholic; rapes Pecola and burns his storefront house down; beats Pauline and gets arrested in Toni Morrison's *The Bluest Eye*.

**Pauline Williams (Polly) Breedlove**   Wife of Cholly; mother of Sammy and Pecola; has a deformed foot; marries Cholly because he is the first man to ever talk to her; works as a cleaning woman for a white family and considers them more desirable than her own in Toni Morrison's *The Bluest Eye*.

**Pecola Breedlove**   Daughter of Cholly and Pauline Breedlove and sister of Sammy; is named after a mulatto character in the movie *Imitation of Life*; considers the three whores who live above her as family over her own; wishes for blue eyes as a remedy to her problems; raped and impregnated by her father, she goes insane in Toni Morrison's *The Bluest Eye*.

**Sammy Breedlove**   Son of Cholly and Pauline Breedlove and brother of Pecola; reacts to his parent's fighting by cursing and trying to hurt Cholly; runs away to escape his parents and his legacy in Toni Morrison's *The Bluest Eye*.

**Yancey Breedlove**   Young deputy who is second-in-command of the hunt for Rato Mustian, the dog, and the snake in Reynolds Price's *A Generous Man*.

**Tony Brenzo**   Liberal white policeman, friend of Joe Market, and eloquent foe of narcissism and nihilism in Hal Bennett's *Lord of Dark Places*.

**Nina Brett**   Chic young woman who interviews Francesca Bolt at an employment agency in Gail Godwin's *Glass People*.

**Father Brice**   Haitian slave trader; works for the Worthingtons; is killed by the Worthingtons in Herbert Gold's *Slave Trade*.

**Carol Brightling**   Presidential science adviser and radical environmentalist in Tom Clancy's *Rainbow Six*.

**John Brightling**   Businessman, founder of the Horizon Group, and radical environmentalist in Tom Clancy's *Rainbow Six.*

**Joseph Brill**   Principal and founder of Edmond Fleg Primary School; Holocaust survivor; is infatuated by Hester Lilt; father of Naphtali in Cynthia Ozick's *The Cannibal Galaxy.*

**Naphtali Brill**   Son of Joseph and Iris Brill; initially wants to be a teacher, but in college decides he wants to go into business in Cynthia Ozick's *The Cannibal Galaxy.*

**Dr. Myron T. Brink**   Second psychiatrist of John Wilder; prescribes large quantities of drugs to treat Wilder's emotional breakdowns in Richard Yates's *Disturbing the Peace.*

**Mr. Briscoe**   Marie Fermoyle's employer; catches Benjy shoplifting in Mary McGarry Morris's *Songs in Ordinary Time.*

**Cecile Bristol**   Daughter of William and Julia; student at Berkeley; elopes to Las Vegas to be married in Susan Cheever's *The Cage.*

**Julia Bristol**   Wife of William; mother of Cecile; imprisons her husband in a cage at their vacation home; shoots him, perhaps accidentally, while waiting to shoot the deer who destroyed her vegetable garden in Susan Cheever's *The Cage.*

**Louise Bristol**   British commoner living off Los Angeles coast; is engaged to and then left by crown prince Lawrence Mayfair; writes tongue-in-cheek exposé in Stanley Elkin's *Van Gogh's Room at Arles.*

**William Bristol**   Writer and editor for a weekly magazine; married to Julia; father of Cecile; after wife has imprisoned him in a cage at their vacation home, realizes he can live only by asserting himself; escapes and is shot, perhaps accidentally, by his wife in Susan Cheever's *The Cage.*

**Wellington (Don Velantén Bristé) Bristow**   American businessman who keeps a list of wanted men in Thornton Wilder's *The Eighth Day.*

**Bill (Billy) Britt**   Stepson of Helen and son of Paul Britt in Gail Godwin's *Evensong.*

**Helen Britt**   Stepmother of Bill Britt, widow of Paul Britt in Gail Godwin's *Evensong.*

**Paul Britt**   Husband of Helen Britt, father of Bill Britt; owned newspapers; dies of a heart attack in Gail Godwin's *Evensong.*

**Cora Brittain**   Surreptitious racial avenger emulated by her grandson Kevin Brittain in Hal Bennett's *Wait Until the Evening.*

**Dolores Brittain**   Adopted daughter of Grandpa Brittain and wife of Henry Robinson, who murders her as she gives birth to her lover's child in Hal Bennett's *Wait Until the Evening.*

**Kevin Brittain**   Son of Minnie and Percy Brittain; narrator of Hal Bennett's *Wait Until the Evening.*

**Minnie Brittain**   Wife of Percy Brittain and mother of eight; frees her family from the despotism of her father-in-law in Hal Bennett's *Wait Until the Evening.*

**Paul Brittain**   Son of Minnie and Percy Brittain; tricked into hanging himself by his brother Kevin Brittain in Hal Bennett's *Wait Until the Evening.*

**Percy Brittain**   Philandering husband of Minnie Brittain and father of eight; marked for death by his son Kevin Brittain in Hal Bennett's *Wait Until the Evening.*

**Shadrach (Grandpa, Mr. Brittain) Brittain**   Former slave and tyrannical owner of the farm on which his family works as sharecroppers; husband of Cora Brittain in Hal Bennett's *Wait Until the Evening.*

**Andrew Broder**   Forty-something journalist and author from Florida who moves to Boulder, Colorado, to be closer to his young daughter, Sara; published one book as a cathartic measure after the death of his son in a car accident; is the ex-husband of Francine "B. B." Brady Broder; develops a deep relationship with Margo Sampson in Judy Blume's *Smart Women.*

**Francine "B. B." Brady Broder**   Successful forty-something realtor in Boulder, Colorado; has one daughter, Sara; marries an older lover on a whim; blames ex-husband for the death of their son, has a mental breakdown in Judy Blume's *Smart Women.*

**Herman Broder**   Member of a well-to-do Polish family who survived World War II by hiding in a hayloft after hearing that the Nazis had killed his wife and children; later marries the servant who hid him and immigrates to America, where he poses as a traveling book salesman in order to have time to spend with his mistress and serve as a ghostwriter for a successful rabbi in Isaac Bashevis Singer's *Enemies, A Love Story.*

**Sara Broder**   Eleven-year-old daughter of Francine "B. B." Brady Broder and Andrew Broder in Judy Blume's *Smart Women.*

**Tamara Luria Broder**   Polish upper-class activist and first wife of Herman Broder; shot and left to die by Nazis but survives her wounds and, subsequently, Russian work camps; learns after the war that her husband is alive and follows him to New York in Isaac Bashevis Singer's *Enemies, A Love Story.*

**Yadwiga Pracz Broder**   Polish Catholic; former servant and later wife of Herman Broder; immigrates with him to America, where she gives birth to a daughter named after his mistress in Isaac Bashevis Singer's *Enemies, A Love Story.*

**Mrs. Brodhag**   Devoted housekeeper of Don and Carol Wanderhope in Peter De Vries's *The Blood of the Lamb.*

**Brodie**   Tattooed bomber and anorexic teenage girl in Paul Theroux's *The Family Arsenal.*

**Ellen Brody**   Wife of Martin Brody; unsympathetic toward her husband's concerns about the Great White Shark; becomes so bored that she has an affair with Matt Hooper in Peter Benchley's *Jaws.*

**Martin Brody**   Chief of police in Amity determined to protect people from the Great White Shark; sole survivor of the attempt to hunt the shark in Peter Benchley's *Jaws.*

**Austin (Irwin Swenson) Bromberg**   See Volume I.

**Chief Broom (Big Chief) Bromden**   Large, half Native American inmate of a mental hospital who hallucinates and pretends to be deaf and mute before Randle McMurphy restores his self-confidence; narrator of Ken Kesey's *One Flew Over the Cuckoo's Nest.*

**Louie Bronk**   Convicted murderer on death row in Texas; admits guilt before being executed, though the validity of the admission is called into question in Mary Willis Walker's *The Red Scream.*

**Charlie Bronski**   Young Los Angeles vice detective in the Red Scalotta case in Joseph Wambaugh's *The Blue Knight.*

**Albert Bronzini**   Retired science teacher and chess tutor living in a decaying neighborhood in New York City; formerly married to Klara Sax; perceives every loss as an echo of Klara's departure; dies himself in the summer of 1992 in Don DeLillo's *Underworld.*

**Mackey Brood**   Friend and lover of Jack Curran; gives birth to a son nine months after her last night with Curran before his death in Mark Steadman's *A Lion's Share.*

**Pierce R. (P. R.) Brooks**   Los Angeles homicide detective sergeant; investigating officer in the death of Ian Campbell in Joseph Wambaugh's *The Onion Field.*

**Broud**   Brutal, brutish youth groomed to be leader of Neanderthal Clan; obsessively vengeful leader who puts his petty dreams of revenge before the interests of the Clan and whose banishment of Ayla devastates the Clan; father of Ayla's son; son of Brun in Jean M. Auel's *The Clan of the Cave Bear.*

**Bo Browder**   Childhood acquaintance of Thomas Eborn; policeman who investigates the break-in at the house of Louise Eborn in Reynolds Price's *Love and Work.*

**Andy Brown**   Radio character jailed for robbing Amos's place; freed from jail by Minnie Yellings in Ishmael Reed's *The Last Days of Louisiana Red.*

**Annie McGairy Brown**   Eighteen-year-old bride of Carl Brown; budding writer and heroine of Betty Smith's *Joy in the Morning.*

**Betty Brown**   See Eliza Mellon Swain.

**Bobby Brown**   See Wilbur Rockefeller Daffodil-11 Swain.

**Buddy Brown**   Rival of Tom More; doctor who defends the use of euthanasia with the elderly in Walker Percy's *Love in the Ruins.*

**Carl (Carlton Braun) Brown**   Struggling law student at a midwestern university in 1927; husband of Annie McGairy Brown in Betty Smith's *Joy in the Morning.*

**Cicely Brown**   Ian Bedloe's high school girlfriend; refuses to marry Ian and moves to California in Anne Tyler's *Saint Maybe.*

**Corporal Brown**   Union soldier who befriends the black child Ticey and renames her Jane in Ernest J. Gaines's *The Autobiography of Miss Jane Pittman.*

**Dan Brown**   Loving husband of Laura Brown, father of Richie; World War II veteran in Michael Cunningham's *The Hours.*

**Dick Brown**   Second-rate commercial artist; married man and first lover of Dorothy Renfrew in Mary McCarthy's *The Group.*

**Esther Brown**   See Esther Brown Braithwaite.

**Fran Brown**   College friend of Renay Davis and babysitter for Denise Davis in Ann Allen Shockley's *Loving Her.*

**Hattie Brown**   Wife of Heck Brown, daughter of Ma Sigafoos, and client of Billy Bumpers in Peter De Vries's *I Hear America Swinging.*

**Helen Brown**   See Angela Sterling.

**Herkimer (Heck) Brown**   Renegade farmer, husband of Hattie Brown, son-in-law of Ma Sigafoos, and client of Billy Bumpers in Peter De Vries's *I Hear America Swinging.*

**Herman (Wimpy) Brown**   Heroin addict and informer for Bumper Morgan in Joseph Wambaugh's *The Blue Knight.*

**Hillman (Hilly) Brown**   Accident-prone ten-year-old son of Bryant and Marie Brown and grandson of Everett (Ev) Hillman; makes younger brother David disappear; then slips into a coma in Stephen King's *The Tommyknockers.*

**Jackie Brown**   Hard-bitten gun dealer who acts as middleman for those who sell guns and those who want them for illegal reasons in George V. Higgins's *The Friends of Eddie Coyle.*

**Jane Brown**   See Miss Jane Pittman.

**Jenny (Jane, Jenny Angel, Johanna Engel) Brown**   American painter traveling with David Scott, with whom she has a tumultuous relationship in Katherine Anne Porter's *Ship of Fools.*

**John Brown**   Christian abolitionist devoted to freeing slaves and helping already freed blacks find work and learn to farm; fathers twenty children, only eight of whom reach adulthood; gets his family deeper into debt with each scheme to sell wool or buy land; hanged when he is captured at Harpers Ferry in Russell Banks's *Cloudsplitter.*

**Johnny Brown**   Sales executive under Andy Kagle in Joseph Heller's *Something Happened.*

**Laura Brown**   Restless, discontented homemaker in 1949 Los Angeles who is reading *Mrs. Dalloway;* wife of Dan, mother of Richie; meets Clarissa Vaughan after her adult son Richard commits suicide in Michael Cunningham's *The Hours.*

**Maureen Brown**   A sophomore at Haddan School who lights black candles on her windowsill and alarms her roommates with the wicked things she says in her sleep in Alice Hoffman's *The River King.*

**Ned Brown**   See Edward Stephen Douglass.

**Owen Brown**   Third son of John Brown and an atheist; tells the story of his father's raid on Harpers Ferry in Virginia in 1859; responsible for Lyman Epp's death; escapes to the California mountains in Russell Banks's *Cloudsplitter.*

**Richard (Richie) Brown**   As a child, sensitive and adores his mother; as an adult, a talented poet and novelist; former lover of Clarissa Vaughan and Louis; dying of AIDS, he commits suicide before Clarissa's party in Michael Cunningham's *The Hours.*

**Sheldon Brown**   Los Angeles deputy district attorney; co-prosecutor in the second murder trial of Gregory Powell and Jimmy Smith in Joseph Wambaugh's *The Onion Field.*

**Sister Brown**   Creepy neighbor of the Bray family; has a sickly, clever daughter in Maureen Howard's *Natural History.*

**Katherine Morley (Kitty) Brownell**   American visitor to Schloss Riva and friend of Warren Howe; possibly (and briefly) Etienne Dulac's mistress in Wright Morris's *Cause for Wonder.*

**Clarissa Browning**   Academy Award–winning actress with a troubled past and secret history in Jackie Collins's *Hollywood Husbands.*

**Hank Browning**   Buys a field from Gram in Joan Chase's *During the Reign of the Queen of Persia.*

**Bruce**   Pan-like bisexual friend and lover of Renate, who travels with her through Mexico and periodically lives with her in Anaïs Nin's *Collages.*

**Walter Bruch**   Sixty-year-old musicologist and baritone who likes to enact his own funeral and is a compulsive masturbator when excited by women's arms, a weakness he confesses regularly to Artur Sammler in Saul Bellow's *Mr. Sammler's Planet.*

**Joseph Brudegher**   A Vineyard native and Vix's first lover; eventually marries Caitlin and has a daughter with her in Judy Blume's *Summer Sisters.*

**Brun**   Stern but fair leader of Neanderthal Clan that adopts the orphaned Cro-Magnon child Ayla; proud father whose love for his son Broud blinds him to Broud's unfitness to succeed him as leader; brother of Creb and Iza in Jean M. Auel's *The Clan of the Cave Bear.*

**Joe Brundige**   Author of a story in the *Evening News* reporting his scientific body transfer with a Mayan so he can destroy the Mayan control machine in William S. Burroughs's *The Soft Machine.*

**Antonio Bruno**   Father of Giovanni and Marcella Bruno; dies in front of a television set in Robert Coover's *The Origin of the Brunists.*

**Emilia Bruno**   Mother of Giovanni and Marcella Bruno in Robert Coover's *The Origin of the Brunists.*

**Giovanni Bruno**   Catholic coal miner who, during a mine disaster, claims to have been visited by the Virgin Mary, thereby inaugurating the chiliastic cult of the Brunists in Robert Coover's *The Origin of the Brunists.*

**Marcella Bruno**   Innocent sister of Giovanni Bruno and Justin Miller's object of infatuation; hit and killed by a car in Robert Coover's *The Origin of the Brunists.*

**James Bruton**   English fiancé, for a brief period, of Jane Clifford in Gail Godwin's *The Odd Woman.*

**Bobby Bryant**   Alcoholic friend of Bill Kelsey; committed to winning government money by becoming the first male to bear a child in Hal Bennett's *Seventh Heaven.*

**Clarke Bryant**   Charismatic white supremacist and political leader against school integration in Julian Mayfield's *The Grand Parade.*

**William Cullen Bryant**   Poet and editor of the *Evening Post* in Gore Vidal's *Burr.*

**Bubbles**   See Richard Wiggins.

**Rosemarie (Rosie) Buchanan**   See Volume I.

**Joe (Cowboy, Tex) Buck**   Would-be hustler and grandson of Sally Buck; travels from Albuquerque to Houston and New York, where he befriends Ratso Rizzo in James Leo Herlihy's *Midnight Cowboy.*

**Sally Buck**   Grandmother of Joe Buck; dies while Joe is in the army in James Leo Herlihy's *Midnight Cowboy.*

**Rachel Buck**   Daughter of Gram and Grandad, sister of Libby, Grace, Elinor, and May; mother of her son, Rossie, aunt of Valery, Jenny, Celia, Anne, and Katie; married for a short, miserable spell at eighteen, remarried to Tom Buck in Joan Chase's *During the Reign of the Queen of Persia.*

**Tom Buck**   Second husband of Rachel, divorces his wife to marry her; stepfather of Rossie; years before was in love with Grace and wanted to marry her in Joan Chase's *During the Reign of the Queen of Persia*.

**Helen Buckle**   Outspoken wife of Slim Buckle in Jack Kerouac's *Visions of Cody*.

**Slim (Ed Buckle) Buckle**   Cross-country traveling companion of Cody Pomeray and Jack Duluoz; husband of Helen Buckle in Jack Kerouac's *Visions of Cody*; also appears in *Book of Dreams*.

**Asher Buckner**   Maternal uncle of Paul Herz; lives an unattached life as a painter in Philip Roth's *Letting Go*.

**Elgin Buell**   Spy and personal cinematographer in Lancelot Lamar's quest to see sin in Walker Percy's *Lancelot*.

**Buffalo Wallow Woman**   Wife of Old Lodge Skins in Thomas Berger's *Little Big Man*.

**John Buford**   Adept cavalry officer who is the first Northern general to arrive at Gettysburg in Michael Shaara's *The Killer Angels*.

**Beety Buggit**   Dennis's wife; often takes care of Bunny and Sunshine; has comedy act that is big hit at annual Christmas pageant in E. Annie Proulx's *The Shipping News*.

**Dennis Buggit**   Jack Buggit's youngest son; married to Beety; does carpentry work; loves to fish in E. Annie Proulx's *The Shipping News*.

**Jack Buggit**   Started newspaper to get out of the nonlucrative fishing business; had one son, Jesson, drown and a second son, Dennis, almost drown; assumed dead from drowning until he sits up in his coffin in E. Annie Proulx's *The Shipping News*.

**Professor Bulgaraux**   Leader of the Autogenists in Susan Sontag's *The Benefactor*.

**Major Rupert Bullock**   Close friend of Judge Clinton McKelva; informs Fay McKelva's family that the judge has died in Eudora Welty's *The Optimist's Daughter*.

**Tennyson Bullock**   Close friend of Becky McKelva; wife of Major Bullock and mother of Tish Bullock in Eudora Welty's *The Optimist's Daughter*.

**Tish Bullock**   Bridesmaid and close friend of Laurel McKelva Hand; daughter of Major and Tennyson Bullock in Eudora Welty's *The Optimist's Daughter*.

**Emil (Satire) Bummer**   German dope dealer and former cat burglar in Thomas Pynchon's *Gravity's Rainbow*.

**Stanley Bumpas**   Policeman who thirteen years before beat Sonny Boy Mosby; an accomplice of Willie Joe Worth in the murder of Lord Byron Jones in Jesse Hill Ford's *The Liberation of Lord Byron Jones*.

**William (Billy) Bumpers**   Marriage counselor who earned a doctorate by submitting a rejected sociology dissertation to the English department as an experimental novel; narrator of Peter De Vries's *I Hear America Swinging*.

**Pauline (Polly) Buncombe**   Wife of Willis Buncombe; helps her husband in their grocery store at Pickerel Beach and hides Bible verses among the vegetables in Doris Betts's *The River to Pickle Beach*.

**Willis Buncombe**   Husband of Pauline Buncombe; proprietor of a small grocery store at Pickerel Beach in Doris Betts's *The River to Pickle Beach*.

**Nat Bundle**   Press agent for Harry Mercury in Peter De Vries's *Through the Fields of Clover*.

**Bunny**   First daughter of Quoyle and Petal Bear; imaginative and fearful; stands up for her friend, Wavy's son, Herry, by pushing a teacher who mimics him in E. Annie Proulx's *The Shipping News*.

**Gloria Bunshaft**   Featherbrained wife of Wally Hines and paramour of Joe Sandwich in Peter De Vries's *The Vale of Laughter*.

**Amanita Buntline**   Wealthy lesbian friend of Caroline Rosewater in Kurt Vonnegut's *God Bless You, Mr. Rosewater*.

**Becky Burgess**   Daughter of a poor fisherman who married into the middle class; found guilty of killing her husband with the assistance of teen lover, Sam; first in family to go to college in Marge Piercy's *The Longings of Women*.

**Milton Burgess**   Owner of a general store and rival merchant of Jasper Lathrop in Wendell Berry's *A Place on Earth* and *The Memory of Old Jack*.

**Richard Burgess**   Guard for the South Eastern Railway who is bribed into helping Edward Pierce in Michael Crichton's *The Great Train Robbery*.

**Beto Burgos**   Son of César Burgos; student of Rafael Beltran; feels responsible for his mother's death; keeps his mother's shawl after her death; helps his father decorate a roadside altar for his family with shells and sea glass in Sandra Benítez's *A Place Where the Sea Remembers*.

**César Burgos**   Fisherman and father of Beto Burgos; his wife and two other sons are killed in a bus accident; builds a roadside altar for his family in Sandra Benítez's *A Place Where the Sea Remembers*.

**Carlyle Burke**   Retired schoolteacher who provokes his former brother-in-law into killing him in L. R. Wright's *The Suspect*.

**Mary Burke**   Former suburban housewife; goes through a bitter divorce; is injured in a fire and later goes to live in California with Leila Landsman's sister in Marge Piercy's *The Longings of Women*.

**Matthew (Matt) Burke**    Teacher who befriends Ben Mears; assists in destroying the evil that surrounds the Marsten House in Stephen King's *'Salem's Lot*.

**Teddy Burke**    Pickpocket who pretends to pick Edgar Trent's pocket, thus permitting Edward Pierce to gain information on safe keys in Michael Crichton's *The Great Train Robbery*.

**Toonker Burkette**    Dentist who tells of Eleanor Fite's murder and Thomas McCutcheon's suicide in Jesse Hill Ford's *Mountains of Gilead*; mentioned in *The Liberation of Lord Byron Jones*.

**Johnnie Price Burkhalter**    Hardware dealer in Somerton and tennis partner of Steve Mundine in Jesse Hill Ford's *The Liberation of Lord Byron Jones*.

**Burl**    Brother of Molly, uncle of Lil; travels to California and New York; his favorite sister was Lil's mother in Joan Chase's *During the Reign of the Queen of Persia*.

**Jean Burling**    Lover of Nicholas Delbanco in Nicholas Delbanco's *In the Middle Distance*.

**Nichole Burnell**    Fourteen-year-old paralyzed survivor of a bus accident; before the accident was frequently molested by her father; lies during her deposition in order to stop the accident victims' lawsuit and get revenge on her father in Russell Banks's *The Sweet Hereafter*.

**Alistair Burnham**    Australian neighbor; lives in a hippie commune with his wife, Julie, and his son, Chen-Yu, in Diane Johnson's *Lying Low*.

**Julie Burnham**    Neighbor who lives with her husband, Alistair, and son, Chen-Yu; creates and sells false identities; makes explosives and stores them in jars in Diane Johnson's *Lying Low*.

**Col. Aaron Burr**    Third vice president of the United States; accused of killing Alexander Hamilton in a duel and arrested for treason in Gore Vidal's *Burr*.

**Theodosia Burr**    Daughter of Aaron Burr and wife of Joseph Alston; believed to have drowned in Gore Vidal's *Burr*.

**Charles (Barton) Burton**    Baylor University pathologist and member of the scientist group at Project Wildfire in Michael Crichton's *The Andromeda Strain*.

**Detective Burton**    Policeman investigating the murders in Donald E. Westlake's *The Ax*.

**Bobby Busco**    Large sixteen-year-old boy in Mary McGarry Morris's *Songs in Ordinary Time*.

**Lucky Buster**    Retarded man who falls into the spillway of the Hoover Dam and is saved by Turtle and Taylor in Barbara Kingsolver's *Pigs in Heaven*.

**Buteo**    Native of South America and king-to-be when the revolution is won; fights alongside Ramón Cordes and feels brotherhood with him in William Herrick's *The Last to Die*.

**Michael X. (Butty) Butler**    First husband of Rozelle Hardcastle; dies in a yachting accident in Robert Penn Warren's *A Place to Come To*.

**Sophia Butler**    Wife of one of Albert's stepsons; sent to jail for slapping the mayor's wife; released on parole as servant to mayor and his family; serves as a role model for Celie in Alice Walker's *The Color Purple*.

**Ann Butterfield**    Wife of Hugh Butterfield and mother of Jade, Sam, and Keith Butterfield in Scott Spencer's *Endless Love*.

**Hugh Butterfield**    Doctor and father of Jade, Sam, and Hugh Butterfield; killed by a taxi while pursuing David Axelrod in Scott Spencer's *Endless Love*.

**Jade Butterfield**    Object of David Axelrod's obsessive love in Scott Spencer's *Endless Love*.

**Keith Butterfield**    Son of Hugh and Ann Butterfield in Scott Spencer's *Endless Love*.

**Sam (Sammy) Butterfield**    Son of Hugh and Ann Butterfield in Scott Spencer's *Endless Love*.

**Elsie Buttrick**    Spirited independent officer in the Rhode Island Natural Resources Department and lover of Dick Pierce; she chooses him to be the father of her child in John Casey's *Spartina*.

**Ben Butts**    Easygoing, homily-quoting Texan; husband of Sophie Butts in Aaron Elkins's *Old Bones*.

**Sophie Butts**    Plain-spoken wife of Ben Butts and aunt of Ray Schaefer in Aaron Elkins's *Old Bones*.

**Earl Butz**    White Landrace boar that is the subject of Dr. Bo Jones's animal science experiment at Moo University; escapes from his pen when the building where he is housed is demolished, and dies while in flight in Jane Smiley's *Moo*.

**Willard Buzzard**    Iowa State wrestler who beats his former teammate George Bender in the championship for the one-hundred-fifty-eight-pound division in John Irving's *The 158-Pound Marriage*.

**Buzzy**    Boyhood tormentor of the unnamed male narrator in Darryl Pinckney's *High Cotton*.

**Eileen Byers**    Wife of Pete Byers in Alice Hoffman's *The River King*.

**Pete Byers**    Husband of Eileen Byers; as the pharmacist, privy to more personal matters than anyone else in Haddan; doesn't gossip or judge in Alice Hoffman's *The River King*.

**Sean Byers**    Nephew of Pete Byers; handsome seventeen-year-old who has stolen two cars; friend of Gus Pierce; falls in love with Carlin Leander in Alice Hoffman's *The River King*.

**Anthony Byrd**    Florist, aspiring writer, and friend of Annie Brown in Betty Smith's *Joy in the Morning*.

**Crowell Byrd**    Father of Susan Byrd and son of Heddy Byrd in Toni Morrison's *Song of Solomon*.

**Heddy Byrd**    Indian woman who finds and rears Jake (Macon Dead I) when he is dropped by his father, the flying African; mother of Sing and Crowell Byrd and grandmother of Susan Byrd in Toni Morrison's *Song of Solomon*.

**Sing Byrd**    Wife of Macon Dead I, daughter of Heddy Byrd, and mother of Pilate Dead and Macon Dead II; dies in childbirth in Toni Morrison's *Song of Solomon*.

**Susan Byrd**    Granddaughter of Heddy Byrd and cousin of Macon (Milkman) Dead III; tells Milkman during his visit to Shalimar, Virginia, of the flying powers of his great-grandfather in Toni Morrison's *Song of Solomon*.

**Raymond Byrne**    Los Angeles deputy district attorney; co-prosecutor in the second murder trial of Gregory Powell and Jimmy Smith in Joseph Wambaugh's *The Onion Field*.

**BZ**    Homosexual film producer and husband of Helene; commits suicide in Joan Didion's *Play It As It Lays*.

**Jan Bzik**    Sickly Polish peasant, father of Wanda Bzik, and owner of the slave Jacob Eliezer in Isaac Bashevis Singer's *The Slave*.

**Mannon Cable**   Prolific movie star and womanizer; husband of Melanie-Shanna in Jackie Collins's *Hollywood Husbands*.

**Melanie–Shanna Cable**   Forgiving wife of womanizing movie-star husband Mannon Cable in Jackie Collins's *Hollywood Husbands*.

**Cacciato**   American infantryman who goes AWOL to travel from Vietnam to Paris and is pursued by his own squad in Tim O'Brien's *Going After Cacciato*.

**Mrs. Cadogan**   Mother of Emma; widow of Lyon the blacksmith, lover of Joe Hart the brewer and the Welshman Cadogan in Susan Sontag's *The Volcano Lover*.

**Abraham (Abe) Cady**   American Jewish author of *The Holocaust*, a book that charges Adam Kelno with sterilizing healthy Jewish patients without the use of an anaesthetic in the Jadwiga concentration camp; defendant in a libel suit; lover of Sarah Wydman in Leon Uris's *QB VII*.

**Ben Cady**   Son of Abe Cady; Israeli pilot killed during the Arab-Israeli conflict in Leon Uris's *QB VII*.

**Dr. Benjamin Cady**   Nobel Prize winner, one of Jesse Vogel's medical heroes, and father of Helene Cady Vogel in Joyce Carol Oates's *Wonderland*.

**Helene Cady**   See Helene Cady Vogel.

**Brian (Art) Caffrey**   Grandson of Katherine Brownell and heir apparent to Etienne Dulac's audacity in Wright Morris's *Cause for Wonder*.

**Liam Cagertown**   Boyfriend of Jean Warner; British psychology professor; Dara makes a pass at him, and he tells Jean about it in Ann Beattie's *My Life, Starring Dara Falcon*.

**Matthew (Matt) Cahn**   Handsome Arab; second husband of Rachel Farrell in William Herrick's *The Itinerant*.

**Anna Oliver Caillet**   Beautiful and artistic older daughter of Thomas Oliver; marries Oliver's adopted son, Robert Caillet, and bears a son to carry on the family name in Shirley Ann Grau's *The Condor Passes*.

**Anthony Caillet**   Son of Anna and Robert Caillet destined to carry on the family name; commits suicide, driving his parents to despair in Shirley Ann Grau's *The Condor Passes*.

**Aurelie Caillet**   Mother of Joan Mitchell and four other daughters from five successive marriages in Shirley Ann Grau's *The House on Coliseum Street*.

**Robert Caillet**   Adopted son of Thomas Oliver; unfaithful husband of Anna Oliver Caillet and father of Anthony Caillet in Shirley Ann Grau's *The Condor Passes*.

**Woodrow Cain**   Boy Frieda MacTeer fights at the school playground to defend Pecola Breedlove in Toni Morrison's *The Bluest Eye*.

**George (Georgie, Daddy George, Junior) Cain**   Harlem basketball star and community hero unable to handle the pressure in a private school, which he attends as a token black; becomes a drug addict and ex-convict; narrator of George Cain's *Blueschild Baby*.

**Keith (Raschid) Cain**   Brother of George Cain; involved in urban street violence; becomes a Muslim in George Cain's *Blueschild Baby*.

**Mom Cain**   Deeply religious mother of George Cain in George Cain's *Blueschild Baby*.

**Pop (Grandad) Cain**  Ambitious government worker and father of George Cain in George Cain's *Blueschild Baby*.

**Cal**  Favorite student of Thomas Eborn; Eborn dreams that Cal has died on the evening Eborn's mother actually dies in Reynolds Price's *Love and Work*.

**Sally Caldwell**  Divorced mother, "lady friend" of Frank Bascombe; owns Curtain Calls, a business that finds Broadway theater tickets for people with terminal illnesses in Richard Ford's *Independence Day*.

**Catherine Kramer (Cassie, Chariclo) Caldwell**  Wife of George Caldwell, mother of Peter Caldwell, and daughter of Pop Kramer in John Updike's *The Centaur*.

**Elias (Old Man) Caldwell**  Dying neighbor of the Holbrooks, who tries to tell Mazie Holbrook what he has learned about life and wills her his books, which her father sells for fifty cents in Tillie Olsen's *Yonnondio*.

**George W. (Chiron, Sticks) Caldwell**  Husband of Cassie Caldwell and father of Peter Caldwell; high school general science teacher and swimming coach preoccupied with death and mythic delusions that he is the perpetually wounded Chiron, noblest of all centaurs; narrates part of John Updike's *The Centaur*.

**Maude Caldwell**  West Indian neighbor of the Coffin family and twelve-year-old best friend of Francie Coffin in Louise Meriwether's *Daddy Was a Number Runner*.

**Peter Caldwell**  Son of George and Cassie Caldwell; cares deeply about his father but is often embarrassed by him; longs to be an artist; narrates part of John Updike's *The Centaur*.

**Rebecca (Becky) Caldwell**  Sixteen-year-old sister of Maude Caldwell and neighbor and friend of Francie Coffin in Louise Meriwether's *Daddy Was a Number Runner*.

**Sam Caldwell**  Railroad man in William Faulkner's *The Reivers*.

**Vallejo (Vallie) Caldwell**  Neighbor of Francie Coffin; arrested and sentenced to die for the robbery and murder of a shoe salesman in Louise Meriwether's *Daddy Was a Number Runner*.

**Jackson Calhoun**  Rutherford's older brother and father figure who cares for their master, Peleg Chandler; asks Chandler to divide his inheritance among the slaves instead of taking all for himself and Rutherford in Charles Johnson's *Middle Passage*.

**Noah Calhoun**  Hardworking lover of poetry, the North Carolina outdoors, and Allie Nelson; his adoration of Allie survives fourteen years of separation, Allie's engagement to Lon Hammond, and Allie's battle with Alzheimer's disease in Nicholas Sparks's *The Notebook*.

**Riley Calhoun**  Rutherford's father; leaves his family to escape from Peleg Chandler's farm; is caught and killed in Charles Johnson's *Middle Passage*.

**Rutherford Calhoun**  Freed slave from southern Illinois who works as petty thief; travels to Louisiana once freed; works on a slave clipper, the *Republic,* to avoid creditor Philippe "Papa" Zeringue and marriage to Isadora Bailey; survives mutiny and shipwreck to be rescued by luxury ship, the *Juno;* rediscovers Isadora and saves her from marriage to Zeringue by marrying her himself; raises Baleka as his own daughter in Charles Johnson's *Middle Passage*.

**Woodrow F. Call**  Former Texas Ranger captain; partner with Augustus McCrae in the Hat Creek Cattle Company; father of Newton Dobbs; gives Newton responsibility over cattle operations in Larry McMurtry's *Lonesome Dove*.

**Deedee (Dolores) Callahan**  Wife of Jack Callahan; heavy marijuana user; has sex with Pablo Tabor on the *Cloud* and is killed by him in Robert Stone's *A Flag for Sunrise*.

**Donald Callahan**  Pastor of Jerusalem's Lot, who seeks to help Matt Burke destroy vampires in Stephen King's *'Salem's Lot*.

**Jack Callahan**  Owner of the *Cloud,* a shrimp boat Pablo Tabor works on; sells guns to the rebels; married to Deedee; is killed by Pablo Tabor in Robert Stone's *A Flag for Sunrise*.

**Thomas Callahan**  Recovering alcoholic, middle-aged law professor at Tulane University; former law clerk of one of the Supreme Court justices who is murdered in John Grisham's *The Pelican Brief;* boyfriend of Darby Shaw, a law student at Tulane; killed in a car bombing.

**Maria Callas**  Singer and girlfriend of Trout Fishing in America in Richard Brautigan's *Trout Fishing in America*.

**Mindy Callender**  Young and pregnant girlfriend of Jake Simms in Anne Tyler's *Earthly Possessions*.

**Dante Callicchio**  Former boxer and wrestler and father of three children; severely beats the federal men in New York so Fred Trumper can flee them in John Irving's *The Water-Method Man*.

**Dutt Callister**  Neighbor who accompanies Elias McCutcheon on the raid of the Horse Pens and later to the Civil War in Jesse Hill Ford's *The Raider*.

**Fancy Callister**  Wife of Dutt Callister; bears several children and constantly complains in Jesse Hill Ford's *The Raider*.

**Callistus**  Servant and bodyguard assigned to Julian Augustus by a cabal of Christian military officers; assassinates Julian at the height of a military skirmish with the Persians in Gore Vidal's *Julian*.

**Caroline Calloway**    Intellectual mother of Louisa Calloway; suffers from periods of depression in Alice Adams's *Families and Survivors*.

**Corrine Calloway**    Stockbroker who desperately wishes to leave professional life to start a family; suffers a miscarriage and separates from her husband, Russell, after he has an affair; feels guilty when Jeff Pierce, the couple's mutual friend and her one-time lover, dies; remains in love with Russell after a divorce in Jay McInerney's *Brightness Falls*.

**Jack Calloway**    Tobacco-rich father of Louisa Calloway; vocal in his prejudice against Franklin Delano Roosevelt, unions, blacks, and Jews; spends life in and out of sanitoriums in Alice Adams's *Families and Survivors*.

**Louisa (Lou, Louisa Jeffreys, Louisa Wasserman) Calloway**    Modern southern belle rebelling against family wealth and tradition; protagonist of Alice Adams's *Families and Survivors*.

**Russell (Crash) Calloway**    Rising young editor at a New York publishing house who lives with his wife, Corrine, in a tiny Manhattan apartment; seeks to overthrow his former mentor; fails, and destroys his marriage; out of a job and divorced, he lands in Los Angeles, working for a movie studio and developing scripts in Jay McInerney's *Brightness Falls*.

**Calvin**    Black gay man who befriends Molly Bolt on her arrival in New York City in Rita Mae Brown's *Rubyfruit Jungle*.

**Calyxa**    Mythical figure who is also a student writing a thesis on *Perseus in the Perseid*, a novella in John Barth's *Chimera*.

**Camara (Princess)**    Six-year-old daughter of Truman Held and Lynne Rabinowitz; dies as the result of a violent, unspecified crime in Alice Walker's *Meridian*.

**Joe Camber**    Owner of Cujo, who neglects to take the dog to the vet for his rabies shots. An independent and alcoholic backwoods mechanic, he offers to fix Donna Trenton's car in Stephen King's *Cujo*.

**Hector Camerando**    Resident of the Towers, a seniors' condominium complex where Mrs. Bliss lives; gives Mrs. Bliss a ride after one of her therapeusist meetings; afterward, places bets on the greyhound races and jai alai games for her in Stanley Elkin's *Mrs. Ted Bliss*.

**Cameron**    Professional killer, companion of Greer, habitual counter, and destroyer of the Hawkline Monster; plans to but does not marry Susan Hawkline in Richard Brautigan's *The Hawkline Monster*.

**Adah Campbell**    Former Las Vegas showgirl; wife of Ian Campbell in Joseph Wambaugh's *The Onion Field*.

**Chrissie Campbell**    Mother of Ian Campbell in Joseph Wambaugh's *The Onion Field*.

**Howard W. Campbell, Jr.**    American playwright turned Nazi propagandist and U.S. spy; narrator of Kurt Vonnegut's *Mother Night*, and the "American Quisling" in *Slaughterhouse-Five*.

**Ian James Campbell**    Los Angeles policeman killed by Gregory Powell and Jimmy Smith in Joseph Wambaugh's *The Onion Field*.

**Kay (Kay-Kay, The Pumpkin) Campbell**    English literature major from Iowa and lover of Alex Portnoy; her refusal to convert to Judaism prompts Portnoy to end their relationship in Philip Roth's *Portnoy's Complaint*.

**Milly Campbell**    Wife of Shep Campbell and mother of their four sons; contented with her suburban life in Richard Yates's *Revolutionary Road*.

**Sheppard Sears (Shep) Campbell**    Well-educated and affluent engineer who adopts a self-created mask of boorish masculinity; secretly in love with April Wheeler in Richard Yates's *Revolutionary Road*.

**Terrence (Terry) Campbell**    Ward of Adam Kelno and friend of Stephan Kelno; medical doctor in Leon Uris's *QB VII*.

**Tunis G. Campbell**    Antislavery activist, author of a memoir, and subject of Sam's research in Nicholas Delbanco's *News*; mentioned in *In the Middle Distance*.

**Virgil Campbell**    Owner and operator of Bound for Hell Grocery and Dry Goods on the outskirts of Tipton, North Carolina; discovers that a child rescued from a roadside creek is a relative of a state official and, with the help of a reporter, declares the rescuer a hero in Fred Chappell's *Brighten the Corner Where You Are*.

**Virgil Campbell**    Wily country storekeeper and school board member who gives David Christopher the job as principal of Cornhill Grammar School in Fred Chappell's *It Is Time, Lord*.

**Dan T. Campion**    Corrupt contractor and important member of the Catholic Church in John Gregory Dunne's *True Confessions*.

**Lieutenant Campos**    Social agent of the Guardia Nacional in Tecan; kills a young hippie girl and confesses to Father Egan about it; watches Sister Justin and later tortures and kills her and confesses it to Father Egan in Robert Stone's *A Flag for Sunrise*.

**Eva Medina (Eve, Sweet) Canada**    Narrator who, as a young woman, is sentenced to a reformatory for having stabbed Moses Tripp in the hand; married for two years to James Hunn; murders her lover, Davis Carter, and is imprisoned in a psychiatric prison in Gayl Jones's *Eva's Man*.

**John Canada**    Husband of Marie Canada and father of Eva Medina Canada in Gayl Jones's *Eva's Man*.

**Marie Canada**    Wife of John Canada, mother of Eva Medina Canada, and lover of Tyrone in Gayl Jones's *Eva's Man*.

**John (Johnny) Candoe**   Puritan soldier and follower of Johnny Church and Thankful Perkins; condemned to death for mutiny but spared in Cromwell's blanket pardon in Mary Lee Settle's *Prisons*.

**Audrey Cannon**   Assistant professor of dance and theater arts who limps because of an accident with a lawnmower; has an affair with Severin Winter in John Irving's *The 158-Pound Marriage*.

**Rinaldo (Ronald) Cantabile**   Flashy criminal and would-be mafia operator who smashes Charlie Citrine's Mercedes over a welched bet and tries to exploit Citrine's writings for personal profit in Saul Bellow's *Humboldt's Gift*.

**Davey Cantor**   Fellow student and friend of Reuven Malter in Chaim Potok's *The Chosen*.

**Benjamin (Ben) Cape**   Son of Caleb and Lizzie Cape; witnesses the murder of his friend Folded Leaf in Jessamyn West's *The Massacre at Fall Creek*.

**Caleb (Cale) Cape**   Husband of Lizzie Cape and unordained preacher to the settlement in Jessamyn West's *The Massacre at Fall Creek*.

**Hannah (Hannay) Cape**   Daughter of Caleb and Lizzie Cape; courted by Charles Fort and Oscar Dilk in Jessamyn West's *The Massacre at Fall Creek*.

**Lizzie Cape**   Wife of Caleb Cape in Jessamyn West's *The Massacre at Fall Creek*.

**Barry Caprio**   Brother of Steve Caprio and former navy boxer; hired by Jackie Cogan to beat a confession out of Mark Trattman in George V. Higgins's *Cogan's Trade*.

**Steve Caprio**   Mafia thug and brother of Barry Caprio; hired by Jackie Cogan to beat a confession out of Mark Trattman in George V. Higgins's *Cogan's Trade*.

**Captain of the Gendarmes**   Man in exile on a mission; mercilessly hunts down Timur in a graphic, labyrinthine chase and ensuing brutal murder; shows no remorse for his actions in Mary Lee Settle's *Blood Tie*.

**Admiral Caracciolo**   Forty-seven-year-old Neapolitan prince who gives decades of service to the Bourbon monarchs; put to death by a verdict requested by The Hero in Susan Sontag's *The Volcano Lover*.

**C. (Eye, Stew Meat) Card**   Spanish Civil War veteran and down-and-out private detective given to daydreaming about Babylon; hired to steal a corpse in Richard Brautigan's *Dreaming of Babylon*.

**Robert Card**   African-American man known as Bobby; joins Civil Rights movement; undergoes horrors in Mississippi while working on voter registration campaign; helped by John Calvin Marshall; lives with African-American woman and has daughter with her; leaves for a white lover; reconciles with mother of his child in Julius Lester's *And All Our Wounds Forgiven*.

**Tert Card**   Managing editor for *Gammy Bird* newspaper in E. Annie Proulx's *The Shipping News;* hires Quoyle; leaves newspaper to write newsletter for oil rig suppliers.

**Antonio Careri**   Venetian autodidact and physician who claims he is following in the footsteps of his uncle, Gemelli Careri, who had experienced many marvels in the Indian jungles in Bharati Mukherjee's *The Holder of the World*.

**Colonel Cargill**   Former marketing executive famed for failure; now troubleshooter for General Peckem in Joseph Heller's *Catch-22*.

**Carl**   Husband of Vera; kills her lover, E. L. Fletcher in Jerry Bumpus's *Anaconda*.

**Carl**   Navy combat veteran whose plan to murder Raditzer is thwarted in Peter Matthiessen's *Raditzer*.

**Carla**   Mental patient who becomes Deborah Blau's friend in Hannah Green's *I Never Promised You a Rose Garden*.

**Clare Carleton-Robbins**   Flamboyant art gallery owner; divorced with one daughter, Puffin; is caught in the middle of a conflict between her friends Margo Sampson and Francine "B. B." Brady Broder; attempts a cautious reconciliation with her husband, Robin, in Judy Blume's *Smart Women*.

**Darlene Mosby Carlisle**   Best friend of Neva Manning and former lover of Calvin Bartley in Hal Bennett's *A Wilderness of Vines*.

**Ida (Cordelia) Carlisle**   Powerful preserver of a social system based on differences in skin color among blacks in Burnside, Virginia; convicted of pretending to be white; dies in a home for the criminally insane; appears in Hal Bennett's *A Wilderness of Vines*, *The Black Wine*, and *Wait Until Evening*.

**Carlos**   Proprietor of a wine cellar in John Edgar Wideman's *Hurry Home*.

**Carlos**   Neighbor of Harry Meyers; often beats his wife, Nydia, and threatens Meyers in Jay Neugeboren's *Listen Ruben Fontanez*.

**Carlotta**   Mother of BZ; gives BZ and Helene money to stay married in Joan Didion's *Play It As It Lays*.

**Bob Carlson**   Sophomore at Moo University; caretaker of Earl Butz, the porcine subject of Dr. Bo Jones's experiment in Jane Smiley's *Moo*.

**Carmen**   Partner of Winston; lived with Ursula and Michael for a year; always preferred exotic men from foreign countries before Winston in Sandra Scofield's *Beyond Deserving*.

**Margaret Carmichael**   See Margaret Carmichael Howland.

**Robert Carmichael**   See Robert Carmichael Howland.

**Jersey Carmody**   Single mother, writer, and helper of the other activists in M. F. Beal's *Amazon One*.

**Joe Carp**   Bakery worker with Charlie Gordon in Daniel Keyes's *Flowers for Algernon*.

**David (Davey) Carpenter**   Infant son of Patsy and Jim Carpenter in Larry McMurtry's *Moving On*.

**James (Jim) Carpenter**   Husband of Patsy White Carpenter and father of Davey Carpenter; leaves Patsy for fellow Rice University graduate student Clara Clark in Larry McMurtry's *Moving On*.

**Patsy White Carpenter**   Wife of Jim Carpenter and mother of Davey Carpenter; takes Hank Malory as a lover and loses her husband to Clara Clark in Larry McMurtry's *Moving On*.

**Carl Carper**   Youngest son of Hildie Carper, half brother of Blue and Peter in Mary McGarry Morris's *Songs in Ordinary Time*.

**Hildie Carper**   Mother of Blue; sells alcohol to minors in Mary McGarry Morris's *Songs in Ordinary Time*.

**Peter Carper**   Son of Hildie Carper, half brother of Blue and Carl in Mary McGarry Morris's *Songs in Ordinary Time*.

**Oswaldo "Pepe" Carreon**   Protégé and possibly son of General Nicasio Ledesma; member of the Philippine security forces that assassinate Senator Domingo Avila; woman-hater who marries into the wealthy Alacran family and neglects his wife, Baby Alacran, in Jessica Hagedorn's *Dogeaters*.

**Carrie**   Mute slave who befriends Dana Franklin and marries Nigel in Octavia E. Butler's *Kindred*.

**James Lawford Carrington**   Nashville sculptor and second husband of Rozelle Hardcastle; dies of a heroin overdose in Robert Penn Warren's *A Place to Come To*.

**Rebecca Carrington**   See Rebecca Carrington Jones-Talbot.

**Rozelle Hardcastle Butler (Beauty Queen of Dugton High, Miss Pritty-Pants, Rose) Carrington**   Wife successively of Michael X. Butler, J. Lawford Carrington, and a black man posing as a swami; lover of Jed Tewksbury in Robert Penn Warren's *A Place to Come To*.

**Willard Carroll**   Paterfamilias and grandfather of Lucy Nelson Bassart in Philip Roth's *When She Was Good*.

**Lowell Carruthers**   Tense, paranoid boyfriend of Ursa Mackenzie; hates his job and his boss at an electronics company in Paule Marshall's *Daughters*.

**Grondine Carson**   Garbage man; engaged to Jozia, but she breaks up with him in Mary McGarry Morris's *Songs in Ordinary Time*.

**Jonah Dean (J. D.) Carson**   Powerful political ally of Angus Cleveland under indictment for theft of political funds; manipulator of anti–school integration demonstrations in Julian Mayfield's *The Grand Parade*.

**Marvin (Marv) Carson**   Banker who encourages Larry Cook to transfer his farm, Harold Clark to buy his tractor, and Tyler Smith to buy the Slurrystore and Harvestore for raising hogs; his refusal to lend Ty the money to plant, coupled with a downturn in agricultural prices, ultimately leads to the demise of the farm in Jane Smiley's *A Thousand Acres*.

**Audrey Carsons**   American child who becomes a wild boy in William S. Burroughs's *The Wild Boys*; creates his lover Jerry in his story, *The Autobiography of a Wolf*, and participates in the attempt to blow up the nerve-gas train in *Exterminator!*

**Ardis Carter**   See Ardis Ross.

**Davis (Davy) Carter**   Kentuckian who is murdered by his lover, Eva Medina Canada in Gayl Jones's *Eva's Man*.

**Faron Carter**   Fishing guide who works out of Key West in Thomas McGuane's *Ninety-Two in the Shade*.

**Dr. Harry Carter**   Teacher of psychology and one of Jacob Horner's interviewers at Wicomico State Teachers College in John Barth's *The End of the Road*.

**William Carter**   See Jackson Yeager.

**Elijah J. (Hookworm) Cartwright**   Sex-driven Tennessee mountain boy who is a member of Big Red Smalley's traveling gospel show in George Garrett's *Do, Lord, Remember Me*.

**Lettie Cartwright**   Midwife of Tangierneck in Sarah E. Wright's *This Child's Gonna Live*.

**Betsy Carver**   Middle-aged Memphis eccentric and oldest daughter of George and Minta Carver; prevented from marrying her Nashville sweetheart, Wyant Brawley; opens a real estate business in Memphis; never marries and carries on an indiscreet social life in Memphis nightclubs in Peter Taylor's *A Summons to Memphis*.

**George Carver, Jr.**   Youngest son of George and Minta Carver; described as an unimaginative and insensitive boy as he seems undisturbed by the family's relocation from Nashville to Memphis; after briefly working in his father's law firm, he lies about being drafted into the army in order to establish his independence from his domineering parent; killed in World War II in Peter Taylor's *A Summons to Memphis*.

**George Carver, Sr.**   Husband of Minta Carver and father of George, Phillip, Betsy, and Josephine; takes his family from

Nashville to Memphis after being betrayed by a friend and business partner; becomes a successful lawyer; he earns the resentment of his family, who address their emotions when he is older and wants to remarry in Peter Taylor's *A Summons to Memphis*.

**Josephine Carver**   Youngest daughter of George and Minta Carver; prevented from marrying Clarkson Manning; opens a real estate business in Memphis with her sister, Betsy; submits to her father's control as a young woman; eventually rebels and evolves into an independent woman in Peter Taylor's *A Summons to Memphis*.

**Minta Carver**   Wife of George Carver, Sr. and mother of Betsy, Josephine, Phillip, and George; tries to maintain the family's spirits when it leaves Nashville for Memphis, but eventually loses her health in Peter Taylor's *A Summons to Memphis*.

**Phillip Carver**   Son of George, Sr., and Minta Carver and brother of Josephine, Betsy, and George, Jr., whose life in New York City is interrupted by his sisters' determination that he become involved in family matters in Memphis. The interruption allows him to address issues he has ignored in Peter Taylor's *A Summons to Memphis*.

**Jock Casey**   Imaginary pitcher who kills Damon Rutherford with a bean ball in Robert Coover's *The Universal Baseball Association, Inc., J. Henry Waugh, Prop.*

**Margaret Casey**   Manipulative Irish-Catholic housekeeper to whom Isabel Moore makes a final conscience payment in Mary Gordon's *Final Payments*.

**Mrs. Casey**   Patient of Jack Flood who dies; ran a smoke shop for forty years in Maureen Howard's *Expensive Habits*.

**Leni Cass**   Unemployed actress living with her son in a Second Avenue apartment managed by Norman Moonbloom in Edward Lewis Wallant's *The Tenants of Moonbloom*.

**Cassandra (Candy)**   Daughter of Skipper and Gertrude, mother of Pixie, and wife of Fernandez; commits suicide by jumping from the top of a lighthouse in John Hawkes's *Second Skin*.

**Cassie**   Fiancée of Bumper Morgan and teacher of French at Los Angeles City College in Joseph Wambaugh's *The Blue Knight*.

**Lou Castelluci**   Former student of Yolanda Garcia; discovers a collection of short stories by Professor Garcia that contains a story strikingly similar to one he wrote in a creative writing class; husband of Penny Ross Castelluci in Julia Alvarez's *Yo!*

**Minnie Castevet**   Wife of Roman Castevet; prepares the mysterious daily drinks for Rosemary Woodhouse during Rosemary's pregnancy with Satan's son in Ira Levin's *Rosemary's Baby*.

**Roman Castevet**   Warlock who poses as a kindly old neighbor of Rosemary and Guy Woodhouse; orchestrates Satan's seduction of Rosemary Woodhouse in Ira Levin's *Rosemary's Baby*. See also Steven Marcato.

**Joe Castiglione**   Miner who initiates a new recruit by sodomizing him with an air hose in Robert Coover's *The Origin of the Brunists*.

**Cesar Castillo**   Older brother of Nestor Castillo and son of Maria and Pedro Castillo; moves to New York from Cuba to become a famous bandleader; drinks himself to death in a hotel room surrounded by his old recordings and photographs in Oscar Hijuelos's *The Mambo Kings Play Songs of Love*.

**Eugenio Castillo**   Son of Nestor and Delores Castillo; as a child, is close to his uncle Cesar, but as an adult, is distant; calls Desi Arnaz to tell him about Cesar's death in Oscar Hijuelos's *The Mambo Kings Play Songs of Love*.

**Maria Castillo**   Wife of Pedro and mother of Cesar and Nestor Castillo; dejected by Nestor's death; thinks Cesar has become a drunkard; lives in Cuba in Oscar Hijuelos's *The Mambo Kings Play Songs of Love*.

**Nestor Castillo**   Younger brother of Cesar Castillo and son of Maria and Pedro Castillo; moves to New York to play in a band with his brother; writes their most famous song, "Beautiful Maria of My Soul"; marries Delores Fuentes and has two children; never gets over his love for Maria Rivera; dies in a car accident in Oscar Hijuelos's *The Mambo Kings Play Songs of Love*.

**Pablo Castillo**   Cousin and immigration sponsor of Cesar and Nestor; works at a meatpacking plant; worries about Cesar after Nestor's death in Oscar Hijuelos's *The Mambo Kings Play Songs of Love*.

**Pedro Castillo**   Husband of Maria and father of Cesar and Nestor Castillo; beats Cesar until he moves to Havana; believes musicians are effeminate; works hard on his farm in Cuba; is not compassionate or kind toward anyone in Oscar Hijuelos's *The Mambo Kings Play Songs of Love*.

**Julian Castle**   Operator of a jungle hospital; Albert Schweitzer-figure in Kurt Vonnegut's *Cat's Cradle*.

**Mr. Castle**   Sexually molests Jill Harrington after she babysits for him; won't let his wife drive his new Lincoln to the store in Alice Hoffman's *Local Girls*.

**Mrs. Castle**   Wife of Mr. Castle; hires Jill Harrington to babysit her children Pearl and Amy in Alice Hoffman's *Local Girls*.

**Philip Castle**   Son of Julian Castle; hotelkeeper and author of a book on San Lorenzo in Kurt Vonnegut's *Cat's Cradle*.

**Uncle Castor**   One of Grandfather Eustace's brothers; visits the unnamed male narrator and main character at boyhood Capital Avenue home; jazz musician; travels with bands across the United States and Europe until his fortunes decline and he relies on relatives for his support in Darryl Pinckney's *High Cotton*.

**Fidel Castro**   Cuban dictator who, in Margaret Reynolds's fantasy, is really a woman disguised as a man in Anne Richardson Roiphe's *Up the Sandbox!*

**Ernesto Cata**   Twelve-year-old Zuni Indian in Tony Hillerman's *Dance Hall of the Dead;* chosen to represent Shulawitsi, the Little Fire God, in an important annual religious ceremony; killed by Chester Reynolds, disguised as a Salamobia, or death spirit, because he stole falsified artifacts from Reynolds's dig site.

**Catalina Kate**   See Kate.

**Governor John (Blackjack) Cates**   Head of Typhon International; great-uncle of Amy Joubert in William Gaddis's *JR.*

**John Vernon Cates**   African-American professor of chemistry at Moo University; married to a woman from Ghana; has one son; discovers the plans for Loren Stroop's machine, thereby saving the university from financial ruin in Jane Smiley's *Moo.*

**Molly Cates**   Headstrong investigative reporter; author of recent crime book based on true-life accounts of Texas death row inmate Louie Bronk; discovers that her book contains potentially false information based on recent evidence, and fights in vain to overturn Bronk's conviction in Mary Willis Walker's *The Red Scream.*

**Colonel Cathcart**   Air force officer whose desire for personal glory causes him to keep raising the number of bombing missions Yossarian's squadron must fly in Joseph Heller's *Catch-22.*

**Catherine**   Wife of Hugh, lover of Cyril, and mother of Meredith, Dolores, and Eveline; once forced by Hugh to wear a chastity belt in an attempt to stop her affair with Cyril; collapses at Hugh's funeral and spends time in a village sanctuary in John Hawkes's *The Blood Oranges.*

**Catherine**   Asthmatic wife of the Cavaliere; the only child of a wealthy Pembrokeshire squire in Susan Sontag's *The Volcano Lover.*

**Doc Cathey**   Physician and small-town philosopher; long-term companion and comforter to Henry Soames in John Gardner's *Nickel Mountain.*

**Cathy**   Boarder at the Geronimo Hotel and a student at the local teacher's college; alternately spies on and flirts with Paco in Larry Heinemann's *Paco's Story.*

**Andy Catlett**   Oldest son of Bess and Wheeler Catlett in Wendell Berry's *A Place on Earth* and *The Memory of Old Jack.*

**Bess Feltner Catlett**   Daughter of Mat and Margaret Feltner; wife of Wheeler Catlett and mother of Andy and Henry Catlett in Wendell Berry's *A Place on Earth* and *The Memory of Old Jack.*

**Henry Catlett**   Youngest son of Bess and Wheeler Catlett in Wendell Berry's *A Place on Earth* and *The Memory of Old Jack.*

**Wheeler Catlett**   Lawyer in Port William, Kentucky, and son-in-law of Mat Feltner; husband of Bess Catlett and father of Andy and Henry Catlett in Wendell Berry's *A Place on Earth* and *The Memory of Old Jack.*

**Debby Catlin**   Daughter of John and Marian Catlin in Wallace Stegner's *All the Little Live Things.*

**Henry (Hank) Catlin**   Depression-era newcomer to California from the Midwest; defeats Walter Knight for a seat in the state legislature in Joan Didion's *Run River.*

**John Catlin**   Husband of Marian Catlin in Wallace Stegner's *All the Little Live Things.*

**Marian Catlin**   Neighbor of the Allstons; dies of cancer while pregnant in Wallace Stegner's *All the Little Live Things.*

**Katherine Cattleman**   Wife of Paul Cattleman; becomes the lover of Iz Einsam, a psychiatrist for whom she works as a research assistant at UCLA in Alison Lurie's *The Nowhere City.*

**Paul Cattleman**   History researcher, husband of Katherine Cattleman, and lover of Ceci O'Connor in Alison Lurie's *The Nowhere City.*

**Charlotte Ann Caulder**   Former girlfriend of Bob Beaudreau, who shoots her after she becomes Phil Elliott's lover in Peter Gent's *North Dallas Forty.*

**Il Cavaliere (Sir William Hamilton)**   Husband of Catherine and, later, of Emma; grandson of a duke, youngest son of a lord, and childhood companion of the king; has a front-rank diplomatic posting abroad in Naples; wherever he is, prone to cast himself in the role of guide or mentor; flees the French army and ends up in Palermo; returns to London with Emma Hart and The Hero; passes away in Susan Sontag's *The Volcano Lover.*

**Melissa Cavanaugh**   Lover of Tommy Douglas in Scott Spencer's *Preservation Hall.*

**Theodore (Ted) Cavanaugh**   President of West Condon's First National Bank who is behind the efforts of the Common Sense Committee to disband the Brunists in Robert Coover's *The Origin of the Brunists.*

**Tommy (Kit, Kitten) Cavanaugh**   Son of Ted Cavanaugh; follows in the footsteps of Justin Miller as a high school basketball star in Robert Coover's *The Origin of the Brunists.*

**Robert Cavendish**   Left-wing professor of political science at Columbia University; uses women sexually and domestically; has an affair with Felicitas Taylor in Mary Gordon's *The Company of Women.*

**Jennifer (Jenny) Cavilleri**   See Jennifer Cavilleri Barrett.

**Philip (Phil) Cavilleri**   Rhode Island pastry chef and father of Jennifer Cavilleri Barrett; approves of his daughter's marriage to Oliver Barrett IV in Erich Segal's *Love Story;* consoles Barrett after Jenny's death in *Oliver's Story.*

**Ceci**   See Cecile O'Connor.

**Cederberge**   Chief inspector in the international marine police; investigates the disappearance of Hellos in Calvin Hernton's *Scarecrow*.

**Celia**   Daughter of Dan and Libby, sister of Jennie; cousin of Anne, Jenny, Rossie, and Valerie; niece of Grace, Rachel, May, and Elinor; engaged to Philip Masterson, but breaks it off when she discovers he has gotten Louanne Price pregnant; marries her old beau, Jimmy; tries to commit suicide with an overdose of pills and loses her baby in Joan Chase's *During the Reign of the Queen of Persia*.

**Celie**   Wife of Albert; older sister of Nettie; writes letters to God and later to Nettie; raped by man she believes to be her father, later discovered to be her stepfather, bears two children by him; loves Shug Avery; discovers sexuality with her; becomes active and independent in Alice Walker's *The Color Purple*.

**Dr. Chadwick**   Black general practitioner who comforts John Wilder during Wilder's last emotional breakdown in Richard Yates's *Disturbing the Peace*.

**Freddy Chaikin**   Agent for Maria Wyeth in Joan Didion's *Play It As It Lays*.

**Chairman Mao's Robot**   Chinese woman delegate to a youth festival in Moscow; kidnapped and sexually exploited by George Levanter and Romarkin in Jerzy Kosinski's *Blind Date*.

**Conrad Chakravorti**   Indian who rents the Adirondack cabin inhabited by Ambrose Clay; mishap prevents his discovery of Clay's suicide in Gail Godwin's *Violet Clay*.

**Celeste Chalfonte**   Cora's employer and friend; sister of Curtis, Spottiswod, and Carlotta; lesbian lover of Ramellekills Brutus Rife; dies at sixty-seven of a fall from a horse in Rita Mae Brown's *Six of One*. Also appears in *Loose Lips*.

**Curtis Chalfonte**   Brother of Celeste Chalfonte; lives in California; has an affair with Ramelle and is father of her daughter in Rita Mae Brown's *Six of One*.

**Spottiswood (Spotty) Chalfonte**   Celeste's youngest brother; is in the army and dies in World War I in Rita Mae Brown's *Six of One*.

**Madame Charles (Anastasia Petrovna Potapov) Chamar**   Russian mother of Armande Chamar Person; product of a noble family ruined by the revolution in Vladimir Nabokov's *Transparent Things*.

**Joshua Lawrence Chamberlain**   Brilliant Union colonel who defends a rocky hill called Little Round Top against a rebel onslaught at Gettysburg in Michael Shaara's *The Killer Angels*.

**Ishmael Chambers**   Owner, publisher, and sole reporter of the *San Piedro Review;* childhood sweetheart of Hatsue Imada; discovers evidence that could exonerate Kabuo Miyamoto of the murder of Carl Heine in David Guterson's *Snow Falling on Cedars*.

**Edith de Chambrolet**   Wealthy expatriate American who takes in McKenna Gallagher after Louisa Gallagher's suicide attempt in James Jones's *The Merry Month of May*.

**Chance (Chauncey Gardiner)**   Gardener, idiot, and hero who is propelled to fame in Jerzy Kosinski's *Being There*.

**Hamijolli Chand**   Wife of the owner of the Hotel Phoenix in Delhi; becomes Lieutenant Corson's lover in Tim O'Brien's *Going After Cacciato*.

**Cathie Chandler**   See Cathie Chandler Finer.

**Reverend Peleg Chandler**   Rutherford's master; a tobacco planter, cared for until his death by Rutherford's brother Jackson; frees Rutherford and Jackson upon his death; gives Rutherford about forty dollars and the family Bible as his share of inheritance in Charles Johnson's *Middle Passage*.

**Tom Chaney**   Hired hand and outlaw who kills two men and who is pursued by Mattie Ross, Rooster Cogburn, and LaBoeuf in Charles Portis's *True Grit*.

**Helen Chang**   Gentle, frail daughter of an aristocratic Shanghai family that secures a student visa for her to flee to the United States during the Chinese revolution in 1949; wife of Ralph Chang in Gish Jen's *Typical American*. In *Mona in the Promised Land*, she is a strict parent whose American-born children's attempts to determine their individual identities often challenge her sense of propriety and her belief that the concerns of family are paramount.

**Mona Chang**   Chinese-American teenager living in an upscale, largely Jewish New York suburb; intelligent and witty daughter who rebels against her immigrant parents by adopting the new popular ideals of late-1960s and early-1970s America; converts to Judaism in Gish Jen's *Mona in the Promised Land*.

**Ralph Chang**   Chinese graduate student stranded in the United States by the 1949 Chinese revolution; dissatisfied engineering professor who becomes an entrepreneur; domineering in times of family crisis; husband of Helen Chang, brother of Theresa Chang in Gish Jen's *Typical American*.

**Theresa Chang**   Studious independent-minded woman who arrives with her friend Helen in the United States during the 1949 Chinese revolution and finds her brother, Ralph, despairing over his poverty and his uncertain status as a foreign student; postpones her medical career to encourage Ralph to complete his doctorate; lonely and unmarried; her affair with Ralph's married colleague estranges her from Ralph and her sister-in-law Helen in Gish Jen's *Typical American*.

**Elizabeth Rockbridge Channing**   Stunningly beautiful artist who moves to the small village of Chatham, Massachusetts; begins a tragic affair with one of the school's married teachers, Leland Reed; is charged with attempted murder and adultery and is convicted and imprisoned for three years for the latter offense in Thomas H. Cook's *The Chatham School Affair*.

**Nancy Dupree (Bugsy) Channing**   Bay Area socialite who marries and divorces Ryder Charming in Joan Didion's *Run River*.

**Ryder Channing**   Entrepreneur and real estate developer; seducer of Martha McClellan and Lily Knight McClellan; murdered by Everett McClellan in Joan Didion's *Run River*.

**Chantal**   Daughter of Papa and Honorine, older sister of Pascal, and lover of Henri for five years; with Henri, an unwilling passenger in the car in John Hawkes's *Travesty*.

**John Chapman**   Lawyer and prestigious private investigator; lonely man who finds solace in his work in Danielle Steel's *Kaleidoscope*.

**John Chapman**   Friend of Thomas Keene and Fanny Cooper; grows apples and is nicknamed Appleseed John; admirer of Emanuel Swedenborg; townspeople think he is a lunatic, but they tolerate him in Hugh Nissenson's *The Tree of Life*.

**Ali Juan (God of Street Boys) Chapultepec**   Street boy in William S. Burroughs's *The Soft Machine;* as Clinch Smith's houseboy, he runs amok and is killed in *Exterminator!;* appears also in *Nova Express*, *The Ticket That Exploded*, and *The Wild Boys*.

**Anna-Maria Charaiambos**   Sister of Orsetta Procopirios in Nicholas Delbanco's *The Martlet's Tale*.

**Lambert Charibon**   Friend of Orkney Vas; owns a trout camp; burly, large, and nervous around women in Howard Norman's *The Bird Artist*.

**John F. (Jack) Charisma**   Martyred United States president and rival of Trick E. Dixon in Philip Roth's *Our Gang*.

**Charity**   Wife of Lazarus and nurse to Johnny Church, his mother, and his aunt, Nell Lacy, in Mary Lee Settle's *Prisons*.

**Charlane**   Tough-talking chef at the Deerslayer Inn in Richard Ford's *Independence Day*.

**Charles**   Son of Clara, brother of Susan, and stepson of Pete; in love with Laura, a married woman who eventually leaves her husband in Ann Beattie's *Chilly Scenes of Winter*.

**Charles**   Young street hustler and drug addict; sent to a school for delinquent boys at age fourteen for stealing; homeless after his release because his mother is hospitalized and his father has disappeared in Alexis Deveaux's *Spirit in the Street*.

**Charles**   Nephew of the Cavaliere; mineralogy is the ruling passion of his life; manages Catherine's estate in Wales; compulsively washes his hands; never marries in Susan Sontag's *The Volcano Lover*.

**Charles II**   See Charles Xavier Vseslav.

**Charlie**   Large, kind, black male nurse on the Men's Violent Ward of Bellevue Mental Hospital, where John Wilder is a patient in Richard Yates's *Disturbing the Peace*.

**Charlie**   Painter from Texas whose affair with Big Lot inspires the male narrator, Charlie's lover, to write in Tennessee Williams's *Moise and the World of Reason*.

**Charlotte**   Daughter of Miss Billie in Gayl Jones's *Eva's Man*.

**Charlotte**   French trainee PaPa LaBas hires to replace Berbelang; becomes an assistant in a stage show and, because she helps Berbelang return art stolen by Western museums to the original owners, is killed by Biff Musclewhite in Ishmael Reed's *Mumbo Jumbo*.

**Charlotte**   Mina and Anatole Krainik's niece; orphaned by an accident in the salmon-canning factory where her parents worked; moves to Toronto; becomes more independent; meets Martha and Bernice, waitresses at a diner she frequents, and invites them to her birthday party in Howard Norman's *Northern Lights*.

**Charlotte**   Viennese prostitute questioned about lust by Jenny Fields; has sex with Garp, becomes a close friend of his, and dies of uterine cancer in John Irving's *The World According to Garp*.

**Charo**   Miss Mary's gun bearer and tracker; protective of her; aware of her deficiencies as a marksman in Ernest Hemingway's *True At First Light*.

**Mark Charon**   Corrupt police detective who works with Henry Tucker; arranges the murder of one of Tucker's contacts, Eddie Morello, is killed by Tucker's associate Tony Piaggi during the final confrontation between Tucker and Kelly in Tom Clancy's *Without Remorse*.

**Chase**   Brief flirtation of Beigh's from a summer archaeology dig in Harvard Yard, with a knack for finding fragments; the first of her friends to win a genius grant in Bharati Mukherjee's *The Holder of the World*.

**Betsy Chase**   Fiancée of Eric Herman, the new photography instructor at Haddan School and houseparent at St. Anne's dormitory; is used to life in the city rather than life in a small town, continually gets lost; orphaned, she possesses a survivor's guilt; becomes the lover of Abel Gray and runs away with him in Alice Hoffman's *The River King*.

**Joseph Raymond (Joe, Joey) Chase**   Brother of Orpha Chase; Quaker minister and faith healer charged with manslaughter in the death of Marie Griswold in Jessamyn West's *The Life I Really Lived*.

**Mary Eliza Chase**   Niece of Eliza Bowen Jumel; marries Nelson Chase in Gore Vidal's *Burr*.

**Nelson Chase**   Nephew by marriage of Eliza Bowen Jumel and husband of Mary Eliza Chase in Gore Vidal's *Burr*.

**Orpha (Mrs. Dudley, Mrs. Hesse, Tumbleweed) Chase**   Novelist; sister of Joseph Chase; wife of Alonzo Dudley, Jacob Hesse, and Ralph Navarro; lover of Tom O'Hara and Gregory McGovern; adoptive mother of Wanda; narrator of Jessamyn West's *The Life I Really Lived*.

**Dean Chasen**   Bond trader on Wall Street who dreams of retiring so that he can become a full-time writer; begins a promising relationship with Alison Poole that is eventually sabotaged by infidelity and the excesses of Alison's lifestyle in Jay McInerney's *Story of My Life*.

**Darryl Louise (DL) Chastain**   Ninja warrior who was trained in Japan while her parents were stationed at a military base; serves as an assassin in a failed attempt to murder Brock Vond; protects Prarie Wheeler from Brock Vond and informs the girl of the political acts of her parents during the 1960s in Thomas Pynchon's *Vineland*.

**Denise Chatillion**   Early settler of Fort Hill and wife of Pettecasockee in Jesse Hill Ford's *The Raider*.

**Chaucer**   Chief writer for comedian Harry Mercury in Peter De Vries's *Through the Fields of Clover*.

**Domingo (Ding) Chavez**   Light-infantry sergeant who volunteers for a covert operation against Colombian drug-smuggling operations; is stranded in Colombia with members of other teams when Cutter cuts off support for their mission; fends off Colombian assaults long enough for Jack Ryan and John Clark to effect their rescue; transfers to CIA at Clark's suggestion in Tom Clancy's *Clear and Present Danger*. Later appears as a CIA field officer and son-in-law to Clark in *Rainbow Six*.

**Mary Cheap**   Elderly Jewish store owner who insists Joe Market end her life as he did his son's in Hal Bennett's *Lord of Dark Places*.

**Annie Chelsea**   Billy Chelsea's five-year-old daughter in Mary McGarry Morris's *A Dangerous Woman*.

**Billy Chelsea**   Widower whom Martha Horgan has a crush on; has two small daughters in Mary McGarry Morris's *A Dangerous Woman*.

**CeeCee Chelsea**   Billy Chelsea's four-year-old daughter in Mary McGarry Morris's *A Dangerous Woman*.

**Albert Chenal**   White merchant in protest of whom the Reverend Phillip Martin is organizing the black community in Ernest J. Gaines's *In My Father's House*.

**Celia Chentshiner**   Intellectual wife of Haiml Chentshiner and lover of Morris Feitelzohn and Aaron Greidinger in Isaac Bashevis Singer's *Shosha*.

**Haiml Chentshiner**   Well-to-do husband of Celia Chentshiner and friend and benefactor of Aaron Greidinger in Isaac Bashevis Singer's *Shosha*.

**Cherry**   See Cherry Melanie.

**Cheryl**   Speech therapist; teaches Theodora not to hiss her s's in Bette Pesetsky's *Midnight Sweets*.

**Charles (Cheswickle) Cheswick**   Blustering but insecure mental patient who apparently drowns himself in Ken Kesey's *One Flew Over the Cuckoo's Nest*.

**Kashi Chetty**   Trader at Fort St. Sebastian in Bharati Mukherjee's *The Holder of the World*.

**Chiang (Elder Gull, The Elder)**   Leader of the flock of seagulls who are perfecting their flying skills; helps Jonathan Livingston Seagull become a better flyer in Richard Bach's *Jonathan Livingston Seagull*.

**Bebe (Francois Parmentier) Chicago**   West Indian homosexual with political connections to the guerrilleros and to Gerardo Strasser-Mendana in Joan Didion's *A Book of Common Prayer*.

**Chicken Little**   Young boy who, during a child's game, slips from Sula's hands and drowns in Toni Morrison's *Sula*.

**Chicken Number Two**   Lifetime convict who, in his dying days, evokes a transforming sympathy in Zeke Farragut that results in Farragut's escape in John Cheever's *Falconer*.

**Clayton (Bloody) Chiclitz**   American industrialist and president of Yoyodyne, Inc. in Thomas Pynchon's *V.* and *The Crying of Lot 49*; toy manufacturer involved in black-marketeering with Major Duane Marvy in *Gravity's Rainbow*.

**Chief Broom**   See Chief Broom Bromden.

**Doctor Reverend Wesley Augustus Chillingworth**   Professor of ethics at the divinity school Thomas Marshfield attended; father of Jane Chillingworth Marshfield in John Updike's *A Month of Sundays*.

**China**   Thinnest of the three prostitutes who live above the Breedloves; so named for her makeup choices; like her roommates, she hates men in Toni Morrison's *The Bluest Eye*.

**China Mary**   Longtime housekeeper for the McClellan family in Joan Didion's *Run River*.

**Chink**   Keeper of the clockworks, shaman of Siwash Ridge, and impregnator of Sissy Hankshaw Gitche in Tom Robbins's *Even Cowgirls Get the Blues*.

**Thomas Chippering**   Professor of linguistics; compulsive womanizer and liar; boyhood friend of Herbie and Lorna Sue Zylstra; serves in Vietnam; marries Lorna Sue; after she leaves, seeks revenge on her and new husband; begins affair with Donna Kooshof; loses his job; agrees to marry Donna Kooshof in Tim O'Brien's *Tomcat in Love*.

**Chippo**    See Erin Simon.

**Edith Chipps**    English radio and television writer; wife, then widow of Gowan McGland and paramour of Alvin Mopworth in Peter De Vries's *Reuben, Reuben*.

**Deputy Warden Chisholm**    Unsympathetic supervisor at Falconer prison whose denial of drugs to Zeke Farragut gives the convict periods of extreme agony in John Cheever's *Falconer*.

**Alcibiades Chitral**    Buys Mrs. Bliss's deceased husband's Buick LeSabre; Mrs. Bliss testifies against him; he is convicted of dealing drugs and is sentenced to one hundred years in prison; Mrs. Bliss later visits him in prison in Stanley Elkin's *Mrs. Ted Bliss*.

**Choh**    Artisan and Tehkohn wife of Gehnahteh; fosters Tien in Octavia E. Butler's *Survivor*.

**Bill Chokee**    Pawnbroker from whom Edward Pierce buys guns and bullets in Michael Crichton's *The Great Train Robbery*.

**Luzana (Old Luze) Cholly**    Legendary bluesman idolized by Scooter in Albert Murray's *Train Whistle Guitar*.

**Chorus**    Ancient chorus upset with Antigone for taking away its lines; shoots Minnie Yellings aboard an airplane she is hijacking; the airplane captain, mistaking Chorus for a hijacker, shoots it to death in Ishmael Reed's *The Last Days of Louisiana Red*.

**Choufleur**    Free mulatto; son of Sieur Maltrot, a wealthy planter of the French colony Saint Domingue; when his father is captured during the slave rebellion of 1792–1802, Choufleur murders him and saves his father's severed penis in a snuff box as a gift for his father's former mistress, Nanon; attempts to seduce Nanon in Madison Smartt Bell's *All Souls' Rising*.

**Chris**    Friend of Gwen Murray in Jenkintown; seriously pretty, with a rope of blond hair and creamy, pale skin in Alice Hoffman's *Here on Earth*.

**Rebecca "Jelly" Christie**    Wife of Thomas Christie; likes to entertain in a grand fashion and is a consummate hostess, circulating among her guests with grace and charm in Frances Sherwood's *Vindication*.

**Thomas Christie**    Thursday-night dinner guest of Joseph Johnson; one of Joseph's lovers; marries Rebecca "Jelly" Christie; dies of fever in Surinam the same year Mary dies in Frances Sherwood's *Vindication*.

**Christine**    Aunt of Katie, sister of June; recently widowed in Sandra Scofield's *Beyond Deserving*.

**Christine**    Worker in a laundry across from Sebastian Dangerfield's house; becomes one of Sebastian's girlfriends in J. P. Donleavy's *The Ginger Man*.

**Black Christopher**    See Christopher Hall.

**Cory Christopher**    Wife of David Christopher, mother of James and Julia Christopher, and daughter of the owners of the farm where the Christophers live in Fred Chappell's *It Is Time, Lord*.

**David (Davy) Christopher**    Husband of Cory Christopher and father critical of his son, James, but indulgent toward his daughter, Julia; teacher fired for his teaching of science but too proud to ask for reinstatement in Fred Chappell's *It Is Time, Lord*.

**James (Jimmy) Christopher**    Son of Cory and David Christopher and husband of Sylvia Christopher; quits his job as production manager of Winton College Press to come to terms with his past and his own identity; eventually starts over by reapplying for his job and returning to his family; narrator of Fred Chappell's *It Is Time, Lord*.

**Julia Christopher**    Younger sister of James Christopher; model child and responsible adult who claims she always has protected James from the consequences of his actions in Fred Chappell's *It Is Time, Lord*.

**Sylvia Christopher**    Understanding wife of James Christopher in Fred Chappell's *It Is Time, Lord*.

**Chrysanthi (Chrýsomou)**    Lover of Sotiris Procopirios in Athens in Nicholas Delbanco's *The Martlet's Tale*.

**Eustace Chubb**    Poet known for his cold war verse in John Updike's *Bech: A Book*.

**Laurence Chubb, Jr.**    Head of Chubb's safe-making company who shows the South Eastern Railway safes to Miss Miriam in Michael Crichton's *The Great Train Robbery*.

**Arkikov Chuchki**    Eskimo reindeer herder; strikes gold at Seven Above mine in Nome; loses claim due to foreign status; discovers first gold on Nome beaches in James Michener's *Alaska*.

**Corporal Jonathan (Johnny) Church**    Young rebel who is disowned by his father and enlists in Cromwell's army at age sixteen; opposes Cromwell's Irish campaign but is offered a pardon if he will recant his democratic views; chooses to be executed by a firing squad; fathers a child by Nell Lacy; narrator of Mary Lee Settle's *Prisons*.

**Roy Church**    Agent for the Kansas Bureau of Investigation; works with Harold Nye in breaking the false story of Richard Hickock in Truman Capote's *In Cold Blood*.

**Soaphead Church**    See Elihue Micah Whitcomb.

**Dowell Churnin**　Neighbor of the Warners; retired high school basketball coach whose son was killed in Vietnam; partner with Tom Van Sant in Snell's Greenhouse; dates and later becomes engaged to Barbara Warner in Ann Beattie's *My Life, Starring Dara Falcon*.

**Isabelle Cigny**　Creole woman of Le Cap, capital city of the French colony Saint Domingue; during the initial days of the slave rebellion of 1791–1802, she shelters Antoine Hébert's mistress, Nanon, who bears Hebert's child in an upstairs room of Isabelle's home; takes his friend Captain Maillart, among other officers, as one of her frequent, casual lovers; escapes Le Cap after the city is subdued in the rebellion in Madison Smartt Bell's *All Souls' Rising*.

**Cipher X**　Designer of hula hoops in Ishmael Reed's *The Free-Lance Pallbearers*.

**Circe**　Midwife and housekeeper on the Butler plantation in Danville, Pennsylvania; secretly cares for Pilate Dead and Macon Dead II after their father is killed in Toni Morrison's *Song of Solomon*.

**Domenico Cirillo**　Official physician to the court and personal physician of the Cavaliere and his wife; hanged because he had welcomed the republic's invitation to carry out much-needed reforms in the organization of hospitals and medical care for the poor in Susan Sontag's *The Volcano Lover*.

**Charles (Charlie) Citrine**　Author of the Broadway play *Von Trenck,* which wins a Pulitzer Prize and becomes a successful film; friend of Von Humboldt Fleisher, jilted lover of Renata Koffritz, and seeker of a quiet life through anthroposophy; narrator of Saul Bellow's *Humboldt's Gift*.

**Claire**　Syphilitic store owner and wife of Jimmy in Jerry Bumpus's *Anaconda*.

**Claire**　Deceased wife of Konrad Vost and mother of Mirabelle in John Hawkes's *The Passion Artist*.

**Clem (Cousin Clem) Clammidge**　Farmhand turned primitive art critic; writes for the *Daily Bugle* in Peter De Vries's *I Hear America Swinging*.

**William de la Touche Clancey**　Tory sodomite and editor of the anti-American magazine *America* in Gore Vidal's *Burr*.

**Clancy**　Displaced archetypal 1890s police officer in William S. Burroughs's *Exterminator!*

**John Jester Clane**　Grandson of Judge Fox Clane and son of Johnny Clane; determined to discover the reason for his father's suicide; loves Sherman Pew in Carson McCullers's *Clock Without Hands*.

**Johnny Clane**　Son of Judge Fox Clane and father of John Jester Clane; commits suicide after he learns the woman he loves, Joy Little, detests him and loves Nigra Jones in Carson McCullers's *Clock Without Hands*.

**Judge Fox Clane**　Prejudiced judge and retired statesman whose idea to convince the government to redeem Confederate money leads to Sherman Pew's rebellion and death in Carson McCullers's *Clock Without Hands*.

**Clara**　Mother of Charles and Susan and wife of Pete; medically and psychologically unstable, demands extra care from those who are close to her in Ann Beattie's *Chilly Scenes of Winter*.

**Clara**　Native American woman who comes to a Montana reservation to care for her bedridden sister Annie George; Clara's relationship with other characters is revealed in the final section of Michael Dorris's *A Yellow Raft in Blue Water*.

**Aunt Clara**　Maternal great aunt of the unnamed male narrator and main character; lives on the margins of both black and white society in Opelika, Alabama; married a doctor, "Uncle Eugene," who was called upon to perform secret abortions on white patients; a landowner with tenants, she is devoted to the isolated dignity of her position in Darryl Pinckney's *High Cotton*.

**Clare**　Mother of Ursula; left her husband when Ursula was fifteen in Sandra Scofield's *Beyond Deserving*.

**Stormy Claridge**　Girlfriend of Ezra Lyttle; uses sex to further her career in Peter Gent's *Texas Celebrity Turkey Trot*.

**Clarie**　See Clarence Henderson.

**Clarissa**　Mira's friend in graduate school; abandons her traditional marriage for a lesbian relationship in Marilyn French's *The Women's Room*.

**Clara Clark**　Rice University graduate student and lover of Jim Carpenter in Larry McMurtry's *Moving On*.

**Howard Clark**　Farmer in Zebulon County, Iowa; father of sons Loren and Jess Clark; best friend, cohort, and neighbor of Laurence Cook; pretends to arrange reconciliation between Rose, Ginny, and their father, but instead orchestrates a public charge of disloyalty against the two older daughters in Jane Smiley's *A Thousand Acres*.

**Jess Clark**　Prodigal son of Harold and Verna Clark, who returns to Cabot, Iowa, after spending thirteen years in Vancouver, British Columbia, to escape the draft; sometime Buddhist; imaginative dreamer of alternative farming techniques and products; lover of both Ginny Cook Smith and Rose Cook Lewis; lives with Rose Lewis after her husband, Pete, dies in Jane Smiley's *A Thousand Acres*.

**John Clark**　CIA field officer who assists in planning and execution of joint CIA and military operations against drug cartels in Colombia; meets Jack Ryan after the passing of their common mentor, James Greer; returns to Colombia to kill or capture intelligence officer turned drug kingpin Felix Cortez; talks James

Cutter into committing suicide; and recruits Domingo Chavez for CIA in Tom Clancy's *Clear and Present Danger*. Also appears in *Without Remorse* and *Rainbow Six*.

**Loren Clark**   Less glamorous son of Harold and Verna Clark, who stays home to help his father farm after Jess moves to Vancouver, British Columbia, during the Vietnam War; imitates his father in mannerisms and habits but not in attitude; friend and neighbor of Ginny Cook Smith and Rose Cook Lewis in Jane Smiley's *A Thousand Acres*.

**Dorothy Clarke**   Senile neighbor of the Martins; wife of Edward; actual murderer of Robert's daughter Amber and wife, Gwen, in Minette Walters's *The Sculptress*.

**Edward Clarke**   Neighbor of the Martins; has affair with both Robert Martin and his daughter, accused murderer Olive Martin; husband of senile wife, Dorothy, the actual murderer of both Olive's mother, Gwen, and sister, Amber, in Minette Walters's *The Sculptress.*

**Helen Clarke**   Only friend of Mary Katherine, Constance, and Julian Blackwood and only regular visitor to the family home in Shirley Jackson's *We Have Always Lived in the Castle.*

**Jim Clarke**   Husband of Helen Clarke in Shirley Jackson's *We Have Always Lived in the Castle.*

**Maxwell E. Clarke**   Principal of Calvin Coolidge High School; manages to stay in his office all day, except for a rare public appearance to give a speech on lofty ideals in Bel Kaufman's *Up the Down Staircase.*

**Jud Clasby**   Hunter, trapper, and instigator of the Indian massacre in Jessamyn West's *The Massacre at Fall Creek.*

**Claudia**   Child vampire whom Louis treats as a daughter; destroyed by Lestat in Anne Rice's *Interview with the Vampire.*

**Anna Clausen**   Sister-in-law of Orin Clausen and neighbor of Chris Van Eenanain and Ellen Strohe in Larry Woiwode's *What I'm Going to Do, I Think.*

**Orin Clausen**   Brother-in-law of Anna Clausen and Michigan-woods neighbor of Chris Van Eenanam and Ellen Strohe in Larry Woiwode's *What I'm Going to Do, I Think.*

**Clay**   College freshman in New Hampshire who returns home to Los Angeles for Christmas vacation and reevaluates the friends and glamour-filled world with which he grew up in Bret Easton Ellis's *Less Than Zero.*

**Ambrose Valentine Clay**   Uncle of Violet Clay; dabbles at writing, is briefly married to Carol Gruber, and shoots himself in Gail Godwin's *Violet Clay.*

**Catherine Clay**   South Carolinian and former lover of Chester Hunnicutt Pomeroy; produces a Panamanian marriage certificate showing her marriage to Pomeroy in Thomas McGuane's *Panama.*

**Henry Clay**   Judge; the mayor of the town thirty years before; dies in Mary McGarry Morris's *Songs in Ordinary Time.*

**Violet Isabel Clay**   Aspiring artist who leaves her unsatisfactory work in New York as an illustrator of gothic novels to work seriously on her painting in an isolated cabin; narrator of Gail Godwin's *Violet Clay.*

**Harry C. Clegg**   Newspaper reporter in Thomas Berger's *Killing Time.*

**Hiram Clegg**   Brunist and eventually bishop of Randolph Junction in Robert Coover's *The Origin of the Brunists.*

**Donald Clellon**   First fiancé of Sarah Grimes Wilson; lies about his age and background, causing the engagement to be broken in Richard Yates's *Easter Parade.*

**Clem**   One of the seven dwarfs who wash windows, make Chinese baby food, and live with Snow White in Donald Barthelme's *Snow White.*

**Sam Clemence**   Boyfriend of Mary Kettlesmith in Bernard Malamud's *The Tenants.*

**Esperanza Clemente**   Nurse and midwife; was raped when she was seventeen; falls in love with and marries Rafael Beltrán in Sandra Benítez's *A Place Where the Sea Remembers.*

**Peter Clemenza**   Gangster who remains loyal to the Corleone family in Mario Puzo's *The Godfather.*

**Clemmie**   Ambitious prostitute who tells Arkie McClellan a lie about her new pimp and so causes him to shoot Zebulon Johns Mackie in Fred Chappell's *The Gaudy Place.*

**Cleo**   Divorced, consumptive, pot-smoking member of the Hippodrome's cast in Cyrus Colter's *The Hippodrome.*

**Angus Cleveland**   Powerful, corrupt seventy-year-old political leader, former mayor of Gainesboro, and benefactor of Douglas Taylor, his successor in Julian Mayfield's *The Grand Parade.*

**Mr. Cleveland**   Chauffeur of Miss Ann and her accomplice in crime in Richard Brautigan's *Dreaming of Babylon.*

**Clevenger**   Car test-track owner who takes the hitchhiking David Bell to Texas at the end of Don DeLillo's *Americana.*

**Clevinger**   Friend and fellow squadron member of Yossarian; Harvard undergraduate with much intelligence and no brains; hounded as a troublemaker by Lieutenant Scheisskopf in Joseph Heller's *Catch-22.*

**Leland Clewes**   Former state department friend whom Walter F. Starbuck betrays; husband of Sarah Wyatt in Kurt Vonnegut's *Jailbird.*

**Jane Clifford**   Teacher of English at a midwestern university and lover of Gabriel Weeks in Gail Godwin's *The Odd Woman.*

**Jerome Clifford**  Lawyer of Barry Muldanno; fears he will be killed by his Mafia-connected client so decides to kill himself before he is killed; tells Mark Sway where the body of a dead senator is buried, then kills himself in John Grisham's *The Client*.

**Percy Clocklan**  Dublin friend of Sebastian Dangerfield; fakes suicide in the Irish Sea and later re-emerges in London as a mysteriously wealthy man in J. P. Donleavy's *The Ginger Man*.

**Cletus James (C. J.) Clovis**  Entrepreneur who builds bat towers for insect control in Thomas McGuane's *The Bushwhacked Piano*.

**Esther Clumly**  Blind wife of Fred Clumly; helps temper his zeal for obedience to laws in John Gardner's *The Sunlight Dialogues*.

**Fred Clumly**  Police chief of Batavia, New York, who finally understands what makes the Sunlight Man behave like a criminal; husband of Esther Clumly in John Gardner's *The Sunlight Dialogues*.

**Bonnie Fox Clutter**  Wife of Herbert Clutter and mother of their four children; ill with emotional and physical ailments, she is the last member of the family to be murdered in Truman Capote's *In Cold Blood*.

**Herbert William Clutter**  Prominent and wealthy owner of River Valley Farm in Holcomb, Kansas; victim of the first and most brutal murder by Perry Smith in Truman Capote's *In Cold Blood*.

**Kenyon Clutter**  Youngest child and only son of Bonnie and Herbert Clutter; shot to death in Truman Capote's *In Cold Blood*.

**Nancy Clutter**  Talented and much admired sixteen-year-old daughter of Bonnie and Herbert Clutter; third murder victim in Truman Capote's *In Cold Blood*.

**Albert Cluveau**  Cajun who is the occasional fishing companion of Miss Jane Pittman and the hired killer of Ned Douglass in Ernest J. Gaines's *The Autobiography of Miss Jane Pittman*.

**Fletcher Coal**  Sinister, ambitious, presidential chief of staff; works to suppress Darby Shaw's damaging brief; is politically ruined when the brief is made public in John Grisham's *The Pelican Brief*.

**Bernice Coates**  Young woman from Massachusetts; joins the WASP to become a pilot during World War II; sister of Jeffrey Coates; occasional lover of Zachary Taylor who assists her in obtaining the legal documents to assume a man's identity; after the war, moves with her partner Florence to Alaska in Marge Piercy's *Gone to Soldiers*.

**Jeff Coates**  Painter who joins the Office of Strategic Services (OSS) during World War II; brother of Bernice Coates; in his work with an active cell of L'Armee Juive, falls in love with Jacqueline Levy-Monot; they are captured; Jeff commits suicide with a cyanide capsule in Marge Piercy's *Gone to Soldiers*.

**Jeremiah Cobb**  Judge who sentences Nat Turner and Hark to be hanged; Job figure and lonely widower in William Styron's *The Confessions of Nat Turner*.

**Maybelline (Mae) Cobb**  Defiant, bedridden wife of Winston Cobb; killed in a fire set by her husband; appears in Hal Bennett's *A Wilderness of Vines, The Black Wine, Wait Until the Evening*, and *Seventh Heaven*.

**Reverend Winston Cobb**  Preacher in Burnside, Virginia; sex-show performer, blackmailer, and perfume salesman; father of David Hunter, mentor of Kevin Brittain, alter ego of Bill Kelsey, and slayer of his wife, Mae Cobb; apprehended in New Jersey for murdering Dolly Anderson and visited in jail by Joe Market; appears in Hal Bennett's *A Wilderness of Vines, The Black Wine, Lord of Dark Places, Wait Until the Evening*, and *Seventh Heaven*.

**James Cobleigh**  Handsome and charming son of financially ruined parents; puts himself through Harvard Law School and marries socialite Winifred Tuttle; has five children, oldest is Nicholas; philanderer and alcoholic in Susan Isaacs's *Almost Paradise*.

**Jane Cobleigh (Heissenhuber)**  Tall, outgoing daughter of Richard Heissenhuber and Sarah Taubman; abused by father and stepmother; studies acting in college but abandons career to support husband, Nicholas Cobleigh, in his acting career; mother of two daughters; develops agoraphobia, which threatens her marriage in Susan Isaacs's *Almost Paradise*.

**Nicholas Cobleigh**  Photogenic scion of New York society mother, Winifred Tuttle, and father, James Cobleigh; excels at sports and studies law; bucks family expectations to become actor; marries Jane Heissenhuber; becomes estranged from family and values by fame in Susan Isaacs's *Almost Paradise*.

**Winifred Cobleigh (Tuttle)**  Awkward and tomboyish daughter of wealthy New York family; marries James Cobleigh; has five children; battles depression and insecurity throughout her life in Susan Isaacs's *Almost Paradise*.

**Wayne Codd**  Cowboy and ranch foreman who hits Nicholas Payne, possibly causing Payne brain damage in Thomas McGuane's *The Bushwhacked Piano*.

**Esperanza Codero**  Thirteen-year-old Mexican-American girl; attends Catholic school; has three brothers and sisters; hopes for a "real house" someday; narrates Sandra Cisneros's *The House on Mango Street*.

**James M. (Jimmy) Cody**  Doctor who concludes that Danny Glick was killed by vampires in Stephen King's *'Salem's Lot*.

**Cindi Coeur**  Lucy Spenser's nom de plume for *Country Daze* magazine in Ann Beattie's *Love Always*.

**Edward R. (Instant) Coffee**  Impulsive presiding judge; character in Osgood Wallop's *The Duchess of Obloquy* in Peter De Vries's *Mrs. Wallop*.

**Mr. Coffee**   Ragman and vagrant in Carlene Hatcher Polite's *The Flagellants*.

**China Doff Coffin**   Older sister of Sukie Maceo and neighborhood prostitute in 1930s Harlem; stabs and kills her pimp in Louise Meriwether's *Daddy Was a Number Runner*.

**Francie Coffin**   Twelve-year-old only daughter and youngest child of Henrietta and Adam Coffin; comes of age in mid-1930s Harlem; narrator of Louise Meriwether's *Daddy Was a Number Runner*.

**Henrietta Coffin**   Wife of Adam Coffin and mother of James Junior, Sterling, and Francie Coffin; becomes the primary support of the family after her husband abandons them in a Harlem tenement in Louise Meriwether's *Daddy Was a Number Runner*.

**James Adam Coffin**   Husband of Henrietta Coffin and father of James Junior, Sterling, and Francie Coffin; becomes a number runner and eventually abandons his family after legal fees for Junior absorb his income in Louise Meriwether's *Daddy Was a Number Runner*.

**James Adam (James Junior, Junior) Coffin, Jr.**   Fifteen-year-old brother of Sterling and Francie Coffin; arrested for the robbery and murder of a white shoe salesman, but released in Louise Meriwether's *Daddy Was a Number Runner*.

**Sterling Coffin**   Fourteen-year-old brother of Francie and James Junior Coffin; quits high school to take a job because he sees no future as a black person with a diploma in Louise Meriwether's *Daddy Was a Number Runner*.

**Jack (Jackie) Cogan**   Mafia enforcer who restores order to mob-run enterprises; kills Frankie, Mark Trattman, and Squirrel Amato in George V. Higgins's *Cogan's Trade*.

**Reuben (Rooster) Cogburn**   United States marshal and bounty hunter who is hired by Mattie Ross to capture Tom Chaney in Charles Portis's *True Grit*.

**Archie Cohen**   Young American volunteer in the Spanish Civil War; eventually denounces the Communist party in William Herrick's *Hermanos!*

**Bernie Cohen**   Jewish-American citizen who works at the Higate winery for Jake and Claire Levy; volunteer soldier with the Lincoln Brigade; rescuer of Marcel Duboise; meets Barbara Lavette in Paris and falls in love with her in Howard Fast's *Second Generation*.

**Gabriel C. (Dutch) Cohen**   Friend of Samuel Paul Berman since grade school in Jay Neugeboren's *Sam's Legacy*.

**Genghis Cohen**   Eminent philatelist hired to appraise Pierce Inverarity's stamp collection in Thomas Pynchon's *The Crying of Lot 49*.

**Morris (Mike Palgrave) Cohen**   Architect who designs a temple for David Dehn; adopts Dehn's daughter, Rachel Dehn, in Jerome Weidman's *The Temple*.

**Rachel Cohen**   Daughter of David Dehn and Bella Biaggi Dehn, and adopted daughter of Morris Cohen; friend of the reporter who discovers the source of David Dehn's wealth in Jerome Weidman's *The Temple*.

**Gene Colder**   Police investigator who is Felicity's lover and vows to find her killer; suspected by Ben Dill as her murderer in Ross Thomas's *Briarpatch*.

**John Grady Cole**   Idealistic sixteen-year-old from west Texas; accomplished horseman, and confident in his abilities to run the family ranch, despite his mother's objections; runs away to Mexico to live out his dreams of being a mythic cowboy; finds love, adventure, and eventual disillusionment in Cormac McCarthy's *All the Pretty Horses*.

**Marion Cole**   Ruth Cole's mother; suffering from grief over the tragic accident that killed her two sons, is drawn into an affair with a much younger man named Eddie O'Hare; affair prompts Marion to leave her husband, Ted, and four-year-old Ruth in John Irving's *A Widow for One Year*.

**Miranda Cole**   High school teacher and girlfriend of Thomas Skelton in Thomas McGuane's *Ninety-Two in the Shade*.

**Ruth Cole**   Protagonist; daughter of Marion Cole; an acclaimed novelist who still bears the emotional scars resulting from Marion's abrupt departure from the family in John Irving's *A Widow for One Year*.

**Ted Cole**   Ruth Cole's father; a children's book author and illustrator with a lustful eye who is left to raise his young daughter when his wife, Marion, leaves them in John Irving's *A Widow for One Year*.

**Colonel Coleman**   General manager of the New Dominion Stone Company; buys Clay Spencer's mountain property so Spencer can send his oldest son of college in Earl Hamner, Jr.'s *Spencer's Mountain*.

**Jewell Coleman**   Glen Davis's longtime girlfriend and the mother of his son David; a hardworking waitress who remains faithful to Glen during the three years he spends in prison in Larry Brown's *Father and Son*.

**Anne-Marion Coles**   College roommate and later correspondent of Meridian Hill in Alice Walker's *Meridian*.

**Andrew Collier**   Journalist and half brother of Daniel Compton Wills; discovers his supposed benefactor, Daniel Cable Wills, is his father and a former member of the OSS and CIA in George V. Higgins's *Dreamland*.

**Audrey Collins**   Oldest child of Theresa and Dan Collins; sister of Lizzy Collins; friend of Emma and Claire Goodwin in Jane Hamilton's *A Map of the World*.

**Clara Collins**    Widow of Ely Collins and leader of the Circle in Robert Coover's *The Origin of the Brunists*.

**Dan Collins**    Husband of Theresa; father of Lizzy and Audrey; friend of Howard; curator for the Dairy Shrine and organist at the Presbyterian Church in Prairie Center in Jane Hamilton's *A Map of the World*.

**Elaine Collins**    Repressed daughter of Ely Collins; falls in love with Carl Dean Palmers in Robert Coover's *The Origin of the Brunists*.

**Ely Collins**    Preacher and coal miner; deceased husband of Clara Collins in Robert Coover's *The Origin of the Brunists*.

**Hannah Ann Collins**    Old and blind Alabama poetess in John Updike's *Bech: A Book*.

**Lieutenant Collins**    Leader of an expedition with Dick Gibson in search of the last living dodo bird on the island of Mauritius during World War II in Stanley Elkin's *The Dick Gibson Show*.

**Lizzy Collins**    Youngest daughter of Dan and Theresa Collins; victim of drowning in Alice Goodwin's pond; child about whom Alice continues to think in Jane Hamilton's *A Map of the World*.

**Theresa Collins**    Psychologist/therapist; wife of Dan and mother of Audrey and Lizzy Collins; best friend of Alice and witness at her trial; with her family, leaves for Montana following her youngest daughter's death; cares for Alice's children and husband, Howard, during Alice's jail stay in Jane Hamilton's *A Map of the World*.

**William David Collins**    Name given to the baby Leslie Collins adopts in Harriette Simpson Arnow's *The Kentucky Trace*.

**William David Leslie Collins II**    Son of Virginia gentry and patriot covertly involved in the American Revolution; shoots his own brother at the battle of Camden; cares for and ultimately adopts a child in Harriette Simpson Arnow's *The Kentucky Trace*.

**Joe Colper**    Sales manager of Harris Towers, a condominium complex in *The Condominium*, a novella in Stanley Elkin's *Searches and Seizures*.

**Alfonso (Al) Columbato**    Birdy's boyhood friend in real life; the male canary in Birdy's fantasy bird life in William Wharton's *Birdy*.

**Bob Comeaux**    Physician who works at Fedville medical facility; with the help of John Van Dorn, secretly taints water supply of Ruhr Valley, Louisiana; contamination decreases violent crime, drug addiction, pregnancy, and the spread of AIDS virus in Walker Percy's *The Thanatos Syndrome*.

**Aycock Comfort**    Friend of Jack Renfro sentenced with him to Parchman State Penitentiary; maintains the balance of Maud Eva Moody's car while it hangs on the edge of Banner Top in Eudora Welty's *Losing Battles*.

**Dan Comisky**    Gambler who promotes free-hanging as a sport and urges Clyde Stout to compete in it in Jack Matthews's *Hanger Stout, Awake!*

**Munn Li Compor**    Councilman of Terminus who aids Mayor Harla Branno in exiling Golan Trevize, then is himself exiled by Branno and assigned to follow Trevize through space and report on his movements; secretly an agent of the Second Foundation who reports to Stor Gendibal in Isaac Asimov's *Foundation's Edge*.

**Jason Lycurgus Compson (II)**    See Volume I.

**Molly Compton**    Lawyer from Washington, D.C.; dates Roger Gaston in Elizabeth Benedict's *Slow Dancing*.

**Edgar Comroe**    Night officer at Vandenberg Air Force Base in Michael Crichton's *The Andromeda Strain*.

**Ralph Comyns**    Physical therapist at Emma Lazarus Retirement Home and lover of Mandy Dattner in Alan Isler's *The Prince of West End Avenue*.

**Jerry Conant**    Designer and animator of television commercials; husband of Ruth Conant and lover of Sally Mathias in John Updike's *Marry Me*.

**Ruth Conant**    Wife of Jerry Conant and lover of Richard Mathias in John Updike's *Marry Me*.

**La Condesa**    Insane, drug-addicted Spanish noblewoman deported from Cuba for her political activities; loved by the ship's doctor, Schumann, in Katherine Anne Porter's *Ship of Fools*.

**Signor (Cee-Pee) Condotti-Pignata**    Painter who imagines Cynthia Pomeroy as Primavera in Wright Morris's *What a Way to Go*.

**Will (Willie) Conklin**    Chief of the Emerald Isle Engine Company; he and his men destroy the Model T of Coalhouse Walker, Jr., and cause the death of many innocent people in E. L. Doctorow's *Ragtime*.

**Conmal (Duke of Aros)**    Renowned translator of Shakespeare into Zemblan; uncle who influences Charles Xavier, the last king of Zembla, to be passionately addicted to literature in Vladimir Nabokov's *Pale Fire*.

**Andrea Biddle Conover**    Washington mistress of Bruce Gold and daughter of Pugh Biddle Conover in Joseph Heller's *Good as Gold*.

**Pugh Biddle Conover**    Member of well-connected Virginia gentry and father of Andrea Biddle Conover in Joseph Heller's *Good as Gold*.

**Sarah (Sally) Conover**    Lover of Ian Sherbrooke in Nicholas Delbanco's *Sherbrookes*.

**Constantin** United Nations simultaneous interpreter and blind date of Esther Greenwood in Sylvia Plath's *The Bell Jar*.

**Carol Constantine** Painter and wife of Eddie Constantine; they participate in couple swapping, with homosexual overtones, with Irene and Ben Saltz in John Updike's *Couples*.

**Eddie Constantine** Airline pilot married to Carol Constantine in John Updike's *Couples*.

**John Converse** American journalist in Vietnam who tries to get rich by smuggling heroin into the United States but is captured by Antheil and forced to locate his wife, Marge Converse, who has the heroin in Robert Stone's *Dog Soldiers*.

**Marge Bender Converse** Wife of John Converse; pursued by Antheil's men in Robert Stone's *Dog Soldiers*.

**Amanda Conway** Young, beautiful fashion model on the rise in New York City who leaves her husband, Jamie Conway, for a more exciting career and life in Paris in Jay McInerney's *Bright Lights, Big City*.

**Dodo Conway** Often-pregnant Catholic housewife and neighbor of Esther Greenwood in Sylvia Plath's *The Bell Jar*.

**Jamie Conway** Young writer working in the Department of Factual Verification at a prominent New York magazine; throughout the course of a few days he tries to outstrip mortality with nothing but good will, controlled substances, and wit; ex-husband of Amanda Conway in Jay McInerney's *Bright Lights, Big City*.

**Cook** Cooks for Mrs. Dawson; sings sad Sicilian songs in a feeble soprano in Frances Sherwood's *Vindication*.

**Mrs. Beatrice Latchett (Bea) Cook** Mistress of Henry Bech following her sister, Norma Latchett; bland and gentle thirty-four-year-old mother of three in the process of divorcing her husband in John Updike's *Bech: A Book*.

**Caroline Cook** Youngest daughter of Laurence Cook; wife of Frank Rasmussen; sister of Ginny Cook Smith and Rose Cook Lewis; lawyer in Des Moines, Iowa; loses her father's allegiance when she voices concern regarding Larry Cook's plans to bequeath property to his daughters, which Larry perceives as a lack of gratitude and loyalty; recovers her father's affections as she helps her father sue his two older daughters in Jane Smiley's *A Thousand Acres*.

**Ginny Cook** See Ginny Cook Smith.

**Laurence (Larry and Daddy) Cook** Alcoholic, tyrannical, and abusive father of Ginny Cook Smith, Rose Cook Lewis, Caroline Cook; friend and arch-competitor of Harold Clark; grandfather of Pammy and Linda; inheritor of land in Iowa; impulsive Lear-like retiree who at Jess Clark's homecoming party announces his plan to transfer his farm to his daughters; accuses Ginny and Rose of casting him off; temporarily disowns and subsequently collaborates with daughter Caroline regarding the transfer of his land in Jane Smiley's *A Thousand Acres*.

**Rose Cook** See Rose Cook Lewis.

**Jasper Coon** Free Soiler who questions why he fights for the Confederacy in Jesse Hill Ford's *The Raider*.

**Coop** Hollis's and Belinda's child, who died of leukemia; the single trait shared by father and son was their dislike of horses in Alice Hoffman's *Here on Earth*.

**Nate Coop** Quiet Alaskan native; marries Flossie Flatch; scouts Japanese bases in Aleutian Islands during World War II; works with Flossie to achieve Alaskan statehood in James Michener's *Alaska*.

**Annabeth Cooper** Belinda Cooper's mother in Alice Hoffman's *Here on Earth*.

**April Cooper** Louise and Nat's daughter and oldest child by nine years; sister of Danny Cooper; gay; well-known singer whose stage name is April Gold; self-centered instigator; is pregnant by artificial insemination in David Leavitt's *Equal Affections*.

**Belinda Cooper** Daughter of Annabeth Cooper and sister of Richard Cooper, a pale, red-haired next-door neighbor of March; keeps injured wild animals and nurses them back to health; inherits Guardian Farm; marries Hollis and dies from his abuse and neglect in Alice Hoffman's *Here on Earth*.

**Cynthia Cooper** Albermarle County deputy in Rita Mae Brown's *Cat on the Scent*.

**Danny Cooper** Louise and Nat's son and youngest child; brother of April Cooper; gay; life partner of Walter Bayles; lawyer; feels both close to and resentful of his sister, April; moves from California to Connecticut in David Leavitt's *Equal Affections*.

**Fanny Cooper** Widow of Henry Cooper, who dies from a snake bite; mother of Carrie, to whom she gives birth after Henry's death, and Sarah; is engaged to and later marries Thomas Keene in Hugh Nissenson's *The Tree of Life*.

**Ivy Cooper** The other new girl on the swim team besides Carlin Leander in Alice Hoffman's *The River King*.

**Louise Cooper** Wife of Danny Cooper and mother of April and Nat Cooper; older sister of Eleanor Friedman; atheist; has a temper, but loses her "fighting spirit" after she is diagnosed with cancer; lives with cancer for twenty years and dies of it in David Leavitt's *Equal Affections*.

**Michael Cooper** Lover of Nell; a reporter for a trade magazine in Elizabeth Benedict's *Slow Dancing*.

**Mr. Cooper**   Father of Richard and Belinda Cooper; disinherited his son and is killed with his wife in a car wreck before he can reverse his rash decision in Alice Hoffman's *Here on Earth.*

**Nat Cooper**   Husband of Louise Cooper and father of April and Nat Cooper; computer scientist; has an affair with and loves Lillian Rubenstein-Kraft in David Leavitt's *Equal Affections.*

**Reverend Cooper**   Minister in Danville, Pennsylvania, who helps Milkman find his family farm in Toni Morrison's *Song of Solomon.*

**Richard Cooper**   Husband of March Murray, father of Gwen Cooper, son of Annabeth Cooper, and brother of Belinda Cooper; estranged from his father; a biologist; rejoices in the odd and unprecedented; married to March Murray for eighteen years until she leaves him for Hollis in Alice Hoffman's *Here on Earth.*

**Brownfield (Brown) Copeland**   Crazed son of Margaret and Grange Copeland; kills his wife, Mem Copeland, and is later murdered by his father in Alice Walker's *The Third Life of Grange Copeland.*

**Daphne (Daffy) Copeland**   Eldest daughter of Mem and Brownfield Copeland; committed to an insane asylum in Alice Walker's *The Third Life of Grange Copeland.*

**Grange Copeland**   Georgia black redeemed by love for his granddaughter, Ruth Copeland; his life is chronicled from Prohibition to the Civil Rights movement in Alice Walker's *The Third Life of Grange Copeland.*

**Josie Copeland**   One-time prostitute and owner of the Dew Drop Inn; vacillates in her allegiance to Grange Copeland, whom she marries, and his son, Brownfield Copeland, in Alice Walker's *The Third Life of Grange Copeland.*

**Margaret Copeland**   First wife of Grange Copeland; commits suicide after poisoning her illegitimate son Star in Alice Walker's *The Third Life of Grange Copeland.*

**Mem R. Copeland**   Teacher demoralized by her husband, Brownfield Copeland, who shoots her to death in front of their children in Alice Walker's *The Third Life of Grange Copeland.*

**Ornette Copeland**   Middle daughter of Mem and Brownfield Copeland; becomes a prostitute in Alice Walker's *The Third Life of Grange Copeland.*

**Ruth Copeland**   Youngest daughter of Mem and Brownfield Copeland; reared by her grandfather, Grange, who is slain by police after attempting to save her from her father's custody in Alice Walker's *The Third Life of Grange Copeland.*

**Cora**   Young, impoverished black student of Eric Eisner's literacy program; suffers from depression and suicidal tendencies in Phillip Lopate's *Confessions of Summer.*

**Aunt Cora Lou**   Sister of Bertha Ann Upshur, mother of Lil Bits and Mamie, and friend of Mariah Upshur; outcast of Tangierneck in Sarah E. Wright's *This Child's Gonna Live.*

**Coransee**   Brother of Teray and son of Rayal and Jansee; challenges his brother for the Pattern, a vast network of mental links in Octavia E. Butler's *Patternmaster.*

**Earlie Corbett**   A young black man murdered by Omar Duvall in Mary McGarry Morris's *Songs in Ordinary Time.*

**Luther Corbett**   Grandfather of Earlie in Mary McGarry Morris's *Songs in Ordinary Time.*

**Myna Corbett**   Overweight health food advocate and occasional companion of Gary Harkness at Logos College in Don DeLillo's *End Zone.*

**Jerome (Corky) Corcoran**   Son of Timothy and Theresa Corcoran; successful businessman, active in local politics; sexually attractive, flirtatious, and unstable in Joyce Carol Oates's *What I Lived For.*

**Sean Corcoran**   Heavy drinker, brother of Timothy, and uncle of Corky in Joyce Carol Oates's *What I Lived For.*

**Theresa Corcoran**   Widow of the murdered Timothy; neurotic alcoholic mother of Corky in Joyce Carol Oates's *What I Lived For.*

**Timothy Patrick Corcoran**   Irish-American man in favor of black workers; murdered on Christmas Eve in front of his own house in Joyce Carol Oates's *What I Lived For.*

**Jonas Cord, Jr.**   Magnate who takes control of Cord Explosives upon the death of his father; develops an aircraft company, an electronics firm, and a movie company; sacrifices personal happiness for power in Harold Robbins's *The Carpetbaggers.*

**Jonas Cord, Sr.**   Father of Jonas Cord, Jr., and founder of Cord Explosives and the Cord fortune; dies of an encephalic embolism in Harold Robbins's *The Carpetbaggers.*

**Rina Marlowe Cord**   See Rina Marlowe.

**Albert Corde**   Dean of a Chicago university and husband of one of the university's astrophysicists, Minna Raresh; a journalist by trade, nationally known for his columns on the ravages of the inner city and American prisons; spends his Christmas vacation in Romania attending to the dying mother of his wife, while escaping the scandal of the murder of a university student in Saul Bellow's *The Dean's December.*

**Minna Raresh Corde**   Romanian-born astrophysicist who is married to her university's dean, Albert Corde; is thin and pensive, with a fierce work ethic; suffers greatly at the sudden illness and subsequent death of her mother, Valeria, in Saul Bellow's *The Dean's December.*

**Ramón (Cortés) Cordes**    Itinerant professional revolutionary with a fatal attraction to lost causes; leader of a band of revolutionaries who is taken prisoner and awaits execution in William Herrick's *The Last to Die*.

**Cordelia Swain Cordiner**    Psychologist who separates the Swain twins, Wilbur and Eliza, in Kurt Vonnegut's *Slapstick*.

**Corey**    Leader of the Indians, a youth movement revolting against an authoritarian United States; his followers disperse and survive in ragtag groups in Marge Piercy's *Dance the Eagle to Sleep*.

**Constanzia (Connie) Corleone**    Daughter of Vito Corleone and wife of the abusive Carlo Rizzi in Mario Puzo's *The Godfather*.

**Kay Corleone**    See Kay Adams.

**Michael Corleone**    Youngest son of Don Corleone; originally determined to stay out of the family business, he takes the place of his father after the old man's death and proceeds to murder all of his family's enemies in Mario Puzo's *The Godfather*.

**Santino (Sonny) Corleone**    Acting head of the family during the convalescence of his father, Don Corleone, until he himself is killed by rival gangsters in Mario Puzo's *The Godfather*.

**Vito (Don Corleone, The Godfather) Corleone**    Head of a powerful family of Sicilian gangsters in Mario Puzo's *The Godfather*.

**Corley**    Sexy boyfriend of Celia in Joan Chase's *During the Reign of the Queen of Persia*.

**Aunt Cornelia (Cornie)**    Aunt of Honey Winthrop; takes over Honey's upbringing, allows her to go to Paris for a year, and enrolls her in the Katie Gibbs Secretarial School in New York in Judith Krantz's *Scruples*.

**Georgie Cornell**    Twenty-first-century man living in a society dominated by women; escapes enslavement by females in a fantasy of role reversals; protagonist of Thomas Berger's *Regiment of Women*.

**Brother Coronett**    Handsome charismatic preacher; Christianna Wheeler has a sexual dream about Brother Coronett and believes it is partially responsible for the difficult and mysterious pregnancy that results in her quintuplets in Bobbie Ann Mason's *Feather Crowns*.

**The Corpse**    Mummified and later plastered body of Jesus Christ stolen from the Vatican by Plucky Purcell; incinerated along with John Paul Ziller and Mon Cul on the Icarus XC solar balloon in Tom Robbins's *Another Roadside Attraction*.

**Corregidora**    Portuguese sea captain who in Brazil is a slave breeder and whoremonger; in fathering two females by his own daughters, he ultimately influences the life of Ursa Corregidora in Gayl Jones's *Corregidora*.

**Correy (Mama) Corregidora**    Daughter of Gram Corregidora and Corregidora; mother by Martin of Ursa Corregidora in Gayl Jones's *Corregidora*.

**Dorita (Great Gram) Corregidora**    Slave of Corregidora, by whom she has Gram Corregidora; great-grandmother of Ursa Corregidora in Gayl Jones's *Corregidora*.

**Gram (Grandmama) Corregidora**    Daughter of Dorita and Corregidora; mother, by Corregidora, of Correy Corregidora; grandmother of Ursa Corregidora in Gayl Jones's *Corregidora*.

**Ursa (U. C., Ursa Corre, Urs, Ursie) Corregidora**    Blues singer descended from the whoremonger Corregidora and instructed by her female forebears to make generations; after her husband, Mutt Thomas, throws her, pregnant, down a flight of stairs, she undergoes a hysterectomy; narrator of Gayl Jones's *Corregidora*.

**Miss Corrie**    See Everbe Corinthia Hogganbeck.

**Corrine**    Wife of Reverend Samuel; unable to have children; fears Olivia and Adam are the children of Nettie and Samuel but is wrong; dies during a mission in Africa in Alice Walker's *The Color Purple*.

**Lieutenant Corson**    Veteran army lieutenant who is disillusioned by the Vietnam War and years for the old army; falls in love with Hamijolli Chand in Delhi in Tim O'Brien's *Going After Cacciato*.

**Felix Cortez**    Cuban emigrant who becomes chief adviser to Colombian drug kingpin Escobedo; seduces FBI director Jacobs's secretary in order to uncover American actions against the Colombian cartels; leads assaults against American light-infantry teams in Colombia; is captured by John Clark and returned to Cuba in Tom Clancy's *Clear and Present Danger*.

**Billy Cosgrove**    Wealthy acquaintance of Father Urban and patron of the Order of St. Clement; offended by Father Urban's attempt to correct his behavior, he abandons both priest and order in J. F. Powers's *Morte D'Urban*.

**Michael Cosman**    General practitioner; best friend and almost lover of Isadora Wing; tells Isadora of her husband's affair in Erica Jong's *How to Save Your Own Life*.

**Edgar Cosset**    Seventy-year-old uncle of Charles Henri Persaud; former soldier, politician, and statesman; married; has an affair with nephew's sister-in-law Isabel Walker; leaves her on the excuse of a mission to Eastern Europe in Diane Johnson's *Le Divorce*.

**Bill Costello**    Sponsor of John Wilder in Alcoholics Anonymous; well-intentioned but platitudinous in Richard Yates's *Disturbing the Peace*.

**Ivan Costello**    First boyfriend of Maria Wyeth in New York in Joan Didion's *Play It As It Lays*.

**Comte Edouard de la Côte de Grace**   Poor French count who refuses to marry Billy Winthrop when he discovers that she has no money in Judith Krantz's *Scruples*.

**Ralph (Ralphie) Cotton**   Rich and snobbish black student, one of only two, at a private academy; his family discourages his association with George Cain in George Cain's *Blueschild Baby*.

**Hannah Coulter**   Wife of Nathan Coulter and mother of Mattie Coulter; widow of Virgil Feltner and mother by him of Little Margaret Feltner in Wendell Berry's *A Place on Earth* and *The Memory of Old Jack*.

**Mathew Burley (Mattie) Coulter**   Son of Nathan and Hannah Coulter in Wendell Berry's *The Memory of Old Jack*.

**The Counselor**   Lawyer, fellow drinker, and close friend of Frederick Exley; his apartment is a place of retreat after Exley is released from one of his stints in a mental hospital; suffers the ignominy of disbarment, but remains optimistic even as Exley sinks into bitter despair in Frederick Exley's *A Fan's Notes*.

**Countess**   Epicene tycoon of feminine hygiene products and owner of the Rubber Rose Ranch; makes Sissy Hankshaw his star model as the Yoni Yum/ Dew Girl in Tom Robbins's *Even Cowgirls Get the Blues*.

**Mont Court**   Parole officer of Gary Gilmore in Norman Mailer's *The Executioner's Song*.

**Mary Courter**   Librarian of River Cover; always calls Geneva first when a book comes in that she thinks Geneva would like in Sandra Scofield's *Beyond Deserving*.

**Adele Courtland**   Neighbor of the McKelvas and sister of Nate Courtland in Eudora Welty's *The Optimist's Daughter*.

**Nate Courtland**   New Orleans eye specialist and family friend of the McKelvas; treats both Clinton and Becky McKelva's vision problems in Eudora Welty's *The Optimist's Daughter*.

**Courtney**   Lover of Patrick Bateman and best friend of his girlfriend Evelyn; has a boyfriend who is unaware that she is having an affair; comes from money and makes a lot of it herself; street smart, but not smart enough to know that Patrick Bateman is a serial killer in Bret Easton Ellis's *American Psycho*.

**Duke Courtney**   Father of Iris and husband of Persia; respected middle-class Irish-American businessman in Hammond; loving and mild-tempered until he gambles away his fortune and his family in Joyce Carol Oates's *Because It Is Bitter, and Because It Is My Heart*.

**Iris Courtney**   Daughter of Duke and Persia Courtney; sensitive and strong-willed; the only witness of the killing of "Little Red"; secret admirer of Jinx; later fiancée of Alan Savage in Joyce Carol Oates's *Because It Is Bitter, and Because It Is My Heart*.

**Leslie Courtney**   Iris's uncle, Duke Courtney's older, bachelor brother; photographer who supports minorities' civil right against a racist community; admirer of Persia in Joyce Carol Oates's *Because It Is Bitter, and Because It Is My Heart*.

**Persia Courtney**   Mother of Iris and wife of Duke Courtney; elegant hostess at Lambert's Tea Room; later divorced from Duke and dies an alcoholic, "loose" woman in Joyce Carol Oates's *Because It Is Bitter, and Because It Is My Heart*.

**Tom Courtney**   *New York Times* reporter who conducts the first interview with Chance in Jerzy Kosinski's *Being There*.

**Major de Coverley**   Magisterially photogenic officer responsible for renting apartments for the use of officers and enlisted men on rest leave in Europe in Joseph Heller's *Catch-22*.

**T. Cowles**   Trainer of horses who helps Michael Banks to steal a horse but who betrays Banks to Larry, the leader of a group of killers and thieves who want to benefit from Banks's theft in John Hawkes's *The Lime Twig*.

**George Cox**   Friend of Nelson Dewey; involves Dewey in mining investments that lead to the wealth of both men in August Derleth's *The Shadow in the Glass*.

**Trina Cox**   Ruthless investment banker who specializes in hostile takeovers; helps an old college friend, Russell Calloway, to initiate a bid to buy the publishing firm where he is an editor; her relentless and eventually successful seduction of Russell leads to the end of his marriage in Jay McInerney's *Brightness Falls*.

**Eddie (Eddie Fingers, Paulie) Coyle**   Convicted small-time criminal who sells out other criminals in order to make a deal with federal authorities in George V. Higgins's *The Friends of Eddie Coyle*.

**Duddy Coyne**   Neighbor of the Bray family; sailor torpedoed and killed in the North Atlantic in Maureen Howard's *Natural History*.

**Caroline (Calamity Jane) Crabb**   Sister of Jack Crabb in Thomas Berger's *Little Big Man*.

**Jack (Little Big Man) Crabb**   One-hundred-eleven-year-old survivor of the Battle of Little Bighorn; picaresque hero and narrator of Thomas Berger's *Little Big Man*.

**Olga Crabb**   Wife of Jack Crabb and mother of their son in Thomas Berger's *Little Big Man*.

**Alice Craddock**   Name that Mary Reed comes to be known by after she is adopted by Dr. Craddock and his wife (see Mary Alice Reed) in Thomas H. Cook's *The Chatham School Affair*.

**Benn Crader**   Maternal uncle of Kenneth Tractenberg in Saul Bellow's *More Die of Heartbreak;* famous botanist and great reader who believes society can be understood by reading

Balzac; abruptly weds socialite Matilda Layamon whom he abandons before their honeymoon in order to study lichens in Antarctica and avoid being used by her family in a scheme to manipulate money from Benn's gangster uncle Harold Vilitzer.

**Mr. Craft**    Partner in Aaron Burr's law firm in Gore Vidal's *Burr*.

**Crainpool**    Dickensian secretary to Alexander Main; forced to flee for his life for jumping bail in *The Bailbondsman*, a novella in Stanley Elkin's *Searches and Seizures*.

**Nurse Cramer**    Freckled army nurse and friend of Sue Ann Duckett in Joseph Heller's *Catch-22*.

**Judson "Jud" Crandall**    Kind-hearted and nostalgic eighty-three-year-old neighbor of the Creed family and husband of Norma Crandall; shows Louis the Micmac burying grounds and helps him to bury Winston Churchill; seemingly omniscient regarding Louis's plans for Gage's body after Gage's death; later killed by Gage after Gage's return from the dead in Stephen King's *Pet Sematary*.

**Norma Crandall**    Arthritic wife of Judson "Jud" Crandall; puts up a healthy facade despite the intense pain of her arthritis; refuses to go to the doctor about her heart condition, and later dies as a result in Stephen King's *Pet Sematary*.

**Lewis Crane**    Army electronics technician who looks for the downed Scoop VII satellite in Michael Crichton's *The Andromeda Strain*.

**Mrs. Amelia Cranston**    Operator of a boardinghouse for Newport servants in Thornton Wilder's *Theophilus North*.

**Wanda Cravens**    Dimwitted widow who is readily seduced by both Justin Miller and Vince Bonali in Robert Coover's *The Origin of the Brunists*.

**Andrew Crawford**    Husband for one summer of Emily Grimes; impotent, he hates Emily's sexuality in Richard Yates's *Easter Parade*.

**Elise Crawford**    Sister of Maija von Einzeedle, wife of Reuben Crawford, and lover of Anthony Hope Harding in Nicholas Delbanco's *Small Rain*.

**Frank Crawford**    Father of Sonny Crawford, former high school principal, and proprietor of a domino parlor in Larry McMurtry's *The Last Picture Show*.

**Haim Crawford**    Cousin of Bannie Upshire Dudley; member of the Paddy Rollers of Mantipico County in Sarah E. Wright's *This Child's Gonna Live*.

**Jack Crawford**    Chief of the Behavioral Science section of the Federal Bureau of Investigation; supervisor of FBI trainee Clarice Starling, whom he selects to interview serial killer Hannibal Lecter, in Thomas Harris's *The Silence of the Lambs*. Crawford also appears in Harris's *Red Dragon* (1981) and *Hannibal* (1999).

**Reuben Crawford**    Husband of Elise Crawford in Nicholas Delbanco's *Small Rain*.

**Sonny Crawford**    Athlete at Thalia High School, roommate of Duane Moore, and lover of Ruth Popper; initiated into adulthood in Larry McMurtry's *The Last Picture Show*.

**Gin Crazed**    Known as G. C.; chief game warden of the district where Ernie is serving as a temporary game warden; admired and liked by both Ernie and Miss Mary; participates in the killing of Miss Mary's lion in Ernest Hemingway's *True At First Light*.

**Lady Creamhair**    See Virginia R. Hector.

**Oscar Crease**    Stepbrother of Christina Lutz and community college teacher and playwright who relies increasingly upon litigation as a means of gaining recognition and capital in William Gaddis's *A Frolic of His Own*.

**Creb**    Powerful Neanderthal shaman, or Mog-ur, whose childhood crippling by a bear is regarded as the source of his mystical potency; teacher and adoptive father of Ayla, who discovers that her mixed-heritage son has a natural Cro-Magnon resilience that is the key to preventing Neanderthal extinction; brother of Brun and Iza in Jean M. Auel's *The Clan of the Cave Bear*.

**Peter Crecy**    Wealthy friend of Lennie; later, Jill's lover who feels that he has to develop her mentally; marries Donna, but abuses her in Marge Piercy's *Braided Lives*.

**Louis Credenza**    Senior member of a large property-owning family in northwest Iowa that controls the radio station that employs Dick Gibson in Stanley Elkin's *The Dick Gibson Show*.

**Foxy (Kennedy) Cree**    Native American cousin of Rayona Taylor who harasses Rayona when she moves onto his Montana reservation in Michael Dorris's *A Yellow Raft in Blue Water*.

**Pauline George Cree**    Native American woman living on a Montana reservation; younger sister of Ida George and mother of Foxy Cree in Michael Dorris's *A Yellow Raft in Blue Water*.

**Eileen "Ellie" Creed**    Adventurous yet emotionally reserved daughter of Louis and Rachel Creed; has visions of future disasters regarding Louis and Gage in Stephen King's *Pet Sematary*.

**Emmett Creed**    Head football coach in his first year at Logos College; has a no-nonsense attitude and reputation for winning in Don DeLillo's *End Zone*.

**Dr. Louis Creed**    Middle-aged methodical and organized physician, employed at the University of Maine; has something of a quick temper; saved Norma Crandal's life when she suffered a heart attack; father of Gage and Ellie and husband of Rachel in Stephen King's *Pet Sematary*.

**Rachel Creed**    City-born wife of Louis Creed and mother of Gage and Eileen; siser Zelda died of spinal meningitis as a child, and Rachel blames herself; is later killed by Gage after Fage's return from the dead and then buried in the Micmac burying grounds in Stephen King's *Pet Sematary*.

**Winston Churchill Creed**   Creed family cat that is killed by a passing truck on the highway near the Creed house; is buried in the Micmac burying grounds behind the Pet Sematary, and returns as a changed cat, sreving as foreshadowing for future events in Stephen King's *Pet Sematary*.

**Fannie Jump Creighton**   Friend and contemporary of Celeste's; plays bridge with Celeste, Fairy, and Ramelle; drinker whose husband leaves her with no money; opens a speakeasy and becomes independent in Rita Mae Brown's *Six of One*.

**Peter Crew**   Unethical solicitor who represents confessed murderer Olive Martin and is later arrested for embezzling Olive's father's legacy in Minette Walters's *The Sculptress*.

**Alicia Crick**   Lover of the Reverend Thomas Marshfield in the first of his many adulterous affairs; later lover of Ned Bork; church organist and divorced mother of three in John Updike's *A Month of Sundays*.

**Peter Cringle**   First mate and quartermaster of the *Republic*, son of an immigrant who earned a fortune and despised the privileged, of which his son is considered part; watches his father dote on an orphan who had a hard beginning similar to that of Cringle's father; comforts Tommy O'Toole after the boy receives abuse from Captain Falcon; asks to be killed and eaten by his starving shipmates; has this wish carried out in Charles Johnson's *Middle Passage*.

**Croaker**   Savage, uneducated sexual brute who rapes Anastasia Stoker in John Barth's *Giles Goat-Boy*.

**Priss Hartshorn Crockett**   Introverted New York socialite and member of the group in Mary McCarthy's *The Group*.

**Charles Croker**   Wealthy real estate developer with overextended credit; agrees to endorse innocence of Fareek Fanon, college football star who is an alleged rapist, in return for settlement of his debts; reneges on the deal; loses wife, money, and property; becomes a televangelist for The Stoic's Hour in Tome Wolfe's *A Man In Full*.

**Martha Croker**   First wife of Charles Croker; mother of three children; educated, intelligent; from an old Virginia family, marries Raymond Peepgas in Tom Wolfe's *A Man In Full*.

**Serena Croker**   Second wife of Charles Croker; mother of one daughter; beautiful; thirty-six years younger than Charles in Tom Wolfe's *A Man In Full*.

**Clarence (Sinbad) Cromwell**   Veteran black Los Angeles police detective; friend of A. M. Valnikov in Joseph Wambaugh's *The Black Marble*.

**Oliver (Ironsides) Cromwell**   Commander of the Parliamentary army; originally appears to consider his soldiers equals but is corrupted by power and property, betraying his promises to the soldiers opposed to his Irish campaign in Mary Lee Settle's *Prisons*.

**Annie Crop**   Young daughter of Gideon and Ida Crop; swept off a country bridge to her death during a flood in Wendell Berry's *A Place on Earth*.

**Gideon Crop**   Tenant farmer of Roger Merchant, husband of Ida Crop, and father of Annie Crop in Wendell Berry's *A Place on Earth*.

**Ida Crop**   Wife of Gideon Crop, mother of Annie Crop, and object of Ernest Finley's unrequited love in Wendell Berry's *A Place on Earth*.

**Hazel (Mom) Crosby**   Hoosier wife of H. Lowe Crosby; sews the U.S. flag in Kurt Vonnegut's *Cat's Cradle*.

**H. Lowe Crosby**   Midwestern entrepreneur and patriot; husband of Hazel Crosby in Kurt Vonnegut's *Cat's Cradle*.

**Nadine Cross**   Woman chosen to bear Randall Flagg's child in Stephen King's *The Stand*.

**Frank Crotty**   Los Angeles policeman and partner of Thomas Spellacy in John Gregory Dunne's *True Confessions*.

**Jonah (J., Jayber, Jaybird) Crow**   Barber of Port William, Kentucky, and self-taught philosopher in Wendell Berry's *A Place on Earth* and *The Memory of Old Jack*.

**Ben Crowder**   Tough-minded manager of the Washington baseball team in Mark Harris's *It Looked Like For Ever*.

**Attila Csycsyry**   Publican in Fort St. Sebastian; an oft-wounded, now philosophical Transylvanian Protestant; since public houses are not permitted, he calls his business a water room in Bharati Mukherjee's *The Holder of the World*.

**Cuckold**   Wife murderer and convict who runs a private commissary and tells of a homosexual relationship that parallels that of Zeke Farragut in John Cheever's *Falconer*.

**Cuffee Ned**   Hero of the poor blacks on Bourne Island; led the largest and most successful slave revolt in the island's history in Paule Marshall's *The Chosen Place, the Timeless People*.

**Cujo**   Friendly Saint Bernard who becomes rabid after being bitten on the muzzle by an infected bat; after killing his owner, Cujo terrorizes Donna and Tad Trenton as he is left to slowly die in Stephen King's *Cujo*.

**Tom Cullen**   Slightly retarded man who, under the influence of Nick Andros's spirit, saves Stuart Redman's life in Stephen King's *The Stand*.

**Norah (Norry) Culligan**   Landlady and lover of Charles Fort in Jessamyn West's *The Massacre at Fall Creek*.

**Captain Cully**   Would-be minstrel and leader of a band of ineffective outlaws in Peter S. Beagle's *The Last Unicorn*.

**Catherine Culpepper**   Daughter of Spence and Lila Culpepper, who lives nearby and provides emotional support to her mother and father when Lila faces a mastectomy in Bobbie Ann Mason's *Spence and Lila*.

**Lee Culpepper**   Son of Spence and Lila Culpepper; has abandoned the family farm for factory work but provides some emotional support to his mother and father when Lila faces a mastectomy in Bobbie Ann Mason's *Spence and Lila*.

**Lila Culpepper**   Mother of Nancy, Catherine, and Lee Culpepper and wife of Spence Culpepper; endures a mastectomy and, as a result of the operation, must rediscover herself as a mother and a wife in Bobbie Ann Mason's *Spence and Lila*.

**Nancy Culpepper**   Daughter of Spence and Lila Culpepper; moved away from her hometown but returns to provide emotional support to her mother and father when Lila faces a mastectomy in Bobbie Ann Mason's *Spence and Lila*.

**Spence Culpepper**   Father of Catherine, Nancy, and Lee Culpepper and husband of Lila Culpepper, who undergoes a mastectomy; is challenged to accept the ways his wife and his marriage might change because of the operation in Bobbie Ann Mason's *Spence and Lila*.

**Candace (Candy, The One Who Is Always Wrapped, The Muffled One) Cunningham**   Blond American second wife of Colonel Ellellov; fellow student with him at McCarthy College in Wisconsin; wears full purdah to survive the coup Ellellov leads against foreigners; leaves him after his own government falls in John Updike's *The Coup*.

**Mr. Cunningham**   Old man cared for until his death by Elizabeth Abbott in Anne Tyler's *The Clock Winder*.

**Billy Cupcake**   Television evangelist who delivers a eulogy for Trick E. Dixon in Philip Roth's *Our Gang*.

**Ed Cupp**   Leslie's father-in-law; six-foot-eleven Californian whose conversation concerns his troubles with his Mercedes in Walker Percy's *The Second Coming*.

**Jason Cupp**   Leslie's fiancé (later husband); a Californian, he too is a born-again Christian in Walker Percy's *The Second Coming*.

**Leslie Barrett Cupp**   Unsmiling daughter of Will and Marion who becomes a born-again Christian and plans to use her mother's money to found a "love-and-faith community" in Walker Percy's *The Second Coming*.

**Marge Cupp**   Leslie's mother-in-law; an athletic woman whose hobby has become her religion; teaches infants to swim in Walker Percy's *The Second Coming*.

**Jack Curl**   Episcopal priest who believes manual labor contributes to his stature as a priest; has so little faith that he cannot even admit a belief in God in Walker Percy's *The Second Coming*.

**Jack Curran**   Son of Kathleen and Johnny Curran; football star of Boniface College, beer truck driver, and wrestler; falls in love with and marries Mary Odell, who later leaves him; dies fighting a fire in Mark Steadman's *A Lion's Share*.

**Johnny (Old Johnny) Curran**   Father of Jack Curran and ex-husband of Kathleen Reilley in Mark Steadman's *A Lion's Share*.

**Kathleen Curran**   See Kathleen Lynch Reilley.

**Mary Cheney Odell Curran**   First real love of Jack Curran; marries Curran against her parents' wishes and later divorces him in Mark Steadman's *A Lion's Share*.

**Honey Curry**   Small-time Irish hoodlum who is involved in Charlie Boy McCall's kidnapping; killed in Newark in a gun battle with the police in William Kennedy's *Billy Phelan's Greatest Game*.

**Marie Curtin**   Asthmatic young socialite and part-time model and writer; lover of Jack Bogardes, Teddy Forster, and Eric Eisner in Phillip Lopate's *Confessions of Summer*.

**Curtis**   Psychologist who marries Gretchen; reads Tarot cards and owns a house in the Berkshires in Elizabeth Benedict's *Slow Dancing*.

**Ephraim Curtis**   Captain who rescues Thomas from the Nipmuc ambush; crawled and ran thirty miles to get troops and supplies from Marlborough in Bharati Mukherjee's *The Holder of the World*.

**Kelly Curtis**   Brainy thirteen-year-old seventh grader; best friend of R. B. "Arby" Benton; student assistant of Richard Levine; stowaway onboard RV trailer destined for dinosaur-infested Costa Rican jungle in Michael Crichton's *The Lost World*.

**George Armstrong Custer**   Army general defeated at Little Bighorn in Thomas Berger's *Little Big Man*.

**Rav Yosef Cutler**   Mashpia of Asher Lev; treats Lev compassionately until Lev exhibits his masterpieces in Chaim Potok's *My Name Is Asher Lev*.

**Emily Bolling Cutrer**   Stoical and aristocratic great aunt and patron of Binx Bolling in Walker Percy's *The Moviegoer*.

**Jules Cutrer**   Worldly and wealthy husband of Emily Bolling Cutrer and father of Kate Cutrer in Walker Percy's *The Moviegoer*.

**Kate Cutrer**   Despairing daughter of Jules Cutrer and stepdaughter of Emily Bolling Cutrer; marries Binx Bolling in Walker Percy's *The Moviegoer*.

**James Cutter**    Vice admiral and national security adviser who urges the president to treat drug smuggling as a terrorist threat and use military force against Colombian cartels; sets up several missions, violates chains of command, and fails to ensure operational security; commits suicide after John Clark shows him the evidence against him in Tom Clancy's *Clear and Present Danger.*

**Joseph Cutter**    CIA agent who was trained by Miles Kendig but leads the team that pursues Kendig in Brian Garfield's *Hopscotch.*

**Leo Cutter**    Anna Dunlap's lover; a passionate, unconventional artist who falls deeply in love with Anna and awakens her sexuality, then becomes a scapegoat accused of child abuse in Sue Miller's *The Good Mother.*

**Cynthia**    Girlfriend, briefly, of Jesse; leaves him just before he joins Lee Mellon at Big Sur in Richard Brautigan's *A Confederate General from Big Sur.*

**Father Cyprian**    Parish priest; in 1932 organized a retreat for working women at which some characters in novel met and became friends; in later years they visit him for three weeks each summer in Mary Gordon's *The Company of Women.*

**Cyril**    Husband of Fiona, lover of Catherine, and employer of Rosella; narrator of John Hawkes's *The Blood Oranges.*

**Sybil Czap**    Mother who sells the story of her son's death to Waldo in Paul Theroux's *Waldo.*

**D**  Passenger on the *Here They Come* who plans to buy the English language in Gregory Corso's *The American Express*.

**Elliott Dabney**  Four-year-old son of Billie Dabney; rival of Jack Duluoz for Billie's attention in Jack Kerouac's *Big Sur*.

**Willamine (Billie) Dabney**  Blond model whose beauty reminds Jack Duluoz of Julien Love; mother of Elliott Dabney, mistress of Cody Pomeray, and lover of Jack Duluoz in Jack Kerouac's *Big Sur*.

**Elaine Dade**  Jamaican lover of Allan and mother of their child in Nicholas Delbanco's *News*.

**Daggett**  Lawyer for the Ross family in Charles Portis's *True Grit*.

**Dagon**  Phoenician fertility god, half man and half fish; subject of Peter Leland's investigations and the deity to whom he is finally sacrificed in Fred Chappell's *Dagon*.

**Howie Dahlberg**  Childhood friend of Jill's; has an affair with Jill, whom he becomes engaged to, but marries Stephanie Barboulis in Marge Piercy's *Braided Lives*.

**O. P. Dahlberg**  Handyman and writer who runs off with Alice Kelcey in Wright Morris's *The Fork River Space Project*. See also P. O. Bergdahl.

**Judith Dale**  Housekeeper who raised March Murray after her mother died when March was little more than a baby; a very private person; Bill Justice's longtime lover in Alice Hoffman's *Here on Earth*.

**Anthony X. (Tony) D'Alessandro**  Lover of Bella Biaggi before and after her marriage to David Dehn; dies with Biaggi in an automobile accident in Jerome Weidman's *The Temple*.

**Stephanie D'Alfonso**  See Stephanie Maria D'Alfonso Oliver.

**Brother Dallas**  See L. Westminster Purcell III.

**Col. Ennis Dalton**  Yankee officer and later husband of Ellen Poe Ashe in Jesse Hill Ford's *The Raider*.

**Mr. Dalzell**  Hospital roommate of Judge Clinton McKelva; convinces himself that the judge is his long-lost son in Eudora Welty's *The Optimist's Daughter*.

**Vern Damico**  Uncle who gives Gary Gilmore a job when Gilmore first gets out of prison in Norman Mailer's *The Executioner's Song*.

**Magda Damrosch**  Beautiful, vital object of Otto Korner's passion and obsession in his youth in Alan Isler's *The Prince of West End Avenue*.

**Dan**  Husband of Libby, father of Jennie and Celia, uncle of Anne, Katie, Rossie, and Valery; has a butcher shop, but has to hire another man to do the actual killing; a Marine during World War II; forever joking, complaining that he never intended to settle in Ohio in Joan Chase's *During the Reign of the Queen of Persia*.

**Dan**  New leader of Snow White's seven dwarfs, after Bill's execution in Donald Barthelme's *Snow White*.

**Seth Dana**  Active telepath who joins the vast network of mental links known as the Pattern in Octavia E. Butler's *Mind of My Mind*.

**Troy Dana**  Hollow actor who plays the mysterious savior in the southern melodrama being filmed in Walker Percy's *Lancelot*.

**Hugh Danaher**   Catholic cardinal and superior of Desmond Spellacy in John Gregory Dunne's *True Confessions*.

**Nichol Dance**   Key West fishing guide whose feud with Thomas Skelton leads to the burning of Dance's boat and the deaths of both Skelton and Dance in Thomas McGuane's *Ninety-Two in the Shade*.

**Doc Daneeka**   Brooding medical officer who introduces Yossarian to Catch-22; because his name falsely appears on the manifest of a crashed plane, he is declared officially dead, despite his obvious continued existence in Joseph Heller's *Catch-22*.

**Nigel Danforth**   Steeplechase jockey who becomes Adelia Valiant's boyfriend shortly before she receives her hefty inheritance; is mysteriously murdered with a dagger to his heart shortly after fighting with Charles Valiant; employed at a local stable at the time of Mary Lou Valiant's disappearance in Rita Mae Brown's *Murder, She Meowed*.

**Marion Dangerfield**   English wife of Sebastian Dangerfield; in exasperation, she leaves him, taking their daughter with her in J. P. Donleavy's *The Ginger Man*.

**Sebastian Dangerfield**   American law student at Trinity College, Dublin, which he flees in order to escape creditors; narrator of J. P. Donleavy's *The Ginger Man*.

**Daniel**   Friend of Clay's who has spent one semester with him in New Hampshire but decides to remain in Los Angeles after the Christmas vacation, though Clay decides to return to New Hampshire in Bret Easton Ellis's *Less Than Zero*.

**Daniel**   Student who serves on the Cinema Committee with Hill Gallagher during the student rebellion in James Jones's *The Merry Month of May*.

**Daniel**   Friend of Fonny Hunt; recently released from prison in James Baldwin's *If Beale Street Could Talk*.

**Robeson Daniels**   Son of Viney Daniels; named for singer Paul Robeson; godson of Ursa Mackenzie; arrested at the age of nine by a racist police officer in Paule Marshall's *Daughters*.

**Vincereta ("Viney") Daniels**   Best friend of Ursa Mackenzie; single mother of one son; assistant vice president at Metropolitan Life Insurance Company in Paule Marshall's *Daughters*.

**Daphne**   Passenger on the *Here They Come* who designs a replacement ship, *There They Go*, in Gregory Corso's *The American Express*.

**Lady Darah**   Patternist who leads a faction against Teray and Amber in Octavia E. Butler's *Patternmaster*.

**George Darby**   Son of Mary and George, brother of Mae and Francis; spoiled; dies in Normandy during World War II in Maureen Howard's *Expensive Habits*.

**George Darby**   Grandfather of Margaret Flood, husband of Mary, father of Mae, George, and Francis; left public school in the seventh grade in order to support his mother; composes eloquent letters to the editor; lives in considerable back pain; eventually he gets an office job in Maureen Howard's *Expensive Habits*.

**Mary Darby**   Grandmother of Margaret Flood, wife of George, mother of Mae, George, and Francis; habitually cups her fragile translucent hands up and around her bulging eyes in Maureen Howard's *Expensive Habits*.

**Jacques d'Argus**   See Jakob Gradus.

**Darlene**   Lovely but stupid employee of Lana Lee in the Night of Joy, a bar on Bourbon Street in New Orleans; wants to be a professional exotic dancer; tries to help coworker Burma Jones make something of himself in John Kennedy Toole's *A Confederacy of Dunces*.

**Darlene**   Performer in the Hippodrome; rescued from a tavern by Bea; attempts to save Jackson Yeager in Cyrus Colter's *The Hippodrome*.

**Mrs. Edward Darley**   See Flora Deland.

**Emil Lazarus (Laz) Darlovsky**   Handsome, mystic, fifteen-and-a-half-year-old brother of Simon Darlovsky in Jack Kerouac's *Desolation Angels*.

**Simon (The Mad Russian) Darlovsky**   Poet, companion, and lover of Irwin Garden, and older brother of Lazarus Darlovsky in Jack Kerouac's *Desolation Angels*.

**Dart**   See D'Artagnan Foxx.

**James W. (Jim) Darwent**   Kindly dean of the law school and friend of Carl and Annie Brown in Betty Smith's *Joy in the Morning*.

**Mahmoud Haji Daryaei**   Iranian religious leader who forms the United Islamic Republic; forges an alliance with China and India; arranges the attempted kidnapping of Jack Ryan's daughter; attempts to cripple America with an Ebola epidemic; invades Saudi Arabia; is executed by cruise missile on Ryan's order in Tom Clancy's *Executive Orders*.

**Mandy Dattner**   Physical therapist at Emma Lazarus Retirement Home whose beauty and youth initially remind Otto Korner painfully of Magda Damrosch; her vapid, childish nature quickly ends the resemblance in Alan Isler's *The Prince of West End Avenue*.

**Edward Daugherty**   Husband of Katrina Daugherty, father of Martin Daugherty, and lover of Melissa Spencer; author of two plays in William Kennedy's *Billy Phelan's Greatest Game*.

**Katrina Daugherty**   Wife of Edward Daugherty and mother of Martin Daugherty; burned in the Delavan Hotel fire and dies from smoke inhalation in the Brothers' School fire in William Kennedy's *Billy Phelan's Greatest Game*.

**Martin Daugherty**    Husband of Mary Daugherty, father of Peter Daugherty, and lover of Melissa Spencer; go-between in Charlie Boy McCall's kidnapping; chastises the McCalls for their treatment of his friend Billy Phelan in William Kennedy's *Billy Phelan's Greatest Game.*

**Mary Daugherty**    Wife of Martin Daugherty and mother of Peter Daugherty in William Kennedy's *Billy Phelan's Greatest Game.*

**Peter Daugherty**    Son of Mary and Martin Daugherty; joins the Catholic priesthood, to his mother's delight and his father's chagrin in William Kennedy's *Billy Phelan's Greatest Game.*

**David**    Illegitimate son of Jewell Coleman and Glen Davis; confused about who his father is; dotes on his grandfather and serves as a means of family reconciliation in Larry Brown's *Father and Son.*

**David**    Old, dying ruler of Israel reflecting on his rise from humble shepherd to powerful king; passionate, powerful man who alienates God by arranging for the death of a rival in order to marry the rival's wife, Bathsheba, but who longs for an end to his estrangement from God in Joseph Heller's *God Knows.*

**Dave Davidoff**    Public relations director first for Typhon International, then for JR's company in William Gaddis's *JR.*

**Helena Davidson**    Highly educated daughter of a wealthy Ohio family; roommate of Kay Leiland Strong and member of the Group in Mary McCarthy's *The Group.*

**Rachel Davidson**    Healer who joins the vast network of mental links known as the Pattern in Octavia E. Butler's *Mind of My Mind.*

**Scott Davidson**    Lover of Hildegaard Falkenstein; pilot killed during the Berlin airlift in Leon Uris's *Armageddon.*

**Davis**    See Davis Carter.

**Barney Davis**    Supervisor of the Deepwater Mine in Robert Coover's *The Origin of the Brunists.*

**Becky Davis**    Schoolgirl who appears slutty to her teacher George Caldwell in John Updike's *The Centaur.*

**Charles (Chappie) Davis**    Coach and spiritual father of the alumni of a black high school athletic team and neighborhood gang, the Junior Bachelor Society, which holds a reunion to celebrate his seventieth birthday in John A. Williams's *The Junior Bachelor Society.*

**Dante Davis**    High school sweetheart of Kippy Strednicki (Dolores's college roommate); becomes a high school teacher rather than the minister he once intended to be; marries Dolores but is then fired for having an affair with one of his students; Dolores divorces him in Wally Lamb's *She's Come Undone.*

**Denise Davis**    Daughter of Renay and Jerome Lee Davis; killed in an automobile accident in Ann Allen Shockley's *Loving Her.*

**Emma Lee Davis**    Vigil's recently dead wife; a bitter woman who mourned the loss of her son Theron and tries desperately to turn her second son, Glen, against his father in Larry Brown's *Father and Son.*

**Glen Davis**    Second legitimate son of Virgil and Emma Davis; filled with hatred and guilt, he cannot love his family, his girlfriend Jewell, or himself; fated to a violent end in Larry Brown's *Father and Son.*

**Helen Davis**    American history teacher at Haddan School for more than fifty years; the senior houseparent of St. Anne's dormitory; had an affair with George Howe when she was a student at Haddan; remorseful over the part she played in Annie Howe's miserable marriage, seeks absolution from Annie before her own death; has a feud with Eric Herman, who teaches ancient history; employs Carlin Leander as a helper, and becomes friends with Abel Gray and Betsy Chase; dies of heart failure in Alice Hoffman's *The River King.*

**Jack Davis**    Convict husband of Judy Davis; beats Preacher Smathers and causes his death in Fred Chappell's *It Is Time, Lord.*

**Jerome Lee Davis**    Ex-athlete; philandering, alcoholic, and abusive husband of Renay Davis, and father of Denise Davis in Ann Allen Shockley's *Loving Her.*

**Judy Davis**    Millworker and prostitute involved first with Preacher Smathers and then also with James Christopher; wife of Jack Davis in Fred Chappell's *It Is Time, Lord.*

**Matthew L. (Matt) Davis**    Newspaper editor, historian, and official biographer of Aaron Burr; conspiratorial political activist in Gore Vidal's *Burr.*

**Randolph (Puppy) Davis**    Third legitimate son of Virgil and Emma Davis; skilled mechanic; married and the father of three children in Larry Brown's *Father and Son.*

**Renay Davis**    Musician, mother of Denise Davis, wife of Jerome Lee Davis, and black lover of Terry Bluvard in Ann Allen Shockley's *Loving Her.*

**Roger Davis**    American novelist and friend of Thomas Hudson in Ernest Hemingway's *Islands in the Stream.*

**Theron Davis**    Oldest legitimate son of Virgil and Emma Davis; a good athlete; as a teenager, his brother Glen accidentally shoots him in Larry Brown's *Father and Son.*

**Virgil Davis**    Negative patriarch of the Davis family; a man wounded by lost love, World War II, and alcohol; hopeful grandfather of Glen's illegitimate son, David, in Larry Brown's *Father and Son.*

**Meredith (Mered) Dawe**    Young counterculture artist, mystic, and prophet who is imprisoned and later defended by lawyer Jack Morrissey in Joyce Carol Oates's *Do with Me What You Will.*

**Tosca Dawidowicz**    Resident of Emma Lazarus Retirement Home and diva of the home's theatrical society; has her moment of glory as Ophelia in the home's production of *Hamlet* in Alan Isler's *The Prince of West End Avenue.*

**Dawn**    Tall, slim high school girl who does housework for Frances Beecham in Mary McGarry Morris's *A Dangerous Woman.*

**Joanna Dawson**    Teenage traveling companion and first wife of Cody Pomeray in Jack Kerouac's *Visions of Cody.*

**Mrs. Dawson**    Employs Mary Wollstonecraft as a lady's companion at Bath when Mary is twenty-one; autocratic and sanctimonious in Frances Sherwood's *Vindication.*

**George Daxter**    Obese, half-white mortician; tries to seduce Meridian Hill in Alice Walker's *Meridian.*

**Diana Day**    Intellectual daughter of Burden Day and wife of Billy Thorne; hopelessly in love with Peter Sanford in Gore Vidal's *Washington, D.C.*

**James Burden Day**    Flawed, idealistic senator whose fall from power drives him to suicide in Gore Vidal's *Washington, D.C.*

**Kitty Day**    Eccentric wife of Burden Day; known for blurting out embarrassing truths in Gore Vidal's *Washington, D.C.*

**Uncle Dayton**    June's elderly uncle in Sandra Scofield's *Beyond Deserving.*

**First Corinthians Dead**    Daughter of Macon Dead II and Ruth Foster Dead; sister of Mary Magdalene Dead and Milkman; falls in love with Henry Porter in Toni Morrison's *Song of Solomon.*

**Hagar Dead**    Cousin and lover of Milkman, granddaughter of Pilate Dead; attempts to kill Milkman after he ends their relationship in Toni Morrison's *Song of Solomon.*

**Macon Dead**    Father of Milkman; brother of Pilate; has strong southern working-class roots; now an upper-class businessman in Toni Morrison's *Song of Solomon.*

**Macon (Jake) Dead I**    Ex-slave whose name was changed erroneously by a drunken Civil War soldier; youngest son of Solomon, the flying African; because of his wealth and independence, he is killed by resentful white landowners in Toni Morrison's *Song of Solomon.*

**Macon Dead II**    Son of Macon Dead I and Sing Byrd; brother of Pilate Dead, husband of Ruth Foster Dead, and father of Milkman, First Corinthians, and Mary Magdalene Dead in Toni Morrison's *Song of Solomon.*

**Macon (Milk, Milkman) Dead III**    Son of Macon Dead II and Ruth Foster Dead; hero who discovers in a journey to Shalimar, Virginia, the history and mythical powers of his African great-grandfather in Toni Morrison's *Song of Solomon.*

**Mary Magdalene (Lena) Dead**    Daughter of Macon Dead II and Ruth Foster Dead; sister of First Corinthians and Milkman Dead in Toni Morrison's *Song of Solomon.*

**Pilate Dead**    Sister of Macon Dead II, daughter of Sing Byrd and Macon Dead I, mother of Hagar and Reba Dead; known for her independence, use of conjure, and absence of a navel in Toni Morrison's *Song of Solomon.*

**Rebecca (Reba) Dead**    Daughter of Pilate Dead and sister of Hagar Dead in Toni Morrison's *Song of Solomon.*

**Ruth Foster (Miss Rufie) Dead**    Daughter of the town's only black doctor; wife of Macon Dead II and mother of Mary Magdalene, First Corinthians, and Milkman Dead in Toni Morrison's *Song of Solomon.*

**The Dead Father**    Abstract hero who slowly loses limbs on the journey to his grave in Donald Barthelme's *The Dead Father.*

**Mr. Deak**    Bracktown store owner in Gayl Jones's *Corregidora.*

**Agatha Dean**    Daughter of Lucy Dean; after Danny dies, takes care of her mother; keeps her mother's jewelry box and refuses to let anyone including her brother look in it; is reared by her stepuncle, Ian, after her mother's death; becomes a dermatologist and moves to California in Anne Tyler's *Saint Maybe.*

**Eliza Dean**    First fiancée of Francis Prescott; broke the engagement after he announced his intention to become a clergyman and educator in Louis Auchincloss's *The Rector of Justin.*

**Hank Dean**    White supremacist follower of Clarke Bryant; assassin of integrationist mayor Douglas Taylor in Julian Mayfield's *The Grand Parade.*

**Jean (Jane Provost) Dean**    Former secretary of John Shade; arranges a disastrous blind date between Hazel Shade and her cousin Pete Dean; supposedly Charles Kinbote's source of information about Hazel in Vladimir Nabokov's *Pale Fire.*

**Lucy Dean**    Wife of Danny and mother of Agatha and Thomas Dean and Daphne Bedloe; after Danny's death, becomes depressed and commits suicide by a pill overdose in Anne Tyler's *Saint Maybe.*

**Thomas Dean**    Son of Lucy Dean; charismatic and popular; when young, accidentally tells the Deans the name of his father; is reared by his stepuncle, Ian, after his mother's death in Anne Tyler's *Saint Maybe.*

**Debba**    Kamba tribeswoman; secondary wife of Ernie, who is pleased by her insolence and impudence; fascinated by trappings of civilization; has pictures of them in her home in Ernest Hemingway's *True At First Light.*

**Paul Decaze**   Husband of Veronique; father of Laurent; attorney; learns of his wife's affair with Ben in Louis Begley's *The Man Who Was Late.*

**Veronique Decaze**   Wife of Paul Decaze; mother of Laurent; cousin of Jack; falls in love with Ben but ultimately rejects him in Louis Begley's *The Man Who Was Late.*

**Daniel (Danny) Deck**   Husband of Sally Bynum Deck, father of Lorena Deck, and lover of Jill Peel; aspiring novelist who travels from Texas to California and back to Texas; disappears into the Rio Grande; narrator of Larry McMurtry's *All My Friends Are Going to Be Strangers.*

**Lorena Deck**   Daughter of Daniel and Sally Deck in Larry McMurtry's *All My Friends Are Going to Be Strangers.*

**Sally Bynum Deck**   Wife of Daniel Deck and mother of Lorena Deck; after her marriage fails, she refuses to permit Daniel to see Lorena in Larry McMurtry's *All My Friends Are Going to Be Strangers.*

**Johnny Dedman**   Delinquent held back in school in John Updike's *The Centaur.*

**Leonard Dedman**   Friend and victim of Leo Feldman in Stanley Elkin's *A Bad Man.*

**Flora Dees**   Foster mother of Tisha Dees and wife of Squire Dees in Arthenia J. Bates's *The Deity Nodded.*

**Heflin (Hef) Dees**   Foster brother of Tisha Dees and legal son of Flora and Squire Dees in Arthenia J. Bates's *The Deity Nodded.*

**Katie Mae (Plump) Dees**   Foster sister of Tisha Dees, legal daughter of Flora and Squire Dees, and wife of Obidiah Funches in Arthenia J. Bates's *The Deity Nodded.*

**Ludd Dees**   Foster brother of Tisha Dees and legal son of Flora and Squire Dees in Arthenia J. Bates's *The Deity Nodded.*

**Lyman Portland (Pa) Dees**   Father of Squire Dees and foster grandfather of Tisha Dees in Arthenia J. Bates's *The Deity Nodded.*

**Squire Dees**   Foster father of Tisha Dees and husband of Flora Dees in Arthenia J. Bates's *The Deity Nodded.*

**Tisha (Chip, Tish) Dees**   Foster daughter of Flora and Squire Dees, teenage bride of Kovel Henry, and Black Muslim convert in Arthenia J. Bates's *The Deity Nodded.*

**Duffy Deeter**   Visitor to the Rattlesnake Roundup from Gainesville, Florida, in Harry Crews's *A Feast of Snakes.*

**Dad Deform**   Hunchbacked passenger on the *Here They Come* who makes bombs for Hinderov and religious statues for Simon in Gregory Corso's *The American Express.*

**Mr. Degré**   See Jakob Gradus.

**Jack Degree**   See Jakob Gradus.

**David (Dave) Dehn**   Builder of a temple and founder and leader of the Beechwood, New York, Jewish community in Jerome Weidman's *The Temple.*

**Ray (Deify) Deifendorf**   Ace swimmer and student of George Caldwell who accidentally breaks the grille on Caldwell's car in John Updike's *The Centaur.*

**Deirdre**   Friend of Theodora Waite mother of Jane; believes her life breaks evenly into when she was with Ben or after she left him or when she was with Ralph and after she left him; life is separated by her moves; once a merchandising assistant for a sportswear wholesaler; obsessed with divorce in Bette Pesetsky's *Midnight Sweets.*

**Del**   Father of Selma; held her hand against a lantern globe until it burned in Joan Chase's *During the Reign of the Queen of Persia.*

**Flora (Mrs. Edward Darley) Deland**   Newspaper gossip writer in Thornton Wilder's *Theophilus North.*

**Grace Delaney**   Managing editor of *Running Dog* and lover of Lomax in Don DeLillo's *Running Dog.*

**Patrick (Packy) Delaney**   Owner of the Parody Club and bartender at the Kenmore Hotel in William Kennedy's *Legs.*

**Delora Delarmi**   Ambitious Speaker of Second Foundation who seeks First Speakership; rival of Stor Gendibal, who attempts to impeach Gendibal, then manipulates him into leaving Trantor to investigate Golan Trevize's mission in Isaac Asimov's *Foundation's Edge.*

**Edward Delatte**   Lawyer hired by Abigail Tolliver to help her keep the Howland fortune intact in Shirley Ann Grau's *The Keepers of the House.*

**Andrea Delbanco**   Sister of Nicholas Delbanco in Nicholas Delbanco's *In the Middle Distance.*

**Barbara Delbanco**   Wife of Nicholas Delbanco in Nicholas Delbanco's *In the Middle Distance.*

**Evelyn (Eve) Delbanco**   Daughter of Nicholas and Barbara Delbanco in Nicholas Delbanco's *In the Middle Distance.*

**Michael Delbanco**   Son of Nicholas and Barbara Delbanco; accidentally killed at age thirteen in Nicholas Delbanco's *In the Middle Distance.*

**Nicholas (Nicky) Delbanco**   Architect and would-be novelist; narrator of Nicholas Delbanco's *In the Middle Distance.*

**Delbert (Delly)**   Owner of the rum shop and leader in the village of Spiretown, center of the poorest section of Bourne Island in Paule Marshall's *The Chosen Place, the Timeless People.*

**Delgado** Former Cuban pickpocket and brothel exhibitionist; member of Ramén Cordes's band of revolutionaries in William Herrick's *The Last to Die.*

**Herminia Delgado** Best friend of Felicia since they were both six; daughter of a Santeria high priest; teaches Felicia Santeria; remembers prerevolution racial divides between her ancestors and the white Cubans in Cristina Garcia's *Dreaming in Cuban.*

**Dr. Delibro** Psychiatrist/gerontologist for John Tremont, Sr.; serves to unravel the complexities of John, Sr., and Bette's relationship that have John, Sr., sinking into a dream-world; helps John, Sr., to understand what is occurring with his senility; diagnoses John, Sr., as a functional schizophrenic in William Wharton's *Dad.*

**Della** African-American woman and daughter of a fortune teller; cleans for Gram in Joan Chase's *During the Reign of the Queen of Persia.*

**Bella Biaggi Delm** First wife of David Dehn and lover of Anthony X. D'Alessandro; owner of the land on which Dehn builds a temple in Jerome Weidman's *The Temple.*

**Gladia Delmarre** Also called Gladia Solaria; previously rescued by Elijah Baley from the planet Solaria, where inhabitants live in extreme isolation; lover of humaniform robot that Dr. Han Fastolfe is accused by his enemies of deactivating; urges Fastolfe to arrange for Baley to come from Earth and investigate the robot's destruction in Isaac Asimov's *The Robots of Dawn.*

**Jason DeLoessian** Jack Sawyer's persona in the alternate world of the Territories, son of Queen Laura's in Stephen King's and Peter Straub's *The Talisman.*

**Laura DeLoessian** Queen of the Territories; twinner of Lily Cavanaugh Sawyer in an alternate world in Stephen King's and Peter Straub's *The Talisman.*

**Del Rio** Boxer and aspiring actor; lives in the 13th Street building managed by Norman Moonbloom in Edward Lewis Wallant's *The Tenants of Moonbloom.*

**Ida (Ida Bitch) Delson** Worker in a textile union office in New Jersey; first wife of Zeke Gurevich; transvestite in William Herrick's *The Itinerant.*

**Angelo DeMarco** Nineteen-year-old pharmacist's assistant; beneficiary of Sammy Kahan's insurance policy in Edward Lewis Wallant's *The Children at the Gate.*

**Ellen DeMarco** Beautiful teenage swimming instructor for the campers at Montana's Bearpaw Lake State Park, whom Rayona Taylor both admires and envies in Michael Dorris's *A Yellow Raft in Blue Water.*

**Esther DeMarco** Widowed mother of Angelo and Theresa DeMarco in Edward Lewis Wallant's *The Children at the Gate.*

**Frank DeMarco** Cousin of Angelo and Theresa DeMarco; owner of a pharmacy and employer of Angelo in Edward Lewis Wallant's *The Children at the Gate.*

**Theresa DeMarco** Mentally retarded sister of Angelo DeMarco and daughter of Esther DeMarco; dies of a congenital heart ailment in Edward Lewis Wallant's *The Children at the Gate.*

**Geraldo De Martino** James Bray's music teacher; becomes the director of the high school marching band in Maureen Howard's *Natural History.*

**Signora De Martino** Mr. De Martino's old mother in Maureen Howard's *Natural History.*

**Alice (Legs) Dembosky** Baton twirler and fiancée of Heshie Portnoy in Philip Roth's *Portnoy's Complaint.*

**Alonzo I. R. Demby** Former linebacker and current teacher of Afro-American studies at a college in upstate New York; office mate of Phil Sorenson and Turner's eventual roommate; dismissed from the college faculty on grounds of moral turpitude in Frederick Busch's *Rounds.*

**Carol Deming** Aspiring actress who plays a role in David Bell's documentary film in Don DeLillo's *Americana.*

**Constantin Demiris** Billionaire with more power than most heads of state; defies the rules of ordinary men in the elaborate games of sex and death he masterminds; husband of Melina Demiris in Sidney Sheldon's *Memories of Midnight.*

**Melina Demiris** Sets out to destroy the husband who once loved her, Constantin Demiris, to save her brother, Spyros Lambrou, in Sidney Sheldon's *Memories of Midnight.*

**Bill Denbrough** Head of The Losers Club; his younger brother, Georgie, is one of "IT's" first victims. First as a child, and then as an adult, he joins the rest of his friends in attempting to defeat "IT" in Stephen King's *IT.*

**Denise** Hard-nosed eleven-year-old daughter of Babette Gladney; is highly critical of her mother's behavior; is the first to discover that Babette is taking the drug Dylar; tries to work with Jack on discovering what the drug is, but is denied explanations; destroys the remaining Dylar pills to Jack's chagrin in Don DeLillo's *White Noise.*

**Norma Denitz** Daughter of a psychiatrist; jealously claims that Callie Wells's pregnancy was entrapment in John Gardner's *Nickel Mountain.*

**Reva Denk** Beautiful blond woman with whom Jesse Vogel falls obsessively in love in Joyce Carol Oates's *Wonderland.*

**Ep Denman** Husband of Jennifer Denman, father of Leroy and Ted Denman, and uncle of Molly Bolt in Rita Mae Brown's *Rubyfruit Jungle.*

**Jennifer (Jenna) Denman**   Wife of Ep Denman, mother of Leroy and Ted Denman, aunt of Molly Bolt; dies of cancer in Rita Mae Brown's *Rubyfruit Jungle.*

**Leroy Denman**   Cousin of Molly Bolt in Rita Mae Brown's *Rubyfruit Jungle.*

**Ted Denman**   Cousin of Molly Bolt in Rita Mae Brown's *Rubyfruit Jungle.*

**Cornet Henry (Harry) Denne**   Chaplain in Cromwell's army and one of two officers to remain with the dissenting soldiers; confesses and implicates Johnny Church and Thankful Perkins; sentenced to death but recants and is pardoned in Mary Lee Settle's *Prisons.*

**Weede Denney**   Television executive and David Bell's boss in Don DeLillo's *Americana.*

**Burke Dennings**   British film director and friend of Chris MacNeil; murdered by Captain Howdy, the demon in William Peter Blatty's *The Exorcist.*

**Mrs. Dennison**   Elderly woman in Franconia said to keep a shotgun in her parlor and hate people; Gretel Samuelson goes to visit her in Alice Hoffman's *Local Girls.*

**Garrett Denniston**   Land speculator who hopes to make Cassville Wisconsin's state capital in August Derleth's *The Shadow in the Glass.*

**William (Wilhelm) Denny**   Chemical engineer from Texas in Katherine Anne Porter's *Ship of Fools.*

**Nelson Denoon**   Forty-something white American anthropologist, dilettante, and social activist guru; love interest of an unnamed white Stanford anthropology graduate student whom he meets in Gaborone, Botswana; creator of the experimental community of Tsau, a socialist, feminist compound for ostensibly outcast African women; is accused of a murder by one of his enemies and must flee; while in exile, is nearly eaten by a wild lion, the experience of which makes him more religious and less attractive to his lover, who conspires to replace herself with another adoring young woman in Norman Rush's *Mating.*

**Jennie (Judy Belden, Sister M. Thomas) Denton**   Young woman, raped as a teenager, who escapes her neighborhood through a nursing school scholarship; turns from nursing to prostitution; becomes a movie star and the lover and fiancée of Jonas Cord, Jr., but breaks the engagement after telling him of her past; becomes a nun in Harold Robbins's *The Carpetbaggers.*

**Denver**   Daughter of Sethe; sister of Beloved; saves her family by working; is college bound in Toni Morrison's *Beloved.*

**Amy Denver**   Indentured servant; encounters Sethe on her escape from Sweet Home Plantation; begins to heal Sethe's beaten back; helps deliver Sethe's baby; is Denver's namesake in Toni Morrison's *Beloved.*

**Edgar Derby**   Former teacher and leader of American prisoners of war in Kurt Vonnegut's *Slaughterhouse-Five.*

**Der Springer**   See Gerhardt von Göll.

**Miriam Desebour**   See Miriam Desebour Kranz.

**Miss Desjardin**   Sympathetic gym teacher of Carrie White in Stephen King's *Carrie.*

**Miss Destiny**   Flamboyant drag queen who dreams of a grand Hollywood-style wedding for herself in John Rechy's *City of Night.*

**Joseph (Joe) Detweiler**   Deranged murderer in Thomas Berger's *Killing Time.*

**Brockhurst (Broc, Broccoli) Detwiler**   Childhood friend of Molly Bolt who exposes himself in a scheme for the two children to make money in Rita Mae Brown's *Rubyfruit Jungle.*

**DeVasher**   Sinister security chief of Mafia-tied law firm in John Grisham's *The Firm.*

**Samantha (Sam) De Vere**   Self-sufficient carpenter in Gail Godwin's *Violet Clay.*

**Devon**   Lover of Beigh who gets her through the first lonely months in London until he disappears and the police find sticks of dynamite and blasting caps in Beigh's closet in Bharati Mukherjee's *The Holder of the World.*

**Buster Devonne**   Former police officer who was taken off the force for assaulting African Americans; is with Paris when he shoots Rosie Sayers, and shoots Mary McNutt himself; gets $1,000 from Harry Seagraves to testify for Paris at the trial in Pete Dexter's *Paris Trout.*

**Betsy Devore**   Nineteen-year-old daughter of Burke and Margaret Devore in Donald E. Westlake's *The Ax.*

**Bill "Billy" Devore**   Eighteen-year-old son of Burke and Margaret Devore, arrested for breaking into a store in Donald E. Westlake's *The Ax.*

**Burke Devore**   Fifty-one-year-old former sales manager and product manager at a paper company, laid-off after twenty years and unemployed for close to two years, who decides to kill off his competition; husband of Margaret and father of Betsy and Bill Devore in Donald E. Westlake's *The Ax.*

**Kyra Devore**   Young daughter of Mattie Devore, who exhibits psychic powers; her love enables Mike Noonan to learn how to love someone in return again; is a surrogate daughter to Mike Noonan, and the pawn in the custody battle between her mother and her paternal grandfather, Max Devore, in Stephen King's *Bag of Bones.*

**Margaret Devore**   Wife of Burke Devore; works two part-time jobs as a dentist's receptionist and a cashier at a movie theater; is ignorant of Burke's murders; has an affair and insists on marriage counseling in Donald E. Westlake's *The Ax*.

**Mattie Devore**   Young widowed mother who helps Mike Noonan to grieve and learn to love in Stephen King's *Bag of Bones*.

**Max Devore**   Powerful millionaire who holds the entire town of Castle Rock in his grasp; the father-in-law of Mattie Devore and grandfather of Kyra Devore, he is determined to win custody of Kyra by any means possible in Stephen King's *Bag of Bones*.

**Cleva Dewar**   Sister of Edith Barnstorff who figures in Jane Clifford's family lore; left the South for New York with a traveling actor in 1905 and died in childbirth, unwed and deserted in Gail Godwin's *The Odd Woman*.

**Dewey**   Name given to three indigent children who live in the home of Eva Peace in Toni Morrison's *Sula*.

**Alvin Adams (Al) Dewey**   Member of the Kansas Bureau of Investigation; appointed chief investigator in the Clutter murder case; breaks the case with the assistance of three other agents in Truman Capote's *In Cold Blood*.

**Charles (Charlie) Dewey**   Elder son of Nelson and Katherine Dewey; his death in childhood causes difficulties between his parents in August Derleth's *The Shadow in the Glass*.

**Katherine Dunn (Kate, Katie) Dewey**   Wife of Nelson Dewey; after being the first lady of Wisconsin she cannot live easily in a lesser role in August Derleth's *The Shadow in the Glass*.

**Katie Dewey**   Daughter of Nelson and Katherine Dewey; becomes the agency by which her mother is able to separate herself from Nelson Dewey in August Derleth's *The Shadow in the Glass*.

**Nelson (Nels) Dewey**   Lawyer, land speculator, mining and railroad investor, and politician who becomes the first governor of Wisconsin; his determination to live as a country squire leads to his disappointment and despair in August Derleth's *The Shadow in the Glass*.

**Nelson (Nettie) Dewey**   Younger son of Nelson and Katherine Dewey; leaves college to seek a fortune in the West, but disappears and is not heard from again in August Derleth's *The Shadow in the Glass*.

**Thomas E. Dewey**   Special public prosecutor appointed to clean up the rackets and targeted by Dutch Schultz's gang in E. L. Doctorow's *Billy Bathgate*.

**Josiah Dexter**   Newport mechanic who buys Theophilus North's car, rents North a bicycle, and sells him a car in Thornton Wilder's *Theophilus North*.

**Evelyn Dial**   Seemingly hard-nosed but kindly woman who works as cook for the campers at Montana's Bearpaw Lake State Park and who takes in the runaway Rayona Taylor; wife of Sky Dial in Michael Dorris's *A Yellow Raft in Blue Water*.

**Sky (Norman) Dial**   Kindhearted middle-aged hippie who operates a gas station near Bearpaw Lake State Park and takes in the runaway Rayona Taylor; husband of Evelyn Dial in Michael Dorris's *A Yellow Raft in Blue Water*.

**Adele Diamond**   Mother of Ann August; married and divorced from Hishan (Ann's father) and Ted Diamond; moves from Bay City, Wisconsin, to Los Angeles with her daughter; vain and manipulative; believes she has to find a husband; threatens to commit suicide after her daughter leaves for college in Mona Simpson's *Anywhere but Here*.

**Alice Diamond**   Wife of Legs Diamond; tends to her husband following the various assassination attempts against him and tolerates his affair with Kiki Roberts in William Kennedy's *Legs*.

**Eddie Diamond**   Brother of Legs Diamond; suffers from tuberculosis and moves to Denver, where he escapes an assassination attempt in William Kennedy's *Legs*.

**John Thomas (Jack, Legs) Diamond**   Husband of Alice Diamond and lover of Kiki Roberts; gangster who survives five assassination attempts before being killed in William Kennedy's *Legs*; also appears in *Billy Phelan's Greatest Game*.

**Ted Diamond**   Adele's second husband; ice-skating instructor; is kind to and loves Ann; Adele leaves him to move to California in Mona Simpson's *Anywhere but Here*.

**Diana**   Flamboyant collector of textiles, paintings, and jewelry; resident of Golconda and friend of Lillian Beye and Fred in Anaïs Nin's *Seduction of the Minotaur*.

**Diane**   First-year student at Moo University; dates Bob Carlson for a time; a social climber concerned with joining the right sorority and learning the right skills to become a corporate woman in Jane Smiley's *Moo*.

**Diane**   Single, twenty-nine-year-old woman obsessed with dieting and staying thin; spends a week with her friend Lanier trying to diet drastically but gets sidetracked by her alcoholic cousin Sandor in Ellen Gilchrist's *Victory over Japan*.

**Diane**   Third wife of Cody Pomeray in Jack Kerouac's *Visions of Cody*.

**Dib**   Contact of Johnny with the wild boys in William S. Burroughs's *The Wild Boys;* also appears in *Exterminator!*

**Rita DiCarlo**   Friend of Daphne Bedloe who organizes houses for a living; wears flannel and bakes her own bread; falls in love and marries Ian Bedloe in Anne Tyler's *Saint Maybe*.

**Dicey**   Common-law wife of Bill Kelsey and mother of seven; slain by white magic in Hal Bennett's *Seventh Heaven*.

**Dick**   Son of Wolfie and Azusa; preys constantly on his father's mind in Peter Matthiessen's *At Play in the Fields of the Lord*.

**Dick**  Personable chauffeur to Robert Druff, who suspects him of being a spy in Stanley Elkin's *The MacGuffin*.

**Dick**  Father of Josie, husband of Felicia; a corporation lawyer in Gail Godwin's *Evensong*.

**Pamela Dickensen**  Actress who performs a lesbian scene with Arabella in Boris Adrian's pornographic movie in Terry Southern's *Blue Movie*.

**Foley Dickinson**  Refugee from an Ivy League college who lives for several months at Pickerel Beach; Bebe Sellars tries to reunite him with his parents in Maryland in Doris Betts's *The River to Pickle Beach*.

**Mr. Diefendorf**  Newport chief of police who is frequently consulted as Theophilus North becomes involved in local conflicts in Thornton Wilder's *Theophilus North*.

**Cathleen Diehl**  Married woman involved in an adulterous love affair with Edwin Locke in Joyce Carol Oates's *Cybele*.

**Dieter**  Drug guru who lives in the desert and provides a hiding place for Marge Converse in Robert Stone's *Dog Soldiers*.

**Paul Digita**  New York University professor of English and lover of Polina Bellantoni and Molly Bolt in Rita Mae Brown's *Rubyfruit Jungle*.

**Oscar Achilles (O. A., Ossie) Dilk**  Assistant prosecutor who courts Hannah Cape in Jessamyn West's *The Massacre at Fall Creek*.

**Benjamin (Ben) Dill**  No-nonsense, divorced former employee of the FBI who travels back to his hometown to investigate the murder of his twin sister, Felicity, in Ross Thomas's *Briarpatch*.

**Marguerite Dill**  Though originally from Georgia, she works as a nurse in Florida; has an affair with Bob Dubois until Bob's son is born and he breaks off their relationship in Russell Banks's *Continental Drift*.

**Bonita Dille**  Daughter of Theodora and Mortimer, sister of John, half sister of Sheryl, Rebecca, and Robert; has a cookie named after her, and gets upset when Theodora changes the recipe; goes to school in Massachusetts; learning Italian in preparation for summer session in Florence in Bette Pesetsky's *Midnight Sweets*.

**John Dille**  Son of Theodora and Mortimer, brother of Bonita, and half brother of Sheryl, Rebecca, and Robert; goes to school in Colorado in Bette Pesetsky's *Midnight Sweets*.

**Mortimer Dille**  First husband of Theodora, father of John and Bonita; well-known artist; on prescription tranquilizers; a vegetarian; completely immodest in Bette Pesetsky's *Midnight Sweets*.

**Dillon**  Full-time bartender and part-time hit man who works for the mob but also snitches to the police when it suits him in George V. Higgins's *The Friends of Eddie Coyle*.

**Grover Ding**  Manipulative, charismatic self-made millionaire who convinces Ralph Chang to purchase a take-out restaurant built on unstable land; seduces Ralph's wife, Helen, while Ralph is immersed with bookkeeping and who causes the Changs' financial woes after Helen eventually rejects him by allowing Ralph to build an addition to the restaurant in Gish Jen's *Typical American*.

**Dint**  Tehkohn tribal leader who marries Alanna Verrick and fathers Tien; narrates part of Octavia E. Butler's *Survivor*.

**Sally Dio**  Narcissistic sociopath and principal villain of the novel; small-time drug trafficker with Mafia connections and delusions of grandeur; tapped by FBI as link to more prominent underworld figures; instigates real estate and mineral lease scam as cover for drug operation in James Lee Burke's *Black Cherry Blues*.

**Disa, Duchess of Payn (Queen Disa)**  Cherished wife of Charles II; once copied into her album a quatrain from a poem by John Shade in Vladimir Nabokov's *Pale Fire*.

**Robert DiSilva**  District attorney for New York County with a vendetta against Jennifer Parker in Sidney Sheldon's *Rage of Angels*.

**Benny Diskin**  Delicatessen counterboy who serves J. Henry Waugh his meals in Robert Coover's *The Universal Baseball Association, Inc., J. Henry Waugh, Prop.*

**Alonzo Divich**  Frequently married carnival owner in Anne Tyler's *Searching for Caleb*.

**Gertie Divine**  Buxom stripper and con artist living in New York City; live-in companion and "nurse" of Matthew Grierson, an aging master con man; becomes part of a complicated confidence scheme to retrieve Grierson's estate from Fred Fitch, the gullible nephew who inherits it; eventually forms a romantic relationship with Fred after he sees through the con in Donald E. Westlake's *God Save The Mark*.

**Jerry Divine**  Sportscaster with whom Henry Wiggen does some announcing in Mark Harris's *It Looked Like For Ever*.

**Trick E. (Tricky, Tricky D) Dixon**  Double-talking United States president who champions the unborn and directs the invasion of Denmark; dies when stuffed naked in a fetal position into a water-filled baggie in Philip Roth's *Our Gang*.

**D. J. (Jellicoe Jethroe, Ranald Jethroe)**  Eighteen-year-old who remembers an Alaskan hunting expedition on the night before going to Vietnam; narrator of Norman Mailer's *Why Are We in Vietnam?*.

**Djuna**  See Volume I.

**Newton Dobbs**  Son of Woodrow F. Call and prostitute named Maggie; raised in foster homes; works for Call and McRae at the Hat Creek Cattle Company; takes over the cattle operations after the drive to Montana in Larry McMurtry's *Lonesome Dove*.

**Dobbs**   Copilot who wrestles the controls from Huple on a fateful bombing mission over Avignon; urges the assassination of Colonel Cathcart in Joseph Heller's *Catch-22*.

**Elaine Dobbs-Jellinek**   Associate vice president for development at Moo University; ex-wife of Dean Jellinek; ruthless social climber interested in powerful men; involved with Arlen Martin's and Dr. Lionel Gift's proposed Costa Rican gold mine in Jane Smiley's *Moo*.

**Mrs. Dockey**   Receptionist and nurse at the Remobilization Farm in John Barth's *The End of the Road*.

**Doctor**   Director of the Remobilization Farm and Jacob Horner's personal psychotherapist in John Barth's *The End of the Road*.

**Frank Dodd**   Psychotic rapist and murderer whose true identity Johnny Smith's psychic ability helps reveal in Stephen King's *The Dead Zone*.

**Henry Dodge**   Territorial governor of Wisconsin and United States senator in August Derleth's *The Shadow in the Glass*.

**Sister Addine Dodgen**   Death row religious counselor and friend of Louie Bronk; believes in Louie's innocence; opposed to death penalty; ingratiates herself to Molly Cates through her support of Louie in Mary Willis Walker's *The Red Scream*.

**William (Little Will) Dogood**   Fifteen-year-old Puritan soldier and follower of Johnny Church; beaten for refusing to sign Cromwell's petition asking pardon and sentenced to death for mutiny; saved by Cromwell's blanket pardon in Mary Lee Settle's *Prisons*.

**Jerry (Digger) Doherty**   Boston criminal and owner of the bar The Bright Red; owes the mob $18,000; resorts to theft and other crimes in George V. Higgins's *The Digger's Game*.

**Paul Doherty**   Catholic priest and brother of Jerry Doherty; attempts to keep his brother out of trouble with the mob and the police in George V. Higgins's *The Digger's Game*.

**Don Doll**   Naive Virginian private in C-for-Charlie Company who is distressed that his cowardice is mistaken for bravery in James Jones's *The Thin Red Line*.

**Mama Doll**   Retarded, half blind, and half deaf; goes to the same speech clinic as Theodora in Bette Pesetsky's *Midnight Sweets*.

**Engelbert Dollfuss**   Chancellor of Austria killed by his brother in John Irving's *Setting Free the Bears*.

**Yakov Ivanovitch Dologushev**   See Yakov Shepsovitch Bok.

**Dolores**   Daughter of Hugh and Catherine, younger sister of Meredith, and twin sister of Eveline in John Hawkes's *The Blood Oranges*.

**Abraham Ulysses (Abe) Dolphin**   Son of William Body and Carrie Trout; grandson of Arlington Bloodworth, Sr., in Leon Forrest's *The Bloodworth Orphans*.

**Domiron**   Spirit contact of Eleanor Norton in Robert Coover's *The Origin of the Brunists*.

**Donald**   Homosexual member of the Hippodrome's cast; solicits Jackson Yeager in Cyrus Colter's *The Hippodrome*.

**Geoffrey (Fife of Fain) Donald**   Established San Francisco poet and benefactor of Jack Duluoz in Jack Kerouac's *Desolation Angels*.

**Gerritt Donaldson**   History professor; Jill has a crush on him from her freshman to senior years; steals money from an African-American prostitute in Marge Piercy's *Braided Lives*.

**Keri Donaldson**   First-year student at Moo University; from a small town in Iowa, where she was Warren County Pork Queen; witnesses the escape and death of Earl Butz in Jane Smiley's *Moo*.

**Nick Donato**   Unconventional painter who is the lover of Janet Belle Smith in Alison Lurie's *Real People*.

**Jim Donell**   Chief of the village fire department; most vocal and only identified individual in an otherwise anonymous crowd of cruel villagers in Shirley Jackson's *We Have Always Lived in the Castle*.

**Ramona Donsell**   Lexington Avenue florist, beautiful divorcée, and graduate student in art history enrolled in Moses Herzog's evening course; resilient survivor and Herzog's mistress and priestess of love in Saul Bellow's *Herzog*.

**Bukka (Make-um-shit) Doopeyduk**   Narrator and resident of HARRY SAM, who wants to become the first black bacteriological warfare expert; flunks out of college, loses his job as a hospital orderly; marries Fannie Mae; has the hoodoo put on him by her grandmother, has it removed by U2 Polyglot; is divorced from his wife, and meets Harry Sam in Ishmael Reed's *The Free-Lance Pallbearers*.

**Doreen**   Cynical fellow guest editor with Esther Greenwood on a New York fashion magazine and Esther's companion during a sexual escapade in Sylvia Plath's *The Bell Jar*.

**Dorfû**   Astute spy for Michaelis Ezana; becomes the new president of Kush and exiles the fallen Colonel Ellelloû in John Updike's *The Coup*.

**Dorine**   Commune-mate of Beth Walker; acquires self-esteem in Marge Piercy's *Small Changes*.

**Doris**   Flirtatious sister of Joan Mitchell and daughter of Aurelie Caillet; dates Michael Kern in Shirley Ann Grau's *The House on Coliseum Street*.

**Doro**   Nubian male who can change bodies and live indefinitely in Octavia E. Butler's *Mind of My Mind*.

**Nancy Dorsey**   Iris's girlfriend in Joyce Carol Oates's *Because It Is Bitter, and Because It Is My Heart.*

**Vanise Dorsinville**   Haitian woman who works as Jimmy Grabow's whore until her nephew kills him before they take Bob Dubois's boat to Florida; the only survivor of the tragedy in Russell Banks's *Continental Drift.*

**Lewis Dorson**   Once a student of Joe Robert Kirkman at the high school in Tipton, North Carolina; returns from World War II a heavily decorated hero; leaves North Carolina for Detroit, where he commits suicide; Lewis's parents, Pruitt and Ginny Dorson, give Kirkman one of Lewis's many medals as a remembrance in Fred Chappell's *Brighten the Corner Where You Are.*

**Olga Sergeievna Doubkov**   Russian dressmaker living in Coaltown; befriends the Ashley and Lansing families; influences George Lansing by teaching him Russian and encouraging his interest in acting in Thornton Wilder's *The Eighth Day.*

**Doug**   Professionally congenial chauffeur for both Robert Druff and the mayor; Druff believes him to be a spy in Stanley Elkin's *The MacGuffin.*

**Banny Douglas**   Religious grandmother of Hosea Douglas; storyteller of the lives of black heroes in Herbert Simmons's *Man Walking on Eggshells.*

**Catherine Douglas**   Survivor of deadly erotic machinations that leave her with amnesia; learns to live again overcoming odds that threaten to destroy her in Sidney Sheldon's *Memories of Midnight.*

**Charlotte Amelia (Char) Douglas**   Wife of Leonard Douglas and formerly of Warren Bogart; mother of Marin Bogart; killed in a coup d'état in Boca Grande in Joan Didion's *A Book of Common Prayer.*

**Helen Douglas**   Sister of Raymond Douglas in Herbert Simmons's *Man Walking on Eggshells.*

**Hosea Douglas**   Husband of Mae Douglas and father of Raymond Douglas; aspiring football player who in 1927 is unable to play professionally because he is black in Herbert Simmons's *Man Walking on Eggshells.*

**Leonard Douglas**   San Francisco attorney, second husband of Charlotte Douglas, and father of their hydrocephalic baby; possible power broker in Boca Grande in Joan Didion's *A Book of Common Prayer.*

**Lillian Belsito Douglas**   See Lillian Belsito Douglas Morgan.

**Mae Douglas**   Wife of Hosea Douglas and mother of Raymond Douglas; becomes insane as a result of her hatred of whites and her son's preference for music over any other career in Herbert Simmons's *Man Walking on Eggshells.*

**Raymond Charles Douglas**   Son of Mae and Hosea Douglas; grows up in St. Louis's black belt during the depression and be- comes a jazz musician in Herbert Simmons's *Man Walking on Eggshells.*

**Thomas (Tom, Tommy) Douglas**   Prisoners' rights activist who is accidentally killed by his stepbrother Virgil Morgan in Scott Spencer's *Preservation Hall.*

**Edward Stephen (Ned, Ned Brown) Douglass**   Son of Big Laura reared by Miss Jane Pittman; murdered for his efforts to improve the condition of his people in Ernest J. Gaines's *The Autobiography of Miss Jane Pittman.*

**Frederick Douglass**   One of the most prominent leaders in the antislavery movement; meets and confers with John Brown numerous times; in their final meeting on the eve of the raid on Harpers Ferry Douglass refuses to join John Brown in his scheme because it would be a senseless risk of lives in Russell Banks's *Cloudsplitter.*

**Hercules Dousman**   Entrepreneur in the early development of Wisconsin; helps Nelson Dewey with railroad investments in August Derleth's *The Shadow in the Glass.*

**The Dove**   See Hilda.

**Kevin Dowd**   Forty-five-year-old interim priest at the Chapel of St. Francis-in-the-Valley; worries about being liked; finally gets to lead a parish at fifty-two in Gail Godwin's *Evensong.*

**Clary "Mittens" Dowdy**   Black wet-nurse and close friend of Christianna Wheeler; lives in Hopewell, Kentucky, with her husband, Sam, in a shack behind Dr. Cooley's house; assists Christianna Wheeler with the quintuplets by offering her own milk; tells Christianna that she is an unacknowledged descendant of the Wheeler family in Bobbie Ann Mason's *Feather Crowns.*

**Kenny Doyle**   Works with Norm Fermoyle and is the toughest man he's ever known; stops on his way home every Friday night to buy ice cream and root beer for his five kids in Mary McGarry Morris's *Songs in Ordinary Time.*

**Sarah Doyle**   Teenage Irish servant girl of the Griswalds; grows friendly with Chatham's teenage son, Henry; admires the beautiful Elizabeth Channing, enlisting her services in literacy tutoring; is killed by Abigail Reed in a freak car accident, in Thomas H. Cook's *The Chatham School Affair.*

**Hella (Helen Drake) Drachenfels**   Nazi at Buchenwald and a prostitute following World War II; second wife of David Dehn, the source of whose money she reveals; murdered by Fanny Mintz in Jerome Weidman's *The Temple.*

**Jonathan Bailey (Johnny B.) Draeger**   Union official who comes from California to Oregon to supervise the suppression of the Stamper family's nonunion logging operation in Ken Kesey's *Sometimes a Great Notion.*

**Ada Dragan**   Active telepath who founds a school for Patternists in Octavia E. Butler's *Mind of My Mind.*

**Dragon**   Guardian of a personal treasure hoard who cynically denies any freedom of will in a world of chance in John Gardner's *Grendel*.

**Augusta Drake**   Friend of Susan Ward and wife of Thomas Hudson; artist living in the East in Wallace Stegner's *Angle of Repose*.

**Alice Draper**   Troubled wife of Jack Draper; has an affair with Jean-Paul La Prade in Richard Yates's *A Good School*.

**Jack Draper**   Polio-crippled, alcoholic, and cynical chemistry master at Dorset Academy; characteristically botches an attempt to hang himself in his lab with a Brooks Brothers belt in Richard Yates's *A Good School*.

**General Dreedle**   Rival of General P. P. Peckem; prevented from pinning a medal on Yossarian when Yossarian appears at the ceremony naked in Joseph Heller's *Catch-22*.

**Samuel Dreff**   Retired Jewish accountant who spends one night in a shelter on an Appalachian mountain trail with Mac Miller in Frederick Busch's *Domestic Particulars*.

**Sam Dreiman**   American builder and investor who leaves his estranged wife and children to live and travel with Betty Slonim; finances Aaron Greidinger's first play, *The Ludmir Maiden*, in Isaac Bashevis Singer's *Shosha*.

**Ruby Drew**   Black cleaning woman who tries to save her fair sister, Savata; narrator of William Goyen's *The Fair Sister*.

**Margaret Jane (Polly) Drewry**   Caretaker, sometime daughter substitute, and sometime mistress of Robinson Mayfield in Reynolds Price's *The Surface of Earth*.

**Dr. Felix Dreyfus**   Plastic surgeon who operates on one of Sissy Hankshaw Gitche's thumbs; later creates the first Cubist nose in Tom Robbins's *Even Cowgirls Get the Blues*.

**Randolph Driblette**   Actor and director who stages a performance of Richard Wharfinger's *The Courier's Tragedy*, in which he delivers a variant line that mentions the Tristero; commits suicide by walking into the ocean in Thomas Pynchon's *The Crying of Lot 49*.

**Dolores Driscoll**   Wife of Abbott Driscoll, an invalid whose advice she heeds; school bus driver who survives the deadly accident; refuses to become a party in a lawsuit with Mitchell Stephens as the lawyer; after the accident, is treated apathetically by her community in Russell Banks's *The Sweet Hereafter*.

**Robert (Bob, Pop) Driscoll**   Assistant English master popular with his students and his colleagues; loves Dorset Academy and tries to believe it is a good school in Richard Yates's *A Good School*.

**Stanley Drobeck**   Captain of the Wilshire Police Station, base of the ten Los Angeles policemen protagonists of Joseph Wambaugh's *The Choirboys*.

**Walter Drogue**   Director of the film *The Awakening* written by Gordon Walker and starring Lee (LuAnne) Verger in Robert Stone's *Children of Light*.

**Drop John**   See Granser.

**Michael (Mikey) Druff**   Thirty-year-old perpetual adolescent, the only child of Robert and Rose Helen; romantically involved with Su'ad al-Najaf, he also delivers the expensive Iranian rugs Su'ad smuggles in Stanley Elkin's *The MacGuffin*.

**Robert (Bobbo, Bob) Druff**   City commissioner of streets; husband of Rose Helen and father of Michael; Druff's recent heart surgery, his boredom with his job, and his suspicion of being dismissed as out-dated by the bureaucracy he works for lead him to conjure up an intricate plot against himself and suspect everyone he comes in contact with in Stanley Elkin's *The MacGuffin*.

**Rose Helen Druff**   Long-suffering wife of Robert and mother of Michael; as a young woman, her self-consciousness about her scoliosis as well as her intense pride leads to a protracted, tension-fraught courtship with Robert in Stanley Elkin's *The MacGuffin*.

**David Drumlin**   Eleanor Arroway's professional nemesis and ultimately, her protective mentor; does not subscribe completely to the existence of intelligent extraterrestrial life; an insider in the bureaucracy of science and politics; one of original members of The Five in Carl Sagan's *Contact*.

**Charlotte Drummond**   Daughter of Corky's wealthy boss, Ross Drummond, the biggest realtor in the region; an actress and divorcée before marrying Corky; stubborn, strong-willed, attractive woman in Joyce Carol Oates's *What I Lived For*.

**Ross Drummond**   Biggest realtor in the region where Corky works; father of Charlotte and later father-in-law of Corky in Joyce Carol Oates's *What I Lived For*.

**Gerald Dubin**   See Gerald Willis.

**Kitty Willis Dubin**   Widow who marries William Dubin; mother of Gerald Willis and Maud Dubin in Bernard Malamud's *Dubin's Lives*.

**Maud Dubin**   Daughter of William and Kitty Dubin; as a college student, becomes pregnant by a much older professor who is both married and of a different race in Bernard Malamud's *Dubin's Lives*.

**William B. Dubin**   Biographer; husband of Kitty Dubin, father of Maud Dubin, and adoptive father of Gerald Willis; has a passionate extramarital affair with the much younger Fanny Bick in Bernard Malamud's *Dubin's Lives*.

**Bob Dubois**   While working at his brother's liquor store, he shoots an intruder; has an affair with Marguerite Dill; later works for his friend Avery Boone on Boone's fishing boat and gets involved in smuggling Haitian refugees; on his first run, causes the deaths of all but one of his passengers in Russell Banks's *Continental Drift*.

**Eddie Dubois**   Successful businessman in Florida, who runs a liquor store and is involved in real estate; owns a large home with a swimming pool as well as a large boat; his business begins to falter and his involvement with dangerous people begins to frighten him; his wife leaves him with the children, and although his brother, Bob, tries to help him out of his depression, Eddie kills himself in Russell Banks's *Continental Drift*.

**Elaine Dubois**   Married to Bob Dubois and mother of Ruthie, Emma, and Bob, Jr., Elaine once had a one-night stand with Bob's best friend, Avery Boone; gets a job as a waitress when they move to Florida just to help make ends meet in Russell Banks's *Continental Drift*.

**Chloe Duboise**   Mistress of both Hans and Alexander Mueller and mother by one of them of Robert Mueller in Nicholas Delbanco's *Fathering*.

**Marcel Duboise**   French citizen; fiancé of American expatriate Barbara Lavette; volunteers as a war correspondent with the Fifteenth Brigade and suffers a bullet wound that turns gangrenous in Howard Fast's *Second Generation*.

**Sue Ann Duckett**   Army nurse and occasionally lover of Yossarian in Joseph Heller's *Catch-22*.

**Alonzo T. (Lon, Lonnie) Dudley**   First husband of Orpha Chase; murders Crit Matthews and then kills himself to prevent Orpha's learning of his homosexuality in Jessamyn West's *The Life I Really Lived*.

**Bannie Upshire Dudley**   White second cousin of Margaret Upshur, lover of Percy Upshur, and mother of Dr. Albert Grene; holds the deed to the Upshur land in Sarah E. Wright's *This Child's Gonna Live*.

**Mrs. Dudley**   See Orpha Chase.

**Leo Duffy**   Composition instructor at Cascadia College; his high standards, radical thinking, and liaison with Pauline Gilley cause his demise at that institution and his eventual suicide in Bernard Malamud's *A New Life*.

**Butch (Monster) Dugan**   Maine state trooper, friend of Ruth McCausland and her late husband's partner; kills himself after going with Ev Hillman to investigate the mysterious power in the woods in Stephen King's *The Tommyknockers*.

**Charlene Duggs**   Girlfriend of Sonny Crawford, who outgrows her in Larry McMurtry's *The Last Picture Show*.

**Dr. Alistair Dukhipoor (Duk)**   Allie's inept psychiatrist, who forces her to undergo electric shock treatments; half British, half Indian, and insecure; like Allie's parents, he succumbs to the temptation of money in Walker Percy's *The Second Coming*.

**Etienne Dulac**   Owner of the Austrian castle Schloss Riva and weaver of fantasies; his alleged death brings the characters together in Wright Morris's *Cause for Wonder*.

**Ange (Angie, Angy, Ma, Memère) Duluoz**   Wife of Emil Duluoz and mother of Gerard, Catherine, and Jean Duluoz in Jack Kerouac's *Doctor Sax, Maggie Cassidy, Book of Dreams, Big Sur, Visions of Gerard*, and *Desolation Angels*.

**Catherine (Nin, Ti Nin) Duluoz**   Older sister of Jean Duluoz in Jack Kerouac's *Doctor Sax, Maggie Cassidy, Book of Dreams, Visions of Gerard, Desolation Angels*, and *Visions of Cody*.

**Emil Alcide (Emilio, Emil Kerouac, Emil Pop, Leo, Pa) Duluoz**   Husband of Ange Duluoz and father of Gerard, Catherine, and Jean Duluoz in Jack Kerouac's *Doctor Sax, Maggie Cassidy, Book of Dreams, Big Sur, Visions of Gerard*, and *Desolation Angels*.

**Gerard (Gerardo, Ti Gerard) Duluoz**   Saintly older brother of Jean Duluoz; dies at age nine of a rheumatic heart in Jack Kerouac's *Visions of Gerard*; appears briefly in *Doctor Sax, Maggie Cassidy, Book of Dreams, Big Sur, Desolation Angels*, and *Visions of Cody*.

**Jean Louis (Jack, Jackie, Jacky, J. D., John, Ti Jean, Ti Loup, Ti Pousse [Little Thumb], Zagg, Zaggo) Duluoz**   Autobiographical French Canadian hero and narrator of Jack Kerouac's *Doctor Sax, Maggie Cassidy, Visions of Gerard, Desolation Angels*, and *Visions of Cody*.

**Jacqueline Dumas**   OAS member who seduces Colonel Saint-Clair of the Presidential Security Corps in order to compromise the investigation into OAS movements and gain inside information about security preparations; is caught speaking to her contact, Valmy, when Lebel taps Saint-Clair's phone, thus allowing Lebel to close the security breach in Frederick Forsyth's *The Day of the Jackal*.

**Mr. Dumas**   One of Adrian's earliest mentors; alcoholic and nerve-damaged from World War II; unemployable, but a simple-hearted, faithful Catholic from a respected family in the area; gets Adrian to hide his empty bottles out in the woods in Gail Godwin's *Evensong*.

**Jack Dumbrowski**   Neighbor and antagonist of Alvin Mopworth; popular novelist whose narrative style is satirically demonstrated in Peter De Vries's *Reuben, Reuben*.

**Kenneth (Snake) Dumpson**   Housing commissioner and former member of the black high school athletic team and neighborhood gang gathering for a birthday testimonial honoring Chappie Davis in John A. Williams's *The Junior Bachelor Society*.

**Dunbar**   Air force lieutenant and friend of Yossarian; malingerer who believes he will live longer if he makes time pass slowly in Joseph Heller's *Catch-22*.

**Anthony Duncan**   Popular author who attempts to fake his disappearance in East Germany; after Tarden exposes him,

Duncan is found dead in his car in Denmark, near the German border in Jerzy Kosinski's *Cockpit*.

**Mary Beth Duncan**　Secretary of James Quinn in Thomas McGuane's *The Sporting Club*.

**Whitey Duncan**　Veteran Los Angeles policeman and alcoholic partner of Roy Fehler; dies of cirrhosis of the liver in Joseph Wambaugh's *The New Centurions*.

**Everett Boyd Dunes**　Respondent to Burke Devore's ad; has worked in the paper industry for twenty-five years; married, with three nearly grown children; run over and murdered by Burke Devore in Donald E. Westlake's *The Ax*.

**Ronald (Strike) Dunham**　Nineteen-year-old brother of Victor Dunham; a cocaine and crack dealer; works for Rodney Little and looks up to him as a father; sees potential in Tyrone Jeeter and tries to employ him; has never killed anyone; after his brother's arrest, leaves drug dealing to travel all over the United States in Richard Price's *Clockers*.

**Victor Dunham**　Older brother of Ronald (Strike) Dunham; husband of ShaRon and father of two young children; lives with his mother, wife, and two children in one apartment in the projects; has two jobs to support his family; is liked and respected; kills Darryl Adams and surrenders to the police in Richard Price's *Clockers*.

**Anna Dunlap**　Single mother of Molly and ex-wife of Brian Dunlap; a devoted mother but otherwise unsure of her identity; experiences a sexual awakening with her lover, Leo, and then finds her relationship with her daughter jeopardized in Sue Miller's *The Good Mother*.

**Brian Dunlap**　Anna's ex-husband and father of Molly; a kind father with traditional values who becomes wrathful and judgmental when he suspects his daughter has been abused in Sue Miller's *The Good Mother*.

**Molly Dunlap**　Three-year-old daughter of Anna and Brian Dunlap; strongly attached to both parents; suffers though their divorce and custody battle in Sue Miller's *The Good Mother*.

**Rosie Dunlup**　Wife of Royce Dunlup and housekeeper for Aurora Greenway in Larry McMurtry's *Terms of Endearment*.

**Royce Dunlup**　Husband of Rosie Dunlup; has an affair and is stabbed to death in Larry McMurtry's *Terms of Endearment*.

**Brigid Dunn**　See Brigid Dunn Kelly.

**Charles Dunn**　Judge who examines Nelson Dewey for the bar and who becomes Dewey's father-in-law in August Derleth's *The Shadow in the Glass*.

**Katherine Dunn**　See Katherine Dunn Dewey.

**Katherine (Kitty) Dunn**　Older and more liberal sister of Theresa Dunn; introduces Theresa to drugs in Judith Rossner's *Looking for Mr. Goodbar*.

**Theresa (Terry, Tessie, Theresita) Dunn**　Young Catholic teacher who frequents bars to meet men; murdered by one of her pickups, Gary Cooper White, in Judith Rossner's *Looking for Mr. Goodbar*.

**Thomas Dunn**　Older brother of Theresa Dunn; dies in Vietnam when Theresa is very young in Judith Rossner's *Looking for Mr. Goodbar*.

**Howard Dunninger**　Lawyer and final lover of Emily Grimes; leaves her to return to his young second wife in Richard Yates's *Easter Parade*.

**Clarence Duntz**　Agent for the Kansas Bureau of Investigation; works with Alvin Dewey to break down the lies of murderer Perry Smith in Truman Capote's *In Cold Blood*.

**Dunyazade (Doony)**　Younger sister of Scheherazade in the *Dunyazadiad*, a novella in John Barth's *Chimera*.

**Lone DuPres**　Eighty-six-year-old midwife and healer in the all-black town of Ruby, Oklahoma; is ostracized by the young women of Ruby after two Fleetwood children die in childbirth; instructs Connie (Consolata) Sosa in the ways of healing; tries and fails to warn the Convent women, a group of mostly black women with sullied pasts who live on the outskirts of town, of the impending raid by the townsmen in Toni Morrison's *Paradise*.

**Sergio (Serge) Duran**　Mexican-American Los Angeles policeman who grows to accept his heritage in Joseph Wambaugh's *The New Centurions*.

**Borsfa Durd**　Slovenian peasant killed by Ustashi terrorists in John Irving's *Setting Free the Bears*.

**Roger Durling**　President running for re-election after replacing President Fowler; faced with economic and military assaults from Japan; relies heavily on Jack Ryan's abilities to end the war and resolve the crisis; appoints Ryan vice president to replace the disgraced Kealty; dies while addressing a joint session of Congress when Torajiro Sato crash-lands an airliner into the Capitol building in Tom Clancy's *Debt of Honor*.

**Reverend Paul Durrell**　Civil rights leader resembling Martin Luther King, Jr., in John A. Williams's *The Man Who Cried I Am*.

**Dr. Walter Durrfeld**　Director of a German industrial conglomerate for which the Auschwitz concentration camp furnishes labor in William Styron's *Sophie's Choice*.

**Birdy Dusser**　Lover of Getso, manager of Kolditis Cleaners; breaks off contact with Martha Horgan although Martha considers Birdy her best friend in Mary McGarry Morris's *A Dangerous Woman*.

**Du Thien**    Fierce survivor who grew up in Vietnamese refugee camps; adopted teenage son of Bud and Jane Ripplemeyer; expert tinkerer in electronics; efficient adapter in Bharati Mukherjee's *Jasmine*.

**Omar Duvall**    Con artist; stabs Earlie to death; convinces Marie Fermoyle that they will get married and make a fortune selling Presto soap; Norm discovers he is altering the amounts on people's checks and Omar tries to murder him in Mary McGarry Morris's *Songs in Ordinary Time*.

**Dori Duz**    Shameless sexual exploiter of men; loved by Yossarian in Joseph Heller's *Catch-22*.

**Inspector Dyce**    Detective who investigates N. Hexam's claim that Evalin McCabe Wilson was murdered in Diane Johnson's *The Shadow Knows*.

**Joan Dyer**    Owner of the stable where Grace Maclean's horse Pilgrim and Judith's horse Gulliver are kept; mother of two sons whose aggressive treatment of Pilgrim is contrasted with Tom Booker's compassion and skill as a horse whisperer; teaches Grace to ride and calls Robert Maclean following Grace's accident in Nicholas Evans's *The Horse Whisperer*.

**Harlan Truth Eagleton**   Faith healer; has affairs with James Savage and Josef Ehelich von Fremd; ex-gambler, beautician, and rock-star manager of Joan Savage; was married to Norvelle Goodling, with whom she traveled to Africa; is stabbed with a knife and heals herself in Gayl Jones's *The Healing.*

**Roy Earle**   See Johnston Wade.

**Easterbrook**   Politician who charges that some Chicano community leaders had registered illegal aliens to vote in Elizabeth Benedict's *Slow Dancing.*

**Elinor (Lakey) Eastlake**   Taciturn brunette beauty who studies art in Paris after graduating from Vassar; believed by other members of the Group to be homosexual in Mary McCarthy's *The Group.*

**Edward Easton**   Older bachelor farmer with education and some money who arrives in Brookfield, Massachusetts, in 1661; marries Rebecca Easton in 1668; his daughter, Hannah Easton, is born in 1670; dies in 1671 of a bee sting in Bharati Mukherjee's *The Holder of the World.*

**Rebecca Easton**   Wife of Edward Easton, mother of Hannah Easton, daughter of Elias Walker; loves to sing; leaves with her Nipmuc lover when the Nipmuc Indians lay siege to Brookfield in August 1675 in Bharati Mukherjee's *The Holder of the World.*

**Athens Ebanks**   Incompetent and insubordinate crew member of the *Lillias Eden;* said to be a thief; jumps ship to join Desmond Eden's crew in Peter Matthiessen's *Far Tortuga.*

**David Eberhardt**   Husband of Lainey and father of the six Eberhardt children; a rational intellectual psychiatrist who drives a wedge in his marriage by judging Lainey as the cause of their son's autism, but also shows a deep and abiding love for his family in Sue Miller's *Family Pictures.*

**Lainey Eberhardt**   Wife of David and mother of the six Eberhardt children; suffers her husband's blame when their third child is diagnosed autistic; tries desperately to prove herself a good mother by continuing to have "healthy" babies and devoting herself to her family in Sue Miller's *Family Pictures.*

**Lydia (Liddie) Eberhardt**   Oldest child of David and Lainey Eberhardt; independent, self-assured, and talented, Liddie escapes from the intense emotional entanglements of the Eberhardt family in Sue Miller's *Family Pictures.*

**Macklin (Mack) Eberhardt**   Son of David and Lainey Eberhardt; a thoughtful but angry young man, deeply troubled by his parents' intense conflicts and his brother's autism; struggles to define himself and find direction in his life in Sue Miller's *Family Pictures.*

**Mary Eberhardt**   One of David and Lainey Eberhardt's youngest daughters; well-adjusted and cheerful—one of the "healthy" children in a family troubled by one child's autism in Sue Miller's *Family Pictures.*

**Nina Eberhardt**   Fourth child of David and Lainey Eberhardt; a photographer living on the fringe of society; Nina's childhood and adolescence are shaped by the illness of her older brother Randall and by her parents' conflicted relationship; works through this history in her adult relationships in Sue Miller's *Family Pictures.*

**Randall Eberhardt**   Third child of David and Lainey Eberhardt; a beautiful but autistic child who cannot communicate or relate normally to others; center of the Eberhardt family's intense dynamics as they struggle to understand and cope with his autism in Sue Miller's *Family Pictures.*

**Sarah Eberhardt**   Youngest child of David and Lainey Eberhardt; one of the "healthy" children in a family troubled by one child's autism in Sue Miller's *Family Pictures.*

**Lionel Eberhart**   Another inmate of the convalescent home; a former gardener, he will help Allie develop her greenhouse in Walker Percy's *The Second Coming*.

**Jane Eborn**   Wife of Thomas Eborn in Reynolds Price's *Love and Work*.

**Jim Eborn**   Father of Todd Eborn and grandfather of Thomas Eborn in Reynolds Price's *Love and Work*.

**Louise Attwater (Lou) Eborn**   Mother of Thomas Eborn; her death sets off her son's questioning of his own life in Reynolds Price's *Love and Work*.

**Thomas (Tom) Eborn**   Professor of English whose elderly mother's death sets in motion the events of Reynolds Price's *Love and Work*.

**Todd Eborn**   Deceased father of Thomas Eborn and husband of Louise Eborn in Reynolds Price's *Love and Work*.

**Echegaray**   Gentle wood-carver of animals who drowns after saving a dog thrown overboard by Ric and Rac in Katherine Anne Porter's *Ship of Fools*.

**Adela Ecklund**   Daughter of Olle; poses as daughter of famous Polish author to trick Lars Andemening into publicizing forged literary masterpiece in Cynthia Ozick's *The Messiah of Stockholm*.

**Heidi Ecklund**   Bookstore owner who befriends Lars Andemening in his quest to prove he is the son of a famous Polish author; colludes with her husband, Olle, and stepdaughter, Adela, to pass off forged literary masterpiece in Cynthia Ozick's *The Messiah of Stockholm*.

**Olle Ecklund**   Posing as a doctor, works with his wife, Heidi, and daughter, Adela, to trick Lars Andemening into publicizing forged literary masterpiece in Cynthia Ozick's *The Messiah of Stockholm*.

**Char Ecktin**   Young dramatist in John Updike's *Bech: A Book*.

**Ecrest**   Psychiatrist who treats David Axelrod in Scott Spencer's *Endless Love*.

**Abonneba Eda**   Physicist held in same regard as Einstein and Newton, responsible for conceptualizing Superunification Theory; Muslim from Nigeria; member of The World Message Consortium and The Five in Carl Sagan's *Contact*.

**Eddie**   Teenage husband of Meridian Hill and father of Eddie Jr.; divorces Meridian in Alice Walker's *Meridian*.

**Eddie**   Baker at La Patisserie; has Theodora Waite fired because he says she gives him the evil eye; wears a red ribbon in Bette Pesetsky's *Midnight Sweets*.

**Eddie Jr. (Rundi)**   Son of Meridian Hill and Eddie; she gives him away so she can resume her education in Alice Walker's *Meridian*.

**Eddy**   Bimini fisherman admired by the Hudsons in Ernest Hemingway's *Islands in the Stream*.

**Captain Desmond Eden**   Outside child of Captain Andrew Avers and half brother of Raib Avers, who hates him; reputed to be a pirate and smuggler; competes with Raib Avers for turtles in Peter Matthiessen's *Far Tortuga*.

**Sister Alma Edgar**   Elderly nun tending to the needy in the Bronx; former teacher in Catholic school; dedicated to her work but often abrasive and has trouble connecting with the younger nuns; troubled by the murder of Esmerelda, a homeless child she had been trying to care for; dies after witnessing an apparently miraculous vision of Esmerelda, which helps restore her faith in Don DeLillo's *Underworld*.

**Homer Edge**   Promoter of Herman Mack's attempt to eat a Ford Maverick at the Hotel Sherman in Harry Crews's *Car*.

**Julian Edge**   Thirty-something owner and publisher of *Businessman's Press* and Macon Leary's editor and employer; marries Macon's sister, Rose; loses her temporarily while she moves back to tend to her brothers and their elderly neighbors, but gains her back by inviting her to reorganize the office work at his publishing company in Anne Tyler's *The Accidental Tourist*.

**Rose Leary Edge**   Sister of Macon Leary; has spent her whole life caring for her brothers after they divorce their respective wives and return to the family home in Baltimore; also cares for the elderly neighbors who live nearby; while Macon is living with her, she meets his publisher (Julian Edge) and develops a relationship with him that ends in marriage in Anne Tyler's *The Accidental Tourist*.

**Carothers (Roth) Edmonds**   See Volume I.

**Carothers McCaslin (Old Cass) Edmonds**   See Volume I.

**Zachary Taylor (Zack) Edmonds**   See Volume I.

**Edmund**   Drunken, fat, illegitimate son in Donald Barthelme's *The Dead Father*.

**King Edumu IV, Lord of Wanjiji**   Aged king of Noire deposed by his adopted son, Colonel Hakim Félix Ellelloû; beheaded by Ellelloû to restore rain to the land; his severed head is used by the Soviets and Ellelloû's enemies as a fake oracle to stir up dissent in John Updike's *The Coup*.

**Edward**   Ex-violinist who lives in a trailer on the beach in Golconda with his many children in Anaïs Nin's *Seduction of the Minotaur*.

**Edward**   One of the seven dwarfs who wash windows, make Chinese baby food, and live with Snow White in Donald Barthelme's *Snow White*.

**Alfonse Edwards**   Black CIA agent involved in undercover counterintelligence activities including assassination, while posing as a writer in John A. Williams's *The Man Who Cried I Am*.

**Mike Edwards**   Meteorologist for joint navy/air force airbase in Keflavik, Iceland, who survives the initial bombing and Soviet invasion of Iceland and escapes to the mountains with a small team of marines; rescues Vigdis Agustdottir, an Icelander, from rape by a Soviet patrol in Tom Clancy's *Red Storm Rising.*

**Wesley Edwards**   Presbyterian minister in Robert Coover's *The Origin of the Brunists.*

**Edwin**   Querulous and conventional father of Waldo in Paul Theroux's *Waldo.*

**Mehmet Effendi**   Turkish friend of Alexis Saranditis and lover of Saranditis's daughter in Nicholas Delbanco's *The Martlet's Tale.*

**Father Charles Egan**   Priest at a mission in Tecan with Sister Justin; Lieutenant Campos confesses to him about a murder; Egan takes the body back to the mission and throws it in the sea; an alcoholic who has been asked to leave Tecan, but instead ministers to the hippies and a child murderer at the Indian ruins in Robert Stone's *A Flag for Sunrise.*

**Frances Egan**   School nurse at Calvin Coolidge High School who sends memos pronouncing poor nutrition is frequently the cause of poor marks in Bel Kaufman's *Up the Down Staircase.*

**Sister Egba**   Leader of a local organization called Heirs of Malcolm in Darryl Pinckney's *High Cotton.*

**Egon**   Wealthy friend of Helmuth; grew up with Helmuth, who designed his country home; is married to Gisela, but has an affair with Rita Tropf-Ulmwehrt; publisher in Walter Abish's *How German Is It.*

**Eblis Eierkopf**   Physically deficient and impotent scientist in John Barth's *Giles Goat-Boy.*

**Thomas Eigen**   Author of an important novel, reduced to doing public relations work for Typhon International in William Gaddis's *JR.*

**Dudley Eigenvalue, D.D.S.**   Practitioner of psychodontia; Herbert Stencil's consultant in Thomas Pynchon's *V.*

**Dr. Isidore (Iz) Einsam**   Psychiatrist, husband of Glory Green, and lover of Katherine Cattleman in Alison Lurie's *The Nowhere City.*

**Harald von Einzeedle**   Husband of Maija von Einzeedle in Nicholas Delbanco's *Small Rain.*

**James von Einzeedle**   Son of Maija and Harald von Einzeedle in Nicholas Delbanco's *Small Rain.*

**Maija von Einzeedle**   Former wife of Harald von Einzeedle and lover of Anthony Hope-Harding in Nicholas Delbanco's *Small Rain.*

**Thomas von Einzeedle**   Son of Harald and Maija von Einzeedle in Nicholas Delbanco's *Small Rain.*

**Eisen**   Ex-husband of Shula Sammler; toeless, handsome, mentally unstable artist manqué who gleefully smashes the head of a black pickpocket with his art objects in Saul Bellow's *Mr. Sammler's Planet.*

**Norman Eisenberg**   White lover of Eloise McLindon, unsuspecting father of Clair Hunter, and self-appointed moral guide of David Hunter in Hal Bennett's *The Black Wine.*

**Ruth Eisenbraun**   English instructor and Lanier Club adviser at a Virginia women's college; arranges for Henry Bech's visit and offers to sleep with him in John Updike's *Bech: A Book.*

**Dwight David Eisenhower**   President of the United States and most recent incarnation of Uncle Sam Slick in Robert Coover's *The Public Burning.*

**Eric Eisner**   Columbia University graduate, former journalist, and current teacher in the New York City literacy program; friend of Jack Borgardes and lover of Marie Curtin; narrator of Phillip Lopate's *Confessions of Summer.*

**Elaine**   Lover of Jesse; they meet in a Monterey bar in Richard Brautigan's *A Confederate General from Big Sur.*

**Elan**   Soul at the seventh aspect of Eleanor Norton in Robert Coover's *The Origin of the Brunists.*

**Donald Merwin (Trashcan Man) Elbert**   Pyromaniac and devoted servant to Randall Flagg; inadvertently destroys Flagg's forces, thus saving The Free Zone in Stephen King's *The Stand.*

**Eleanor**   Friend of Gerda Mulvaney in Chicago; tells Jane Clifford the story of her marriage and her husband's new fiancée in Gail Godwin's *The Odd Woman.*

**Benjamin Eliezer**   Son of Jacob Eliezer and Wanda Bzik; grows up in Jerusalem and becomes a teacher in the yeshiva and the father of three children in Isaac Bashevis Singer's *The Slave.*

**Jacob (Reb Jacob) Eliezer**   Jewish slave of Polish peasants after the Chmielnicki massacres in which his wife and children were murdered; falls in love with Wanda Bzik and lives in Pilitz with her until she dies in childbirth; when he dies two decades later, he is buried next to her in Isaac Bashevis Singer's *The Slave.*

**Elinor**   Daughter of Gram and Grandad, sister of Libby, Grace, Rachel, and May; aunt of Anne, Katie, Jenny, Celia, Rossie, and Valery; plays the piano; art director of a large advertising agency; a Christian Scientist who believes Grace can be cured of terminal cancer in Joan Chase's *During the Reign of the Queen of Persia.*

**Elizabeth**   Part-time prostitute and Lee Mellon's part-time lover; visits Mellon and Jesse at Big Sur in Richard Brautigan's *A Confederate General from Big Sur.*

**Colonel Hakim Félix (Bini, Happy) Ellelou**   Ill-fated, American-trained creator and dictator president of the imaginary African nation of Kush; struggles with the meaning of freedom and identity in John Updike's *The Coup*.

**Tex Ellery**   See Dick Gibson.

**Elliot**   Journalist at the *Post;* gnomelike, crookbacked mite of a fellow with rimless glasses in Maureen Howard's *Natural History*.

**Jim Elliott**   Secretary of the West Condon Chamber of Commerce in Robert Coover's *The Origin of the Brunists*.

**Peter (Spider) Elliott**   New York fashion photographer who, after being fired from various jobs, moves to California with his partner, Valentine O'Neill, to run Scruples, Billy Ikehorn Orsini's boutique in Judith Krantz's *Scruples*.

**Phillip J. (Bertrand, Phil) Elliott**   Dallas Cowboy wide receiver and loner who is released from the team for behavior detrimental to professional football in Peter Gent's *North Dallas Forty*.

**Dr. Ellis**   Research physician at Duke who diagnoses Will Barrett's physical problem as Hausmann's Syndrome and gives Leslie the opportunity to "put her father away" in Walker Percy's *The Second Coming*.

**John Ellis**   Neurosurgeon who performs the stage-three operation on Harold Benson in Michael Crichton's *The Terminal Man*.

**Puss Ellis**   Town's loose woman in Reynolds Price's *A Generous Man*.

**Steve Ellis**   Television producer and sugar daddy to Ida Scott in James Baldwin's *Another Country*.

**Alice Ellish**   Roommate of Natalie Novotny in Thomas Berger's *Who Is Teddy Villanova?*

**Amy Ellison**   A roommate of Carlin Leander; sleeps with Harry McKenna in Alice Hoffman's *The River King*.

**Ted Elmer**   See Dick Gibson.

**Lorna Elswint**   Old fortune-teller and storyteller; friend of Riddley who gives him advice; foretells that Riddley will be important in Russell Hoban's *Riddley Walker*.

**Elvira**   See Elvira Moody.

**Elvira Jane**   Great-granddaughter of Veenie Goodwin and, through an affair with Robinson Mayfield, mother of Rover Walters in Reynolds Price's *The Surface of Earth*.

**Andrew Emerson**   Son of Pamela Emerson; one of seven Emerson siblings and twin of the ill-fated Timothy Emerson; brother-in-law of Elizabeth Abbott in Anne Tyler's *The Clock Winder*.

**Gillespie Emerson**   See Elizabeth Abbott.

**Margaret Emerson**   Daughter of Pamela Emerson; one of seven Emerson siblings and sister-in-law of Elizabeth Abbott in Anne Tyler's *The Clock Winder*.

**Matthew Emerson**   Newspaperman; son of Pamela Emerson and, eventually, husband of Elizabeth Abbott and father of their two children in Anne Tyler's *The Clock Winder*.

**Pamela Emerson**   Baltimore matron and mother of four sons and three daughters; saved from neglect by Elizabeth Abbott, who becomes her daughter-in-law in Anne Tyler's *The Clock Winder*.

**Peter Emerson**   Vietnam veteran; youngest child of Pamela Emerson and brother-in-law of Elizabeth Abbott in Anne Tyler's *The Clock Winder*.

**Timothy Emerson**   Medical student who shoots himself; son of Pamela Emerson and twin of Andrew Emerson in Anne Tyler's *The Clock Winder*.

**Emile**   Taxi driver, friend of the French consul, and painter from Marseilles in Anaïs Nin's *Collages*.

**Emma (Em)**   Ibo woman who can heal herself and shift her shape and thus live indefinitely in Octavia E. Butler's *Mind of My Mind*.

**Emma**   Secretary shared by Lexi Steiner and Mark in Elizabeth Benedict's *Slow Dancing*.

**Emma**   Mean-spirited, one-eyed mother of Waldo in Paul Theroux's *Waldo*.

**Emma**   Buxom daughter of The Dead Father in Donald Barthelme's *The Dead Father*.

**Miss Emma**   Elderly African-American godmother of Jefferson, a young man facing execution in 1948 rural Louisiana; former servant in white homes who urges Grant Wiggins to help Jefferson die with dignity in Ernest J. Gaines's *A Lesson Before Dying*.

**Reverent Emmett**   Minister at the Church of the Second Chance, which Ian Bedloe attends; wants Ian to be his replacement when he retires in Anne Tyler's *Saint Maybe*.

**Emmy (Mary Elizabeth)**   Charming Southern matriarch who lives in Brooklyn with her second husband, Pop; mother of a recently deceased son and grandmother of a fifteen-year-old boy; is moved by the letter of admonishment and loving advice her son leaves his son in Joseph McElroy's *The Letter Left to Me*.

**Alberta Emory**   Gypsylike mother of Amos, Saul, Linus, and Julian Emory in Anne Tyler's *Earthly Possessions*.

**Amos Emory**   Musician brother of Saul Emory and would-be lover of Saul's wife, Charlotte Emory in Anne Tyler's *Earthly Possessions*.

**Catherine (Selinda) Emory**  Daughter of Charlotte and Saul Emory, who adopts the name and identity of an imaginary playmate in Anne Tyler's *Earthly Possessions*.

**Charlotte Ames Emory**  Wife of Saul Emory, mother of Selinda Emory, and foster mother of Jiggs Emory; photographer whose longing to travel is fulfilled only when she is kidnapped by Jake Simms in Anne Tyler's *Earthly Possessions*.

**Jiggs Emory**  Foster son of Charlotte and Saul Emory in Anne Tyler's *Earthly Possessions*.

**Julian Emory**  Shiftless but mechanically talented brother of Saul Emory and brother-in-law of Charlotte Emory in Anne Tyler's *Earthly Possessions*.

**Linus Emory**  Carver of dollhouse furniture; brother of Saul Emory and brother-in-law of Charlotte Emory in Anne Tyler's *Earthly Possessions*.

**Saul Emory**  Bible-toting pastor of Holy Basis Church in Clarion, Maryland; oldest and gravest of Alberta Emory's sons; husband of Charlotte Emory, father of Selinda Emory, and foster father of Jiggs Emory in Anne Tyler's *Earthly Possessions*.

**Empire State**  Townsman who never speaks; member of a racial revenge group called the Seven Days in Toni Morrison's *Song of Solomon*.

**Dane Tarrant Empson**  Former magazine writer, wife of John Empson, and stepmother of Robin Empson in Gail Godwin's *The Perfectionists*.

**John Dominick Empson**  Unconventional psychotherapist, husband of Dane Empson, and father, by an earlier liaison, of Robin Empson in Gail Godwin's *The Perfectionists*.

**Robin (Robin Redbreast) Empson**  Three-year-old illegitimate son of John Empson; silent child who engages in a battle of wills with his new stepmother, Dane Empson, in Gail Godwin's *The Perfectionists*.

**Melissa Endicott**  Recently divorced from Phil Endicott, a philandering psychologist; cries all the time and takes Prozac and any other antidepressant she can get her hands on in Alice Hoffman's *The River King*.

**Henrik Endor**  Mathematician for Field Experiment Number One who becomes disillusioned and retreats to a hole in the ground for the rest of his life in Don DeLillo's *Ratner's Star*.

**Lou Engel**  Lover of classical music and steak; attempts to save J. Henry Waugh's job in Robert Coover's *The Universal Baseball Association, Inc., J. Henry Waugh, Prop.*

**Martin Engle**  English professor who becomes Theresa Dunn's first lover in Judith Rossner's *Looking for Mr. Goodbar*.

**Enid**  Blond lesbian prostitute who anticipates becoming Mina Morgan's next victim when the disintegration of Peter Leland is completed in Fred Chappell's *Dagon*.

**Donny Ennis**  Mentally handicapped boy befriended by Tim Neumiller in Larry Woiwode's *Beyond the Bedroom Wall*.

**Enos Enoch**  First grand tutor of New Tammany College, whose influence has weakened in John Barth's *Giles Goat-Boy*.

**Father Enright**  Confessor of the young Joe Sandwich in Peter De Vries's *The Vale of Laughter*.

**Reverend Wilbur Entwistle**  See Stingo.

**Oberst Enzian**  Leader of the Herero group known as the Schwarzkommando, who attempt to build a rocket in occupied Germany; half brother of Vaslav Tchitcherine and former lover of Lieutenant Weissmann in Thomas Pynchon's *Gravity's Rainbow*.

**Jaja Enzkwu**  African diplomat assassinated for uncovering a CIA contingency plan for removing the minority population of the United States into concentration camps in John A. Williams's *The Man Who Cried I Am*.

**Max Epperson**  Also called Bob Weir; old "friend" of Dick McMahon; gun runner who sets up Elena McMahon in Joan Didion's *The Last Thing He Wanted*.

**Reverend Alexander Eppes**  Backwoods preacher who buys Nat Turner from Samuel Turner and hires him out to his congregation; eventually sells him back into slavery in William Styron's *The Confessions of Nat Turner*.

**Lyman Epps**  Family friend of the Browns, Lyman and his wife, Sarah, live with them in North Elba until their child dies stillborn and they return to Timbuctoo; assists the Browns on the farm and in maintaining their link in the Underground Railroad, transporting escaped slaves to Canada; kills himself accidentally in Russell Banks's *Cloudsplitter*.

**Nathan Epstein**  Philosophy professor at Marlowe College; campus favorite whose students refer to him as God in Richard Yates's *Disturbing the Peace*.

**Margherita (Greta, Gretel) Erdmann**  German actress and star of Gerhardt von Göll's semipornographic horror films; sometime lover of Tyrone Slothrop in Thomas Pynchon's *Gravity's Rainbow*.

**Lars Ericson**  Handsome merchant marine who leaves Emily Grimes for a male lover in Richard Yates's *Easter Parade*.

**Vladimir Ermelov**  Arrogant Russian naval officer sent to oversee merchant activities in Alaska; instrumental in dishonoring Aleksandr Baranov and prompting Russian government to sell Alaskan territory to United States; husband of Natasha Ermelova in James Michener's *Alaska*.

**Ernie**   Fictionalized Ernest Hemingway; first-person narrator; married to Miss Mary; quasi-married to Debba, a Kamba woman, following the local custom of having more than one wife; feels responsible for well-being of his wife, Debba, his employees, and the animals he hunts; strict ethical codes govern his behavior toward humans, animals, and the landscape in Ernest Hemingway's *True At First Light*.

**Estelle**   Sister of Mildred Sutton in Reynolds Price's *A Long and Happy Life*.

**Annabel Eubanks**   Mother of Gus; constantly puts Gus down in Gail Godwin's *Evensong*.

**Augusta (Gus) Eubanks**   Forty-two-year-old local architect; marries Charles Tye in Gail Godwin's *Evensong*.

**Smathers Eubanks**   Cousin of Gus Eubanks and partner of the Eubanks Construction Company; gay lover of Edmund Gallatin; attractive in a quicksilvery, patrician way in Gail Godwin's *Evensong*.

**Eusebia**   Roman empress who intercedes with her husband, Constantius, on behalf of Julian in Gore Vidal's *Julian*.

**Eva**   See Eva Medina Canada.

**Carrie Evans**   Wife of Richard and mother of Jenna; along with Richard, answers ad from Mary for lodging and meal preparation; becomes very close to Mary and learns valuable advice about parenting in Richard Evans's *The Christmas Box*.

**Charlotte Evans**   Best friend and next-door neighbor of Lois Jeremy; mother of Melissa in Alice Hoffman's *The River King*.

**Elsa Rausch Evans**   Oldest child and only daughter of Sally Cochran Rausch and Ludwig Rausch; president of the local bank in Waynesboro, Ohio, in Helen Hooven Santmyer's *". . . And Ladies of the Club."*

**Harold Evans**   First husband of Lucy Henley; archaeologist working in Kenya; dies young in Shirley Ann Grau's *Evidence of Love*.

**Jenny Evans**   Widowed aunt of Fern Smith; takes her and sons in after Fern leaves husband in William Maxwell's *So Long, See You Tomorrow*.

**June Evans**   See June.

**Loiselle Evans**   Soft-haired, soft-eyed woman who lives for any kind of love—dogs, cats, men, soap operas, and God—in Mary McGarry Morris's *A Dangerous Woman*.

**Lucy Evans**   See Lucy Roundtree Evans Henley.

**M (Em, Thelma Postgate) Evans**   Eccentric bald woman who has rejected her former name; hires Francesca Bolt as an amanuensis in Gail Godwin's *Glass People*.

**Ricardo S. (Rick) Evans**   Black nationalist figure in Ed Bullins's *The Reluctant Rapist*.

**Richard Evans**   Aspiring entrepreneur; married to Carrie, father of Jenna; experiences disturbing dreams of an angel visiting him; learns the mysteries behind an old Christmas box and ultimately what is really important in life in Richard Evans's *The Christmas Box*.

**Eveline**   Daughter of Hugh and Catherine, younger sister of Meredith, and twin sister of Dolores in John Hawkes's *The Blood Oranges*.

**Evelyn**   Girlfriend of Patrick Bateman; has an addiction to Valium and other prescription pills as well as to cocaine; unaware of her boyfriend's secret life of sexual liaisons and serial killings in Bret Easton Ellis's *American Psycho*.

**Floyd Evenwrite**   Bumbling local union leader in conflict with the Stamper family in Ken Kesey's *Sometimes a Great Notion*.

**Everett**   First-person narrator; author writing fictionalized version of the story of Sarah Blumenthal's father and theft of cross from Thomas Pemberton's church; divorced from Trish vanden Meer; skeptical inquirer into religious views of Pemberton and Blumenthal in E. L. Doctorow's *City of God*.

**Elwood Everett**   Crass businessman and father of Richard Everett in Joyce Carol Oates's *Expensive People*.

**Farah Everett**   Wife of Junior Everett; leaves him for Mabry Jenkins in Peter Gent's *Texas Celebrity Turkey Trot*.

**Jace Everett**   Wealthy Texan whose business empire includes the radio station where Mabry Jenkins works, the chemical company that Titus Bean is trying to expose, and the celebrity tournaments that George Billings oversees in Peter Gent's *Texas Celebrity Turkey Trot*.

**Jace (Junior) Everett, Jr.**   Son of Jace Everett; leaves his wife and son for Stephano Valentine, who helps him perpetuate a massive swindle in Peter Gent's *Texas Celebrity Turkey Trot*.

**Jason (Trey) Everett III**   Son of Junior and Farah Everett; watches television no matter what is happening around him in Peter Gent's *Texas Celebrity Turkey Trot*.

**Natashya Romanov (Nada, Tashya) Everett**   Mother of Richard Everett; self-centered, destructive woman and object of her son's murderous fantasies in Joyce Carol Oates's *Expensive People*.

**Richard (Dickie) Everett**   Son of Nada and Elwood Everett; teenage memoirist who recounts his childhood experiences in the affluent suburbs of Detroit in Joyce Carol Oates's *Expensive People*.

**Eli Everjohn**   Private detective from Caro Mill, Maryland; hired to locate Daniel Peck's missing half brother, Caleb, in Anne Tyler's *Searching for Caleb*.

**Herbert Coleman Everly**    Job seeker; a former manager for a paper manufacturer with an intense history in the production and sales of specialized polymer paper products, twenty-three years' experience, unemployed for two years; forty-nine years old, but looks older; a murder victim shot by Burke Devore in Donald E. Westlake's *The Ax*.

**Cudjo Evers**    Prosperous blue-collar worker and former member of the black high school athletic team and neighborhood gang gathering for a birthday testimonial honoring Chappie Davis in John A. Williams's *The Junior Bachelor Society*.

**Vemon Dilbert (Blue Nose) Evers**    Experienced sailor aboard the *Lillias Eden* and sometime drunkard; left by Captain Raib Avers in Nicaragua when Evers leaves the boat overnight in Peter Matthiessen's *Far Tortuga*.

**Charles Everson**    Editor and publishing company executive living in New York City; a long-standing friend of the novelist Bill Gray; pushes Bill to produce long-awaited third novel; also leads an international committee on free expression, and persuades Bill to travel to London to take part in a press conference intended to free a poet being held hostage in Lebanon in Don DeLillo's *Mao II*.

**Richard Everton**    Determined American who reclaims grandfather's copper mine in rural Mexico; husband of Sara Everton; dying of leukemia but resists disease up to the end; compassionate toward natives, but distrustful of their superstitions in Harriet Doerr's *Stones for Ibarra*.

**Samantha-Marie (Sam) Everton**    Expatriate American who has affairs with Dave Weintraub, Hill Gallagher, and Harry Gallagher in James Jones's *The Merry Month of May*.

**Sara Everton**    American who moves with husband, Richard Everton, to small village in rural Mexico to reclaim abandoned copper mine; speaks Spanish poorly but grows to understand natives; resorts to fantasy to escape reality of husband's impending death from leukemia in Harriet Doerr's *Stones for Ibarra*.

**Richard (Dick, Baldy) Ewell**    Southern general whose recent loss of a leg affects his self-confidence in Michael Shaara's *The Killer Angels*.

**Walter Ewell**    See Volume I.

**Ewka**    Daughter of Makar and first sexual partner of the narrator; also has sex with goats and her brother Anton in Jerzy Kosinski's *The Painted Bird*.

**Earl Exley**    Father of Frederick Exley; hard-nosed former football star who remains a local celebrity in Watertown, New York; dies of lung cancer at forty, but bequeaths to his son a hunger for fame and adulation in Frederick Exley's *A Fan's Notes*.

**Frederick (Fred, Freddy) Exley**    Alcoholic writer and avid fan of the New York Giants; father was a local sports legend; envious and passionate fan of football star Frank Gifford, who was one of his classmates at the University of Southern California; obsessed with achieving fame; married and the father of two sons; seeks the comfort of outcasts and drunks; narrator of Frederick Exley's autobiographical novel *A Fan's Notes*.

**Patience Exley**    Wife of Frederick Exley and mother of their two sons; works for a family court judge, writing reports on child custody cases; meets Exley while he is in a mental hospital, and supports him while he works as a writer; his alcoholism destroys not only his career but also their marriage in Frederick Exley's *A Fan's Notes*.

**Hauck Curtis Exman**    Ex-marine who responds to Burke Devore's ad; murdered with a hammer by Burke Devore in Donald E. Westlake's *The Ax*.

**Michaelis Ezana**    Fastidious minister of the interior under Colonel Ellelloû; specializes in statistics and regulations and loves forbidden luxuries from the West; imprisoned by Ellelloû, he escapes to help overthrow the government; becomes the lover of Angelica Gibbs in John Updike's *The Coup*.

**Ben Fagan**   Poet, Buddhist, and drinking companion of Jack Duluoz in Jack Kerouac's *Big Sur*.

**Jinx (Verlyn Rayburn) Fairchild**   Black American; high school basketball player; friend from Iris's childhood; killed "Little Red" in a fight while trying to protect Iris; tortured by his secret crime ever since; later secretly loved by Iris in Joyce Carol Oates's *Because It Is Bitter, and Because It Is My Heart*.

**Minnie Fairchild**   Black American housewife; mother of Sugar Baby and Jinx; assistant to Dr. O'Shaughnessy with whom she had an affair in Joyce Carol Oates's *Because It Is Bitter, and Because It Is My Heart*.

**Sugar Baby Fairchild**   Black boy; brother of Jinx Fairchild in Joyce Carol Oates's *Because It Is Bitter, and Because It Is My Heart*.

**Sir Thomas (Black Tom) Fairfax**   Second-in-command to Oliver Cromwell at the Battle of Naseby and one of those present when Johnny Church and Thankful Perkins are condemned to death and executed in Mary Lee Settle's *Prisons*.

**Grace Fairfield**   Writer for Chatelaine West who wants to interview Francesca Bolt in Gail Godwin's *Glass People*.

**Father Fairing**   Jesuit priest who attempts to convert the rats in the New York sewers of the 1930s; keeps a journal that mentions a specific rat, Veronica, whom he refers to as V.; also involved with Sydney Stencil and Veronica Manganese in the politics of Valetta, Malta, in 1919 in Thomas Pynchon's *V.*

**Ulysses S. (Mistah Baseball) Fairsmith**   Devout Christian manager of the Ruppert Mundys and baseball missionary to Africa; dies in the dugout after a stupid play by one of his players in Philip Roth's *The Great American Novel*.

**Dara Falcon**   Actress and friend of Jean Warner whose real name is Darcy Fisher; has affairs with Frank Warner and Tom Van Sant; self-involved, controlling, and a liar; has a twin sister; dies of pancreatic cancer in Ann Beattie's *My Life, Starring Dara Falcon*.

**Ebenezer Falcon**   Dwarflike, fierce captain of the Republic who works for the ship's owner, Papa Zeringue, to bring to the states Allmuseri tribesmen; strikes fear into hearts of all crew members; requires Rutherford to spy on others aboard ship and report back to him the goings-on; shoots himself when Allmuseri slaves overtake ship in Charles Johnson's *Middle Passage*.

**Charles Falkenroth**   Owner of *The Clarion*, who sells the local newspaper but re-establishes it soon afterward, helping Nicole Smith to maintain her position as editor of the local news in Rita Mae Brown's *Bingo*.

**Ernestine (Erna) Falkenstein**   Niece and caretaker of Ulrich Falkenstein, sister of Hildegaard Falkenstein, and lover of Sean O'Sullivan; bears the brunt of Nazi guilt and commits suicide in Leon Uris's *Armageddon*.

**Hildegaard (Hilde Diehl) Falkenstein**   Niece of Ulrich Falkenstein, sister of Ernestine Falkenstein, and lover of Scott Davidson; reformed prostitute from post–World War II Berlin in Leon Uris's *Armageddon*.

**Ulrich Falkenstein**   Uncle of Ernestine and Hildegaard Falkenstein; survivor of Schwabenwald; pre-Nazi head of the Social Democrats; post–World War II head of the new Democratic party in Berlin in Leon Uris's *Armageddon*.

**Upton "Ralph" Fallon**   Production line manager at Arcadia Processing, whose job Burke Devore wants; divorced three times, with three grown-up kids and two younger children who visit him in the summer and at Christmas; suffocated by Burke Devore in Donald E. Westlake's *The Ax*.

**Mike Fallopian**   Member of the Peter Pinguid Society involved with an alternate mail system in Thomas Pynchon's *The Crying of Lot 49*.

**Peter Fallow**   Reporter on *The City Light;* British, living in New York; alcoholic with a fading career; covers the story of Sherman McCoy's involvement in hit-and-run accident and subsequent trial; wins Pulitzer Prize for coverage of the case in Tom Wolfe's *The Bonfire of the Vanities*.

**Fannie Mae**   Wife of Bukka Doopeyduk; divorces him in Ishmael Reed's *The Free-Lance Pallbearers*.

**Fanny**   Wife of The Hero, stepmother of Josiah; a dignified widow; lives in England in Susan Sontag's *The Volcano Lover*.

**Fareek Fanon**   Georgia Tech football star; African American; grew up in ghetto area; arrogant; obnoxious; because of athletic prowess thinks he can do no wrong; allegedly raped Elizabeth Armholtz in Tom Wolfe's *A Man In Full*.

**Shirley Fanon**   Attorney for the condominium where Marshall Preminger lives after his father's death in *The Condominium*, a novella in Stanley Elkin's *Searches and Seizures*.

**Morad Farah**   Most ruthless commander of Nawab Haider Beg; a mercenary Moor from the Barbary Coast who has battled infidels on both sides of the Mediterranean, the Black Sea, and up and down the Malabar Coast; killed by Hannah in Bharati Mukherjee's *The Holder of the World*.

**Farley**   Computer specialist at Autotronics who allows Robert Morris to examine Harold Benson's desk in Michael Crichton's *The Terminal Man*.

**Madelyn (Maddy) Farley**   Friend of Margaret's mother with whom Margaret lives with for a while in Greenwich Village; a set designer and creator of controversial pieces; when Margaret was six, Madelyn destroyed Margaret's parents' marriage and robbed Margaret of her mother; has a successful triple bypass; dies later in Gail Godwin's *Evensong*.

**Mr. Farley**   Father of Madelyn; cantankerous; selfish, foul-mouthed painter; either has a heart attack or falls asleep and freezes to death on his front porch in Gail Godwin's *Evensong*.

**Nate Farmer**   Tough, young black Los Angeles police detective in Joseph Wambaugh's *The Black Marble*.

**Hubert H. (Skeeter) Farnsworth**   Black radical Vietnam veteran arrested for drug pushing; escapes and hides at Rabbit Angstrom's house in John Updike's *Rabbit Redux*.

**Burrell Farnum**   Son of the tenant farmer, Hob Farnum, on the property of Joe Robert Kirkman; Hob forces his son to challenge Jess Kirkman to a fight which Jess refuses; eventually Jess confronts Burrell in the barn, fights him, and removes from his own imagination the scorn of being a coward in Fred Chappell's *Brighten the Corner Where You Are*.

**Ivy Faro**   Lucille Faro's blond infant twin in Mary McGarry Morris's *A Dangerous Woman*.

**Lucille Faro**   Runs a beauty parlor in her basement; mother of twins Ivy and Rose in Mary McGarry Morris's *A Dangerous Woman*.

**Rose Faro**   Lucille Faro's redhead infant twin in Mary McGarry Morris's *A Dangerous Woman*.

**Eben Farragut**   Selfish brother who hates Zeke Farragut from childhood and who even in death is the agent of Zeke's betrayal in John Cheever's *Falconer*.

**Ezekiel (Zeke) Farragut**   University professor and drug addict who accidentally kills his insufferable brother, Eben Farragut; achieves a new vision of life based on his association with other convicts in Falconer prison in John Cheever's *Falconer*.

**Marcia Farragut**   Narcissistic wife of Zeke Farragut, whose contempt for him is one of the destructive forces in his life in John Cheever's *Falconer*.

**Farrell**   Northern Irish Protestant and mercenary soldier in Jamaica, where he masterminds the raid on the Rasta camp; rival of Marshall Pearl in Mark Helprin's *Refiner's Fire*.

**Rachel Mary Conyngham Farrell**   Young Irish girl, twice married, and enduring love of Zeke Gurevich in William Herrick's *The Itinerant*.

**Simon Xavier Farrell**   Sickly photographer, painter, and sculptor; first husband of Rachel Farrell in William Herrick's *The Itinerant*.

**Captain Farren**   Protector of Jack in the alternate world of the Territories in Stephen King's and Peter Straub's *The Talisman*.

**Farris**   Judge who spies against Randall Flagg in Stephen King's *The Stand*.

**Gene Farrow**   Husband of Lois Farrow and father of Jacy Farrow; rich from oil leases, but hard-pressed to remain rich in Larry McMurtry's *The Last Picture Show*.

**Jacy Farrow**   Daughter of Gene and Lois Farrow; spoiled and naive girlfriend of Duane Moore; elopes with Sonny Crawford, although the marriage is annulled in Larry McMurtry's *The Last Picture Show*.

**Lois Farrow**   Wife of Gene Farrow, mother of Jacy Farrow, and lover of Sam the Lion; cynical drunk who is practical in matters of sex in Larry McMurtry's *The Last Picture Show*.

**Fast Horse**   Boastful friend of Fools Crow whose loud bragging alerts the Crows during a Pikuni horse raid on their camp;

lies after he deserts Yellow Kidney in the Crow camp; is banished when Yellow Kidney returns to camp and joins a band of renegades lead by Owl Child; is later killed in retribution by whites in James Welch's *Fools Crow*.

**Han Fastolfe**   Political leader and preeminent theoretical roboticist on the planet Aurora; accused of roboticide to prevent political rivals from replicating his design, he arranges for Elijah Baley to come from Earth to prove his innocence; supporter of Earth's inclusion in colonization of unsettled worlds; designer of R. Daneel Olivaw; father of Vasilia Fastolfe in Isaac Asimov's *The Robots of Dawn*.

**Vasilia Fastolfe**   Also called Vasalia Aliena; estranged roboticist daughter of Dr. Han, she opposes Fastolfe's position of permitting Earth to colonize unsettled worlds; early in her career, she accidentally and unknowingly endows R. Giskard with telepathic powers during a lab experiment in Isaac Asimov's *The Robots of Dawn*.

**Father**   Carpenter; takes cold baths to relieve his back pain; engages in extramarital affairs but loves his wife and daughter; constructs a steamer trunk for his daughter and sends her to school in England in Jamaica Kincaid's *Annie John*.

**Father**   Harvard graduate and Wall Street financier who dies three years after he writes an undelivered letter of loving advice and admonishment to his son; forward-thinking man whose death prompts all around him to rethink their own life paths and relationships in Joseph McElroy's *The Letter Left to Me*.

**Father**   Husband of Mother and father of Little Boy; owner of a company that makes flags, buntings, and fireworks; accompanies Admiral Peary's expedition to the North Pole; intermediary during Coalhouse Walker, Jr.'s siege at the Morgan Library; dies on the *Lusitania* in E.L. Doctorow's *Ragtime*.

**Sam Fathers**   See Volume I.

**Fatima**   Favorite maid of Emma; a beautiful black Copt in Susan Sontag's *The Volcano Lover*.

**Lois Fazenda**   Prostitute and murder victim in John Gregory Dunne's *True Confessions*.

**Feather Woman**   Pikuni woman who lives in exile in the spiritual realm, having been punished for digging up a sacred turnip, leaving a hole in the sky; formerly, she married the Morning Star, the son of Sun and Moon, and gave birth to Scarface, who brought the Sun Dance ceremony to the Pikuni; she paints prophetic scenes on a tanned hide for Fools Crow to give him knowledge about the future of his people during his vision quest in James Welch's *Fools Crow*.

**Beatrice (Bea, Bee) Fedder**   Wife of Niles Fedder in Thomas Berger's *Reinhart in Love*.

**Niles Fedder**   Neighbor of Carl Reinhart in Vetsville in Thomas Berger's *Reinhart in Love*.

**Cheops Feeley**   Scientist who wants to implant an electrode in Billy Twillig's head to boost the power of his left brain in Don DeLillo's *Ratner's Star*.

**Sister Justin (May) Feeney**   Twenty-eight-year-old nun and nurse at a mission in Tecan with Father Egan; is sexually attracted to Father Godoy; has been asked to leave Tecan, but instead joins the rebels; sleeps with Frank Holliwell; is tortured and killed by Lieutenant Campos in Robert Stone's *A Flag for Sunrise*.

**Lionel Feffer**   Former reader for poor-sighted Artur Sammler; academic operator who arranges Sammler's Bloomsbury talk at Columbia University; causes a violent street scene by photographing the black pickpocket who menaces Sammler in Saul Bellow's *Mr. Sammler's Planet*.

**Roy Fehler**   Recovered alcoholic and Los Angeles policeman; killed at the end of Joseph Wambaugh's *The New Centurions*.

**Hannah Portnoy Feibish**   Sister of Alex Portnoy in Philip Roth's *Portnoy's Complaint*.

**Mendel (The Ox) Feinstein**   Weightlifter and Legs Diamond's henchman; dies from a heart attack in William Kennedy's *Legs*.

**Morris Feitelzolm**   Agnostic philosopher and lecturer, woman-chaser, and zloty-borrowing friend of Aaron Greidinger in Isaac Bashevis Singer's *Shosha*.

**Billy Feldman**   Son of Leo Feldman in Stanley Elkin's *A Bad Man*.

**Isidore Feldman**   Jewish peddler and father of Leo Feldman; teaches Leo the fundamentals and ethics of selling in Stanley Elkin's *A Bad Man*.

**Leo Feldman**   Department store owner and purveyor of The Basement, where he does favors; sentenced to a year in prison for the crime of being himself in Stanley Elkin's *A Bad Man*.

**Lilly Feldman**   Wife of Leo Feldman in Stanley Elkin's *A Bad Man*.

**Murray Feldstein**   Young Jewish American man from Detroit who signs up with the marines during World War II; survives the brutal battles of Guadalcanal to come home and marry his sweetheart, Ruthie Siegal, in Marge Piercy's *Gone to Soldiers*.

**Ruthie Siegal Feldstein**   Young Jewish American woman living in Detroit during World War II; sister of Duvey Siegal, cousin to Naomi Levy-Monot; works in a factory during the war and attends night school to become a social worker; marries Murray Feldstein and achieves her career goal in Marge Piercy's *Gone to Soldiers*.

**Franny Feldstone**   Dara's twin sister; Dara moves in with her in Provincetown in Ann Beattie's *My Life, Starring Dara Falcon*.

**Luke (Paragon) Fellinka**   Head guide on Rusty Jethroe's hunting expedition into the Brooks Range in Norman Mailer's *Why Are We in Vietnam?*

**Ben Feltner**   Father of Mat Feltner and husband of Nancy Beechum Feltner in Wendell Berry's *The Memory of Old Jack.*

**Bess Feltner**   See Bess Feltner Catlett.

**Hannah Feltner**   See Hannah Coulter.

**Margaret (Little Margaret) Feltner**   Daughter of Virgil and Hannah Feltner; born after the death of her father in Wendell Berry's *A Place on Earth;* also appears in *The Memory of Old Jack.*

**Margaret Finley Feltner**   Wife of Mat Feltner and mother of Virgil Feltner and Bess Feltner Catlett; brings her daughter-in-law, Hannah Feltner, to live with her family following the death of Virgil in Wendell Berry's *A Place on Earth;* also appears in *Nathan Coulter* and *The Memory of Old Jack.*

**Mat Feltner**   Subsistence tobacco farmer in Port William, Kentucky; son of Ben and Nancy Feltner and husband of Margaret Feltner; centered consciousness of Wendell Berry's *A Place on Earth;* also appears in *Nathan Coulter* and *The Memory of Old Jack.*

**Nancy Beechum Feltner**   Wife of Ben Feltner, mother of Mat Feltner, and sister of Old Jack Beechum in Wendell Berry's *The Memory of Old Jack.*

**Virgil Feltner**   Son of Mat and Margaret Feltner, first husband of Hannah Coulter, and father of Little Margaret Feltner; dies in World War II in Wendell Berry's *A Place on Earth.*

**Dr. Robert (Frank X. Barlow, Kilgore Trout) Fender**   Prisoner with Walter F. Starbuck; writes science fiction pseudonymously in Kurt Vonnegut's *Jailbird.*

**Feng Wo**   Chinese accountant in San Francisco; father-in-law of Dan Lavette in Howard Fast's *Second Generation.*

**Edward B. (Ed, Eddie) Fenig**   Writer who lives upstairs from Bucky Wunderlick in Don DeLillo's *Great Jones Street.*

**Julian Fenn**   Colleague of Holman Turner in the English department at Convers College in Alison Lurie's *Love and Friendship.*

**Miranda Fenn**   Wife of Julian Fenn in Alison Lurie's *Love and Friendship.*

**Charles Fenwick**   Proud and arrogant youth with stunted social development; aided by Theophilus North in Thornton Wilder's *Theophilus North.*

**Eloise Fenwick**   Sister of Charles Fenwick; introduces her brother to Theophilus North, who has been her tennis instructor in Thornton Wilder's *Theophilus North.*

**Feral**   Senegalese actor who performs in a sex scene with Angela Sterling in Boris Adrian's pornographic movie in Terry Southern's *Blue Movie.*

**Ferguson (Fergy)**   Worker at the Cane Vale sugar factory in Bournehills, the poorest section of Bourne Island in Paule Marshall's *The Chosen Place, the Timeless People.*

**Swoop Ferguson**   Corrupt policeman never allowed to join his contemporaries in the Junior Bachelor Society; tries to humiliate them by arresting Moon Porter at the testimonial for Chappie Davis in John A. Williams's *The Junior Bachelor Society.*

**Alice Fermoyle**   Seventeen-year-old sister of Benjamin and Norm, daughter of Sam Fermoyle; has limp brown hair; dates and then breaks up with Les Stoner; gets involved with Joe, a priest; is caught in the act by a monsignor; has a breakdown; goes to college in Mary McGarry Morris's *Songs in Ordinary Time.*

**Benjamin (Benjy) Fermoyle**   Twelve-year-old brother of Norm and Alice; son of Sam Fermoyle in Mary McGarry Morris's *Songs in Ordinary Time.*

**Bridget Fermoyle**   Mother of Helen and Sam; lives in her dining room in an enormous crib; wears diapers and needs to be fed in Mary McGarry Morris's *Songs in Ordinary Time.*

**Marie Fermoyle**   Ex-wife of Sam Fermoyle, mother of Alice, Norm, and Benjamin; secretary at Briscoe's Sporting Goods; becomes engaged to Omar in Mary McGarry Morris's *Songs in Ordinary Time.*

**Norm Fermoyle**   Sixteen-year-old brother of Benjamin and Alice; man of the house for ten years; son of Sam Fermoyle; steals money from Lonzo Thayer to give to Kenny Doyle when Kenny loses at gambling; attacks Jarden Greene when he evicts Joey Seldon in Mary McGarry Morris's *Songs in Ordinary Time.*

**Sam Fermoyle**   Brother of Helen LaChance, ex-husband of Mary Fermoyle, father of Benjamin, Norm, and Alice; an alcoholic; goes to Applegate and sobers up in Mary McGarry Morris's *Songs in Ordinary Time.*

**Fernandez**   Husband of Cassandra and son-in-law of Skipper; leaves Cassandra for Harry and is found dead by Skipper, strangled by a guitar string in John Hawkes's *Second Skin.*

**Jaimito Fernandez**   Farmer and businessman in the Dominican Republic during the reign of Trujillo; husband of Dede Mirabal, he does not want his wife to join her sisters in their underground political activities in Julia Alvarez's *In the Time of the Butterflies.*

**Joseph (Joe) Ferone**   Problem student at Calvin Coolidge High School whom Sylvia Barrett works desperately to help; very bright teenager who is a product of the streets in Bel Kaufman's *Up the Down Staircase.*

**Earl Fetner**   Husband of Tweet Fetner, brother of Bebe Sellars, and owner of a used car lot in Doris Betts's *The River to Pickle Beach*.

**Grace Fetner**   Mother of Bebe Sellars; disapproves of her daughter's marriage, fearing that Jack Sellars has inherited mental problems in Doris Betts's *The River to Pickle Beach*.

**Mary Ruth Packard Fetner**   Wife of Troy Fetner and mother of Randy Fetner in Doris Betts's *The River to Pickle Beach*.

**Randy Fetner**   Young son of Troy and Mary Ruth Fetner; nearly drowns in a pond during a family outing in Doris Betts's *The River to Pickle Beach*.

**Treva (Tweet) Fetner**   Wife of Earl Fetner; her home exhibits multiple decorating clichés in Doris Betts's *The River to Pickle Beach*.

**Troy Fetner**   Brother of Bebe Sellars and Earl Fetner; family jester who writes ads for Earl's used car business in Doris Betts's *The River to Pickle Beach*.

**Fiammetta**   French prostitute who, regardless of the amount of money, refuses Tarden in Jerzy Kosinski's *Cockpit*.

**Alonzo Fiber**   See Belt.

**Charles (Charlie) Fielding**   Musician, conductor, and composer; begins writing symphonies but never finishes them; first lover of Isadora Wing after her first marriage in Erica Jong's *Fear of Flying*.

**Jenny (Jennifer) Fields**   Tough-as-nails nurse and single mother of T. S. Garp; the black sheep of a wealthy New England family; head nurse at an all-boys prep school; writes a wildly successful autobiography, *A Sexual Suspect,* and becomes a guru to countless feminists and women in need of care; in her later years, runs a compound on her seaside estate for women until her murder by a madman in John Irving's *The World According to Garp*.

**Corporal Fife**   Clerk in C-for-Charlie Company and close friend of Private Witt; his combat experiences cause a series of recurring nightmares in James Jones's *The Thin Red Line*.

**Angela Figueroa**   Oldest child in the Figueroa family; physically abused by her father; escapes from a girls' shelter to which she has been sent and hides out with her sixteen-year-old boyfriend, Buddy Rivers, in June Jordan's *His Own Where*.

**Charlie Filetti**   Friend of Legs Diamond; involved in the Hotsy Totsy Club shootout in William Kennedy's *Legs*.

**Mikhail Semyonovich (Misha) Filitov**   Colonel in the Soviet Army and veteran of World War II; spies for the Americans despite being a patriotic Russian; discovered, arrested, and interrogated at length by Vatutin before being freed by Gerasimov when Jack Ryan coerces the KGB chairman into defection in Tom Clancy's *The Cardinal of the Kremlin*.

**Mahmoud Fils–Aimé**   Haitian who recommends Sid to the Worthingtons; follows Sid to Paris; kills Lucien and is killed by Sid in Herbert Gold's *Slave Trade*.

**Filthy Herman**   Double amputee and sexual pervert in Joseph Wambaugh's *The Choirboys*.

**Miss Finch**   Blind, elderly woman to whom Ruth Grey is a paid companion; loves to listen to books on tape; becomes one of Ruth's best friends; is placed in a nursing home after Ruth graduates from high school in Jane Hamilton's *Book of Ruth*.

**Sadie Finch**   Chief clerk at Calvin Coolidge High School, who sends out memos such as "Please ignore the bells"; signs in for Paul Barringer so he can slip in late undetected in Bel Kaufman's *Up the Down Staircase*.

**Cathie Chandler Finer**   Wife of Sam Finer; a lover, briefly, of Ron Grant; caught in adultery with Al Bonham in a motel in James Jones's *Go to the Widow-Maker*.

**Sam Finer**   Wisconsin businessman who loans Al Bonham money to buy the schooner *Naiad;* marries Cathie Chandler in James Jones's *Go to the Widow-Maker*.

**Eddie Fingers**   See Eddie Coyle.

**Morris Fink**   Handyman and resident of the apartment house also occupied by Stingo, Nathan Landau, and Sophie Zawistowska in William Styron's *Sophie's Choice*.

**Dauphine Finkel**   Second wife of Jed Tewksbury; introduces Tewksbury to all the ideas that were going to redeem the world in the early 1940s in Robert Penn Warren's *A Place to Come To*.

**Judith Finkel**   Grandmother of Jerry Kaplan and one of only two whites living in the black Cousinville, New Jersey, ghetto in Hal Bennett's *The Black Wine*.

**Sanford (Sandy, Zed) Finkelstein**   Owner of Krishna Bookshop and lover of Erica Tate in Alison Lurie's *The War between the Tates*.

**Ernest (Shamble) Finley**   Crippled brother of Margaret Feltner; commits suicide because of unrequited love for Ida Crop in Wendell Berry's *A Place on Earth*.

**Jacob Finney**   Young, honest hired gun who befriends and protects orphaned Johannes Verne and Miss Nesselrode in Louis L'Amour's *The Lonesome Gods*.

**Samson Finney**   Lawyer and old friend of Judah Sherbrooke in Nicholas Delbanco's *Possession* and *Sherbrookes*.

**Alvin Finque**   Los Angeles police lieutenant in the Wilshire Station in Joseph Wambaugh's *The Choirboys*.

**Julius Finsberg**   Old business partner of Ben Flesh's father in the costume industry; father of the eighteen Finsberg children;

grants to Ben the gift of the prime interest rate in Stanley Elkin's *The Franchiser*.

**Patty Finsberg**    One of eighteen children of Julius Finsberg and favorite god-cousin of Ben Flesh; cannot hear loud noises in Stanley Elkin's *The Franchiser*.

**Finsberg children**    Eighteen children of Julius Finsberg, four sets of triplets and three sets of twins, all named for musical stage personalities (Patty, LaVerne, Maxene, Oscar, Ethel, Lorenz, Jerome, Irving, Noel, Gertrude, Kitty, Helen, Sigmund-Rudolf, Mary, Moss, Gus-Ira, Lotte, and Cole); all suffer from strange, mortal diseases in Stanley Elkin's *The Franchiser*.

**Fiona**    Sensual wife of Cyril and lover of Hugh; departs with Meredith, Dolores, and Eveline after Hugh's death and Catherine's collapse in John Hawkes's *The Blood Oranges*.

**Jack Fiori**    See Jack Flowers.

**Carol Ann Firebaugh**    College student who spends a summer as a Red Cross Grey Lady in Kilrainey Army Hospital during World War II; becomes involved with Marion Landers and later, more seriously, with Martin Winch in James Jones's *Whistle*.

**Gary Fish**    Friend and business associate of Tracy Morgan in Scott Spencer's *Preservation Hall*.

**Bruno Fisher**    Classmate of Eric Eisner at Columbia University and New York social worker; finds Eric a job with the literacy program for the disadvantaged in Phillip Lopate's *Confessions of Summer*.

**Carter Fisher**    Eighteen-year-old son of Ursula and Michael, brother of Juliette Fisher; works at a produce market; after he graduates from high school, opens his own pizza parlor with his girlfriend Annabel in Sandra Scofield's *Beyond Deserving*.

**Evelyn Fisher**    Sister of Gulsvig and Michael, older by one year; daughter of Geneva and Gully; died from a botched abortion in Sandra Scofield's *Beyond Deserving*.

**Geneva Fisher**    Wife of Gully Fisher for fifty years, mother of Gulsvig and Michael, grandmother of Juliette, Carter, and Rhea; leaves Gully to spend time with her sister, Ruby, in Sandra Scofield's *Beyond Deserving*.

**Gulsvig "Fish" Fisher**    Husband of Katie, twin brother of Michael; a Vietnam vet; becomes violent when he drinks; spends a year in jail for a joyride in a Porsche; a carpenter, his work is an artisan's, but he is undependable; dislikes authority, suspicious of promises in Sandra Scofield's *Beyond Deserving*.

**Juliette Fisher**    Fifteen-year-old daughter of Ursula and Michael, sister of Carter Fisher; wants to go to dance school and dances fifteen hours a week; does not get along with her brother in Sandra Scofield's *Beyond Deserving*.

**Katie Fisher**    Wife of Gulsvig Fisher, mother of Rhea, daughter of June; decides to take Rhea temporarily to stay with her mother

and aunt in Texas when Gulsvig punches her in the face; goes back to him and leaves Rhea with June; while Gulsvig is in jail, takes a lover named Jeff in Sandra Scofield's *Beyond Deserving*.

**Michael Fisher**    Twin brother of Gulsvig, husband of Ursula; a teacher; a great believer in waiting things out, especially kids; careful, thorough, loyal, uncritical; bears responsibility for his aging parents; never shows what he is thinking; has a propensity for taciturnity; forty-five in Sandra Scofield's *Beyond Deserving*.

**Michael "Gully" Fisher**    Seventy-three-year-old husband of Geneva Fisher for fifty years, father of Gulsvig and Michael, grandfather of Juliette, Carter, and Rhea; used to build heavy equipment for road construction; handyman at the fishing lodge; a reformed alcoholic who stopped drinking after his house burned down; spent months in the state mental hospital in Sandra Scofield's *Beyond Deserving*.

**Rhea Fisher**    Daughter of Katie and Gulsvig Fisher in Sandra Scofield's *Beyond Deserving*.

**Ursula "Ursie" Fisher**    Wife of Michael, sister-in-law of Gulsvig; her job is looking out for people who don't have the sense to look out for themselves, was Gulsvig's lover before she married Michael; has a master's degree in counseling and is a social worker; habitually messy in Sandra Scofield's *Beyond Deserving*.

**Wally Fisher**    Owner of a West Condon hotel; rents the ground on which the Brunists believe they will ascend to heaven to the operators of a fair in Robert Coover's *The Origin of the Brunists*.

**Warden Fisher**    Warden of a surreal prison; terrorizes Leo Feldman in Stanley Elkin's *A Bad Man*.

**Johann Fist**    Captain of a motley crew of smugglers and a Satanic/Faustian figure in *The Smugglers of Lost Souls' Rock*, the interior novel within John Gardner's *October Light*.

**Fred Fitch**    Freelance researcher living alone in New York City; has been the victim of hundreds of con games; originally from Montana, but fled to the anonymity of New York to avoid being embarrassed by his continual victimization; for the same reason, has avoided romantic relationships and has few friends aside from Jack Reilly, the cop he reports his losses to; inherits $300,000 from a previously unknown uncle who had lived as a con man; must learn distrust in order to extricate himself from a particularly complex con in Donald E. Westlake's comic novel *God Save The Mark*.

**Robert Fitch**    Foster father of Hannah Easton, husband of Susannah, father of Thomas; a slow, clumsy, tender, arthritic man; moves from Brookfield to Salem after King Philip's War and takes up cabinet making in Bharati Mukherjee's *The Holder of the World*.

**Susannah Fitch**    Foster mother of Hannah Easton, wife of Robert, mother of Thomas; a slow, clumsy, tender arthritic woman; moves from Brookfield to Salem after King Philip's War and takes up sewing in Bharati Mukherjee's *The Holder of the World*.

**Thomas Fitch**   Grown son of Robert and Susannah Fitch; injured in a Nipmuc ambush, never walks again; moves with his family from Brookfield to Salem after King Philip's War and takes up cabinet making in Bharati Mukherjee's *The Holder of the World*.

**Eleanor Fite**   Memphis socialite engaged to Gratt Shafer; murdered at her wedding by Thomas McCutcheon in Jesse Hill Ford's *Mountains of Gilead*.

**Ann Fitzgerald**   Photographer who travels with her lover Nicholas Payne, but marries another; her photographs of Payne receive critical acclaim in Thomas McGuane's *The Bushwhacked Piano*.

**Duke and Edna (La) Fitzgerald**   Parents of Ann Fitzgerald; dislike Nicholas Payne in Thomas McGuane's *The Bushwhacked Piano*.

**Atty Fitzpatrick**   Lover of Conor Larkin and member of the Irish Republican Brotherhood in Leon Uris's *Trinity*.

**Mrs. Fitzpatrick**   Heavy drinker who becomes blasphemous and makes a fool of herself when drunk in Carlene Hatcher Polite's *The Flagellants*.

**Charles Evans (Charlie) Flagg**   Communist Party organizer, civil rights activist, and coworker of Zeke Gurevich in William Herrick's *The Itinerant;* battalion commander of loyalist forces in the Spanish civil war in *Hermanos!*

**Randall Flagg**   Former faceless entity materialized into human form; leads the forces of evil in Stephen King's *The Stand*.

**Jack Flaherty**   Student in Benjamin Fermoyle's class; his voice has just deepened in Mary McGarry Morris's *Songs in Ordinary Time*.

**Patrick Flaherty**   Insensitive government bureaucrat who helps the government buy Colleton Island for a nuclear arms factory and installation in Pat Conroy's *The Prince of Tides*.

**John (Jack) Flanders**   Divorced poet who takes Emily Grimes with him when he accepts a teaching post at the University of Iowa Writers' Workshop; she rejects his marriage proposal and returns to New York without him in Richard Yates's *Easter Parade*.

**Elmer Flatch**   Destitute Minnesota farmer who moves family to settlement in Matanuska Valley, Alaska; husband of Hilda, father of LeRoy and Flossie; runs hunting tourism business; injured while driving bulldozers on Alcan Highway project in James Michener's *Alaska*.

**LeRoy Flatch**   Adventurous son of Elmer Flatch; renowned bush pilot; flies cargo for Air Corps to help build defense airstrips in Alaska during World War II in James Michener's *Alaska*.

**Kathleen (Kathleen Tigler) Fleisher**   Wife of Von Humboldt Fleisher and friend of Charlie Citrine, with whom she shares the money collected from the lawsuit against literary pirates who stole the *Caldofredo* script in Saul Bellow's *Humboldt's Gift*.

**Von Humboldt Fleisher**   Friend and literary father of Charlie Citrine, author of *Harlequin Ballads,* and collaborator with Citrine on the film script for *Caldofredo,* later pirated and the subject of a lawsuit; "poet, thinker, problem drinker, pill-taker, man of genius, manic depressive intricate schemer," and compulsive talker, whose body Citrine arranges to have moved from an obscure pauper's grave in New Jersey to Valhalla Cemetery and whose wisdom—"Remember: we are not natural beings but supernatural beings"—Citrine receives as a gift in Saul Bellow's *Humboldt's Gift*.

**Carla Fleming**   Pilot who transports Miles Kendig and whose zest for life is communicated to Miles Kendig, giving him reason to end his provocation of the CIA and foreign government forces in Brian Garfield's *Hopscotch*.

**Benjamin (Ben) Flesh**   Franchiser who travels to his businesses throughout America; god-cousin to the eighteen Finsberg children and sufferer from multiple sclerosis in Stanley Elkin's *The Franchiser*.

**Adaline Fletcher**   Disturbed, eccentric wife of E. L. Fletcher in Jerry Bumpus's *Anaconda*.

**Alice (Quiet Alice) Fletcher**   Wife of Harrison Fletcher; has an affair with T. S. Garp; unable to finish her second novel; dies in an airplane crash in John Irving's *The World According to Garp*.

**E. L. Fletcher**   Oil-field roughneck, husband of Adaline Fletcher, and lover of Vera; killed by Vera's husband, Carl in Jerry Bumpus's *Anaconda*.

**Harrison (Harry) Fletcher**   Husband of Alice Fletcher and professor who has affairs with his students; dies in an airplane crash in John Irving's *The World According to Garp*.

**Alice Flett**   Eldest daughter of Daisy and Barker; author of several works on Chekhov; resident of England following marriage to Ben Downing; mother of two; later known as Alice Goodwill-Spanner following name change precipitated by publication of very poorly received novel published under birth name in Carol Shields's *The Stone Diaries*.

**Barker Flett**   Son of Clarentine and Magnus; professor of botany; becomes director of agricultural research for Canadian government; husband of Daisy Goodwill; father of Alice, Warren, and Joan; dies of a brain tumor in Carol Shields's *The Stone Diaries*.

**Clarentine Flett**   Neighbor of Cuyler and Mercy Goodwill; adopted mother of Daisy after Mercy's death; mother of three sons; wife of Magnus, whom she leaves without explanation to take Mercy and live with son, Barker; owner of flower shop;

killed by teenage bicyclist who later builds a park in her memory in Carol Shields's *The Stone Diaries*.

**Magnus Flett**   Husband of Clarentine and father of Simon, Andrew, and Barker; Canadian immigrant who returns to Orkney Islands at age sixty-five after becoming completely estranged from his family; later famous for ability to recite all of *Jane Eyre* from memory and for being the oldest living person in the British Isles in Carol Shields's *The Stone Diaries*.

**Kate (Kate Harrington) Flickinger**   Red-haired childhood friend of Louisa Calloway; happily married in Alice Adams's *Families and Survivors*.

**Flip**   Coworker who warns Will Harris that if southern blacks do not accept subservience, they will suffer the consequences in Junius Edwards's *If We Must Die*.

**Flo**   Manager of a charity rummage shop in Jay Neugeboren's *Sam's Legacy*.

**Renata Flonzaley**   See Renata Koffritz.

**Charles Curtis (Curt) Flood**   Baseball player who leaves the Washington Senators; charged by Trick E. Dixon with attempting to destroy baseball and corrupt the youth of America in Philip Roth's *Our Gang*.

**Ginger Flood**   Jake Flood's second wife, daughter of his chief of staff; worships Daddy; self-absorbed in Maureen Howard's *Expensive Habits*.

**Jack (Johnny, John Sarsfield) Flood**   Margaret's first husband; a thoracic surgeon who wears all the accoutrements of his profession as often as he can; sleeps with his nurse; divorces Margaret; remarries; has two daughters and an affair with the head nurse in pediatrics, then more casual affairs; decides to leave his second wife, Ginger, in Maureen Howard's *Expensive Habits*.

**Lily Flood**   Favorite daughter of Jack Flood in Maureen Howard's *Expensive Habits*.

**Margaret (Maggie) Flood**   Woman who at forty-five is reflecting on her life; in her twenties she was an aspiring novelist married to Jack Flood, a thoracic surgeon; wrote a successful book based on her failing marriage; divorced; begins works on a book about people in the American Communist Party; her son, Bayard Strong, is stabbed to death in Maureen Howard's *Expensive Habits*.

**Rose Flood**   Older daughter of Jack Flood in Maureen Howard's *Expensive Habits*.

**Florence**   Cousin of Libby, Grace, Elinor, Rachel, and May; takes in ironing to help support more than a dozen children in Joan Chase's *During the Reign of the Queen of Persia*.

**Florence**   Student who serves on the Cinema Committee with Hill Gallagher during the student rebellion in James Jones's *The Merry Month of May*.

**Florence**   Friend of Theodora Waite, wife of Jack; attacked by a man, hits him over the head with a wine bottle in Bette Pesetsky's *Midnight Sweets*.

**Justo Flores**   Birdman who keeps and trains performing birds; father of Justina and Ernestina, whom he never sees; lives near Marta Rodríguez; feels that his dog and his birds are his family; cannot read and is an ex-alcoholic who goes on a binge on the evening one of his daughters dies in Sandra Benítez's *A Place Where the Sea Remembers*.

**Flossie (Floss, Queen of Stars)**   Beautiful prostitute and friend of Legs Diamond and Marcus Gorman in William Kennedy's *Legs*.

**Bill Flower**   Bombastic and rotund former accountant who becomes a millionaire when he splits a lottery ticket with his friend Willie Stone; maintains a random and haphazard collection of historical objects including the ruins of a fifteenth-century Irish castle; tyrannically exacting in the reconciling of accounts, he enslaves John Nashe and Jack Pozzi when they lose a poker game in Paul Auster's *The Music of Chance*.

**Jack Flowers (Fiori)**   American pimp, philosopher, and romantic visionary in Singapore in Paul Theroux's *Saint Jack*.

**Rachel Rebecca Carpenter (Sister Rache) Flowers**   Blind priestess and mother of Industrious and Carl-Rae Bowman in Leon Forrest's *The Bloodworth Orphans*.

**Mr. Floyd**   Bracktown resident who attempts to court Correy Corregidora in Gayl Jones's *Corregidora*.

**Mrs. Floyd**   Boardinghouse operator in Charles Portis's *True Grit*.

**Captain Flume**   Squadron public relations officer frightened of his tent mate, Chief White Halfoat, in Joseph Heller's *Catch-22*.

**Terry Flynn**   Handsome, swaggering, athletic student who is two years behind his classmates in reading skills in Richard Yates's *A Good School*.

**Joe (Speed) Fogarty**   Principal sidekick of Legs Diamond in William Kennedy's *Legs*.

**Eliezer Fogel**   Anti-Zionist Jewish professor whose ideas Daniel Ginsberg admires but disagrees with in Jay Neugeboren's *An Orphan's Tale*.

**Margie Fogg**   Attractive, middle-aged woman whose desire to escape her bleak existence as a waitress in a small town diner initially drives her to seek a new life with her troubled, alcoholic boyfriend, Wade; one of the few who directly contributes to the account of the final days of Wade Whitehouse in Russell Banks's *Affliction*.

**Penny Fogleman**   Girlfriend of Peter Caldwell in John Updike's *The Centaur*.

**Folded Leaf**   Seneca Indian boy taught by Black Antler and murdered by George Benson in Jessamyn West's *The Massacre at Fall Creek*.

**Dave (Foles) Foley**   Pragmatic federal agent who listens to the snitching of Eddie Coyle and the other punks in George V. Higgins's *The Friends of Eddie Coyle*.

**Mary Pat Foley**   CIA field agent who (with her husband Ed) is "running" Misha Filitov; notices signs that operational security has been endangered and urges Washington to help him escape to America; is compromised and expelled from the USSR when Filitov is arrested, and assists in planning his rescue in Tom Clancy's *The Cardinal of the Kremlin*.

**Glenn Follett**   CIA agent in France who directs the European pursuit of Miles Kendig in Brian Garfield's *Hopscotch*.

**Roy Foltrigg**   Egotistical, publicity-driven U.S. district attorney; seeks to be governor of Louisiana through the prosecution of Mafia members for the murder of a U.S. senator; thwarted in his attempts to force information out of Mark Sway by the legal efforts of Reggie Love; he must capitulate to the demands of Reggie on behalf of her client before he is given the information he needs to proceed with his prosecution in John Grisham's *The Client*.

**Eleonora de Fonseca Pimentel**   Poet and journalist executed during the White Terror; turns to her fellow prisoners as they are waiting to be taken to the gallows and utters a line from Virgil, "Perhaps one day even this will be a joy to recall," in Susan Sontag's *The Volcano Lover*.

**Johnny Fontane**   Popular singer whose career is promoted by Don Corleone in Mario Puzo's *The Godfather*.

**Ruben Fontanez**   Troublesome Puerto Rican student of Harry Meyers; becomes Meyers's friend in Jay Neugeboren's *Listen Ruben Fontanez*.

**Fools Crow**   Title character of James Welch's novel, *Fools in Crow*; originally name is White Man's Dog of the Lone Eaters band of Pikuni Blackfeet; changes name when he performs honorably during battle; he knows from his vision quest that his people will ultimately survive despite the horrific experiences they will endure due to colonization.

**Clinton Foote**   Universally hated general manager and director of player personnel of the Dallas Cowboys in Peter Gent's *North Dallas Forty*.

**Dr. Foote**   Doctor from Hopewell, Kentucky, who delivers James and Christianna Wheeler's quintuplets in 1900; when Christianna first visits him in 1899, he tells her that her unusual pregnancy is the result of fibroid tumors and sends her home with a tonic; after the quintuplets are born he offers his services for free while capitalizing on their fame in Bobbie Ann Mason's *Feather Crowns*.

**Foppl**   Plantation owner in Germany's Protectorate in South-West Africa in 1922; holds a Siege Party, which includes Kurt Mondaugen, Lieutenant Weissmann, and Vera Meroving and fondly recalls the extermination of the native Herero population in Thomas Pynchon's *V*.

**Eva Grumbauer Forbes**   Plain, conventional older sister of Alice Prentice; both praises and chides Alice's independence of spirit in Richard Yates's *A Special Providence*.

**Janie Forbes**   Star student of Joe Robert Kirkman at the high school in Tipton, North Carolina; must keep her marriage and pregnancy a secret because of a prohibition against married students attending high school; had at one time ambition to attend college, but now reserves that hope for her children in Fred Chappell's *Brighten the Corner Where You Are*.

**John Kingsgrant Forbes**   New England novelist of manners who receives the Medal for Modern Fiction in John Updike's *Bech: A Book*.

**Owen Forbes**   Lumbering, drunken husband of Eva Grumbauer Forbes; claims to be writing a history of World War I in Richard Yates's *A Special Providence*.

**W. W. W. (C. C. C., W. A. D., W. F.) Ford**   Spiritualist and master of disguises in Leon Forrest's *The Bloodworth Orphans*.

**Astral Forde**   Manager of the Mile Trees resort hotel on the fictional Caribbean island of Triunion; has an affair with politician Primus Mackenzie in Paule Marshall's *Daughters*.

**Dr. George Fordyce**   Thursday-night dinner guest of Joseph Johnson; a physician and a member of the Royal College of Surgeons; a dour, silent man in Frances Sherwood's *Vindication*.

**Paulette Foreman**   Friend and neighbor of Marzala and Nathan Spenser; nurse in Atlanta; goes to Miami and leaves fliers about Sonny, missing son of the Spensers, at hospital and in the community; through flyer, Sonny is recognized after arrival at hospital unable to speak or identify himself in Toni Cade Bambara's *These Bones Are Not My Child*.

**Linda Forloines**   Wife of Will and a former jockey; employed by the richest family in the county but fired for embezzling funds; a cocaine user and dealer, is a prime suspect in two murders until she is found by a cat named Pewter, decomposing in a stream in Rita Mae Brown's *Murder, She Meowed*.

**Will Forloines**   Husband of Linda, but not as bright as his wife and does not know she was skimming profits from their cocaine sales; discovered upstream from his dead wife, both apparent victims of the cocaine trade in Rita Mae Brown's *Murder, She Meowed*.

**Cynthia Forrest**   Yale University graduate student teaching English in high school during the summer; Mary Knapp is one of her students; waiting for return of her lover, Peter Spangle, who has gone to Spain; discovers he has returned without seeing her, but accepts him when he returns to her in Ann Beattie's *Falling in Place*.

**Kyla Forrester**   Mira's friend in graduate school; leaves her husband for a lesbian lover in Marilyn French's *The Women's Room*.

**Teddy Forster**   Canadian living in London; talent agent, drug dealer, and former lover of Marie Curtin; introduces Eric Eisner to the beautiful people of London in Phillip Lopate's *Confessions of Summer*.

**Dr. Abdul Forsythe**   Villain who changes people into shadows in C. Card's latest daydream of Babylon in Richard Brautigan's *Dreaming of Babylon*.

**Charles (Charlie) Fort**   Defense lawyer who successfully courts Hannah Cape in Jessamyn West's *The Massacre at Fall Creek*.

**Fortescue**   Centennial Club member who collects military miniatures and heads up a group to track down and punish Earl Olive in Thomas McGuane's *The Sporting Club*.

**Don Fortgang**   Member of the Beechwood community before David Dehn builds a temple; opposes Dehn's plans and commits suicide after losing an election to Dehn in Jerome Weidman's *The Temple*.

**Mommy Fortuna**   Witch who captures the unicorn (Lady Amalthea) for her Midnight Carnival in Peter S. Beagle's *The Last Unicorn*.

**Billy Fosnacht**   Son of Peggy Fosnacht and friend of Nelson Angstrom in John Updike's *Rabbit Redux*.

**Peggy Fosnacht**   Mother of Billy Fosnacht and lover for one night of Rabbit Angstrom in John Updike's *Rabbit Redux*.

**Foster**   Library employee, cave worker, and friend of Vida Kramar and the narrator in Richard Brautigan's *The Abortion*.

**Anne Foster**   Married mother of two; very maternal; working on a catalogue for exhibition of the works of Caroline Watson, early twentieth-century American painter; hires Laura Post as nanny but dislikes and fires her; after Laura's suicide, realizes that children cannot and should not be protected from every danger and horror in the world in Mary Gordon's *Men and Angels*.

**Kenneth Foster**   University art teacher and friend of Janet Belle Smith in Alison Lurie's *Real People*.

**Michael Foster**   Husband of Anne Foster; professor at Selby College, Massachusetts; on leave on a fellowship in France in Mary Gordon's *Men and Angels*.

**Roger Foster**   Librarian and intermittent suitor of Fanny Bick in Bernard Malamud's *Dubin's Lives*.

**Roger Foster**   Impersonator of Colonel Sanders; teaches Ben Flesh lessons in salesmanship in Stanley Elkin's *The Franchiser*.

**Claire Fougeray**   Timid daughter of Claude and Leona Fougeray; blooms in the presence of Ray Schaefer in Aaron Elkins's *Old Bones*.

**Claude Fougeray**   Disagreeable former Nazi collaborationist; poisoned with arsenic in Aaron Elkins's *Old Bones*.

**Leona Fougeray**   Hot-tempered Italian wife of Claude Fougeray and mother of Claire; initially suspected of her husband's murder because of her unconcealed hatred of him in Aaron Elkins's *Old Bones*.

**Annawake Fourkiller**   Intelligent, sharp, and strong-willed interning law school graduate who notices that Taylor's adoption of Turtle is against the Indian Child Welfare Act; believer in Native American tribal rights; pained by the tragic experience of her brother Gabriel who was adopted by white foster parents in Barbara Kingsolver's *Pigs in Heaven*.

**Henry Fowler**   General manager of the banking firm of Huddleston & Bradford, who unwittingly gives information to Edward Pierce in Michael Crichton's *The Great Train Robbery*.

**Brother Fowles**   Nathan Price's respected, well-liked predecessor at the Kilanga Mission; lives on a boat with his Congolese wife, Celine, and some of their children, ministering and administering medical supplies along the Congo in Barbara Kingsolver's *The Poisonwood Bible*.

**Georgie (Syph) Fox**   Small-time hoodlum who bungles a robbery and is ostracized by the McCalls; commits suicide by leaping from a viaduct in William Kennedy's *Billy Phelan's Greatest Game*.

**Mardou (Irene May) Fox**   See Volume I.

**D'Artagnan (Dart) Foxx**   Concert singer and former member of the black high school athletic team and neighborhood gang gathering for a birthday testimonial honoring Chappie Davis in John A. Williams's *The Junior Bachelor Society*.

**Foxy Lady**   Transsexual scion of an influential Moslem family; lover of George Levanter in Jerzy Kosinski's *Blind Date*.

**Juan Reyes Fragua**   Albino killed by Abel in N. Scott Momaday's *House Made of Dawn*.

**Eve Frame**   Beautiful silent film and radio actress who marries the brash and outspoken leftist radio actor, Ira Ringold; couldn't accept her husband's brother, Murray, and his wife for their "obvious" Jewishness; married three times previously, with one daughter, Sylphid, who dominates Eve; after learning of infidelities, publishes a memoir, *I Married a Communist*, that ruins the career and reputation of her husband in Philip Roth's *I Married a Communist*.

**Fran**   Friend of Pauline; her first husband, Nathaniel, leaves her and takes their boys in Bette Pesetsky's *Midnight Sweets*.

**Dr. Francis**   Famous humanitarian of the Babylon of C. Card's daydreams in Richard Brautigan's *Dreaming of Babylon*.

**Edwin Francis**   Editor, writer, and critic of children's books; homosexual, sharp-witted, and socially active in London; friend of Vinnie, Rosemary, and Fred in Alison Lurie's *Foreign Affairs*.

**Francisco**    Illegitimate son of Fray Nicolfis; Abel's grandfather in N. Scott Momaday's *House Made of Dawn*.

**Albert B. Francoeur**    Second of seven Francoeur brothers; marine officer who provides money to his parents and for his brothers' education; strives to keep the family together in David Plante's *The Family*.

**André J. Francoeur**    Fifth of seven Francoeur brothers; aspiring singer and amateur painter, he tries a business career before joining the navy in David Plante's *The Family*.

**Aricie Melanie Atalie Lajoie (Reena) Francoeur**    Wife of Arsace Francoeur and mother of seven sons; devotes herself to her family and her house; becomes emotionally ill after her husband disowns their son Philip Francoeur in David Plante's *The Family*.

**Arsace Louis Pylade (Jim) Francoeur**    Husband of Aricie Francoeur and father of seven sons; loses his foreman's job because of union pressure and becomes a day laborer; fails to be elected as a state representative in David Plante's *The Family*.

**Daniel R. Francoeur**    Sixth of seven Francoeur brothers; struggles to understand his father's failures, his mother's emotional illness, and the conflicts between his sexuality and Catholicism in David Plante's *The Family*.

**Edmond R. Francoeur**    Third of seven Francoeur brothers; because he thinks that the family takes him for granted, he tries, unsuccessfully, to break from the family in David Plante's *The Family*.

**Julien E. Francoeur**    Youngest of seven Francoeur brothers; quiet and unassertive in a family that is often emotional and talkative in David Plante's *The Family*.

**Philip P. Francoeur**    Fourth of seven Francoeur brothers; after graduating from MIT, he joins the air force; breaks with his father after marrying and failing to honor a promise to help buy a house for his parents in David Plante's *The Family*.

**Richard A. Francoeur**    Eldest of seven Francoeur brothers; fails in his business ambitions in David Plante's *The Family*.

**Frank**    Car thief and boyfriend of Rosie in Jim Harrison's *A Good Day to Die*.

**Anne Frank**    See Amy Bellette.

**Frankie**    Partner of Squirrel Amato and Russell in robbing a mob-run card game; killed by Jackie Cogan in George V. Higgins's *Cogan's Trade*.

**Edana (Dana) Franklin**    Contemporary black woman pulled into the past by the needs of her white ancestor; narrator of Octavia E. Butler's *Kindred*.

**Kevin Franklin**    White husband of Dana Franklin in Octavia E. Butler's *Kindred*.

**Thomas Franklin**    Young lawyer who evicts Chance and subsequently comes closest to guessing the identity of Chauncey Gardiner in Jerzy Kosinski's *Being There*.

**Cora Frawley**    Mother of Ralph Frawley; gossipmongering acquaintance of Emma Wallop in Peter De Vries's *Mrs. Wallop*.

**Fred**    Stuttering minister who plays poker with Thomas Marshfield at the retreat in John Updike's *A Month of Sundays*.

**Fred**    Student from the University of Chicago who works at the hotel in Golconda translating letters from prospective guests; friend of Lillian Beye and Diana in Anaïs Nin's *Seduction of the Minotaur*.

**Freddie**    Janitor of a local department store and neighborhood handyman and messenger in Toni Morrison's *Song of Solomon*.

**Dr. Freedman**    Physician who provides illegal drugs and abortions to Leo Feldman in Stanley Elkin's *A Bad Man*.

**Buddy Freegood**    Member of Margaret's church; owns a gem shop in Gail Godwin's *Evensong*.

**Freeman**    Drifter who commits himself to helping people along the way, making them his substitute family in John Gardner's *The Sunlight Dialogues*.

**Jerry Freeman**    Young newspaper feature writer who is assigned to interview Cameron Bolt and later goes to work for him in Gail Godwin's *Glass People*.

**Abagail (Abby, Mother Abagail) Freemantle**    Prophetess chosen by God to establish forces in the Free Zone against Randall Flagg in Stephen King's *The Stand*.

**Arthur Lyon Fremantle**    Englishman who sympathizes with the Confederate cause and offers advice and good cheer to the rebel leaders in Michael Shaara's *The Killer Angels*.

**Josef Ehelich von Fremd**    African from Germany, where he was treated like a migrant; polylingual; is paranoid and keeps his wife in Berlin; owns horses and meets Harlan at the racetrack; introduces Harlan and Nicholas in Gayl Jones's *The Healing*.

**Gabe French, Sr.**    Wheelchair-bound invalid who isolates himself in one room of his house with a black servant to wait on him in Jesse Hill Ford's *Mountains of Gilead*.

**Gabriel (Gabe) French**    Land speculator in Jesse Hill Ford's *The Raider*; ancestor of Gabe French, Sr., in Jesse Hill Ford's *Mountains of Gilead*.

**Mattie French**    Unmarried daughter of Gabe French and best friend of Patsy Jo McCutcheon; works in a jewelry store in Jesse Hill Ford's *Mountains of Gilead*.

**Babette Freniere**    Louisianian whom Louis loves after he becomes a vampire; she thinks that he is an evil monster in Anne Rice's *Interview with the Vampire*.

**Willard Freund**   Father of a son, Jimmy, by Callie Wells; abandons both mother and child to free himself for college and a career in John Gardner's *Nickel Mountain*.

**Wilhelm Freytag**   Aryan oilman who is refused seating at the captain's table because he admits to having a Jewish wife in Katherine Anne Porter's *Ship of Fools*.

**Frick and Frack**   Team of Los Angeles homicide investigators in Joseph Wambaugh's *The Black Marble*.

**Christiana Friebourg**   Beautiful daughter of Danish hoteliers; arrives in New York City after the death of her parents; works as a maid for *The Sun* newspaper owner Harry Penn; marries sailor Asbury Gunwillow in Mark Helprin's *Winter's Tale*.

**Doctor Fried**   German psychiatrist who treats Deborah Blau at the mental hospital in Hannah Green's *I Never Promised You a Rose Garden*.

**Ella Friedenberg**   Guidance counselor at Calvin Coolidge High School who keeps extensive records on students and insists that teachers acquaint themselves with the PPP of each student's PRC and believes that everything will be OK if teachers write a CC for student records; also uses many Freudian terms in Bel Kaufman's *Up the Down Staircase*.

**Eleanor Friedman**   Louise's younger sister who had polio as a child; writes a cooking column; sends Louise articles about homosexuality; cooks well and sees the beauty in insignificant things in David Leavitt's *Equal Affections*.

**Frog**   Youth who learned the art of tightrope walking from a European circus performer in Carlene Hatcher Polite's *The Flagellants*.

**Desmond Frogget**   Drinking buddy of Jack Flowers at the Bandung in Singapore in Paul Theroux's *Saint Jack*.

**Jackson Frost**   Husband to Regina Frost, who has an affair with and impregnates Nicole Smith, Regina's best friend in Rita Mae Brown's *Bingo*.

**Regina Frost**   Wife of Jackson Frost and best friend of Nicole Smith, who forgives Nicole for having an affair with Jackson, teaching Nicole the true meaning of friendship in Rita Mae Brown's *Bingo*.

**Lilly Frost**   Tweed-wearing spinster and botanist who rooms with the Dangerfields in Dublin; later Sebastian Dangerfield's reluctant lover in J. P. Donleavy's *The Ginger Man*.

**Horatio (Sgarlotto) Frump**   Detective who seeks to uncover the plans of the passengers on the *Here They Come* in Gregory Corso's *The American Express*.

**Adam Fry**   Father of Gideon Fry; leaves the ranch to his son and commits suicide in Larry McMurtry's *Leaving Cheyenne*.

**Garth Fry**   Husband of Karen; surgeon; meticulous and orderly; takes wife for granted; competent domestically and annoyed by Karen's apparent slothfulness; accepts her departure with equanimity if not relief in Diane Johnson's *Loving Hands at Home*.

**Gideon (Gid) Fry**   Son of Adam Fry, husband of Mabel Peters Fry, father of Jimmy, lover of Molly Taylor White, and friend of Johnny McCloud; owner of a large Texas ranch; dies after falling from a windmill; narrates part of Larry McMurtry's *Leaving Cheyenne*.

**Joan Fry**   Wife of Mahonri; has seven children; paragon of domesticity; unknown to anyone, sleeps with delivery men and workers who come to her home; eighth pregnancy a result of adultery; admits this to family's horror but agrees to undergo psychotherapy and husband stays with her in Diane Johnson's *Loving Hands at Home*.

**Karen Fry**   Married to Garth; two children; feels her straitlaced Mormon in-laws dislike her; eventually blamed by them for transgressions of family members; seduced by brother-in-law Sebastian; leaves marriage and goes to live in a truck at the beach with her two children in Diane Johnson's *Loving Hands at Home*.

**Mabel Peters Fry**   Wife of Gideon Fry in Larry McMurtry's *Leaving Cheyenne*.

**Mahonri Fry**   Husband of Joan; has seven children; brother of Garth and Sebastian; attorney; reviles wife when he discovers eighth pregnancy is result of adulterous sex; agrees to stay with her as she undergoes psychotherapy in Diane Johnson's *Loving Hands at Home*.

**Patty Fry**   Wife of Sebastian; jealous of his employer and time he spends with her; learns that Sebastian has seduced employer, but after initial anger, permits marriage to continue in Diane Johnson's *Loving Hands at Home*.

**Sebastian Fry**   Husband of Patty; brother of Garth and Mahonri; works as factotum for wealthy art collector; loves her and the collection he has amassed in her home; seduces sister-in-law Karen; reveals this to employer; who then permits him to seduce her; wife learns of affair with employer but marriage continues in Diane Johnson's *Loving Hands at Home*.

**Ben Frye**   Handsome high school biology teacher who falls in love with Gillian Owens despite her dangerous past in Alice Hoffman's *Practical Magic*.

**Dulcie Fu**   Working-class immigrant woman living in San Francisco's Chinatown; subject of gossip because of her failed first marriage, an affair during her second marriage, and the death of her second daughter; mother of Leila Louie, Ona Leong, and Nina Leong; wife of Leon Leong in Fae Myenne Ng's *Bone*.

**Leila Fu**   See Leila Louie.

**Alistair Fuchs-Forbes**   Spiritual con man whose pop transcendentalism seduces Doris More in Walker Percy's *Love in the Ruins*.

**Delores Fuentes**   Meets Nestor Castillo at a bus stop; originally from Cuba; marries Nestor when she becomes pregnant; mother of Eugenio and Leticia; wants to go to college, but Nestor will not allow her; after Nestor dies, marries Pedro Ponce, an accountant; eventually goes to college and has an affair with a literature student in Oscar Hijuelos's *The Mambo Kings Play Songs of Love.*

**Luis Fuentes**   Local villager hired by Americans Richard and Sara Everton as their gardener in Harriet Doerr's *Stones for Ibarra.*

**Padre Fuentes**   Roman Catholic missionary murdered by the Niaruna Indians he comes to serve in Peter Matthiessen's *At Play in the Fields of the Lord.*

**Isabelle de Fuentes**   Bryce Proctorr's lover; a divorced woman of thirty-four, the daughter of a Spanish diplomat; her ex-husband is Spanish, divorced her in Spain, and has custody of their three children; a copywriter for an ad agency in Donald E. Westlake's *The Hook.*

**Dino Fulgoni**   Los Angeles prosecutor in the second murder trial of Jimmy Smith in Joseph Wambaugh's *The Onion Field.*

**Professor George Orson Fuller**   Doctor of phrenology who patents a cap to mould the shape of the head, thereby influencing mental capabilities in Gore Vidal's *Burr.*

**Dr. Joel Fuller**   Veterinarian who threatens to put Rato Mustian's dog to sleep in Reynolds Price's *A Generous Man.*

**Obidiah Funches**   Husband of Katie Mae Dees in Arthenia J. Bates's *The Deity Nodded.*

**Fuqua**   Police captain who tries to use the Fazenda murder to further his career in John Gregory Dunne's *True Confessions.*

**Reverend Jethro (Furb) Furber**   Preacher haunted by sexual passion and obsessed by the seemingly impenetrable ease of Brackett Omensetter; Furber's roiling stream of consciousness dominates part of William Gass's Omensetter's *Luck.*

**Eddy Furlong**   Police officer investigating "Little Red's" murder case in Joyce Carol Oates's *Because It Is Bitter, and Because It Is My Heart.*

**Loretta Furlong**   See Loretta Botsford Wendall.

**Patrick (Pat) Furlong**   Brutish man who marries Loretta Wendall and badly beats his stepdaughter, Maureen Wendall, in Joyce Carol Oates's *them.*

**Frank Fusco**   Art critic who prepares a retrospective exhibit of the photography of Maude Coffin Pratt in Paul Theroux's *Picture Palace.*

**Henry Fuseli**   Thursday-night dinner guest of Joseph Johnson until he mistreats Mary Wollstonecraft; rumored, though married, to like men as well as women; Mary Wollstonecraft loses her virginity to him and has an affair with him in Frances Sherwood's *Vindication.*

**Sophia Fuseli**   Plump, pretty woman, a fat little sparrow; brown and perky, but without a trace of intelligence in her face; gap-toothed in Frances Sherwood's *Vindication.*

**Kemp Tomaso Fuselli**   Boy from town Jill Stuart dates; good cook; Jill joins him in robbing a warehouse for money in Marge Piercy's *Braided Lives.*

**Allen Fuso**   American anthropologist who is second in command on the research project designed to help poor blacks on Bourne Island in Paule Marshall's *The Chosen Place, the Timeless People.*

**Gagnon**   Bird lover; friend and killer of Konrad Vost in John Hawkes's *The Passion Artist.*

**Wendy (Wendee) Gahaghan**   Graduate student and lover of Brian Tate in Alison Lurie's *The War Between the Tates.*

**Jean Gail**   White lesbian ex-lover of Terry Bluvard; jealous of the relationship between Bluvard and Renay Davis in Ann Allen Shockley's *Loving Her.*

**Georgie Gaines**   Husband of Harriet; dubbed The Blimp by Harriet back when she would have killed anyone who suggested she might marry him; makes money in real estate in Gail Godwin's *Evensong.*

**Greedy Gaines**   Father of Georgie Gaines; leveled half the hills in Romulus with his condo developments; made a lot of money in real estate in Gail Godwin's *Evensong.*

**Harriet MacGruder Gaines**   Oldest friend of Margaret; has a falling out with Margaret because she isn't invited to Margaret's wedding; a pathologist at the Disease Center in Atlanta in Gail Godwin's *Evensong.*

**Lawrence Mason (Larry) Gaines**   Handsome, intelligent, popular student council president at Dorset Academy; joins the merchant marines, has a tender sexual initiation with Edith Stone, and dies when his ship explodes ten miles out of New York Harbor in Richard Yates's *A Good School.*

**Bill Gains**   See Volume I.

**Paul Lloyd Galambos**   Psychologist kidnapped to work at NESTER; narrator of Scott Spencer's *Last Night at the Brain Thieves' Ball.*

**Gloria Galanter**   Occasional nursemaid and lover of Nathan Zuckerman (a member of his "harem"); mother of two and wife of Zuckerman's accountant, Marvin; indulgent of her lovers and unwilling to leave her husband in Philip Roth's *The Anatomy Lesson.*

**Dimitri Galich**   Former Russian Orthodox priest now living as an exile in tiny Arctic town of Tumsk in Siberia; is seduced by Ludmilla Samsonov, a KGB agent posing as the wife of a famous dissident; kills a police officer who has stumbled upon the relationship; eventually confronted by Porfiry Petrovich Rostnikov, another policeman; seeks to kill Rostnikov but is instead shot dead by Emil Karpo, Rostnikov's associate in Stuart M. Kaminsky's *A Cold Red Sunrise.*

**Gallagher**   One of the men killed in the firefight at Fire Base Harriet in Vietnam; a fellow soldier of Paco, the only man to survive the attack; instigates a gang rape of a captured Viet Cong woman, whom he later shoots at point blank range in Larry Heinemann's *Paco's Story.*

**Harry Gallagher**   Expatriate American screenwriter; married to Louisa Gallagher; has an affair with Samantha Everton and follows her from Paris to Rome and then to Tel Aviv in James Jones's *The Merry Month of May.*

**Hill Gallagher**   Son of Harry Gallagher; becomes involved in student riots in Paris, has an affair with Samantha Everton, and moves to Spain to live in a cave in James Jones's *The Merry Month of May.*

**Louisa Dunn Hill Gallagher**   Wife of Harry Gallagher; suffers brain damage after a suicide attempt in James Jones's *The Merry Month of May.*

**Matt Gallagher**   Partner of Piet Hanema and husband of Terry Gallagher in John Updike's *Couples.*

**McKenna Hartley Gallagher**   Young daughter of Harry and Louisa Gallagher; godchild of Jack Hartley in James Jones's *The Merry Month of May.*

**Terry Gallagher**   Potter and musician; wife of Matt Gallagher in John Updike's *Couples.*

**Edmund Gallatin**   Man with whom Augusta Eubanks was infatuated until he fell in love with her cousin Smathers Eubanks; good-looking with an oblivious, self-absorbed manner in Gail Godwin's *Evensong.*

**Gallen (Gallen von St. Leonhard)**   Lover of Hannes Graff; helps Graff free the animals in John Irving's *Setting Free the Bears.*

**Gallus**   Ambitious, violent-tempered brother of Julian; elevated to the position of Caesar by Constantius but ultimately executed by him in Gore Vidal's *Julian.*

**Trinidad Gamboa**   Plain twenty-eight-year-old woman who desperately loves her boyfriend Romeo Rosales; after he is randomly chosen by the government as a scapegoat for its assassination of an opposition leader, she proclaims his innocence in the media and subsequently "disappears" in Jessica Hagedorn's *Dogeaters.*

**Virginia Gamely**   Intelligent, insightful, and controversial writer for *The Sun* newspaper; mother of Martin Gamely from failed marriage to Boissy d'Anglais; marries Hardesty Marratta and has daughter Abby Marratta in Mark Helprin's *Winter's Tale.*

**Gilbert (Gil) Gamesh**   Egocentric but unbeatable pitcher who kills umpire Mike Masterson with a pitch; banished from baseball but later returns to expose Communist influence in the Patriot League in Philip Roth's *The Great American Novel.*

**General Aubrey T. Gammage**   Friend and confidant of Daniel Cable Wills and principal agent in a program of industrial sabotage and trade sanctions against the Nazis during World War II in George V. Higgins's *Dreamland.*

**Gamow**   Psychoanalyst whom Will Barrett entertains by playing the ideal patient in Walker Percy's *The Last Gentleman.*

**Joe Gannon**   Priest involved in a clandestine relationship with Alice Fermoyle; is caught in the act by the monsignor in Mary McGarry Morris's *Songs in Ordinary Time.*

**Eddie (Uncle Ganooch) Ganucci**   Organized crime leader who is caught in a five-car pileup when Stephen Ro Jack throws Deborah Ro Jack's body from a window in Norman Mailer's *An American Dream.*

**Garbos**   Farmer who hangs the narrator from the ceiling and tortures him with a dog in Jerzy Kosinski's *The Painted Bird.*

**Carla Garcia**   Eldest daughter of Carlos and Laura, sister of Sandra, Yolanda, and Sofia; becomes a child psychologist; second husband is a therapist; consistently analyzes herself and her family for damage from past transgressions in Julia Alvarez's *How the Garcia Girls Lost Their Accents.* Also appears in *Yo!*

**Carlos Garcia**   Husband of Laura, father of Carla, Sandra, Yolanda, and Sofia; a doctor in the Dominican Republic recruited by American CIA to perform a military coup on the existing Communist government; after political exile to America, works as a medical clerk until eventually achieving medical status; insists his married, adult daughters leave their husbands at home for his yearly birthday celebrations in Julia Alvarez's *How the Garcia Girls Lost Their Accents.* Also appears in *Yo!*

**Doctor Garcia**   Tijuana abortionist who performs an abortion on Vida Kramar in Richard Brautigan's *The Abortion.*

**Julian Garcia**   Bandleader of the first band Cesar Castillo is in; takes Cesar into his home and treats him like a son; is loving and affectionate toward Cesar; is pleased when Cesar marries his niece, but later does not like the way Cesar treats her in Oscar Hijuelos's *The Mambo Kings Play Songs of Love.*

**Laura (Mami) de la Torre Garcia**   Wife of Carlos, mother of Carla, Sandra, Yolanda, and Sofia; comes from old monied family in Dominican Republic; as the wife of a political activist, she is constantly harassed and interrogated by Communist guerillas until her family's escape; educated in expensive American boarding schools; an independent woman in Julia Alvarez's *How the Garcia Girls Lost Their Accents;* in *Yo!,* she is deeply upset by her third daughter's novel about the family.

**Luisa Garcia**   Niece of Julian Garcia; a schoolteacher; Cesar courts and marries her; after three years of marriage, when Cesar cheats on her, she leaves him in Oscar Hijuelos's *The Mambo Kings Play Songs of Love.*

**Sandra (Sandi) Garcia**   Immigrant from the Dominican Republic; second daughter of Carlos and Laura, sister of Carla, Yolanda, and Sofia; grows up in New York; as an adult becomes obsessed with losing weight and dying; has a breakdown in Julia Alvarez's *How the Garcia Girls Lost Their Accents.* In *Yo!,* she wants to have a child and conceives one using in vitro fertilization.

**Sofia (Fifi) Garcia**   Youngest and most independent of four sisters who immigrated to the United States from the Dominican Republic, she runs away to Germany and marries Otto, creating a tremendous rift between herself and her father in Julia Alvarez's *How the Garcia Girls Lost Their Accents.* She is the family peacemaker in Julia Alvarez's *Yo!*

**Yolanda Garcia**   Third daughter of Dominican immigrants Carlos and Laura, sister of Carla, Sandra, and Sofia; nicknamed Yo-Yo; first marriage ends when she has a breakdown; discovers that she is neither American nor Dominican in her split self in Julia Alvarez's *How the Garcia Girls Lost Their Accents.* In *Yo!,* she is a professor and writer who has upset her family with her first novel, which is based on the family's experience of immigrating from the Dominican Republic to New York City.

**Irwin Garden**   Homosexual poet and friend of Jack Duluoz in Jack Kerouac's *Visions of Cody*; also appears in *Book of Dreams, Big Sur,* and (as the author of the poem "Howling") in *Desolation Angels.*

**James (Jim, Gard) Gardener**   Alcoholic, antinuclear power activist, and poet; believes he is immune to the mysterious power of the Tommyknockers because of steel plate in head; friend and lover of Bobbi Anderson with whom he excavates the mysterious power in the woods in Stephen King's *The Tommyknockers.*

**Rev. Sunlight Gardener**   Evil director of the Sunlight Gardener Scripture Home for Wayward Boys in which Jack Sawyer and Wolf are incarcerated in Stephen King's and Peter Straub's *The Talisman.*

**Jason Gardens**   Magazine editor and husband of Salley Gardens; their marriage presents the central problem in Susan Cheever's *Looking for Work.*

**Salley Gardens**   Protagonist and dissatisfied wife who finds marriage a trap from which serious employment is conceived of as an escape in Susan Cheever's *Looking for Work.*

**Chauncey Gardiner**   See Chance.

**Cameron Gardner**   Brother of Lottie, brought up by an abusive and alcoholic mother; is a reserved intellectual who aspires to overcome his low-class upbringing; maintains a single-minded, dangerous passion for his wealthy childhood neighbor Elizabeth in Sue Miller's *For Love.*

**Charlotte (Lottie) Gardner**   Middle-aged writer; sister of Cameron Gardner, mother of Ryan, and newly married to Jack; spends a summer playing the reluctant audience to her brother's passionate love affair with their wealthy childhood friend Elizabeth; contemplates her childhood with an alcoholic mother, the viability of her new marriage, and the meaning of love in Sue Miller's *For Love.*

**Ryan Gardner**   Young adult son of Lottie Gardner; an undergraduate at Stanford and just beginning to develop an awareness of himself as an adult; spends the summer with his mother as they renegotiate the terms of their close and sometimes conflicted relationship in Sue Miller's *For Love.*

**Critchwood Laverne (Chick, Chicken, Chicky) Garfield**   Football coach of Jack Curran at Boniface College in Mark Steadman's *A Lion's Share.*

**Jordan Garfield**   English professor at Commodore College; frequently serves as a reference for graduate school for Yolanda Garcia; mentor to Yolanda Garcia in Julia Alvarez's *Yo!*

**"Little Red" (Patrick Wesley) Garlock**   Sixteen-year-old son of Vernon and Vesta Garlock; retarded street drifter; obnoxious for his sexual jokes; picked a fight with Jinx and killed in Joyce Carol Oates's *Because It Is Bitter, and Because It Is My Heart.*

**Vernon Garlock**   Poor white worker living in Hammond; husband of Vesta and father of "Little Red"; a hot-tempered hard drinker in Joyce Carol Oates's *Because It Is Bitter, and Because It Is My Heart.*

**Vesta Garlock**   Mother of "Little Red" and wife of Vernon Garlock; deranged woman who hallucinates about sexually abusive men following her in the street in Joyce Carol Oates's *Because It Is Bitter, and Because It Is My Heart.*

**Joe (José) Garms**   Street fighter, army deserter, and volunteer in an American battalion in the Spanish Civil War; friend of Jake Starr in William Herrick's *Hermanos!*

**Paul D. Garner**   Escaped slave of Sweet Home Plantation; works on a chain gang; lives with Indians; friend and lover of Sethe; is forced out of the house and seduced by Beloved; returns to help Sethe after Beloved leaves in Toni Morrison's *Beloved.*

**Desmond Garnet**   Sonny Garnet's brother; deals amphetamines and crystal meth; served time in the Nassau County jail for eighteen months in Alice Hoffman's *Local Girls.*

**Sonny Garnet**   Gretel Samuelson falls for him when she is seventeen; has been picked up for questioning by the police half a dozen times; keeps odd hours; Gretel leaves him when she discovers he deals amphetamines and crystal meth in Alice Hoffman's *Local Girls.*

**Richard Brooke (Dick) Garnett**   Southern general accused of cowardice for withdrawing from an encounter with Union troops; placed in charge of the second of George Pickett's brigades in Michael Shaara's *The Killer Angels.*

**Duncan Garp**   First child of T. S. Garp and Helen Holm; loses an eye in an automobile crash and an arm in a motorcycle accident; marries one of Roberta Muldoon's transsexual friends; chokes to death on an olive while laughing too hard at one of his own jokes in John Irving's *The World According to Garp.*

**Helen Holm Garp**   See Helen Holm.

**Jenny Garp**   Only daughter of T. S. and Helen Holm Garp; born after the death of the Garps' second child, Walt; becomes a medical doctor; marries and divorces; gives her three children her own last name in John Irving's *The World According to Garp.*

**Technical Sergeant Garp**   Father of T. S. Garp; dies from a flak wound in John Irving's *The World According to Garp.*

**T. S. Garp**   Only son of Jenny Fields and a dying World War II soldier; a wrestling coach and writer who often finds himself unable to write; husband of Helen Holm and father of three children, Duncan, Walt, and Jenny Garp; battles his lust for other women; friend of Ellen James; reaches dubious notoriety with the publication of his third book, *The World According to Bensenhaver*, which gets him murdered by Pooh Percy in John Irving's *The World According to Garp.*

**Walt Garp**   Second child of T. S. Garp and Helen Holm; dies in an automobile accident in John Irving's *The World According to Garp.*

**Moon Garrett**   Member of Ned Pepper's outlaw gang that holds captive Mattie Ross, Rooster Cogburn, and LaBoeuf in Charles Portis's *True Grit.*

**Albert Charles Garson**   Son of Iris Garson; is not bright; lies about being in college because he actually works at a garage; does not like Naphtali, his stepbrother, in Cynthia Ozick's *The Cannibal Galaxy.*

**Iris Garson**   Secretary at Edmond Fleg Primary School; mother of Albert Charles Garson; marries Brill and they have a son, Naphtali; is about thirty years younger than her husband in Cynthia Ozick's *The Cannibal Galaxy.*

**Roger Gaston**   Old friend of David Wiley; writes about immigration for the L.A. *Times;* has stopped smoking, and gained weight; Lexi Steiner's next-door neighbor in Elizabeth Benedict's *Slow Dancing.*

**Andy Gately**   Bank president in Mary McGarry Morris's *A Dangerous Woman.*

**Tom Gately**   Seventeen-year-old member of a gang of twelve boys who rip Martha Horgan's clothes off, pour beer on her, and poke her with sticks in Mary McGarry Morris's *A Dangerous Woman.*

**Frenesi Gates**   Attractive political radical of the 1960s who falls for patriarchial and domineering FBI agent Brock Vond; marries Zoyd Wheeler and gives birth to Prairie Wheeler, but leaves both of them over her obsession with Brock; later lives near her mother and tries to re-establish contact with her daughter in Thomas Pynchon's *Vineland.*

**Seymour Gatz**   Salvage expert and patron of Warren Howe in Wright Morris's *Cause for Wonder.*

**Norman Gaul**   Drunken college halfback who spits into the punch bowl at the party Jane and Thomas Eborn chaperone in Reynolds Price's *Love and Work.*

**Gavin**   Lover of Beigh Masters who seems interchangeable with Giles in Bharati Mukherjee's *The Holder of the World.*

**Gavrila**   Political officer who befriends and indoctrinates the narrator and gives him Gorky's *Childhood* in Jerzy Kosinski's *The Painted Bird.*

**Gawaine**   Nephew of Arthur, faithful husband of Ragnell, dutiful father, proven warrior, and the finest man in Thomas Berger's *Arthur Rex.*

**Ralph C. (Rafie) Gawber**   Middle-aged accountant who fears and witnesses apocalyptic turmoil in Paul Theroux's *The Family Arsenal.*

**Bernard Geffen**   Shady Detroit businessman who hires Jules Wendall as his driver; through Geffen, Wendall meets Geffen's niece, Nadine Greene, in Joyce Carol Oates's *them.*

**Gehl**   Garkohn huntress who befriends Alanna Verrick in Octavia E. Butler's *Survivor.*

**Gehnahteh**   Artisan and Tehkohn husband of Choh; fosters Tien in Octavia E. Butler's *Survivor.*

**Phil Gelvin**   Mundane shoe salesman whose unimaginative lovemaking drives Bab Masters to fantasy and prolonged complaint about the unconscientiousness of lovers and readers alike in William Gass's *Willie Masters' Lonesome Wife.*

**Susan Gender**   Girlfriend of Duffy Deeter; student at the University of Florida in Harry Crews's *A Feast of Snakes.*

**Stor Gendibal**   Youngest Speaker of Second Foundation whose quick rise is resented by fellow Speakers; discoverer of force capable of manipulating the Second Foundation; his revelation allows rival Speaker Delora Delarmi to attempt to impeach him; his successful defense is followed by Delarmi's maneuver to send him into exile to investigate Golan Trevize's mission, but he is named as the First Speaker's successor before he departs in Isaac Asimov's *Foundation's Edge.*

**Genial**   See Terrence Weld.

**Genie**   Fantastic character who must devise a new approach to the writing of fiction in the *Dunyazadiad,* a novella in John Barth's *Chimera.*

**Ed Gentry**   Graphic artist who achieves complete renewal by identifying himself with nature; narrator and protagonist of James Dickey's *Deliverance.*

**George**   Black employee of Joe Lon Mackey; brother of Lummy in Harry Crews's *A Feast of Snakes.*

**George**   Female impersonator and dancer at the Iron Horse in Harry Crews's *Karate Is a Thing of the Spirit.*

**Ida George**   Seemingly hard and sullen Native American woman living on a Montana reservation; mother of Christine George Taylor and Lee George, who call her "Aunt Ida"; Ida's relationship with other characters is revealed only in the final section of Michael Dorris's *A Yellow Raft in Blue Water.*

**Lee George**   Handsome and talented young Native American who grows up on a Montana reservation and is killed in action in Vietnam; son of Ida George and brother of Christine George Taylor in Michael Dorris's *A Yellow Raft in Blue Water.*

**Gerald (Gerry)**   Party host from whose point of view the party is described; adulterer with a wife and son, Mark; in love with Alison and best friend of Vic, whom he later shoots out of compassion in Robert Coover's *Gerald's Party.*

**Geraldine**   Wife of Louis, mother of Junior, but gives her affection and attention to her cat; comes from the nameless group of black women who are college-educated and achieve middle class, reject their blackness, and guard their homes from even their families in Toni Morrison's *The Bluest Eye.*

**Gerald's wife**   Gerald's nameless wife and mother of Mark; hostess who is consumed with feeding the crowd and doesn't think parties are as much fun as they used to be in Robert Coover's *Gerald's Party.*

**Nikolay Borissovich Gerasimov**   Power-hungry KGB chairman who manipulates other ministry officials and Politburo members in his rivalry with General Secretary Narmonov; Jack Ryan pressures him into releasing Misha Filitov and defecting, narrowly escaping recapture by his own subordinates in Tom Clancy's *The Cardinal of the Kremlin.*

**Gerhard**   Computer specialist at the Neuropsychiatric Research Unit who designs the computer that is implanted in Harold Benson in Michael Crichton's *The Terminal Man.*

**Valentine (Val) Gersbach**   Radio personality; false friend of Moses Herzog and adulterous lover of Madeleine Herzog in Saul Bellow's *Herzog.*

**Rav Gershenson**   Orthodox Talmudic scholar who teaches both Danny Saunders and Reuven Malter in Chaim Potok's *The Chosen;* persuades Rav Jacob Kalman to ordain Saunders as a rabbi in *The Promise.*

**Gershon**   Arrogant, ignorant, and nepotistic tax collector, town bully, foe of Jacob Eliezer, and warden of the burial society who forbids the performance of sacred rituals on the body of Jacob's wife, Wanda Bzik, in Isaac Bashevis Singer's *The Slave.*

**Will Gerstenslager**   Widowed lawyer; friend, financial adviser, and suitor of Emma Wallop in Peter De Vries's *Mrs. Wallop.*

**Gertrude**   Wife of Skipper and mother of Cassandra; commits suicide sixteen months after the birth of her granddaughter, Pixie, in John Hawkes's *Second Skin.*

**"Getso" Getsobiski**   Lover of Birdy Dusser who cheats on her with Birdy's coworker Mercy; a laundry truck driver for Kolditis Cleaners who steals money from the register and blames Martha Horgan; divorced twice; former boxer; murdered by Martha during an attempted rape in Mary McGarry Morris's *A Dangerous Woman.*

**Millie Muldoon Gharoujian**   Owner of a miniature schnauzer used by Philo Skinner in his dognapping scheme in Joseph Wambaugh's *The Black Marble.*

**The Ghosts**   Collective voice of the men who died at Fire Base Harriet that narrates the story; Paco is haunted by the ghosts in his dreams; The Ghosts narrate Paco's current situation as well as what happened to them all in Vietnam in Larry Heinemann's *Paco's Story.*

**Nathaniel Gibb**   Freshman from Ohio who shares the attic in Chalk House with Gus Pierce; starts coughing up blood after he witnesses Harry McKenna's murder of Gus Pierce; confesses the murder to Abe Grey even though his classmates have tried violently to prevent him from doing so in Alice Hoffman's *The River King.*

**Peter (Jingles) Gibbons**   Maine state trooper who, with partner Benton Rhodes, investigates mysterious explosion in Haven, Maine, in Stephen King's *The Tommyknockers.*

**Lester (Les) Gibbons**   Cowardly and envious neighbor of the Stamper family in Ken Kesey's *Sometimes a Great Notion.*

**Angelica Gibbs**   Blond American widow of Donald Gibbs; comes to Kush to avenge her husband's death and instead stays to adopt an African lifestyle as Michaelis Ezana's lover in John Updike's *The Coup.*

**Donald X. Gibbs**   Immolated USAID officer burned on a pyre of cereal and junk food meant as relief for famine victims of Kush but rejected by Colonel Ellellou; after Ellellou is ousted, the new government memorializes Gibbs by naming a shopping center after him in John Updike's *The Coup.*

**Jack Gibbs**   Failed writer and polymath; once worked for the General Roll Corporation, but now teaches science and plays the horses in William Gaddis's *JR.*

**Stanley Gibbs**   Gravedigger for Port William, Kentucky, in Wendell Berry's *A Place on Earth.*

**Gibby**   American heiress and lover of Woytek; slain with him and others in a Charles Manson-style massacre in Jerzy Kosinski's *Blind Date.*

**Dick (Tex Ellery, Ted Elmer, Ted Elson, Ellery Loyola, Marshall Maine, etc.) Gibson**   Itinerant radio announcer on a lifelong apprenticeship in search of the meaning of America; adopts numerous aliases in Stanley Elkin's *The Dick Gibson Show;* also appears in *The Franchiser.*

**Drag Gibson**   Western capitalist who French-kisses a green horse; orders brides through the mail and kills them by feeding them to his swine; dying from having been poisoned by Mustache Sal until he recovers miraculously upon learning that the pope is visiting the West in Ishmael Reed's *Yellow Back Radio Broke-Down.*

**Max Gideon**   Historical character once active in the American Communist Party; claimed he was born in Russia, although born in New York; is studying to become an engineer and married to the widow of a covered-button manufacturer; becomes Dotty Schwartz's lover; marries Hannah Brandt in Maureen Howard's *Expensive Habits.*

**Gifford (Gip)**   White leader of a group of militant black revolutionaries; commits suicide in Nicholas Delbanco's *News.*

**Frank Gifford**    All-American football star at the University of Southern California and legendary hero of the New York Giants; figure of obsessive contemplation by Frederick Exley, who was his college classmate in Frederick Exley's *A Fan's Notes*.

**Dr. Lionel Gift**    Professor of economics at Moo University; plans with Moo U. donor and Texas tycoon Arlen Martin to build a gold mine in the last remaining virgin cloud forest in Costa Rica; plans disintegrate in Jane Smiley's *Moo*.

**Gigi (Grace)**    Young woman who finds her way to Ruby, Oklahoma, and the Convent, the home of a group of mostly black women fleeing their sullied pasts; has brief affair with K. D. Morgan, the youngest member of one of the founding families of the all-black town of Ruby; becomes a strong, independent woman by the end of Toni Morrison's *Paradise*.

**Giles**    Lover of Beigh Masters who seems interchangeable with Gavin; aspires to immigration to New Zealand or the Yukon; a pure air and water fetishist in Bharati Mukherjee's *The Holder of the World*.

**George (Billy Bocksfuss, Georgie, Goat-Boy) Giles**    Hero, raised as a goat, who becomes the Grand Tutor; narrator of John Barth's *Giles Goat-Boy*.

**Stoker (Giles Stoker) Giles**    Supposed son of George Giles, whereabouts unknown, existence questionable; claims to be the editor of the text of John Barth's *Giles Goat-Boy*.

**Romeo Gilette**    Store owner; son of Dalton Gilette; had planned on becoming a doctor, but returned to Witless Bay after his father's heart attack; August's murder hearing is held in Gilette's store in Howard Norman's *The Bird Artist*.

**Serena Gill**    Friend since girlhood of Maggie Moran; unconventional; flamboyant; a realist; husband, Max, has just died; Ira and Maggie Moran attend the funeral in Anne Tyler's *Breathing Lessons*.

**Kenny Gill**    Thief and partner of Russell in a dogstealing racket; betrays Russell to Jackie Cogan in George V. Higgins's *Cogan's Trade*.

**Dr. Gerald Gilley**    Director of composition and later chair of the English Department at Cascadia College; husband of Pauline Gilley in Bernard Malamud's *A New Life*.

**Pauline Gilley**    Wife of Gerald Gilley; has affairs with Leo Duffy and Seymour Levin in Bernard Malamud's *A New Life*.

**Dr. Gillies**    Best physician in Coaltown, whose wisdom is often sought; introduces at a turn-of-the-century party the idea that men of the new century were children of the eighth day in Thornton Wilder's *The Eighth Day*.

**Joan Gilling**    Fellow inmate with Esther Greenwood at a private mental hospital; hangs herself in Sylvia Plath's *The Bell Jar*.

**Bessie Gilmore**    Mother of Gary Gilmore in Norman Mailer's *The Executioner's Song*.

**Gary Mark Gilmore**    First American to be executed after a ten-year moratorium; protagonist of Norman Mailer's *The Executioner's Song*.

**Mikal Gilmore**    Brother of Gary Gilmore in Norman Mailer's *The Executioner's Song*.

**Anthony Gilray**    English judge who presides over the libel suit between Adam Kelno and Abe Cady in Leon Uris's *QB VII*.

**Ginger**    Friend of Mortimer and Theodora; carries a copy of *The Life of Saint Therese of Avigne*; has a very young lover in Bette Pesetsky's *Midnight Sweets*.

**Ginny**    Lover of Shawn; develops a skill for raising vegetables and has the first Indian baby after the dispersment of the Indians in Marge Piercy's *Dance the Eagle to Sleep*.

**Daniel (Charles Fogelstein, Danny) Ginsberg**    Orphan at the Maimonides Home for Jewish Boys who wants Charlie Sapistein to adopt him; author of a diary in Jay Neugeboren's *An Orphan's Tale*.

**Jack Gioncarlo**    Sailor befriended by Charlie Stark; helps thwart the murder of Raditzer in Peter Matthiessen's *Raditzer*.

**Terry Gionoffrio**    Young runaway chosen to be the mother of Satan's son; killed when she refuses to consent to the plan in Ira Levin's *Rosemary's Baby*.

**Gisela**    Egon's wife; crouches in corners when under pressure in Walter Abish's *How German Is It*.

**Giskard**    See R. Giskard Reventlov.

**Julian Gitche**    Full-blooded Mohawk Indian pianist and New York/Yale wimp who marries Sissy Hankshaw; she leaves him and he turns to drink in Tom Robbins's *Even Cowgirls Get the Blues*.

**Sissy Hankshaw Gitche**    Big-thumbed model and hitchhiker extraordinaire who marries Julian Gitche; lover of Bonanza Jellybean, the Chink, and Delores del Ruby; jumpsuited heroine of Tom Robbins's *Even Cowgirls Get the Blues*.

**Howard Givings**    Husband of Helen Givings; reads newspapers and turns off his hearing aid whenever he tires of listening to her in Richard Yates's *Revolutionary Road*.

**John Givings**    Paranoid schizophrenic son of Helen and Howard Givings; perceiving and commenting on the falsehoods in other people's lives and plans, he ends up friendless in a mental institution in Richard Yates's *Revolutionary Road*.

**Mrs. Helen Givings**    Garrulous real estate agent; neighbor who befriends the Wheelers in a vain effort to find companions for her schizophrenic son in Richard Yates's *Revolutionary Road*.

**Gladia**    See Gladia Delmarre.

**Babette Gladney**    Neurotic and absentminded forty-something woman married to Jack Gladney; has three children from previous marriages and is stepmother of two of Jack's children; shares Jack's obsessive fear of dying; tries unsuccessfully to alleviate her chronic fear by swapping sexual favors for the failed experimental drug Dylar with charlatan Willie Mink (aka "Mr. Gray") in Don DeLillo's *White Noise*.

**Heinrich Gladney**    Jack Gladney's aloof fourteen-year-old son; comes into his own as a messenger of ominous and terrible information during the evacuation of the northern midwestern town of Blacksmith in Don DeLillo's *White Noise*.

**Jack Gladney**    Fifty-one-year-old college professor and chairman of the department of Hitler studies; married to Babette, his fourth wife; has three children by previous marriages (Steffie, Heinrich, and Bee), and is stepfather of two of Babette's (Denise and Wilder); has obsessive fear of dying; is exposed in a chemical spill to a toxic waste (Nyodene D.); botches a plan to murder the creator of failed experimental drug Dylar, Willie Mink, with whom his wife has traded sex for the drug in Don DeLillo's *White Noise*.

**Steffie (Stephanie Rose) Gladney**    Jack Gladney's adolescent daughter; rarely sees her biological mother, Dana Breedlove, a CIA operative; ultimately finds a satisfactory outlet for her neuroses by playing a victim in a simulated evacuation of her hometown in Don DeLillo's *White Noise*.

**Gladys**    Prostitute in Jack Flowers's stable in Singapore in Paul Theroux's *Saint Jack*.

**Diana Moon Glampers**    Patient of Eliot Rosewater in Kurt Vonnegut's *God Bless You, Mr. Rosewater*.

**Zahn Glanz**    High school lover of Hilke Marter; Vienna taxi driver who disappears after apparently driving into Hungary in John Irving's *Setting Free the Bears*.

**Brian Glassic**    Young executive at the waste management company that also employs Nick Shay; conducting illicit affair with Shay's wife, Marian; distanced from his own wife and children; playful, teasing personality; narrowly escapes a violent confrontation with Nick during a business trip to Russia in Don DeLillo's *Underworld*.

**Vera Glavanakova**    Bulgarian poet of warmth and intelligence; Henry Bech falls in love with her in John Updike's *Bech: A Book*.

**Josh Glazer**    Aging playwright, lyricist, and Broadway wit in John Updike's *Bech: A Book*.

**Judith Glazer**    Wealthy, manipulative, and moderately insane woman; has six months to live because of pancreatic cancer; married to Sam Glazer with two daughters (Milly and Mary); employs the lower-class George Mills as her manservant while she unsuccessfully seeks cancer treatments in Mexico in Stanley Elkin's *George Mills*.

**Glenda**    James Bray's agent for twenty years in Maureen Howard's *Natural History*.

**Glenda (Gilded Girl)**    Stripper and informer for Bumper Morgan in Joseph Wambaugh's *The Blue Knight*.

**Daniel Francis (Danny) Glick**    Brother of Ralphie Glick; becomes a vampire after being bitten by his brother in Stephen King's *'Salem's Lot*.

**Ralphie Glick**    Brother of Danny Glick; killed by the vampire Barlow in Stephen King's *'Salem's Lot*.

**Johnny Glimmergarden**    Second husband of Evelyn Marvel in Peter De Vries's *Through the Fields of Clover*.

**Globke**    Manager of Bucky Wunderlick and employee of Transparanoia organization in Don DeLillo's *Great Jones Street*.

**Karl Glocken**    Hunchbacked tobacco salesman from Mexico City who is returning to Germany in Katherine Anne Porter's *Ship of Fools*.

**Margaret Glorio**    Buyer of men's sportswear for several department stores and purchaser of some of Su'ad al-Najaf's smuggled rugs; she and Robert Druff have a one-night stand in Stanley Elkin's *The MacGuffin*.

**Glynda, Girl of the Glen**    See Arista Prolo.

**Glyp**    Ancient Egyptian tomb robber in a dream experienced by Alexander Main in *The Bailbondsman*, a novella in Stanley Elkin's *Searches and Seizures*.

**Goat-Boy**    See George Giles.

**Goat Lady (Mother)**    Cryptic figure who takes her cart to the road in search of her son and is accidentally killed by George Loomis in John Gardner's *Nickel Mountain*.

**God of Street Boys**    See Ali Juan Chapultepec.

**Evan Godolphin**    Son of Hugh Godolphin; aids his father and encounters Victoria Wren and Sydney Stencil in Florence in 1899; after extensive plastic surgery, becomes Veronica Manganese's caretaker on Malta in 1919 in Thomas Pynchon's *V.*

**Hugh Godolphin**    Explorer of the Antarctic and father of Evan Godolphin; may have discovered the mythical land of Vheissu in 1884; encounters V. as Victoria Wren in Florence in 1899 and as Vera Meroving in South-West Africa in 1922 in Thomas Pynchon's *V.*

**Ma Godolphin**    Rural tycoon and land baroness; reigning celebrity and competitor of Ma Sigafoos; client and briefly paramour of Billy Bumpers in Peter De Vries's *I Hear America Swinging*.

**Rusty (Ace Mann) Godowsky**    Macho boyfriend of Mary-Ann Pringle; anally raped by Myra Breckinridge; later a successful movie star and lover of Letitia Van Allen in Gore Vidal's *Myra Breckinridge.*

**Father Xavier Godoy**   Tecanecan priest who asks Justin to be involved with the revolution of Tecan; goes to the mountains to be with the rebels in Robert Stone's *A Flag for Sunrise.*

**William Godwin**   Thursday-night dinner guest of Joseph Johnson; eventually marries Mary Wollstonecraft; comes from a dissenting family and was a dissenting minister; becomes a philosopher and writer; author of *Political Justice* and the novel *Caleb Williams;* remarries after Mary's death and dies in 1836 in Frances Sherwood's *Vindication.*

**Amon Goeth**   German commander of Plazsow, a forced labor camp outside Cracow; manipulates system for personal gain by selling prisoners' food and personal effects on the black market, and by accepting bribes from businessmen like Oskar Schindler; arrested by Gestapo near the end of World War II; after the war he is imprisoned, found guilty of war crimes and executed in Thomas Keneally's *Schindler's List.*

**Goethe**   Famous poet, writer, and philosopher; attends a party at the Cavaliere's home in Susan Sontag's *The Volcano Lover.*

**Luke (Luke the Loner) Gofannon**   Legendary Patriot League center fielder and the only man Angela Whittling Trust ever loved in Philip Roth's *The Great American Novel.*

**Belle Gold**   Patient wife of the social climbing Bruce Gold in Joseph Heller's *Good as Gold.*

**Bruce Gold**   Dissatisfied college professor and aspiring cabinet officer; at work on a book on the Jewish-American experience in Joseph Heller's *Good as Gold.*

**Gussie Gold**   Slightly crazed stepmother of Bruce Gold; descended from Richmond and Charleston Jewish aristocracy in Joseph Heller's *Good as Gold.*

**Jackson (Crazy Jack) Gold**   Sixteen-year-old playmate of Abeba Torch during her childhood in rural North Carolina in Ellease Southerland's *Let the Lion Eat Straw.*

**Julius Gold**   Irascible father of Bruce Gold in Joseph Heller's *Good as Gold.*

**Sid Gold**   Older brother and irritant of Bruce Gold in Joseph Heller's *Good as Gold.*

**Sam Goldberg**   Family friend and lawyer of Dan Lavette in Howard Fast's *Second Generation.*

**Rabbi Goldfarb**   Rabbi of the synagogue the young David Dehn attends; murdered on the day of Dehn's bar mitzvah in Jerome Weidman's *The Temple.*

**Dory Goldman**   Wife of Irwin and mother of Rachel Creed; tries to smooth things over between Irwin and Dr. Louis Creed; comforts and consoles Rachel after Gage's death because Louis finds himself unable to do so in Stephen King's *Pet Sematary.*

**Emma (Red Emma) Goldman**   Anarchist who gives Evelyn Nesbit a massage and influences the political ideas of Mother's Younger Brother in E. L. Doctorow's *Ragtime.*

**Irwin Goldman**   Jewish father of Rachel Creed; hates Dr. Louis Creed, and tried to bribe him into not marrying Rachel; blames Louis for Gage's death in Stephen King's *Pet Sematary.*

**Jòrgen Josiah (Goldy) Goldschmidt**   English publisher of Henry Bech in John Updike's *Bech: A Book.*

**Frances (Frannie) Goldsmith**   Pregnant woman concerned that her child will develop the disease that has destroyed most of humanity in Stephen King's *The Stand.*

**Britt Goldstein**   Film producer who wants to obtain the screen rights to Isadora Wing's novel *Candida Confesses* in Erica Jong's *How to Save Your Own Life.*

**Judge Hugh Warren Goldsworth**   Distinguished authority on Roman law and intended target of a madman's bullet that kills John Shade by mistake; rents his house to Charles Kinbote, thus making Kinbote a neighbor of John Shade in Vladimir Nabokov's *Pale Fire.*

**Gerhardt (Der Springer) von Göll**   German filmmaker and black-marketeer; symbolized by a knight chess piece in Thomas Pynchon's *Gravity's Rainbow.*

**Marfa Vladimirovna Golov**   Mother of Zhenia Golov in Bernard Malamud's *The Fixer.*

**Zhenia (Zhenechka) Golov**   Twelve-year-old boy murdered in Bernard Malamud's *The Fixer.*

**Altagracia Gomez**   Works as a maid for Sue Ames; emerges from preadolescence as an extremely beautiful woman; leaves Ames and goes to work for Bert Loomis; becomes pregnant by him and later marries him in Harriett Doerr's *Consider This, Senora.*

**(Cura) Juan Gomez**   Catholic priest in village of Ibarra; holds out hope of converting agnostic Americans Sara and Richard Everton in Harriet Doerr's *Stones of Ibarra.*

**Pucha Gonzaga**   Daughter of a less wealthy branch of her Manila family; would-be social climber wishing to marry into the wealthy and powerful Alacran family in order to realize her Hollywood-inspired dreams of materialism; older cousin of Rio Gonzaga in Jessica Hagedorn's *Dogeaters.*

**Rio Gonzaga**   Daughter in a moderately wealthy, somewhat well-connected Manila family who observes the crass hypocrisy and excesses of those of her class; daughter of Freddie Gonzaga; younger cousin of Pucha Gonzaga in Jessica Hagedorn's *Dogeaters.*

**Pedrito Gonzalez**   Political activist in the Dominican Republic during the reign of Trujillo; imprisoned by Trujillo regime;

husband of Patria Mirabal; father of Nelson and Noris in Julia Alvarez's *In the Time of the Butterflies*.

**Joxer Goode**    Buyer of Dick Pierce's fishing hauls and owner of a successful crab-packing plant; embezzlement of his plant's money by an employee alters his decision to loan Dick money in John Casey's *Spartina*.

**Norvelle Goodling**    Harlan's ex-husband; medical anthropologist who took Harlan with him to Africa to record medical lore; lives in Africa in Gayl Jones's *The Healing*.

**Adrian Goodlove**    English psychoanalyst and lover of Isadora Wing in Erica Jong's *Fear of Flying*.

**Abel Goodparley**    Traveling puppeteer who plays Eusa; Orfing's partner; tells Riddley about Punch and performs the Punch and Pooty play; has the same birthday as Riddley; later is blinded and is not allowed by Orfing to play Eusa anymore in Russell Hoban's *Riddley Walker*.

**Clyde Goodson**    Baptist minister who teaches Latin to Clay-Boy Spencer to help him qualify for admission to the University of Richmond in Earl Hamner, Jr.'s *Spencer's Mountain*.

**Cuyler Goodwill**    Stonecutter from Stonewall Township, Manitoba; builder of famous tower of small stones over first wife Mercy's grave; later resident of Bloomington, Indiana, and partner in stonecutting firm; renowned orator; husband in later years to Maria whom he met and abruptly married during vacation to Italy; father of Daisy, the narrator of Carol Shields's *The Stone Diaries*.

**Daisy Goodwill**    Born 1905 in Manitoba, daughter of Cuyler and Mercy Goodwill; married in 1927 to Harold A. Hoad; widowed on honeymoon when drunken Harold falls out of window; marries Barker Flett, son of her adopted mother, Clarentine; mother of three children by Barker; author of newspaper gardening column under the pseudonym Mrs. Green Thumb; later resident of Florida. Dies in nursing home sometime in the 1990s; narrator of Carol Sheilds's *The Stone Diaries*.

**Mercy Goodwill**    Orphan raised in Stonewall Orphans Home and named Mercy Stone after the building. Devoted cook and homemaker; wife of Cuyler, who builds stone tower in her memory after she dies giving birth to first child, Daisy, the narrator of Carol Shields's *The Stone Diaries*.

**Alice Gardner Goodwin**    Wife of Howard Goodwin; school nurse and mother of two daughters, five-year-old Emma and three-year-old Claire; best friend of Theresa Collins and responsible when Theresa's daughter drowns; convicted of child abuse, she struggles to connect with and understand fellow inmates; cartographer of imaginary world of Tangalooponda, from which the novel takes its name; narrator of the first and last third of Jane Hamilton's *A Map of the World*.

**Claire Goodwin**    Relaxed, old-soul, three-year-old daughter of Howard and Alice Goodwin; younger sister of Emma Good-win; friend of Lizzy and Audrey Collins; granddaughter of Nellie Goodwin in Jane Hamilton's *A Map of the World*.

**Dawn Goodwin**    Best friend of Samantha Hughes, who gets pregnant and begins to settle down, a path that Samantha considers but rejects in Bobbie Ann Mason's *In Country*.

**Emma Goodwin**    Anxious, frequently angry five-year-old daughter of Howard and Alice Goodwin; sister of Claire Goodwin; friend of Audrey and Lizzy Collins; the child whose imminent birth prompts the marriage of her parents; the child whose frustration at the world her mother comprehends and shares in Jane Hamilton's *A Map of the World*.

**Felicia Goodwin**    Wife of Les Goodwin in Joan Didion's *Play It As It Lays*.

**Howard Goodwin**    Even-tempered husband of Alice Goodwin; father of Claire and Emma Goodwin; struggles to care for daughters and work the farm after Alice's arrest; son of and debtor to Nellie Goodwin; funds Alice's legal battle; friend of Dan Collins; friend and lover of Theresa Collins; narrator of the middle third of Jane Hamilton's *A Map of the World*.

**Les Goodwin**    Husband of Felicia Goodwin; lover of Maria Wyeth and father of her aborted baby in Joan Didion's *Play It As It Lays*.

**Nellie Goodwin**    Mother of Howard; mother-in-law to Alice Gardner Goodwin; grandmother of Emma and Claire Goodwin; lends money to son Howard and daughter-in-law Alice for their farm; missionary to Romanian babies in Jane Hamilton's *A Map of the World*.

**Veenie Goodwin**    Elderly black woman who has worked for the Mayfield family in the past; great grandmother of Walter Grainger and grandmother of Rover Walters in Reynolds Price's *The Surface of Earth*.

**Lorenz T. Goodykuntz**    Proprietor of the Universal College of Metaphysical Knowledge, a mail order degree mill, in Thomas Berger's *Reinhart in Love*.

**Paul (the Armourer) Goossens**    Belgian machinist and arms merchant with an august record as a partisan and saboteur in World War II before being imprisoned for embezzlement, who becomes a key figure in underworld arms deals; designs the sniper rifle and concealing crutches for the Jackal in Frederick Forsyth's *The Day of the Jackal*.

**Gopi**    Cripple from birth whom Jack Flowers helps in Singapore in Paul Theroux's *Saint Jack*.

**Ephram Gorchak**    Most reliable and best teacher at Edmond Fleg Primary School; usually teaches seventh and eighth grades; detests laziness and taunts lazy students; becomes principal when Brill retires in Cynthia Ozick's *The Cannibal Galaxy*.

**Abraham Gordon**    Excommunicated Jewish scholar whose books questioning the literal truth of the Bible cause his son,

Michael Gordon, to become catatonic in Chaim Potok's *The Promise.*

**Anne Alexander Gordon**  1868 graduate of Waynesboro Female College; charter member of Waynesboro Woman's Club; married to Dr. John Gordon; close friend of Sally Cochran Rausch in Helen Hooven Santmyer's "*. . . And Ladies of the Club.*"

**Charles (Charlie) Gordon**  Author of progress reports; retarded man whose intelligence quotient is raised to over 200, although he loses the new intelligence in Daniel Keyes's *Flowers for Algernon.*

**Doctor Gordon**  Male psychiatrist who administers shock treatments to Esther Greenwood before her suicide attempt in Sylvia Plath's *The Bell Jar.*

**John ("Dock") Gordon**  Former Civil War surgeon; married to Anne Alexander Gordon; prominent doctor in Waynesboro, Ohio, in Helen Hooven Santmyer's "*. . . And Ladies of the Club.*"

**Johnny Gordon**  Son of Dr. John and Anne Alexander Gordon; doctor in Waynesboro, Ohio, in Helen Hooven Santmyer's "*. . . And Ladies of the Club.*"

**Joseph Gordon**  Father of Rachel Gordon and brother of Abraham Gordon in Chaim Potok's *The Promise.*

**Michael Gordon**  Disturbed son of Abraham Gordon; his catatonia is treated by Danny Saunders in Chaim Potok's *The Promise.*

**Rachel Gordon**  Wife of Danny Saunders in Chaim Potok's *The Promise.*

**Sarah Gordon**  Wife of Joseph Gordon and mother of Rachel Gordon in Chaim Potok's *The Promise.*

**Marcus Gorman**  Criminal lawyer and friend of Legs Diamond; narrator of William Kennedy's *Legs*; also appears in *Billy Phelan's Greatest Game.*

**Heine Gortz**  Leader of Gottlob Wut's German Motorcycle Unit Balkan 4 when Wallner is relieved of command; helps kill Wut in an outhouse in John Irving's *Setting Free the Bears.*

**Gottfried**  Pawn in Lieutenant Weissmann's sexual intrigues; launched by Weissmann in rocket 00000, known as the Schwarzgerdt in Thomas Pynchon's *Gravity's Rainbow.*

**Max Gottlieb**  Behaviorist psychiatrist and best friend of Tom More in Walker Percy's *Love in the Ruins.*

**Max Gottlieb**  Friend and fellow physician of Tom More; defends More's desire to continue in private practice against Comeaux's plot to force More to join the staff at Fedville, where Comeaux can monitor More's actions; a reluctant conspirator in the "Blue Boy" project, a rogue pilot experiment run by Bob Comeaux and John Van Dorn in Walker Percy's *The Thanatos Syndrome.*

**Brindle Gower**  Lives with her brother, Morgan, since she was widowed by her first husband, Horace; rejects old sweetheart, Robert Roberts; ends up living with Morgan and Emily until they move to Tindell, Maryland; moves back with Bonny, Morgan's first wife in Anne Tyler's *Morgan's Passing.*

**Louisa Gower**  Morgan's increasingly forgetful mother who lives with him; follows Morgan when he moves in with Emily, but eventually moves back with Bonny, Morgan's first wife, when Morgan moves to Tindell, Maryland; near the end of the novel, she has a hard time even recognizing Morgan as her son in Anne Tyler's *Morgan's Passing.*

**Morgan Gower**  Eccentric man who has a fancy for hats, he absentmindedly manages Cullen Hardware; he and his first wife, Bonny, have seven daughters; divorces Bonny for Emily Meredith, a woman whom Morgan befriends after he drives her to the hospital with her husband to deliver her baby; Emily and Morgan then have a child, Josh, in Anne Tyler's *Morgan's Passing.*

**Reginald Gower**  Printer and bookstore owner who wants to print a pamphlet for Charles Schuyler in Gore Vidal's *Burr.*

**Ruth Gower**  Mother of Margaret; went straight from her southern women's college to her older husband's rectory; leaves her husband when she is twenty-eight; has an aptitude for parody and caricature, which she had to repress in her role as rector's wife; killed in an automobile accident in England in Gail Godwin's *Evensong.*

**Walter Gower**  Father of Margaret; a chaplain; Adrian's former spiritual director; suffers from depression, called "Father Melancholy" behind his back; dies of a stroke when he is sixty in Gail Godwin's *Evensong.*

**Doc Graaf**  Mennonite physician who examines Mary Robinson after her attack in John Updike's *Of the Farm.*

**Coach Graber**  Norm's baseball coach; kicks Norm off the team for beating up a boy making fun of his father and brother in Mary McGarry Morris's *Songs in Ordinary Time.*

**Grace "Grady"**  Daughter of Gram and Grandad; mother of Anne and Katie, wife of Neil, sister of Elinor, Libby, Rachel, and May; aunt of Celia, Jenny, Valery, and Rossie; has had a mastectomy, dies of cancer in Joan Chase's *During the Reign of the Queen of Persia.*

**Jakob (Jacques d'Argus, James de Gray, Mr. Degré, Jack Degree, Jacques de Grey, G, Jack Grey, Ravenstone, Ravus, Vinogradus) Gradus**  Assassin who stalks Charles II, the exiled King of Zembla, and mistakenly kills John Shade, according to Charles Kinbote; may be a figment of Kinbote's imagination in Vladimir Nabokov's *Pale Fire.*

**Delbert Grady**  Former winter caretaker of the Overlook Hotel, who kills his wife and daughters; appears as a ghost to John Torrance in Stephen King's *The Shining.*

**Rosemary Grady**   Housemother of Alice Fermoyle in Mary McGarry Morris's *Songs in Ordinary Time.*

**Harold Graebner**   Army friend of Binx Bolling; saves Bolling's life during the Korean War in Walker Percy's *The Moviegoer.*

**Wilibald Graf**   Dying religious fanatic who perceives himself as a faith healer in Katherine Anne Porter's *Ship of Fools.*

**Hannes Graff**   Friend of Siggy Javotnik and lover of Gallen; frees the animals; narrator of John Irving's *Setting Free the Bears.*

**Walter S. Grainger**   Son of Rover Walters; becomes a combination servant and friend of Forrest and Rob Mayfield in Reynolds Price's *The Surface of Earth.*

**Grammy**   Grandmother of Waldo; ate dandelions during the depression in Paul Theroux's *Waldo.*

**George Francis Granberry**   Husband of Myra Granberry; his wealth keeps him from finding an outlet for his energies; his claims for being an inventor are shown to be false; seeks help from Theophilus North for Myra in Thornton Wilder's *Theophilus North.*

**Myra Granberry**   Wife of George Granberry; confined to home because she is pregnant following two miscarriages; Theophilus North reads to her and helps improve her education in Thornton Wilder's *Theophilus North.*

**Noah Ridgerook Grandberry**   Son of Pourty Bloodworth and half brother of Amos-Otis Thigpen, LaDonna Scales, Regal Pettibone, and Jonathan Bass; associate of Nathaniel Turner Witherspoon in Leon Forrest's *The Bloodworth Orphans.*

**Grandfather Eustace**   Grandfather of the unnamed male narrator and main character; South Carolina native and black descendant of a plantation family; graduate of Harvard and Brown; Baptist preacher; after losing his position as Congregational minister, moves to Boston; eventually returns to second wife in Darryl Pinckney's *High Cotton.*

**Grandma Frieda**   Mother of Frances, grandmother of Gretel and Jason Samuelson; goes to Atlantic City with her canasta-playing cronies for the annual Tri-State Championships; dies that night at the Copper Penney Motel; her spirit sabotages Sam and Theo's food after she dies in Alice Hoffman's *Local Girls.*

**Granser**   Also known as Drop John; Abel Goodparley tries to kill him, but instead is healed by him; is killed by an explosion in Russell Hoban's *Riddley Walker.*

**Alan Grant**   Forty-year-old paleontologist; colleague of Ellie Sattler; guest of John Hammond; uses his ingenuity to battle genetically engineered dinosaurs during weekend stay at Isla Nublar, a remote Costa Rican island resort in Michael Crichton's *Jurassic Park.*

**Lucia Angelina Elena Videndi (Lucky) Grant**   Lover and wife of Ron Grant and daughter of a New York bootlegger; holds a master's degree in political philosophy in James Jones's *Go to the Widow-Maker.*

**Ron Grant**   Famous playwright and naval veteran; marries Lucky Videndi and suspects her of adultery with Jim Grointon; protagonist of James Jones's *Go to the Widow-Maker.*

**Gray Grantham**   Reporter for *Washington Herald* in John Grisham's *The Pelican Brief;* becomes involved in the investigation of the murder of two Supreme Court justices at the request of Darby Shaw; exposes the connection of the office of the president and the murders of the justices through a cover story on the case.

**Gerald (Gerry) Grass**   Young antiestablishment poet in Alison Lurie's *Real People.*

**Detective Grasso**   Los Angeles police detective investigating the murder of Lucie Proctorr in Donald E. Westlake's *The Hook.*

**Robert Graves**   Patient, compliant husband and observer of Annie Graves Maclean; adoring father of Grace Maclean; attorney in New York City law firm; his visit to the Booker ranch at the conclusion of Grace and Annie's visit precipitates Tom Booker's argument that Annie must return to her husband in Nicholas Evans's *The Horse Whisperer.*

**Abel "Abe" Gray**   Thirty-eight-year-old detective on the Haddan police force who has been best friends since second grade with his partner, Joey Tosh; unwittingly co-owns Helen Davis's cat, Midnight; becomes the lover of Betsy Chase and runs away with her in Alice Hoffman's *The River King.*

**Bill Gray**   American novelist who has become famous for being reclusive; born as Willard Skansky Jr., later changed name; attempts to take part in a press conference to free a kidnapped poet in Lebanon; tries to go to Beirut to trade his own freedom for the hostages after a bombing disrupts the original plan; dies along the way when he is hit by a car in Athens in Don DeLillo's *Mao II.*

**Ernest Gray**   Father of Abel Gray, son of Annie and George Howe; police chief of Haddan until his retirement in Florida in Alice Hoffman's *The River King.*

**Florence Gray**   Wife of Wright Gray; good-natured and plain in Alice Hoffman's *The River King.*

**Frank Gray**   Brother of Abel Gray, son of Ernest Gray, and grandson of Wright Gray; was the valedictorian at Hamilton High and was scheduled to go off to Columbia University, but committed suicide with a shotgun at the age of seventeen in Alice Hoffman's *The River King.*

**James de Gray**   See Jakob Gradus.

**Margaret Gray**   Wife of Ernest Gray, mother of Abel and Frank Gray in Alice Hoffman's *The River King.*

**Thomas R. Gray**    Defense attorney who reads Nat Turner's confession to the court in William Styron's *The Confessions of Nat Turner.*

**Wright Gray**    Nonbiological father of Ernest Gray and non-biological grandfather of Abel Gray; police chief of Haddan for thirty years; knew Annie Howe all her life in Alice Hoffman's *The River King.*

**Peter Gerald Grayson**    Known as Mr. Pierre, a gay man and the town hairdresser, whose business is a social center and who marries Nicole Smith to become a father of her two children in Rita Mae Brown's *Bingo.*

**Great White Shark**    Enormous shark that terrorizes the town of Amity in Peter Benchley's *Jaws.*

**Wodie Greaves**    One-eyed believer in magic; joins the crew of the *Lillias Eden* to escape someone who seeks his death but dies when the boat wrecks on Misteriosa Reef in Peter Matthiessen's *Far Tortuga.*

**Mrs. Greco**    Lonely white neighbor of Bill Kelsey; after the death of her only friend, allows cockroaches to overrun her apartment in Hal Bennett's *Seventh Heaven.*

**Elijah Green**    Follower who calls the Reverend Phillip Martin "our Martin Luther King" in Ernest J. Gaines's *In My Father's House.*

**Glory Green**    Actress and wife of Iz Einsam in Alison Lurie's *The Nowhere City.*

**Jack Green**    Head of market research, rival of Andy Kagle, and boss and principal antagonist of Bob Slocum in Joseph Heller's *Something Happened.*

**Ned Green**    Mississippi-born expatriate black poet in Copenhagen in Cecil Brown's *The Life and Loves of Mr. Jiveass Nigger.*

**Tony Green**    Member of the Nova Mob in William S. Burroughs's *Nova Express* and *The Soft Machine;* appears also in *The Wild Boys.*

**Beatrice (Babe) Greene**    Black singer at Jimbo's bar; befriends Jill Pendleton and sends her to live with Harry Angstrom in John Updike's *Rabbit Redux.*

**David Greene**    Divorced and estranged from his wife and son; returns to hometown and enters a landscape business with his sister; has an affair with Judith Silver; runs for town selectman; becomes involved with Crystal Sinclair; realizes after Crystal's death he has been used by her; marries Judith after her husband's death in Marge Piercy's *Storm Tide.*

**Francesca Greene**    Childhood friend of Alison Poole; despite being from a wealthy and powerful family, she is obsessed with status and celebrity; less attractive than her circle of friends, she is their equal in consuming drugs and circulating at trendy clubs in Jay McInerney's *Story of My Life.*

**Jarden Greene**    Department of Public Works head and alderman; evicts Joey Seldon in Mary McGarry Morris's *Songs in Ordinary Time.*

**Nadine Greene**    Mentally unstable young woman from the affluent Detroit suburb Grosse Pointe; shoots her lover, Jules Wendall, in Joyce Carol Oates's *them.*

**Peter (Pete) Greene**    Optimistic innocent, but self-reliant and selfish American in John Barth's *Giles Goat-Boy.*

**General Lewis (Colonel) Greenfield**    Citizen of Saint Louis who leads the expedition against the wild boys in William S. Burroughs's *The Wild Boys.*

**Lionel (Bulldog) Greenspan**    Jewish FBI agent who tails Bruce Gold in Joseph Heller's *Good as Gold.*

**Aurora Starrett Greenway**    Widowed mother of Emma Horton, mother-in-law of Thomas Horton, grandmother of Melanie, Teddy, and Tommy Horton, and lover of General Hector Scott in Larry McMurtry's *Terms of Endearment.*

**Alice Greenwood**    See Alice Greenwood Weylin.

**Esther (Elly Higginbottom) Greenwood**    Brilliant college student and aspiring writer who attempts suicide after a 1953 summer stint as a college guest editor of a New York fashion magazine; narrator of Sylvia Plath's *The Bell Jar.*

**Mrs. Greenwood**    Mother of Esther Greenwood; finds her daughter in the crawl space under the house after Esther attempts suicide with an overdose of sleeping pills in Sylvia Plath's *The Bell Jar.*

**Greer**    Professional killer; companion of Cameron, and lover and briefly husband of Jane Hawkline; hired by the Hawkline sisters to destroy the monster created by their father in Richard Brautigan's *The Hawkline Monster.*

**Alice Greer (Harland/Stillwater)**    Strong independent woman raised on a hog farm during the depression; works as a housemaid after leaving her first husband; then unhappily married to a TV addict for two years; later marries Johnny Cash Stillwater, the biological grandfather of her adopted granddaughter, Turtle; mother of Taylor in Barbara Kingsolver's *Pigs in Heaven.*

**James Greer**    Admiral (and future CIA director in Clancy's other Jack Ryan books) who, with "Dutch" Maxwell and Cas Podulski, works to liberate American POWs from a camp in Vietnam; calls on John Kelly to assist in the mission; and survives the political fallout of the abortive mission to assist Kelly in his fake death and escape into a new life as Clark in Tom Clancy's *Without Remorse.* Also appears in *Hunt for Red October* and *Patriot Games.*

**Taylor Greer**  Daughter of Alice Greer; stubborn, independent, free-spirited; runs away with her adopted Cherokee daughter, Turtle Stillwater, for fear of having to give her back to the tribe; girlfriend of Jax Thibodeaux in Barbara Kingsolver's *Pigs in Heaven.*

**Al Gregory**  American scientist working on an antiballistic missile project; is kidnapped by Soviet agents after being betrayed by Bea Taussig; is rescued by Gus Werner's Hostage Rescue Team after being held for several days in Tom Clancy's *The Cardinal of the Kremlin.*

**Aaron (Arele, Tsutsik) Greidinger**  Playwright and novelist in Warsaw prior to and during Hitler's regime; forms sexual liaisons with Dora Stolnitz, Betty Slonim, Celia Chentshiner, and Tekla, but marries his childhood love, Shosha; narrator of Isaac Bashevis Singer's *Shosha.*

**Grendel (Cowface)**  Enlightened monster who seeks brotherhood with the Scyldings, who assign him the role of ravager; narrator of John Gardner's *Grendel.*

**Dr. Albert Grene**  Black physician of Calvertown; son of Bannie Upshire Dudley and Percy Upshur and father of Mariah Upshur's daughter, Bardetta Tometta Upshur, in Sarah E. Wright's *This Child's Gonna Live.*

**Gretchen**  Ex-wife of David Wiley, a clinical psychologist; her homespun wisdom is never profound but always on the mark; marries Curtis in Elizabeth Benedict's *Slow Dancing.*

**Elmer Grey**  Second husband of May Grey and father of Matt and Ruth Grey; silent man who rarely fights with his wife or tells his children that he loves them; leaves suddenly one evening and never comes back in Jane Hamilton's *Book of Ruth.*

**Jack Grey**  See Jakob Gradus.

**Jacques de Grey**  See Jakob Gradus.

**Jason Grey**  Quiet but warm father of Richard Grey; husband of Helen; Shinnecock Indian migrant worker; supports son's marriage to Lila Grey in Alice Hoffman's *Fortune's Daughter.*

**Lila Grey**  Fortune-teller; abandoned by her parents as a teenager for becoming pregnant, she is separated from her newborn daughter and sent to live with a relative; marries Richard Grey but cannot have more children; is thrown back to grieving for lost daughter when she meets Rae Perry in Alice Hoffman's *Fortune's Daughter.*

**Matt Grey**  Exceptionally intelligent brother of Ruth Grey and son of May Grey; attractive and popular in school; wants to distance himself from his rural upbringing in Honey Creek, Illinois, in Jane Hamilton's *Book of Ruth.*

**May Grey**  Unattractive, bitter woman who can only show flashes of love to her children; mother of Ruth and Matt Grey; hardened by the death of her first husband; abandoned by Elmer Grey, her second husband and father of her children in Jane Hamilton's *Book of Ruth.*

**Richard Grey**  Husband of psychic Lila Grey; mechanic; son of ostracized mixed-race couple; desperately loves wife but walled off from her by secret of her past; supports Rae Perry in his wife's absence in Alice Hoffman's *Fortune's Daughter.*

**Ruth Grey**  Daughter of Elmer and May Grey; sister of Matt Grey; plagued by low self-esteem as a result of her mother's coldness toward her and her brother Matt's inability to accept her because she is not intelligent; witty narrator of Jane Hamilton's *Book of Ruth.*

**Irma Griese**  See Zofia Maria Bieganska Zawistowska.

**Julius Griffin**  Los Angeles psychiatrist; treats Karl Hettinger after the murder of Hettinger's partner in Joseph Wambaugh's *The Onion Field.*

**Harold Griffiths**  Melodramatic poet and newspaper columnist in Gore Vidal's *Washington, D.C.*

**L. J. Griggs**  See Big Red Smalley.

**Mr. Griggs**  Ouida's boyfriend; African American in his fifties; Ouida cleans his house; needs money for his son, Lonnie, who has curvature of the spine in Diane Johnson's *Lying Low.*

**Mrs. Griggs**  Lives in Claire Mayo's boardinghouse; served as secretary for the recreation department for forty-five years in Mary McGarry Morris's *A Dangerous Woman.*

**Carrol Grilhiggen**  Passenger on the *Here They Come* who plans to return Lucifer to heaven in Gregory Corso's *The American Express.*

**The Grim Reaper**  See John Sallow.

**Edie Grimes**  Rich, unpredictable daughter of an influential businessman and a schoolgirl friend of Elizabeth Booth; may function in a plot to divest Elizabeth of her fortune in William Gaddis's *Carpenter's Gothic.*

**Emily (Emmy) Grimes**  Younger sister of Sarah Grimes Wilson; pursues a series of love affairs, but late in life is friendless and alone, relying on a nephew as a guardian in Richard Yates's *Easter Parade.*

**Esther (Pookie) Grimes**  Mother of Sarah Grimes Wilson and Emily Grimes; childish yet ambitious for social status; falls while drunk and dies in a state hospital in Richard Yates's *Easter Parade.*

**Walter Grimes**  Estranged husband of Esther Grimes; writes headlines for the *New York Sun* and dotes on his daughters, Sarah Grimes Wilson and Emily Grimes, in Richard Yates's *Easter Parade.*

**David (Davey) Griscam**   Wall Street lawyer and early graduate of Justin Martyr School whose efforts as trustee and fundraiser lead to institutional growth but loss of the original vision of the school; author of notes compiled by Brian Aspinwall in Louis Auchincloss's *The Rector of Justin.*

**Jules Griscam**   Son of David Griscam and graduate of Justin Martyr School; bitter young man who dies in an automobile crash and is Francis Prescott's greatest failure as headmaster in Louis Auchincloss's *The Rector of Justin.*

**Nikolay Yevgeniyevich (Kolya) Grishanov**   Soviet Air Force officer in charge of questioning American POWs at the Sender Green camp in Vietnam; successfully breaks Robin Zacharias with kindness and alcohol; risks his career to protect the lives of the prisoners he works with; is captured by John Kelly during the abortive raid; gives information that ensures the safety and ultimate release of the POWs in Tom Clancy's *Without Remorse.*

**Arthur Griswald**   Headmaster of the Chatham School for boys; withstands the disdain of his son, Henry, and the anger of his wife, Mildred; must watch his school be destroyed in the wake of the tragic affair carried on by two of its teachers, Elizabeth Channing and Leland Reed; ultimately maintains a compassionate feeling toward Channing when she is jailed for adultery in Thomas H. Cook's *The Chatham School Affair.*

**Henry Griswald**   Son of Arthur; New England bachelor attorney who has carried into his old age a dark secret about certain deaths that took place in 1927; as a youth, has his world and his spirit enlarged upon meeting Chatham School's new art teacher, Elizabeth Channing; grows friendly with Channing and her lover, Leland Reed, a married teacher at the school; is ultimately responsible for the tragic death of Reed's wife, Abigail, in Thomas H. Cook's *The Chatham School Affair.*

**Mildred Griswald**   Wife of Arthur Griswald and mother of Henry; a woman made bitter by suspicions of infidelity and betrayal; was girlhood friends with Abigail Reed and thus sensitive when Reed's husband, Leland, begins an affair with Elizabeth Channing; is gratified when Channing is prosecuted for adultery in 1927 in Thomas H. Cook's *The Chatham School Affair.*

**Burt Griswold**   Husband of Marie Griswold; testifies against Joseph Chase in Jessamyn West's *The Life I Really Lived.*

**Marie Shields Griswold**   Wife of Burt Griswold; her death from cancer prompts the manslaughter charges against Joseph Chase in Jessamyn West's *The Life I Really Lived.*

**Mrs. Grogan**   Knitter who makes Irish sweaters for Margaret Flood and Bayard Strong; invents Gaelic names and tales about her sweaters in Maureen Howard's *Expensive Habits.*

**Jim Grointon**   American skin diver out of Kingston, Jamaica; takes Lucky and Ron Grant diving and asks Lucky to leave Ron and marry him in James Jones's *Go to the Widow-Maker.*

**Gregor Gronfein**   Wealthy prisoner who offers to smuggle letters out of prison for Yakov Bok and later turns in Bok to the warden in Bernard Malamud's *The Fixer.*

**LD Groover**   Roommate of Mabry Jenkins; member of the Dallas Cowboys who writes in his spare time and is cut from the team at the end of the season in Peter Gent's *Texas Celebrity Turkey Trot.*

**Dora Grossbart**   Fantasy friend of Margaret Reynolds and fellow worker in Another Mother for Peace; travels with Reynolds to Vietnam to spread the word about the peace movement in Anne Richardson Roiphe's *Up the Sandbox!*

**William (Bill) Grove**   Shy, awkward student who develops a measure of self-confidence by becoming chief writer and editor of the *Dorset Academy Chronicle* in Richard Yates's *A Good School.*

**Bob Grover**   Undertaker and recent veteran of an acrimonious divorce in Gail Godwin's *Evensong.*

**Grown Boy**   Retarded nephew of Verily; accidentally killed by mill hands and a policeman when Jester Clane chases him in Carson McCullers's *Clock Without Hands.*

**Maureen Grube**   Small-town girl living in New York City; easy sexual conquest for Frank Wheeler in Richard Yates's *Revolutionary Road.*

**Carol M. Gruber**   Successful owner of several factories; married briefly to Ambrose Clay in Gail Godwin's *Violet Clay.*

**Vladislav Grigorievitch Grubeshov**   Prosecuting attorney and procurator of the Kiev Superior Court; tries to convict Yakov Bok of murder in Bernard Malamud's *The Fixer.*

**Joe Grubner**   Great high school athlete on whom Pookie Adams has a crush; dies in an automobile accident while on a date with Pookie in John Nichols's *The Sterile Cuckoo.*

**Molly Grue**   Cook for Captain Cully's outlaws; leaves Cully to join the unicorn in Peter S. Beagle's *The Last Unicorn.*

**Joshua Gruen**   Rabbi at Synagogue of Evolutionary Judaism on roof of which cross stolen from Thomas Pemberton's church is found; married to Rabbi Sarah Blumenthal; beaten to death outside abandoned synagogue in Vilnius while searching for lost ghetto archive connected with Sarah's father in E. L. Doctorow's *City of God.*

**Mose Grundy**   Bracktown barber in Gayl Jones's *Corregidora.*

**Angela Gruner**   Niece of Artur Sammler and estranged daughter of Arnold Gruner; confesses to Sammler her sexual exploits and her indifference to her father's disapproval in Saul Bellow's *Mr. Sammler's Planet.*

**Dr. Arnold (Elya) Gruner**   Physician and benevolent Jewish patriarch who disapproves of his son's schemes and his daughter's sexual liberation; provides care and security for Artur and

Shula Sammler and, apparently, abortions for the Mafia; dies of a brain aneurysm in Saul Bellow's *Mr. Sammler's Planet*.

**Nels Gudmundsson**   Attorney; seventy-nine years old; physically failing but shrewd and humane; appointed to defend Kabuo Miyamoto in David Guterson's *Snow Falling on Cedars*.

**Bea Guerin**   Wife of Roger Guerin and lover of Piet Hanema in John Updike's *Couples*.

**Pauline Guerin**   Black woman who gains small material and emotional amenities as the mistress of Sidney Bonbon in Ernest J. Gaines's *Of Love and Dust*.

**Roger Guerin**   Independently wealthy husband of Bea Guerin in John Updike's *Couples*.

**Barbara Gugelstein**   Generous and loyal classmate and best friend of Mona Chang, whose luxurious home becomes a refuge for Alfred Knickerbocker and African-American friends; civil rights idealist who finds she cannot help suspecting one of her guests when a valuable piece of silver turns up missing in Gish Jen's *Mona in the Promised Land*.

**Philomena Guinea**   Wealthy patroness of scholarship student Esther Greenwood; finances Esther's psychiatric recovery from suicidal depression in a private sanitarium in Sylvia Plath's *The Bell Jar*.

**Guinevere**   Wife of King Arthur and mistress of Launcelot in Thomas Berger's *Arthur Rex*.

**Bernard (Bernar', Bernie) Guizot**   Young hustler and, briefly, lover of Leslie McGivers; tries unsuccessfully to come between McGivers and her friend Honor Rogers in Marge Piercy's *The High Cost of Living*.

**Gumsto**   Brave, forty-three-year-old clan leader in South Africa; instinctive antelope hunter; has a wandering eye and knows he can have any woman in the tribe that he wants; married to Kharu in James A. Michener's *The Covenant*.

**Gunstone**   Client for whom Jack Flowers provides women in Paul Theroux's *Saint Jack*.

**Betty June Gunter**   Adolescent friend of Todd Andrews and his first sexual partner; later, as a prostitute, attacks Andrews in a Baltimore brothel in John Barth's *The Floating Opera*.

**Theda Gunther**   Secretary and mistress of Adrian Lynch in Joseph Wambaugh's *The Choirboys*.

**Asbury Gunwillow**   Sailor drawn to New York City by promise to dying father; becomes pilot of *The Sun* newspaper's launch, and marries Christiana Friebourg in Mark Helprin's *Winter's Tale*.

**Arnold Gupton**   Oldest Gupton brother; bachelor with no palate in his mouth; cheats at cards in Reynolds Price's *A Long and Happy Life*.

**Frederick Gupton**   Infant son of Marise and Macey Gupton; plays Baby Jesus to Rosacoke Mustian's Virgin Mary in Reynolds Price's *A Long and Happy Life*.

**Macey Gupton**   Childhood friend of Milo Mustian in Reynolds Price's *A Long and Happy Life*; joins Milo in sexual experimentation with an unnamed black girl in *A Generous Man*.

**Marise Gupton**   Sister of Willie Duke Aycock; married to Macey Gupton in Reynolds Price's *A Long and Happy Life* and *A Generous Man*.

**Pacifici Bartola Ahmed Gurevich**   Second wife of Zeke Gurevich and mother of his children in William Herrick's *The Itinerant*.

**Samuel Ezekiel (Jakie, Red, Zeke) Gurevich**   Son of a poor Jewish family in New York City; civil rights activist; itinerant soldier in the Spanish Civil War and World War II; lover and rebel in William Herrick's *The Itinerant*.

**Fred Gustav**   Husband of Molly Gustav; his son, Perry, went to school with Jack Wagner in Donald E. Westlake's *The Hook*.

**Molly Gustav**   Wife of Fred Gustav; her son, Perry, went to school with Jack Wagner in Donald E. Westlake's *The Hook*.

**Eleanor Guthrie**   Wealthy Texas heiress and lover of Sonny Shanks in Larry McMurtry's *Moving On*.

**Father Gutstadt**   Catholic villain who follows the trail of The Corpse to the zoo in Tom Robbins's *Another Roadside Attraction*.

**El Comandante Rulino Guzmán**   Prefect of Oriente State bent on forcibly bringing the Niaruna Indians under his control over the objections of the missionaries in Peter Matthiessen's *At Play in the Fields of the Lord*.

**Fausto Guzmán**   Son of Comandante Guzmán in Peter Matthiessen's *At Play in the Fields of the Lord*.

**Sefiora Dolores Estella Carmen Maria Cruz y Peralta Guzmán**   Wife of Comandante Guzmán in Peter Matthiessen's *At Play in the Fields of the Lord*.

**Gwen**   Annie's first best friend and first replacement figure for Annie's mother; spends every afternoon with Annie until they are sixteen and Annie moves to another scholastic level in Jamaica Kincaid's *Annie John*.

**Mamma Habblesham**   Midwife who rears Abeba Torch before the six-year-old child's mother takes her to New York in Ellease Southerland's *Let the Lion Eat Straw.*

**Astrid Haddad**   Wife of Robert Haddad; former Las Vegas showgirl; has soap parties in Mary McGarry Morris's *Songs in Ordinary Time.*

**George Haddad**   Professor living in Athens with his wife and daughter; serves as contact between Abu Rashid's Lebanese terrorist group and Charles Everson's committee on free expression; lures famously reclusive novelist Bill Gray to travel to Lebanon in a doomed attempt to trade himself for the poet held hostage in Don DeLillo's *Mao II.*

**Robert Haddad**   Husband of Astrid Haddad; insurance agent who loses his clients' money gambling; is shot by Joey Seldon when he tries to rob a bank in Mary McGarry Morris's *Songs in Ordinary Time.*

**Sol Hadden**   Member of the National Academy of Engineering; eccentric and gluttonously wealthy business tycoon; unlikely ally for Eleanor Arroway in Carl Sagan's *Contact.*

**Ellen Shipp Hadley**   Wife of Daniel Compton Wills, daughter of a well-to-do Boston family, and graduate of Wellesley College; discovers her husband has seduced the wife of Andrew Collier in George V. Higgins's *Dreamland.*

**Reba (Dickless Tracy, No-Balls) Hadley**   Intelligent, articulate, and courageous Los Angeles policewoman in Joseph Wambaugh's *The Choirboys.*

**Mr. Haecker**   Retired high school principal and resident of the Dorset Hotel in John Barth's *The Floating Opera.*

**Alonso Hagan**   Frustrated fisherman who never caught a trout; his fishing diary is found in his sister's attic by the narrator of Richard Brautigan's *Trout Fishing in America.*

**Hagar**   See Hagar Dead.

**Thomas (Tom) Hagen**   Lawyer and counselor to the Corleone family; taken in and reared by the Corleones after being orphaned in Mario Puzo's *The Godfather.*

**King Haggard**   Ruler of Hagsgate in Peter S. Beagle's *The Last Unicorn.*

**Hal**   Mrs. Waite's lover in Bette Pesetsky's *Midnight Sweets.*

**Lisa Halder**   Jamaican wife of René Halder; engineers the wedding of Lucky Videndi and Ron Grant in James Jones's *Go to the Widow-Maker.*

**René Halder**   Owner of Grand Hotel Crount, Kingston; old friend of Lucky Videndi in James Jones's *Go to the Widow-Maker.*

**Christopher (Black Christopher) Hall**   Harlem radical; lover and valet of Leo Proudhammer in James Baldwin's *Tell Me How Long the Train's Been Gone.*

**Cubsy Hall**   Seven-year-old preacher whom Ruby Drew tries to take from Orondo McCabe in William Goyen's *The Fair Sister.*

**Ed Hall**   Father of the boy Glen Davis drunkenly ran down and killed three years before the immediate action of Larry Brown's *Father and Son.*

**Judy Hall**   Mother of the boy Glen Davis drunkenly ran down and killed three years before the immediate action of Larry Brown's *Father and Son.*

**Mark William Hall**   Surgeon who is the "odd man" member of the scientist group at Project Wildfire in Michael Crichton's *The Andromeda Strain.*

**Willie (Littleman) Hall**   Angry, crippled, young black man who plots to lynch a white policeman in John Edgar Wideman's *The Lynchers.*

**Gary Hallett**   Astute and weathered investigator for attorney general's office on the trail of Gillian Owens's dead boyfriend; is inexplicably drawn to Gillian's sister, Sally Owens, and falls in love with her in Alice Hoffman's *Practical Magic.*

**Dick Hallorann**   Black chef at the Overlook Hotel who uses his psychic ability to rescue Daniel Torrance and Daniel's mother from John Torrance in Stephen King's *The Shining.*

**Halmea**   Black housekeeper at Homer Bannon's ranch, which she leaves after being raped by Hud in Larry McMurtry's *Horseman, Pass By.*

**Bob Halpin**   Businessman who employs Virgil Morgan in Scott Spencer's *Preservation Hall.*

**Phil Halpin**   Los Angeles deputy district attorney; second prosecutor of Gregory Powell and Jimmy Smith in Joseph Wambaugh's *The Onion Field.*

**James Halstead**   Former banker turned Mercedes salesman with whom Margaret Devore has an affair in Donald E. Westlake's *The Ax.*

**Benno Hamburger**   Resident of Emma Lazarus Retirement Home and best friend of Otto Korner; he woos and wins Hermoine Perlmutter, convincing her to return a treasured letter stolen from Otto in Alan Isler's *The Prince of West End Avenue.*

**Abdul Hamid**   Black Muslim leader who believes that in the United States something is successful in direct proportion to how it is put over; murdered in Ishmael Reed's *Mumbo Jumbo.*

**Alexander Hamilton**   Leader who persuades the Federalist party to vote for Thomas Jefferson over Aaron Burr for president after an election tie in 1800; killed by Burr in a duel in Gore Vidal's *Burr.*

**Milo (Arabella Stone) Hamilton**   Close friend of Violet Clay and writer of gothic novels in Gail Godwin's *Violet Clay.*

**Uncle Hamilton**   Wealthy maternal uncle and frequent houseguest of Joe Sandwich; becomes infatuated with and later marries Laura Pribble in Peter De Vries's *The Vale of Laughter.*

**John Hamlin**   Lover of Audrey Carsons in William S. Burroughs's *The Wild Boys.*

**Agnis Hamm**   Quoyle's aunt; convinces Quoyle to move to Newfoundland after his wife's death; lives with Quoyle and his family in Newfoundland until opening a yacht upholstering business elsewhere; raped by Quoyle's father when she was a child in E. Annie Proulx's *The Shipping News.*

**Laila Hammad**   Belly dancer and prostitute who asks Bumper Morgan for help when she is pregnant in Joseph Wambaugh's *The Blue Knight.*

**Ambrose Hammer**   Retired postal worker researching and writing a book on black history; boarder of Clotilda Pilgrim; adopts Lester Parker after Pilgrim's death in Cyrus Colter's *The Rivers of Eros.*

**Marietta Drum Hammer**   Wife of Paul Hammer; tender toward him only when there is a public disaster in John Cheever's *Bullet Park.*

**Paul Hammer**   Warped idealist who seeks to wake up the world by the attempted sacrifice of a model citizen (later substituting the citizen's son) in John Cheever's *Bullet Park.*

**John Hammond**   Septuagenarian creator/owner of *Jurassic Park,* theme park located on Isla Nublar, remote Costa Rican island; grandfather of Tim and Alexis "Lex" Murphy; creates genetically engineered dinosaurs that spell danger for park visitors and himself in Michael Crichton's *Jurassic Park.*

**Liz Hammond**   Large animal veterinarian who locates Tom Booker when Annie Graves Maclean asks her to find a "horse psychiatrist" in Nicholas Evans's *The Horse Whisperer.*

**Lon Hammond**   Ambitious, career-driven lawyer engaged to Allie Nelson in Nicholas Sparks's *The Notebook.*

**Ruby Hammond**   Younger sister of Geneva, a good-looking woman who was favored by her stepfather; well-off widow of Gordon in Sandra Scofield's *Beyond Deserving.*

**Opel Hampson**   Drug-using rock groupie who dies suddenly in bed; her New York apartment is a refuge for Bucky Wunderlick in Don DeLillo's *Great Jones Street.*

**Hope (Hub) Hampton (1)**   See Volume I.

**Hope (Little Hub) Hampton**   See Volume I.

**Winfield Scott Hancock**   Former hero in the Mexican War and friend of Lewis Armistead; Northern general who takes Possession of Cemetery Hill during the Battle of Gettysburg in Michael Shaara's *The Killer Angels.*

**Laurel McKelva (Polly) Hand**   Chicago fabric designer; daughter of Clinton and Becky McKelva and widow of Philip Hand in Eudora Welty's *The Optimist's Daughter.*

**Philip Hand**   Husband of Laurel McKelva Hand; killed during World War II in Eudora Welty's *The Optimist's Daughter.*

**Enoch Handle**   Margaret's father; drives the mail boat; part Beothuk Indian; helps Fabian and his family escape after the murder in Howard Norman's *The Bird Artist.*

**Margaret Handle**   Daughter of Enoch Handle; lover and eventual wife of Fabian Vas; as a young girl, she crashes into and kills Dalton Gillette while riding her bicycle; later crashes into Alaric Vas in a fatal boat accident; starts drinking when she is not working as an accountant; seems to settle down after her father's death and her marriage in Howard Norman's *The Bird Artist*.

**Martin Handson**   Uncle and manager of Putsy Handson in Calvin Hernton's *Scarecrow*.

**Orville Handson**   Racist, sadistic, and murderous army sergeant; killed in Korea by Scarecrow in Calvin Hernton's *Scarecrow*.

**Putsy Handson**   Successful model, daughter of Orville Handson, and lover of Wantman Krane in Calvin Hernton's *Scarecrow*.

**Beatrice (Billy) Handy**   Loyal's girlfriend; redheaded nightclub singer; will not have sex with Loyal; wants to move away from a small town; is killed by Loyal and is buried in an abandoned fox den in E. Annie Proulx's *Postcards*.

**Angela Hanema**   Wife of Piet Hanema and mother of Ruth and Nancy Hanema in John Updike's *Couples*.

**Foxy Hanema**   See Elizabeth Fox Whitman.

**Nancy Hanema**   Younger daughter of Piet and Angela Hanema in John Updike's *Couples*.

**Piet Hanema**   Philandering husband of Angela Hanema and later of Foxy Whitman; father of Ruth and Nancy Hanema in John Updike's *Couples*.

**Ruth Hanema**   Older daughter of Piet and Angela Hanema in John Updike's *Couples*.

**Hanes**   Assistant to Globke in Transparanoia organization; steals a mysterious drug in Don DeLillo's *Great Jones Street*.

**Hania**   Redheaded prison companion of Eva Laubenstein and seducer of Laubenstein's son, Konrad Vost, in John Hawkes's *The Passion Artist*.

**Ariadne Hanim**   American woman who leaves her ordinary life behind for adventure in Turkey; target of malicious rumors that she killed her estranged husband; watches the sacrifice at the beginning of the novel and witnesses the aftermath of murder and mayhem near the novel's end in Mary Lee Settle's *Blood Tie*.

**Melek Hanim**   Munci's mother; a beautiful woman, compared to Medea; called Lady Melek by many; she harbors a resentment for her old husband and focuses on her beloved Munci in Mary Lee Settle's *Blood Tie*.

**Munci Hanim (Monkey)**   Called a "useful Ceramian" by Basil; a strong diver who must retrieve the bodies of the drowned students, including the beautiful Lale; becomes too close to Ariadne Hanim, causing her much heartache and shame in Mary Lee Settle's *Blood Tie*.

**Sissy Hankshaw**   See Sissy Hankshaw Gitche.

**Ray Hanley**   Law partner and friend of Calvin Jarrett in Judith Guest's *Ordinary People*.

**Mike Hanlon**   One of few black residents in Derry, Mike is also a member of The Losers Club; as an adult, Mike stays in Derry to work as a librarian and to keep an eye on "IT," who hibernates for twenty seven years before returning again to destroy the children of Derry in Stephen King's *IT*.

**Ben Hanscomb**   Overweight member of The Losers Club; his rational thought aids the club in their attacks on "IT" in Stephen King's *IT*.

**Andrew Jackson (Chip) Hansen**   Army general, superior to Sean O'Sullivan, and first military governor of post–World War II Germany in Leon Uris's *Armageddon*.

**Arne Hansen**   Volatile Swede in Katherine Anne Porter's *Ship of Fools*.

**Mr. Hansen**   Tall, blond Austrian who owns the Black Pearl nightclub in Golconda, where Lillian Beye plays piano in Anaïs Nin's *Seduction of the Minotaur*.

**Margo Hansmon**   Friendly landlady; baker of Annie and Carl Brown's wedding cake in Betty Smith's *Joy in the Morning*.

**George (Georgette) Hanson**   Transvestite and homosexual almost aggressively defensive about his sexuality; becomes a creature for pity after rejection by his beloved Vinnie in Hubert Selby, Jr.'s *Last Exit to Brooklyn*.

**Elizabeth Harbour**   Born into a wealthy intellectual Cambridge family, a dramatic and self-centered wife and mother of three; stung by her husband's philandering, she spends a summer rekindling a dangerous romance with Cameron Gardner in Sue Miller's *For Love*.

**Rozelle Hardcastle**   See Rozelle Hardcastle Butler Carrington.

**John Wesley Hardin**   Racist hired by Drag Gibson to defeat the Loop Garoo Kid, but unable to do so in Ishmael Reed's *Yellow Back Radio Broke-Down*.

**Angela Harding**   Friend and former roommate of Karen Randall; steals drugs from the hospital; performs abortion on Karen Randall that kills her in Jeffery Hudson's *A Case of Need*.

**Dale Harding**   Most intelligent and articulate of the intimidated mental patients who respond to Randle McMurphy's example in resisting Big Nurse in Ken Kesey's *One Flew Over the Cuckoo's Nest*.

**Sarah Harding**   Beautiful, independent thirty-three-year-old animal behaviorist; former lover of Ian Malcolm; journeys to Costa Rican jungle to investigate dinosaur sightings in Michael Crichton's *The Lost World*.

**Dennis Hardy**    Geometry teacher at Haddan School in Alice Hoffman's *The River King.*

**Walter Hardy**    Semifamous novelist; smug sycophant who Clarissa unwillingly invites to her party in Michael Cunningham's *The Hours.*

**Gisela Hargenau**    Ten-year-old daughter of Helmuth Hargenau, who moves in with him when he leaves his wife in Walter Abish's *How German Is It.*

**Helmuth von Hargenau**    Brother of Ulrich Hargenau; father was executed by Hitler in 1944; drops the "von" in his name; well-known and much-admired architect; playboy who separates from his wife, Maria; has his brother shot in Walter Abish's *How German Is It.*

**Ulrich von Hargenau**    German writer; brother of Helmuth Hargenau; father was executed by Hitler in 1944; drops the "von" in his name; former political activist with the Einzieh group, along with his ex-wife, Paula, in Walter Abish's *How German Is It.*

**Christine (Chris) Hargensen**    Classmate who torments Carrie White in Stephen King's *Carrie.*

**Manson Hargrove**    Man who shoots Estelle in the chest without killing her in Reynolds Price's *A Long and Happy Life.*

**Mary Minor (Harry) Haristeen**    Full-time postmistress and part-time sleuth of Crozet, Virginia; divorced owner of a cat, a dog, and a horse farm, she solves mysteries with the unsolicited help of her pets in Rita Mae Brown's *Cat on the Scent* and *Murder at Monticello.*

**Pharamond Haristeen**    Tall, blond giant of a man; veterinarian; formerly married to Mary Minor Haristeen, with whom he is still good friends; is still in love with her and wants her back in Rita Mae Brown's *Murder at Monticello.*

**Hark (Hercules)**    Slave and closest friend of Nat Turner; Hark's wife and son are sold to another plantation in William Styron's *The Confessions of Nat Turner.*

**Gary Harkness**    Football halfback for Logos College who is preoccupied by nuclear cataclysm; narrator of Don DeLillo's *End Zone.*

**Frances (Frankie) Harlow**    Member of Thomas Marshfield's congregation who complains of too much music in the services and not enough excitement in her marriage; Marshfield is unable to make love to her in John Updike's *A Month of Sundays.*

**Gerald (Gerry) Harlow**    Husband of Frankie Harlow; banker and a deacon of Thomas Marshfield's church in John Updike's *A Month of Sundays.*

**Effie (Mamma Effie) Harmon**    Wife of Pop Harmon and mother of Mariah Upshur in Sarah E. Wright's *This Child's Gonna Live.*

**Pop Harmon**    Husband of Effie Harmon and father of Mariah Upshur in Sarah E. Wright's *This Child's Gonna Live.*

**Harold**    Father of a child by the young May Alice in Gayl Jones's *Corregidora.*

**A. J. Harper**    Abusive lover of Evalin McCabe Wilson in Diane Johnson's *The Shadow Knows.*

**Andrew T. Harper**    Father of Linn Harper and husband of Katherine Harper; assistant professor of history at William Watson College and reluctant collaborator in Zebulon Johns Mackie's history of Bunker County in Fred Chappell's *The Gaudy Place.*

**Henry Harper**    Nine-year-old orphan who calls a late-night radio talk show in Stanley Elkin's *The Dick Gibson Show.*

**Katherine (Katy) Harper**    Mother of Linn Harper, wife of Andrew Harper, and niece of Zebulon Johns Mackie; insists on calling Mackie to get Linn out of jail in Fred Chappell's *The Gaudy Place.*

**Linn Harper**    Seventeen-year-old son of Andrew and Katherine Harper; inspired by the works of Albert Camus to commit the gratuitous act of breaking into the Spartan Stock Feed Products Mill to steal chicken feed in Fred Chappell's *The Gaudy Place.*

**Col. Looseleaf Harper**    Pilot who dropped the atomic bomb on Nagasaki; Eliot Rosewater's pilot in Kurt Vonnegut's *Breakfast of Champions.*

**Edward Harranby**    Scotland Yard man who captures Edward Pierce in Michael Crichton's *The Great Train Robbery.*

**Harriet (Harry the Rapist)**    Lover of Georgie Cornell in Thomas Berger's *Regiment of Women.*

**Harrington**    Customer at Jerry Doherty's bar; becomes an accomplice with Doherty in a fur theft and turns him into the FBI when he feels cheated with his share of the take in George V. Higgins's *The Digger's Game.*

**Jill Harrington**    Best friend and neighbor of Gretel Samuelson in Franconia; gets pregnant from Eddie LoPacca and marries him; doesn't finish eleventh grade; has sons named Leonardo and Eddie Jr., and a daughter named Angela in Alice Hoffman's *Local Girls.*

**Kate Harrington**    See Kate Flickinger.

**Mrs. Harrington**    Jill's mother, head of the PTA; doesn't speak for several months after hospital stay; eventually begins to talk again as if she hasn't had a lapse of any sort in Alice Hoffman's *Local Girls.*

**Bernadine Harris**    Thirty-something African-American real estate firm controller whose husband, John, divorces her to marry a younger white woman (Kathleen); unfulfilled but wealthy mother of adolescents John, Jr., and Onika and resident of Scottsdale, Arizona; old friends with Savannah Jackson; forces her husband's cheating hand and receives a hefty divorce settlement and eventually, with a new love, some piece of mind in Terry McMillan's *Waiting to Exhale.*

**Pod Jo (Pod J) Harris**   White kidnapper, ex-convict, and gambler in Shelby Foote's *September September.*

**Sid Harris**   Condominium president who duns Marshall Preminger for back rent in *The Condominium*, a novella in Stanley Elkin's *Searches and Seizures.*

**Stink Harris**   Army infantryman in Vietnam noted for his toughness, pettiness, and distrust in Tim O'Brien's *Going after Cacciato.*

**Will Harris**   Veteran who returns from Korea to the South to live and become an active citizen; prevented from registering to vote because he is black in Junius Edwards's *If We Must Die.*

**Harrison (Hal, Harry)**   White organizer of the Irredentist movement in Mexico; murdered by Mexican police in Nicholas Delbanco's *News.*

**C. D. Harrison**   Necrophiliac father of Les Harrison; essentially owns Metropolitan Pictures in Terry Southern's *Blue Movie.*

**Charlie Harrison**   Friend and coworker of Georgie Cornell in Thomas Berger's *Regiment of Women.*

**Fido Harrison**   Head broker at MacNaughton and Blair; friend and supervisor of Joe Sandwich in Peter De Vries's *The Vale of Laughter.*

**John Harrison**   Suicide for whose death Inspector Lee blames Terrence Weld in William S. Burroughs's *The Ticket That Exploded.*

**Les (Rat Prick) Harrison**   Son of C. D. Harrison and vice president of Metropolitan Pictures; kept under sedation to prevent his learning about explicit sex scenes in Boris Adrian's pornographic movie in Terry Southern's *Blue Movie.*

**Dalton (Diddy) Harron**   Public relations man determined to discover whether he has actually committed a murder; his dying fantasies upon his suicide constitute the events of Susan Sontag's *Death Kit.*

**Joan Harron**   Ex-wife of Dalton Harron in Susan Sontag's *Death Kit.*

**Paul Harron**   Younger brother of Dalton Harron; concert pianist who likes to drop in on Diddy without calling, in Susan Sontag's *Death Kit.*

**Harry**   Chronically cold passenger on the *Here They Come* who plans to make the world warmer in Gregory Corso's *The American Express.*

**Harry**   Elderly resident of the Golden Years Community; pays a janitress to permit him to shave her pubic hair with his electric shaver in Jerzy Kosinski's *Cockpit.*

**Harry**   Clerk in a record store with extensive knowledge of jazz; contributor to Renate's planned magazine in Anaïs Nin's *Collages.*

**Harry**   Gunner's mate for whom Fernandez leaves Cassandra; dies in a hotel room, trying to save Fernandez in John Hawkes's *Second Skin.*

**Harry the Rapist**   See Harriet.

**Alvine Harshawe**   Successful novelist; had employed Connie Birch as a typist; thought to be one candidate for his true father by John Jaimison in Dawn Powell's *The Golden Spur.*

**Ivar Harstad**   Provost of Moo University, well-intentioned administrator who lives in fear of his secretary, Mrs. Walker; has a long-standing and clandestine relationship with Helen Levy of the foreign language department (whom he eventually marries); is the twin brother of Nils Harstad, dean of extension in Jane Smiley's *Moo.*

**Nils Harstad**   Dean of extension at Moo University, a land-grant college in the Midwest; twin brother of Ivar Harstad, provost; member of the Creation Science church; tries to marry fellow church member Marly Hellmich in order to create his ideal benevolent family; when Marly leaves both him and her father, he invites the old man to live with him in Jane Smiley's *Moo.*

**Emma Hart (Emma Hamilton)**   Lover and eventually second wife of the Cavaliere; never forgives herself for sacrificing life with her daughter for life with the Cavaliere; participation in the White Terror that follows the suppression of the Neapolitan Republic shows her to be cunning, cruel, and bloodthirsty; never tells her daughter that she is her mother, even when her daughter nurses her through the debilitating effects of her alcoholism in Susan Sontag's *The Volcano Lover.*

**Henrietta Hart**   Maternal elderly widow who befriends Dane Empson in Majorca in Gail Godwin's *The Perfectionists.*

**Jesse (Jesse Pedersen, Jesse Vogel) Harte**   Boy who escapes his father's murderous rampage and as an adult becomes a brain surgeon; having legally changed his name, he pursues the American dream and the mystery of his own identity; husband of Helene Cady Vogel in Joyce Carol Oates's *Wonderland.*

**Nelson Hartis**   Presbyterian minister who marries Ellen Strohe and Chris Van Eenanam in Larry Woiwode's *What I'm Going to Do, I Think.*

**Eleanor Hartley**   Ex-wife of Jack Hartley in James Jones's *The Merry Month of May.*

**Jonathan James (Jack) Hartley III**   Editor of the *Two Islands Review* and friend of the Gallagher family; narrator of James Jones's *The Merry Month of May.*

**Willard Hartman**   Wayne Prentice's agent in Donald E. Westlake's *The Hook*.

**Bess Harvill**   Close friend of N. Hexam in Diane Johnson's *The Shadow Knows*.

**Esther Harvitz**   Roommate of Rachel Owlglass; has an affair with the plastic surgeon who performs her nose job in Thomas Pynchon's *V*.

**Freddy Harwood**   Intellectual bookstore owner; independently wealthy; falls head-over-heels in love with Nora Jane Whittington in Ellen Gilchrist's *Victory Over Japan*.

**Daphne Hasendruck**   American neighbor of Ulrich Hargenau who is studying philosophy at the university; has an affair with Ulrich; infiltrates the Einzieh group and becomes friends with Paula in Walter Abish's *How German Is It*.

**Eva Hassel**   Classmate and early love interest of Henry Bech in John Updike's *Bech: A Book*.

**Jake Hasty**   Dog-show handler at the fair in Reynolds Price's *A Generous Man*.

**Hat**   Oldest sister of Lil in Joan Chase's *During the Reign of the Queen of Persia*.

**Hatcher**   American engineer who comes to Mexico to forget his past, but cannot in Anaïs Nin's *Seduction of the Minotaur*.

**Theresa Haug**   See Theresa Bigoness.

**Bobby Hauser**   Son of Sherman and Carol Hauser; dies accidentally in Edward Lewis Wallant's *The Tenants of Moonbloom*.

**Carol Hauser**   Wife of Sherman Hauser and mother of Bobby Hauser; lives in the 70th Street building managed by Norman Moonbloom in Edward Lewis Wallant's *The Tenants of Moonbloom*.

**Horse Hauser**   Foul-mouthed and hilarious ne'er-do-well friend of Ralph Sandifer in Thomas Berger's *Sneaky People*.

**Sherman Hauser**   Husband of Carol Hauser and father of Bobby Hauser; tenant in the 70th Street building managed by Norman Moonbloom in Edward Lewis Wallant's *The Tenants of Moonbloom*.

**Captain Havermeyer**   Sharpshooter and lead bombardier in Yossarian's squadron; refuses to take evasive action in battle in Joseph Heller's *Catch-22*.

**Horace Havistock**   Wealthy American expatriate and esthete living in Paris; schoolmate and boyhood friend of Francis Prescott and author of *The Art of Friendship* about their relationship in Louis Auchincloss's *The Rector of Justin*.

**Hawk**   Black gunman and professional thug working in Boston; enforcer for loan shark King Powers; former heavyweight boxer; is warned by Spenser of a police trap and saves Spenser's life in return in Robert B. Parker's *Promised Land* and most of Parker's other Spenser novels.

**Hal Hawkesley**   Ex-policeman who arrested accused murderer Olive Martin; chef and restaurateur; is framed for health violations and extorted to foreclose business; falls in love with writer Rosalind Leigh and collaborates with her to vindicate Olive Martin in Minette Walters's *The Sculptress*.

**Sadie Hawkins**   Daughter of a taverner; tricks Leslie Collins into marrying her and gives birth to another man's son six months later in Harriette Simpson Arnow's *The Kentucky Trace*.

**Jane Hawkline**   Twin sister of Susan Hawkline and daughter of Professor Hawkline; hires Cameron and Greer to destroy the Hawkline Monster in Richard Brautigan's *The Hawkline Monster*.

**Professor Hawkline**   Father of Susan and Jane Hawkline; Harvard chemistry professor whose experiments create the Hawkline Monster, which turns him into an elephant-foot umbrella stand, from which transformation he is rescued by Greer and Cameron in Richard Brautigan's *The Hawkline Monster*.

**Susan Hawkline**   Twin sister of Jane Hawkline and daughter of Professor Hawkline; hires Cameron and Greer to destroy the Hawkline Monster; plans to but does not marry Cameron in Richard Brautigan's *The Hawkline Monster*.

**Hawkline Monster**   Sentient, malevolent creature of light, accompanied by a beneficent if inept shadow; created in Professor Hawkline's chemistry experiments and destroyed by Cameron in Richard Brautigan's *The Hawkline Monster*.

**Ethan Allen (Eth) Hawley**   Grocery clerk at Marullo's Fruit and Fancy Groceries, who regains ownership of the store by having Alfio Marullo deported; son of a formerly prominent family who takes possession of the most valuable land in New Baytown by manipulating his childhood friend in John Steinbeck's *The Winter of Our Discontent*.

**Mary Hawley**   Devoted wife of Ethan Allen Hawley; encourages her husband to rise above the level of grocery clerk so their family will have the financial status to be respected among the people of New Baytown in John Steinbeck's *The Winter of Our Discontent*.

**Jack Haxby**   Jealous husband of Lucille Haxby; celebrity dentist who maliciously pulls the wrong tooth from Gowan McGland, precipitating McGland's suicide in Peter De Vries's *Reuben, Reuben*.

**Lucille Haxby**   Wife of Jack Haxby and paramour of Gowan McGland in Peter De Vries's *Reuben, Reuben*.

**Dr. Kenneth Hale Hayden**   Jewish physician who diagnoses and treats J. T. Malone for leukemia; exposes Malone's prejudice in Carson McCullers's *Clock Without Hands*.

**Taylor Hayes**   Young college professor in New York who hires Jasmine Vijh to be his child's nanny; begins a relationship with Jasmine, which is cut short when her husband's killer, Sukhwinder Singh, unexpectedly appears; three years later he accepts a teaching position in California and convinces Jasmine, who is a pregnant housewife hiding in Iowa, to join him and his daughter in Bharati Mukherjee's *Jasmine*.

**Val Hayes**   Mentor of Cody Porneray and friend at Columbia University of Jack Duluoz; introduces Duluoz to Pomeray in Jack Kerouac's *Visions of Cody*.

**Charles Hayman**   Pioneer who in 1876 settled beside a creek that now bears his name in Richard Brautigan's *Trout Fishing in America*.

**Miss Haynsworth**   Winner of the poetry contest Henry Bech judges at a Virginia women's college in John Updike's *Bech: A Book*.

**Dexter Hays**   American man who travels to the Dominican Republic to court Yolanda Garcia; suitor of Yo in Julia Alvarez's *Yo!*

**Arnold Hayward**   White lawyer of Formy Hunt in James Baldwin's *If Beale Street Could Talk*.

**Billy Hazard**   Younger brother of George Hazard; first lieutenant in the Confederate forces; settled in Washington, D.C., to do work as an engineer; newly married and deeply in love with Brett Main Orry Main's sister in John Jakes's *Love and War*.

**Brett Hazard**   Pretty, headstrong Southern belle from South Carolina; sister of Orry Main; devoted wife of Billy Hazard; must fight loneliness and the prejudice of Pennsylvania, where she lives with George Hazard and his wife while Billy is away in the Civil War in John Jake's *Love and War*.

**George Hazard**   West Point graduate; Union supporter; owner of an iron works in his Pennsylvania town; best friend of Confederate supporter Orry Main; employed by the War Department in Washington, D.C., after the outbreak of the Civil War in John Jakes's *Love and War*.

**Sarah Bracknell Hazlett**   Girlfriend of Johnny Smith; marries another man while Smith is in a coma following an automobile accident in Stephen King's *The Dead Zone*.

**Neal Hazzard**   Commandant for the American sector of Berlin in Leon Uris's *Armageddon*.

**Gerald Healey**   Minister who marries Earl Morgan and Lillian Douglas in Scott Spencer's *Preservation Hall*.

**Jane Healy**   Semiautobiographical fictional character created by Margaret Flood in her novel *Child's Play;* wife of Tim Healy; works at a library in Maureen Howard's *Expensive Habits*.

**Michael Healy**   African-American mariner; heavy drinker with an uncontrollable temper, yet respected force of justice and morality in lawless Alaskan coastal waters in James Michener's *Alaska.*

**Richard Healy**   First-year law student at UCLA who works part-time in Lexi Steiner's office in Elizabeth Benedict's *Slow Dancing*.

**Tim Healy**   Semiautobiographical fictional character created by Margaret Flood in her novel *Child's Play;* husband of Jane Healy; a medical intern; awarded a Silver Star in the Pacific in Maureen Howard's *Expensive Habits*.

**Ruth Heaper**   Lover of Jack Duluoz in New York in Jack Kerouac's *Desolation Angels*.

**The Heavy Metal Kid**   See Uranian Willy.

**Heavy Shield Woman**   Wife of Yellow Kidney, who takes a sacred vow to act as Medicine Woman during the Pikuni Sun Dance in order to assure her husband's safe return in James Welch's *Fools Crow*.

**Antoine Hébert**   Middle-aged doctor from Leon, France; travels to the French colony Saint Domingue in search of his sister, Elise Thibodet; falls in love with a professional mulatto mistress, Nanon, who bears his child; captured during the slave rebellion on Saint Domingue between 1791 and 1802; works with Toussaint in a field hospital where he learns to be an expert in herbal medicine in Madison Smartt Bell's *All Souls' Rising*.

**Marshall Hebert**   White plantation owner whose past criminal activities are known by Sidney Bonbon and Aunt Julie Rand in Ernest J. Gaines's *Of Love and Dust*.

**Don Hector**   Hacendado of the La Purisima Ranch; doubts John Grady's innocence in the stolen horse fiasco perpetrated by Jimmy Blevins, but is later impressed by John Grady's obvious abilities regarding horses in Cormac McCarthy's *All the Pretty Horses*.

**Virginia R. (Lady Creamhair, Creamie) Hector**   Virgin mother of George Giles, whom he almost rapes; daughter of the former chancellor of New Tammany College in John Barth's *Giles Goat-Boy*.

**Sybil Hedden**   Date of Todd Eborn on the day he meets Louise Attwater in Reynolds Price's *Love and Work*.

**Oman Hedgepath**   Most prominent lawyer in Somerton and nephew and law partner of Steve Mundine; hired by Lord Byron Jones to win a divorce from Emma Jones; narrates part of Jesse Hill Ford's *The Liberation of Lord Byron Jones*.

**Virgil (Virge) Hedgepath**   Marine colonel and friend of the Meecham family; godfather of Ben Meecham in Pat Conroy's *The Great Santini*.

**Robert Thomas Hedrick IV**   School friend of Susie Schnitzer; their dates are a pretense that allows her to visit her maternal grandmother in Harriette Simpson Arnow's *The Weedkiller's Daughter*.

**Carl Heine**   Fisherman found drowned in his nets at sea; Kabuo Miyamoto is accused of killing him; bought land Kabuo Miyamoto believes is rightfully his; World War II veteran; married to Susan Marie in David Guterson's *Snow Falling on Cedars*.

**Heinie**   See Vahine.

**Jimmy Heinze**   Police officer in Mary McGarry Morris's *Songs in Ordinary Time*.

**Dorothy Heissenhuber (Rhodes)**   Plain but assertive and ambitious second wife of Richard Heissenhuber; abuses stepdaughter, Jane, and dotes on son Rhodes in Susan Isaacs's *Almost Paradise*.

**Rhodes Heissenhuber**   Devastatingly handsome homosexual stepbrother of Jane Cobleigh; loving and supportive of stepsister; companion and lover of older wealthy businessman in Susan Isaacs's *Almost Paradise*.

**Richard Heissenhuber**   Stolid son of German immigrants; marries first Sarah Taubman, then Dorothy Rhodes; has unremarkable career as accountant; abuses daughter, Jane, in Susan Isaacs's *Almost Paradise*.

**Truman (True) Held**   Artist and civil rights activist; husband of Lynne Rabinowitz, father of Camara, and friend and occasional lover of Meridian Hill in Alice Walker's *Meridian*.

**Ana Helein**   Viennese social worker raped and murdered by a Russian checkpoint guard in John Irving's *Setting Free the Bears*.

**Helen (Helena, Helen of Troy)**   Greek heroine mysteriously transported to Egypt for the duration of the Trojan War in H. D.'s *Helen in Egypt*.

**Helena**   Wife of Julian and sister of Constantius; after learning that her infant children have been secretly murdered by Eusebia, Helena encourages Julian to overthrow Constantius in Gore Vidal's *Julian*.

**Helene**   Wife of BZ; has an affair with Carter Lang in Joan Didion's *Play It As It Lays*.

**Heller**   Old Dutch janitor at Olinger High School in John Updike's *The Centaur*.

**Anna Heller**   Teacher who has an affair with Helmuth Hargenau; Gisela's favorite teacher; also has an affair with Ulrich Hargenau in Walter Abish's *How German Is It*.

**Marly Hellmich**   Cafeteria server at Moo University; a member of the Creation Science church, where she meets and agrees to marry Nils Harstad; abandons him after finding out about his plans to have six children and move to Eastern Europe; moves to California in Jane Smiley's *Moo*.

**Hellos**   Voluptuous woman of supernatural powers; murdered by Scarecrow in Calvin Hernton's *Scarecrow*.

**Ken Helm**   Handyman for the Murray family in Alice Hoffman's *Here on Earth*.

**Trish Helmsley**   Rich and shallow friend of Oscar Crease and Christina Lutz who flaunts her wealth in William Gaddis's *A Frolic of His Own*.

**William Hencher**   Boarder who induces Michael Banks to help him to steal a horse, Rock Castle, to win one race in John Hawkes's *The Lime Twig*.

**Brooks Hendell**   Divorced Jewish lawyer who marries and divorces Katherine Dunn in Judith Rossner's *Looking for Mr. Goodbar*.

**Katherine Dunn Hendell**   See Katherine Dunn.

**Clarence (Clarie) Henderson**   Professor of English at the University of California; former member of the black high school athletic team and neighborhood gang gathering for a birthday testimonial honoring Chappie Davis in John A. Williams's *The Junior Bachelor Society*.

**Johnny Henderson**   Humorless young man who does Frances Beecham's yard work in Mary McGarry Morris's *A Dangerous Woman*.

**Mrs. (Suzy) Hendrick**   Owner of the small-town Kentucky hotel in which Old Jack Beechum lives out his final days in Wendell Berry's *A Place on Earth* and *The Memory of Old Jack*.

**Billy Hendricks**   Tall senior first baseman on Norm Fermoyle's baseball team; Norm beats him up for making fun of his father and brother in Mary McGarry Morris's *Songs in Ordinary Time*.

**Eddy Hendricks**   Father of Billy Hendricks in Mary McGarry Morris's *Songs in Ordinary Time*.

**Pamela (Pam) Hendricks**   Sexually aggressive young mistress of John Wilder; encourages him to make a movie about his mental hospital experiences in Richard Yates's *Disturbing the Peace*.

**Abigail Morton Henley**   First wife of Edward Henley; divorces him after he pays a sixteen-year-old Irish woman $10,000 to bear his child in Shirley Ann Grau's *Evidence of Love*.

**Edward Milton Henley**   Veteran of several marriages and numerous love affairs; focal character who narrates part of Shirley Ann Grau's *Evidence of Love*.

**Eleanor Halsey Henley**   Second wife of Edward Henley in Shirley Ann Grau's *Evidence of Love*.

**Lucy Roundtree Evans Henley**   First wife of Stephen Henley; narrates part of Shirley Ann Grau's *Evidence of Love*.

**Stephen Henley**    Son of Edward Henley and a young Irish woman; becomes a Unitarian minister; narrates part of Shirley Ann Grau's *Evidence of Love*.

**Thomas Henley**    Son of Lucy and Stephen Henley; takes after his promiscuous grandfather, Edward Henley; lives in Chicago and collects art in Shirley Ann Grau's *Evidence of Love*.

**Tom Hennessey**    Judge at Martha Horgan's trial who refuses to make her have an abortion in Mary McGarry Morris's *A Dangerous Woman*.

**Lloyd Henreid**    Aide to Randall Flagg in Stephen King's *The Stand*.

**Henri**    Chef for the Paradise Inn who is dazzled by the past; contributes recipes to Renate's planned magazine in Anaïs Nin's *Collages*.

**Henri**    Lover of Chantal and Honorine; poet, former mental patient, and closest friend of Papa; with Chantal, an unwilling passenger in the car in John Hawkes's *Travesty*.

**William Henriksen**    Former FBI Hostage Rescue Team agent, founder of Global Security, and environmental radical who works with Brightling's Horizon Group; plans and supervises the failed attempt to infect the crowds at the Olympics with the Shiva virus; is exiled by John Clark into the rain forest outside the Project compound in Brazil in Tom Clancy's *Rainbow Six*.

**Francisco (Pancho, Papancho) Henriquez**    Dominican-American citizen who studies medicine in France for four years; briefly president of the Dominican Republic; husband of Salome Urena and father of Salome Camila in Julia Alvarez's *In the Name of Salome*.

**Henry**    Crusty but benevolent grocer; friend of Annie Brown and inspiration for her first paid piece of writing in Betty Smith's *Joy in the Morning*.

**Henry**    Crew member on Thomas Hudson's antisubmarine patrol boat in Ernest Hemingway's *Islands in the Stream*.

**Henry**    One of the seven dwarfs who wash windows, make Chinese baby food, and live with Snow White in Donald Barthelme's *Snow White*.

**Byron Henry**    Son of Victor and Rhoda; brother of Warren and Madeline; married to Natalie; father of Louis; serves in submarines during World War II; reunited with wife at war's end; through his efforts his missing son is located in Herman Wouk's *War and Remembrance*.

**James Lee Henry**    Husband of Velma; father of James Lee; nicknamed Obie; runs the 7 Arts Academy; upset by his wife's increasing distance from him and her suicide attempt; has a hopeful vision of the future as his wife is healed in Toni Cade Bambara's *The Salt Eaters*.

**Janice Henry**    Daughter of a senator; married to Warren Henry; mother of Vic; after husband's death has an affair with Carter Aster, her brother-in-law's commanding officer; returns to Washington, D.C., and attends law school in Herman Wouk's *War and Remembrance*.

**Jubal Henry**    Longtime janitor at the high school in Tipton, North Carolina, where Joe Robert Kirkman is a teacher; runs a still and has secret room in school basement to memorialize the war dead among former students; claims to have clairvoyant powers in Fred Chappell's *Brighten the Corner Where You Are*.

**Kovel (Shot) Henry**    Husband of Tisha Dees in Arthenia J. Bates's *The Deity Nodded*.

**Lil James Henry**    Teenage son of Velma and James Lee; known also as Jibari in Toni Cade Bambara's *The Salt Eaters*.

**Louis Henry**    Son of Natalie and Byron; survives concentration camp by escape organized by his great-uncle's cousin; postwar whereabouts unknown; eventually located by father and reunited with mother in Herman Wouk's *War and Remembrance*.

**Madeline Henry**    Daughter of Victor and Rhoda; sister of Warren and Byron; works as an aide and writer to married radio comedian, with whom she is having an affair; eventually leaves him and marries a Navy officer in Herman Wouk's *War and Remembrance*.

**Natalie Jastrow Henry**    Niece of Aaron Jastrow, wife of Byron, mother of Louis; stranded in Europe with her uncle during World War II; transported to Auschwitz; as German war effort disintegrates, found by Russian troops; suffers from disease and mental distress but begins to recover when son is found by Byron in Herman Wouk's *War and Remembrance*.

**Rhoda Henry**    Victor's wife; mother of Warren, Madeline, and Byron; having affair with a physicist; asks husband for divorce but rescinds request after Warren's death; suspects husband is having an affair with Pamela Tudsbury; begins platonic relationship with Harrison Peters; divorces husband and marries Peters in Herman Wouk's *War and Remembrance*.

**Susan Henry**    Lover of Jade Butterfield before Jade's reunion with David Axelrod in Scott Spencer's *Endless Love*.

**Tisha Dees Henry**    See Tisha Dees.

**Velma Henry**    Wife of James Lee; mother of Lil James; computer consultant, activist in civil rights, environmental, and feminist causes; attempts suicide; healed by Minnie Ransom and comes into her heritage as a person capable of spiritual and psychic knowledge to help self and others in Toni Cade Bambara's *The Salt Eaters*.

**Victor "Pug" Henry**    Husband of Rhoda; father of Warren, Madeline, and Byron; has long loved Pamela Tudsbury but will not have an affair with her; learns of his wife's infidelity and divorces her; during World War II, becomes naval attaché of President Truman; after the war translates work of a German historian; marries Pamela in Herman Wouk's *War and Remembrance*.

**Warren Henry**    Son of Victor and Rhoda; brother of Byron and Madeline; married to Janice Henry; father of Vic; naval aviator; after successful bombing runs at Midway, dies when plane is hit during mop-up operation to destroy an already crippled ship in Herman Wouk's *War and Remembrance*.

**Conrad Hensely**    Worker in warehouse of Crocker Global Foods; after being laid off, series of circumstances results in his imprisonment; while in jail reads Epictetus and other Stoic philosophers; escapes from jail; flees to Atlanta and becomes a home care worker; converts Charles Croker to Stoicism in Tom Wolfe's *A Man In Full*.

**John Everett Henshaw**    Rancher and first husband of Tasmania Orcino in Jessamyn West's *A Matter of Time*.

**Andrew (Jake) Hepburn III**    Close friend of Robert Mueller; killed in a mugging in Nicholas Delbanco's *Fathering*.

**Mr. Herald**    Apartment building manager who tells Terry Bluvard to get rid of her black friend or leave in Ann Allen Shockley's *Loving Her*.

**Binky Herebonde**    Husband of Velma Herebonde, father of two babies; a poor relation of Frances Beecham in Mary McGarry Morris's *A Dangerous Woman*.

**Velma Herebonde**    Wife of Binky Herebonde, mother of two babies, burned out from drugs in Mary McGarry Morris's *A Dangerous Woman*.

**Leon Herlitz**    Ironic psychologist who counsels James Boswell to become a strongman; the result is a fate in direct opposition to Boswell's character in Stanley Elkin's *Boswell*.

**Eric Herman**    Fiancé of Betsy Chase; senior proctor and teacher of ancient history at Haddan School; has a feud with Helen Davis; cares much more about his career advancement than his students; Betsy dumps him for Abel Gray in Alice Hoffman's *The River King*.

**Doctor Hernandez**    Mexican physician of Golconda who becomes a friend of Lillian Beye and is murdered for opposing drug trafficking in his community in Anaïs Nin's *Seduction of the Minotaur*.

**The Hero (Lord Nelson)**    British admiral; husband of Fanny; has stepson, Josiah, he takes to sea with him; becomes Emma's lover; participation in the White Terror that follows the suppression of the Neapolitan Republic shows him to be vindictive and self-righteous; fathers Emma's child; is made second in command of the Channel Fleet; dies in battle in Susan Sontag's *The Volcano Lover*.

**Kenneth der Herr**    Biologist; presidential science adviser regarding the alien palimpsest and building of the Machine; Eleanor Arrowyay's love interest for majority of Carl Sagan's *Contact*.

**George Herrold**    Black man who hears George Giles crying in the computer and pulls him out; later rendered insane in John Barth's *Giles Goat-Boy*.

**Sam Herschberger**    War comrade who loans C. Card five dollars in Richard Brautigan's *Dreaming of Babylon*.

**Elizabeth DeWitt (Libby) Herz**    Unhealthy and unhappy young woman married to Paul Herz; finds some measure of contentment in her role as an adoptive mother in Philip Roth's *Letting Go*.

**Karen Herz**    Young farm woman involved in an obsessive love affair in Joyce Carol Oates's *With Shuddering Fall*.

**Mr. Herz**    Stern farmer and father of Karen Herz in Joyce Carol Oates's *With Shuddering Fall*.

**Paul Herz**    Aspiring novelist and professor of English whose marriage to Libby DeWitt alienates his parents and creates many responsibilities and difficulties for him in Philip Roth's *Letting Go*.

**Hermann Herzenbrecher**    Pharmacist and employer of Konrad Vost in John Hawkes's *The Passion Artist*.

**June (Junie) Herzog**    Precocious small daughter of Moses Herzog who loves his "most of every type" stories and whose ostensible vulnerability to emotional pain almost leads Herzog to murder Val Gersbach in Saul Bellow's *Herzog*.

**Madeleine Pontritter (Mady) Herzog**    Unfaithful second wife of Moses Herzog, mother of June Herzog, and lover of Val Gersbach; intelligent, beautiful, haughty, histrionic, unpredictable, and vindictive in Saul Bellow's *Herzog*.

**Mim Herzog**    School board member accidentally discovered by George Caldwell to be having an affair with Louis Zimmerman in John Updike's *The Centaur*.

**Moses Elkanah (Butterfingers, Fishbones, Fuckyknuckles, Ikey-Fishbones, Ikey-Moe, Mose, Moshe) Herzog**    Unemployed history professor with a Ph.D., wealthy siblings, displaced children, an adulterous second wife, an important scholarly book (*Romanticism and Christianity*), a faithful friend, a devoted mistress, a disorderly career, and assorted problems that intensify the central conflict between his intellect and his sensibilities; tormented protagonist and "suffering joker" of Saul Bellow's *Herzog*.

**Harvey Hess**    Pool player who thinks he can beat Billy Phelan; wears expensive suits and atrocious ties and socks in William Kennedy's *Billy Phelan's Greatest Game*.

**Mrs. Hess**   Old woman whose room is directly below Martha Horgan's in Claire Mayo's boardinghouse in Mary McGarry Morris's *A Dangerous Woman*.

**Jacob (Jake) Hesse**   Owner of a chain of shoe stores and second husband of Orpha Chase in Jessamyn West's *The Life I Really Lived*.

**Mrs. Hesse**   See Orpha Chase.

**Hester**   Would-be love of Tom More in the counterculture, who has rejected technology to live in the swamps in Walker Percy's *Love in the Ruins*.

**Helen (Moms) Hettinger**   Wife of Karl Hettinger in Joseph Wambaugh's *The Onion Field*.

**Karl Hettinger**   Los Angeles policeman and partner of Ian Campbell; kidnapped and nearly killed by Gregory Powell and Jimmy Smith in Joseph Wambaugh's *The Onion Field*.

**Jack Hewitt**   Handsome young former pro-baseball player whose sports injury returns him to the very small-town life he sought to escape; in his attempts to transcend the barriers of class he earns the antagonism that results in his own murder; boyfriend of Hettie Rodgers and close friend of Wade Whitehouse in Russell Banks's *Affliction*.

**Gavin Hexam**   Lawyer and former husband of N. Hexam in Diane Johnson's *The Shadow Knows*.

**N. Hexam**   Paranoid narrator who believes someone is plotting to kill her; lover of Andrew Mason and former wife of Gavin Hexam in Diane Johnson's *The Shadow Knows*.

**Karl Heykoop**   Dutch husband of Polly Heykoop and philanderer who has an affair with Penelope MacMahon in Gail Godwin's *The Perfectionists*.

**Polly Heykoop**   American wife of Karl Heykoop and mother of twin girls; keeps a secret photograph album of her husband's sexual conquests in Gail Godwin's *The Perfectionists*.

**Marvin Heywood**   Owner of the Pink Dragon Bar, watering hole for petty criminals on patrolman Bumper Morgan's beat in Joseph Wambaugh's *The Blue Knight*.

**Sophie Heywood**   Godmother of Velma Henry; has magic and spiritual knowledge and powers; present at Velma's healing and realizes Velma is now ready for psychic and spiritual training in Toni Cade Bambara's *The Salt Eaters*.

**Li Van Hgoc**   Major in the Fourth Viet Cong Battalion who is in charge of the tunnel system; a condemned deserter who believes that the land is America's enemy in Vietnam in Tim O'Brien's *Going after Cacciato*.

**Preston Hibbard**   Former prep school classmate of Bing Lockwood; marries Tina Lockwood in John O'Hara's *The Lockwood Concern*.

**Alonzo Zuber Hickman**   Black Baptist minister; was a jazz musician and ladies' man before his brother was lynched and his mother died; raises Adam Sunraider to be a boy preacher; stays with Sunraider in the hospital after Sunraider is shot in Ralph Ellison's *Juneteenth*.

**James Butler (Duck Bill, Wild Bill) Hickok**   Nervous gunslinger of the American West and friend of Jack Crabb in Thomas Berger's *Little Big Man*.

**Richard Eugene (Dick) Hickock**   Mastermind of the crime against the Clutter family; persuades Perry Smith to become his partner in robbery and murder in Truman Capote's *In Cold Blood*.

**Dickey Hicks**   Son adopted by Lewis and Ginny Hicks in an attempt to assuage the loss after the suicide of her brother, Richard Page, in John Gardner's *October Light*.

**Raymond (Cap, Ray) Hicks**   American sailor who smuggles heroin into the United States for John Converse; chased into hiding by Antheil in Robert Stone's *Dog Soldiers*.

**Uwis Hicks**   Swamp Yankee and part-Indian handyman whose closeness to the rhythms of nature helps restore a sense of balance in the conflict between James Page and Sally Page Abbott in John Gardner's *October Light*.

**Virginia Page (Ginny) Hicks**   Sensible daughter of James Page; her unintentional near-death at the hands of Sally Page Abbott quiets the violence within the family in John Gardner's *October Light*.

**Walter (Wally) Hicks**   Left-leaning National Security Agency staffer who betrays Clark Kelly's mission to rescue American POWs to the Russians through his friend and fellow spy, Peter Henderson; dies when Kelly forces him to take an overdose of heroin in Tom Clancy's *Without Remorse*.

**Samuel Higginbottham**   Second factor in Fort St. Sebastian; takes over Cephus Prynne's job as chief factor when he is murdered in Bharati Mukherjee's *The Holder of the World*.

**Sarah Higginbottham**   Wife of Samuel; arrived on a company allowance to find a mate and accepted his proposal one week before she would have had to return to England; dies when she is bitten by a rabid flying fox in Bharati Mukherjee's *The Holder of the World*.

**Elly Higginbottom**   See Esther Greenwood.

**Doc Higgins**   Proprietor of Doc Higgins's Tonsorial Palace; bribes his friend, a postmaster, to prevent Jack Jackson's being fired in Richard Wright's *Lawd Today*.

**Hondo Higgins**   Television star and pornographic movie mogul who helps Stormy Claridge further her career in return for sexual favors in Peter Gent's *Texas Celebrity Turkey Trot*.

**Janet Higgins**   Friend of Lucie Proctorr; the director of Jack Wagner's play, a native Floridian who has directed half a dozen off-Broadway plays and has considerable experience in regional theater in Donald E. Westlake's *The Hook.*

**Frances Highsmith**   Aggressive woman who dominates Johnny Strange and causes his belated sexual awakening in James Jones's *Whistle.*

**Robert Highsmith**   Lawyer for Adam Kelno, member of the House of Commons, and head of the British office of Sanctuary International in Leon Uris's *QB VII.*

**Dr. Hilarius**   Psychotherapist of Oedipa Maas; conducts experiments with LSD; formerly worked at Buchenwald in Thomas Pynchon's *The Crying of Lot 49.*

**Hilda (The Dove)**   Fellow guest editor with Esther Greenwood for a New York fashion magazine; pleased that the Rosenbergs will be executed in Sylvia Plath's *The Bell Jar.*

**Mrs. Hildebrand**   Housekeeper for Bryce Proctorr when he moves to Connecticut; a widow in her late sixties; formerly a nutritionist in a private school; a quiet, efficient woman in Donald E. Westlake's *The Hook.*

**Hildon**   Maureen's husband and Lucy Spenser's lover and friend; began *Country Daze* magazine, but sells it and remains editor until he resigns; Maureen divorces him and he moves from Vermont to Boston in Ann Beattie's *Love Always.*

**Maureen Hildon**   Hildon's wife and Matt Smith's lover; jealous of Lucy Spenser; perfectionist; joins a militant feminist group and files for divorce in Ann Beattie's *Love Always.*

**Ambrose Powell Hill**   Irritable Southern general in Michael Shaara's *The Killer Angels.*

**Dr. Hill**   Well-meaning young obstetrician who unknowingly turns Rosemary Woodhouse over to devil worshippers when she comes to him for help in Ira Levin's *Rosemary's Baby.*

**Fiorio (Fifi) Hill**   Brilliant film director who wins an Oscar as best director for his work on Vito Orsini's *Mirrors* in Judith Krantz's *Scruples.*

**Gertrude Hill**   Former teacher, mother of Meridian Hill, and earliest source of her daughter's feelings of guilt in Alice Walker's *Meridian.*

**Meridian Hill**   Compassionate civil rights activist who suffers from psychosomatic paralysis in Alice Walker's *Meridian.*

**Ev Hillman**   Grandfather of Hilly and David Brown; tries to warn others about the mysterious force in Haven; goes with trooper Butch (Monster) Dugan to investigate the site of the force in Stephen King's *The Tommyknockers.*

**Joshua Isaiah (Josh) Hillman**   Lawyer for Billy Orsini; handles all of her business affairs and falls in love with Valentine O'Neill in Judith Krantz's *Scruples.*

**Ralph Himebaugh**   Sexually repressed attorney whose numerological model of the end of the world is merged with Eleanor Norton's mystic model in Robert Coover's *The Origin of the Brunists.*

**Sandor Himmelstein**   Chicago lawyer of Madeleine Herzog; provides temporary lodging and fierce advice to the displaced Moses Herzog in Saul Bellow's *Herzog.*

**Hinderov**   Passenger on the *Here They Come* who plans to use an American Express office as a distribution center for bombs in Gregory Corso's *The American Express.*

**Bernard (Bernie) Hinds**   Young cousin of the monsignor; ill with cancer; tries to refuse chemotherapy in Mary McGarry Morris's *Songs in Ordinary Time.*

**Cleveland Hinds**   Lover of Hildie Carper in Mary McGarry Morris's *Songs in Ordinary Time.*

**Nora Hinds**   Cousin of the monsignor; mother of Bernie in Mary McGarry Morris's *Songs in Ordinary Time.*

**Mother Hines**   Possessive mother of Wally Hines in Peter De Vries's *The Vale of Laughter.*

**Wally Hines**   Psychology instructor at Wilton College, theorist of comedy and laughter, and former teacher of Joe Sandwich; Sandwich cuckolds him and later marries his widow; narrates part of Peter De Vries's *The Vale of Laughter.*

**Big Hing**   See Chop Hing, Kheng Fatt.

**Horace Hinton**   Black director of the social services office where Bruno Fisher and Eric Eisner work; carries a gun in order to intimidate students in Phillip Lopate's *Confessions of Summer.*

**Hippolyte**   Narrator who recounts his dream and real life in Susan Sontag's *The Benefactor.*

**Heinrich Hirsch**   Secretary of education, culture, and information in post–World War II Berlin, who defects to the American sector in Leon Uris's *Armageddon.*

**Mr. Hirsch**   Uncle of Aaron Lublin; moves into the Lublin family's 70th Street apartment in Edward Lewis Wallant's *The Tenants of Moonbloom.*

**Hishan (John)**   Adele's ex-husband and Ann August's father; Egyptian who had been Adele's professor in college; leaves them when Jill is about two years old to move to California; Ann sees him only twice after he leaves them in Mona Simpson's *Anywhere but Here.*

**Mr. and Mrs. Hoaglund**    Managers of N. Hexam's apartment in Diane Johnson's *The Shadow Knows.*

**Hoak**    Sailor who helps Charlie Stark save Raditzer from murder in Peter Matthiessen's *Raditzer.*

**Bob Hobart**    Seventeen-year-old classmate of Martha Horgan who is the gang leader in a group of twelve boys who rip her clothes off, pour beer on her, and poke her with sticks in Mary McGarry Morris's *A Dangerous Woman.*

**Pie Hobson**    Roommate of Carlin Leander in Alice Hoffman's *The River King.*

**Hock**    Resident of Harmony House, a home for retarded adults in Mary McGarry Morris's *A Dangerous Woman.*

**Arthur Taggert (Old Man) Hodge, Sr.**    Patriarch known for his tolerance of each of his children's search for selfhood—the equivalent of his view, as a congressman, of democracy—in John Gardner's *The Sunlight Dialogues.*

**Benjamin (Ben) Hodge, Sr.**    Foster father of Indian brothers after the death of his own son in Korea in John Gardner's *The Sunlight Dialogues.*

**Kathleen Paxton Hodge**    Wife of Taggert Hodge; driven into a catatonic state by her father, Clive Paxton, in John Gardner's *The Sunlight Dialogues.*

**Luke Hodge**    Son of Millie and William Hodge, Sr.; sacrifices his life to reunite his parents; his death persuades his uncle, Taggert Hodge, to surrender to the law in John Gardner's *The Sunlight Dialogues.*

**Mildred Jewel (Millie) Hodge**    Divorced wife of William Hodge, Sr., and mother of Luke Hodge; almost committed as insane by William because she understands the complexities of love, which seems clear and simple to him in John Gardner's *The Sunlight Dialogues.*

**Taggert Faeley (The Sunlight Man, Tag) Hodge**    Husband of Kathleen Paxton Hodge; returns to Batavia, New York, to avenge her brutalization by Clive Paxton in John Gardner's *The Sunlight Dialogues.*

**William B. (Will) Hodge, Sr.**    Lawyer enraged that he is only the second choice of his wife, Millie Hodge; love for their son, Luke, redeems him in John Gardner's *The Sunlight Dialogues.*

**Marion (Sister Mary) Hodgkiss**    Intellectual Marine radio operator and friend of Danny Forrester; killed at Saipan in Leon Uris's *Armageddon.*

**Dr. Luther Hodler**    Swiss physician who imagines Cynthia Pomeroy as Nausicaä in Wright Morris's *What a Way to Go.*

**Harry Hoekstra**    Native from Amsterdam who meets and then weds Ruth Cole; an ex-cop, he provides Ruth with the un-conditional love she needs after being abandoned by her mother, Marion, in John Irving's *A Widow for One Year.*

**Angela (Mrs. Harrison C. Conners) Hoenikker**    Saxophonist and sister of Newton and Frank Hoenikker in Kurt Vonnegut's *Cat's Cradle.*

**Dr. Felix Hoenikker**    Father of the atom bomb, Ice-9, and Frank, Angela, and Newton Hoenikker in Kurt Vonnegut's *Cat's Cradle.*

**Franklin (Frank) Hoenikker**    Older brother of Newton and Angela Hoenikker and adviser to President Papa Monzano in Kurt Vonnegut's *Cat's Cradle.*

**Newton (Little Newt) Hoenikker**    Midget brother of Frank and Angela Hoenikker; painter in Kurt Vonnegut's *Cat's Cradle.*

**Ferenc Hofmann-Beck**    Employee of a French publishing company and friend of the Gallaghers; appears for many of the gatherings of expatriate Americans at the Gallagher home in James Jones's *The Merry Month of May.*

**Major Hogan**    Antagonistic and disapproving doctor at Kilrainey Army Hospital whose responsibility it is to return wounded men to duty as soon as possible in James Jones's *Whistle.*

**Miranda Hogendobber**    Elderly, Bible-thumping widow who is good friends with Mary Minor Haristeen and plays matchmaker for her; knows Monticello like the back of her hand in Rita Mae Brown's *Murder at Monticello.* In *Cat on the Scent,* she works without pay as the postmistress.

**Boon Hogganbeck**    See Volume I.

**Everbe Corinthia (Miss Corrie) Hogganbeck**    Prostitute who marries Boon Hogganbeck in William Faulkner's *The Reivers.*

**Lucius Priest Hogganbeck**    See Volume I.

**Anna Holbrook**    Wife of Jim Holbrook and mother of Mazie and other Holbrook children; inspires her poor family with her poetic yearnings in Tillie Olsen's *Yonnondio.*

**Jim Holbrook**    Bitter husband and father of a 1920s family brutalized by poverty; searches from mining town to farm to industrial city for a better way of life in Tillie Olsen's *Yonnondio.*

**Mazie (Big-eyes) Holbrook**    Oldest Holbrook child who, though often terrified by life, still wonders and dreams about the world in Tillie Olsen's *Yonnondio,* much of which is told from Mazie's point of view.

**Billie Holiday**    Singer whose life and music are invoked in Alice Adams's *Listening to Billie.*

**Grandma Holland**    Takes care of her granddaughter, Dolores, after her daughter Bernice is institutionalized and later killed in a car accident; Dolores inherits her house in Westerly, Rhode Island, in Wally Lamb's *She's Come Undone.*

**Jay Hollander**   Falconing expert in William Bayer's *Peregrine;* brought in to assist Pam Barrett with her investigation of the killer peregrine falcon; trains his peregrine falcon to kill pretty young girls.

**Cora Holley**   Fabian Vas's fourth cousin and wife by an arranged marriage; they never see each other after the wedding in Howard Norman's *The Bird Artist.*

**Hollis**   Man March Murray has been in love with for most of her life; becomes the richest man in Jenkintown through insurance fraud schemes; called Mr. Death behind his back; loses his wife and his son, Coop; he and March move in together, but she eventually leaves because of his abusive behavior; dies in a car wreck in Alice Hoffman's *Here on Earth.*

**Blix Murphy Hollister**   Younger sister of Tasmania Ofcino; enlists Tasmania's help in dying when her cancer becomes unbearable in Jessamyn West's *A Matter of Time.*

**Captain Hollister**   Head of the secret government organization called the Shop; has Charlie and Andrew McGee pursued across the country so he can control Charlie's powers to influence world leaders in Stephen King's *Firestarter.*

**Milt Hollister**   Young widower who becomes Blix Hollister's husband in Jessamyn West's *A Matter of Time.*

**Frank Holliwell**   Anthropologist, professor, Vietnam veteran, and heavy drinker; is asked by American Intelligence to travel to Tecan to find out what is going on; travels to Compostela to give a lecture, and afterward, travels to Tecan; meets Sister Justin while snorkeling and falls in love with her; is in Tecan when the revolution starts and escapes with Pablo Tabor in the mission's boat; kills Pablo in Robert Stone's *A Flag for Sunrise.*

**Charles Hollopeter**   Pasadena attorney who defends Jimmy Smith in Smith's second murder trial in Joseph Wambaugh's *The Onion Field.*

**Holly**   Lover and coworker of Molly Bolt in New York City in Rita Mae Brown's *Rubyfruit Jungle.*

**Ernie Holm**   Divorced father of Helen Holm; Steering School wrestling coach who dies while reading a pornographic magazine in John Irving's *The World According to Garp.*

**Helen Holm**   Daughter of Steering Academy wrestling coach; wife of T. S. Garp and mother of Duncan, Walt, and Jenny Garp; respected college English teacher who has an affair with Michael Milton; cremated in John Irving's *The World According to Garp.*

**Ben Holmes**   Black friend of Susie Schnitzer in Harriette Simpson Arnow's *The Weedkiller's Daughter.*

**Tina Marie (Teeny Marie) Holt**   Bald, breastless, one-legged, and one-eyed actress in Terry Southern's *Blue Movie.*

**Konrad Holzapfel**   German tourist baited by Jewish Adrien Perkheimer in Wright Morris's *What a Way to Go.*

**Sim Homby**   Half-breed and one of Jane Nail's attackers; killed in the raid on the Horse Pens in Jesse Hill Ford's *The Raider.*

**Jacob (Jake) Homer**   Teacher of prescriptive grammar at Wicomico State Teachers College and lover of Rennie Morgan; narrator of John Barth's *The End of the Road.*

**Morris Homestead**   Aristocratic fraternity brother of Abraham Lockwood; later Lockwood's banker and investment partner in John O'Hara's *The Lockwood Concern.*

**Charles Ames Homey**   Educator and author; fearfully eschews the past in Wright Morris's *Cause for Wonder.*

**Honest Lil (Lillian)**   Cuban prostitute and friend of Thomas Hudson in Ernest Hemingway's *Islands in the Stream.*

**Jason Honeygale**   Tennessee writer in John Updike's *Bech: A Book.*

**Clarence Honeywell**   Black mechanic employed by Buddy Sandifer in Thomas Berger's *Sneaky People.*

**Honorine**   Mother of Pascal and Chantal, wife of Papa, and lover of Henri; has a tattoo of pale purple grapes with yellow stems below her navel; sleeps at home, unaware of her husband's grisly plan in John Hawkes's *Travesty.*

**Wayne Hoobler**   Prison parolee drawn to Dwayne Hoover in Kurt Vonnegut's *Breakfast of Champions.*

**Valentine (Val) Hood**   Fugitive American consul in Vietnam; involved with gunrunners and would-be terrorists in London in Paul Theroux's *The Family Arsenal.*

**Charlie Hooker**   Lover of Neva Manning and farmworker intent on founding a religion based on honesty, self-acceptance, and racial reconciliation in Hal Bennett's *A Wilderness of Vines.*

**Skipper (Cap, Hipless) Hooker**   Fanatical deep-sea fisherman and Los Angeles police captain of Hollywood Station's detective division in Joseph Wambaugh's *The Black Marble.*

**Alvin Hooks**   Prosecuting attorney in the trial of Kabuo Miyamoto in David Guterson's *Snow Falling on Cedars.*

**Bentley T. Hooks**   Disillusioned son of a revival preacher; offers Brooke Kincaid her one chance to live authentically in Lee Smith's *Something in the Wind.*

**Hookworm**   See Elijah J. Cartwright.

**Matthew (Matt) Hooper**   Oceanographer who helps identify and hunt the Great White Shark in Peter Benchley's *Jaws.*

**Hank Hoos**   Kansas primitive sanitorium roommate of Don Wanderhope in Peter De Vries's *The Blood of the Lamb.*

**Celia Hoover**   Wife of Dwayne Hoover and mother of Bunny Hoover; commits suicide in Kurt Vonnegut's *Breakfast of Champions*.

**Dwayne Hoover**   Husband of Celia Hoover, father of Bunny Hoover, and Pontiac dealer who goes insane in Kurt Vonnegut's *Breakfast of Champions*.

**George (Bunny) Hoover**   Homosexual pianist and son of Dwayne and Celia Hoover in Kurt Vonnegut's *Breakfast of Champions*.

**Anthony (Jeeves) Hope-Harding**   Frame-maker and lover of two sisters, Maija von Einzeedle and Elise Crawford; dies of cancer in Nicholas Delbanco's *Small Rain*.

**Janet Hope-Harding**   Mother of Anthony Hope-Harding in Nicholas Delbanco's *Small Rain*.

**Sally Thwaites Hopwood**   Fallen-away Catholic and daughter of Mrs. Andrew Thwaites; alone on an island in a small lake with Father Urban she proposes a swim in the nude and disrobes in front of him; insulted by his refusal of the seduction, she maroons him in J. F. Powers's *Morte D'Urban*.

**Floyd Horgan**   Martha Horgan's father, who dies when she is thirty-one; widowed when Martha is a year and a half old; Horace Beecham's caretaker; brother of Frances Beecham in Mary McGarry Morris's *A Dangerous Woman*.

**Martha Horgan**   Woman tormented by a gang of boys at the age of seventeen who grows to be a tormented adult; takes a job at Kolditis Cleaners and a room in Claire Mayo's boardinghouse until she is fired and moves back in with her aunt Frances; gets pregnant with Colin "Mack" Mackey's child; is kicked out of her aunt's house; moves in with Ben Weilman until she murders Getso and is arrested in Mary McGarry Morris's *A Dangerous Woman*.

**Mrs. Horowitz**   Superstitious neighbor of the Luries who leaves David Lurie a collection of books on higher Biblical criticism in Chaim Potok's *In the Beginning*.

**Horst**   German member of the CIA in Ceramos under the guise of an archaeological dig in Mary Lee Settle's *Blood Tie*.

**Emma Greenway Horton**   Daughter of Aurora Greenway, wife of Thomas Horton, and mother of Melanie, Teddy, and Tommy Horton; following the collapse of her marriage, she dies of cancer in Larry McMurtry's *Terms of Endearment;* appears in *Moving On* and *All My Friends Are Going to Be Strangers*.

**Melanie, Teddy, and Tommy Horton**   Children of Emma and Thomas Horton and grandchildren of Aurora Greenway in Larry McMurtry's *Term of Endearment;* Teddy and Tommy also appear in *Moving On;* Tommy appears in *All My Friends Are Going to Be Strangers*.

**Thomas (Flap) Horton**   Husband of Emma Greenway Horton, father of Melanie, Teddy, and Tommy Horton, and son-in-law of Aurora Greenway; second-rate graduate student and professor of English; appears in Larry McMurtry's *Terms of Endearment, Moving On,* and *All My Friends Are Going to Be Strangers*.

**Hospital Tommy**   Co-owner of a local barbershop and member of the racial revenge group known as the Seven Days in Toni Morrison's *Song of Solomon*.

**Rudolph Franz Höss**   Commandant of Auschwitz concentration camp and employer of Sophie Zawistowska for a brief period; sentenced and executed during the Nuremberg trials in William Styron's *Sophie's Choice*.

**Harry (Erich Weiss) Houdini**   Magician and escape artist who stops at Father's house and who tries to contact his dead mother through séances in E. L. Doctorow's *Ragtime*.

**Ted Houlihan**   Recently widowed, retired engineer who puts his remodeled American farmhouse in Penns Neck, New Jersey, on the real estate market; is moving to Tucson for cancer treatment and to live with his surgeon son; is nostalgic and touchingly sentimental about his home, but also proves to be a shrewd businessman in Richard Ford's *Independence Day*.

**Howard**   Art critic; husband of Tania, an artist, who is killed at the party in Robert Coover's *Gerald's Party*.

**Howard**   Only black member of the board of review for the post office in Richard Wright's *Lawd Today*.

**Rosanna Howard**   Wealthy student of Isadora Wing and her lover in Erica Jong's *How to Save Your Own Life*.

**Sara Howard**   Brave, determined New York City police department secretary who assists psychologist Dr. Lazlo Kriezler and crime reporter John Moore in solving a series of grisly adolescent murders in Caleb Carr's *The Alienist*.

**Captain (Nowonmai, Satan) Howdy**   Overpowering demonic possessor of Regan MacNeil's mind and body in William Peter Blatty's *The Exorcist*.

**Annie Jordan Howe**   Wife of Dr. George Howe; once the most beautiful girl in the village of Haddan; George tells her he will release her from their unhappy marriage if she can turn a white rose red, but he fails to do so when she covers a white rose with her blood; hangs herself while pregnant in Alice Hoffman's *The River King*.

**Elena Ross (Elena Kármán) Howe**   Beautiful young blonde married to the domineering lawyer Marvin Howe; seeks to define herself through an adulterous affair with Jack Morrissey in Joyce Carol Oates's *Do with Me What You Will*.

**Dr. George Howe**   Husband of Annie Jordan; one of the first headmasters in Haddan School history; after marriage is found to be jealous and vindictive and turns local people, including his wife's relatives, away from his doors; dies when he nears the century mark in Alice Hoffman's *The River King*.

**Marvin Howe**   Brilliant but ruthless attorney who marries Elena Ross in Joyce Carol Oates's *Do with Me What You Will.*

**Marybeth Howe (Lynn Lord)**   Student radical and fugitive who boards with Anton and Theo Wait under the assumed name of Lynn Lord in Diane Johnson's *Lying Low.*

**Warren P. Howe**   Author and television writer; narrator of events taking place at Schloss Riva in Wright Morris's *Cause for Wonder.*

**Abigail Howland**   See Abigail Howland Mason.

**Margaret Carmichael Howland**   Black housekeeper, mistress, and later wife of William Howland; mother of Robert Carmichael in Shirley Ann Grau's *The Keepers of the House.*

**Robert Carmichael Howland**   Mulatto son of William Howland and Margaret Carmichael; reveals his parents' secret marriage to the press and thereby ruins the political career of John Tolliver in Shirley Ann Grau's *The Keepers of the House.*

**William Howland**   Patriarch of the Howland family secretly married to his black housekeeper; narrates part of Shirley Ann Grau's *The Keepers of the House.*

**Hrothgar**   King of the Scyldings, who, having conquered all adjacent lands, seeks the meaning of life in his old-age ruminations in John Gardner's *Grendel.*

**Hrothulf**   Orphaned nephew of Hrothgar; becomes a pretender to Hrothgar's throne in John Gardner's *Grendel.*

**An-Mei Hsu**   Mother of Rose Hsu Jordan; her mother is a concubine who dies of intentional opium poisoning; immigrates to America; loses faith in God after son, Bing, drowns in Amy Tan's *The Joy Luck Club.*

**Bull (Big Bull) Hubbard**   Novelist and drug addict; accidentally shoots and kills his wife, June, in Jack Kerouac's *Visions of Cody;* also appears in *Doctor Sax, Book of Dreams,* and (as the author of *Nude Supper*) in *Desolation Angels.*

**Caroline Weed Hubble**   Daughter of Frederick Weed, wife of Roger Hubble, mother of Jeremy Hubble, and friend of Conor Larkin in Leon Uris's *Trinity.*

**Jeremy Hubble**   Son of Caroline and Roger Hubble; friend, protégé, and fellow athlete of Conor Larkin; lover of a Catholic woman in Leon Uris's *Trinity.*

**Roger Hubble**   Owner of Hubble Manor, who heads and supports the Ulster Protestants against Irish Catholics; husband of Caroline Weed Hubble and father of Jeremy Hubble in Leon Uris's *Trinity.*

**Hubby**   Exhibitionist who periodically disrobes before his front window during his wife's pregnancy in Carlene Hatcher Polite's *Sister X and the Victims of Foul Play.*

**Andy Huben**   American missionary and wife of Leslie Huben; gradually disillusioned by her husband's childish radical Christianity in Peter Matthiessen's *At Play in the Fields of the Lord.*

**Leslie (Les) Huben**   American missionary, husband of Andy Huben, and bitter foe of Roman Catholicism; mistakenly believes he can convert the Niaruna Indians of South America to his brand of Protestant Christianity in Peter Matthiessen's *At Play in the Fields of the Lord.*

**Hubert**   Twenty-four-year-old man who appears much older; researcher with the Royal Society; is attacked and disfigured by Gabriel's men when Gabriel returns in Bharati Mukherjee's *The Holder of the World.*

**Hubert**   One of the seven dwarfs who wash windows, make Chinese baby food, and live with Snow White in Donald Barthelme's *Snow White.*

**Huck (Old Huck)**   Friend from New York of Bull Hubbard and Irwin Garden; develops boils while visiting Hubbard in Jack Kerouac's *Visions of Cody;* also appears in *Book of Dreams* and *Desolation Angels.*

**Hud (Huddie)**   Son of Jewel Bannon and stepuncle of Lonnie Bannon; rapes Halmea and kills his stepfather, Homer Bannon, in Larry McMurtry's *Horseman, Pass By.*

**Andrew Hudson**   Son of Thomas Hudson; killed in an automobile accident in Ernest Hemingway's *Islands in the Stream.*

**David (Dave, Davy, Mr. David) Hudson**   Son of Thomas Hudson; almost catches a huge fish off Bimini; killed in an automobile accident in Ernest Hemingway's *Islands in the Stream.*

**Thomas Hudson**   Husband of Augusta Drake; Susan Ward's editor in Wallace Stegner's *Angle of Repose.*

**Thomas (Mr. Tom, Tomfis) Hudson**   American painter who helps track down German U-boat sailors in the Caribbean in Ernest Hemingway's *Islands in the Stream.*

**Tom Hudson**   Vietnam vet and older man who falls for Samantha Hughes but suffers from impotence as a result of his war experiences in Bobbie Ann Mason's *In Country.*

**Tom (Schatz) Hudson**   Eldest son of Thomas Hudson; visits his father in Bimini and is later killed in World War II in Ernest Hemingway's *Islands in the Stream.*

**Isaac Huffacre**   Man who teaches Leslie Collins woods skills for survival in Harriette Simpson Arnow's *The Kentucky Trace.*

**Clifford Huffley**   Ordinary but effective successor of the Reverend Jethro Furber after Furber's breakdown in William Gass's *Omensetter's Luck.*

**Allison (Allie) Huger**   Daughter of Will's Barrett's old girlfriend Kitty Vaught; Allie has "made straight A's and flunked ordinary living"; escapes from Valleyhead, the mental hospital where her parents have placed her, claims an inheritance, and begins to build a life based on love with Will Barrett in Walker Percy's *The Second Coming.*

**Katherine (Kitty) Vaught Huger**   Middle-aged, suntanned, gold-braceleted socialite who puts her desire for money ahead of concern for her daughter in Walker Percy's *The Second Coming.*

**Walter Huger**   Kitty's dentist husband who has "passionate and insane views on every subject" in Walker Percy's *The Second Coming.*

**Hugh**   One-armed husband of Catherine, father of Meredith, Dolores, and Eveline, and lover of Fiona; photographer and collector of pornography; forces Catherine to wear a chastity belt in an attempt to stop her affair with Cyril; accidentally hangs himself in his photography studio in John Hawkes's *The Blood Oranges.*

**Charles Windham Hughes**   Friend whom Brooke Kincaid says made her mind; his death precipitates the action of Lee Smith's *Something in the Wind.*

**Dwayne Hughes**   Father of Samantha Hughes and killed in Vietnam before the action of the book but whose journal plays a part in helping Samantha understand her father and uncle Emmet in Bobbie Ann Mason's *In Country.*

**Elbert Hughes**   Youth with remarkable skill at duplicating the handwriting of others; trapped in a scheme to forge famous letters and documents in Thornton Wilder's *Theophilus North.*

**Mamaw Hughes**   Mother of Dwayne Hughes, who travels with Samantha Hughes and Emmet Smith to visit the Vietnam War memorial and may thereby come to terms with the death of her son in Vietnam in Bobbie Ann Mason's *In Country.*

**Ronny (Root) Hughes**   Youngster responsible for the unjust punishment of Jan Anderson; later imprisoned by Anderson in a box supposedly filled with poisonous spiders but actually filled with mice in Fred Chappell's *The Inkling.*

**Samantha Hughes**   Young woman who must come to terms with the impact on her life of the Vietnam War, which changed her uncle Emmet and took the life of her father, whom she never met in Bobbie Ann Mason's *In Country.*

**Alain Hugues**   Husband of Chantal Hugues and guardian of the young Robert Mueller in Nicholas Delbanco's *Fathering.*

**Chantal Hugues**   Wife of Alain Hugues and guardian of Robert Mueller as a child in Nicholas Delbanco's *Fathering.*

**Boon Hulburt**   Father of Lilah Lee and husband of Hetsie, managed Lilah Lee in the rodeo in Maureen Howard's *Natural History.*

**Hetsie Hulburt**   Mother of Lilah Lee and wife of Boon Hulbert; cleans houses and picks almonds in Maureen Howard's *Natural History.*

**Claude Humbold**   Real estate huckster and employer of Carl Reinhart in Thomas Berger's *Reinhart in Love.*

**Al Hummel**   Owner of Hummel's Garage and school board member responsible for George Caldwell's appointment as a teacher; husband of Vera Hummel and nephew of Pop Kramer in John Updike's *The Centaur.*

**Vera Hummel**   Girls' physical education teacher at Olinger High School, widely rumored to have had numerous affairs; wife of Al Hummel in John Updike's *The Centaur.*

**Hump**   Cheyenne war chief in Thomas Berger's *Little Big Man.*

**Hungry Joe**   Hero who holds an air force record for flying the most combat tours of duty; has nightmares when grounded in Joseph Heller's *Catch-22.*

**James (Hawk) Hunn**   Husband of Eva Medina Canada; kills a man in a dispute over a woman in Gayl Jones's *Eva's Man.*

**Cora Zepp Hunsenmeir**   Mother of Louise and Julia Ellen; friend and employer to Celeste Chalfonte and lover to Aimes Rankin; practical and patient; helps Celeste cheat at cards in Rita Mae Brown's *Loose Lips.* Dies of a heart attack at seventy-nine in *Six of One.*

**Hansford Hunsenmeir**   Louise and Julia's father and Cora's husband, who left them when they were young; returns with lung cancer to Cora after thirty-four years away; dies in Rita Mae Brown's *Loose Lips.*

**Adrienne Hunt**   Older of Fonny Hunt's uppity sisters in James Baldwin's *If Beale Street Could Talk.*

**Alonzo (Fonny) Hunt**   Aspiring sculptor and lover of Tish Rivers; sent to prison for rape in James Baldwin's *If Beale Street Could Talk.*

**Frank Hunt**   Father of Fonny Hunt in James Baldwin's *If Beale Street Could Talk.*

**Laura Hunt**   Black fiancée of Roy Fehler; helps him recover from divorce and alcoholism in Joseph Wambaugh's *The New Centurions.*

**Mrs. Hunt**   Pious wife of Frank Hunt and mother of Fonny Hunt in James Baldwin's *If Beale Street Could Talk.*

**Sheila Hunt**   Younger of Fonny Hunt's uppity sisters in James Baldwin's *If Beale Street Could Talk.*

**Thomas Hunt**   Husband of Alma S. Wheeler Hunt; a salesman who travels through the South selling women's underwear; his identity is almost completely subsumed by his domineering wife; has an affair with his sister-in-law, Amanda Wheeler; abandons the Wheeler family and moves to Texas in Bobbie Ann Mason's *Feather Crowns.*

**Clair Hunter**    Daughter of Eloise McLindon and Norman Eisenberg and half sister of David Hunter; seized and killed by an eagle in Hal Bennett's *The Black Wine*.

**Conrad R. Hunter**    Wealthy owner of the Dallas Cowboys in Peter Gent's *North Dallas Forty*.

**David Hunter**    Troubled son of Eloise McLindon and Winston Cobb; his initiation into adulthood is the central focus of Hal Bennett's *The Black Wine*.

**Eloise Hunter**    See Eloise McLindon.

**Emmett John Hunter**    Fiancé of Joanne Remington; business failure who is made president of the Dallas Cowboys by his brother, Conrad Hunter in Peter Gent's *North Dallas Forty*.

**Henry Hunter**    Common-law husband of Eloise McLindon and Korean War veteran dispirited by the segregated North; leaves an ambiguous legacy for his putative son, David Hunter, in Hal Bennett's *The Black Wine*.

**Huple**    Fifteen-year-old pilot who lied about his age to join the air force; lives with his cat in a tent with Hungry Joe in Joseph Heller's *Catch-22*.

**Father Hurlburt**    Part-Seneca Catholic priest on a Montana Indian reservation, whose trustworthiness enables him to befriend and help Ida George and her family in Michael Dorris's *A Yellow Raft in Blue Water*.

**Dana McManus Hurst**    Wife of David Hurst with whom she shares a dental practice; mother of Lizzie, Stephanie, and Leah; sings opera in community productions; leaves David for several days only to return to him, admitting an affair in Jane Smiley's *The Age of Grief*.

**David McManus Hurst**    Husband of Dana McManus Hurst with whom he shares a dental practice; father of Lizzie, Stephanie, and Leah; a participatory father who shares all aspects of child rearing with wife; is obsessed with Dana and suspects her of having an affair; takes her back when eventually she confesses in Jane Smiley's *The Age of Grief*.

**Leah Hurst**    Youngest daughter of Dana and David Hurst; learned to crawl at ten months, and first word was "song," a request for her mother to sing; has recently developed a complete infatuation with David to the point that she refuses to touch or speak to her mother at all in Jane Smiley's *The Age of Grief*.

**Lizzie Hurst**    Oldest daughter of Dana and David Hurst; suffers perpetual stomach problems that are her way of dealing with stress; according to her father has a good sense of humor, distinct fashion tastes, and is naturally graceful in Jane Smiley's *The Age of Grief*.

**Stephanie Hurst**    Middle daughter of Dana and David Hurst; according to her father she is the tomboy in the family and looks at kindergarden as a liberating mechanism; prefers to play at a friend's house rather than her own in Jane Smiley's *The Age of Grief*.

**Anatole Husac**    Father of Neo-Figurism in John Updike's *Bech: A Book*.

**Edward (Hutch) Hutchins**    English-born New York novelist who befriends Rosemary Woodhouse and is killed trying to protect her from devil worshippers in Ira Levin's *Rosemary's Baby*.

**Rachel Hutchins**    Beautiful, seriously disturbed woman who marries Rob Mayfield and dies in childbirth in Reynolds Price's *The Surface of Earth*.

**Raven Hutchins**    Father of Rachel Hutchins in Reynolds Price's *The Surface of Earth*.

**Lyle Hutson**    Most successful lawyer on Bourne Island and a senator in the legislature in Paule Marshall's *The Chosen Place, the Timeless People*.

**Hutten**    Professor married to Käthe Hutten in Katherine Anne Porter's *Ship of Fools*.

**Käthe Hutten**    Childless wife of Professor Hutten; speaks publicly against her husband in Katherine Anne Porter's *Ship of Fools*.

**Rufus (Rufe) Hutton**    White kidnapper and exconvict killed in Shelby Foote's *September September*.

**Yellowbeard Huyghen**    Pirate who had been a butcher in Batavia in Bharati Mukherjee's *The Holder of the World*.

**Gottfried (Son of Gutsy, Texas) Hyde, Jr.**    Best friend of D. J.; goes on the Alaskan hunting expedition in Norman Mailer's *Why Are We in Vietnam?*

**Gottfried (Gotsie, Gutsy) Hyde, Sr.**    Undertaker and father of Tex Hyde in Norman Mailer's *Why Are We in Vietnam?*

**Hygmod**    Lord of the Helmings; overcome in battle, he surrenders his sister, Wealtheow, to the victorious Hrothgar in John Gardner's *Grendel*.

**I**   As a boy, has brief friendship with Cletus Smith; after Smith's father is accused of murder, Smith stops seeing him; encounters Smith in high school after move to Chicago; does not speak to him; feels guilty; as a mature man, researches, reconstructs, and imagines story of Cletus's family in William Maxwell's *So Long, See You Tomorrow*.

**I&I**   See The Intolerable Kid.

**Duncan Idaho**   Reincarnated from the cells of the original Duncan Idaho, this Duncan Idaho has been constantly recreated to keep Leto II company and also serve as a breeding base through the emperor's 3,000-year reign; the present Duncan becomes discontent faster than the previous ones, and teams up with Siona Atreides to slay Leto II; he is also head of Leto's elite guard of women warriors called the Fish Speakers in Frank Herbert's *God Emperor of Dune*.

**Ideal**   Young woman who explores the mental and physical dimensions of love with her lover, Jimson; together they constitute the title characters in Carlene Hatcher Polite's *The Flagellants*.

**The Idiot**   Retarded white lover of Dolores Brittain; slain by black women of Burnside, Virginia, during an Easter pageant in Hal Bennett's *Wait Until the Evening*.

**Billy Ikehorn**   See Wilhelmina Hunnenwell Winthrop Ikehorn Orsini.

**Ellis Ikehorn**   Wealthy businessman who marries his secretary, Billy Winthrop, and who leaves her his fortune in Judith Krantz's *Scruples*.

**Ikkemotubbe (Doom)**   See Volume I.

**Hatsue Imada**   Wife of Kabuo Miyamoto, childhood sweetheart of Ishmael Chambers; brought up to believe in Japanese traditions and values; ends relationship with Chambers when her family is interned during World War II; appeals to Chambers's sense of fairness during the trial of Kabuo Miyamoto in David Guterson's *Snow Falling on Cedars*.

**Gilbert Imlay**   American lover of Mary Wollstonecraft; meets her in France during the French Revolution; originally from New Jersey although he presents himself as a frontiersman; fathers Mary's child, Fanny; leaves her for his lover, Agnes; dies in 1828 in Frances Sherwood's *Vindication*.

**Art Immelmann**   Mephisophelean funding officer who tempts Tom More to pursue a life of abstraction and eroticism in Walker Percy's *Love in the Ruins*.

**Angelo (Joe) Incardona**   Railroad trackman and husband of Myra Incardona; killed by Dalton Harron in Susan Sontag's *Death Kit*.

**Myra Incardona**   Widow of the murdered Angelo Incardona in Susan Sontag's *Death Kit*.

**Indian Jenny**   Solitary old woman who drinks, dabbles in the occult, and carries a grudge against the Stamper family in Ken Kesey's *Sometimes a Great Notion*.

**Inez**   Notorious character in Ideal's neighborhood; dies a bloody, unsolved death while her neighbors sleep in Carlene Hatcher Polite's *The Flagellants*.

**The Informer**   Government police informer who serves as a go-between for messages from Ernie to Debba in Ernest Hemingway's *True At First Light*.

**Tory Ingersoll**  Homosexual anthologist of new 1960s poetry in John Updike's *Bech: A Book.*

**Allen Ingram**  Teacher of creative writing on the faculty at Convers College in Alison Lurie's *Love and Friendship.*

**Andrew Ingram**  Friend and teacher of Conor Larkin and Seamus O'Neill in Leon Uris's *Trinity.*

**Ingstrom**  David Wiley's editor; a nervous type, new to the job, and eager to keep up with his reporters in Elizabeth Benedict's *Slow Dancing.*

**Inman**  Native of western North Carolina mountains and Confederate soldier who is seriously wounded near Petersburg and in 1864 deserts and makes his way home to Cold Mountain; psychologically damaged veteran haunted by war memories; lover to Ada Monroe in Charles Frazier's *Cold Mountain.*

**Innocent (Pope)**  Pope who appears in the West to fight the Loop Garoo Kid, which he does successfully; rejects Drag Gibson's request to kill Loop in Ishmael Reed's *Yellow Back Radio Broke-Down.*

**The Intolerable Kid (I&I)**  Member of the Nova Mob who spreads havoc through slander in William S. Burroughs's *Nova Express.*

**Pierce Inverarity**  California real estate mogul who names Oedipa Maas as executrix of his estate, which contains a stamp collection that leads Oedipa into her search for the meaning of Tristero in Thomas Pynchon's *The Crying of Lot 49.*

**Invicta**  Black-cloaked, melodramatic actress who informs Tony Smith of Moise's financial needs and searches for Big Lot, her missing lover, in Tennessee Williams's *Moise and the World of Reason.*

**Iray**  Young wife of Teray in Octavia E. Butler's *Patternmaster.*

**Hettie Irden**  Frowsy B-girl whom J. Henry Waugh entertains in Robert Coover's *The Universal Baseball Association, Inc., J. Henry Waugh, Prop.*

**Iris**  Daughter of Bea; hawker of cigarettes; old beyond her years in Cyrus Colter's *The Hippodrome.*

**Aunt Irma**  Cousin of Joel Munger; adopted Grace after her parents died in Gail Godwin's *Evensong.*

**Washington Irving**  Pseudonym used by Yossarian and Major Major Major Major in Joseph Heller's *Catch-22.*

**Irwin**  Professor from Cambridge, Massachusetts, whom Esther Greenwood seduces and to whom she loses her virginity on an overnight release from a mental hospital in Sylvia Plath's *The Bell Jar.*

**Ted Isaacs**  White anthropology graduate research assistant of Chester Reynolds; chooses his work and the potential for respect and fame that it may bring over his love for a young, homeless woman, Susanne, in Tony Hillerman's *Dance Hall of the Dead.*

**Daniel Isaacson**  See Daniel Isaacson Lewin.

**Paul (Pauly) Isaacson**  Husband of Rochelle Isaacson and father of Daniel Isaacson Lewin and Susan Isaacson Lewin; radio shop operator who becomes a member of the Communist Party; convicted as a spy and electrocuted in E. L. Doctorow's *The Book of Daniel.*

**Rochelle Isaacson**  Wife of Paul Isaacson and mother of Daniel Isaacson Lewin and Susan Isaacson Lewin; becomes a member of the Communist Party and is convicted as a spy and electrocuted in E. L. Doctorow's *The Book of Daniel.*

**Susan Isaacson**  See Susan Isaacson Lewin.

**Isabel (Bel)**  Daughter of Annette Blagovo and Vadim Vadimovich; marries a self-proclaimed revolutionary and flees to Russia, where she becomes ill and poverty-stricken; Vadim rushes in vain to help the daughter he neglected most of her life in Vladimir Nabokov's *Look at the Harlequins!*

**(Don) Isidro**  Vengeful and influential Spanish nobleman in early Los Angeles; grandfather of Johannes Verne; disowns his daughter when she marries sailor Zachery Verne and ultimately has his son-in-law killed in Louis L'Amour's *The Lonesome Gods.*

**Doug Ismaileh**  Playwright from Hunt Hills Theatre Group and imitator of Ron Grant; invited by Carol Abernathy to skindive in Jamaica with the group in James Jones's *Go to the Widow-Maker.*

**Isold of the White Hands**  Look-alike of La Belle Isold; Tristram marries her but is not happy with only the image of his true love, La Belle Isold, in Thomas Berger's *Arthur Rex.*

**Isolde (Iso)**  Lesbian prominent among Mira's friends in graduate school in Marilyn French's *The Women's Room.*

**Issetibbeha**  See Volume I.

**Ives**  Silent, elderly linguist whom Tom More saves from enforced euthanasia in Walker Percy's *Love in the Ruins.*

**Padma S. Iyer**  Venn's mother; operates her own fertility clinic in Boston; born a half hour's ride from the old White Town of Fort St. George in Bharati Mukherjee's *The Holder of the World.*

**Venn Iyer**  Lover of Beigh Masters; born in India; father of fractals and designer of inner space; is working at MIT on a grid for time travel in Bharati Mukherjee's *The Holder of the World.*

**Iza** Nurturing, maternal Neanderthal medicine woman who discovers and saves the injured and hungry Cro-Magnon orphan Ayla after a devastating earthquake; loving adoptive mother who trains Ayla to be a skilled healer; sibling of Creb and Brun in Jean M. Auel's *The Clan of the Cave Bear*.

**Izzy the Push** Member of the Nova Mob in William S. Burroughs's *Nova Express* and *The Ticket that Exploded*.

**Grandmother Jaboti**  Harlan's grandmother; worked as "The Turtle Woman" in a carnival before she met her husband; had traveled to Brazil, where she got the name Jaboti in Gayl Jones's *The Healing*.

**Jack**  Middle-aged doctor and father of three; formerly married to a woman essentially brain-dead due to multiple strokes; carries on a long-term affair with Lottie Gardner and finally marries her when his first wife dies, but then struggles to redefine the now socially sanctioned relationship in Sue Miller's *For Love*.

**Jack**  Husband of Florence in Bette Pesetsky's *Midnight Sweets*.

**Jack**  With Danny Turnbow and Harley Osgood, collects wolf-bounties by fair and foul means in 1890s eastern Oregon; Blue Odell sees him shoot a neighbor's cow, initiating a feud with Blue Odell and Tim Whiteaker; spends one entire summer playing euchre and five-card in Molly Gloss's *The Jump-Off Creek*.

**Jack**  Magazine writer and journalist; best friend of Ben; cousin of Ben's beloved Veronique Decaze; Ben's executor; married to Prudence; narrates Ben's story in Louis Begley's *The Man Who Was Late*.

**Jack**  Son of Utch Thalhammer and the unnamed narrator, brother of Bart, and playmate and friend of Dorabella and Fiordiligi Winter in John Irving's *The 158-Pound Marriage*.

**Jack**  The Cavaliere's East Indian monkey; has an intelligent, very black face, set off by a light brown beard; an extraordinarily sweet and trusting disposition; dies during a cold winter in Susan Sontag's *The Volcano Lover*.

**The Jackal ("le Chacal")**  English contract assassin and master of disguise hired by the French OAS to assassinate Charles de Gaulle for half a million dollars; seduces and kills a French countess and a homosexual artist in order to use their homes as cover; attempts the assassination with a high-powered rifle concealed in a set of crutches, only to be killed by Lebel in Frederick Forsyth's *The Day of the Jackal*.

**Albert (Ajax) Jacks**  Town dandy and lover of Sula in Toni Morrison's *Sula*.

**Jackson**  Murderer of Gil Santini; captured by Harry Meyers in Jay Neugeboren's *Listen Ruben Fontanez*.

**Alice Jackson**  See Alice Greenwood Weylin.

**Chester (Ches) Jackson**  Porter; brother-in-law of Clotilda Pilgrim and father of their daughter, Ruby Parker; deceased in Cyrus Colter's *The Rivers of Eros*.

**Dorrie Jackson**  Mother of Perry Jackson; sympathetic and considerate; comes to live with her son in Alison Lurie's *The Last Resort*.

**Douglas MacArthur Jackson**  Lover of Miriam Berg; intellectual who is occasionally emotionally abusive in Marge Piercy's *Small Changes*.

**Ezzard (Chops, Ezz) Jackson**  Assistant editorial director of Lawrence Publications and former member of the black high school athletic team and neighborhood gang gathering for a birthday testimonial honoring Chappie Davis in John A. Williams's *The Junior Bachelor Society*.

**Jake Jackson**  Postal worker who is deeply in debt; wife beater, card player, and heavy drinker in Richard Wright's *Lawd Today*.

**Lil Jackson**   Wife of Jake Jackson and frequent victim of his physical abuse; needs an operation in Richard Wright's *Lawd Today*.

**Martha Jackson**   Friend who encourages Mira to return to college in Marilyn French's *The Women's Room*.

**Mary Jackson**   First-year African-American student at Moo University; the first in her Chicago family to go to college; under much pressure from her sister Carol to succeed and thus raise the family out of its working class; sees herself as a "woman" at the beginning of a relationship with an older graduate student; has difficulty finding her sense of identity amid her black and white friends in Jane Smiley's *Moo*.

**Myra Jackson**   Aunt of Perry Jackson; materialistic and interfering manipulator in Alison Lurie's *The Last Resort*.

**Pearl (Pearlie) Jackson**   Wife of Chester Jackson and sister of Clotilda Pilgrim in Cyrus Colter's *The Rivers of Eros*.

**Perry Jackson**   Owner of house he inherited from his wealthy older lover; rents it to Wilkie and Jenny Walker; professional landscape gardener; has AIDS in Alison Lurie's *The Last Resort*.

**Peter Jackson**   Sixty-nine-year-old man who survives the Andromeda Strain attack in Michael Crichton's *The Andromeda Strain*.

**Robert (Robby) Jackson**   Admiral in charge of air operations for the navy in the Pacific; briefs Jack Ryan and the president on navy assets and abilities in the Pacific, and is appointed to head the Stennis carrier group in operations against the Japanese in Tom Clancy's *Debt of Honor*.

**Savannah Jackson**   Thirty-something African-American public relations specialist who moves to Arizona to be closer to her college friend, Bernadine Harris; dissatisfied with her lack of options in eligible black men and annoyed with the incessant meddling of her mother and her married sister, Sheila; manages to "detoxify" her life of cigarettes, bad men, and unfulfilling work in Terry McMillan's *Waiting to Exhale*.

**Sheldon Jackson**   Small but powerfully charismatic Presbyterian missionary; defies superiors to sail with Capt. Michael Healy to organize Protestant religion in Alaskan territory in James Michener's *Alaska*.

**Jacob**   See Jacob Eliezer.

**Bob (Satan) Jacobs**   Black American hairdresser in Copenhagen; married to a rich Swedish woman in Cecil Brown's *The Life and Loves of Mr. Jiveass Nigger*.

**Paul Jacobson**   Family friend of the Steiners; proud of Lexi Steiner; recent widower, has lost thirty pounds since his wife, Berthe, died after forty years of marriage in Elizabeth Benedict's *Slow Dancing*.

**Lena Jacobson**   Old woman saved by Marshall Preminger from drowning in *The Condominium*, a novella in Stanley Elkin's *Searches and Seizures*.

**Arnold Jacoby**   Tenant of the 70th Street building managed by Norman Moonbloom; lives with his common-law wife, Betty Jacoby, in Edward Lewis Wallant's *The Tenants of Moonbloom*.

**Betty Jacoby**   Common-law wife of Arnold Jacoby and tenant of the 70th Street building managed by Norman Moonbloom in Edward Lewis Wallant's *The Tenants of Moonbloom*.

**Janos Jacoby**   Lover of Margot Lamar and codirector of the film being shot at Belle Isle in Walker Percy's *Lancelot*.

**Sid Jaffe**   Respectable and responsible lawyer whose pursuit of Martha Reganhart involves him in doing free legal work for Paul and Libby Herz in Philip Roth's *Letting Go*.

**Jaga**   Polish nurse who works at Anton Associates Trichological Clinic, a treatment center for hair problems, where she meets Nathan Zuckerman; becomes one of Zuckerman's "harem" of nursemaids in Philip Roth's *The Anatomy Lesson*.

**Jaggers**   Reconnaissance photography interpreter who examines the film taken by Samuel Wilson in Michael Crichton's *The Andromeda Strain*.

**Jonathan Jaimison, Jr.**   Son of Constance Birch; naive and impressionable; leaves Ohio to go to New York to find out who his real father is; discovers his father was Major Wedburn, who leaves him money with which he becomes a partner in art gallery with Cassie Bender in Dawn Powell's *The Golden Spur*.

**Jake**   See Macon Dead I.

**Jake ("Kneebone")**   War buddy of Fisher; Blackfoot Indian, lives in a houseboat in Sausalito; soft-spoken except when he is drunk in Sandra Scofield's *Beyond Deserving*.

**James**   Dead husband of June, father of Katie; drew away from his wife after Katie was born; a tire salesman in Sandra Scofield's *Beyond Deserving*.

**James I (James VI of Scotland)**   King of England who was King James VI of Scotland in George Garrett's *Death of the Fox*.

**Celestine James**   Part-Chippewa woman who works in the Argus, North Dakota, butcher shop; best friend of Mary Adare and mother of Dot Adare in Louise Erdrich's *The Beet Queen*.

**Ellen James**   Rape victim whose attackers cut off her tongue; martyr for the Ellen Jamesians, whom she does not admire; drowns at Dog's Head Harbor in John Irving's *The World According to Garp*.

**Jesse James**   Gunfighter and legendary outlaw, whose death Chester Pomeroy denies; appears to Pomeroy at the end of Thomas McGuane's *Panama*.

**Lyle James**   Husband to Sandy James and friend of Joe Paterson, who is killed for being a company operative in E. L. Doctorow's *Loon Lake*.

**Nathan James**   Young missionary doctor in Octavia E. Butler's *Survivor*.

**Raglan James**   Exiled member of the Talamasca, a secret organization dedicated to the worldwide study of occult, paranormal, and metaphysical phenomenon; trades bodies with the vampire Lestat and goes on a wild killing and robbery spree; steals David Talbot's body and is killed upon Lestat's discovery of this in Anne Rice's *The Tale of the Body Thief*.

**Sandy James**   Wife of Lyle James, who marries Joe Paterson after her husband, Lyle, is killed for being a company operative in E. L. Doctorow's *Loon Lake*.

**Professor Doctor Laszlo Jamf**   German scientist who developed Imipolex G and conducted Pavlovian experiments that presumably conditioned Tyrone Slothrop's responses to the V-2 rocket in Thomas Pynchon's *Gravity's Rainbow*.

**Oliver (O. J.) Jamison**   Reform school buddy of Jake Simms in Anne Tyler's *Earthly Possessions*.

**Jane**   Pretentious older woman; sometime companion and lover of Vivaldo Moore in James Baldwin's *Another Country*.

**Jane**   Daughter of Deirdre and Ben; goddaughter of Theodora Waite; lives with Deirdre until she is ten, then decides to stay in New York with Ben when Deirdre moves to California with Ralph in Bette Pesetsky's *Midnight Sweets*.

**Jane**   Promiscuous pilot who becomes involved with drug dealers in *The Smugglers of Lost Souls' Rock*, the interior novel within John Gardner's *October Light*.

**Jane**   See Jane Villiers de l'Isle-Adam.

**Frank Janek**   Fifty-four-year-old police detective; haunted by memories of having to shoot a former partner; finds redemption in the thought of leading Pam Barrett back to sanity after she is kidnapped and "trained" by the falconer in William Bayer's *Peregrine*.

**Janey**   Lover of Vernor Stanton in Thomas McGuane's *The Sporting Club*.

**Fred Janklow**   Boy who is killed when he escapes from the Sunlight Home for Wayward Boys in Stephen King's and Peter Straub's *The Talisman*.

**Karen Janney**   Young, highly sensitive woman living with the reclusive novelist Bill Gray and his assistant Scott Martineau; goes to New York to look for Bill after he disappears, but becomes fascinated by the world of the city's homeless and poor and begins to remember her Moonie training as she attempts to save them; eventually returns to Scott with Brita Nilsson's pictures of Bill in Don DeLillo's *Mao II*.

**Jansee**   Lead wife and sister of Patternmaster Rayal in Octavia E. Butler's *Patternmaster*.

**Beth Jarrett**   Wife of Calvin Jarrett and mother of Jordan and Conrad Jarrett in Judith Guest's *Ordinary People*.

**Calvin (Cal) Jarrett**   Successful tax attorney, husband of Beth Jarrett, and father of Jordan and Conrad Jarrett in Judith Guest's *Ordinary People*.

**Conrad Keith (Con) Jarrett**   Younger son of Calvin and Beth Jarrett; returns home a year after his suicide attempt in Judith Guest's *Ordinary People*.

**Jordan (Buck, Bucky) Jarrett**   Older son of Calvin and Beth Jarrett; dies in a boat accident in Judith Guest's *Ordinary People*.

**Roberta Jaskiewicz**   Runs a tattoo parlor across the street from Grandma Holland's house; was once married to "the Canuck"; moves in with Dolores when she is older and she and Dolores begin a delivery service for the local Chinese restaurant in Wally Lamb's *She's Come Undone*.

**Aaron Jastrow**   Uncle of Natalie; scholar and historian who also writes popular works about history of religion; refuses to believe danger he is in living in Europe during early days of World War II; taken to Terezin concentration camp; where he recovers his Jewish faith; ultimately gassed at Auschwitz in Herman Wouk's *War and Remembrance*.

**Berel Jastrow**   Cousin of Aaron; Polish Jew but pretends to be Russian; is eventually caught and sent to Terezin; escapes with Louis Henry from Terezin camp, but does not survive in Herman Wouk's *War and Remembrance*.

**Siegfried (Siggy) Javotnik**   Friend of Hannes Graff; persuades Graff to help free the animals; stung to death by bees in John Irving's *Setting Free the Bears*.

**Vratno Javotnik**   Husband of Hilke Marter-Javotnik and father of Siggy Javotnik; linguist and friend of Gottlub Wut; murdered by Todor Slivinca in John Irving's *Setting Free the Bears*.

**Jay**   See Volume I.

**Jay Cee**   Brainy literary editor of a New York fashion magazine and supervisor who tries to nurture Esther Greenwood's literary aspirations in Sylvia Plath's *The Bell Jar*.

**Hamilton Jaynes**   Deputy director of the FBI; pursues Patrick Lanigan as a federal fugitive; coerces Jack Stephano into handing Patrick over to the federal government and cooperating with the FBI; indicts and arrests Benny Aricia and the partners of Patrick's law firm for conspiracy and fraud in John Grisham's *The Partner*.

**Leon Jazinski**   Employee of Piet Hanema's construction firm in John Updike's *Couples.*

**J. B.**   See James Black.

**Jealous**   Miller who removes his ploughboy's eyes with a spoon in Jerzy Kosinski's *The Painted Bird.*

**Jean**   Masochistic wife of Alfonso in Gayl Jones's *Eva's Man.*

**Jeanette**   Regular at The Melody Coast and a favorite of Betty; a back-up singer on the skids whose only lasting celebrity is among the regulars of the bar itself; bums drinks and constantly complains about the difficulty she has with her agent; a temporary infatuation of the unnamed male narrator and main character in Darryl Pinckney's *High Cotton.*

**Jean-Jacques**   Struggling writer, part-time prostitute and petty thief, and best friend of Hippolyte in Susan Sontag's *The Benefactor.*

**Jeannie**   Childhood friend and roommate of Alison Poole; assistant editor at a fashion magazine in New York; after discovering her fiancé in bed with another woman, becomes involved with Alison's former boyfriend, Alex; blames her own financial irresponsibility on Alison in order to coax more money from her wealthy father in Jay McInerney's *Story of My Life.*

**Tyrone Jeeter**   Twelve-year-old boy Strike Dunham likes and employs; his mother does not like Strike and tries to protect him from drugs and drug dealers; shoots Erroll Barnes with Strike's gun in Richard Price's *Clockers.*

**Jeff**   Lover of Katie Fisher; an agricultural geneticist in Sandra Scofield's *Beyond Deserving.*

**Jeff**   Attacker who attempts to castrate Will Harris in Junius Edwards's *If We Must Die.*

**Jefferson**   Twenty-one-year-old African-American rural Louisiana man; illiterate; sentenced to death for being bystander at shooting of white man; questions his human worth; learns to face his impending death with dignity from schoolteacher Grant Wiggins in Ernest J. Gaines's *A Lesson Before Dying.*

**Frannie Jefferson**   Teacher, community leader, and wife of Ol Jefferson in Sarah E. Wright's *This Child's Gonna Live.*

**Ol Jefferson**   Husband of Frannie Jefferson; eccentric peddler and spreader of community history in Sarah E. Wright's *This Child's Gonna Live.*

**Thomas Jefferson**   Principal author of the Declaration of Independence and third president of the United States; orders Aaron Burr arrested for treason in Gore Vidal's *Burr.*

**Woodrow Wilson Jefferson**   Black Marxist who believes that Marx and Engels are alive and wants to meet them; makes the Negro Viewpoint in Hinckle Von Vampton's novel-within-the-novel *The Benign Monster,* but is saved by his preacher father in Ishmael Reed's *Mumbo Jumbo.*

**Jeffrey**   Ophthalmologist; married; seduces Audrey and has sex with her at each visit for contact lens check in Lynne Sharon Schwartz's *Leaving Brooklyn.*

**John Jeffreys**   Older, silver-haired second husband of Louisa Calloway in Alice Adams's *Families and Survivors.*

**Louisa Jeffreys**   See Louisa Calloway.

**Jeffy (Jeff)**   Young teenage girl who makes sexual advances toward Ursa Corregidora in Gayl Jones's *Corregidora.*

**Dean Jellinek**   Professor of animal science at Moo University, ex-husband of Elaine Dobbs-Jellinek; neglectful of his girlfriend, Joy Pfisterer; obsessed with being the first to publish groundbreaking research in cloning cows; unsuccessfully tries to "milk" four companies out of grant money to do research on calf-free lactation techniques in Jane Smiley's *Moo.*

**Bonanza (Sally Elizabeth Jones) Jellybean**   Cutest and best cowgirl and the first cowgirl to die; leads the revolt on the Rubber Rose Ranch; lover of Sissy Hankshaw Gitche in Tom Robbins's *Even Cowgirls Get the Blues.*

**George Jenkins**   Actor interested in doing a series of cop movies based on a Bryce Proctorr novel in Donald E. Westlake's *The Hook.*

**Mabry Jenkins**   Dallas Cowboy defensive back whose life falls apart when he is cut from the team in Peter Gent's *Texas Celebrity Turkey Trot.*

**Sarah Jenkins**   Black woman who delivers the Wingo twins and sacrifices her own life for those of the children during a hurricane in Pat Conroy's *The Prince of Tides.*

**Jenny**   Friend and occasional lover of Nathan Zuckerman (a member of his "harem"); the only woman who possesses qualities of his three ex-wives and thereby is the only one Zuckerman can envision marrying in Philip Roth's *The Anatomy Lesson.*

**Jenny**   Daughter of Dan and Libby, sister of Celia; cousin of Anne, Jenny, Rossie, and Valerie, niece of May, Grace, and Rachel, Elinor; has to protect her sister and cousins in Joan Chase's *During the Reign of the Queen of Persia.*

**Lois Jeremy**   Best friend and next-door neighbor of Charlotte Evans; mother of alcoholic son AJ; a member of the Haddan Garden Club in Alice Hoffman's *The River King.*

**Beach Jernigan**   Operates the Haven Lunch restaurant; vaporizes two state troopers in order to mislead investigation of strange happenings in Haven, Maine, in Stephen King's *The Tommyknockers.*

**Jero** African in Copenhagen who injures George Washington in a fight in Cecil Brown's *The Life and Loves of Mr. Jiveass Nigger*.

**Melvin (Doc) Jerrell** Philosophical black homosexual physician in Copenhagen in Cecil Brown's *The Life and Loves of Mr. Jiveass Nigger*.

**Jerry (the Lemon Kid)** Wolf mate of Audrey Carsons in Audrey's story "The Autobiography of a Wolf" in William S. Burroughs's *Exterminator!*

**Jerry** Easygoing Italian-American and, for a short time, lover of Barbara King in James Baldwin's *Tell Me How Long the Train's Been Gone*.

**Jesse** Lover of Elaine, friend of Lee Mellon, and narrator of Richard Brautigan's *A Confederate General from Big Sur*.

**Jesse** Vietnam veteran who wanders into the Texas Lunch and converses with Ernest Monroe and Paco Sullivan about his war experiences in a way that Paco cannot in Larry Heinemann's *Paco's Story*.

**Jessica** Pretty young college student working as a summer nanny for Elizabeth Harbour's three children; is the unwitting victim of the dangerous and self-serving passion between Elizabeth and Cameron Gardner in Sue Miller's *For Love*.

**Jessup** Self-centered and dangerous boyfriend of Rae Perry; chases after sequence of get-rich-quick schemes and abandons Rae, later to discover that she is pregnant with his child in Alice Hoffman's *Fortune's Daughter*.

**Jesus Christ** See The Corpse.

**Jethro** Black slave and childhood companion of Leslie Collins; later given to Leslie in Harriette Simpson Arnow's *The Kentucky Trace*.

**Alice Hallie Lee (Death-row Jethroe) Jethroe** Mother of D. J. in Norman Mailer's *Why Are We in Vietnam?*

**Ranald Jethroe** See D. J.

**Rusty (David Rutherford Jethroe, Jellicoe Jethroe, Sir Jet-Throne) Jethroe** Husband of Alice Jethroe and father of D. J.; organizes the Alaskan hunting expedition in Norman Mailer's *Why Are We in Vietnam?*

**Helen Jewett** Mistress of Charles Schuyler; murdered at the brothel of Rosanna Townsend in Gore Vidal's *Burr*.

**Jill** Friend of Susan Prenctice; a sweet, rather vague woman with many small, unimportant problems in Donald E. Westlake's *The Hook*.

**Jimmy** Store owner and husband of Claire in Jerry Bumpus's *Anaconda*.

**Jimmy (Jim)** Cousin of Mutt Thomas in Gayl Jones's *Corregidora*.

**Jimmy** Husband of Celia in Joan Chase's *During the Reign of the Queen of Persia*.

**Jimmy** Illegitimate son of Molly Taylor White and Gideon Fry and half brother of Joe; killed in World War I in Larry McMurtry's *Leaving Cheyenne*.

**Jimmy** Illegitimate son of Callie Wells and Willard Freund; reared by Henry Soames in John Gardner's *Nickel Mountain*.

**Aunt Jimmy** Raises Cholly after his mother abandoned him; continuously reminds him that she saved him and even named him; dies, it is rumored, from eating peach cobbler in Toni Morrison's *The Bluest Eye*.

**Jimson (Jim)** Lover of Ideal; together they constitute the title characters in Carlene Hatcher Polite's *The Flagellants*.

**Joab** Chief of Israelite army under his uncle, King David; kills enemies of the state and rivals to his position with equal swiftness and decisiveness; against David's orders, slays David's son Absalom after Absalom leads a rebellion to depose his father in Joseph Heller's *God Knows*.

**Joachim** Housemaster to whom Teray is apprenticed in Octavia E. Butler's *Patternmaster*.

**Jo-Ann** Daughter of Monica Winthrop and, it is later revealed, Jonas Cord, Jr., in Harold Robbins's *The Carpetbaggers*.

**Joanna** Member of the Indians and lover of Corey; captured and brainwashed to embrace Freudian femininity in Marge Piercy's *Dance the Eagle to Sleep*.

**Jody** Con man and homosexual lover of Zeke Farragut; makes a dramatic escape from Falconer prison in John Cheever's *Falconer*.

**Jody** Divorced from Wayne; mother of Will; supports self by doing wedding photography; lover and eventual wife of Mel Anthis; through his efforts has her first gallery show; becomes a successful and world-traveling photographer in Ann Beattie's *Picturing Will*.

**Joe** Highway patrolman and boyfriend of Junell Mack in Harry Crews's *Car*.

**Joe** Illegitimate son of Molly Taylor White and Johnny McCloud and half brother of Jimmy; killed in World War I in Larry McMurtry's *Leaving Cheyenne*.

**Joel** Buddy of Carter in Sandra Scofield's *Beyond Deserving*.

**Johann** Nurse who despises his dying uncle, Wilibald Graf, in Katherine Anne Porter's *Ship of Fools*.

**John (Jonah)**   Fiancé of Mona Aamons Monzano and narrator of Kurt Vonnegut's *Cat's Cradle.*

**John**   Clairvoyant film critic and contributor to Renate's planned magazine in Anaïs Nin's *Collages.*

**John (Harry, Harry Hotspur, Northumberland, Parsifal, Percival, Prince Hal, Pussy)**   Priest-physician whose virtual silence enables his longtime friend Lancelot Lamar to confess; narrator of Walker Percy's *Lancelot.*

**John**   Fantasy lover of Margaret Reynolds; leader of PROWL, a secret subversive organization whose plan is to blow up the George Washington Bridge to isolate Manhattan for black solidarity in Anne Richardson Roiphe's *Up the Sandbox!*

**John**   Lover of Patricia and finder of the Logan brothers' bowling trophies, which he keeps in the apartment he shares with Patricia beneath the apartment of Constance Marlow and Bob in Richard Brautigan's *Willard and His Bowling Trophies.*

**Annie John**   Lives in Antigua; at age twelve she acquires a mysterious illness that keeps her in bed for almost four months; upon her return to school, she finds herself changed, distant from her former friends; leaves Antigua for school in England in Jamaica Kincaid's *Annie John.*

**Johnny**   Narrator who goes to find the wild boys in William S. Burroughs's *The Wild Boys;* also appears in *Exterminator!*

**Albert (Al) Johnson**   Overweight friend of Jake Jackson and fellow postal worker in Richard Wright's *Lawd Today.*

**Albertine Johnson**   Granddaughter of Nector and Marie Kashpaw; half Chippewa and half Swedish; never knew her father; runs away at age fifteen; has one-night affair with Henry Lamartine, Jr.; works at a construction site weighing trucks; studies medicine in Louise Erdrich's *Love Medicine.*

**Amos (Brick) Johnson**   Star pitcher with the Brooklyn Royal Dodgers and teammate of Mason Tidewater, of whom Johnson is jealous in Jay Neugeboren's *Sam's Legacy.*

**Arthur Johnson**   New York homicide detective investigating the murder of Lucie Proctorr; a tall, rangy African-American man with a calm and gentle voice in Donald E. Westlake's *The Hook.*

**Canaan Johnson**   Teacher at and business manager of the Light of the World Holiness Church; deserts Savata in William Goyen's *The Fair Sister.*

**Earl Johnson**   Poolroom companion of Cody Poineray in Denver in Jack Kerouac's *Visions of Cody.*

**Elmira Johnson**   Wife of July Johnson; former prostitute; restless woman who leaves Johnson in search of a former love; bears Johnson's child at Clara Allen's ranch and then goes off with a buffalo skinner; both are killed by Indians in Larry McMurtry's *Lonesome Dove.*

**Francesca Johnson**   War bride of Richard Johnson, with whom she lives in Madison County, Iowa; taught literature in private girls school in Italy and briefly in high school in Iowa; mother of Michael and Carolyn; falls in love with Robert Kincaid; stays with her husband and family out of sense of responsibility, but never forgets Kincaid in Robert James Waller's *The Bridges of Madison County.*

**Dr. Graham Johnson**   Executive of the Institute of Man in Washington, D.C., for the study and preservation of medical phenomena; after abandoning Mr. W. Greenberry McCain, the Wheelers take the quintuplets to Dr. Johnson's institute, where the remains will be preserved in Bobbie Ann Mason's *Feather Crowns.*

**Helen Johnson**   Wyoming native; wife of Earl Johnson in Jack Kerouac's *Visions of Cody.*

**Jade Johnson**   Supermodel and face of Cloud Cosmetics in Jackie Collins's *Hollywood Husbands.*

**Jeremy Johnson, Sr.**   Owner of fighting dogs who sells a dog to Edward Pierce in Michael Crichton's *The Great Train Robbery.*

**Joseph Johnson**   Publisher of Mary Wollstonecraft's books and of the journal the *Analytical Review;* searches for Mary when she is missing and rescues her from Bedlam, cares for her after her suicide attempt; Mary becomes infatuated with him, but he is homosexual; dies in 1809 in Frances Sherwood's *Vindication.*

**July Johnson**   Sheriff in Fort Smith, Arkansas; goes in quest of Jake Spoon, who accidentally shot his brother-in-law; then searches for his wife, Elmira, who has run away from him; finds his newborn son at Clara Allen's ranch, but wife has gone with a buffalo hunter in Larry McMurtry's *Lonesome Dove.*

**Lionel Boyd (Bokonon) Johnson**   Guru, philosopher, priest, and author in Kurt Vonnegut's *Cat's Cradle.*

**Lyin' B. Johnson**   United States president before Trick E. Dixon in Philip Roth's *Our Gang.*

**Oscar Johnson**   Cold, hard, tough, collected African-American sergeant in the Third Squad with a mysterious past; persists relentlessly in the search for Cacciato in Tim O'Brien's *Going After Cacciato.*

**Sherri Johnson**   First-year student at Moo University; roommates with three other girls (Mary, Diane, and Keri) in Dubuque House; from a large, small-town family; has lost sixty-two pounds in an effort to become beautiful and popular in Jane Smiley's *Moo.*

**Wade Johnson**   Teacher who lives in a Second Avenue apartment managed by Norman Moonbloom in Edward Lewis Wallant's *The Tenants of Moonbloom.*

**Malcolm Johnsprang**   Realtor, suitor of Lee Mercury; chauvinistic New Englander from the Deep South; an interesting bore, an intelligent ass in Peter De Vries's *Through the Fields of Clover.*

**Jolene**　Small-town beauty who entangles George Levanter in her divorce proceedings in Jerzy Kosinski's *Blind Date*.

**Lucien Joly**　Chief inspector of the Police Nationale's Provincial Department of Criminal Investigation; initially sceptical of Gideon Oliver's deductions in Aaron Elkins's *Old Bones*.

**Jonah**　See John.

**Jonathan**　Second husband of Kate and stepfather of Francesca Fox Bolt in Gail Godwin's *Glass People*.

**Jondalar**　Strong, blond companion and love of Ayla; wishes to return home to his people, the Zelandonii, after living with the Mammoth Hearth so that he can begin his new life with Ayla in Jean Auel's *The Plains of Passage*. Also appears in *The Valley of Horses and The Mammoth Hunters*.

**Alpha Jones**　See Alpha Jones Neumiller.

**Dr. Bo Jones**　Eccentric professor of animal sciences at Moo University, specializes in the study of hogs; owner of Earl Butz, a Landrace boar who is the subject of Jones's experiment; is obsessed with all things related to hogs; disappears in Russia while hunting exotic boars in Jane Smiley's *Moo*.

**Burma Jones**　Young, black New Orleanian, often in trouble with the police; finds a low-paying job as a janitor at a bar on Bourbon Street; discovers the pornography ring that his boss, Lana Lee, is running and leads the police to it; after the bar is raided and shut down, he is lauded as a hero and is offered a job by Gus Levy, an old employer of Ignatius J. Reilly in John Kennedy Toole's *A Confederacy of Dunces*.

**Conrad Jones**　Son of Ed and Electra Jones; killed in a car-train accident in Larry Woiwode's *Beyond the Bedroom Wall*.

**Edward (Ed) Jones**　Crusty, baseball-obsessed husband of Electra Jones and father of Alpha Jones Neumiller and four sons in Larry Woiwode's *Beyond the Bedroom Wall*.

**Electra Jones**　Wife of Ed Jones and mother of Alpha Jones Neumiller and four sons in Larry Woiwode's *Beyond the Bedroom Wall*.

**Elling Jones**　Son of Ed and Electra Jones; killed in a car-train accident in Larry Woiwode's *Beyond the Bedroom Wall*.

**Emma Lee Lessenbery Jones**　Wife of Lord Byron Jones and lover of the white police officer Willie Joe Worth, by whom she bears a son in Jesse Hill Ford's *The Liberation of Lord Byron Jones*.

**Eric Jones**　Disenfranchised rich kid from Alabama who becomes an international actor; lover and patron of Yves and lover of Cass Silenski in James Baldwin's *Another Country*.

**George Gordon Lord Byron (L. B.) Jones**　Black undertaker in Somerton who seeks a divorce from Emma Jones; brutally murdered and his body mutilated by Willie Joe Worth in Jesse Hill Ford's *The Liberation of Lord Byron Jones;* also appears in *Mountains of Gilead*.

**Hilary Jones**　Married man with a daughter; almost runs away with Diana Bell before Theophilus North intervenes in Thornton Wilder's *Theophilus North*.

**Jefferson Jones**　Ohio State University wrestler who defeats Severin Winter for sixth place in the national championship; becomes the wrestling coach at a Cleveland high school in John Irving's *The 158-Pound Marriage*.

**Jerome Jones**　Son of Ed and Electra Jones; victim of a childhood drowning accident in Larry Woiwode's *Beyond the Bedroom Wall*.

**Lamont Cranston Jones**　Black homosexual and writer driven to suicide by Joe Market in Hal Bennett's *Lord of Dark Places*.

**Lionell Jones**　Son of Ed and Electra Jones in Larry Woiwode's *Beyond the Bedroom Wall*.

**Lou Jones**　Cynical assistant and boy-of-all-work to Justin Miller; loses his job when he photographs Miller's failed attempt to seduce Marcella Bruno in Robert Coover's *The Origin of the Brunists*.

**Marvin Cora Jones**　Barbed-wire drummer who shares a stagecoach with Greer, Cameron, and Magic Child in Richard Brautigan's *The Hawkline Monster*.

**Nigra Jones**　Black man accused of murdering Ossie Little and defended by Johnny Clane; lover of Joy Little and father of Sherman Pew in Carson McCullers's *Clock Without Hands*.

**Captain Osborn Jones**　Retired oyster dredger and a resident of the Dorset Hotel in John Barth's *The Floating Opera*.

**Sally Elizabeth Jones**　See Bonanza Jellybean.

**Sherman Jones**　See Sherman Pew.

**Rebecca Carrington (Dee-Dee, Mrs. David McInnis) Jones-Talbot**　Aunt of J. Lawford Carrington; leaves her English husband for an Italian lover and eventually returns to Nashville society in Robert Penn Warren's *A Place to Come To*.

**Lindo Jong**　Mother of Waverly Jong; enters an arranged marriage at the age of two; is married at age sixteen and treated as a servant; devises a plan to force her husband's family to release her; immigrates to America in Amy Tan's *The Joy Luck Club*.

**Amos Jordan**　See Amos Winthrop.

**Rose Hsu Jordan**　Daughter of An-Mei Hsu; studies fine arts at UC Berkeley; feels responsible for her brother, Bing's, drowning; husband asks her for a divorce based on her inability to make decisions in Amy Tan's *The Joy Luck Club*.

**Jose**   Friend of George Cain; disillusioned when Cain does not become a successful role model for youngsters in the community in George Cain's *Blueschild Baby*.

**Chief Joseph**   Brilliant military strategist and leader of the Nez Perce Indians in Jim Harrison's *A Good Day to Die*.

**Josiah**   Tayo's maternal uncle, who nurtures him after his mother's death and whose face Tayo sees among those of the Japanese soldiers his unit is shooting in World War II; Josiah's relationship with Tayo is in harmony with traditional Laguna roles, while his sister's (Auntie) is not, in Leslie Marmon Silko's *Ceremony*.

**Palmer Joss**   Charismatic carnival roustabout turned evangelical guru; not tied to full conventions of religion; provides spiritual balance to scientific logic while demonstrating a critical inquisitiveness for both in Carl Sagan's *Contact*.

**Amy Moncrieff Joubert**   Wealthy heiress and JR's teacher; has a brief affair with Jack Gibbs in William Gaddis's *JR*.

**Joy**   Hippie; girlfriend of Stanley and traveling companion of Floyd Warner and Kermit Oelsligle in Wright Morris's *Fire Sermon*.

**Mary Joy**   See Naomi Sandifer.

**Joyce**   Coworker of Katie who attends Al-Anon; boyfriend is an alcoholic and wants to move from the area in Sandra Scofield's *Beyond Deserving*.

**JP**   Eastern European fencing champion imprisoned and tortured for refusing to become a spy; avenged by his friend George Levanter in Jerzy Kosinski's *Blind Date*.

**Juanita**   First girlfriend of Scarecrow; moves from Chattanooga, Tennessee, to New York, where she becomes a heroin addict and dies of an overdose in Calvin Hernton's *Scarecrow*.

**Jude**   Husband of Nel Wright in Toni Morrison's *Sula*.

**Judge Harry**   Corrupt white judge who awards wife-slayer Brownfield Copeland custody of his daughter, Ruth Copeland, in Alice Walker's *The Third Life of Grange Copeland*.

**Judith**   Depraved young woman who joins Big Red Smalley's traveling gospel show in George Garrett's *Do, Lord, Remember Me*.

**Judith**   Fourteen-year-old friend of Grace Maclean; owner of a horse named Gulliver; neighbor of the Maclean family in Chatham, New York; girl whose death contributes to Grace Maclean's feelings of guilt and anxiety in Nicholas Evans's *The Horse Whisperer*.

**Fred (Old Man) Judkins**   Old-timer, folk philosopher, and diner habitué in John Gardner's *Nickel Mountain*.

**Julia**   Pregnant psychology professor, partner of Angel Stone, and lover of Kat Alcazar; helps Kat unravel the secret of Angel in M. F. Beal's *Angel Dance*.

**Julian**   Elementary school friend of Clay who had been a drug dealer and, because of debt to his suppliers, is enrolled as a male prostitute and cannot escape in Bret Easton Ellis's *Less Than Zero*.

**Julie**   Motherless daughter of The Dead Father in Donald Barthelme's *The Dead Father*.

**Eliza Bowen Jumel**   Second wife of Aaron Burr; divorces him in Gore Vidal's *Burr*.

**June**   Mother of Katie, sister of Christine; recently widowed, she had been devoted to her husband, James; owns a small dress shop; has a lover who is a physician; offers to take Rhea Fisher on the condition that it be permanent in Sandra Scofield's *Beyond Deserving*.

**June**   Tall Girl Scout from Pennsylvania in Maureen Howard's *Natural History*.

**June (June Evans)**   Benzedrine addict accidentally shot and killed by her husband, Bull Hubbard, in Jack Kerouac's *Visions of Cody*; also appears in *Book of Dreams* and *Desolation Angels*.

**Junior**   Son of Geraldine and Louis; hates his mother's cat because it gets more affection than he does; transfers his hatred to Pecola Breedlove; tries to kill the cat and blames it on Pecola in Toni Morrison's *The Bluest Eye*.

**Junior**   Brutish man who plays host to Inman and Solomon Veasey on their westward journey, only to betray them to the Home Guard in Charles Frazier's *Cold Mountain*.

**Bill "the Judge" Justice**   March Murray's father's old friend and partner, an attorney for fifty years and a judge for thirty; husband of Louise, father of Susie; was in love with Judith Dale in Alice Hoffman's *Here on Earth*.

**Louise Justice**   Wife of Bill Justice and mother of Susie Justice, she has known for almost thirty-two years that Bill was in love with Judith Dale in Alice Hoffman's *Here on Earth*.

**Susanna "Susie" Justice**   Daughter of Bill "the Judge" and Louise; March Murray's oldest friend; a reporter for the local newspaper; worries about March's relationship with Hollis in Alice Hoffman's *Here on Earth*.

# K

**Kadongolimi**  Obese first wife of Colonel Elleloû; marries him when he is an unproven boy and tries to preserve the African ways of their youth in John Updike's *The Coup.*

**Harry Kagan**  Self-styled political leader of students at Calvin Coolidge High School; accomplished apple polisher in Bel Kaufman's *Up the Down Staircase.*

**Andy Kagle**  Head of the sales department, rival of Jack Green, and friend and colleague of Bob Slocum until Slocum supplants him and has him pensioned off in Joseph Heller's *Something Happened.*

**Louise Kahan**  Romance writer, pen name Annette Hollander Sinclair, who becomes a war correspondent during World War II; ex-wife of Oscar Kahan, mother of Kay Kahan; conducts a long affair with Daniel Balaban during the war, but is reunited with Oscar at the end of the war in Marge Piercy's *Gone to Soldiers.*

**Oscar Kahan**  Professor at Columbia University, he joins the Office of Strategic Services during World War II; ex-husband of Louise, he has an affair with Abra Scott during the war; Oscar and Louise are reunited at the end of World War II in Marge Piercy's *Gone to Soldiers.*

**Samuel Abel (Sammy) Kahan**  Jewish orderly at Sacred Heart Hospital who sells drugs to patients; dies in a freak accident on the hospital steps in Edward Lewis Wallant's *The Children at the Gate.*

**Jacob Kahn**  Nonreligious Jewish sculptor who becomes Asher Lev's art teacher and mentor in Chaim Potok's *My Name Is Asher Lev.*

**Tanya Kahn**  Russian wife of Jacob Kahn; encourages her husband's artistic endeavors in Chaim Potok's *My Name Is Asher Lev.*

**John Kaimon**  Drifter who joins Belt's dojo; leaves with Gave Nell Odell at the end of Harry Crews's *Karate Is a Thing of the Spirit.*

**Kaisa**  Garrulous aspiring actress; roommate of Hellos aboard the *Castel Felice* in Calvin Hernton's *Scarecrow.*

**Albert Kalandyk**  See Alberto Mogadiscio.

**Rav Jacob Kalman**  Holocaust survivor and Talmudic scholar who almost refuses to ordain Reuven Malter in Chaim Potok's *The Promise.*

**Moussa Kamara**  Young tribal friend and servant of Michael Killigan; possesses pictures taken by Michael that might solve the enigma of his disappearance; killed by a tribal mob after being identified as a thief by a local tribal chief in Richard Dooling's *White Man's Grave.*

**Kamikazee**  See Heritage Wright.

**Irving Kanarek**  Los Angeles defense attorney; second defender of Jimmy Smith in Joseph Wambaugh's *The Onion Field.*

**Morton L. (Morty) Kanovitz**  Production manager of Boris Adrian's pornographic movie in Terry Southern's *Blue Movie.*

**Sol (Uncle Sol) Kantor**  Friend of Charlie Sapistein; travels the country visiting friends he knew at the Maimonides Home for Jewish Boys in Jay Neugeboren's *An Orphan's Tale.*

**Holly Kaplan**  Life partner of Phillip Carver, whose support during his father's old age helps him to come to terms with his family's complex past in Peter Taylor's *A Summons to Memphis.*

**Jerry Kaplan**   Grandson of Judith Finkel; spends a summer exploring race, sexuality, and friendship with David Hunter in Hal Bennett's *The Black Wine*.

**Rabo Karabekian**   Minimalist painter in Kurt Vonnegut's *Breakfast of Champions*.

**Karen**   Wealthy ex-wife of Gifford in Nicholas Delbanco's *News*.

**Karloff**   Huge 104-year-old Russian immigrant who dies in a Thirteenth Street apartment managed by Norman Moonbloom in Edward Lewis Wallant's *The Tenants of Moonbloom*.

**Igor Karlovy**   Russian colonel and chief of engineers in post–World War II Berlin; friend of Sean O'Sullivan and lover of Lotte Böhm in Leon Uris's *Armageddon*.

**Ardis Kármán**   See Ardis Ross.

**Elena Kármán**   See Elena Ross Howe.

**Karmin**   Soul at the seventh aspect of Carl Dean Palmers in Robert Coover's *The Origin of the Brunists*.

**Emil Karpo**   Deputy inspector with the MVD, the Moscow police department; sent to Siberia by KGB to monitor Rostnikov's handling of a sensitive case, but ultimately refuses to give evidence against him in Stuart M. Kaminsky's *A Cold Red Sunrise*.

**Damien Karras**   Jesuit priest, psychiatrist, and counselor who is forced to confront his faith in God in the presence of the demonic possession of Regan MacNeil in William Peter Blatty's *The Exorcist*.

**Marina (Rina) Karsh**   Activist on the run after an explosion; escapes the country with the aid of her father in M. F. Beal's *Amazon One*.

**Max Kasavubu**   Professor and agent for the Louisiana Red Corporation who believes that Richard Wright's Bigger Thomas was not executed but was smuggled out of prison; dreams that he is Mary, about to be raped by Thomas, and then sees himself as Thomas and kills Nanny Lisa, his Louisiana Red coconspirator in Ishmael Reed's *The Last Days of Louisiana Red*.

**Fitz John Kasch**   Reclusive writer and academic who becomes obsessed with an impoverished rural family, the Bartletts, especially teenage Laney Bartlett in Joyce Carol Oates's *Childwold*.

**Sid Kasdan**   Ex-private investigator in San Francisco; recently divorced from Priscilla Kasdan, whom he still loves; Korean and Vietnam veteran; is hired by the Worthingtons to be a slave courier for white slavery; kills Mahmoud Fils-Aimé in Herbert Gold's *Slave Trade*.

**Lilly Kase**   Beautiful young wife of Duncan Kase and confidant of Fanny Yellin; begins to regret marrying for money in Ellen Gilchrst's *Victory Over Japan*.

**June Kashpaw**   Daughter of Lucille Lazarre, who dies when June is young; taken in by Marie Kashpaw at age nine; later raised by Eli Kashpaw; marries Gordie Kashpaw; has an affair with Gerry Nanapush; mother of King Kashpaw and Lipsha Morrisey; studies to be a beautician; dies walking in a snowstorm in Louise Erdrich's *Love Medicine*.

**King Kashpaw**   Son of June and Gordie Kashpaw; husband of Lynette and father of King Jr.; is awarded June's inheritance and buys a car; Gerry Nanapush's cellmate who snitches on him in Louise Erdrich's *Love Medicine*.

**Marie Lazarre Kashpaw**   Comes from a "bad" white family; is abused by a nun and consequently worshipped for her wounds resembling the stigmata; wife of Nector Kashpaw; raises June Kashpaw and Lipsha Morrisey; befriends Lulu Lamartine in her old age in Louise Erdrich's *Love Medicine*.

**Nector Kashpaw**   Brother of Eli Kashpaw; husband of Marie Lazarre Kashpaw; chairman of the tribe in 1952; carries on an extended affair with Lulu Lamartine; accidentally burns down Lulu's house; loses his mind in his old age; dies choking on a turkey heart intended as love medicine in Louise Erdrich's *Love Medicine*.

**Russell Kashpaw**   Chippewa half brother of the mixed-blood Celestine James; disabled veteran of World War II and Korea in Louise Erdrich's *The Beet Queen*.

**Eddie Kaspbrak**   Asthmatic member of The Losers Club, and one of Bill Denbrough's best friends; although Eddie's asthma is not real (his mother has made him a hypochondriac), his inhaler serves as a talisman in wounding "IT" in Stephen King's *IT*.

**Katje**   See Katje Borgesius.

**Kate (Catalina Kate)**   Young black woman who gives birth to a child by Skipper on the night of All Saints in John Hawkes's *Second Skin*.

**Kate (Katie)**   Mother of Francesca Fox Bolt; lives in the mountains with Ware Smith and bears their child in Gail Godwin's *Glass People*.

**Aunt Kate**   Alice Gardner Goodwin's "adoptive mother"; friend of Alice's real mother, Mrs. Gardner, whose will requests that Aunt Kate act as caretaker; the confidante who dies as Alice goes off to college and the woman for whom Alice longs after Lizzy's death in Jane Hamilton's *A Map of the World*.

**Katherine**   Lover of Harry Miller; breaks off their relationship after her ex-husband beats him up in Frederick Busch's *Domestic Particulars*.

**Katie**   Sister of Anne, daughter of Grace and Neil, niece of Dan and Libby, Elinor, May, and Rachel, cousin of Jennie, Celia, Rossie, and Valerie; youngest of the cousins in Joan Chase's *During the Reign of the Queen of Persia*.

**Ari Katz**   Fiancé of Daniela Rubin, who is killed in a Nazi concentration camp; he locates Jacqueline Levy-Monot, Daniela's best friend, at the end of World War II and encourages her to join him in Israel in Marge Piercy's *Gone to Soldiers*.

**Joe Katz**   Bryce Proctorr's editor in Donald E. Westlake's *The Hook*.

**Joshua Katz**   Eleven-year-old son of Joe and Shelly Katz in Donald E. Westlake's *The Hook*.

**Sam Katz**   Nine-year-old son of Joe and Shelly Katz in Donald E. Westlake's *The Hook*.

**Shelly Katz**   Wife of Joe Katz; a tiny dynamo of a woman, compact, with tightly curled black hair; an easy, comic, relaxed manner; employed as a computer programmer in Donald E. Westlake's *The Hook*.

**Stanley Katz**   Trumpet player who lives with Jer Sidone in the 70th Street building managed by Norman Moonbloom; attempts suicide in Edward Lewis Wallant's *The Tenants of Moonbloom*.

**Christina Kavanaugh**   Corky's lover; attractive wife of a sexually disabled judge in Joyce Carol Oates's *What I Lived For*.

**Harry Kavanaugh**   Former federal court justice who suffers from multiple sclerosis; friend of Corky in Joyce Carol Oates's *What I Lived For*.

**Kay-Kay**   See Kay Campbell.

**Kazak**   See Volume I.

**Tracy Keating**   See Tracy Keating Morgan.

**Mrs. Doris Keefe**   Landlady of Theophilus North in Thornton Wilder's *Theophilus North*.

**Jeb Keeler**   Athletic young lawyer drawn to Alaska by big game hunting and opportunities created by tribal corporations in James Michener's *Alaska*.

**Thomas Keene**   Educated artist and widower who keeps a diary that is the narrative of the novel; an ex-pastor and an alcoholic; has an affair with Lettiece Shipman, but is engaged to and later marries Fanny Cooper in Hugh Nissenson's *The Tree of Life*.

**Rolfe Keepsake**   Fascist son ignored by Rolfe Ruskin; killed in the Spanish Civil War in William Herrick's *Hermanos!*

**Kegerise**   Brightest student of George Caldwell in John Updike's *The Centaur*.

**Mitchell Kelb**   Detective who arrests Fabian Vas in Halifax; acts as representative magistrate for the preliminary hearing about Botho August's murder; acquits Fabian and takes Margaret Handle to a sanitarium after the trial in Howard Norman's *The Bird Artist*.

**Kelcey (Serenus Vogel)**   Magazine writer who investigates the Fork River Project; narrator of Wright Morris's *The Fork River Space Project*.

**Alice Kelcey**   Wife of Kelcey; runs off with O. P. Dahlberg to parts unknown in Wright Morris's *The Fork River Space Project*.

**John (Jack) Kelleher**   Priest of the Order of St. Clement; exiled along with Father Urban to Duesterhaus, Minnesota, to help convert a sanitarium into a retreat house in J. F. Powers's *Morte D'Urban*.

**Kelly Kelleher**   Beautiful, ambitious, and intense; daughter of protective parents; outstanding college graduate working for a major political journal; idealistic believer in politics; infatuated admirer of "The Senator" in Joyce Carol Oates's *Black Water*.

**Bert Keller**   Peter's father; likes Ann August and offers to help her financially; allows Adele Diamond to live in his beach house after Ann leaves and Nan Keller is killed in Mona Simpson's *Anywhere but Here*.

**Nan Keller**   Peter's mother; does not like Adele Diamond; hires Adele as a maid, but fires her; allows Adele and her daughter, Ann, to live in her art studio behind the house; is run over and killed by a snowplow years later in Mona Simpson's *Anywhere but Here*.

**Peter Keller**   Friend of Ann August's in California; Ann and her mother move in with his family; Ann loses her virginity to him in Mona Simpson's *Anywhere but Here*.

**Beata Kellerman-Ashley**   Wife of John Ashley, by whom she has four children; moves to California long after her husband's death in Thornton Wilder's *The Eighth Day*.

**John Harvey Kellog**   Dubious doctor of cures; always present but not always seen in T. Coraghessan Boyle's *The Road to Wellville*.

**Dr. Kellsey**   Literature professor; Connie Birch had been a student in his class; thought to be one candidate for Connie's true father by John Jaimison in Dawn Powell's *The Golden Spur*.

**Barney Oswald Kelly**   Father of Deborah Kelly Rojack; multimillionaire who wishes to appear with Stephen Rojack at his daughter's funeral in Norman Mailer's *An American Dream*.

**Brigid Dunn Kelly**   Younger sister of Theresa Dunn; happily married mother of three children in Judith Rossner's *Looking for Mr. Goodbar*.

**Deborah Caughlin Mangaravidi Kelly**   See Deborah Kelly Rojack.

**Frank James (Jim, Geam) Kelly**    Survival-wise black man who vainly counsels Marcus Payne; narrator of Ernest J. Gaines's *Of Love and Dust*.

**John Kelly**    Also called John Clark; retired Navy SEAL who engages in a one-man war against drug dealers who kill his lover, Pamela Madden; helps Maxwell, Podulski and James Greer plan an abortive attempt to rescue American POWs in Vietnam; captures Soviet colonel Grishanov; fakes own death at sea and becomes Clark; marries nurse Sandy O'Toole in Tom Clancy's *Without Remorse*.

**Mike Kelly**    Unemployed, unambitious lower-class urban male, supported by his wife in Hubert Selby, Jr.'s *Last Exit to Brooklyn*.

**Adam Kelno**    Former doctor at Jadwiga concentration camp, where he performed sterilization experiments on Jewish prisoners; knighted doctor in London; plaintiff in a libel suit against author Abe Cady in Leon Uris's *QB VII*.

**Angela Brown Kelno**    British nurse and wife of Adam Kelno in Leon Uris's *QB VII*.

**Stephan Kelno**    Architect son of Adam and Angela Kelno in Leon Uris's *QB VII*.

**Bill Kelsey**    Self-satisfied middle-aged hustler and dreamer fought over and controlled by female conjurers; submits to the will of Maria Befies in Hal Bennett's *Seventh Heaven*.

**Serena Kelsey**    Mother of Bill Kelsey and practitioner of juju; defeated by the superior magic of Aunt Keziah in Hal Bennett's *Seventh Heaven*.

**Zachary Kelsey**    Schizophrenic father of Bill Kelsey in Hal Bennett's *Seventh Heaven*.

**Kelso**    Allie's only friend at Valleyhead, who warns Allie that her parents are out "to screw her" in Walker Percy's *The Second Coming*.

**Detroit (Pumpkin Kitty) Kemp**    Friend of Tisha Dees in Arthenia J. Bates's *The Deity Nodded*.

**Miss Sally Kemp**    Friend of the Hugers who leaves Allie her valuable estate in Walker Percy's *The Second Coming*.

**Ken**    Opium addict and early lover of Bruce in Anaïs Nin's *Collages*.

**Bedford Kendal**    Father of Eva Kendal in Reynolds Price's *The Surface of Earth*.

**Charlotte Watson Kendal**    Mother of Eva Kendal; commits suicide by drinking a glass of lye on hearing that Eva has had a child; leaves a letter blaming Eva for the suicide in Reynolds Price's *The Surface of Earth*.

**Eva Kendal**    Protagonist, whose elopement with her Latin teacher sets events in motion in Reynolds Price's *The Surface of Earth*.

**Kennerly Kendal**    Brother of Eva Kendal, whom he blames for the suicide of their mother in Reynolds Price's *The Surface of Earth*.

**Rena Kendal**    Sister of Eva Kendal; first Eva's ally and then her enemy in Reynolds Price's *The Surface of Earth*.

**Candy Kendall**    Young woman who comes with her fiancé, Wally Worthington, to St. Cloud's in order to obtain an abortion; during the war, she and Homer Wells work together in the cider house and eventually fall in love in John Irving's *The Cider House Rules*.

**Gretchen Kendall**    Feminist lawyer and close friend of Isadora Wing in Erica Jong's *How to Save Your Own Life*.

**Miles Kendig**    Retired CIA agent who misses the excitement of espionage until he induces the agency, and foreign government forces, to pursue him when he writes a book and threatens to publish government secrets in Brian Garfield's *Hopscotch*.

**Richard Kennington**    Successful pianist who is the musical idol and the lover of Paul Porterfield in David Leavitt's *The Page Turner*.

**Kenny**    Father of Carl and Peter; Hildie calls him her husband although there has probably never been a marriage in Mary McGarry Morris's *Songs in Ordinary Time*.

**Caroline Kent**    Proprietor of Illyria in Alison Lurie's *Real People*.

**Vance Kenton**    Wealthy white artist, owner of Sherwood Forest Inn, and lesbian in Ann Allen Shockley's *Loving Her*.

**Al Keochakian**    Gordon Walker's screenwriting agent in Robert Stone's *Children of Light*.

**David Alan (Dave) Kepesh**    Professor of comparative literature who is transformed into a six-foot-long breast; narrator of Philip Roth's *The Breast*.

**Michael Kern**    Young college professor who has an affair with Joan Mitchell; she destroys his career by revealing that he is having an affair with an undergraduate in Shirley Ann Grau's *The House on Coliseum Street*.

**Emil Kerouac**    See Emil Duluoz.

**Jean-Louis Lebris (Jack, John Louis Kerouac) de Kérouac**    American writer visiting France in search of his family origins; narrator of Jack Kerouac's *Satori in Paris*.

**John (Jack) Kerouac**    Dreamer and narrator of Jack Kerouac's *Book of Dreams*.

**Alexis Kessler**  Musician and music professor at Woodslee University; becomes involved in a turbulent love affair with fellow academic Brigit Stott in Joyce Carol Oates's *Unholy Loves.*

**Eugene Kessler**  Supposedly Jason's best friend, but has more in common with Gretel Samuelson; they are in business together selling term papers; when they are caught and suspended, he runs off to San Francisco; publishes a magazine in Menlo Park, and Gretel is hired as associate editor in Alice Hoffman's *Local Girls.*

**Kevin**  One of the seven dwarfs who wash windows, make Chinese baby food, and live with Snow White in Donald Barthelme's *Snow White.*

**Aunt Keziah**  Powerful Burnside, Virginia, conjurer; surrogate mother and sexual enslaver of Bill Kelsey in Hal Bennett's *Seventh Heaven.*

**Kharu**  Tough old wife of clan leader Gumsto; cunning and possessive of him because of his wandering eye and position as clan leader; wishes her son to marry a young woman in the clan that Gumsto has his eye on in James A. Michener's *The Covenant.*

**Chop Hing Kheng Fatt (Big Hing)**  Ship chandler and Chinese boss of Jack Flowers in Paul Theroux's *Saint Jack.*

**Blanche Kibbee**  Passive and wraithlike daughter of Madge and Ned; closely resembles her grandmother; Cora Atkins; taken off the farm by her aunt Sharon to go to school in Chicago, but misses her father and willingly returns to spend her life helping her mother in Wright Morris's *Plains Song for Female Voices.*

**Caroline Kibbee**  Assertive second daughter of Madge and Ned; sister of Blanche; rebels against and criticizes her grandmother (Cora Atkins) and mother for their passive acceptance of the restrictions farm life imposes on women in Wright Morris's *Plains Song for Female Voices.*

**Ned Kibbee**  Carpenter, marries Madge Atkins; father of Blanche, Caroline and Rosalene; runs a building business that deteriorates after World War II in Wright Morris's *Plains Song for Female Voices.*

**Susan Kidwell**  Closest friend and confidante of Nancy Clutter; discovers Nancy's body the morning after the crime in Truman Capote's *In Cold Blood.*

**Kiki**  Homosexual street boy in William S. Burroughs's *The Soft Machine;* possessed by Ali in *The Ticket That Exploded;* serves as a deep trance medium to the Mayan Death God in *The Wild Boys;* also appears in *Nova Express.*

**Bugs Kilken**  Son of a Dachau survivor, the Hollywood producer-director of five slug-and-chase movies; collects colonial American art and asks Beigh Masters to be his private art adviser in Bharati Mukherjee's *The Holder of the World.*

**John Killgore**  Doctor and environmental radical working for the Horizon Group, who develops and tests the Shiva virus for the Project; reports Popov's disappearance to Brightling and flees with other Project staff to the compound in Brazil, where he dies in a firefight against the Rainbow team in Tom Clancy's *Rainbow Six.*

**Thomas Killian**  Attorney with Dershkin Bellavita, Fishbein & Schlossel; defends Sherman McCoy in Tom Wolfe's *The Bonfire of the Vanities.*

**Michael Killigan**  American Peace Corps volunteer who works with a tribe of the Mendes people of Sierra Leone, West Africa; participated in a secret-society ritual and disappeared into the bush; known within the tribe as Lamin Kaikai; gradually comes to hate the consumerism of the West in favor of the subsistence-living of the tribal communities in Richard Dooling's *White Man's Grave.*

**Randall Killigan**  Ruthless senior partner of a law firm specializing in bankruptcy; a hypochondriac who experiences emotional and physical ill effects of "ndilei," a package of black magic sent to him from Sierra Leone; father of Michael in Richard Dooling's *White Man's Grave.*

**Andy Kilvinsky**  Veteran Los Angeles policeman, partner of Gus Plebesly, philosopher, and eventual suicide in Joseph Wambaugh's *The New Centurions.*

**Kyung-hee Kim**  Nine-year-old Korean cellist and student of Renne Sundheimer; his mother is overbearing and his father would rather he work in the family business than play the cello; relates music to architecture in Mark Salzman's *The Soloist.*

**Merle Kinbona**  Emotionally unstable but strongminded Bourne Island woman who dreams of a better life for the poor blacks of Bournehills in Paule Marshall's *The Chosen Place, the Timeless People.*

**Dr. Charles (K.) Kinbote**  Mad editor of John Shade's poem *Pale Fire;* his commentaries interpret the work as the story of his own life as an exiled monarch, Charles Xavier Vseslav, last king of Zembla, in Vladimir Nabokov's *Pale Fire.*

**Brooke Kincaid**  College student who divides herself into Brooke, her real self, and Brooke Proper, her social persona; desperately seeks a language of the heart and then throws away her one chance for it in Bentley T. Hooks; narrator of Lee Smith's *Something in the Wind.*

**Carolyn Kincaid**  Ephemeral and emotionally unavailable mother of Brooke Kincaid in Lee Smith's *Something in the Wind.*

**Carter Kincaid**  Cynical brother of Brooke Kincaid in Lee Smith's *Something in the Wind.*

**Robert Kincaid**  Professional photographer; travels on assignments; believes he is an example of an earlier type of man, freer and stronger than those in the modern technological world; falls in love with Francesca Johnson when he is sent to photograph covered bridges in Madison County, Iowa; leaves her his belongings in his will in Robert James Waller's *The Bridges of Madison County*.

**Sharon Kincaid**   Girlfriend of Binx Bolling in Walker Percy's *The Moviegoer*.

**T. Royce Kincaid**   Lawyer father of Brooke Kincaid; shields himself from his children by clichés in Lee Smith's *Something in the Wind*.

**Andrew Kincannon**   Lover of Maggie Sherbrooke in Nicholas Delbanco's *Sherbrookes*.

**William F. Kinderman**   Persevering and insatiably curious homicide detective whose investigation of a bizarre murder leads him to the MacNeil family in William Peter Blatty's *The Exorcist*.

**Lydia Kindle**   University of Iowa student with whom Fred Trumper is unable to make love in John Irving's *The Water-Method Man*.

**King**   Black bisexual lover of Louisa Calloway; outspoken about the rich South in Alice Adams's *Families and Survivors*.

**Barbara King**   White actress from a well-to-do Kentucky family; becomes the friend, lover, and eventually lifelong companion of Leo Proudhammer in James Baldwin's *Tell Me How Long the Train's Been Gone*.

**Ed King**   Middle-aged homosexual who has a brief paid sexual encounter with the unnamed protagonist of John Rechy's *City of Night*.

**Lady Kingsborough**   Employer of Mary Wollstonecraft when she works as a governess in Ireland in Frances Sherwood's *Vindication*.

**Richard Kingsborough**   Sixteen-year-old son of Lady Kingsborough; becomes Mary Wollstonecraft's lover in Frances Sherwood's *Vindication*.

**William Kingsborough**   Seven-year-old son of Lady Kingsborough and brother of Richard Kingsborough in Frances Sherwood's *Vindication*.

**J. Kinnear**   Government agent who has infiltrated a terrorist group plotting to bomb the New York Stock Exchange in Don DeLillo's *Players*.

**Alice Kinnian**   Teacher who selects Charlie Gordon for an experiment involving increased intelligence in Daniel Keyes's *Flowers for Algernon*.

**Eben Kinship**   Black husband of Martha Kinship and father of Teddy and Lucinda Kinship in Shelby Foote's *September September*.

**Lucinda (Sister Baby) Kinship**   Six-year-old younger sister of Teddy Kinship in Shelby Foote's *September September*.

**Martha Wiggins Kinship**   Black wife of Eben Kinship, daughter of Theo Wiggins, and mother of Teddy and Lucinda Kinship in Shelby Foote's *September September*.

**Theo (Ted, Teddy) Kinship**   Eight-year-old son of Martha and Eben Kinship; kidnapped in Shelby Foote's *September September*.

**Athanasius Kircher**   Volcano enthusiast who was lowered into the craters of Etna and Vesuvius by a pulley in Susan Sontag's *The Volcano Lover*.

**Christian Kirke**   Yale University anthropologist whose appendicitis attack prevents him from joining the group of scientists at Project Wildfire in Michael Crichton's *The Andromeda Strain*.

**Mary-Jane (Madeleine) Saxon Kirkland**   Widow of a wealthy industrialist; dies of cancer after her marriage to George Levanter in Jerzy Kosinski's *Blind Date*.

**Jess Kirkman**   Son of Joe Robert Kirkman; narrates his father's adventures over a two-day period in Fred Chappell's *Brighten the Corner Where You Are*.

**Joe Robert Kirkman**   Thirty-six-year-old teacher at a country high school living on a farm outside of Tipton, North Carolina; hired to replace the high school's principal; summoned to an examination by the school board for his practical jokes and for teaching the theory of evolution, he decides to quit rather than endure the indignity of being fired in Fred Chappell's *Brighten the Corner Where You Are*.

**Leo Kirsch**   Repressed mama's boy and used car salesman in Thomas Berger's *Sneaky People*.

**Kisu-Mu**   See Meriwether Lewis Moon.

**Thayer Kitchen**   Father of a thirteen-year-old son, Jemal, from his first marriage, Thayer meets Dolores in their English composition course at a community college; agrees to fix her roof cheap; later marries Dolores in Wally Lamb's *She's Come Undone*.

**Opal Kitchener**   Sculptress and sometime member of a ménage á trois with Heck and Hattie Brown in Peter De Vries's *I Hear America Swinging*.

**Kitty**   Attractive neighbor of Laura Brown; kisses Laura in Michael Cunningham's *The Hours*.

**Michael Kitz**   Assistant secretary of defense for C3I, whose concern for national security outweigh those of scientific discovery in Carl Sagan's *Contact*.

**Patty Klein**   Wife of Rocco Klein and mother of Erin; met him when she was almost arrested because of a crank phone call to a radio show; does not like police officers in Richard Price's *Clockers*.

**Rocco Klein**   Homicide detective who loves his job; husband of Patty Klein and father of Erin; does not believe in Victor Dunham's guilt and works hard at investigating the murder in Richard Price's *Clockers*.

**Tanya Klein**   Pro bono lawyer assigned to help Louie Bronk in the appeal process for his death sentence; convinced of Louie's guilt and of the futility of his appeal; does not change her opinion, despite the urgings of Molly Cates regarding new evidence she discovers in the case in Mary Willis Walker's *The Red Scream*.

**R. V. Kleppmann**   Confidence man and gangster in John Gardner's *The Sunlight Dialogues*.

**Dr. Klinger**   Psychoanalyst of David Kepesh in Philip Roth's *The Breast*.

**Menasha Klinger**   Companion of Waldemar and ancient tenor who sings arias over Von Humboldt Fleisher's last resting place in Saul Bellow's *Humboldt's Gift*.

**Mr. Klipspringer**   United States government contact of Michaelis Ezana; responsible for new international investments in Kush; becomes adviser to the new government when Colonel Elleloû is overthrown in John Updike's *The Coup*.

**Zachary Klinger**   Rich and powerful owner of Orpheus Studios in Hollywood; father of Silver Anderson's daughter, Heaven, in Jackie Collins's *Hollywood Husbands*.

**John Klope**   Serious, young Idaho farmer; leaves impoverished family to seek fortune in Yukon gold rush; after perilous journey and many years of labor hits rich vein and shares wealth with friends Tom Venn, Matthew Murphy, and Missy Peckham in James Michener's *Alaska*.

**Dotty Schwartz Klotz**   Historical character Margaret has met and is writing about; once active in the American Communist Party; former lover of Max Gideon; nurses the wounded in the Spanish Civil War; marries Red Klotz in Maureen Howard's *Expensive Habits*.

**Red Klotz**   Deceased husband of Dotty; met her when he was shot in a skirmish in the Spanish Civil War; taught English at Erasmus Hall High School in Maureen Howard's *Expensive Habits*.

**Jessie Klubock**   Mother of Louie; plays the piano and sings in a high, sweet voice in Mary McGarry Morris's *Songs in Ordinary Time*.

**Louis (Louie) Klubock**   Chubby six-year-old boy who lives next door to Benjamin and is his only friend in Mary McGarry Morris's *Songs in Ordinary Time*.

**Mr. Klubock**   Father of Louie, a butcher in Mary McGarry Morris's *Songs in Ordinary Time*.

**Brandt Knapp**   Five-year-old son of John and Louise; brother of Mary and John Joel; lives with father's mother; father stays with them during the week in Ann Beattie's *Falling in Place*.

**John Knapp**   Advertising writer; married to Louise; father of Mary, John Joel, and Brandt; loves Nina, with whom he is having an affair; after John Joel shoots Mary, realizes he cannot take responsibility for everyone's happiness and becomes optimistic about a married future with Nina in Ann Beattie's *Falling in Place*.

**John Joel Knapp**   Ten-year-old son of John and Louise; brother of Mary and Brandt; overweight; shoots Mary, who teases him constantly, when he believes gun is not loaded in Ann Beattie's *Falling in Place*.

**Louise Knapp**   Married to John; mother of Mary, John Joel, and Brandt; does not love her husband; still mourning the death of their dog years earlier; envious of her only friend, a feminist and teacher; asks John for a divorce after John Joel shoots Mary in Ann Beattie's *Falling in Place*.

**Mary Knapp**   Fifteen-year-old daughter of John and Louise; sister of John Joel and Brandt; hates and teases John Joel; after he shoots her, decides she no longer hates him in Ann Beattie's *Falling in Place*.

**Zivan Knezevich**   Olympic wrestler and Chetnik freedom fighter who flees Tito's Yugoslavia to live in Vienna; teaches his nephew, Severin Winter, to wrestle in John Irving's *The 158-Pound Marriage*.

**Alfred Knickerbocker**   African-American cook at Mona Chang's family's restaurant who seems to be due a promotion but who is fired after Barbara Gugelstein's mother discovers he had been living in her house and having an affair with Barbara's cousin; plaintiff whose threatened discrimination lawsuit against the Changs contributes to Mona's estrangement from her mother in Gish Jen's *Mona in the Promised Land*.

**Edith Knight**   Wife of Walter Knight and mother of Lily Knight McClellan in Joan Didion's *Run River*.

**Gaylord Knight**   Superintendent for the four Moonbloom Realty buildings managed by Norman Moonbloom in Edward Lewis Wallant's *The Tenants of Moonbloom*.

**Walter Knight**   Rancher and father of Lily Knight McClellan; once hoped to become governor of California in Joan Didion's *Run River*.

**K9**   Agent for the Nova Police in William S. Burroughs's *Nova Express*, *The Soft Machine*, and *The Ticket That Exploded*.

**W. Alcott (Old Bottle-ass) Knoedler**   Headmaster of Dorset Academy; spends most of his time trying to recruit students and secure funding for the ill-fated school in Richard Yates's *A Good School*.

**Carter Knott**   Likable, wealthy resident of Haddam, New Jersey; member of the now defunct "Divorced Men's Club" and friend of Frank Bascombe; retired at forty-something to a garish Greek revival house where he spends his time managing his sizable portfolio in Richard Ford's *Independence Day.*

**Deborah Knott**   Savvy, single, thirty-four-year-old North Carolina attorney cum sleuth; uncovers dangerous, decades-old secrets while investigating a senseless, never-solved, eighteen-year-old murder in Margaret Maron's *Bootlegger's Daughter.*

**Carl Knox**   Police detective in Thomas Berger's *Who Is Teddy Villanova?*

**Dr. Schlichter von Koenigswald**   Reformed Nazi and physician in Julian Castle's hospital in Kurt Vonnegut's *Cat's Cradle.*

**Renata (Fat-Tits, Renata Flonzaley, Miss Universe) Koffritz**   Earthy and beautiful hedonist and interior decorator who serves as Charlie Citrine's mistress until she dumps her son on him and marries a wealthy undertaker named Flonzaley in Saul Bellow's *Humboldt's Gift.*

**Molly Kohm**   Older, assertive graduate student of Professor Jack Schiff; organizes graduate student party at his house in the novella *Her Sense of Timing* in Stanley Elkin's *Van Gogh's Room at Arles.*

**Kojak**   Dog of Glen Bateman; helps save Stuart Redman in Stephen King's *The Stand.*

**John Kolditis**   Dishonest owner of Kolditis Cleaners in Mary McGarry Morris's *A Dangerous Woman.*

**Ko-li**   Soul at the seventh aspect of Colin Meredith in Robert Coover's *The Origin of the Brunists.*

**Mathilde Kollwitz**   School teacher and companion to Winifred Throop in Wright Morris's *What a Way to Go.*

**Donna Kooshof**   Mrs. Robert Kooshof; kind and decent; falls in love with Thomas Chippering while husband is in jail; attempts to make Thomas see what he really is; saves him from obsession with former wife; convinces Thomas to agree to marry her in Tim O'Brien's *Tomcat in Love.*

**Cardinal von Kopf**   Official of the Liechtenstein Catholic Church who confiscates Boris Arian's pornographic movie in Terry Southern's *Blue Movie.*

**Kori**   Leader of an outcast band of Niaruna Indians who live on the generosity of the missionaries in Peter Matthiessen's *At Play in the Fields of the Lord.*

**Lieutenant Colonel Korn**   Scheming assistant to Colonel Cathcart in Joseph Heller's *Catch-22.*

**Meta Korner**   Cousin and first wife of Otto Korner; she urges Otto to leave Nazi Germany before it is too late but he ignores her pleas; she dies insane in a cattle car en route to Auschwitz in Alan Isler's *The Prince of West End Avenue.*

**Otto Korner**   Guilt-ridden survivor of Auschwitz who is unable to let go of romantic obsessions, betrayals, and bitterness of unfulfilled potential; resident of Emma Lazarus Retirement Home, he takes over as director and star of the home's production of *Hamlet* following the demise of Nahaum Lipschitz in Alan Isler's *The Prince of West End Avenue.*

**Joe Korzeniowski**   Also known as Joe Paterson, whose journeys from home take him past and back to Loon Lake, where he establishes an ambiguous relationship with the glorious and greedy industrialist F. W. Bennett, who may eventually have adopted Joe and left the lake to him in E. L. Doctorow's *Loon Lake.*

**Anna Kossowski**   Drunken childhood guardian of Konrad Vost in John Hawkes's *The Passion Artist.*

**Stanley Koteks**   Engineer at Yoyodyne, Inc.; tells Oedipa Maas about the Nefastis machine in Thomas Pynchon's *The Crying of Lot 49.*

**Dr. Bernard M. (Bernie) Kotelchuk**   Veterinarian who becomes Danielle Zimmern's lover in Alison Lurie's *The War Between the Tates.*

**Nat Kott**   Childhood friend and schoolmate of Nicholas Delbanco in Nicholas Delbanco's *In the Middle Distance.*

**Fritzie Kozka**   Thin chain-smoking Polish woman who owns and operates the Argus, North Dakota, butcher shop with her husband, Pete Kozka; mother of Sita Kozka, sister of Adelaide Adare, and foster mother of Mary Adare in Louise Erdrich's *The Beet Queen.*

**Pete Kozka**   Polish man who owns and operates the Argus, North Dakota, butcher shop with his wife, Fritzie Kozka; father of Sita Kozka in Louise Erdrich's *The Beet Queen.*

**Sita Kozka**   Pretty and selfish only child of Pete and Fritzie Kozka, who resents the intrusion of her cousin Mary Adare; neurotic and frail woman who marries Jimmy Bohl and Louis Tappe in Louise Erdrich's *The Beet Queen.*

**George Kraft**   Soviet spy and friend of Howard Campbell in Kurt Vonnegut's *Mother Night.*

**Anatole (Anthony) Krainik**   Cartographer, musician, and absent husband and father; leaves his family and lives in the woods, where he keeps various musical instruments and cartographic equipment; eventually confronts his son in the woods, almost drowns himself, and then runs away again in Howard Norman's *Northern Lights.*

**Mina Krainik**   Wife of Anatole Krainik, mother of Noah Krainik; moves, along with her niece Charlotte, to Toronto, where she gets a job at the movie theater Northern Lights; buys theater after the owner leaves, and runs it with her niece and her son in Howard Norman's *Northern Lights*.

**Noah Krainik**   Electronically talented son of Anthony and Mina Krainik; struggles to deal with his father's frequent absences (and eventual abandonment) and his friend Pelly Bay's senseless death; eventually moves to Toronto to help his mother and cousin run the Northern Lights movie theater in Howard Norman's *Northern Lights*.

**Kram**   Hunchbacked artist who lives in a Mott Street apartment managed by Norman Moonbloom in Edward Lewis Wallant's *The Tenants of Moonbloom*.

**Vida Kramar**   Nineteen-year-old beauty and lover of Mr. Librarian; has an abortion in Tijuana in Richard Brautigan's *The Abortion*.

**Lawrence Kramer**   Assistant Bronx district attorney; married to Rhoda; has an infant son, Joshua; attempts to improve his position in the D.A.'s office and to attract women by his power while prosecuting Sherman McCoy in Tom Wolfe's *The Bonfire of the Vanities*.

**Pop Kramer**   Elderly father of Cassie Caldwell, grandfather of Peter Caldwell, and father-in-law of George Caldwell in John Updike's *The Centaur*.

**Wantman Krane**   Beat poet, lover of Hellos and later of Putsy Handson, and friend of Scarecrow in Calvin Hernton's *Scarecrow*.

**Miriam Desebour Kranz**   Hospital nurse in Morristown, New Jersey, who teaches Dick Gibson the secret of the dead room in Stanley Elkin's *The Dick Gibson Show*.

**Krasnikov**   Discredited general in Russian army, now living in exile in Siberia; has written a manuscript attacking the Russian aggression in Afghanistan, which he hopes to smuggle to the West in Stuart M. Kaminsky's *A Cold Red Sunrise*.

**Sidney H. (Sid) Krassman**   Film producer who arranges the financing for Boris Adrian's pornographic movie, and acts in one of its sex scenes in Terry Southern's *Blue Movie*.

**Gunther Kraus**   German Roman Catholic priest who saves Henry Wingo's life after his plane goes down during World War II; his act of guilty compassion motivates Henry Wingo's conversion to Catholicism in *The Prince of Tides*.

**Jacob "Grandad" "Jake" Krauss**   Husband of Gram; father of May, Elinor, Libby, Rachel, and Grace, grandfather of Rossie, Anne, Katie, Jenny, Celia, Rossie, and Valerie; used to beat Libby and Rachel when he was drunk; dies of heart failure in Joan Chase's *During the Reign of the Queen of Persia*.

**Lil "Gram" "Queenie" Krauss**   The Queen of Persia, wife of Jacob Krauss, mother of May, Elinor, Grace, Rachel, and Libby, grandmother of Rossie, Anne, Katie, Celia, Valerie, and Jenny;

inherits money from her uncle Burl and buys the farm, three houses, four places of business, and another couple of farms in Joan Chase's *During the Reign of the Queen of Persia*.

**Alice (Contessa) Krebs**   Wealthy second wife of Otto Korner; her lusty nature is somewhat dampened by Otto's fastidiousness and scorn, but she leaves her fortune to him when she dies in Alan Isler's *The Prince of West End Avenue*.

**Jozef Muck-Horch von Kretschmann**   Half brother of Wanda Muck-Horch von Kretschmann and lover of Sophie Zawistowska; assassin for the Polish resistance forces in Warsaw; murdered by Ukrainian guards in William Styron's *Sophie's Choice*.

**Wanda Muck-Horch von Kretschmann**   Half sister of Jozef Muck-Horch von Kretschmann; Polish resistance leader captured by Nazis and confined in Birkenau in William Styron's *Sophie's Choice*.

**Minor Kretz**   Owner of Minor's Luncheonette; fearful of communism in John Updike's *The Centaur*.

**Lazlo Kriezler**   Intellectual forensic psychology expert in late 1890s New York City; founder of Kriezler Institute for Children; labeled "alienist" by psychiatry skeptics; enlisted by Theodore Roosevelt to construct a serial murderer's psychological profile in Caleb Carr's *The Alienist*.

**Reb Yudel Krinsky**   Russian-born Jew who is rescued from Siberia by Aryeh Lev and who encourages Asher Lev's interest in art in Chaim Potok's *My Name Is Asher Lev*.

**Kristel**   Assistant to Anna Kossowski and would-be seducer of Konrad Vost in John Hawkes's *The Passion Artist*.

**Charles (Charlie) Kroegel**   Friend and classmate of Eric Eisner at Columbia University and presently a graduate student at Columbia; lends Eric his New York apartment in Phillip Lopate's *Confessions of Summer*.

**Marie Krull**   Wife of Charles Neumiller (1) and cousin of Father Krull in Larry Woiwode's *Beyond the Bedroom Wall*.

**Mary Krull**   Professor at New York University, queer theorist; infatuated with Julia Vaughan; intellectually and morally intense in Michael Cunningham's *The Hours*.

**Selmer Krull**   Catholic priest and spiritual adviser to Martin Neumiller in Courtenay, North Dakota; performs the marriage ceremony of Neumiller and Alpha Jones in Larry Woiwode's *Beyond the Bedroom Wall*.

**Sofia (Cidaq) Kuchovskaya**   Determined Aleut girl from Lapak Island; abandons dying tribe to seek survival through slavery on Russian trading ship; converts to Christianity; marries Russian Orthodox priest Vasili Voronov and has one son, Arkady; runs orphanage in Kodiak in James Michener's *Alaska*.

**Kudashvili**   Russian captain who discovers Utch Thalhammer inside a dead cow's carcass and becomes Utch's guardian; killed in Budapest in John Irving's *The 158-Pound Marriage;* also appears in *Setting Free the Bears.*

**Eddie Kulanski**   Catholic neighbor of the Luries; his virulent anti-Semitism takes the form of endlessly tormenting David Lurie in Chaim Potok's *In the Beginning.*

**Larry Kulik**   Gangster lawyer in Joan Didion's *Play It As It Lays.*

**Sue (Biggie) Kunft**   See Sue Kunft Trumper Bennett.

**Gerhardt Kunstler**   New arrival at the Emma Lazarus Retirement Home whose presence disturbs Otto Korner in Alan Isler's *The Prince of West End Avenue.*

**Freida Kurtz**   Friend and former coworker of Nell Bray; a power at the Board of Education; drinks and smokes a lot, and sleeps around with married men in Maureen Howard's *Natural History.*

**PaPa (Papa) LaBas**   God of the crossroads in the New World and an astro-detective in Ishmael Reed's *Mumbo Jumbo* and *The Last Days of Louisiana Red*.

**Labina**   Halfhearted prostitute who finds the narrator frozen in the woods and takes him home in Jerzy Kosinski's *The Painted Bird*.

**LaBoeuf**   Texas Ranger who hunts the murderer Tom Chaney in Charles Portis's *True Grit*.

**Zozo Labrique**   Charter member of the American Hoo-Doo Church in Ishmael Reed's *Yellow Back Radio Broke-Down*.

**Nate Lace**   Exotic-foods restaurateur whose establishment is intended as the gathering place for The Club in Stanley Elkin's *Boswell*.

**Helen Fermoyle LaChance**   Wife of Renie LaChance; poisoned her husband's nice dog Riddles and made Howard bury it in the back of the yard in Mary McGarry Morris's *Songs in Ordinary Time*.

**Renie LaChance**   Husband of Helen LaChance, ex-brother-in-law of Marie Fermoyle; his only friend is his cat, Tom, which disappears; tries to force himself on Marie, who turns him in to the IRS in Mary McGarry Morris's *Songs in Ordinary Time*.

**Lactamaeon**   Tormentor of Deborah Blau in Yr, the mental world of Deborah's creation in Hannah Green's *I Never Promised You a Rose Garden*.

**Nell Lacy**   Younger sister of Johnny Church's mother, wife of Sir Valentine Lacy, and mother of Peregrine Lacy and of a child by Johnny Church in Mary Lee Settle's *Prisons*.

**Peregrine Lacy**   Son of Nell and Sir Valentine Lacy; cousin and childhood playmate of Johnny Church; dies fighting with the king's army at the siege of Bristol in Mary Lee Settle's *Prisons*.

**Sir Valentine Lacy**   Husband of Nell Lacy and father of Peregrine Lacy; befriends Johnny Church despite political and religious differences; expresses a dying wish for another child and so causes the sexual encounter between Nell and Johnny in Mary Lee Settle's *Prisons*.

**Lady of the Lake**   Benevolent mythic character in Thomas Berger's *Arthur Rex*.

**Zoot Lafferty**   Street bookie for Red Scalotta and informer for Bumper Morgan in Joseph Wambaugh's *The Blue Knight*.

**Timothy (Snail) Laird**   Free black man who works for both sides in the Civil War by selling stolen goods, helping runaway slaves, and running guns in Jesse Hill Ford's *The Raider*.

**Julia Lake**   Fifty-year-old secretary to Todd Andrews in John Barth's *The Floating Opera*.

**Peter Lake**   Orphaned immigrant raised by the Baymen, expert machinist and burglar, and former member of the Short Tails gang; marries Beverly Penn, daughter of wealthy publisher Isaac Penn; is pursued by nemesis Pearly Soames across time; reemerges as savior of New York City in Mark Helprin's *Winter's Tale*.

**Dr. V. Govinda Lal**   Space scientist, author of the book *Future of the Moon*, and advocate of inhabitation of the moon; Shula Sammler steals his lecture notes and Artur Sammler subsequently holds philosophical discussions with him in Saul Bellow's *Mr. Sammler's Planet*.

**Lancelot Andrewes (Lance) Lamar**   Crazed lawyer who tells how he wreaked apocalyptic vengeance for his wife's adultery; narrator of Walker Percy's *Lancelot*.

**Lily Lamar**   Mother of Lancelot Lamar, who suspects her of having committed adultery with her distant cousin in Walker Percy's *Lancelot*.

**Lucy Lamar**   Daughter of Lancelot and Lucy Cobb Lamar; plans to join the ménage of Raine Robinette and Troy Dana in Walker Percy's *Lancelot*.

**Lucy Cobb Lamar**   Dead and highly romanticized first wife of Lancelot Lamar in Walker Percy's *Lancelot*.

**Mary Margaret Reilly (Margot) Lamar**   Second wife of Lancelot Lamar; stars in a movie codirected by Robert Merlin, her former lover, and Janos Jacoby, her latest lover in Walker Percy's *Lancelot*.

**Maury Lamar**   Feckless and politically corrupt father of Lancelot Lamar in Walker Percy's *Lancelot*.

**Henry Lamartine, Jr.**   Son of Lulu Lamartine; named for his dead "father" but more likely the son of Beverly Lamartine; has one-night affair with Albertine Johnson; is deeply affected by his Vietnam war experiences; intentionally drowns in Louise Erdrich's *Love Medicine*.

**Lulu Lamartine**   Widow of Henry, who intentionally parks his car on railroad tracks; mother of eight boys and one girl; has affair with and eventually marries Henry's brother; has an extended affair with Nector Kashpaw; some speculate she is a witch in Louise Erdrich's *Love Medicine*.

**Lyman Lamartine**   Son of Lulu Lamartine and Nector Kashpaw; first to drive a convertible on the reservation; runs the tribal souvenir factory in Louise Erdrich's *Love Medicine*.

**Oliver Lambert**   Senior partner of Bendini, Lambert and Locke law firm in John Grisham's *The Firm*; despite grandfatherly persona and sociability, is deeply involved with illegal Mafia activities of the firm; reluctant to murder junior members of the firm who may be cooperating with the FBI, but is too afraid of the more powerful Mafia members to stop the murders.

**Coty Lamont**   Best steeplechase jockey of the decade; helped bury Mary Lou Valiant's body five years earlier; became the second recent murder victim of Arthur Tetrick after he was caught attempting to exhume Mary Lou's remains buried in Orion's stall in Rita Mae Brown's *Murder, She Meowed*.

**Maurice Lamotta**   Unscrupulous business manager for Thomas Oliver; arranges Oliver's marriage to Stephanie D'Alfonso in Shirley Ann Grau's *The Condor Passes*.

**Rabbi Milton Lampert**   Noted scholar whose publications and lectures are written for him by Herman Broder; grows wealthy from ventures in real estate, gambling, and the stock market in Isaac Bashevis Singer's *Enemies, A Love Story*.

**Lance**   Attractive black figure skater who dies of a drug overdose while skating; first lover of the male narrator of Tennessee Williams's *Moise and the World of Reason*.

**Nathan Landau**   Paranoid schizophrenic posing as a research biologist; befriends Stingo; commits double suicide with his lover, Sophie Zawistowska, in William Styron's *Sophie's Choice*.

**Marion Landers**   Company clerk who returns from duty in the South Pacific with an injured ankle and, once in the United States, stays in trouble because of his chronic violent behavior and disrespect for the army; kills himself by stepping in front of a moving car in James Jones's *Whistle*.

**John Landro**   Young reporter for *Bangor Daily News* who goes to Haven to interview citizens about the strange goings-on; killed when he gets too close to the awful truth in Stephen King's *The Tommyknockers*.

**Timothy G. Landry**   Armed robber against whom patrolman Bumper Morgan offers perjured testimony in Joseph Wambaugh's *The Blue Knight*.

**Stewart Landshorough**   Publisher of war books who is temporarily mistaken by Violet Clay for a publisher of pornography in Gail Godwin's *Violet Clay*.

**Leila Landsman**   Successful professor and author who writes about abused women; she becomes attracted to the Becky Burgess murder case and begins to write a book about it; finally trades cheating husband for cats in Marge Piercy's *The Longings of Women*.

**Nick Landsman**   Leila's ex-husband; a theater director and a philanderer; Leila divorces him after he begins traveling with a young actress in Marge Piercy's *The Longings of Women*.

**Rachel Lane**   Pious, kind, middle-aged woman who serves as a World Tribes missionary in the Pantanal region of Brazil; illegitimate daughter of Troy Phelan and heiress to his 11-billion-dollar fortune in John Grisham's *The Testament*.

**Silvia Lane**   Dishonest secretary to Leo Feldman in Stanley Elkin's *A Bad Man*.

**Carter Lang**   Womanizing movie director and husband of Maria Wyeth in Joan Didion's *Play It As It Lays*.

**Kate Lang**   Institutionalized retarded daughter of Maria Wyeth and Carter Lang in Joan Didion's *Play It As It Lays*.

**Mrs. Lang**   Name Maria Wyeth never calls herself in Joan Didion's *Play It As It Lays*.

**Susan Lang**   Prostitute who gets information about gold shipments from her client Henry Fowler in Michael Crichton's *The Great Train Robbery*.

**Torquemada Langguth**   California writer in John Updike's *Bech: A Book*.

**Ninel Ilinishna (Ninella, Nonna) Langley**   Landlady of Annette Blagovo and Vadim Vadimovich; perishes along with Annette in floods caused by a hurricane in Vladimir Nabokov's *Look at the Harlequins!*

**Lewis Lanier**   Ex-husband of Violet Clay in Gail Godwin's *Violet Clay*.

**Patrick Lanigan**   Youngest partner of a Biloxi, Mississippi, law firm; married to an unfaithful wife; fakes his own death; discovers the fraudulent nature of Benny Aricia's case under the False Claims Act and steals the subsequent reward; the woman he entrusted with the fortune disappears and leaves him with nothing in John Grisham's *The Partner*.

**Trudy Lanigan**   Unfaithful wife of Patrick Lanigan; maintained her high school lover, Lance, throughout her marriage; once Patrick returns, plots with her lover to kill him so that she will not lose the life insurance money she has collected in John Grisham's *The Partner*.

**Anne Lansing**   Youngest Lansing child and her father's favorite; becomes deeply attached to her brother George Lansing in Thornton Wilder's *The Eighth Day*.

**Breckenridge (Breck) Lansing**   Loud and boisterous managing director of some of Coaltown's mines; murder victim in Thornton Wilder's *The Eighth Day*.

**Eustacia Sims (Eustachie, Stacey) Lansing**   Wife of Breckenridge Lansing; native of St. Kitts, where she operated a store; endures much from her husband but remains faithful to him even after his death in Thornton Wilder's *The Eighth Day*.

**Fisher Lansing**   Iowa farmer who is the brother of Breckenridge Lansing; takes charge of much of Eustacia Lansing's business after his brother's murder; manages to sell some of the inventions of John Ashley as if they were Breck's work in Thornton Wilder's *The Eighth Day*.

**Félicité Marjolaine Dupuy Lansing**   Second Lansing daughter; has ambitions of becoming a nun; uncovers the mystery of her father's death and marries Roger Ashley in Thornton Wilder's *The Eighth Day*.

**George Sims Lansing**   Troubled son of Breckenridge and Eustacia Lansing; becomes fascinated with the Russian language and the theater and runs away to pursue both interests; admits to having killed his father in Thornton Wilder's *The Eighth Day*.

**Heidi Lansing**   Senior at Haddan School so nervous about college applications that she pulls out half the hair on her head in Alice Hoffman's *The River King*.

**Jean-Paul (Frenchy) La Prade**   Self-centered, wonderfully Gallic French master at Dorset Academy; has an affair with Alice Draper and then in a self-dramatizing gesture joins the Office of Strategic Services during World War II in Richard Yates's *A Good School*.

**Dr. Wilbur Larch**   Aging and ether-addicted doctor who looks upon Homer Wells as a son; performs private abortions on unwed mothers and runs the St. Cloud's Orphanage, and is determined to pass on his medical knowledge to Homer in John Irving's *The Cider House Rules*.

**Gordon LaRiviere**   Ruthlessly enterprising small-town businessman, he amasses a fortune in local real estate, dominates the local mining industry, and controls the Lawford city government; a perfectionist and consummate diplomat, he has a casual affair with the wife of his future employee Wade Whitehouse in Russell Banks's *Affliction*.

**Mlle Ida (Mlle L., Guillaume de Monparnasse) Larivière**   Governess of Ada and Lucette Veen who, using a pseudonym, becomes a famous author in Vladimir Nabokov's *Ada*.

**Brigid Larkin**   Sister of Conor Larkin; runs the family farm in Leon Uris's *Trinity*.

**Conor Larkin**   Blacksmith, Gaelic football player, and revolutionary for the Irish Catholics; lover of Shelley MacLeod and Atty Fitzpatrick in Leon Uris's *Trinity*.

**Dary Larkin**   Catholic priest; helps his brother Conor Larkin escape from prison in Leon Uris's *Trinity*.

**Karl Larkin**   Active telepath and husband of Mary Larkin in Octavia E. Butler's *Mind of My Mind*.

**Liam Larkin**   Brother of Conor Larkin; moves to Australia to farm his own land in Leon Uris's *Trinity*.

**Mary Larkin**   Wife of Karl Larkin, daughter of Doro, and granddaughter of Emma; establisher of the vast network of mental links known as the Pattern and narrator of parts of Octavia E. Butler's *Mind of My Mind*.

**Maude Larkin**   Affluent but impractical friend who encourages Alice Prentice to live beyond her means in Richard Yates's *A Special Providence*.

**Larry**   Friend of Wayne Prentice; a crotchety old bachelor with a sardonic sense of humor in Donald E. Westlake's *The Hook*.

**Larry**   Leader of a group of killers and thieves who want to benefit from Banks's theft in John Hawkes's *The Lime Twig*.

**Larry**   See Volume I.

**Lars**   Lover of Joseph Johnson; towheaded, boyish, with heavy brown eyes, short and shaggy as a pony in Frances Sherwood's *Vindication*.

**Donny LaRue**   Seventeen-year-old boy whom Martha Horgan has a crush on until he and his friends rip her clothes off, pour beer on her, and poke her with sticks in Mary McGarry Morris's *A Dangerous Woman*.

**Ken LaSalle**   Attorney to Larry Cook who helps arrange the transfer and the incorporation of the farm; helps Caroline Cook Rasmussen and Larry Cook sue Rose Cook Lewis and Ginny Cook Smith to get the farm back in Jane Smiley's *A Thousand Acres*.

**Richard Lasker**   Publisher and editor of *Great Naval Battles*; Tarden exposes Lasker's involvement in a plot to boost book sales by faking the disappearance of one of his authors behind the Iron Curtain in Jerzy Kosinski's *Cockpit*.

**Norma Latchett**   Thirty-six-year-old mistress of Henry Bech for two and a half years; tense, critical woman with a sharp tongue; replaced as mistress by her sister, Bea Latchett Cook, in John Updike's *Bech: A Book*.

**Frank Lathrop**   Lifetime farming friend and neighbor of Mat Feltner; together they own the building used by Jasper Lathrop for his general store, the central meeting place for many of the conversations in Wendell Berry's *A Place on Earth* and *The Memory of Old Jack*.

**Jasper Lathrop**   Son of Frank Lathrop and owner of a general store in Port William, Kentucky, in Wendell Berry's *A Place on Earth* and *The Memory of Old Jack*.

**John Lau**   Stolid, good-natured FBI detective and friend of Gideon Oliver in Aaron Elkins's *Old Bones*.

**Eva Laubenstein**   Mother of Konrad Vost imprisoned for murdering Konrad Vost the father; engineers her son's sexual liberation during a revolt of women prisoners in John Hawkes's *The Passion Artist*.

**Harold Emery Lauder**   Adolescent in love with Frances Goldsmith; joins forces with Randall Flagg in Stephen King's *The Stand*.

**Launcelot**   Lover of Guinevere and antagonist of Arthur; describes himself as "not a leader, but . . . always led" in Thomas Berger's *Arthur Rex*.

**Count Laundromat**   Austrian who runs a laundromat near Renate's home in Anaïs Nin's *Collages*.

**Laura**   Married woman who has had an affair with Charles, eventually leaves her husband, and seems to begin a more permanent relationship with Charles in Ann Beattie's *Chilly Scenes of Winter*.

**Natividad (Tivisita) Lauranzon**   Former student of Salome Urena's who comes to live with her; marries Francisco Henriquez when Salome dies; stepmother of Salome Camila in Julia Alvarez's *In the Name of Salome*.

**Meghan Laurel**   Beautiful and intelligent daughter of a sea captain who falls in love with Johannes Verne in Louis L'Amour's *The Lonesome Gods*.

**Laurie**   Sexual conquest of Carol Severin Swanson in Jim Harrison's *Wolf*.

**Albert (Kid Lousy, Lousse, Kid Louso, Lousy) Lauzon**   See Volume I.

**Eleanor Lavery**   Lifelong friend who helps liberate Isabel Moore from bondage to the past in Mary Gordon's *Final Payments*.

**Barbara Lavette**   Heiress of a wealthy San Francisco banker, she leaves Sarah Lawrence College to volunteer at a union soup kitchen on the Embarcadero, then moves to Paris to work as a magazine correspondent in Howard Fast's *Second Generation*.

**Dan Lavette**   Former shipbuilder and captain of industry, he abandons his first family to marry a Chinese woman and work as a fisherman; father of Tom, Barbara, and Joe Lavette in Howard Fast's *Second Generation*.

**Eloise Clawson Lavette**   Unhappy wife of Tom Lavette; she suffers painful migraine headaches and an abusive husband in Howard Fast's *Second Generation*.

**Joe Lavette**   Chinese-American son of Dan Lavette and May Ling; is the stepbrother of Tom and Barbara Lavette and the object of Sally Levy's affection in Howard Fast's *Second Generation*.

**Tom Lavette**   Spoiled rich son of Dan Lavette and Jean Lavette Whittier; relies on his stepfather, John Whittier, to bail him out of trouble in Howard Fast's *Second Generation*.

**Angela Williams Lavoisier**   Fierce mother of Abeba Torch, her only child in Ellease Southerland's *Let the Lion Eat Straw*.

**Arthur Lavoisier**   Loving stepfather of Abeba Torch in Ellease Southerland's *Let the Lion Eat Straw*.

**Mama Lavorn**   Operator of a black café and tourist home, a front for prostitution; dying of cancer, she narrates part of Jesse Hill Ford's *The Liberation of Lord Byron Jones*.

**Jack Laws**   Lover of Ethan Segal and friend of Pammy Wynant; commits suicide while the three are vacationing in Maine in Don DeLillo's *Players*.

**Catherine (Cat, Catty) Lawson**   Hair straightener who tends to Ursa Corregidora following Ursa's operation in Gayl Jones's *Corregidora*.

**Lawyer Bob**   Bryce Proctorr's divorce attorney; he lacks a sense of humor in Donald E. Westlake's *The Hook*.

**William Layamon**   Father of Benn Crader's bride, Matilda; a wealthy physician with political aspirations, he encourages

Matilda's marriage as a means of manipulating Benn to sue for his lost inheritance and thereby have the substantial funds necessary to support Matilda in Saul Bellow's *More Die of Heartbreak*.

**Lazarus**  Ex-insurance salesman; bouncer at the Iron Horse and student at Belt's dojo in Harry Crews's *Karate Is a Thing of the Spirit*.

**Lazarus**  Servant of Johnny Church's family; sent to fight in Cromwell's army; captured by the king's army, who cut off his ears and his tongue in Mary Lee Settle's *Prisons*.

**Joe (Joey, Laze) Lazenby**  High school friend of Conrad Jarrett in Judith Guest's *Ordinary People*.

**Clark Lazlo**  Great-grandson of Clarence and Stella Wilmot; the unexpected result of Essie Wilmot's brief affair with Hollywood scriptwriter Matt Lazlo; joins a doomsday cult led by Jesse Smith; saves some of the cult children from the government's attack on the cult's headquarters; dies as his grandfather, Teddy Wilmot, watches the horrifying event unfold on television; central figure in the fourth and last part of John Updike's saga of the Wilmot family, *In the Beauty of the Lilies*.

**Joan Lazio**  Sister of John Jr., daughter of John Sr. and Bette; lives in Los Angeles with her husband, Mario, and her two children; after her mother's heart attack, she helps John Jr. take care of her mother and father in William Wharton's *Dad*.

**Rose Wise (Mrs. Rose, Rosey) Lazuli**  San Francisco socialite who directs poetry readings and entertains Jack Duluoz in Jack Kerouac's *Desolation Angels*.

**Paul Lazzaro**  Prisoner of war and murderer of Billy Pilgrim in Kurt Vonnegut's *Slaughterhouse-Five*.

**Eddie Lazzutti**  Private in the Third Squad who pursues Cacciato; music lover who carries the radio and sings to the men in the Third Squad; a follower of Oscar Johnson in Tim O'Brien's *Going After Cacciato*.

**Zelda Leah**  First wife of Jacob Eliezer, engaged to him at the age of ten, and mother of their three children; killed with her children in the Chmielnicki massacre in Isaac Bashevis Singer's *The Slave*.

**Carlin Leander**  Girl who has never left home before she wins a swimming scholarship to Haddan School; has a father she has never met and a mother who is a clerk at Value Mart; tells other students that her mother and father travel the world; a friend of Gus Pierce; works for Helen Davis; dates Harry McKenna in Alice Hoffman's *The River King*.

**Joe Leaphorn**  Navajo Indian policeman with the New Mexico Navajo Tribal police; thorough detective and an excellent tracker; figures out the motive for the murder of Ernesto Cata, but is too late to save George Bowlegs in Tony Hillerman's *Dance Hall of the Dead*.

**Charles Leary**  Divorced brother of Macon Leary; lives with his siblings Rose Leary Edge and Porter Leary in the family home in Baltimore, Maryland, in Anne Tyler's *The Accidental Tourist*.

**Macon Leary**  Forty-something resident of Baltimore, Maryland, and travel writer for the Accidental Tourist series of guidebooks; brother of Charles and Porter Leary and Rose Leary Edge, who are all like him in personality; suffers a mental breakdown and finds solace in the disorder and wackiness of his dog's trainer, Muriel Pritchett, in Anne Tyler's *The Accidental Tourist*.

**Porter Leary**  Good-looking, vibrant brother of Macon Leary; divorced father of Danny, Susan, and Liberty in Anne Tyler's *The Accidental Tourist*.

**Sarah Leary**  Forty-something resident of Baltimore, Maryland, and wife of Macon Leary; leaves her husband and files for divorce but finds herself missing him and moves back, only to have him leave her in Anne Tyler's *The Accidental Tourist*.

**Woodrow (Woody) Leathers**  World War II friend of Orlando Pratt; sleeps with Maude Coffin Pratt, who thinks Leathers is her brother, Orlando, in Paul Theroux's *Picture Palace*.

**Peter Leavitt**  Clinical microbiologist and member of the scientist group at Project Wildfire in Michael Crichton's *The Andromeda Strain*.

**Nikolai Maximovitch Lebedev**  Owner of a brickyard; hires Yakov Bok as foreman after Yakov saves his life in Bernard Malamud's *The Fixer*.

**Zinaida Nikolaevna (Zina) Lebedev**  Daughter of Nikolai Lebedev; tries to seduce Yakov Bok and later testifies against him in Bernard Malamud's *The Fixer*.

**Dmitri Lebedov**  Elderly Russian orderly at Sacred Heart Hospital; confesses to Angelo DeMarco that he attempted to rape Maria Alvarez in Edward Lewis Wallant's *The Children at the Gate*.

**Claude Lebel**  Deputy to head of the Criminal Brigade, called "the best detective in France," who tracks down and exposes several of the Jackal's false identities; alerts the French police to the Jackal's last identity; follows a hunch to discover the Jackal, whom he kills in a firefight in Frederick Forsyth's *The Day of the Jackal*.

**Ulysse Lebris**  Restaurateur in Brittany and distant relative discovered by Jean-Louis Lebris de Kérouac in Jack Kerouac's *Satori in Paris*.

**Hannibal Lecter (Hannibal the Cannibal)**  Cannibalistic serial killer and former psychiatrist; from his cell in a mental hospital, he draws FBI trainee Clarice Starling into a dark psychological game that helps her track down another serial killer in *The Silence of the Lambs* by Thomas Harris. Lecter also is a central character in Harris's *Red Dragon* (1981) and *Hannibal* (1999).

**Nicasio Ledesma**   Head of Philippine security forces who arranges for the assassination of opposition leader Senator Domingo Avila; expert on torture who has Daisy Avila interrogated and gang-raped; coldly dominating and highly jealous lover of Manila's top movie starlet in Jessica Hagedorn's *Dogeaters*.

**Arthur Lee**   Obstetrician; friend of John and Judith Berry and husband of Betty Lee; performs abortions; is arrested for the murder of Karen Randall in Jeffery Hudson's *A Case of Need*.

**Carol Lee**   Friend of Fish Fisher; had a child at sixteen and gave her up for adoption; stays with Sky and Prudence in Sandra Scofield's *Beyond Deserving*.

**Lana Lee**   Beautiful and cold-hearted owner of the Night of Joy, a bar on Bourbon Street in New Orleans; the mastermind of a pornography ring; accidentally propositions patrolman Mancuso and gets arrested in John Kennedy Toole's *A Confederacy of Dunces*.

**Mavis (China Doll) Lee**   Prostitute in Decatur, New Jersey; becomes involved with murder and drug dealing in Hal Bennett's *Lord of Dark Places*.

**Mr. Lee**   School janitor and crossing guard in Mary McGarry Morris's *Songs in Ordinary Time*.

**Robert Lee**   Friend of Theodora Waite in college; leaves school with Theodora and moves to New York; steals from the bakery cash drawer; they break up after she hits him in Bette Pesetsky's *Midnight Sweets*.

**Robert Edward Lee**   Confederate general commanding the Army of Northern Virginia; hopes to destroy Union forces through a second invasion of the North, but loses decisively at Gettysburg in Michael Shaara's *The Killer Angels*.

**Washington Lee**   African-American literary editor who regularly fends off cuckolded husbands and angry authors; forcibly removes Rasheed Jamaal, an African-American writer, from his office, which angers African-American activists; works with fellow editor Russell Calloway in an attempt to engineer a leveraged buyout of their publishing firm in Jay McInerney's *Brightness Falls*.

**William (Bill, Billy, Lee the Agent, El Hombre Invisible, Inspector J. Lee, Klinker, William Seward) Lee**   See Volume I.

**Mary Agnes LeFabre**   Creole black woman who rejects the advances of white Tee Bob Samson in Ernest J. Gaines's *The Autobiography of Miss Jane Pittman*.

**Gordon Lefferts**   Husband of Myra Lefferts and father of Connie and Kate; wealthy gynecologist who owns a vacation home in Jamaica; has a one-night stand with Sondra Pressman and offers to leave his wife for her in Judy Blume's *Wifey*.

**Myra Lefferts**   Older sister of Sandy Pressman and wife of Gordon Lefferts; mother of Connie and Kate, twins; is wealthy and concerned with appearances; enjoys going to the country club and is a very good tennis player; gains her identity through being a doctor's wife in Judy Blume's *Wifey*.

**Natalie LeFrance**   Healer located in a shopping mall in Glades beside the Dunkin' Donuts in Alice Hoffman's *Local Girls*.

**Felicity "Fleece" Legge**   Wife of Morgan Legge, mother of seven children; a former serving girl in Bharati Mukherjee's *The Holder of the World*.

**Gabriel Legge**   Claims to be the son of the owner of the ship the *Swallow*, but his father turns out to be an indebted drunk; courts Hester Manning; after she commits suicide, courts and marries Hannah Easton; murders Cephus Prynne and isn't caught; joins the marquis as a pirate; Hannah leaves him when she discovers his relationship with Zeb-un-Nissa, his black bibbi; he dies in 1720 and is buried in the British Cemetery in Calcutta in Bharati Mukherjee's *The Holder of the World*.

**Hannah Easton Fitch Legge**   Also known as the Salem Bibi; a Puritan woman from Salem who ends up in the Mughal Emperor's court; marries Gabriel Legge and moves to England in 1692; gets a reputation as a healer; sails with Gabriel to India, but leaves him when she hears about his mistress; is rescued from an angry mob by the Raja Jadav Singh, and when Singh is killed, returns to Salem with her daughter and ekes out a living as a nurse, veterinarian, and occasionally, a doctor in Bharati Mukherjee's *The Holder of the World*.

**Morgan Legge**   Far older, dull-witted brother of Gabriel; husband of Felicity; squat, short, fair, and balding, with seven children in Bharati Mukherjee's *The Holder of the World*.

**William Leggett**   Consumptive editor of the *Evening Post*; invites Charles Schuyler to write Aaron Burr's story; convinced that Martin Van Buren is Burr's illegitimate son in Gore Vidal's *Burr*.

**Rosalind Leigh**   Successful writer; emotionally exhausted after the death of her daughter and divorce; investigates Olive Martin's gruesome murder of her mother and sister, believing Olive to be innocent; collaborates and falls in love with ex-policeman Hal Hawksley in Minette Walters's *The Sculptress*.

**William Leigh**   Friend of Jack Flowers; dies suddenly in Paul Theroux's *Saint Jack*.

**Lekh**   Bird catcher and lover of Stupid Ludmila; paints the bird in the title of Jerzy Kosinski's *The Painted Bird*.

**Annie Leland**   Grandmother of Peter Leland; forces her grandson to look at his manacled father and later wills him the house where his father was imprisoned in the attic in Fred Chappell's *Dagon*.

**Peter Leland**   Methodist minister, author of *Remnants of Pagan Forces in American Puritanism*, and drunken subject of Mina Morgan's humiliations, mutilations, and human sacrifice; protagonist of Fred Chappell's *Dagon*.

**Sheila Leland**　Wife of Peter Leland; presumably murdered by him in Fred Chappell's *Dagon*.

**Len**　Second husband of Deidre in Bette Pesetsky's *Midnight Sweets*.

**Lena**　See Mary Magdalene Dead.

**Lenard (Len)**　Lover of Lou Ellen and party host in Ed Bullins's *The Reluctant Rapist*.

**Judith (Judy) Lengel**　Stupid but determined student of George Caldwell in John Updike's *The Centaur*.

**Lenore**　Radical left-wing contact of Kat Alcazar; recommended Kat to Angel Stone in M. F. Beal's *Angel Dance*.

**Leola**　Second cousin by marriage to Shokotee McNeilly; comes to live with Elias McCutcheon and Jane Nail at the birth of their first child and remains in Jesse Hill Ford's *The Raider*.

**Leona (Anne)**　Poor white woman from Georgia whom Rufus Scott loves and abuses in James Baldwin's *Another Country*.

**Tawny Leonard**　Raised by Darlene, Tawny is convinced she can offer a better life to her children Vix, Lanie, Nathan, and Lewis; however, eventually leaves the family to take care of her boss, the Countess; ends up in Florida with Myles, a retired navy man, in Judy Blume's *Summer Sisters*.

**Victoria (Vix) Leonard**　Originally from Santa Fe, Vix befriends Caitlin Somers and her life changes; she vacations on Martha's Vineyard, begins attending a private school, discovers sex with Bru, and ends up at Harvard; marries and has a child with Gus, another guest at the Somers's Vineyard house in Judy Blume's *Summer Sisters*.

**Dulcie Leong**　See Dulcie Fu.

**Leon Leong**　Merchant seaman whose restlessness on land drives him constantly to go on long voyages but who does not abandon his wife and family; Chinese immigrant for whom the American Dream has failed; moves out of his home after one of his daughters dies; second husband of Dulcie Fu, stepfather of Leila Louie, and father of Ona and Nina Leong in Fae Myenne Ng's *Bone*.

**Nina Leong**　Youngest child of a San Francisco immigrant Chinese family who moves to New York to avoid her parents' pressures and demands; tour guide on trips from the United States to China; youngest half sister of Leila Louie in Fae Myenne Ng's *Bone*.

**Ona Leong**　Middle child of immigrant parents who either accidentally or intentionally plunges to her death from an upper story of a San Francisco Chinatown housing project; her unexpected death haunts the surviving members of her family, who wonder how they might have prevented the tragedy; half sister of Leila Louie in Fae Myenne Ng's *Bone*.

**Leontine**　Black singer at the Paradise Inn nightclub in Anaïs Nin's *Collages*.

**J. T. Leopold**　Retired painter and husband of Milly Leopold; occupies a Second Avenue apartment managed by Norman Moonbloom in Edward Lewis Wallant's *The Tenants of Moonbloom*.

**Milly Leopold**　Wife of J. T. Leopold; lives in a Second Avenue apartment managed by Norman Moonbloom in Edward Lewis Wallant's *The Tenants of Moonbloom*.

**Jack Lerner**　Frances Samuelson's oncologist; holds his patients' hands when he has to deliver bad news, and weeps in his car while he drives home in Alice Hoffman's *Local Girls*.

**Harry LeSabre**　Transvestite Pontiac salesman in Kurt Vonnegut's *Breakfast of Champions*.

**Thomas Le Sage**　Los Angeles Superior Court judge who replaces Arthur Alarcon in the second trial of Gregory Powell and Jimmy Smith in Joseph Wambaugh's *The Onion Field*.

**Harry Lesser**　Jewish novelist struggling to finish his third novel; criticizes the writing of Willie Spearmint and falls in love with Irene Bell in Bernard Malamud's *The Tenants*.

**Lestat**　Vampire who makes Louis a vampire; kills Claudia and Madeleine in Anne Rice's *Interview with the Vampire*. Famed vampire-hero and writer; depressed and suicidal because of his long years (200+) as a vampire; is haunted by the memory of the child vampire, Claudia; trades bodies with the thieving spirit, Raglan James; regains his body with the help of his only human friend, David Talbot, but betrays Talbot by turning him into a vampire in Anne Rice's *The Tale of the Body Thief*.

**Abe (Lynx) Letterman**　Agent for Angela Sterling and for Dave and Debbie Roberts in Terry Southern's *Blue Movie*.

**George Letwin**　New husband of Theodora's stepmother; asks Theodora to call him Dad; a decent man, but alien to Theodora; has two boys, ages eight and ten, in Bette Pesetsky's *Midnight Sweets*.

**Pauline Waite Letwin**　Deserted wife of Abner Waite, wife of George, stepmother of Theodora; married three times; after Abner leaves, becomes a babysitter until she meets her new husband, George, and moves to Florida; ages early and moves to a long-term care home in Bette Pesetsky's *Midnight Sweets*.

**Madame Leuwen**　Pseudonym under which one of Tarden's unidentified lovers checks into Hotel de la Mole in Jerzy Kosinski's *Cockpit*.

**Lev (Arich Ben Barak)**　Husband of Katrina Perlk and father of Marshall Pearl; Russian Jew who commands the Israeli Second Mountain Brigade in Mark Helprin's *Refiner's Fire*.

**Aryeh Lev**　Father of Asher Lev; breaks with his son over Asher's art; assists European Jews in Chaim Potok's *My Name Is Asher Lev*.

**Asher Lev**    Narrator whose art causes his rejection by the Jewish community in Chaim Potok's *My Name Is Asher Lev.*

**Rivkeh Lev**    Mother of Asher Lev; torn between her son's artistic talent and her husband's disdain of that talent in Chaim Potok's *My Name Is Asher Lev.*

**Yitzchok Lev**    Supportive uncle of Asher Lev in Chaim Potok's *My Name Is Asher Lev.*

**George (Lev) Levanter**    Russian emigré, international businessman, and adventurer; protagonist of Jerzy Kosinski's *Blind Date.*

**Irving Levenspiel**    Jewish landlord who wants Harry Lesser to move so he can tear down the building in Bernard Malamud's *The Tenants.*

**Seymour (Sam, Sy) Levin**    Thirty-year-old composition instructor at Cascadia College who has an affair with Pauline Gilley that eventually leads to his resignation from the college; central character in Bernard Malamud's *A New Life.*

**Holly Levine**    Literary critic and friend of Leslie Braverman in Wallace Markfield's *To an Early Grave.*

**Richard Levine**    Fossil-hunting zoologist whose disappearance sparks a dangerous manhunt through dinosaur-infested Costa Rican jungle in Michael Crichton's *The Lost World.*

**Tannie Levitt**    Pathetic old lady in the "convalescent home" where Will Barrett is taken after his diagnosis; Jack Curl uses Tannie and Tod to demonstrate the efficacy of the system in Walker Percy's *The Second Coming.*

**Tod Levitt**    Old man, married to Tannie in the "convalescent home" where Will Barrett is taken after his diagnosis. Jack Curl uses Tod and Tannie to demonstrate the efficacy of the system in Walker Percy's *The Second Coming.*

**Dawn Levov**    Wife of Seymour Levov; former Miss New Jersey and Miss America contestant; Irish Catholic; claims to have entered beauty contests only to earn scholarship money and dislikes being reminded of her title; mother of Meredith; owns and manages a beef cattle operation; suffers suicidal depression after daughter becomes a fugitive; emerges from it with help of her husband and plastic surgery; has an affair with William Orcutt in Philip Roth's *American Pastoral.*

**Jerry Levov**    Younger brother of Seymour Levov; successful cardiac surgeon, married four times; aggressive, outspoken; when Seymour calls him in despair, instead of comforting him, tells Seymour he never understood anything about himself or those around him in Philip Roth's *American Pastoral.*

**Meredith (Merry) Levov**    Daughter of Seymour and Dawn Levov; beautiful and intelligent child but has a severe stutter; at age sixteen, kills a man when she bombs a local store and post office as a Vietnam war protest; becomes a fugitive; hides from her family; becomes a Jain and loses stutter in Philip Roth's *American Pastoral.*

**Seymour "Swede" Levov**    Blond, handsome Jewish former high school star athlete; runs a Newark glove factory; kind, respectable, dislikes violence; distraught when his daughter, Meredith, becomes a fugitive; searches for her obsessively; first marriage destroyed by wife's affair with William Orcutt five years after Meredith's disappearance in Philip Roth's *American Pastoral.*

**Adam Levy**    Son of Jake and Clair Levy; he falls in love with Eloise Clawson Lavette in Howard Fast's *Second Generation.*

**Clair Levy**    Wife of Jake Levy; co-owner of Higate winery in the Napa Valley; mother of Joshua, Adam, and Sally Levy in Howard Fast's *Second Generation.*

**Mr. Gus Levy**    Owner of the failing Levy Pants, a manufacturer of men's trousers in New Orleans; is hen-pecked by his wife, Mrs. Levy, and forever under the shadow of his domineering, though deceased, father; tries to avoid confrontation and his factory whenever possible; changes the scope of Levy Pants to Levy Shorts and gives Burma Jones a high-profile job in John Kennedy Toole's *A Confederacy of Dunces.*

**Helen Levy**    Professor of foreign languages at Moo University; involved fourteen years earlier with Dr. Bo Jones; has a long-standing and clandestine relationship with provost Ivar Harstad, whom she later marries; the kind and gentle soul of the university community; friends with Margaret Bell and Joy Pfisterer in Jane Smiley's *Moo.*

**Jake Levy**    Friend of Dan Lavette; winemaker in the Napa Valley; father of Joshua, Adam, and Sally Levy in Howard Fast's *Second Generation.*

**Joshua Levy**    Son of Jake and Clair Levy; he is killed in action in World War II in Howard Fast's *Second Generation.*

**Lydia Levy**    American Jew who is the sister of Paul Levy and the wife of Marshall Pearl; understands her husband's visions and supports his search for his family in Mark Helprin's *Refiner's Fire.*

**Paul Levy**    American Jew who is the brother of Lydia Levy and the protector of Marshall Pearl; navy officer who, as captain of the *Lindos Transit,* tries unsuccessfully to help transport European Jews to Palestine in Mark Helprin's *Refiner's Fire.*

**Sally Levy**    Daughter of Jake and Clair Levy, as a teenager she falls madly in love with family friend Joe Lavette in Howard Fast's *Second Generation.*

**Chava Levy-Monot**    Wife of Martin Levy-Monot, mother of Jacqueline, Naomi, and Rivka; dies at Dora/Nordhausen concentration camp in World War II in Marge Piercy's *Gone to Soldiers.*

**Jacqueline Levy-Monot**    Also known by her Jewish name, Yakova, and her code name, Gingembre; daughter of Martin and

Chava Levy-Monot, older sister of twins Naomi and Rivka Levy-Monot; Jewish-French citizen at the beginning World War II, she loses all but one of her immediate family members during the war; a member of the French Resistance; falls in love with an American OSS soldier, Jeff Coates; survives Auschwitz and the death march to Magdenberg; when the war ends, she reunites with her one living sister, Naomi, in Marge Piercy's *Gone to Soldiers*.

**Martin Levy-Monot**  Jewish-French citizen, he is known by the code name Lapin as a leader in the French Resistance; husband of Chava, father of Jacqueline, Naomi, and Rivka; he is killed in the massacre on Montange Noire in Marge Piercy's *Gone to Soldiers*.

**Naomi Levy-Monot**  Younger sister of Jacqueline and twin of Rivka Levy-Monot; Naomi is sent to live with her extended family in Detroit, Michigan, during World War II; adopted by her aunt and uncle; molested by her cousin Duvey Siegal, raped and impregnated by a boarder named Lieb; she leaves the United States for Israel with her one surviving sister, Jacqueline, in Marge Piercy's *Gone to Soldiers*.

**Rivka Levy-Monot**  Jewish-French citizen; younger sister of Jacqueline and twin of Naomi Levy-Monot; Rivka and her mother are sent to a concentration camp during World War II; Rivka dies after trying to escape in Marge Piercy's *Gone to Soldiers*.

**Daniel Isaacson (Danny) Lewin**  Son of Paul and Rochelle Isaacson, reared by Robert and Lise Lewin following his parents' execution; Ph.D. candidate at Columbia University who physically abuses his wife and is a radical protester; narrates parts of E. L. Doctorow's *The Book of Daniel*.

**Lise Lewin**  Wife of Robert Lewin and foster-mother of Daniel Isaacson Lewin and Susan Isaacson Lewin in E. L. Doctorow's *The Book of Daniel*.

**Robert Lewin**  Husband of Lise Lewin and foster father of Daniel Isaacson Lewin and Susan Isaacson Lewin; Boston College law professor who knows that the Isaacsons' trial was a travesty in E. L. Doctorow's *The Book of Daniel*.

**Susan Isaacson (Susy, Susyanna) Lewin**  Daughter of Paul and Rochelle Isaacson reared by Robert and Lise Lewin following her parents' execution; institutionalized after attempting suicide; retreats into her madness and dies in E. L. Doctorow's *The Book of Daniel*.

**Linda Lewis**  Daughter of Rose Cook Lewis and Pete Lewis; sister of Pammy Lewis; student sent to Quaker boarding school in West Branch, Iowa; niece of Ginny Cook Smith and Caroline Cook; granddaughter of Larry Cook in Jane Smiley's *A Thousand Acres*.

**Peter (Pete) Lewis**  Charismatic musician who meets and marries Rose Cook in college; urban transplant to Iowa; disappointed farmer; father of Pammy and Linda; son-in-law of Larry Cook, with whom he argues fiercely and whose rule he resists;

continues to remain an outsider until his suicide in Jane Smiley's *A Thousand Acres*.

**Rose Cook Lewis**  Sister of Ginny Cook Smith and Caroline Cook; feisty daughter who occasionally stands up to her father Larry Cook; lover of Jess Clark; wife and then widow of Pete Lewis; victim of breast cancer in Jane Smiley's *A Thousand Acres*.

**Sam Lewis**  Peace Corps agricultural volunteer nearing the end of his two-year commitment in the Pujehun district of Sierra Leone; a cynic who dismisses the Mende culture for its superstition and lack of science-based medicine, but warily understands that consequences in West Africa are dictated by both in Richard Dooling's *White Man's Grave*.

**Shepherd (Shep) Lewis**  Black schoolteacher and friend of Eli Jah Green; takes a special but not necessarily benevolent interest in Robert X in Ernest J. Gaines's *In My Father's House*.

**Tony Lewis**  Good-looking gay man in his thirties; lover of Sebastian Michael and friend of Johnny Rio in John Rechy's *Numbers*.

**Lieutenant Leznicki**  New York detective who first accuses Stephen Rojack of murdering Deborah Rojack in Norman Mailer's *An American Dream*.

**Mélanie (La Jarretière) L'Heuremaudit**  Young French ballet star; has an affair with V. in Paris in 1913; dies during a performance as the result of an accident or suicide in Thomas Pynchon's *V.*

**Libanius**  Hellenist scholar and philosopher whose teachings are much admired by Julian; narrates part of Gore Vidal's *Julian*.

**Libby**  Wife of Dan, mother of Jennie and Celia, aunt of Anne, Katie, Rossie, and Valery, sister of Grace, Rachel, Elinor, and May; has stomach trouble in Joan Chase's *During the Reign of the Queen of Persia*.

**Mr. Librarian (Candyman)**  Caretaker of an unusual San Francisco library and lover of Vida Kramar; narrator of Richard Brautigan's *The Abortion*.

**Abraham Licht**  Confidence man and schemer; father of Thurston and Harwood by Arabella Jenkins, Millie by Morna Hirshfield, Darian and Esther by Sophia; rescues black foundling Elisha and raises him as a son; in old age weds Rosamund Grille and fathers Melanie; having become paranoid, burns the memoir of all the details of his schemes, triumphs, and losses in Joyce Carl Oates's *My Heart Laid Bare*.

**Darian Licht**  Youngest son of Abraham Licht; unlike his older siblings, never allowed to know of or participate in his father's schemes; becomes a composer of modern music ahead of its time; falls in love with his father's wife, Rosamund; their affair not consummated until one month before Abraham's death in Joyce Carol Oates's *My Heart Laid Bare*.

**Elisha Licht**   Black foundling raised by Abraham Licht; extremely talented at confidence schemes Abraham involves him in; falls in love with Millicent Licht; banished by Abraham, reappears years later as Prince Elihu, leader of the World Negro Betterment and Liberation Union in Joyce Carol Oates's *My Heart Laid Bare.*

**Emily Licht**   Nurse Jack Flood has an affair with in Maureen Howard's *Expensive Habits.*

**Esther Licht**   Youngest daughter of Abraham Licht; unlike older siblings, never allowed to know of or participate in her father's schemes; compassionate, warm, loving; becomes a nurse and then a crusader for birth control in Joyce Carol Oates's *My Heart Laid Bare.*

**Harwood Licht**   Second son of Abraham Licht; surly, untalkative; murders a woman during a quarrel with his brother Thurston; sent to Colorado, engineers a confidence scheme in which he murders a wealthy man and takes his place; when the man's relatives discover the scheme, he is killed, dismembered, and parts of his body are sent to his father in gift boxes in Joyce Carol Oates's *My Heart Laid Bare.*

**Millicent Licht**   Oldest daughter of Abraham Licht; accomplished and beautiful confidence artist; falls in love with adopted brother, Elisha Licht, and wishes to marry him; father forbids this; weds the son of a confidence scheme victim in Joyce Carol Oates's *My Heart Laid Bare.*

**Thurston Licht**   Oldest son of Abraham Licht; submits to arrest and trial for murder of a woman killed by his brother; undergoes a religious conversion in jail; apparently executed, but actually escapes to Canada; reappears as a traveling minister and evangelist in Joyce Carol Oates's *My Heart Laid Bare.*

**Lieb**   Jewish-American man, he dates Ruthie Siegal but marries her best friend, Trudi; loses a foot from a war injury while serving in World War II; when Trudi and Lieb move in with the Siegal family, Lieb seduces and rapes Naomi Levy-Monot in Marge Piercy's *Gone to Soldiers.*

**Maxwell (Skip) Lieberman**   Coney Island schoolmate of Bruce Gold and now manager of a small intellectual magazine that publishes Gold's articles in Joseph Heller's *Good as Gold.*

**The Lie Detector**   See Volume I.

**Lietta**   Oldest daughter of Edward in Anaïs Nin's *Seduction of the Minotaur.*

**Will Lightbody**   Desperate patient with an enigmatic stomach problem; he's looking for a miracle cure, and a special turn-of-the-century sanitarium promises to offer it in T. Coraghessan Boyle's *The Road to Wellville.*

**Lightborne**   Owner of a Soho gallery and erotic art dealer in Don DeLillo's *Running Dog.*

**Charlie Lightfoot**   Veteran Los Angeles police detective and former partner of A. M. Valnikov; a suicide in Joseph Wambaugh's *The Black Marble.*

**Ruth Lightwood**   Bitter wife of Jack Beechum; refuses to sleep with her husband after the birth of their daughter, Clara Beechum, in Wendell Berry's *The Memory of Old Jack.*

**Lil Bits**   Daughter of Aunt Cora Lou and sister of Mamie in Sarah E. Wright's *This Child's Gonna Live.*

**Lillian**   Mother of Adele Diamond and grandmother of Ann August; was married to Art, who has died; her home is a place of peace for Ann and Adele; enjoys the outdoors and collects rocks with Ann in Mona Simpson's *Anywhere but Here.*

**Lillian**   See Honest Lil.

**Beulah Lilt**   Daughter of Hester Lilt; as a child, is dull and never talks; moves to Paris as a teenager, and as an adult becomes a famous and influential artist in Cynthia Ozick's *The Cannibal Galaxy.*

**Hester Lilt**   Imagistic linguistic logician; single mother of Beulah; very direct and patronizing; friend of Joseph Brill in Cynthia Ozick's *The Cannibal Galaxy.*

**Lily**   Mira's friend; driven insane by the cruelty of her father, husband, and son in Marilyn French's *The Women's Room.*

**Mr. Lincoln**   Black Philadelphian who raises canaries and teaches Birdy about breeding them in William Wharton's *Birdy.*

**David Linden**   Freshman who shares the attic in Chalk House with Gus Pierce; his great-grandfather had been governor of the Commonwealth; develops a stutter because of his treatment by other boys in Alice Hoffman's *The River King.*

**May Ling**   Chinese wife of American Dan Lavette; mother of Joe Lavette in Howard Fast's *Second Generation.*

**Mr. Linnehan**   High school principal of Henry Bech in John Updike's *Bech: A Book.*

**Colonel Linscomb**   Horse owner in William Faulkner's *The Reivers.*

**Lestat de Lioncourt**   See Lestat.

**Lip Lipranzer**   Homicide detective on special command with the Kindle County Prosecuting Office; Rusty Sabich's best friend, who helps Rusty out when he is accused of murder in Scott Turow's *Presumed Innocent.*

**Nahum Lipschitz**   Resident of Emma Lazarus Retirement Home whose decisions as director of the home's production of *Hamlet* infuriate Otto Korner; Otto initially regards his death with suspicion in Alan Isler's *The Prince of West End Avenue.*

**Lucy Lipscomb**   Distant cousin of Tom More; owner of family plantation Pantherburn; she and More discover that molar sodium 24 (NA 24) is being pumped into the Ratlif intake; helps More to expose the child pornography ring at John Van Dorn's private school in Walker Percy's *The Thanatos Syndrome*.

**Jane Lées Lipton**   World traveler and philanthropist; sufferer from lupus erythematosus; friend of Brewster Ashenden in *The Making of Ashenden*, a novella in Stanley Elkin's *Searches and Seizures*.

**Prince Lir**   Adopted son of King Haggard; falls in love with Lady Amalthea and performs heroic deeds to win her favor in Peter S. Beagle's *The Last Unicorn*.

**Lisa**   Exotic woman in Acapulco who looks like a combination of a Toulouse-Lautrec painting and the jungle; moves back to New York with her lover Bill; friend of Renate in Anaïs Nin's *Collages*.

**Lissener**   Twelve-year-old boy born on the same day as Riddley Walker; blind; friend of the dogs; Riddley meets him while running away in Russell Hoban's *Riddley Walker*.

**Binky Lister**   Secretary of David Bell at a New York television network; while on the road, Bell calls her regularly for home office news in Don DeLillo's *Americana*.

**Craig Lister**   Seventeen-year-old who is part of a gang of twelve boys who rip Martha Horgan's clothes off, pour beer on her, and poke her with sticks in Mary McGarry Morris's *A Dangerous Woman*.

**Barry Little**   Black American student at McCarthy College in Wisconsin who befriends the young Hakim Elleloû in John Updike's *The Coup*.

**Joy (Mrs. Ossie Little) Little**   Wife of Ossie Little, lover of Nigra Jones, and mother by Jones of the mulatto Sherman Pew; Johnny Clane falls in love with her and commits suicide after she gives birth to her son in Carson McCullers's *Clock Without Hands*.

**Ossie Little**   Preacher whom Nigra Jones is accused of murdering; husband of Joy Little in Carson McCullers's *Clock Without Hands*.

**Rodney Little**   Thirty-seven-year-old cocaine dealer who owns a grocery store, Rodney's Place; employer of Darryl Adams, Erroll Barnes, and Strike Dunham; mentor and father figure to Strike; wants Strike to take over as the dealer at Ahab's in Richard Price's *Clockers*.

**Little Big Man**   See Jack Crabb.

**Little Boy**   Son of Father and Mother; becomes a star in "Our Gang" comedies in E. L. Doctorow's *Ragtime*.

**Little Brother Leaping Fish**   Lone young Indian whom Leslie Collins meets in the forest and names in Harriette Simpson Arnow's *The Kentucky Trace*.

**Norman (Norm) Littlefield**   Head of the English Department at Polycarp College; dies of stress from paying life insurance premiums in Peter De Vries's *Let Me Count the Ways*.

**The Little Girl**   Daughter of Mameh and Tateh; befriended by Evelyn Nesbit in E. L. Doctorow's *Ragtime*.

**Little Horse**   Heemaneh Indian in Thomas Berger's *Little Big Man*.

**Littleman**   See Willie Hall.

**Angel Litwak**   Son of Anna and Ladislaw "Lala" Litwak, big and fair in Maureen Howard's *Natural History*.

**Anna Banana Litwak**   Marries Ladislaw "Lala" Litwak, plain and hardy; bright-black, clever eyes, a thatch of short black hair; Puerto Rican in Maureen Howard's *Natural History*.

**Eddie Litwak**   Nineteen-year-old blond, baby-faced private first class shot four times at close range and killed by Isabelle Poole in Maureen Howard's *Natural History*.

**Jadwiga Litwak**   Wife of Wiltold Litwak and mother of Ladislaw "Lala" and Eddie Litwak, Polish immigrant in Maureen Howard's *Natural History*.

**Ladislaw ("Lala," "Lawrence") Litwak**   Brother of Private First Class Litwak; foundry foreman who eventually owns his own tool and die company in Maureen Howard's *Natural History*.

**Nilda Litwak**   Daughter of Anna and Ladislaw "Lala" Litwak, small and dark in Maureen Howard's *Natural History*.

**Wiltold Litwak**   Husband of Jadwiga Litwak and father of Ladislaw "Lala" and Eddie Litwak, Polish immigrant in Maureen Howard's *Natural History*.

**Livingston (Lischinsky)**   Harvard-educated Russian Jew reared in New York and Arizona; successful businessman who supports the attempts of his adopted son, Marshall Pearl, to locate Pearl's family in Mark Helprin's *Refiner's Fire*.

**Mary Livingston**   Friend of the mother of Ginny, Rose, and Caroline Cook; first person to hint to Ginny that her mother had worried about the way the girls would deal with their father, Larry Cook, after the mother's death from breast cancer when Ginny was fourteen, Rose twelve, and Caroline six in Jane Smiley's *A Thousand Acres*.

**Fulgencio Llanos**   Photographer who hopes to make his fortune with a picture of a famous wrestler; thinks an American who gives him a ride is going to kidnap and rob him; takes pictures of Tonito Marroquín, Richard Rodriguez, and Rafael Beltran and Esperanza Clemente in Sandra Benítez's *A Place Where the Sea Remembers*.

**Lobo**    See Carl Logan.

**Cynthia Locke**    Wife of adulterous Edwin Locke in Joyce Carol Oates's *Cybele*.

**Edwin Locke**    Husband of Cynthia Locke involved in tragicomic midlife crisis; seeks salvation through series of romantic obsessions and marital infidelities in Joyce Carol Oates's *Cybele*.

**Nathan Locke**    Menacing senior partner, center of illegal Mafia activities of the firm; suspects Mitchell McDeere's cooperation with the FBI; confirms the murder order of two junior partners as well as the attempted elimination of Mitch in John Grisham's *The Firm*.

**Townsend Pederson (Towny) Locke**    Visiting conventioneer whom Joe Buck beats up and robs for money with which to take Ratso Rizzo to Florida in James Leo Herlihy's *Midnight Cowboy*.

**Abraham Lockwood**    Son of Moses Lockwood and the first Lockwood to attend college; expands the family wealth by investing outside the town of Swedish Haven; conceives of his family as the Concern in John O'Hara's *The Lockwood Concern*.

**Adelaide Hoffner Lockwood**    Pennsylvania Dutch wife of Abraham Lockwood in John O'Hara's *The Lockwood Concern*.

**Agnes Wynne Lockwood**    Invalid first wife of George Lockwood; mother of Bing and Tina Lockwood in John O'Hara's *The Lockwood Concern*.

**Ernestine (Tina) Lockwood**    Daughter of Agnes and George Lockwood; returns from Europe in John O'Hara's *The Lockwood Concern*.

**George Bingham Lockwood**    Scion of a wealthy rural Pennsylvania family; consolidates the family fortunes and builds a large country estate outside Swedish Haven in John O'Hara's *The Lockwood Concern*.

**George Bingham (Bing) Lockwood, Jr.**    Son of Agnes and George Lockwood; expelled from Princeton; makes his fortune in California oil in John O'Hara's *The Lockwood Concern*.

**Geraldine Lockwood**    Second wife of George Lockwood in John O'Hara's *The Lockwood Concern*.

**Moses Lockwood**    First Lockwood in Swedish Haven, Pennsylvania; suspicious and violent, he amasses a fortune in real estate, coal-dredging, bank stock, and a distillery; builds a large house surrounded by a high wall in John O'Hara's *The Lockwood Concern*.

**Penrose Lockwood**    Younger brother of George Lockwood and his partner in Lockwood & Co. in John O'Hara's *The Lockwood Concern*.

**Wilma Lockwood**    Wife of Penrose Lockwood in John O'Hara's *The Lockwood Concern*.

**Mike Loesser**    Jill's first boyfriend at college; reads her poems, but doesn't like the way she writes; tries to mold her into the type of poet he believes she should be; breaks up with her after her abortion in Marge Piercy's *Braided Lives*.

**Carl (Lobo) Logan**    Gang leader and schoolmate of Raymond Douglas; murders a policeman out of revenge in Herbert Simmons's *Man Walking on Eggshells* and *Corner Boy*.

**Harry Logan**    Veterinarian for Judith's horse Gulliver; caretaker for Pilgrim when Maclean family vet Liz Hammond is not immediately available following the horse's accident; first defers to Annie Maclean's demand to save the horse and later resigns the case in frustration in Nicholas Evans's *The Horse Whisperer*.

**Jesse Logan**    Drifter/cowhand on Homer Bannon's ranch, which he is forced to leave following the slaughter of Homer's diseased cattle herd in Larry McMurtry's *Horseman, Pass By*.

**Mr. Valentino (Val) Logan**    Neighbor who saves the young Eva Medina Canada from sexual molesting, but who makes his own sexual advances toward her in Gayl Jones's *Eva's Man*.

**Logan brothers**    Three brothers whose lifetime of bowling success is destroyed when their trophies are stolen; turn to crime in search of the trophies, eventually shooting Constance Marlow and Bob under the impression they are the trophy thieves in Richard Brautigan's *Willard and His Bowling Trophies*.

**Robbie Lokyar**    Youthful Puritan soldier who turns the soldiers' secret meetings from religion to politics; admired by Johnny Church for his impassioned hatred of all forms of neglect of man; shot for mutiny, becoming a martyr and uniting opposition to Cromwell in Mary Lee Settle's *Prisons*.

**Lomax**    Employee of Earl Mudger in Radial Matrix, an intelligence organization fronting as a business in Don DeLillo's *Running Dog*.

**Michael Lomax**    Twenty-nine-year-old American who owns a house in an ancient city four hours from Golconda to which he brings Lillian Beye; has buried all his emotions in Anaïs Nin's *Seduction of the Minotaur*.

**Buck (Ted Percey) Loner**    Uncle of Myra/Myron Breckinridge and owner of an acting school; his tape-recorded reports reveal that Myra and Myron are the same person in Gore Vidal's *Myra Breckinridge*.

**Walter Longknife**    Indian to whom Meridian Hill's father tries unsuccessfully to give farmland containing sacred Indian burial mounds in Alice Walker's *Meridian*.

**James (Old Pete, The Dutchman) Longstreet**    Southern general who is the right-hand man of Robert E. Lee; opposes Lee's plan to undertake the offensive against the Union army at Gettysburg in Michael Shaara's *The Killer Angels*.

**Emanuel Isidore (E. I., Manny) Lonoff**  Jewish literary hero of Nathan Zuckerman; invites the younger writer to spend the night at his house; feels he has lived his life only in the fantasy of his works in Philip Roth's *The Ghost Writer*.

**Hope (Hopie) Lonoff**  Unhappy wife of E. I. Lonoff; offers to leave Lonoff and Amy Bellette to live together when she feels unloved by Lonoff in Philip Roth's *The Ghost Writer*.

**Bert Loomis**  Facing tax evasion charges in United States; flees to Mexico and becomes a partner in land ownership with Susan Ames; has an affair with Altagracia Gomez, impregnates and marries her; enters ranching venture with Don Enrique Ortiz De Leon in Harriett Doerr's *Consider This, Señora*.

**George Loomis**  One-armed, gimpy veteran of the Korean War who nevertheless manages his own farm; accidentally kills Goat Lady in John Gardner's *Nickel Mountain*.

**Howie Loomis**  Local merchant who helps sponsor Big Red Smalley's traveling gospel show in George Garrett's *Do, Lord, Remember Me*.

**Loop Garoo Kid**  Black cowboy who fights with whips and Hoo-Doo and who is an antagonist of the pope; believes that a novel can be anything it wants to be in Ishmael Reed's *Yellow Back Radio Broke Down*.

**Eddie LoPacca**  Boyfriend of Jill Harrington; gets her pregnant and marries her; the boy whom everyone wanted, but not for keeps; gorgeous and stupid; works in the same deli department as Jason in Alice Hoffman's *Local Girls*.

**Terry LoPacca**  Dates Jason and works in fruits and vegetables at the Food Star in Alice Hoffman's *Local Girls*.

**Tony Lopanto**  Parking garage employee who picks up Theresa Dunn in a bar and becomes her sexual partner in Judith Rossner's *Looking for Mr. Goodbar*.

**Earl Scheib Lopez**  Eleven-year-old Cuban bicycle thief in Joseph Wambaugh's *The Black Marble*.

**Dr. Maria Lopez**  Fantasy female chief of Havana Main Hospital who is interviewed by Margaret Reynolds the journalist; introduces Reynolds to Fidel Castro, who is really a woman disguised as a man in Anne Richardson Roiphe's *Up the Sandbox!*.

**Sarita Lopez**  Successful doctor of sports medicine; immigrant to New York from the Dominican Republican; daughter of Primi and niece of Laura Garcia in Julia Alvarez's *Yo!*.

**Aggie Lopin**  Spinster and gossip; owns a dry goods store in Betty Smith's *Joy in the Morning*.

**Goldie Lopin**  Common-law wife of an Indian storekeeper; adviser on pregnancy and motherhood to Annie Brown in Betty Smith's *Joy in the Morning*.

**Fran LoPresti**  Sculptor and neighbor of Joe Allston in Wallace Stegner's *All the Little Live Things*.

**Julie LoPresti**  Daughter of Fran LoPresti; becomes pregnant at Jim Peck's commune in Wallace Stegner's *All the Little Live Things*.

**LoQuadro**  Mathematician who secretly sells excess time on the Space Brain computer in Don DeLillo's *Ratner's Star*.

**Harry Lorbeer**  Plumber; proprietor and mentor-priest of the Space Project in Wright Morris's *The Fork River Space Project*.

**Cal Lord**  Husband of Lucinda Lord; drinks too much in Gail Godwin's *Evensong*.

**Eric Lord**  Dates Nell; an associate professor of music who moonlighted with a big-name quartet, played Carnegie Hall, Alice Tully Hall, and Tanglewood; a world-class lover in Elizabeth Benedict's *Slow Dancing*.

**Lucinda Lord**  Wife of Cal Lord; cochair of All Saint's Welcoming Committee; gets Alzheimer's disease in Gail Godwin's *Evensong*.

**Lynn Lord**  See Marybeth Howe.

**Horace L'Ordinet**  Professor of English and father of Elizabeth Bean's baby; kidnaps the infant and, after his arrest, pleads temporary insanity; his black ancestry is discovered when the baby is found to have sickle-cell anemia in Frederick Busch's *Rounds*.

**Lori**  Friend of Gwen Murray in Jenkintown; trendy brunette in Alice Hoffman's *Here on Earth*.

**Laverne Linda Hogan Lorraine**  Mistress of Buddy Sandifer and lover of Ralph Sandifer in Thomas Berger's *Sneaky People*.

**Lottie Mae**  Maid of Big Joe Mackey and murderer of Buddy Matlow in Harry Crews's *A Feast of Snakes*.

**Lou Ann**  Daughter of Isabelle Pool; lives with her father in Texas in Maureen Howard's *Natural History*.

**Lou Ellen**  Lover of Lenard and party hostess in Ed Bullins's *The Reluctant Rapist*.

**Leila Louie**  Eldest child who uses her knowledge of English to translate for her working-class immigrant parents; responsible daughter who moves in with her boyfriend in order to break away from feeling trapped at home; daughter of Dulcie Fu, stepdaughter of Leon Leong, half sister of Ona and Nina Leong in Fae Myenne Ng's *Bone*.

**Mason Louie**  Boyfriend, then husband of Leila Louie; auto mechanic; strong, confident, reliable man who supports the Leong family with his presence during its tragedies and crises and who willingly acts as an intermediary during its disputes in Fae Myenne Ng's *Bone*.

**Louis**   Former lover of Richard; fifty-three-year-old drama teacher prone to tears in Michael Cunningham's *The Hours*.

**Louis**   Louisiana plantation owner who, after being made a vampire by Lestat, seeks out other vampires; morally disturbed by his need to kill in order to survive; tells his story to an interviewer in Anne Rice's *Interview with the Vampire*. In *The Tale of the Body Thief*, he vows never to make another vampire and so refuses to perform the "Dark Trick" to help the human Lestat recover his vampire body; is part of the coven that emerges after David Talbot is made a vampire.

**Maria de Lourdes**   Local villager hired as housekeeper by Americans Richard and Sara Everton; uses native superstitions to protect the couple despite their resistance in Harriet Doerr's *Stones for Ibarra*.

**Louvinie**   Slave and storyteller whose tongue is cut out by the plantation owner; her buried tongue nourishes a fabled magnolia tree in Alice Walker's *Meridian*.

**Julien Love**   Friend of Bull Hubbard and Jack Duluoz in Jack Kerouac's *Visions of Cody*; also appears in *Book of Dreams*, *Big Sur*, and *Desolation Angels*.

**Nicholas Jess Love**   Harlan's faith-healing "witness"; very tall; was Josef's bodyguard; buys land in Alaska in Gayl Jones's *The Healing*.

**Reggie Love**   Middle-aged recovering alcoholic, low-income lawyer; becomes eleven-year-old Mark Sway's lawyer by chance; battles the high-profile U.S district attorney, Roy Foltrigg, to help her client protect his family from the Mafia in John Grisham's *The Client*.

**Eddie Lovell**   Unreflecting investor and husband of Nell Lovell in Walker Percy's *The Moviegoer*.

**Nell Lovell**   Glibly humanistic cousin of Binx Bolling and wife of Eddie Lovell in Walker Percy's *The Moviegoer*.

**Butch Lovemaiden**   Deputy in William Faulkner's *The Reivers*.

**Jimmy Low**   Friend of Cody Pomeray; participates in the taped conversations of Jack Kerouac's *Visions of Cody*.

**David Lowe**   Professor Joseph Moore's prize student; Lowe's dalliance with Moore's daughter presumably causes Moore's stroke in Mary Gordon's *Final Payments*.

**Hope Lowell**   Muse and fairy godmother of Isadora Wing in Erica Jong's *How to Save Your Own Life*.

**Johnny Lowell**   Job supervisor of Jimson in Carlene Hatcher Polite's *The Flagellants*.

**Susan Lowenstein**   Savannah Wingo's Jewish psychiatrist in New York, who with the help of Tom Wingo, rescues Savannah from madness, Tom from self-absorption, and herself, temporarily, from a bad marriage in Pat Conroy's *The Prince of Tides*.

**Julius Lowenthal**   Jewish manufacturer of Catholic religious objects and church furnishings who isolates himself from Gentiles, whom he distrusts and dislikes in Katherine Anne Porter's *Ship of Fools*.

**Edna Lown**   Colleague and lover of Robert Softly; works on a project for developing a cosmic language based on mathematical principles in Don DeLillo's *Ratner's Star*.

**Dongan Lowndes**   Magazine feature writer on assignment on the set of the film *The Awakening*, written by Gordon Walker, starring Lee (LuAnne) Verger in Robert Stone's *Children of Light*.

**Lowry**   Lover of Clara Walpole and father of her son, Swan Revere, in Joyce Carol Oates's *A Garden of Earthly Delights*.

**Ellery Loyola**   See Dick Gibson.

**Aaron Lublin**   Husband of Sarah Lublin and father of their two children; Jewish refugee who lives in one of the 70th Street apartments managed by Norman Moonbloom in Edward Lewis Wallant's *The Tenants of Moonbloom*.

**Sarah Lublin**   Wife of Aaron Lublin and mother of their two children; tenant in one of the apartments managed by Norman Moonbloom in Edward Lewis Wallant's *The Tenants of Moonbloom*.

**Luciana**   Voluptuous and independent Italian woman whose back was scarred in an air raid; Yossarian falls in love with her in Joseph Heller's *Catch-22*.

**Lucien**   Handsome Haitian boy made into a slave; rescued by Sid from the sadistic man who purchased him; is killed by Mahmoud in Haiti in Herbert Gold's *Slave Trade*.

**Walter Luckett**   Industrial analyst living in Haddam, New Jersey; recently abandoned by his wife, Yolanda, who has gone to Bimini with another man; fellow member, with Frank Bascombe, of an informal "Divorced Men's Club"; has an unexpected homosexual encounter with an acquaintance; eventually commits suicide in Richard Ford's *The Sportswriter*.

**Lucrezia**   Daughter of Frau Anders and later mistress of Hippolyte in Susan Sontag's *The Benefactor*.

**Ludus**   Black livery stable worker in William Faulkner's *The Reivers*.

**Luke**   Attacker who joins Jeff and Tom in an attempt to castrate Will Harris in Junius Edwards's *If We Must Die*.

**Corporal Lumbowski**   Army corporal whom Columbato strikes in William Wharton's *Birdy*.

**William Wigglesworth (Billy) Lumkin**    Dean of Convers College in Alison Lurie's *Love and Friendship*.

**Lummy**    Black employee of Joe Lon Mackey; brother of George in Harry Crews's *A Feast of Snakes*.

**Vaily (Vagay) Gregorovich Lunacharsky**    Dynamic Soviet physicist whose close relationships with Western scientists and the global community makes the Soviet government uncomfortable; close associate and friend of Eleanor Arroway; member of the World Message Consortium and The Five in Carl Sagan's *Contact*.

**Kabba Lundo**    Aging paramount chief of the Mendes people in Sierra Leone, West Africa; brought the "witchfinder" to Boone Westfall's village to identify the witches and locate the evil medicine in Richard Dooling's *White Man's Grave*.

**Marvin Lundy**    Retired widower and collector of baseball memorabilia; sees complex connections between baseball and the political realities of the cold war; spends his life in search for the home run ball hit by Bobby Thomson to win the pennant for the Giants in 1951; eventually obtains the ball, though he cannot prove it is real; loses his wife, who had shared in the travels the search entailed, and learns that he himself is dying; eventually sells the ball to Nick Shay in Don DeLillo's *Underworld*.

**Claire (Misty) de Lune**    Secretary to Artie Pringle; marries Billy Bumpers in Peter De Vries's *I Hear America Swinging*.

**Lurene**    Mother of Jeffy; works the night shift at a factory in Gayl Jones's *Corregidora*.

**Alex Lurie**    Brother of David Lurie; his love of English literature and his tendency to act rather than think draw him away from his Jewish faith in Chaim Potok's *In the Beginning*.

**David (Davey) Lurie**    Narrator who overcomes a series of childhood illnesses and misfortunes and goes on to apply his brilliant mind and thirst for knowledge to higher biblical criticism despite his family's disapproval in Chaim Potok's *In the Beginning*.

**Max Lurie**    Father of David Lurie; after serving in the Polish army in World War I, he founds an organization to bring Polish Jews to the United States in Chaim Potok's *In the Beginning*.

**Meyer Lurie**    Brother of Max Lurie; follows Max to the United States and serves with him in an organization to bring Polish Jews to America in Chaim Potok's *In the Beginning*.

**Ruth Lurie**    Wife of Max Lurie and mother of David Lurie in Chaim Potok's *In the Beginning*.

**Sarah Lurie**    Wife of Meyer Lurie; helps comfort the Polish Jewish community during their struggles in the United States in Chaim Potok's *In the Beginning*.

**Saul (Rav Shaul) Lurie**    Son of Meyer Lurie; cares for his cousin David Lurie while they are in school together; becomes a rabbi in Chaim Potok's *In the Beginning*.

**Vonda Lusk**    Thirty-three-year-old receptionist; fiercely loyal to the memory of her murdered best friend and coworker, Clair DeVane, and vigilant in her efforts to keep the office mindful that her friend's killer is still on the loose in Richard Ford's *Independence Day*.

**Luster**    See Volume I.

**Christina Lutz**    Stepsister of Oscar Crease, who attempts to help Oscar regain his health and manage both his finances and himself in William Gaddis's *A Frolic of His Own*.

**Darrel Lutz**    Struggling twenty-three-year-old hog farmer who commits suicide after being overwhelmed by his responsibilities; attracted to his neighbor Jane Ripplemeyer; dreamer who wants to sell his Iowa farm and move to New Mexico to open an electronics store in Bharati Mukherjee's *Jasmine*.

**Harry Lutz**    Corporate lawyer and husband of Christina Lutz, he argues that law is about money, not justice, but who sympathizes with and offers law advice to Oscar Crease, his brother-in-law. He dies mysteriously in a car crash in William Gaddis's *A Frolic of His Own*.

**Heinrich Lutz**    Swiss hotelier who is traveling with his wife and their unattractive daughter in Katherine Anne Porter's *Ship of Fools*.

**Louie Lutz**    Son of Naomi Lutz; accompanies George Swiebel to Africa and gets into trouble trying to learn obscenities in Swahili in Saul Bellow's *Humboldt's Gift*.

**Naomi Lutz**    Childhood sweetheart of Charlie Citrine; persuades George Swiebel to take her son, Louie Lutz, with him to Africa in Saul Bellow's *Humboldt's Gift*.

**Lykin**    Astronaut who crash-lands with Bradly and later turns into a Green Fish Boy in William S. Burroughs's *The Ticket That Exploded*.

**Adrian Lynch**    Deputy chief of the Los Angeles Police Department; sloganeer and buffoon in Joseph Wambaugh's *The Choirboys*.

**John Mosley Lynch**    Attorney and real estate developer; runs town affairs; defeated in attempt to develop property by political actions of David Greene; attempts revenge by inciting Crystal Sinclair to confront David about his relationship with Judith Silver in Marge Piercy's *Storm Tide*.

**Mrs. Lynch**    Mother of Margaret Flood; died young of pneumonia in Maureen Howard's *Expensive Habits*.

**Ned Lynch**   Father of Margaret Flood; an insurance agent at Mutual Insurance Agency; bland, neat widower in dark downtown suits in Maureen Howard's *Expensive Habits.*

**Lynda**   High-spirited teenager who is suspended from school and sent to a detention home for girls for slapping a teacher; after her release, she hangs out on the street, smoking cigarettes and drinking wine in Alexis Deveaux's *Spirits in the Street.*

**Ezra Lyttle**   Boyfriend of Stormy Claridge; Dallas Cowboy defensive back whose business ventures collapse after he is caught exposing himself in Peter Gent's *Texas Celebrity Turkey Trot.*

**Arthur Ma**  Son of a prominent Chinatown family in San Francisco; friend and companion of Loren Monsant and Jack Duluoz in Jack Kerouac's *Big Sur*.

**Atlas Androgyne (Atlas Atlantis) Maartens**  Usually stoned security guard and friend of Kam Wright; aids the activists in M. F. Beal's *Amazon One*.

**Oedipa (Oed) Maas**  Wife of Wendell Maas; becomes executrix of Pierce Inverarity's will and searches for the meaning of the mysterious Tristero system; heroine of Thomas Pynchon's *The Crying of Lot 49*.

**Wendell (Mucho) Maas**  Husband of Oedipa Maas; disk jockey on a California radio station who experiments with LSD in Thomas Pynchon's *The Crying of Lot 49*.

**Elizabeth (Libby) MacAusland**  Translator of Italian for a literary agent; eventually marries an actor; member of the Group in Mary McCarthy's *The Group*.

**MacDoon**  Undergarment designer and London friend of Sebastian Dangerfield in J. P. Donleavy's *The Ginger Man*.

**Sukie Maceo**  Sister of China Doll Maceo and friend of Grancie Doffin in Louise Meriweather's *Daddy Was a Number Runner*.

**Maggie (Shirley Silverstein) MacGregor**  Journalist and television personality who makes a living interviewing and reporting on celebrities including Billy Inkehorn Orsini, Vito Orsini, and Spider Elliott in Judith Krantz's *Scruples*.

**Ben MacGruder**  Younger brother of Harriet and former lover of Margaret; insists he has loved her since he was three and Margaret was six; spent his early childhood at diplomatic posts with his parents in Africa and the Middle East in Gail Godwin's *Evensong*.

**Oliver Cromwell MacIvor**  Minister who incites Protestants against Catholics in Leon Uris's *Trinity*.

**Easton (Easy) Mack**  Father of Herman Mack and owner of AutoTown and Salvage House; kills himself in a car crusher in Harry Crews's *Car*.

**Harrison A. Mack, Jr.**  Manager of his father's canning empire and heir to his fortune; friend of Todd Andrews and husband of Jane Mack in John Barth's *The Floating Opera*.

**Herman Mack**  Son of Easy Mack; tries to eat a Ford Maverick bumper to bumper in Harry Crews's *Car*.

**Jane Paulsen Mack**  Wife of Harrison Mack and mother of Jeannine Mack; occasional mistress of Todd Andrews between 1932 and 1937 in John Barth's *The Floating Opera*.

**Jeannine Paulsen Mack**  Daughter of Jane Mack by either Harrison Mack or Todd Andrews in John Barth's *The Floating Opera*.

**Junell Mack**  Daughter of Easy Mack and girlfriend of Joe; drives the tow truck for AutoTown in Harry Crews's *Car*.

**Mister Mack**  Son of Easy Mack; replaces Herman Mack in trying to eat a Ford Maverick in Harry Crews's *Car*.

**Gideon MacKarkle**  Highland Scot who introduces Johnny Church to the realities of war; remains loyal to democratic ideals and is sentenced to death for mutiny, but is saved by Cromwell's blanket pardon; tells others about Virginia but insists he will not move his nine sons and seven grandchildren in Mary Lee Settle's *Prisons*.

**Estelle Mackenzie**  Wife of Primus Mackenzie and mother of Ursa; a former teacher who moved from the United States to the fictional Caribbean island of Triunion; supports her husband's political ambitions and believes in his ideals in Paule Marshall's *Daughters*.

**Primus Mackenzie**   Husband of Estelle and father of Ursa; nicknamed PM; wants to help the poor and suffering among his people; elected prime minister of Triunion, a fictional Caribbean island; voted out of office after the exposure of his scheme to use government lands to build a resort in Paule Marshall's *Daughters*.

**Ursa Mackenzie**   Only child of Primus and Estelle Mackenzie; born on the fictional Caribbean island of Triunion; raised and educated in the United States; wrote a master's thesis on the relationships between slave men and women; has a strong social conscience and feminist sensibilities in Paule Marshall's *Daughters*.

**Robbie MacKessy**   Troubled, lonely kindergartener; accomplished liar; witnesses his mother's promiscuity with fear and misunderstanding; accuser who charges school nurse Alice Goodwin with child abuse in Jane Hamilton's *A Map of the World*.

**Beatriz Dargan (Beeder) Mackey**   Sister of Joe Lon Mackey; driven crazy after finding her mother's body in Harry Crews's *A Feast of Snakes*.

**Big Joe Mackey**   Brutal father of Joe Lon Mackey in Harry Crews's *A Feast of Snakes*.

**Colin "Mack" Mackey**   Handyman for Frances Beecham; impregnates Martha Horgan; becomes Frances Beecham's lover because he wants her to fund his career as an aspiring writer; a former high school English teacher who published one unsuccessful book in Mary McGarry Morris's *A Dangerous Woman*.

**Joe Lon Mackey**   Former Boss Rattler; murders Luther Peacock and Berenice Sweet in a shooting spree in Harry Crews's *A Feast of Snakes*.

**Mabel Mackey**   Harlem neighbor of the Coffin family; frequent number player who runs poker games; Adam Coffin moves in with her when he leaves his family in Louise Meriwether's *Daddy Was a Number Runner*.

**Zebulon Johns (Zeb) Mackie**   City councilman, political boss, owner of construction and sewage companies awarded city contracts, purchaser of Gimlet Street property, and would-be historian of Bunker County in Fred Chappell's *The Gaudy Place*.

**Annie Graves Maclean**   British wife of Robert Maclean; distant mother of Grace Maclean; high-profile journalist and editor of a chic New York magazine; lover of horse whisperer Tom Brooks, whose influence helps heal mother and daughter following the latter's near fatal accident in Nicholas Evans's *The Horse Whisperer*.

**Grace Maclean**   Thirteen-year-old daughter of Robert Maclean and Annie Graves Maclean; friend of Judith; healing

from a serious accident in which her horse and an eighteen-wheel semi-truck collide and she loses leg; witnesses Tom Booker's fatal encounter with wild horse in Nicholas Evans's *The Horse Whisperer*.

**Shelley MacLeod**   Protestant lover of Conor Larkin; killed by Protestant fanatics for loving a Catholic in Leon Uris's *Trinity*.

**Bonnie MacMahon**   Cocktail waitress who serves Breakfast of Champions in Kurt Vonnegut's *Breakfast of Champions*.

**Penelope MacMahon**   Unhappy but hopeful young woman who vacations in Majorca with her psychotherapist and his wife, John and Dane Empson; has an affair there with Karl Heykoop in Gail Godwin's *The Perfectionists*.

**Dan MacNamara**   Child of Ellen and Vincent's dead son, John, who was killed in World War II; raised by his grandparents who took him away from his mother; successful lawyer in Mary Gordon's *The Other Side*.

**Ellen Costelloe MacNamara**   Angry, dying ninety-year-old matriarch of a four-generation Irish-American family; an immigrant from Ireland who stole money from her hated tavern-keeper father for her passage; settled in Queens, New York; married to Vincent for sixty-six years in Mary Gordon's *The Other Side*.

**Vincent MacNamara**   Gentle eighty-eight-year-old husband of Ellen; patriarch of his four-generation Irish-American family; recuperating from a broken hip but reluctant to return home to his family in Mary Gordon's *The Other Side*.

**MacNaughton**   Partner in MacNaughton Blair brokerage; father-in-law and employer of Joe Sandwich in Peter De Vries's *The Vale of Laughter*.

**Betty (Naughty) MacNaughton**   Fiancée, long-suffering wife, then widow of Joe Sandwich; ultimately marries Wally Hines in Peter De Vries's *The Vale of Laughter*.

**Chris MacNeil**   Celebrated actress and divorced, frantic mother of Regan MacNeil, who is possessed by a demon in William Peter Blatty's *The Exorcist*.

**Regan Teresa (Rags) MacNeil**   Eleven-year-old daughter of Chris MacNeil; victim of demonic possession in William Peter Blatty's *The Exorcist*.

**Claudia MacTeer**   Playmate of Pecola Breedlove; narrator of Toni Morrison's *The Bluest Eye*.

**Frieda MacTeer**   Sister of Claudia McTeer in Toni Morrison's *The Bluest Eye*.

**Mama MacTeer**   Mother of Claudia and Frieda; is prone to soliloquies in which she chides "some folks" for household misconduct; sometimes sings the blues in Toni Morrison's *The Bluest Eye*.

**Mr. MacTeer**    Hardworking husband and father; hits Mr. Henry in the head with a tricycle when he discovers the man touched Frieda in Toni Morrison's *The Bluest Eye*.

**Robert (Ray) MacWay**    Orphan who advertises for a wife in the newspaper; meets Mernelle because of her letter and marries her; kind man who takes care of Mernelle and Jewell; dies of cancer in E. Annie Proulx's *Postcards*.

**Madame Zoe**    Palm reader who predicts for Sissy Hankshaw Gitche marriage, good sex, and children—but not all with the same man, or woman—in Tom Robbins's *Even Cowgirls Get the Blues*.

**Pamela (Pam) Madden**    Prostitute who flees Henry Tucker's drug and prostitution ring; with John Kelly's help, breaks her drug addiction; is on her way to give a statement to the police about Tucker when she is abducted from Kelly's vehicle, beaten, raped, and murdered in Tom Clancy's *Without Remorse*.

**Madeleine**    Parisian vampire, friend of Louis, and surrogate mother of Claudia; killed by Lestat in Anne Rice's *Interview with the Vampire*.

**Robert (Bob) Madison**    Fellow postal worker and friend of Jake Jackson; suffers from venereal disease in Richard Wright's *Lawd Today*.

**Mara Madoff**    Daughter of a clothier; murdered by Hitler's Brownshirts; her body is found in the Vienna State Opera House in John Irving's *Setting Free the Bears*.

**Mae**    Unidentified woman whose name Wesley Beavers calls out while making love to Rosacoke Mustian in Reynolds Price's *A Long and Happy Life*.

**Feather Mae**    Great-grandmother of Meridian Hill; fought to preserve sacred Indian burial mounds in Alice Walker's *Meridian*.

**Maestro**    Old and lecherous lover of Lucrezia in Susan Sontag's *The Benefactor*.

**Mag**    Black servant in the Kendal household in Reynolds Price's *The Surface of Earth*.

**Eric (Cop) Magee**    White policeman determined to prove Kevin Brittain guilty of murder in Hal Bennett's *Wait Until the Evening*.

**Janet Magee**    Invalid sister of Cop Magee and unintended murder victim of Cora Brittain in Hal Bennett's *Wait Until the Evening*.

**Magic Child**    Temporary identity of one of the Hawkline sisters (whether Susan or Jane is never revealed) while under the influence of the Hawkline Monster, whom she hires Greer and Cameron to destroy in Richard Brautigan's *The Hawkline Monster*.

**Fausto Maijstral**    Maltese poet and father of Paola Maijstral; recounts his encounter with the Bad Priest in his confessions in Thomas Pynchon's *V*.

**Paola (Ruby) Maijstral**    Daughter of Fausto Maijstral; keeps the ivory comb of the lady V.; gives Herbert Stencil the Confessions of Fausto and thereby convinces Stencil to go to Malta in Thomas Pynchon's *V*.

**Captain Maillart**    Officer of the Regiment Le Cap protecting the capital city of the French colony Saint Domingue; reunited with childhood friend of Antoine Hebert from Leon, France; introduces Antoine to Nanon; after Le Cap is subdued during the slave rebellions between 1791 and 1802, Captain Maillart defects to the Spanish army and ultimately serves as an officer under slave leader Toussaint in Madison Smartt Bell's *All Souls' Rising*.

**Alexander (the Bailbondsman, Phoenician) Main**    Cincinnati bailbondsman obsessed by life's mysteries; claims descent from the ancient Phoenicians; narrator of *The Bailbondsman*, a novella in Stanley Elkin's *Searches and Seizures*.

**Ashton Main**    Promiscuous, strikingly beautiful older sister of Brett Hazard and sister of Orry Main; stuck in an unfulfilling marriage to businessman James Huntoon; engages in an affair with the unprincipled Lamar Powell in John Jakes's *Love and War*.

**Charles Main**    Determined, impatient captain of a rough and rowdy misfit troop of soldiers in a North Carolina Confederate regiment; Orry Main's young cousin; becomes friends with Billy Hazard during his time at West Point in John Jakes's *Love and War*.

**Cooper Main**    Brother of Brett Hazard and Orry Main; forty-one years old; shipbuilder who lives in Great Britain during the Civil War and works with the government of Great Britain in order to obtain goods to support the Confederate army in John Jakes's *Love and War*.

**Orry Main**    Confederate supporter living in South Carolina; best friend of George Hazard, whom he met at West Point; slave owner, but a kind and compassionate man; in love with another man's wife in John Jakes's *Love and War*.

**Marshall Maine**    See Dick Gibson.

**Raymond (Captain Bruno Storm) Mainwaring**    Son of Splendor Mainwaring in Thomas Berger's *Vital Parts*.

**Splendor Gallant Mainwaring**    Black friend of Carlo Reinhart in Thomas Berger's *Reinhart in Love* and *Vital Parts*.

**Major Major Major Major**    Painfully shy squadron commander named by a father fond of practical jokes and promoted by an I.B.M. machine with a sense of humor in Joseph Heller's *Catch-22*.

**Makar**    Farmer and rabbit expert at whose house the narrator is introduced to sex, incest, and bestiality in Jerzy Kosinski's *The Painted Bird*.

**Milo Maki**    Son of Jimmy Yamamoto and stepson of Teddy Maki; Japanese rock star and rebel; has a rocky relationship with his stepfather; learns that Teddy is a product of a harsh war and begins to accept him in Richard Wiley's *Soldiers in Hiding.*

**Teddy Maki**   Japanese-American jazz musician and star of Japanese television who grew up in Los Angeles and considers himself an American; is in Japan during World War II and must fight for the Japanese in the Philippines; his wartime experiences poison his relationships with both his wife and his son in Richard Wiley's *Soldiers in Hiding.*

**Levon Makowisite**   Cree man who becomes the projectionist for the Northern Lights theater; moves his wife, Philomene, and two daughters into the projection room at the movie house as an apartment in exchange for his work in Howard Norman's *Northern Lights.*

**Tony Malarkey**   Dublin friend of Sebastian Dangerfield; barricades himself in his flat to prevent eviction in J. P. Donleavy's *The Ginger Man.*

**Ian Malcolm**   Thin, balding, and wise-cracking thirty-five-year-old mathematician; guest of John Hammond at Isla Nublar, a remote island resort; correctly predicts genetic engineering of extinct dinosaurs as "an accident waiting to happen" in Michael Crichton's *Jurassic Park.* Also appears in *The Lost World.*

**Malkah**   Shira's brilliant grandmother, who raised her; a scientist in her seventies, one of the creators of Yod who gives him human emotions in Marge Piercy's *He, She and It.*

**Elsbeth Malkas**   Supposed artist who gives a venereal disease to Fred Trumper and Cuthbert Bennett in John Irving's *The Water-Method Man.*

**King Mallison (Jr.)**   Son of Crystal Weiss from her first marriage; handsome, troubled, and extremely rebellious teenager who can also be lovable and charming in Ellen Gilchrist's *Victory Over Japan.*

**Professor Mallory**   Visiting geographer from Princeton who is a member of Margaret's church in Gail Godwin's *Evensong.*

**J. T. Malone**   Pharmacist dying of leukemia who tries to deny the truth about his impending death; refuses to bomb the house of Sherman Pew in Carson McCullers's *Clock Without Hands.*

**Lonnie Malone**   Boyfriend of Samantha Hughes who does not understand her preoccupation with the Vietnam War in Bobbie Ann Mason's *In Country.*

**Martha Malone**   Wife of J. T. Malone, she helps nurse her husband while he dies of leukemia; owns Coca-Cola stock in Carson McCullers's *Clock Without Hands.*

**Nathan (Lips) Malone**   Accountant and gopher for Sid Krassman; procures corpses for C. D. Harrison to have sex with in Terry Southern's *Blue Movie.*

**Hank Malory**   Rice University graduate student and lover of Patsy Carpenter in Larry McMurtry's *Moving On.*

**Hubert Maloy**   Member of Legs Diamond's gang in William Kennedy's *Legs;* a kidnapper of Charlie Boy McCall in *Billy Phelan's Greatest Game.*

**David Malter**   Renowned Zionist and Talmudic scholar who teaches his son Reuven to find his own way between old beliefs and new scholarship in Chaim Potok's *The Chosen* and *The Promise.*

**Reuven (Bobby) Malter**   Son of David Malter; helps his friend Danny Saunders come to terms with his intelligence and his Jewish heritage in Chaim Potok's *The Chosen,* which he narrates; chooses to become a rabbi rather than a mathematician in *The Promise.*

**Mama (Ma)**   Impoverished widow and mother of Thomas Henry Oliver in Shirley Ann Grau's *The Condor Passes.*

**Mameh**   Wife of Tateh and mother of The Little Girl; becomes a prostitute in E. L. Doctorow's *Ragtime.*

**Mamie**   Daughter of Aunt Cora Lou and sister of Lil Bits in Sarah E. Wright's *This Child's Gonna Live.*

**Mamut**   Wise medicine man/shaman of the Lion Camp. He continues the work that Ayla had begun with Creb in Jean Auel's *The Mammoth Hunters.*

**Arthur Manchek**   Officer in charge at Vandenberg Air Force Base who declares a state of emergency in Michael Crichton's *The Andromeda Strain.*

**Fu Manchu**   Chinese ambassador to America who stands about the height of a thumb because China has developed a way to shrink people to accommodate their growing numbers; visits the president of the United States to find some secret essays in Kurt Vonnegut's *Slapstick.*

**Angelo Mancuso**   Bungling patrolman on the New Orleans police force; meets the Reilly family while trying to arrest Ignatius as a suspicious character; accidentally wins acclaim and respect by uncovering the Night of Joy bar's pornography ring in John Kennedy Toole's *A Confederacy of Dunces.*

**Celia Mandel**   Has an affair with Rudolf Tinker; teaches kindergarten in Bette Pesetsky's *Midnight Sweets.*

**Seth Mandel**   Intellectual high school graduate who lives ascetically in a teepee in his parents' backyard; affable and iconoclastic nonpracticing Jew who volunteers to work on the local Temple Youth Group crisis hotline; Mona Chang's boyfriend in Gish Jen's *Mona in the Promised Land.*

**Irv and Norma Manders**   Elderly couple who operate a farm in Hastings Glen, New York; they housed Andy and Charlie McGee when they were running from the shop, and later on allowed Charlie to stay with them for several months after the death of Andy in Stephen King's *Firestarter.*

**Homer (Purple Better One) Mandrill**   Presidential candidate presented by A. J. to the Democratic National Convention in William S. Burroughs's *Exterminator!*

**Veronica Manganese**   See V.

**Corey Manley**   American teenager who travels to the Dominican Republic with her father; stepdaughter of Yo Garcia; daughter of Douglas Manley in Julia Alvarez's *Yo!*

**Douglas (Doug) Manley**   Yo Garcia's third husband; father of Corey in Julia Alvarez's *Yo!*

**Doctor Mann**   Israeli who tracks down female writers and is preparing an art exhibition in Israel in Anaïs Nin's *Collages.*

**Justin G. Mannerly**   Denver schoolteacher; benefactor of Cody Pomeray in Jack Kerouac's *Visions of Cody.*

**Dudley Manning**   Father of Rhoda Manning; powerful, hard-working businessman; grew up in the Deep South; struggles with guilt over an extramarital affair and tries to reform his rebellious daughter in Ellen Gilchrist's *Victory Over Japan.*

**Henry Manning**   Town smith; father of Hester Manning; disapproves of Gabriel Legge's courtship of Hester in Bharati Mukherjee's *The Holder of the World.*

**Hester Manning**   Closest friend of Hannah Easton in Salem; daughter of the smith; commits suicide in Bharati Mukherjee's *The Holder of the World.*

**Janus Manning**   Black plantation owner, husband of Neva Stapleton, and leader in an effort to unseat the head of the color hierarchy in Burnside, Virginia, in Hal Bennett's *A Wilderness of Vines.*

**Janus Eugene (Gene) Manning II**   Slow-witted adolescent sexually attracted to his mother, Neva Stapleton Manning, in Hal Bennett's *A Wilderness of Vines.*

**Neva Blanche Stapleton Manning**   Widow of Janus Manning, mother of Gene Manning, and lover of Charlie Hooker; abandons the South and sexual repression at the close of Hal Bennett's *A Wilderness of Vines.*

**Otha Manning**   Son of Janus Manning; killed in France during World War I in Hal Bennett's *A Wilderness of Vines.*

**Phelan Manning**   Brother of Crystal Weiss and inheritor of the Manning fortune; a powerful, competitive, athletic man who loves to drink and hunt big game in Ellen Gilchrist's *Victory Over Japan.*

**Rhoda Manning**   Headstrong, smart, and spoiled daughter of wealthy businessman Dudley Manning and southern belle Ariane Manning; Rhoda is first depicted as an aspiring young writer and rebellious teenager, later as a pampered southern dilettante who wishes for independence but doesn't want to give up the privilege of her wealthy married life in Ellen Gilchrist's *Victory Over Japan.*

**Manon**   Retired psychiatrist who counsels against the stage-three operation on Harold Benson in Michael Crichton's *The Terminal Man.*

**Bernadette Mansaw**   Seventeen-year-old high school dropout with two children, Merry and Noelle, and a boyfriend in jail in Mary McGarry Morris's *Songs in Ordinary Time.*

**Joseph Mansourian**   Agent and lover of Richard Kennington, he becomes the older lover of Paul Porterfield in David Leavitt's *The Page Turner.*

**Signor Rafael Mantissa**   Italian intriguer; enlists the aid of the Gaucho in the aborted attempt to steal Botticelli's Venus in Florence in 1899 in Thomas Pynchon's *V.*

**Manuel**   Helper in Emil Duluoz's print shop in Jack Kerouac's *Visions of Gerard.*

**Manya**   Russian housekeeper for David and Reuven Malter in Chaim Potok's *The Chosen* and *The Promise.*

**Charles Maple**   Los Angeles public defender of Gregory Powell during Powell's second trial for the murder of Ian Campbell in Joseph Wambaugh's *The Onion Field.*

**Steven (Roman Castevet) Marcato**   Son of an infamous devil worshipper in the 1890s; changes his name and carries on his father's practices in Ira Levin's *Rosemary's Baby.*

**Reverend March**   Unmarried minister of the Reformed Church in Olinger; interested in Vera Hummel in John Updike's *The Centaur.*

**Ruth (Roo) March**   Passionate, crude, and unconventional; young American photographer; wife of Fred Turner and daughter of Professor Zimmern in Alison Lurie's *Foreign Affairs.*

**Marco**   Peruvian, woman-hating escort of Esther Greenwood to a country club dance; she bloodies his nose to prevent his sexual advances in Sylvia Plath's *The Bell Jar.*

**Marcus**   Leader of a black ghetto youth gang who takes his group to the Catskills; distrusts the Indians but joins them after his group members are killed in Marge Piercy's *Dance the Eagle to Sleep.*

**Elaine Mardell**   Wealthy and arty occasional call-girl and girl-friend of Matt Scudder in Lawrence Block's *A Dance at the Slaughterhouse.*

**Katrina Marek**   Viennese actress who takes the paintings of her husband, Kurt Winter, to London; mother of Severin Winter in John Irving's *The 158-Pound Marriage.*

**Margaret (Maggie)**   Teenage girl found having sex with Billy Benoit during a vice raid on a homeless encampment; rescued by Detective Horner, who later becomes her lover; run out of town by Welshinger; moves to Washington, where she marries Billy and raises a son fathered by Horner in Robert Clark's *Mr. White's Confession.*

**Margaret (Margo)**   Prostitute and girlfriend of Herman Mack in Harry Crews's *Car.*

**Margawse**   Mother of Agravaine, Gawaine, and Mordred; half sister of Arthur and sister of Morgan la Fey in Thomas Berger's *Arthur Rex.*

**Greta Margolin**   Nurse in ghetto hospital; lover of Joseph Barbanel; temporary custodian of Joseph Barbanel's secret ghetto archive in E.L. Doctorow's *City of God.*

**Marguerite**   Native of South America and a tough professional revolutionary; loved by Ramón Cordes but used by his superiors to seduce him into submission in William Herrick's *The Last to Die.*

**Marguerite**   Mary Wollstonecraft and Gilbert Imlay's French maid in Frances Sherwood's *Vindication.*

**Maria**   Beautiful and exotic mistress of Henry Zuckerman; mother of one child, Phoebe; married to an Englishman; has a brief affair with Henry's brother, Nathan, in Philip Roth's *The Counterlife.*

**Maria**   Brilliant and talented twenty-five-year-old black woman who holds a law degree from Columbia University and has the image of a she-fox on her belly; masochistic lover of Scarecrow, who kills her in Calvin Hernton's *Scarecrow.*

**Maria**   Mexican wife of Hatcher in Anaïs Nin's *Seduction of the Minotaur.*

**Marie**   Wife of Sean; an heiress, takes aerobics and paints in Elizabeth Benedict's *Slow Dancing.*

**Miss Marie (Maginot Line)**   Physically formidable prostitute in Toni Morrison's *The Bluest Eye.*

**Marilyn**   Rudolf Tinker's lover and Theodora Waite's former accountant; in Bette Pesetsky's *Midnight Sweets.*

**Marita**   Wealthy European nicknamed "Heiress"; introduces herself to David and Catherine Bourne in a cafe in Cannes; has sexual relations with Catherine; falls in love with David; realizes Catherine is going mad and tries to calm her; stays with David after Catherine leaves in Ernest Hemingway's *The Garden of Eden.*

**Harvey Marker**   Author of *Naked and the Doomed* and husband of Jack Duluoz's old flame in Jack Kerouac's *Desolation Angels.*

**Madame Eudora Market**   Founder of the Church of Stephen Martyr and grandmother of Joe Market in Hal Bennett's *Lord of Dark Places.*

**Joe Market**   Son of Titus and Ramona Market; picaresque hero who appears as Naked Disciple, prostitute, student, husband, soldier, detective, Christ figure, and condemned murderer in Hal Bennett's *Lord of Dark Places* and *Wait Until the Evening.*

**Odessa Barton Market**   Wife of Joe Market; believes she is responsible for their son's death in Hal Bennett's *Lord of Dark Places.*

**Ramona Market**   Self-sacrificing wife of Titus Market and mother of Joe Market in Hal Bennett's *Lord of Dark Places.*

**Roosevelt Market**   Nephew, husband, and disciple of Madame Eudora Market; his lynching and castration are witnessed by his son, Titus Market, in Hal Bennett's *Lord of Dark Places.*

**Titus Market**   Son of Madame Eudora and Roosevelt Market; prophet of black salvation through moral inversion and worship of his son, Joe Market, in Hal Bennett's *Lord of Dark Places* and *Wait Until the Evening.*

**Bo Jack Markham**   Longtime black housekeeper for the Shafer family; prays to live until Gratt and Patsy Jo Shafer's baby is born; dies one month after the birth of Adam Gideon Shafer in Jesse Hill Ford's *Mountains of Gilead.*

**Joe Markham**   Middle-aged nonconformist potter; sells his hand-hewn Vermont home and decides to move his wife, Phyllis, and young daughter, Sonja, to the more solid, stable community of Haddam, New Jersey; meets overwhelming frustration on his mission to find a suitable piece of real estate in Richard Ford's *Independence Day.*

**Phyllis Markham**   Sweet-natured but determined, previously divorced wife of Joe Markham, whose talent at the pottery wheel she successfully marketed and grew into a booming business in Richard Ford's *Independence Day.*

**Virginia (Virgin) Markowitz**   Twenty-one-year-old receptionist in the insurance company where Bob Slocum had his first job; always imagined by Slocum as seated under a Western Union clock, she remains his lifelong image of feminine seductiveness in Joseph Heller's *Something Happened.*

**Sonia Marks**   Friend of Jane Clifford; teaches a women in literature course in Gail Godwin's *The Odd Woman.*

**Lester Marlow**   Native of Wichita Falls who uses his friend Jacy Farrow to enter the fast crowd in Thalia in Larry McMurtry's *The Last Picture Show.*

**Geraldine Marlowe**   Adoptive mother of Rina Marlowe in Harold Robbins's *The Carpetbaggers.*

**Harrison (Harry) Marlowe**   Adoptive father of Rina Marlowe; adopts her after her mother, his cook, dies in Harold Robbins's *The Carpetbaggers*.

**Rina (Katrina Osterlaag) Marlowe**   Orphan adopted by Harrison and Geraldine Marlowe; marries Jonas Cord, Sr., whom she meets while dating his son; later, widowed, she marries Nevada Smith and becomes a movie star; confesses on her deathbed her longstanding love for Jonas Cord, Jr., in Harold Robbins's *The Carpetbaggers*.

**Ronald (Laddie) Marlowe**   Adoptive brother and first lover of Rina Marlowe in Harold Robbins's *The Carpetbaggers*.

**Hardesty Marratta**   Ascetic, quiet, and widely knowledgeable son of wealthy San Francisco leader Vittorio Marratta; leaves father's fortune to seek destiny in New York City; marries Virginia Gamely and has daughter, Abby, in Mark Helprin's *Winter's Tale*.

**Candelario Marroquín**   Husband of Rosario (Chayo) and father of Tonito; volunteers to take his sister-in-law's baby after it is born; tableside Caesar salad chef who is fired because a patron does not like the salad in Sandra Benítez's *A Place Where the Sea Remembers*.

**Rosario (Chayo) Marroquín**   Wife of Candelario and mother of Tonito; sister of Marta Rodriguez; makes and sells paper flowers on the beach; refuses to talk to Marta after Marta puts a curse on Chayo's unborn baby, even though she later retracts it with the help of Remedios in Sandra Benítez's *A Place Where the Sea Remembers*.

**Beverly Marsh**   Sole female of The Losers Club, Beverly is the link that bonds the group together in their childhood attempt to kill "IT"; Beverly is also the adolescent love interest of Bill Denbrough and Ben Hanscomb in Stephen King's *IT*.

**Andrea Williams Marshall**   African-American graduate of Radcliffe; marries John Calvin Marshall; expects to live quiet academic life as wife of philosophy professor; instead caught in midst of civil rights struggle as husband's confidante; becomes public figure after his assassination in Julius Lester's *And All Our Wounds Forgiven*.

**John Calvin Marshall**   African American; Harvard Ph.D.; married to Andrea Williams; teaches philosophy at Spellman College; leads freedom marches, becomes spokesperson for civil rights movement; heads Southern Coalition for Racial Justice; assassinated while leaving hotel where he spent night with his Caucasian lover Elizabeth Adams; dies in her arms in Julius Lester's *And All Our Wounds Forgiven*.

**Little Buddy Marshall**   Friend of Scooter in a series of boyhood adventures in Albert Murray's *Train Whistle Guitar*.

**Jane Chillingworth Marshfield**   Wife of Thomas Marshfield and mother of Martin and Stephen Marshfield; takes a liberal, ethical approach to living and enjoys long, boozy discussions with Ned Bork in John Updike's *A Month of Sundays*.

**Martin Marshfield**   Sixteen-year-old son of Tom and Jane Marshfield; unhappy bully in John Updike's *A Month of Sundays*.

**Stephen Marshfield**   Fourteen-year-old son of Tom and Jane Marshfield; worldly, good-looking young man in John Updike's *A Month of Sundays*.

**Reverend Thomas (Tom) Marshfield**   Adulterous Episcopal minister who sleeps with a number of his parishioners; rationalizes all sex as creative and positive and defines himself as a believing unbeliever; husband of Jane Chillingworth Marshfield and father of Martin and Stephen Marshfield; narrator-diarist of John Updike's *A Month of Sundays*.

**Marta**   Old woman whom the narrator accidentally immolates at the beginning of Jerzy Kosinski's *The Painted Bird*.

**Mrs. Martello**   Private nurse for the hospitalized Judge Clinton McKelva in Eudora Welty's *The Optimist's Daughter*.

**Marter**   Father of Hilke Marter; head librarian at the International Student House and later postmaster at Kaprun; commits suicide by riding his mail sled down the Kitzsteinhorn in John Irving's *Setting Free the Bears*.

**Muttie Marter**   Mother of Hilke Marter; accidentally killed by a Russian machine gunner as she shouts from a window about her grandson's birth in John Irving's *Setting Free the Bears*.

**Hilke Marter-Javotnik**   High school sweetheart of Zahn Glanz; wife of Vratno Javotnik and mother of Siggy Javotnik in John Irving's *Setting Free the Bears*.

**Martha**   Mad typist whom Bob Slocum finally has removed from his office in Joseph Heller's *Something Happened*.

**Martin**   See Mr. Bradly Mr. Martin.

**Martin**   Father, by Correy Corregidora, of Ursa Corregidora in Gayl Jones's *Corregidora*.

**Alma Martin**   Wife of the Reverend Phillip Martin in Ernest J. Gaines's *In My Father's House*.

**Arlen Martin**   Texas billionaire tycoon; a major donor to Moo University, owner of TransNationalAmerica Corporation; plans with Dr. Lionel Gift to build a gold mine in the last remaining virgin cloud forest in Costa Rica; loses TNA and other ill-gotten corporations when the gold mine plans disintegrate in Jane Smiley's *Moo*.

**Cotter Martin**   Black adolescent living in Harlem in the early 1950s; skips school to sneak into the final, famous playoff game between the Brooklyn Dodgers and the New York Giants at the Polo Grounds on October 3, 1951; in outfield bleachers, forms friendly acquaintance with Bill Waterson, a white businessman and fellow Giants fan; recovers the winning home run ball hit by Bobby Thomson, wrestling it out of Waterson's grasp, then foils

Waterson's pursuit; shows the ball proudly to his father, who steals it to sell after Cotter falls asleep, in Don DeLillo's *Underworld*.

**Mr. Bradly Mr. Martin (Bradly, Martin, Mr. & Mrs. D, The Ugly Spirit)**   Leader of the Nova Mob; heavy-metal addict, inventor of the double cross, biggest operator in any universe, and a master of transfer in William S. Burroughs's *Nova Express, The Soft Machine,* and *The Ticket That Exploded.*

**Laodocious Martin**   Friend of Johnny Church at Oxford; arrested with him for writing "Astrologia non est scientia" on the door of Lauds College in Mary Lee Settle's *Prisons.*

**Olive Martin**   Obese young woman who confesses to the gruesome murder of her sister, Amber, and mother, Gwen; she is vindicated by writer Rosalind Leigh, who believes her to be insecure and protective of the true murderer, her lover Edward Clarke; title character of Minette Walters's *The Sculptress.*

**Reverend Phillip J. Martin**   Black leader losing the influence he had during the civil rights movement who is surprised by the appearance of his philosophically antagonistic, illegitimate son, Robert X, whom Martin has not seen since infancy in Ernest J. Gaines's *In My Father's House.*

**Shago Martin**   Black jazz singer in Norman Mailer's *An American Dream.*

**Shep Martin**   Boyfriend of Berenice Sweet; student at the University of Georgia in Harry Crews's *A Feast of Snakes.*

**Lieutenant Sidney Martin**   Army lieutenant in Vietnam; believes that effectiveness means valuing mission over men; killed by his own men in Tim O'Brien's *Going After Cacciato.*

**Sister Martin**   Benjamin Fermoyle's teacher; a young nun in Mary McGarry Morris's *Songs in Ordinary Time.*

**Martine**   Mistress of a wealthy banker connected with the French government; passes along some of her inside information to her lover, Jack Hartley, in James Jones's *The Merry Month of May.*

**Scott Martineau**   Young assistant to Bill Gray, a reclusive novelist with an obsessive following; lives with Bill and Karen Janney, his lover; opposes Bill's participation in Brita Nilsson's project of photographing writers, though he has a sexual tryst with Nilsson; after Bill disappears and Karen goes in search of him, remains in Bill's house, arranging and rearranging ream after ream of records, drafts, and correspondence in Don DeLillo's *Mao II.*

**Martinez**   Los Angeles policeman who beats up Abel after attempting to rob him in N. Scott Momaday's *House Made of Dawn.*

**Marty**   Latino proud of his Indian heritage; cares for the ill Harry Meyers and takes him to a black magic ritual in Jay Neugeboren's *Listen Ruben Fontanez.*

**Alfio Marullo**   Italian Catholic immigrant and owner of Marullo's Fruit and Fancy Groceries who sells the store to his seemingly good and faithful clerk Ethan Allen Hawley; deported as the result of an anonymous phone call to immigration officials in John Steinbeck's *The Winter of Our Discontent.*

**Alma (Moo Moo) Marvel**   Wife of Ben Marvel and mother of Elsie, Evelyn, Bushrod, and Cotton Marvel; celebrates her fortieth wedding anniversary in Peter De Vries's *Through the Fields of Clover.*

**Ben Marvel**   Husband of Alma Marvel, with whom he is celebrating their fortieth wedding anniversary, and father of Elsie, Evelyn, Bushrod, and Cotton Marvel; author of the Edgewise column in the Hickory, Massachusetts, *Blade* in Peter De Vries's *Through the Fields of Clover.*

**Bushrod Marvel**   Son of Alma and Ben Marvel; stereotypical comic liberal and secretary of the Civil Liberties League in Peter De Vries's *Through the Fields of Clover.*

**Clara Marvel**   Wife of Bushrod Marvel; guilt-ridden for her prejudice after objecting to Bushrod's kissing the black maid in Peter De Vries's *Through the Fields of Clover.*

**Cotton Marvel**   Twenty-six-year-old divorced youngest child of Ben and Alma Marvel; lives at home working on *The Seven Who Stank,* a play in Peter De Vries's *Through the Fields of Clover.*

**Elsie Marvel**   Daughter of Alma and Ben Marvel; former wife of Harry Mercury and others in Peter De Vries's *Through the Fields of Clover.*

**Evelyn Shaw Glimmergarden Marvel**   Daughter of Ben and Alma Marvel; her father's favorite, a golden feminine flame in Peter De Vries's *Through the Fields of Clover.*

**Marx Marvelous**   Ex–think tanker, later just a thinker and manager of the zoo; suffers hemorrhoids, lust for Amanda Ziller, and doubt; brilliant but frivolous author in Tom Robbins's *Another Roadside Attraction.*

**Marvin**   Female impersonator and dancer at the Iron Horse in Harry Crews's *Karate Is a Thing of the Spirit.*

**Major Duane Marvy**   Fat American officer stationed in the Zone; involved in black-marketeering with Bloody Chiclitz; nemesis of Tyrone Slothrop and Oberst Enzian; eventually castrated because of mistaken identity in Thomas Pynchon's *Gravity's Rainbow.*

**Mary**   Nurse to Paul and Dalton Harron as children in Susan Sontag's *Death Kit.*

**Mary**   One of Sebastian Dangerfield's girlfriends; leaves her sadistic father and follows Sebastian to London, where she has a promising start as an actress in J. P. Donleavy's *The Ginger Man.*

**Miss Mary**   Wife of Ernie; photographer and journalist; too short to be a good lion hunter because she cannot see over vegetation; has been hunting a specific lion for six months; eventually shoots lion, which is finished off by shots from Ernie and G. C.; thinks Ernie shot the lion before she did and becomes sad in Ernest Hemingway's *True At First Light*.

**Mary Agnes**   Friend of Alice Fermoyle since second grade in Mary McGarry Morris's *Songs in Ordinary Time*.

**Mary Ann**   Elderly lady who seeks a young couple to live in her house and help with light chores; shares the true meaning of Christmas with Richard and Carrie Evans; lives with the memory of her deceased daughter in Richard Evans's *The Christmas Box*.

**Abigail Howland Mason**   Daughter of William Howland by his first wife and mother of Abigail Mason Tolliver in Shirley Ann Grau's *The Keepers of the House*.

**Andrew Mason**   Lawyer and lover of N. Hexam in Diane Johnson's *The Shadow Knows*.

**Gregory Edward Mason**   Englishman who marries Abigail Howland; father of Abigail Mason Tolliver in Shirley Ann Grau's *The Keepers of the House*.

**Mrs. Mason**   Housekeeper for Joseph Johnson; has the brisk manner of her employer, but is easily twice his size; has nine or ten children, buried three in Frances Sherwood's *Vindication*.

**Babs Masters**   Lyrical babbler who gives instructions in patience and attentiveness in the loving of a woman and the reading of a book, which are revealed as equivalent activities, as she narrates William Gass's *Willie Masters's Lonesome Wife*.

**Beigh Masters**   Researches the life of the Salem Bibi; spent her twenties in grad school and in travel and short-term affairs that took her wherever she wanted to go; enters Hannah Legge's world through a virtual reality program constructed by Venn Iyer in search of the Emperor's Tear, Aurangzeb's perfect diamond, in Bharati Mukherjee's *The Holder of the World*.

**Lavinia Masterson**   Lover of William Body in Leon Forrest's *The Bloodworth Orphans*.

**Michael (Mike, Mike the Mouth) Masterson**   Respected and feared umpire whose arguments with Gil Gamesh lead to Masterson's death; killed by a pitched ball in Philip Roth's *The Great American Novel*.

**Tio Mate**   Mexican pistolero in William S. Burroughs's *The Wild Boys*; participates in the attempt to blow up the nerve gas train in *Exterminator!*

**Benjamino (Benjy, Mino) Matera**   Young man who loses his feet in an accident; Theophilus North helps him adjust to his handicap and meet young women in Thornton Wilder's *Theophilus North*.

**Phillip Materson**   Gains Libby's confidence; plans to study law at college; gets Louanne Price pregnant while he is engaged to Celia in Joan Chase's *During the Reign of the Queen of Persia*.

**Richard (Dick) Mathias**   Liquor store owner, husband of Sally Mathias, and lover of Ruth Conant in John Updike's *Marry Me*.

**Sally Mathias**   Wife of Richard Mathias and lover of Jerry Conant in John Updike's *Marry Me*.

**Buddy Matlow**   Lecherous sheriff and Public Safety Director of Lebeau County in Harry Crews's *A Feast of Snakes*.

**Alice Matthews**   Friend of Rachel Hutchins at whose father's sanitarium Rachel has recovered from her nerves; only person to advise Rachel strongly against marrying Rob Mayfield in Reynolds Price's *The Surface of Earth*.

**Crit Matthews**   Neighbor murdered by Alonzo Dudley in Jessamyn West's *The Life I Really Lived*.

**Ebon Matthews**   Homosexual lover of Alonzo Dudley in Jessamyn West's *The Life I Really Lived*.

**Gloria Matthews**   Thirty-something African-American hairdresser who owns one of the only black beauty salons in Scottsdale, Arizona; single mother of teenager Tarik, who becomes a temporary discipline problem as he learns to be a man; finds support in her friends Bernadine Harris and Robin Stokes and a group called Black Women on the Move; begins to move her own life forward, complete with a new love interest, in Terry McMillan's *Waiting to Exhale*.

**Vince Mattiuzzio**   Felix's boyhood friend and business partner in Joyce Carol Oates's *You Must Remember This*.

**Cecil Mature (Wooley)**   Orphan who becomes accomplice of Reverend Mootfowl and Jackson Mead in their efforts to create miraculous bridges throughout time in Mark Helprin's *Winter's Tale*.

**Sarah Abbott (The Pilgrim) Maulsby**   Massachusetts debutante and lover of Alex Portnoy in Philip Roth's *Portnoy's Complaint*.

**Maureen**   Friend and neighbor of Katie; cooks in a vegetarian deli; used to be in Alcoholics Anonymous, still goes to Al-Anon because she keeps falling for substance abusers and worrying too much; keeps inspirational sayings all over her apartment in Sandra Scofield's *Beyond Deserving*.

**Maurice**   Formerly worked in the production arm of a Manhattan publishing firm where the unnamed male narrator and main character is hired as an editorial assistant; following threats by the Black Caucus, the company's "Big Boss" promotes him in order to fend off a lawsuit; discovers that his management position actually has no function; becomes embittered and works to disrupt the company internally in Darryl Pinckney's *High Cotton*.

**Detective Maurice**    Los Angeles police detective investigating the murder of Lucie Proctorr in Donald E. Westlake's *The Hook*.

**Mavis**    Sister of Judy Davis and companion of James Christopher at the Apex Longleaf Club; tells Christopher about Jack Davis's beating of Preacher Smathers and accuses him of being ultimately responsible for Smathers's injuries in Fred Chappell's *It Is Time, Lord*.

**Max**    Photographer and contributor to Renate's planned magazine in Anaïs Nin's *Collages*.

**Max**    Argentinian and second in command of the revolutionary forces in South America; strong intelligent, and intuitive man who loves power in William Herrick's *The Last to Die*.

**Max**    Obese, megalomaniacal auto race manager in Joyce Carol Oates's *With Shuddering Fall*.

**Maximus**    Magician, seer, and pseudophilosopher who ingratiates himself with Julian, to the dismay of Julian's more scholarly friends in Gore Vidal's *Julian*.

**Seth Maxwell**    Party-loving Dallas Cowboy starting quarterback and friend of Phil Elliott in Peter Gent's *North Dallas Forty*.

**May**    Mother of Valerie, oldest daughter of Gram and Grandad, sister of Elinor, Libby, Rachel, and Grace; aunt of Rossie, Anne, Katie, Jenny, and Celia; widowed at forty; becomes a Christian Scientist and marries one in Joan Chase's *During the Reign of the Queen of Persia*.

**May Alice**    Girlhood friend of Ursa Corregidora; sexually active at a young age, she has a baby by Harold in Gayl Jones's *Corregidora*.

**(Prince) Lawrence Mayfair**    Jaded but respectful crown prince of England; proposes to, then breaks with commoner Louise Bristol in the novella *Town Crier Exclusive, Confessions of a Princess Manque: How Royals Found Me Unsuitable to Marry Their Larry,* in Stanley Elkin's *Van Gogh's Room at Arles*.

**Anna Goodwin Mayfield**    Dead mother of Forrest Mayfield in Reynolds Price's *The Surface of Earth*.

**Eva Kendal Mayfield**    See Eva Kendal.

**Forrest Mayfield**    Latin teacher who elopes with his sixteen-year-old pupil Eva Kendal in Reynolds Price's *The Surface of Earth*.

**Hattie (Hatt Shorter) Mayfield**    Sister of Forrest Mayfield and wife of the deceased James Shorter in Reynolds Price's *The Surface of Earth*.

**Aunt Mannie Mayfield**    Elderly aunt of Mildred Sutton in Reynolds Price's *A Long and Happy Life*.

**Rachel Hutchins Mayfield**    See Rachel Hutchins.

**Raven Hutchins (Hutch) Mayfield**    Child of Rachel Hutchins and Rob Mayfield in Reynolds Price's *The Surface of Earth*.

**Robinson Mayfield**    Estranged father of Forrest Mayfield in Reynolds Price's *The Surface of Earth*.

**Robinson (Rob) Mayfield**    Son of Eva Kendal and Forrest Mayfield in Reynolds Price's *The Surface of Earth*.

**Caroline Peck Mayhew**    Hypochondriac mother of Justine Peck and wife of Sam Mayhew; commits suicide after her husband's death in Anne Tyler's *Searching for Caleb*.

**Sam Mayhew**    Husband of Caroline Peck Mayhew in Anne Tyler's *Searching for Caleb*.

**Mayo (May, Sandra)**    Lover of Valentine Hood and wife of Sweeney in Paul Theroux's *The Family Arsenal*.

**Claire Mayo**    Martha Horgan's landlady for eight months, an old lady who runs a boardinghouse in Mary McGarry Morris's *A Dangerous Woman*.

**May Mayo**    Owner of a boardinghouse with her younger sister, Claire; has bluish-white hair and a shy, giggly voice in Mary McGarry Morris's *Songs in Ordinary Time*.

**The Mayor of the Twentieth Century**    Murderer who once disguised himself as Trout Fishing in America in Richard Brautigan's *Trout Fishing in America*.

**Larry Mazilli**    Homicide detective and partner of Rocco Klein; does not like Sean Touhey; owns deli and liquor store in Rodney Little's neighborhood; has many connections in the neighborhood in Richard Price's *Clockers*.

**Ewell McBee**    Former "covite" who has become "a new Southerner" concerned with making money through the manufacture and sale of pornographic videos; he tries to force Will Barrett to invest in his business in Walker Percy's *The Second Coming*.

**Dean McCabe**    First husband of Peggy McCabe Robinson; assistant dean at Yale University in John Updike's *Of the Farm*.

**Earl McCabe**    Marine deserter who, as a partner of Lionel Boyd Johnson, becomes ruler of San Lorenzo in Kurt Vonnegut's *Cat's Cradle*.

**Orondo McCabe**    Owner of a Philadelphia nightclub and manager of Cubsy Hall in William Goyen's *The Fair Sister*.

**Richard McCabe**    Eleven-year-old stepson of Joey Robinson and son of Peggy McCabe Robinson and Dean McCabe; serious boy with a passion for reading and for knowledge of the natural world in John Updike's *Of the Farm*.

**Alonzo (Lon) McCaferty**    Exactor and alcoholic tramp; returns to his hometown to die in Jerry Bumpus's *Anaconda*.

**Daniel X. McCafferty**   Skipper of USS *Chicago,* he discovers a minefield closing off the White Sea; intercepts Soviet submarines in the North Sea headed for North Atlantic; leads mission into Barents Sea to launch cruise missiles against Soviet airfields, from which only the *Chicago* returns in Tom Clancy's *Red Storm Rising.*

**Mr. W. Greenberry McCain**   Agent with whom James and Christianna Wheeler contract to tour the South with the remains of their quintuplets for $100 a week in Bobbie Ann Mason's *Feather Crowns.*

**Bindy McCall**   Brother of Patsy and Matt McCall and father of Charlie Boy McCall; controls Albany's nighttime world, which he closes to Billy Phelan because Phelan refused to spy on Morrie Berman in William Kennedy's *Billy Phelan's Greatest Game.*

**Charlie Boy McCall**   Son of Bindy McCall; kidnap victim in William Kennedy's *Billy Phelan's Greatest Game.*

**Matt McCall**   Brother of Patsy and Bindy McCall and uncle of Charlie Boy McCall; political strategist and spokesman in William Kennedy's *Billy Phelan's Greatest Game.*

**Patsy McCall**   Brother of Bindy and Matt McCall and uncle of Charlie Boy McCall; establishes the powerful Irish Democratic McCall political machine in William Kennedy's *Billy Phelan's Greatest Game.*

**Mrs. McCamb**   Midwife for Mary Wollstonecraft Godwin when she gives birth to Mary Godwin; replacement for Mary's regular midwife, Mrs. Colin, who is assisting her own daughter in Frances Sherwood's *Vindication.*

**Mr. McCandles**   Jaded if idealistic owner of the house rented by Paul and Elizabeth Booth, he has been disappointed by the value others ascribe to his knowledge of geology and the sciences in William Gaddis's *Carpenter's Gothic.*

**Mickey McCane**   Former Army buddy of Jack Sellars; makes passes at Bebe Sellars and finally goes berserk, murdering the idiot boy Pinhead and Miss Whitaker, his black nurse, in Doris Betts's *The River to Pickle Beach.*

**Issac (Ike) McCaslin**   See Volume I.

**Lucius Quintus Carothers (Old Carothers) McCaslin**   See Volume I.

**Ned McCaslin**   Grandson of Carothers McCaslin in William Faulkner's *The Reivers.*

**Theophilus (Uncle Buck) McCaslin**   See Volume I.

**Ruth McCausland**   Beloved town constable and doll collector in Haven, Maine; widow of state trooper Ralph; community activist; blown apart in an explosion staged to call attention to the strange goings-on in Haven in Stephen King's *The Tommyknockers.*

**Reba McClain**   Girlfriend of Red Scalotta and bet recorder in Joseph Wambaugh's *The Blue Knight.*

**Everett Currier McClellan**   Hop farmer and husband of Lily Knight McClellan; murders Ryder Charming before shooting himself in Joan Didion's *Run River.*

**James Parker (Arkie) McClellan**   Fourteen-year-old Gimlet Street hustler who shoots Zebulon Johns Mackie in a misguided attempt to protect Clemmie in Fred Chappell's *The Gaudy Place.*

**Julia Knight (Julie) McClellan**   Daughter of Everett and Lily Knight McClellan in Joan Didion's *Run River.*

**Knight McClellan**   Son of Everett and Lily Knight McClellan in Joan Didion's *Run River.*

**Lily Knight McClellan**   Wife of Everett McClellan and daughter of Walter and Edith Knight; has several affairs, most importantly with Ryder Channing in Joan Didion's *Run River.*

**Martha Currier McClellan**   Sister of Everett McClellan and lover of Ryder Charming; buried on the family farm by Everett after her possibly suicidal drowning in Joan Didion's *Run River.*

**Jonathan (Johnny) McCloud**   Lover of Molly Taylor White, father of Joe White, and friend of Gideon Fry; cowboy on Fry's ranch; narrates part of Larry McMurtry's *Leaving Cheyenne.*

**Mark McCluskey**   Police captain in the pay of Virgil Sollozzo; killed by Michael Corleone in revenge for the shooting of Vito Corleone in Mario Puzo's *The Godfather.*

**Codene McClusky**   Girlfriend of Raymond Douglas in Herbert Simmons's *Man Walking on Eggshells.*

**Alexander Hamilton McCone**   Stuttering son of Daniel McCone and patron of Walter F. Starbuck in Kurt Vonnegut's *Jailbird.*

**Daniel McCone**   Industrialist and father of Alexander McCone in Kurt Vonnegut's *Jailbird.*

**Edith (Babe) McCord**   Youngest child of Frank and Eleanor McCord and playmate to Anna Dunlap; Babe is a free spirit whom Anna loves and admires, but she is forced to conform to the family rules and becomes an alcoholic whose life is cut tragically short in Sue Miller's *The Good Mother.*

**Eleanor McCord**   Grandmother of Anna Dunlap and wife of Frank McCord; a very quiet and seemingly passive woman who loves babies and young children; finally stands up to her husband in Sue Miller's *The Good Mother.*

**Frank McCord**   Anna Dunlap's grandfather and husband of Eleanor; a "self-made" man and patriarch of a large family; uses his money to influence and control his children and grandchildren in Sue Miller's *The Good Mother.*

**Tadpole (Crawdad, Tad, Taddy) McCormick**   Owner of Happy's Café, where Ursa Corregidora sings; tends to Ursa following her operation, and then marries her; because of his affair with Vivian, he and Ursa are divorced in Gayl Jones's *Corregidora*.

**Sherman McCoy**   Investment banker on Wall Street; lives in Park Avenue apartment with his wife, Judy, and daughter, Campbell; owner of Mercedes Benz involved in a hit-and-run accident in the Bronx while his mistress is at the wheel; becomes entangled in legal difficulties and loses his job, position, and family as a result of the accident in Tom Wolfe's *The Bonfire of the Vanities*.

**Augustus McCrae**   Former Texas Ranger captain; partner with Woodrow F. Call in the Hat Creek Cattle Company; goes on cattle drive to Montana to see his former sweetheart in Nebraska; after renegade Indian shoots him with an arrow, contracts gangrene that causes his death in Larry McMurtry's *Lonesome Dove*.

**Mary McCullogh**   White prostitute, pawn of J. D. Carson and proponents of school segregation, whose allegation of rape by three blacks leads to racial violence in Julian Mayfield's *The Grand Parade*.

**Skinny McCullough**   Foreman of Drag Gibson's ranch in Ishmael Reed's *Yellow Back Radio Broke Down*.

**Elias McCutcheon**   Fort Hill settler who becomes a wealthy landowner, common-law husband of Jane Nail, and a leader of Confederate raiders in Jesse Hill Ford's *The Raider*.

**Isaac McCutcheon**   First-born son of Elias McCutcheon and Jane Nail; kills a man in a duel and is injured in the Civil War in Jesse Hill Ford's *The Raider*.

**Jake McCutcheon**   Slave given to Elias McCutcheon by Shokotee McNeilly; becomes McCutcheon's faithful friend and companion in Jesse Hill Ford's *The Raider*.

**Patsy Jo McCutcheon**   See Patricia Josephine McCutcheon Shafer.

**Thomas Gideon (Tom) McCutcheon**   Father of Patsy Jo McCutcheon and longtime member of the Sligo County community; murders Eleanor Fite at her wedding to Gratt Shafer before killing himself in Jesse Hill Ford's *Mountains of Gilead*; apparently descended from Elias McCutcheon in *The Raider*.

**Willy McCutcheon**   Second son of Elias McCutcheon and Jane Nail; marries Sallie Parham before being killed in the Civil War in Jesse Hill Ford's *The Raider*.

**Abby McDeere**   Elementary schoolteacher and strong-willed wife of Mitchell McDeere; questions the intrusive activities of her husband's law firm from the beginning of McDeere's association with the firm; considers leaving Mitch when she discovers he's had an affair but instead chooses to assist him in exposing illegal actions of the firm in John Grisham's *The Firm*.

**Mitchell McDeere**   Ambitious young lawyer from a lower-class, broken home; married to his high school sweetheart, Abby; recruited by an exclusive, well-paying, mysterious Memphis law firm that ostensibly handles tax cases; realizes Mafia connections of firm; despite danger to him and his family, gives vital information to the FBI; enters the witness protection program in John Grisham's *The Firm*.

**Ray McDeere**   Imprisoned older brother of Mitchell McDeere; criminal record and incarceration kept secret by Mitchell from his legal firm's security team; obtains parole through Mitchell's deal with the FBI; works to protect Mitchell from the Mafia in John Grisham's *The Firm*.

**Sandy McDermott**   Old law school friend of Patrick Lanigan in John Grisham's *The Partner*; Patrick hires Sandy as his attorney to prove that he did not kill anyone when he faked his own death; provides the federal government information that proves the culpability of the senior partners of Patrick's law firm as well as Benny Aricia and a U.S. senator in the defrauding of the government.

**Sheen McEvoy**   Deformed and retarded man who tries to throw Mazie Holbrook down a mine shaft in Tillie Olsen's *Yonnondio*.

**Alison McFarland**   Twenty-two-year-old daughter of Charlie McFarland; big fan of Molly Cates's recent book; supposedly saw her mother's murderer; turns out to be the original perpetrator in Mary Willis Walker's *The Red Scream*.

**Andrea Wendell McFarland**   Known as "Tiny" McFarland; first wife of Charlie McFarland; was very wealthy before marriage; supposedly murdered by Louie Bronk; body was found by David Serrano, with whom she was having an affair in Mary Willis Walker's *The Red Scream*.

**Charlie McFarland**   West Texas native; former manual laborer, now wealthy and extravagant real estate developer; widower of two women, one of whom is the apparent victim of Louie Bronk, the other a victim of a "copy-cat" murderer; father of Stuart and Alison McFarland in Mary Willis Walker's *The Red Scream*.

**Georgia McFarland**   Second wife of Charlie McFarland; had been a friend of Tiny McFarland's; murdered by stepdaughter Alison; her body was found at her home by Molly Cates in Mary Willis Walker's *The Red Scream*.

**Stuart McFarland**   Stoic, loner son of Charlie Mcfarland; protective of his sister, Alison; medical student in Dallas in Mary Willis Walker's *The Red Scream*.

**Annie McGairy**   See Annie McGairy Brown.

**Andrew McGee**   Charlie's father and husband of Vicky Tomlinson, who is killed by the Shop; takes part in a psychology experiment where he is administered a drug called Lot Six from which he gains the ability to mentally influence people; meets wife during this experiment; tries to protect his daughter from the Shop, but fails when he dies at the hands of John Rainbird in Stephen King's *Firestarter*.

**Charlene (Charlie) McGee**    Daughter of Andrew and Vicky McGee; has pyrokinetic abilities due to the experiment her parents went through in college; captured and held by the Shop; eventually escapes by killing John Rainbird and hiding out with the Manders in upstate New York; tells her story to *Rolling Stone* magazine as a way of exposing the Shop in Stephen King's *Firestarter*.

**Leslie (Red) McGivers**    Graduate student in history who moves to Detroit when her thesis adviser changes universities; studies karate, befriends Bernie Guizot, and tries to expose Honor Rogers to feminist ideas in Marge Piercy's *The High Cost of Living*.

**Gowan McGland**    Womanizing alcoholic Scotch-Welsh poet on a personal appearance tour in America; commits suicide in Peter De Vries's *Reuben, Reuben*.

**Gregory (Greg) McGovern**    Movie actor and lover of Orpha Chase; marries Chase's daughter Wanda in Jessamyn West's *The Life I Really Lived*.

**Jamie McGregor**    Indomitable man who risks death to retrieve a fortune in diamonds from the South African coast; bitter man whose life aims revolve around revenge; father of Kate Blackwell in Sidney Sheldon's *Master of the Game*.

**Sims McGrother**    Greedy neighbor of Old Jack Beechum; abuses other people, his animals, and his land for profit in Wendell Berry's *The Memory of Old Jack*.

**Sam McGuire**    Friend to Charles who loses his job as a suit salesman, his optimism, and his charisma and eventually moves in with Charles in Ann Beattie's *Chilly Scenes of Winter*.

**James J. (Admiral Ass) McHabe**    Administrative assistant at Calvin Coolidge High School; spends time writing circulars and keeping everyone innundated with paperwork, little of which makes any sense in Bel Kaufman's *Up the Down Staircase*.

**Clay McInnis**    Country doctor of Port William, Kentucky, in Wendell Berry's *The Memory of Old Jack*.

**David McInnis**    Financial manager of Rebecca Carrington's estate and subsequently her husband in Robert Penn Warren's *A Place to Come To*.

**Maria McInnis**    See Maria McInnis Beaufort.

**Rose McInnis**    Wife and widow of Clay McInnis and lover of Jack Beechum; burns to death when her house catches fire in Wendell Berry's *The Memory of Old Jack*.

**Reverend Kenneth McIntoch**    Shady, unctuous minister aboard the *Castel Felice* in Calvin Hernton's *Scarecrow*.

**Joy McIntyre**    Lee (LuAnne) Verger's stand-in on the set of the movie *The Awakening* in Robert Stone's *Children of Light*.

**Becky Thurston McKelva**    First wife of Judge Clinton McKelva and mother of Laurel McKelva Hand; West Virginia native who loses her vision and dies after an eye operation in Eudora Welty's *The Optimist's Daughter*.

**Clinton (Clint, Judge Mac) McKelva**    Seventy-one-year-old judge in Mt. Salus, Mississippi; father of Laurel McKelva Hand and widower of Becky McKelva; marries Wanda Fay Chisom McKelva one and a half years before his eye operation and subsequent death in a New Orleans hospital in Eudora Welty's *The Optimist's Daughter*.

**Wanda Fay Chisom McKelva**    Second wife of Judge Clinton McKelva; inherits the McKelva family home in Eudora Welty's *The Optimist's Daughter*.

**Harry McKenna**    Good-looking senior at Haddan School; dates Carlin Leander until she realizes what he is like and dumps him; cuts one of the eyes out of Abel Gray's and Helen Davis's black cat, Midnight; murders Gus Pierce; expelled after Abe Gray plants an exam in his room in Alice Hoffman's *The River King*.

**Peace McKnight**    Nineteenth-century Scots woman who teaches school on the Great Plains, marries Scranton Roy, and dies in childbirth in Louise Erdrich's *The Antelope Wife*.

**Patrick (Pat) McLear**    Handsome San Francisco poet and friend of Jack Duluoz, who admires McLear's unpublished poem "Dark Brown" in Jack Kerouac's *Big Sur*; also appears in *Desolation Angels*.

**Betty McLeod**    Mousy and distrustful young mother who leads an increasingly reclusive life with her African-American husband, Larry, and their two young children; is rarely seen outside of her home; infuriatingly evasive tenant in one of Frank Bascombe's rental properties in Richard Ford's *Independence Day*.

**Larry McLeod**    Former Green Beret and African American who is a tenant with his white wife, Betsy, and their two children, in one of Frank Bascombe's rental properties; works in the mobile home construction industry and is unreliable about paying his rent on time in Richard Ford's *Independence Day*.

**Eloise (Eloise Hunter) McLindon**    Struggling single parent of David Hunter; moves from Virginia to New Jersey following the death of her daughter, Clair Hunter, in Hal Bennett's *The Black Wine*.

**Dick McMahon**    Father of Elena McMahon; seemingly unscrupulous deal-maker and hustler who secures his daughter's help for one last deal in arms trafficking; dies under mysterious circumstances in Joan Didion's *The Last Thing He Wanted*.

**Elena McMahon**    Former *Washington Post* reporter and political campaign worker who naively becomes caught up in mysterious gun dealings, global intrigue, and conspiracy in the mid-1980s; daughter of Dick McMahon, who enlists his daughter's support for one last deal; ex-wife of Wynn Janklow; mother of Catherine; stranded with a false passport on an island off the coast of Costa Rica and killed in Joan Didion's *The Last Thing He Wanted*.

**Randle Patrick (Mack, McMurry, R. P.) McMurphy**   Fast-talking and irrepressible inmate who challenges Big Nurse's dictatorial control of a mental hospital ward in Ken Kesey's *One Flew over the Cuckoo's Nest*.

**McNab**   See Vadim Vadimovich.

**Shokotee McNeilly**   Chickasaw leader and father of Pettecasockee; gives Jane Nail to Elias McCutcheon for a wife in Jesse Hill Ford's *The Raider*.

**Ann McNulty**   Lives in Claire Mayo's boardinghouse; after twenty-nine years of marriage, her husband, Willis, left her for a handsome young cabana boy they'd both taken a shine to in Clearwater, Florida, in Mary McGarry Morris's *A Dangerous Woman*.

**Mary McNutt**   Older African-American woman who rescues Rosie from Alvin Crooms; Mother of Linda, Jane Ray, Thomas, and Henry Ray; married to Lyle McNutt, Jr.; shot by Paris Trout and Buster Devonne over Henry Ray's car bill, but is not killed in Pete Dexter's *Paris Trout*.

**McPherson**   Dispatcher for the South Eastern Railway whose office is broken into in Michael Crichton's *The Great Train Robbery*.

**Roger A. (Rog) McPherson**   Head of the Neuropsychiatric Research Unit who authorizes the stage-three operation on Harold Benson in Michael Crichton's *The Terminal Man*.

**Ev McTaggart**   Smart but mediocre former catcher for the New York Mammoths; becomes manager of the team when Dutch Schnell dies in Mark Harris's *It Looked Like For Ever*.

**Anthony McVay**   White lawyer who supports the civil rights efforts of the Reverend Phillip Martin in Ernest J. Gaines's *In My Father's House*.

**McWatt**   Air force pilot and showoff; commits suicide by crashing his plane into a mountainside after buzzing the squadron and accidentally killing Kid Sampson in Joseph Heller's *Catch-22*.

**Mollie Catharine (Katy) McWhorter**   Flutist, high school senior, and close friend of Susie Schnitzer; her father is accused of being a Communist during the McCarthy era in Harriette Simpson Arnow's *The Weedkiller's Daughter*.

**McWillie**   Jockey in William Faulkner's *The Reivers*.

**Jackson Mead**   Mysterious and timeless master bridge builder who attempts to build a bridge into the heavens in New York City in Mark Helprin's *Winter's Tale*.

**George Gordon Meade**   Union general who assumes command of the Army of the Potomac shortly before the Battle of Gettysburg in Michael Shaara's *The Killer Angels*.

**Harry Meadows**   Editor of the *Amity Leader*, who agrees to conceal the facts about Christine Watkins's death from the public; discloses the truth after the Great White Shark kills two more people in Peter Benchley's *Jaws*.

**O. B. Meadows**   Obnoxious defensive lineman for the Dallas Cowboys who teams with Jo Bob Williams to make life miserable for Phil Elliott in Peter Gent's *North Dallas Forty*.

**Minerva (Minnie Mouse) Means**   Owner of the Adirondacks cabin rented by Ambrose Clay; informs *Violet Clay* of Ambrose's suicide in Gail Godwin's *Violet Clay*.

**Benjaman (Ben) Mears**   Unemployed writer who returns to Jerusalem's Lot to write a book based on the haunted Marsten House in Stephen King's *'Salem's Lot*.

**Benny (Ben) Measey**   Son of Carol and Jimmy; Ann August's friend who plays with her when she lives in Wisconsin; dies in a car accident when he is eighteen in Mona Simpson's *Anywhere but Here*.

**Carol Measey**   Adele Diamond's older sister by eleven years; married to Jimmy and mother of Hal and Beny; lives in Wisconsin; next door to her mother; fights with Adele in Mona Simpson's *Anywhere but Here*.

**Hal Measey**   Son of Carol and Jimmy; does not do well in school; marries Mary and has one daughter, Tina; uses drugs and is abusive toward his wife and daughter; divorces and later does not use drugs in Mona Simpson's *Anywhere but Here*.

**Jimmy Measey**   Husband of Carol and father of Ben and Hal; likes to tell risque stories; lives in Wisconsin in Mona Simpson's *Anywhere but Here*.

**The Medic**   Medic from Bravo Company who finds Paco, the only surviving American soldier of an attack on Fire Base Harriet in Vietnam; after the war he is haunted by the memory of finding Paco badly burned and injured and blames this particular memory for his alcoholism in Larry Heinemann's *Paco's Story*.

**Principessa Margaret dei Medici**   Woman James Boswell marries in a hopeless attempt to attain immortality through family life and in denial of his basically solitary nature in Stanley Elkin's *Boswell*.

**Medina**   Gypsy woman with seductive eyes in Gayl Jones's *Eva's Man*.

**Lewis (Lew) Medlock**   Physical fitness devotée who believes himself capable of withstanding the wilderness in its most primitive state; group leader during the canoe trip in James Dickey's *Deliverance*.

**Medusa**   Abductor of Perseus after his shipwreck in the *Perseid*, a novella in John Barth's *Chimera*.

**Benjamin (Ben) Meecham**   Elder son of Bull and Lillian Meecham; protagonist of Pat Conroy's *The Great Santini.*

**Karen Meecham**   Younger daughter of Bull and Lillian Meecham in Pat Conroy's *The Great Santini.*

**Lillian Meecham**   Wife of Bull Meecham and mother of Ben, Mary Anne, Karen, and Matt Meecham in Pat Conroy's *The Great Santini.*

**Mary Anne Meecham**   Elder daughter of Bull and Lillian Meecham in Pat Conroy's *The Great Santini.*

**Matthew (Matt) Meecham**   Younger son of Bull and Lillian Meecham in Pat Conroy's *The Great Santini.*

**W. P. (Bull) Meecham**   Marine lieutenant colonel; exacting husband of Lillian Meecham and father of Ben, Mary Anne, Karen, and Matt Meecham in Pat Conroy's *The Great Santini.*

**Rev. Bartholomew Luther Meeks**   Preacher who came to Somerton in 1842 to hold a protracted camp meeting and named the mounds outside town the Mountains of Gilead; predicted Christ's return in 1843 in Jesse Hill Ford's *Mountains of Gilead.*

**Trish vanden Meer**   Former wife of Thomas Pemberton; re-married; daughter of highly placed official in Lyndon Johnson's administration in E. L. Doctorow's *City of God.*

**Cherry Melainie**   Nightclub singer and lover of Stephen Rojack in Norman Mailer's *An American Dream.*

**Augustus Mellon**   Confederate soldier believed by Lee Mellon to be his great-grandfather and a general in Richard Brautigan's *A Confederate General from Big Sur.*

**Lee Mellon**   Dropout and small-time criminal who claims to be the great-grandson of a Confederate general; living hand-to-mouth, he eventually moves to Big Sur in Richard Brautigan's *A Confederate General from Big Sur.*

**Bernard (Bernie) Melman**   Billionaire corporate raider who initially backs Russell Calloway's efforts to seize control of the publishing firm where he is a junior editor; takes pride in his reputation as a "dark outsider" and uses anti-Semitism as fuel for his desire to live regally from the profits of his many successful deals; supports Trina Cox as a fellow outsider in the financial world; increases his profits by eventually betraying Russell and cutting him out of the deal in Jay McInerney's *Brightness Falls.*

**Henry Webster Melrose**   Lawyer of Joseph Detweiler in Thomas Berger's *Killing Time.*

**Austin Melroy**   Friend of Gully Fisher; an elderly man who lives with more than a dozen dogs, mostly mongrels he has rescued; was a depression-era farm boy and then spent thirty years on oil rigs before heading to the Northwest; had two wives in Sandra Scofield's *Beyond Deserving.*

**Anita Mendelsohn**   Headmistress of a Jewish school and lover of Charlie Sapistein after the death of her husband, Murray Mendelsohn, in Jay Neugeboren's *An Orphan's Tale.*

**Ephraim Mendelsohn**   Son of Murray and Anita Mendelsohn; Daniel Ginsberg sends him a short story in Jay Neugeboren's *An Orphan's Tale.*

**Hannah Mendelsohn**   Daughter of Murray and Anita Mendelsohn; kissing partner of Daniel Ginsberg in Jay Neugeboren's *An Orphan's Tale.*

**Murray (Moses, Moshe) Mendelsohn**   Husband of Anita Mendelsohn and friend of Charlie Sapistein; headmaster at a Jewish school who dies playing football in Jay Neugeboren's *An Orphan's Tale.*

**Yehoshua Mendelssohn**   Name given to Sarah Blumenthal's father in Kovno ghetto after disappearance of parents; serves as runner/messenger for ghetto's ruling council; delivers portions of secret ghetto archive to Greta Margolin; later smuggles entire manuscript to Father Petrauskas at his church; survives war; goes to America; dies believing archive is lost in E. L. Doctorow's *City of God.*

**Josephine (Fina) Mendoza**   Young Puerto Rican woman who befriends Benny Profane; involved with street gangs in New York in the 1950s in Thomas Pynchon's *V.*

**Valerie (Val) Mendoza**   Lover of Leslie McGivers; chooses to stay behind in Grand Rapids, Michigan, when McGivers moves to Detroit in Marge Piercy's *The High Cost of Living.*

**Howard Menka**   Twin of Jozia; the monsignor's handyman at St. Mary's in Mary McGarry Morris's *Songs in Ordinary Time.*

**Jozia Menka**   Twin of Howard; housekeeper for the Fermoyle family for thirty years; gets engaged to Grondine but breaks up with him when he shoots Howard in the leg in Mary McGarry Morris's *Songs in Ordinary Time.*

**Valencia Merble**   See Valencia Merble Pilgrim.

**Mercedes**   Indian prostitute under the protection of Comandante Guzmán in Peter Matthiessen's *At Play in the Fields of the Lord.*

**Alex Mercer**   Friend of Phillip Carver who serves as liaison between Phillip in New York City and his family in Memphis in Peter Taylor's *A Summons to Memphis.*

**Roger Merchant**   Degenerate Kentucky landowner and distant cousin of Mat Feltner in Wendell Berry's *A Place on Earth.*

**Chester Mercury**   Teenage son of Harry Mercury and Elsie Marvel; affects Elizabethan speech in Peter De Vries's *Through the Fields of Clover.*

**Harry Mercury**   Television comedian, the latest Last of the Clowns; former husband of Elsie Marvel and father of Lee and Chester Mercury in Peter De Vries's *Through the Fields of Clover*.

**Lee Mercury**   Nineteen-year-old daughter of Harry Mercury and Elsie Marvel; apprentice at Smuggler's Cove Theatre; courted by Malcolm Johnsprang, Bill Prufrock, and Neil Sligh in Peter De Vries's *Through the Fields of Clover*.

**Meredith**   Suspicious and ill-tempered oldest daughter of Hugh and Catherine and older sister of twins Dolores and Eveline in John Hawkes's *The Blood Oranges*.

**Colin Meredith**   Student and follower of Eleanor Norton; attempts suicide after being forcibly removed from the Brunists' influence and made an example by the Common Sense Committee in Robert Coover's *The Origin of the Brunists*.

**Emily Meredith**   Makes puppets and performs with them at local events and parties; marries Morgan Gower and has a boy, Josh, with him in Anne Tyler's *Morgan's Passing*.

**Leon Meredith**   Emily Meredith's first husband; reluctantly agrees to perform puppet shows with her; divorces her and works for his father's bank in Anne Tyler's *Morgan's Passing*.

**Merlin**   Wizard who aspires to spiritual powers in Thomas Berger's *Arthur Rex*.

**Robert Merlin**   Former lover of Margot Lamar; producer and codirector of the film being shot at Belle Isle in Walker Percy's *Lancelot*.

**Vera Meroving**   See *V*.

**Merissa Merrill**   Twenty-seven-year-old British society columnist who has an eight-year-old son in boarding school, a rich father, a Spanish maid, and an American husband she is divorcing; inspires Henry Bech as a model for the heroine of his next novel, *Think Big*, in John Updike's *Bech: A Book*.

**Lankester Merrin**   Elderly Jesuit priest, philosopher, and paleontologist who is called on to exorcise the demon possessing Regan MacNeil in William Peter Blatty's *The Exorcist*.

**Cornell Messenger**   Forty-five-year-old English professor at a university in St. Louis, Missouri; husband of Paula, father of Harve and Jeanne; spends much of his time in a marijuana stupor; reluctantly goes to visit Judith Glazer, the curmudgeonly dying wife of one of the deans, takes over her Meals-on-Wheels route; he meets the Mills couple and their infirm father, eventually connecting George with Glazer in her final time of need and developing a crush on Mills's wife, Louise, in Stanley Elkin's *George Mills*.

**Franz Metz**   Ex-employee of the von Hargenau family who wore red suspenders and was a meticulous eater, but was fired by Mrs. von Hargenau when she found him naked with the maid, Doris; marries Doris; works as a waiter at Pflume; has one son, Obbie, from a previous marriage; is making a model of Durst concentration camp out of matchsticks in Walter Abish's *How German Is It*.

**Metzger (Baby Igor)**   Lawyer and coexecutor with Oedipa Maas of the estate of Pierce Inverarity; former child actor in Thomas Pynchon's *The Crying of Lot 49*.

**Roger Mexico**   Young English statistician and lover of Jessica Swanlake; with Seaman Bodine, an active member of The Counterforce in Thomas Pynchon's *Gravity's Rainbow*.

**Harry (Mad-Man) Meyers**   Jewish teacher of Hebrew who captures Jackson and wins the respect of Ruben Fontanez; narrator of Jay Neugeboren's *Listen Ruben Fontanez*.

**Sarah Meyers**   Dead wife of Harry Meyers, who often imagines that she is alive in Jay Neugeboren's *Listen Ruben Fontanez*.

**Miami**   Former stripper and pornographic movie actress; member of Big Red Smalley's traveling gospel show in George Garrett's *Do, Lord, Remember Me*.

**Michael**   Journeyman in Rayal's House in Octavia E. Butler's *Patternmaster*.

**Sebastian Michaels**   Middle-aged gay writer; lover of Tony Lewis and friend of Johnny Rio in John Rechy's *Numbers*.

**Michelle**   Intelligent teenager with great potential; becomes belligerent after being hit by a teacher; lives at home with her mother, aunt, younger sisters, and brother in Alexis Deveaux's *Spirits in the Street*.

**Midass**   Nineteenth-century Ojibwa woman; mother of Blue Prairie Woman, she raises her twin granddaughters and twin great-granddaughters (Zosie and Mary Shawano) in Louise Erdrich's *The Antelope Wife*.

**Miguelito**   Young bullfighter humiliated when a bull tears his pants during a bullfight in Anaïs Nin's *Seduction of the Minotaur*.

**Milkman**   See Macon Dead III.

**Phil Millard**   White homosexual photographer and friend of Terry Bluvard in Ann Allen Shockley's *Loving Her*.

**Anna Miller**   Wife of Harry Miller; later divorces him; narrates part of Frederick Busch's *Domestic Particulars*.

**Catherine Miller**   Young woman whose infant son dies and who adopts the Adare infant (Jude Miller) kidnapped by her husband in Louise Erdrich's *The Beet Queen*.

**Claire Miller**   Jewish freelance editor; wife of Mac Miller and mother of Harry Miller; narrates part of Frederick Busch's *Domestic Particulars*.

**Dick Miller**  Lutheran pastor; suggests to Margaret that they have an evensong to welcome in the millennium in Gail Godwin's *Evensong.*

**Esmerelda Miller**  Black American student at McCarthy College in Wisconsin; middle-class woman who adopts Marxism and exposes Hakim Elleloû, her occasional lover, to it as well in John Updike's *The Coup.*

**Eva Miller**  Owner of the boardinghouse where Ben Mears stays; vampires seek refuge in her dark basement during the day in Stephen King's *'Salem's Lot.*

**Harry Miller**  Son of Mac and Claire Miller; lover of Katherine and later husband of Anna Miller, who divorces him; maintains minimal contact with his parents, returning to see his mother only after his father dies; narrates part of Frederick Busch's *Domestic Particulars.*

**Henry Miller**  Famous writer with whom a drunken Jack Duluoz breaks an appointment in Jack Kerouac's *Big Sur.*

**Howard Miller**  Homosexual orderly suspected of an attempted rape of Maria Alvarez at Sacred Heart Hospital in Edward Lewis Wallant's *The Children at the Gate.*

**Janice Miller**  Sister of Weeb Miller; gets pregnant and marries her boyfriend in Mary McGarry Morris's *Songs in Ordinary Time.*

**Jude Miller**  Infant son of Adelaide Adare, kidnapped and raised by Martin and Catherine Miller; red-haired Catholic priest in Louise Erdrich's *The Beet Queen.*

**Justin (Tiger) Miller**  High school basketball wonder and editor of the West Condon *Chronicle;* makes fun of the Brunist cult while becoming sexually obsessed with the prophet's sister, Marcella Bruno, in Robert Coover's *The Origin of the Brunists.*

**Mac Miller**  Professor of English, husband of Claire Miller, and father of Harry Miller; suffers and later dies from heart disease; narrates part of Frederick Busch's *Domestic Particulars.*

**Martin Miller**  Young man who kidnaps Adelaide Adare's infant son (Jude Miller) from a Minneapolis fairgrounds in Louise Erdrich's *The Beet Queen.*

**Mr. Miller**  Father of Weeb Miller; a serious red-faced man who always looks worried; a venereal disease specialist with the state health department; has a scar from a war wound from his groin to his neck in Mary McGarry Morris's *Songs in Ordinary Time.*

**Mrs. Miller**  Mother of Weeb Miller, nurse of Mrs. Stoner in Mary McGarry Morris's *Songs in Ordinary Time.*

**Otis Miller**  Also known as Callanwolde to the Wingo children; a sexual monster, he brings absolute evil into their lives in Pat Conroy's *The Prince of Tides.*

**Sean Miller**  Irish terrorist, member of the Ulster Liberation Army; has a vendetta against Jack Ryan; persuades Kevin O'Donnell to try to kill the Ryans in Tom Clancy's *Patriot Games.*

**Weeb Miller**  Best friend of Norm Fermoyle; assistant manager of the baseball team in Mary McGarry Morris's *Songs in Ordinary Time.*

**Willard Miller**  Boss Snake of the Mystic High School Rattlers in Harry Crews's *A Feast of Snakes.*

**George Mills**  Doomed by his great-grandfather, George Mills, to mediocrity and a life in low-level service to wealthier others; works for moving company that collects the furnishings of evicted people; married to Louise; becomes the manservant of a dying woman, Judith Glazer, during her final trip to Mexico in Stanley Elkin's *George Mills.*

**Howard Mills**  Deacon in the Reverend Phillip Martin's church; active in the civil rights struggle in Ernest J. Gaines's *In My Father's House.*

**Louise Mead Mills**  Lascivious and mocking wife of George Mills; is distrustful of George's newfound religious sentiment; becomes friends with Cornell Messenger after the death of her father (who was one of Messenger's stops on his new Meals-on-Wheels route) in Stanley Elkin's *George Mills.*

**Vera Mills**  Diner waitress, Eliot-quoting feminist, and briefly love object of Billy Bumpers in Peter De Vries's *I Hear America Swinging.*

**Milly**  Los Angeles social worker and Abel's girlfriend in N. Scott Momaday's *House Made of Dawn.*

**Margaret Rose Peck (Meg, Meggie) Milsom**  Daughter of Justine and Duncan Peck; married to a minister in Anne Tyler's *Searching for Caleb.*

**Ed Milton**  Lover of Susie Justice; the police chief of Jenkintown in Alice Hoffman's *Here on Earth.*

**Michael Milton**  Graduate student who has an affair with his teacher, Helen Holm; Walt Garp dies when T. S. Garp crashes into Milton's car in John Irving's *The World According to Garp.*

**Milo Minderbinder**  Squadron mess officer who creates the megalithic and multinational M & M Enterprises to put the war on a businesslike basis in Joseph Heller's *Catch-22.*

**Selig Mindish**  Friend of the Isaacsons who testifies against them at their espionage trial in E. L. Doctorow's *The Book of Daniel.*

**Virginia (Vinnie) Miner**  Ivy League college professor in her fifties; specializes in children's literature; often uses imagination to relieve her insecurity and loneliness; plain but refined, cynical about love until she meets Chuck in Alison Lurie's *Foreign Affairs.*

**Minister Q**   Black Muslim leader in John A. Williams's *The Man Who Cried I Am.*

**Myrna Minkoff**   Graduate school friend and nemesis of Ignatius J. Reilly; a proponent of sex therapy to cure all individual and social ills; lives in New York City; believing Ignatius to be on the verge of a nervous breakdown, she travels to New Orleans and at his request, takes him back to New York in John Kennedy Toole's *A Confederacy of Dunces.*

**Minnie**   Pregnant heroin addict who convinces Terry Wilson to become a prostitute in order to support their drug addictions in Donald Goines's *Dopefiend.*

**Minnie**   See Volume I.

**Claire Minton**   Wife of Horlick Minton; together they form a Duprass in Kurt Vonnegut's *Cat's Cradle.*

**Horlick Minton**   Liberal diplomat who with his wife, Claire Minton, forms a Duprass in Kurt Vonnegut's *Cat's Cradle.*

**Fanny Mintz**   Secretary of David Dehn; kills Hella Drachenfels, Dehn's wife, when Drachenfels reveals the source of Dehn's money; commits suicide in Jerome Weidman's *The Temple.*

**Mira (née Ward)**   College professor who recounts her life as daughter, wife, mother, divorcée, graduate student, lover, and friend in Marilyn French's *The Women's Room.*

**Dede Mirabal**   Raises her nieces and nephews after her sisters Patria, Minerva, and Maria Teresa are killed; wife of Jaimito in Julia Alvarez's *In the Time of the Butterflies.*

**Enrique Mirabal**   Farmer in the Dominican Republic; father of four recognized daughters and four illegitimate daughters; husband of Mercedes in Julia Alvarez's *In the Time of the Butterflies.*

**Maria Teresa (Mate, Mariposa #2) Mirabal**   Political activist in the Dominican Republic; tortured and killed by Trujillo regime; sister of Patria, Minerva, and Dede Mirabal; wife of Leandro and mother of Jacqueline in Julia Alvarez's *In the Time of the Butterflies.*

**Mercedes Reyes (Mama) Mirabal**   Mother of four daughters, three of whom are political activists in the Dominican Republic during the Trujillo regime; wife of Enrique Mirabal in Julia Alvarez's *In the Time of the Butterflies.*

**Minerva (Mariposa #1) Mirabal**   Law student and political activist in the Dominican Republic; imprisoned and kept under house arrest; killed by Trujillo regime; sister of Patria, Maria Teresa, and Dede Mirabal; wife of Manolo and mother of Minou and Manolito in Julia Alvarez's *In the Time of the Butterflies.*

**Patria Mercedes (Mariposa #3) Mirabal**   Older sister of Minerva, Maria Teresa, and Dede Mirabal; political activist in the Dominican Republic; killed by the Trujillo regime; wife of Pedrito Gonzalez; mother of Nelson and Noris in Julia Alvarez's *In the Time of the Butterflies.*

**Mirabelle**   Nubile daughter of Konrad Vost and Claire; Vost reports her to police for prostitution in John Hawkes's *The Passion Artist.*

**Miranda**   Asthmatic widow in whose house Skipper, Cassandra, and Pixie live for ten months on the gentle island in John Hawkes's *Second Skin.*

**Eva Miranda**   Brazilian lawyer and lover of Patrick Lanigan; takes sole control of the vast fortune that Patrick stole from his law firm in order to keep it secure from his captors; works with Sandy McDermott to free Patrick from the various legal suits filed against him; after evading her own capture and ensuring Patrick's release from prison, disappears with the remaining multimillion-dollar fortune in John Grisham's *The Partner.*

**Sergei Mirasnikov**   Elderly caretaker in the tiny Siberian town of Tumsk; witnesses the murder of a police officer; terrified, refuses to give his information to Porfiry Petrovich Rostnikov, the officer sent to investigate the crime; eventually attempts to save Rostnikov from a sniper and is shot himself, after which he finds the courage to tell the truth in Stuart M. Kaminsky's *A Cold Red Sunrise.*

**Miriam**   One-handed first cousin and first lover of Zeke Gurevich in William Herrick's *The Itinerant.*

**Miriam**   Black friend and coworker of Eliza Quarles in Alice Adams's *Listening to Billie.*

**Miss (Brigid Lawson, Lady Charlotte Simms) Miriam**   Mistress and accomplice of Edward Pierce in Michael Crichton's *The Great Train Robbery.*

**Mrs. Miriam**   Eighty-one-year-old woman to whom Harry Miller turns for help in remembering his youth in Frederick Busch's *Domestic Particulars.*

**Missouri**   Longtime housekeeper for the McKelvas in Eudora Welty's *The Optimist's Daughter.*

**Mister Man**   See Scooter.

**Mitch**   Mafia hit man hired by Jackie Cogan to kill Frankie, Squirrel Amato, and Mark Trattman; turned in to police by Cogan for parole violation in George V. Higgins's *Cogan's Trade.*

**Anthony Mitchell**   Father of Joan Mitchell and first husband of Aurelie Caillet; dies following his divorce from Aurelie in Shirley Ann Grau's *The House on Coliseum Street.*

**Bernie (Itchy Mitch) Mitchell**   Car thief and burglar; plagued by hives in Joseph Wambaugh's *The Black Marble.*

**Cassandra Mitchell**   Single, middle-aged librarian who befriends an elderly murderer and dates the investigating police detective in L. W. Wright's *The Suspect.*

**Joan Claire Mitchell**   Daughter of Aurelie Caillet and Anthony Mitchell; protagonist who becomes pregnant after a brief love affair and has an abortion in Shirley Ann Grau's *The House on Coliseum Street.*

**Miss Mitchell**   Violence coordinator for NESTER in Scott Spencer's *Last Night at the Brain Thieves' Ball.*

**Mitka (the Cuckoo, the Master)**   Crippled sharpshooter who reads poetry aloud to the narrator of Jerzy Kosinski's *The Painted Bird.*

**Max Mittleman**   Vulgar real estate agent at whose house Daniel Ginsberg stays; fond of crude Jewish jokes in Jay Neugeboren's *An Orphan's Tale.*

**Kabuo Miyamoto**   Defendant on trial for the murder of Carl Heine; fisherman; kendo master; served in the 442nd regiment in World War II; believes Carl Heine's mother cheated him out of land belonging to his family; married to Hatsue Imada in David Guterson's *Snow Falling on Cedars.*

**M/Neighbor**   Neighbor of Bukka Doopeyduk; his mother lost his name in a lottery in Ishmael Reed's *The Free-Lance Pallbearers.*

**Woodenlips Mockett**   Befuddled Los Angeles police lieutenant in Joseph Wambaugh's *The Black Marble.*

**Ilse Moeller**   German immigrant who lives in a Second Avenue apartment managed by Norman Moonbloom in Edward Lewis Wallant's *The Tenants of Moonbloom.*

**Alberto (Albert [Bert, Bertie] Kalandyk) Mogadiscio**   Italian owner of the Hippodrome; connected with the Syndicate in Cyrus Colter's *The Hippodrome.*

**Orang Mohole**   Kingpin of alternate physics and twice winner of the Cheops Feeley Medal in Don DeLillo's *Ratner's Star.*

**Moise**   Eccentric female painter who announces her withdrawal from the world of reason because of her inability to function as an artist in society in Tennessee Williams's *Moise and the World of Reason.*

**Idrissa Moiwo**   Educated in Europe and America, then returned to Sierra Leone to become a section chief in the Pujehun district and a candidate for the office of paramount chief; accepted money, medicines, and goods from Randall Killigan in return for locating his son Michael; manipulated the local tribes' fear of the supernatural to achieve his goals in Richard Dooling's *White Man's Grave.*

**Jenisa Moiwo**   Young, native "love-wife" of Section Chief Idrissa Moiwo; lover of Michael Killigan; secretly selected to be sacrificed to perpetuate the malignant power of an evil medicine known as "bofima" in Richard Dooling's *White Man's Grave.*

**Margot Molinaro**   Best friend of Frances; cousin of Gretel and Jason Samuelson; gets divorced; starts a catering company; strange geomagnetic storm damages her house, then an unusual infestation of small brown spiders, next a hailstorm; marries Mike Sutton; has a son named Frankie in Alice Hoffman's *Local Girls.*

**Mrs. Molinaro**   Mother of Tony Molinaro; always preferred her daughter-in-law, Margot, to her own son; when they divorced, she took to her bed and was dead by the following spring in Alice Hoffman's *Local Girls.*

**Tony Molinaro**   Ex-husband of Margot Molinaro in Alice Hoffman's *Local Girls.*

**Molly**   Aunt of Lil in Joan Chase's *During the Reign of the Queen of Persia.*

**Molly**   Bountiful waitress whom J. Henry Waugh tries to seduce for Lou Engel in Robert Coover's *The Universal Baseball Association, Inc., J. Henry Waugh, Prop.*

**Mona**   Empty-headed, occasional girlfriend of Waldo in Paul Theroux's *Waldo.*

**Christine (Eva McLoch) Monahan**   See Volume I.

**Sean (Kevin McLoch) Monahan**   See Volume I.

**Timothy Monahan**   Associate professor of English at Moo University, fiction writer, vain but uninspired; has brief affair with Ceceila Sanchez and tries to rekindle the relationship; finds renewed strength in helping to expose the Arlen Martin/Dr. Lionel Gift gold mine proposal in Jane Smiley's *Moo.*

**Mon Cul**   Baboon extraordinaire; dies with John Paul Ziller and The Corpse on the Icarus XC solar balloon in Tom Robbins's *Another Roadside Attraction.*

**Kurt Mondaugen**   German radio electronics engineer; employee of Yoyodyne, Inc.; tells Herbert Stencil about his adventures in Africa in 1922, where he met Lieutenant Weissmann at the Siege Party on Foppl's plantation; works for Weissmann on the V in Thomas Pynchon's *V..*

**Gloria Monday**   Kindhearted prostitute and comforter of Carl Reinhart in Thomas Berger's *Reinhart in Love* and *Vital Parts.*

**Daphne Monet**   Elusive "missing" woman sought by private detective Easy Rawlins; formerly Ruby Hanks, born to African-American mother and white father; leaves Louisiana home and adopts a new persona; passes for white; becomes companion to wealthy businessmen and underworld figures; has short-lived affair with Rawlins in Walter Mosley's *Devil in a Blue Dress.*

**Wes Money**   Bartender, drug dealer, and scam artist who comes clean to marry television star Silver Anderson in Jackie Collins's *Hollywood Husbands.*

**Monique**   Second mistress of Hippolyte in Susan Sontag's *The Benefactor.*

**Dr. Talbot Waller (Trick) Monk**   Disturbed young physician and poet; acquaintance of Jesse Vogel in Joyce Carol Oates's *Wonderland*.

**The Monkey**   See Mary Jane Reed.

**Jacques Monod**   Nobel Prize–winning French biologist and philosopher; attended in his final days by George Levanter in Jerzy Kosinski's *Blind Date*.

**Guillaume de Monparnasse**   See Mlle Ida Larivière.

**Monroe**   Educated, cultured minister from Charleston who moves to western North Carolina and buys Black Cove farm near Cold Mountain; admirer of Emerson; father of Ada Monroe in Charles Frazier's *Cold Mountain*.

**Ada Monroe**   Educated, independent-minded young woman from Charleston who moves with her father to Black Cove farm near Cold Mountain but who has learned no survival skills; daughter of Monroe and lover of Inman in Charles Frazier's *Cold Mountain*.

**Ernest Monroe**   World War II veteran, he served as a Marine on Guadalcanal and Iwo Jima; owner and operator of the Texas Lunch in Boone; he hires Paco as a dishwasher and finds him a place to stay in Larry Heinemann's *Paco's Story*.

**James (Roe) Monroe**   High school flame of Yo Garcia and Lucinda de la Torre in Julia Alvarez's *Yo!*

**Max Monroe**   Owner of the Spider Club in Gayl Jones's *Corregidora*.

**Lorenz (Lorry) Monsant**   San Francisco poet and bookstore owner whose remote cabin Jack Duluoz uses for periodic retreats in Jack Kerouac's *Big Sur*.

**Dr. Randolph Spenser Montag**   Psychoanalyst of Myra/Myron Breckinridge in Gore Vidal's *Myra Breckinridge*.

**Ts'eh Montao**   Woman/spirit with whom Tayo falls in love; is an integral part of Tayo's ceremony to reconnect with the earth and his people and to interfere with the cycle of destruction set loose on creation by evil witches in Leslie Marmon Silko's *Ceremony*.

**Montezuma Montez**   Gambler and macho police detective in Joseph Wambaugh's *The Black Marble*.

**Basil de Montfort**   Medieval scholar now sixty-eight years old and somewhat zany; shows strong emotion throughout the novel about his archaeological digs and eyewitness accounts of tragedy in Mary Lee Settle's *Blood Tie*.

**Miguel (Papa) Monzano**   President of San Lorenzo and adoptive father of Mona Aamons Monzano in Kurt Vonnegut's *Cat's Cradle*.

**Mona Aamons Monzano**   Adopted daughter of Papa Monzano and fiancée of John in Kurt Vonnegut's *Cat's Cradle*.

**Colonel Moodus**   Despised son-in-law of General Dreedle in Joseph Heller's *Catch-22*.

**Elvira Moody**   Cellmate of Eva Medina Canada in a psychiatric prison; kills three men with bad whiskey in Gayl Jones's *Eva's Man*.

**Maud Eva Moody**   Wife of Judge Oscar Moody; her car accidentally ends up hanging on the edge of Banner Top in Eudora Welty's *Losing Battles*.

**Oscar Moody**   Judge in Boone County, Mississippi, who sentences Jack Renfro to Parchman State Penitentiary in Eudora Welty's *Losing Battles*.

**Moon**   See Walter Porter.

**Alvin (Joe Redcloud) Moon**   Father of Lewis Moon; becomes for his son a symbol of the lost power and dignity of his Indian ancestors in Peter Matthiessen's *At Play in the Fields of the Lord*.

**Carolina Moon**   Prostitute and police groupie in Joseph Wambaugh's *The Choirboys*.

**Dolly Moon**   Comic actress who becomes a close friend of Billy Orsini during the filming of Vito Orsini's *Mirrors*, for which she wins an Oscar in Judith Krantz's *Scruples*.

**Irma (Big Irma) Moon**   Mother of Lewis Moon in Peter Matthiessen's *At Play in the Fields of the Lord*.

**Meriwether Lewis (Kisu-Mu) Moon**   American mercenary, part Cheyenne Indian, who parachutes into the jungle village of the Niaruna Indians and, posing as Kisu-Mu, Spirit of Rain, attempts to organize them against the encroachment of the white men in Peter Matthiessen's *At Play in the Fields of the Lord*.

**Irwin Moonbloom**   Owner of I. Moonbloom Realty Corp.; employs his brother, Norman, as agent for four tenements in Edward Lewis Wallant's *The Tenants of Moonbloom*.

**Norman (Norm) Moonbloom**   Agent and rent collector for four tenements owned by his brother, Irwin, in Edward Lewis Wallant's *The Tenants of Moonbloom*.

**Kathleen Mooney**   Younger friend and coworker of Eliza Quarles in Alice Adams's *Listening to Billie*.

**Kyle Mooney**   Brother of Blue; serving time in jail in Mary McGarry Morris's *Songs in Ordinary Time*.

**Travis (Blue) Mooney**   Brother of Bernadette's boyfriend Kyle, son of Hildie Carper; his father died in a roofing fall soon after Blue's birth; a full moon is tattooed on his back in Mary McGarry Morris's *Songs in Ordinary Time*.

**Daniel Vivaldo (Viv) Moore**    Bohemian novelist from Brooklyn who falls in love with Ida Scott; friend of Rufus Scott, Eric Jones, and Cass and Richard Silenski in James Baldwin's *Another Country*.

**Reverend Duncan Moore**    Successor to Francis Prescott as rector of Justin Martyr School in Louis Auchincloss's *The Rector of Justin*.

**Duane Moore**    Star athlete at Thalia High School who rooms with Sonny Crawford; joins the army in Larry McMurtry's *The Last Picture Show*.

**Isabel Moore**    Guilt-ridden daughter of a possessive father; begins her life at age thirty when her father dies; narrator of Mary Gordon's *Final Payments*.

**John Moore**    Los Angeles deputy public defender; first to defend Gregory Powell in Joseph Wambaugh's *The Onion Field*.

**John Schuyler Moore**    Shrewd *New York Times* police reporter; former Harvard classmate of Dr. Lazlo Kriezler; knowledgeable about criminal underworld; enlisted by Theodore Roosevelt to help solve a series of grisly New York City murders in Caleb Carr's *The Alienist*.

**Joseph Moore**    Archconservative Catholic father of Isabel Moore and a professor who, though dead at the novel's beginning, dominates much of the action in Mary Gordon's *Final Payments*.

**Julia Moore**    Stepdaughter of Baron R. and friend of Armande Chamar Person; has a one-night affair with Hugh Person in Vladimir Nabokov's *Transparent Things*.

**Rosemary Moore**    Mistress of Lyle Wynant; linked to a terrorist group planning to bomb the New York Stock Exchange in Don DeLillo's *Players*.

**Thomas Moore**    Farmer who buys Nat Turner from Alexander Eppes for $450 in William Styron's *The Confessions of Nat Turner*.

**Myron Moorhen**    Accountant who keeps books in a bait shack in Thomas McGuane's *Ninety-Two in the Shade*.

**Reverend Mootfowl**    Eccentric genius with machines and tools who is one of three leaders of the Overweary Home for orphaned boys; mentors young Peter Lake and assists bridge builder Jackson Mead in Mark Helprin's *Winter's Tale*.

**Alvin Mopworth**    English television actor; friend and aspiring posthumous biographer of Gowan McGland; widely suspected of homosexuality; marries Geneva Spofford in Peter De Vries's *Reuben, Reuben*.

**Virgilio (Lio) Morales**    Political activist in the Dominican Republic who is involved with Dede and Minerva Mirabal in Julia Alvarez's *In The Time of the Butterflies*.

**Daisy Moran**    Daughter of Ira and Maggie; about to leave for college in Anne Tyler's *Breathing Lessons*.

**Fiona Moran**    Divorced from Jesse; mother of daughter Leroy; beautician in Anne Tyler's *Breathing Lessons*.

**Ira Moran**    Husband of Maggie; father of Jesse and Daisy; runs retired father's framing shop business; did not fulfill dream of going to medical school because of marriage and then caring for aged father and eccentric sisters in Anne Tyler's *Breathing Lessons*.

**Jesse Moran**    Son of Ira and Maggie; divorced from Fiona; father of daughter Leroy; lives in the present and unable to see future consequences of actions; unable to hold a job or sustain a relationship; put in awkward situations by his mother's attempts to manipulate lives in Anne Tyler's *Breathing Lessons*.

**Maggie Moran**    Born Margaret Daly; wife of Ira Moran; mother of Jesse and Daisy; works in a nursing home; meddles in the lives of family and strangers, hoping to make everyone, including herself, happy in Anne Tyler's *Breathing Lessons*.

**Mordred**    Illegitimate son of Arthur and Margawse; kills and is killed by his father in Thomas Berger's *Arthur Rex*.

**Doris More**    First wife of Tom More; leaves him to follow the English guru Alistair Fuchs-Forbes in Walker Percy's *Love in the Ruins*.

**Samantha More**    Dead daughter of Tom More; her faith and love inspire her father in Walker Percy's *Love in the Ruins*.

**Tom More**    Psychiatrist who has recently returned home to Feliciana, Louisiana, from federal prison in Alabama; previously convicted for facilitating the sale of prescription drugs at a Louisiana truck stop; wife, Ellen, has become a competitive bridge player with partner John Van Dorn; children Tommy and Margaret attend Van Dorn's private school; with the help of cousin Lucy Lipscomb, he discovers and shuts down a rogue pilot experiment run by Bob Comeaux and Van Dorn that secretly distributes molar sodium (NA 24) in the water supply in Walker Percy's *The Thanatos Syndrome*.

**Thomas (Doc, Tom, Tommy) More, Jr.**    Psychiatrist who tries to save America from self-destruction; narrator of Walker Percy's *Love in the Ruins*.

**T. K. Morehouse**    United States deputy marshal from Memphis who serves warrants on several prominent white citizens of Somerton for violating a black person's civil rights in denying access to a park; narrates part of Jesse Hill Ford's *The Liberation of Lord Byron Jones*.

**Michael Moretti**    Silent, handsome, New York City godfather on trial for murder; love interest of Jennifer Parker in Sidney Sheldon's *Rage of Angels*.

**Deek (Deacon) Morgan**    Twin brother of Steward Morgan and husband of Soane Morgan; member of one of the founding families of the all-black town of Ruby, Oklahoma; has affair with Connie (Consolata) Sosa, the only white woman living in the

Convent; leads the raid on the Convent and is responsible in part for Connie's death in Toni Morrison's *Paradise*.

**Earl Morgan**   Husband of Lillian Douglas Morgan and father of Virgil Morgan; music teacher and composer in Scott Spencer's *Preservation Hall*.

**Ed Morgan**   Bootlegger, muskrat trapper, and tenant on the farm Peter Leland inherits in Fred Chappell's *Dagon*.

**Genevieve Morgan**   Middle-aged night waitress at Thalia's café who listens to Sonny Crawford in Larry McMurtry's *The Last Picture Show*.

**George Morgan**   Husband of Marilyn, father of Laura Morgan in Mary McGarry Morris's *Songs in Ordinary Time*.

**Henry Morgan**   British businessman and contact of Daniel Cable Wills; reveals Wills's career as a spy and the blood kinship of Andrew Collier and Daniel Compton Wills in George V. Higgins's *Dreamland*.

**Joseph (Joe) Morgan**   Colleague of Jacob Horner and husband of Rennie Morgan in John Barth's *The End of the Road*.

**J. Pierpont Morgan**   Multimillionaire whose library is besieged by Coalhouse Walker, Jr., and his insurrectionists in E. L. Doctorow's *Ragtime*.

**Laura Morgan**   Alice's new roommate at college; wants to be a veterinarian in Mary McGarry Morris's *Songs in Ordinary Time*.

**Lillian Belsito Douglas (Lil) Morgan**   Mother of Tommy Douglas and wife of Earl Morgan in Scott Spencer's *Preservation Hall*.

**Marilyn Morgan**   Wife of George, mother of Laura Morgan in Mary McGarry Morris's *Songs in Ordinary Time*.

**Mina Morgan**   Fishlike daughter of Ed Morgan, priestess of Dagon, object of Peter Leland's obsession, and agent of Leland's psychological and physical destruction in Fred Chappell's *Dagon*.

**Mr. Morgan**   Butler to the Hawkline family; sixty-eight-year-old, seven-foot, two-inch tall giant killed by the Hawkline Monster and revivified upon the monster's destruction in Richard Brautigan's *The Hawkline Monster*.

**Renée MacMahon (Rennie) Morgan**   Wife of Joseph Morgan and lover of Jacob Horner; dies while undergoing an abortion in John Barth's *The End of the Road*.

**Rosalie Morgan**   Lover of Sammy in Joan Chase's *During the Reign of the Queen of Persia*.

**Soane Morgan**   Wife of Deek (Deacon) Morgan; mother of sons Easter (nineteen) and Scout (twenty-one), both of whom were killed in the Vietnam War; had an abortion at the Convent, the home of a group of mostly black women with sullied pasts who live on the outskirts of the all-black town of Ruby, Oklahoma; is friends with Connie (Consolata) Sosa; is one of the few women in Ruby who is sympathetic to the Convent women in Toni Morrison's *Paradise*.

**Steward Morgan**   Twin brother of Deek (Deacon) Morgan and husband of Dovey Morgan; member of one of the founding families of the all-black town of Ruby, Oklahoma; leads the raid on the Convent, the home of a group of mostly black women with sullied pasts who live on the outskirts of Ruby; is responsible in part for the death of Convent woman Connie (Consolata) Sosa in Toni Morrison's *Paradise*.

**Cardinal Thaddeus Morgan**   Church dignitary who visits the prison and helps Jody escape, an action that inspires Zeke Farragut in John Cheever's *Falconer*.

**Tracy Keating Morgan**   Book designer married to Virgil Morgan in Scott Spencer's *Preservation Hall*.

**Virgil (Fatboy, Vernon) Morgan**   Businessman who accidentally kills his stepbrother Tommy Douglas; narrator of Scott Spencer's *Preservation Hall*.

**William A. (Bumper) Morgan**   Twenty-year veteran Los Angeles beat patrolman; protagonist and narrator of Joseph Wambaugh's *The Blue Knight*.

**Morgan la Fey**   Evil sister of Margawse and aunt of Mordred in Thomas Berger's *Arthur Rex*.

**Anders Morganof**   Orris's livery man in the Territories; befriends Jack Sawyer and Richard Sloat and helps them get to the West Coast to procure the Talisman in Stephen King's and Peter Straub's *The Talisman*.

**Lionel Morgen**   Psychiatrist husband of Lee (LuAnne) Verger in Robert Stone's *Children of Light*.

**Morning Star**   Son of Little Big Man and Sunshine in Thomas Berger's *Little Big Man*.

**Joey (Morph) Morphy**   Friend of Ethan Allen Hawley and teller at the First National Bank in New Baytown who unknowingly gives Hawley the idea of robbing the bank in John Steinbeck's *The Winter of Our Discontent*.

**Arthur Morris**   Computer programmer who checks the computers at Project Wildfire and misses a simple mechanical problem that keeps the teleprinter from alerting the scientists to important information in Michael Crichton's *The Andromeda Strain*.

**Corinne Morris**   Mistress of Thomas Spellacy in John Gregory Dunne's *True Confessions*.

**Edward Morris**   Commander of antisubmarine frigate USS *Pharris,* which is crippled by a torpedo; reluctantly accepts command of USS *Reuben James;* overcomes guilt over lives lost under his command to successfully escort a critical supply convoy to aid NATO forces in Tom Clancy's *Red Storm Rising.*

**Robert Morris**    Surgeon and member of the Neuropsychiatric Research Unit in Michael Crichton's *The Terminal Man.*

**James Morrisey**    Irish lawyer who falls in love with Theresa Dunn but is incapable of satisfying her sexually in Judith Rossner's *Looking for Mr. Goodbar.*

**Lipsha Morrisey**    Son of June Kashpaw and Gerry Nanapush; half brother of King Kashpaw; grandson of Lulu Lamartine; raised by Marie Kashpaw; does not know his parents' identities until he is an adult; joins the army but regrets it and does not go back for his physical; able to heal with his hands; meets his father and drives him to Canada in Louise Erdrich's *Love Medicine.*

**Treat Morrison**    American ambassador-at-large, "crisis junkie," and possible CIA agent with a mysterious past; in trying to extricate Elena McMahon from danger, falls in love with her; during assassination attempt is severely injured while Elena is killed in Joan Didion's *The Last Thing He Wanted.*

**Wendell Morrison**    Former writing student of Henry Bech; appears on Martha's Vineyard and gets Bech, Norma Latchett, and Bea Cook high on marijuana in John Updike's *Bech: A Book.*

**Jack Morrissey**    Idealistic young lawyer who becomes romantically involved with Elena Howe in Joyce Carol Oates's *Do with Me What You Will.*

**Julia Mortimer**    Unmarried, retired teacher of Banner School who sends Gloria Short Renfro to the normal school for training teachers and tries to discourage her from marrying Jack Renfro; cared for in retirement by Lexie Renfro in Eudora Welty's *Losing Battles.*

**Jeannie Morton**    Friend of Isadora Wing; housewife and poet awarded the Pulitzer Prize for her third book of poems, *Holy Fool's Day;* commits suicide in Erica Jong's *How to Save Your Own Life.*

**Darlene Mosby**    See Darlene Mosby Carlisle.

**William (Sonny Boy) Mosby**    Large black man returning from Kansas City to Somerton, where thirteen years before he was beaten by Stanley Bumpas; soon after arriving, he beats Jimmy Bivens to death and offers to become the bodyguard of Lord Byron Jones in Jesse Hill Ford's *The Liberation of Lord Byron Jones.*

**Moses (Moze)**    Shell-shocked veteran, who may or may not be a Jew; member of Big Red Smalley's traveling gospel show in George Garrett's *Do, Lord, Remember Me.*

**Vincent Mosley**    Husband of Lisbeth Mosley; English professor; is supposed to sleep with other women with his wife's consent to improve his marriage, but other women make him impotent; tries to have sex with Sandy Pressman but cannot in Judy Blume's *Wifey.*

**Zelda (Lisbeth) Mosley**    Born Zelda Rabinowitz; Sandy Pressman's oldest and dearest friend and first lover; wife of Vincent Mosley; is free-spirited and has sex with other men with her husband's consent in order to improve their marriage; is not liked by Norman, Sandy's husband, in Judy Blume's *Wifey.*

**Hector Moss**    Stupid commander in the Los Angeles Police Department; concerned with regulations and his IQ score of 107 in Joseph Wambaugh's *The Choirboys.*

**Kevin Moss**    Seventeen-year-old who is part of a gang of twelve boys who rip Martha Horgan's clothes off, pour beer on her, and poke her with sticks in Mary McGarry Morris's *A Dangerous Woman.*

**Sarah (Suki) Moss**    Girlfriend of Bayard Strong; sleeps with him after he tutors her in math and her grades improve; a Trinity senior in Maureen Howard's *Expensive Habits.*

**Delaney Mossbacher**    Naturalist and writer; married to Kyra, his second wife accidentally hits Candido Rincon with his car; believes Candido responsible for problems encountered; tracks him down intending to shoot him but is swept away by mud slide in T. Coraghessan Boyle's *The Tortilla Curtain.*

**Kyra Mossbacher**    Previously divorced; mother of Jordan; now married to Delaney; extremely health conscious; main source of the family's income in T. Coraghessan Boyle's *The Tortilla Curtain.*

**Jerry Mossman**    Bryce Proctorr's New York agent in Donald E. Westlake's *The Hook.*

**Mother**    Born in Dominica and left for Antigua at sixteen; believes that one of her husband's mistresses has put a spell on their house and attempts to exorcise it; when her daughter becomes mysteriously ill, she stays by her bedside to care for her in Jamaica Kincaid's *Annie John.*

**Mother**    Recently widowed musician and mother of a contemplative and enigmatic fifteen-year-old; is touched significantly by the letter she discovers in her husband's effects, a hidden letter of loving advice and admonishment written three years earlier to their son in Joseph McElroy's *The Letter Left to Me.*

**Mother**    Wife of Father and mother of Little Boy; marries Tateh after the death of Father in E. L. Doctorow's *Ragtime.*

**Mother's Younger Brother (Younger Brother)**    Brother of Mother, lover of Evelyn Nesbit, and admirer of Emma Goldman and socialism; designs fireworks and bombs; joins the gang of Coalhouse Walker, Jr., but drives to Mexico to join Francisco Villa's revolutionaries; dies in a skirmish with government in E. L. Doctorow's *Ragtime.*

**Rims Mott**   Forty-five-year-old house painter and lover of Miss Margaret Treasure in Alice Walker's *Meridian*.

**Dr. Stewart Rawlings Mott**   Physician who oversees Eliza and Wilbur Swain when they are thought to be retarded; he discovers the Swain children are in fact geniuses; later moves to an Eskimo settlement in Vermont; his son becomes the king of Michigan in Kurt Vonnegut's *Slapstick*.

**Wesley Mount**   Funeral director who has a crush on Martha Horgan in Mary McGarry Morris's *A Dangerous Woman*.

**Father Mountjoy**   Director and alumnus of Adrian's orphanage; entered the seminary at age sixteen; makes Adrian haul Mr. Dumas's empty bottles out of the woods in Gail Godwin's *Evensong*.

**Mtesa**   Traitorous driver for Colonel Elleloû; when Mtesa refuses to identify him to a mob, Elleloû is deposed in John Updike's *The Coup*.

**Lieutenant Mudd**   Replacement pilot killed in combat before being checked into Yossarian's squadron; because his death is unofficial, his belongings cannot be removed from Yossarian's tent in Joseph Heller's *Catch-22*.

**Earl Mudger**   Head of Radial Matrix, an intelligence organization, and one of many interested in a movie rumored to include footage of Hider at an orgy in Don DeLillo's *Running Dog*.

**Alexander Mueller**   Son of Hans and Elizabeth Mueller and possible father of Robert Mueller; blinded in a suicide attempt in Nicholas Delbanco's *Fathering*.

**Elizabeth Mueller**   Wife of Hans Mueller and mother of Alexander Mueller; killed when hit by an automobile, a possible suicide in Nicholas Delbanco's *Fathering*.

**Hans Mueller**   Husband of Elizabeth Mueller, father of Alexander Mueller, and possible father of Robert Mueller; killed in an automobile accident in Nicholas Delbanco's *Fathering*.

**Marian Mueller**   First wife of Alexander Mueller; dies of cancer at age twenty-one in Nicholas Delbanco's *Fathering*.

**Robert Mueller**   Actor of ambiguous paternity, the son of Chloe Duboise and either Hans or Alexander Mueller; adopted by Alexander and Susan Mueller in Nicholas Delbanco's *Fathering*.

**Susan Mueller**   Second wife of Alexander Mueller in Nicholas Delbanco's *Fathering*.

**Sidi Mukhtar**   Shrewd caravan leader who transports contraband goods through Kush; guides Colonel Elleloû and Sheba through the Balak in search of King Edumu's severed head in John Updike's *The Coup*.

**Arnold Mulcahy**   Federal man who arranges for Fred Trumper to return to the United States and who wants to hire Dante Callicchio in John Irving's *The Water-Method Man*.

**Father Mulcahy**   Pastor, counselor, and friend of the Moores in Mary Gordon's *Final Payments*.

**Barry (The Blade) Muldanno**   Quick-tempered, dangerous Mafia hit man; kills a U.S. senator and hides the body under the boathouse of his lawyer, Jerome Clifford; attempts to kill Mark Sway because he knows where the senator's body is buried in John Grisham's *The Client*.

**Roberta (Captain Energy, Robert) Muldoon**   Professional football player who becomes a transsexual; bodyguard for Jenny Fields and friend of the Garps; dies after doing wind sprints in John Irving's *The World According to Garp*.

**Blanshard Muller**   Widower who wants Myra Nelson to divorce her departed husband and marry him in Philip Roth's *When She Was Good*.

**Mrs. Muller**   Reference librarian who smells of rotten apples in Maureen Howard's *Natural History*.

**Mr. Mullins**   Owner and operator of the funeral parlor in Hopewell, Kentucky; after James and Christianna Wheeler's quintuplets die, he mummifies the quintuplets and places them in an air-tight glass display case; requests that the remains of the quintuplets remain on display in his funeral parlor indefinitely in Bobbie Ann Mason's *Feather Crowns*.

**Tommy Mullins**   His father owns the bakery, and he always has money, so Norm picks up Mullins to buy beer for him in Mary McGarry Morris's *Songs in Ordinary Time*.

**Gerda Miller Mulvaney**   Longtime friend of Jane Clifford and publisher of the feminist newspaper *Feme Sole* in Gail Godwin's *The Odd Woman*.

**Charles (Chuck) Mumpson**   Retired engineer from Tulsa specializing in waste-disposal systems; warm but coarse and clumsy in Vinnie's refined eyes; develops interests in genealogy after meeting Vinnie on his trip to England; husband of a scornful, workaholic wife, and lover of Vinnie in Alison Lurie's *Foreign Affairs*.

**Carl Munchin**   Wealthy California movie producer who wants to revise John Wilder's autobiographical movie *Bellevue* by having the central figure suffer a complete mental breakdown (wipe him out) in Richard Yates's *Disturbing the Peace*.

**Nella Liseth Mundine**   Half-Scandinavian wife of Steve Mundine; appalled by the racial prejudice in Somerton; narrates part of Jesse Hill Ford's *The Liberation of Lord Byron Jones*.

**Steve Mundine**   Nephew and law partner of Oman Hedgepath; he and his wife, Nella Liseth Mundine, shock Somerton with their liberal racial views in Jesse Hill Ford's *The Liberation of Lord Byron Jones*.

**Louise Munez**   Security guard at the Towers; daughter of Elaine Munez, who also lives in the Towers; while looking for her mother, helps Mrs. Bliss during a hurricane in Stanley Elkin's *Mrs. Ted Bliss*.

**Grace Munger**    Organizer of the Millennium Birthday March for Jesus; her father may have burned himself and his wife in a house fire when she was ten or eleven, or Grace may have set the fire; is seduced by a psychologist at an Episcopal boarding school and talked into getting an abortion by her adoptive parents; fired by an ad agency for touring abortion clinics and causing disturbances in Gail Godwin's *Evensong*.

**Joel Munger**    Father of Grace Munger; pastor of Free Will Baptist Church until he was sentenced to federal prison for embezzlement; he may have burned himself and his wife in their house when Grace was ten or eleven, or Grace may have set the fire in Gail Godwin's *Evensong*.

**Mrs. Munkey**    Loquacious cleaning woman for Joe and Naughty Sandwich in Peter De Vries's *The Vale of Laughter*.

**Ismael Munoz**    AIDS-infected leader of a group of street artists in the Bronx who work to benefit the needy members of the community; works with Sister Edgar and her fellow nuns; creator of the Wall, a communal art project where dead children are memorialized with painted angels; along with the sisters, mourns the senseless and violent death of a street youth named Esmerelda in Don DeLillo's *Underworld*.

**Jefferson Davis Munroe**    Midget and legendary karate master in Harry Crews's *Karate Is a Thing of the Spirit*.

**Dr. Barker Munsing**    Father of Eunice Munsing in Thomas Berger's *Vital Parts*.

**Eunice Munsing**    Secretary of Robert Sweet in Thomas Berger's *Vital Parts*.

**Munt**    Police lieutenant who investigates the death of Tommy Douglas in Scott Spencer's *Preservation Hall*.

**Murf**    Bat-faced cockney sidekick of Valentine Hood in Paul Theroux's *The Family Arsenal*.

**Albert Murillio**    Pimp and racketeer who controls the section of Harlem where Sol Nazerman has his pawnshop in Edward Lewis Wallant's *The Pawnbroker*.

**Calvin Murks**    Immovable handyman of millionaires, Murks controls the fates of two poker hustlers who are the hapless victims of his eccentric employers in Paul Auster's *The Music of Chance*.

**Basil (Blackie) Murphy**    Brother of Tasmania Orcino and Blix Hollister in Jessamyn West's *A Matter of Time*.

**Ike (Mr. Ike) Murphy**    Night desk clerk for the Somerton police department; aids Stanley Bumpas and Willie Joe Worth in their violation of civil rights, especially those of blacks, in Jesse Hill Ford's *The Liberation of Lord Byron Jones*.

**Le Cid (Cid) Murphy**    Brother of Tasmania Orcino and Blix Hollister in Jessamyn West's *A Matter of Time*.

**Marmion Murphy**    Brother of Tasmania Orcino and Blix Hollister in Jessamyn West's *A Matter of Time*.

**Maude Hobhouse Murphy**    Mother of Tasmania Orcino and Blix Hollister in Jessamyn West's *A Matter of Time*.

**Mrs. Murphy ("Sneaky Pie")**    Harry's self-absorbed gray tiger cat; solves most aspects of the murders and disappearances, then must find ways to communicate the clues to her "slow" owner; locates the missing plane, presents the incriminating map to the authorities, and drives a wounded man's Porsche to safety after the man is shot in the head in Rita Mae Brown's *Cat on the Scent*.

**Orland Murphy**    Father of Tasmania Orcino and Blix Hollister in Jessamyn West's *A Matter of Time*.

**Alan Murray**    Estranged brother of March Murray; inherits all of Fox Hill upon Henry Murray's death; his wife dies in a house fire; thereafter he calls himself the Coward; sells Fox Hill for drinking money and ends up living in the marshes in a ramshackle house in Alice Hoffman's *Here on Earth*.

**Daniel Murray**    FBI deputy assistant director who manages the investigation of the assassination of FBI Director Emil Jacobs by a Colombian drug cartel; heads an investigation of the covert operations in Colombia while advising Jack Ryan on the legality of various CIA actions; travels to Colombia to assist Ryan and John Clark in extracting the light-infantry teams abandoned in-country in Tom Clancy's *Clear and Present Danger*.

**Gwen Murray**    Pretty fifteen-year-old daughter of March Murray; becomes Hank Murray's girlfriend; moves in with Hollis and March under threat; eventually leaves the abusive household and goes to live with her father in Alice Hoffman's *Here on Earth*.

**Hank Murray**    Hollis's adopted nephew, Alan Murray's son; he never does anything right in Hollis's eyes; becomes Gwen Murray's boyfriend in Alice Hoffman's *Here on Earth*.

**Henry Murray**    March Murray's father, a well-loved lawyer who dies when March is fourteen; has been dead for nearly twenty-five years when March returns to Jenkintown in Alice Hoffman's *Here on Earth*.

**Julie Murray**    Wife of Alan Murray, dies young in a house fire in Alice Hoffman's *Here on Earth*.

**Marcheline "March" Murray**    Returns to Jenkintown after living in California for nineteen years to attend Judith Dale's funeral; wife of Richard Cooper, mother of Gwen Cooper, daughter of Henry Murray, and sister of Alan Cooper; a jewelry designer; grew up with Hollis and is his former lover in Alice Hoffman's *Here on Earth*.

**Patrick Murray**    Unemployed until he saves people from the church fire and becomes a local hero; becomes Gus Eubanks's and Jennifer Tye's general manager of Eubanks and Tye construction in Gail Godwin's *Evensong*.

**Mr. Murtagh**  Dishonest butcher who has known Nell Bray since she was a bride and gives her bacon for free in Maureen Howard's *Natural History*.

**Biff Musclewhite**  Ruthless guardian of European values in America; former European serf, former police commissioner, and curator of the Center of Art Detention who boards the *Titanic* in Ishmael Reed's *Mumbo Jumbo*.

**Norman Mushari**  Avaricious lawyer who seeks to prove Eliot Rosewater insane in Kurt Vonnegut's *God Bless You, Mr. Rosewater*.

**Marquis de Mussy**  Alsatian gunner of promiscuous employment, born a baker's son from Aachen named Klaus Engelhardt; killed by some of Nawab's soldiers for sacking a Mecca-bound pilgrim ship in Bharati Mukherjee's *The Holder of the World*.

**Mustache Sal**  Mail-order wife of Drag Gibson; lover of the Loop Garoo Kid, who brands her with a Hell's bat; poisons Gibson, but he discovers her action and feeds her to his swine in Ishmael Reed's *Yellow Back Radio Broke-Down*.

**Charles Joanthan Samuel Muster**  Ancestor of Beigh Masters; born in Morpeth, Northumberland; in 1632, at seventeen, Charles stows away to Salem; by 1640 he is the proprietor of a 300-acre tract that he leases to an in-law; returns to Salem and the life of sea trade in Bharati Mukherjee's *The Holder of the World*.

**Baby Lou (Baby Sister) Mustian**  Youngest of the Mustian children in Reynolds Price's *A Long and Happy Life* and *A Generous Man*.

**Horatio (Rato) Mustian, Jr.**  Brother of Rosacoke Mustian in Reynolds Price's *A Long and Happy Life*; runs off to keep his rabid dog from being put to sleep in *A Generous Man*.

**Jasper (Papa) Mustian**  Grandfather of the Mustian children in Reynolds Price's *A Long and Happy Life* and *A Generous Man*.

**Milo Mustian**  Brother of Rosacoke and Rato Mustian in Reynolds Price's *A Long and Happy Life*; loses his virginity to Lois Provo and searches for his brother in *A Generous Man*.

**Pauline Mustian**  Dead wife of Papa Mustian, often quoted by him in Reynolds Price's *A Long and Happy Life* and *A Generous Man*.

**Rosacoke Mustian**  Female protagonist whose fierce love for Wesley Beavers forms the plot of Reynolds Price's *A Long and Happy Life*; appears as a child in *A Generous Man*.

**Sissie Abbott Mustian**  Pregnant wife of Milo Mustian; gives birth to a dead child in Reynolds Price's *A Long and Happy Life*; mentioned in *A Generous Man*.

**Vincente Pesola (Vince) Muzguiz**  Relative who provides shelter, support, and help for Kat Alcazar in California; janitor and nursing student in M. F. Beal's *Angel Dance*.

**Myerson**  CIA bureau chief who fires Miles Kendig and then heads the pursuit of Miles Kendig in Brian Garfield's *Hopscotch*.

**Myrna**  See Vahine.

**Myshkin**  Soviet Writers' Union official in charge of Henry Bech's itinerary in Russia in John Updike's *Bech: A Book*.

**Jane Nail** Common-law wife of Elias McCutcheon, a gift to McCutcheon of Shokotee McNeilly, and mother of Isaac and Willy McCutcheon; her cheek is slashed open by a group of marauders, and she becomes reclusive as a result in Jesse Hill Ford's *The Raider.*

**Eliot Nailles** Suburbanite and model citizen with an ideal family, though unable to function except under the effect of drugs; foil to the fanatic Paul Hammer in John Cheever's *Bullet Park.*

**Nellie Nailles** Model but mindless suburban wife and mother in John Cheever's *Bullet Park.*

**Tony Nailles** Son of Eliot and Nellie Nailles; psychosomatic youth who is saved from sacrificial death at the hands of Paul Hammer in John Cheever's *Bullet Park.*

**Su'ad al-Najaf** Young Shiite Muslim who smuggled costly Iranian rugs into the United States before being killed by a hit-and-run driver; her death sparks Robert Druff's intricate imaginings in Stanley Elkin's *The MacGuffin.*

**Nameless** Adolescent girl raped by George Levanter at a Russian youth camp in Jerzy Kosinski's *Blind Date.*

**Nana-dirat** Young woman who inhabits C. Card's fantasies of Babylon in Richard Brautigan's *Dreaming of Babylon.*

**Gerry Nanapush** Son of Lulu and Moses Pillager; has an affair with June Kashpaw; father of Lipsha Morrisey; famous protester who is imprisoned and often escapes; shoots a state trooper and goes to penitentiary; escapes and Lipsha drives him to Canada in Louise Erdrich's *Love Medicine.*

**Nandy** Woman devoted to George Cain; helps him break his drug addiction in George Cain's *Blueschild Baby.*

**Nanny Lisa** White woman who poses as a black nanny; works for the Louisiana Red Corporation and brings up Minnie Yellings to hate black men; murders Ed Yellings and is killed by Max Kasavubu in Ishmael Reed's *The Last Days of Louisiana Red.*

**Miss Naomi** Former slave and keeper of Tangierneck's slave history in Sarah E. Wright's *This Child's Gonna Live.*

**Andrey Il'ych Narmonov** Soviet secretary-general who undertakes a program of political and economic relaxation designed to reduce tensions and allow the USSR a chance to rebuild; manages a tenuous coalition in the Politburo against the ambitious Nikolay Borissovich Gerasimov; honors Misha Filitov by approving a secret funeral with full military honors in Tom Clancy's *The Cardinal of the Kremlin.*

**Marcie Binnendale Nash** Owner, through inheritance, of a major department store; falls in love with Oliver Barrett IV, but drives him away with her shallowness and her unethical business practices in Erich Segal's *Oliver's Story.*

**John Nashe** Thirty-two-year-old fireman who squanders his unexpected inheritance from his father during a two-year road trip across the United States; befriends poker hustler Jack Pozzi; rediscovers the simple pleasures of existence through this unexpected friendship in Paul Auster's *The Music of Chance.*

**Natahk** Leader of the Garkohn tribe in Octavia E. Butler's *Survivor.*

**Lieutenant Nately** Patriotic companion of Yossarian; despises his wealthy father, falls in love with an Italian prostitute, and dies on a bombing mission in Joseph Heller's *Catch-22.*

**Ralph Navarro** Lawyer for Joseph Chase and third husband of Orpha Chase in Jessamyn West's *The Life I Really Lived.*

**Hester Nayburn**   Stoical young woman blinded by her mother; seduced by Dalton Harron on her way to an operation to restore her sight; niece of Jessie Nayburn in Susan Sontag's *Death Kit.*

**Jessie Nayburn**   Aunt who rears Hester Nayburn after Hester is blinded by her mother in Susan Sontag's *Death Kit.*

**Ruth Nazerman**   Deceased wife of Sol Nazerman in Edward Lewis Wallant's *The Pawnbroker.*

**Sol (Pawnbroker, Solly) Nazerman**   Polish survivor of the Holocaust and Harlem pawnbroker embittered by the deaths of his wife and children in a concentration camp in Edward Lewis Wallant's *The Pawnbroker.*

**Nearly Normal Jimmy**   Ambitious businessman who tells Marx Marvelous about the zoo; shows Tarzan's Triumph in the holy city of Lhasa in Tom Robbins's *Another Roadside Attraction.*

**Jimmy Needles**   Jockey and member of a group of killers and thieves who trick Michael Banks and benefit from his stealing a horse, Rock Castle, whom they expect to win one race in John Hawkes's *The Lime Twig.*

**John Nefastis**   Inventor of the Nefastis machine, which he claims contains a Demon that can violate the Second Law of Thermodynamics in Thomas Pynchon's *The Crying of Lot 49.*

**Drexa Neff**   Viennese housekeeper and laundress for Captain Kudashvili; teaches Utch Thalhammer how to be a Russian in John Irving's *The 158-Pound Marriage;* also appears in *Setting Free the Bears.*

**Sol Negaly**   Margarett Flood's former lover and the director of her movie based on *Child's Play;* marries Tina; a hairy, audacious, powerful man in Maureen Howard's *Expensive Habits.*

**Tina Negaly**   Wife of Sol Negaly; knows Nazi trivia in Maureen Howard's *Expensive Habits.*

**Freddy Negus**   Head crewman on the *Cloud;* doesn't trust Pablo Tabor; is killed by Pablo in Robert Stone's *A Flag for Sunrise.*

**Stu Neihardt**   High school classmate of David Axelrod in Scott Spencer's *Endless Love.*

**Neil**   Separated husband of Grace, father of Anne and Katie; captain of the baseball team in college; sleeps with other women; drinks too much in Joan Chase's *During the Reign of the Queen of Persia.*

**Nell**   Friend of Lexi Steiner, former college roommate; in love with Lexi; becomes Michael Cooper's lover and moves to New York to be with him in Elizabeth Benedict's *Slow Dancing.*

**Nelson**   Cheerful, intelligent, orphaned twelve-year-old Congolese boy whom Anatole sends to the Prices as Mama Tataba's replacement; lives in the Price's chicken house in Barbara Kingsolver's *The Poisonwood Bible.*

**Alice Nelson**   Mistress of Robert Agar; turns Agar in to the police in Michael Crichton's *The Great Train Robbery.*

**Allie Nelson**   Reluctant socialite who abandons the promise of a money-gilded life with Lon Hammond in order to marry Noah Calhoun and fulfill her early promise as a talented painter; stricken by Alzheimer's disease in her later years, but sustained by Noah's love in Nicholas Sparks's *The Notebook.*

**Duane (Whitey) Nelson**   Ne'er-do-well husband of Myra Carroll, who loves him, and father of Lucy Nelson, who detests him, in Philip Roth's *When She Was Good.*

**Lucy Nelson**   See Lucy Nelson Bassart.

**Myra Carroll Nelson**   Daughter of Willard Carroll, wife of Duane Nelson, and mother of Lucy Nelson Bassart in Philip Roth's *When She Was Good.*

**Nicole Nelson**   Fourteen-year-old daughter of Jane Spenser and niece of Lucy Spenser; actress who plays Stephanie Sykes on a soap opera; stays with Lucy for the summer and enjoys Vermont; has an affair with Harry Woods; when her mother dies, moves in with Lucy in Ann Beattie's *Love Always.*

**Sterling Nelson**   Urbane English businessman with whom Alice Prentice has an affair while her son is a child; Nelson's wealth, artistic tastes, and fidelity to Alice all prove fraudulent in Richard Yates's *A Special Providence.*

**Professor Nemur**   Research psychologist who, pushed by his wife for material success, designs an experiment for increasing intelligence and who, with Dr. Strauss, conducts the experiment on Charlie Gordon in Daniel Keyes's *Flowers for Algernon.*

**Evelyn Nesbit**   Wife of Harry K. Thaw; seduced by Stanford White; becomes the lover of Mother's Younger Brother in E. L. Doctorow's *Ragtime.*

**(Miss) Nesselrode**   Graceful, resourceful, and respected Russian immigrant who advises and educates Johannes Verne as he grows up; astute and independent businesswoman in early Los Angeles in Louis L'Amour's *The Lonesome Gods.*

**Nettie**   Younger sister of Celie; runs away and finds work with Reverend Samuel and his wife, Corinne; helps raise Olivia and Adam, Celie's children; marries Samuel after Corrine's death; returns to United States with Samuel and children; reunited with Celie in Alice Walker's *The Color Purple.*

**Eric Neuhoffer**   Managing editor of the newspaper where Jerry Freeman works in Gail Godwin's *Glass People.*

**Alpha Jones Neumiller**   First wife of Martin Neumiller; a victim of uremia in Larry Woiwode's *Beyond the Bedroom Wall.*

**Augustina Neumiller**    Unmarried daughter of Otto Neumiller; nurse to her father in old age and at his death in Larry Woiwode's *Beyond the Bedroom Wall.*

**Becky Neumiller**    Daughter of Charles Neumiller (II) and Katherine Neumiller in Larry Woiwode's *Beyond the Bedroom Wall.*

**Charles John Christopher Neumiller (I)**    Son of Otto Neumiller and inheritor of the Neumiller family farm; father of Martin Neumiller in Larry Woiwode's *Beyond the Bedroom Wall.*

**Charles (Chuck, Chuckie) Neumiller (II)**    Middle son of Martin and Alpha Jones Neumiller; actor living in Greenwich Village and doing voice-overs for commercials in Larry Woiwode's *Beyond the Bedroom Wall.*

**Cheri Neumiller**    Wife of Tim Neumiller in Larry Woiwode's *Beyond the Bedroom Wall.*

**Davey Neumiller**    Son of Charles Neumiller (I) and Marie Krull in Larry Woiwode's *Beyond the Bedroom Wall.*

**Elaine Neumiller**    Oldest daughter of Charles Neumiller (I) and Marie Krull in Larry Woiwode's *Beyond the Bedroom Wall.*

**Emil Neumiller**    Son of Charles Neumiller (I) and Marie Krull in Larry Woiwode's *Beyond the Bedroom Wall.*

**Fred Neumiller**    Son of Charles Neumiller (I) and Marie Krull in Larry Woiwode's *Beyond the Bedroom Wall.*

**Jay Neumiller**    Son of Charles Neumiller (I) and Marie Krull in Larry Woiwode's *Beyond the Bedroom Wall.*

**Jerome Neumiller**    Oldest son of Martin and Alpha Jones Neumiller; physician in Illinois in Larry Woiwode's *Beyond the Bedroom Wall.*

**Katherine Neumiller**    Wife of Charles Neumiller (II) in Larry Woiwode's *Beyond the Bedroom Wall.*

**Laura Neumiller**    Second wife of Martin Neumiller; dies of breast cancer in Larry Woiwode's *Beyond the Bedroom Wall.*

**Lucy Neumiller**    Daughter of Otto Neumiller and wife of a cattle buyer in Larry Woiwode's *Beyond the Bedroom Wall.*

**Marie Neumiller**    Oldest daughter of Martin and Alpha Jones Neumiller in Larry Woiwode's *Beyond the Bedroom Wall.*

**Martin Neumiller**    Son of Charles Neumiller (I) and Marie Krull; husband of Alpha Jones Neumiller; teacher-principal, caretaker, and insurance salesman; twice a widower in Larry Woiwode's *Beyond the Bedroom Wall.*

**Otto Neumiller**    Patriarch of the Neumiller family; builder of the family farm in North Dakota; buried by his son, Charles Neumiller (I) in Larry Woiwode's *Beyond the Bedroom Wall.*

**Rose Marie Neumiller**    Daughter of Charles Neumiller (1) and Marie Krull in Larry Woiwode's *Beyond the Bedroom Wall.*

**Susan Neumiller**    Youngest daughter of Martin and Alpha Jones Neumiller in Larry Woiwode's *Beyond the Bedroom Wall.*

**Timothy (Tim) Neumiller**    Poet and youngest son of Martin and Alpha Jones Neumiller in Larry Woiwode's *Beyond the Bedroom Wall.*

**Tom Neumiller**    Son of Charles Neumiller (I) and Marie Krull in Larry Woiwode's *Beyond the Bedroom Wall.*

**Vince Neumiller**    Son of Charles Neumiller (I) and Marie Krull in Larry Woiwode's *Beyond the Bedroom Wall.*

**Isabel Newbury**    Reese Newbury's first wife, a social snob who, dying of cancer, mandates that Reese marry Lila Wingo in Pat Conroy's *The Prince of Tides.*

**Reese Newbury**    Representative of the social and financial elite in Colleton; a brutal and unscrupulous manipulator who becomes stepfather of the Wingo children in Pat Conroy's *The Prince of Tides.*

**Todd Newbury**    Spoiled, obnoxious son of the Newburys whom Tom Wingo beats up when they are both in high school; Todd ignores his mother when she is dying in Pat Conroy's *The Prince of Tides.*

**Victor (Prof) Newcool**    Encouraging English professor; friend and mentor to Annie Brown in Betty Smith's *Joy in the Morning.*

**Alyce (Ecstasy Pie) Newman**    Astute Jewish lover and roommate of Jack Duluoz in New York in Jack Kerouac's *Desolation Angels.*

**Dr. Charlie Newman**    Protégé of Jack; a talented surgeon chosen to operate on Margaret; tells Margaret his horror stories of Africa in Maureen Howard's *Expensive Habits.*

**New Person**    Probably the son of Lewis Moon and Pindi, though his paternity is attributed by the Niaruna Indians to the warrior Aeore in Peter Matthiessen's *At Play in the Fields of the Lord.*

**Ralph Newsome**    Washington spokesman whose favor Bruce Gold courts in Joseph Heller's *Good as Gold.*

**Rudy Newton**    Friend of Francis Phelan; homeless alcoholic; sometimes works with Francis, when they can find employment; has cancer and dies after being hit with a baseball bat in William Kennedy's *Ironweed.*

**Nezzie**    Strong, outspoken headwoman of the Lion Camp; wife of Talut and fiercely protective adoptive mother of Rydag; acts as an adoptive mother to Ayla in Jean Auel's *The Mammoth Hunters.*

**Ngui**   Ernie's gunbearer and tracker; shares his feelings about animals and ethical hunting in Ernest Hemingway's *True At First Light*.

**Nicholas**   Lover of Theodora Waite; discovers she is a thief, likes to vandalize houses while she burglarizes them; dies when his car hits a concrete pillar in Bette Pesetsky's *Midnight Sweets*.

**Nichole**   Italian-American white activist exploited by George Cain; gives birth to their child in George Cain's *Blueschild Baby*.

**Alec Nichols**   Member of Parliament and on the board of one of the world's largest companies, Roffe and Sons, by way of marriage; conniving and weak man with an addiction to his wife, Vivian Nichols, that leads to financial ruin in Sidney Sheldon's *Bloodline*.

**Vivian Nichols**   Irresponsible and unfaithful wife whose gambling leads to her family's financial ruin and downfall; wife of Alec Nichols in Sidney Sheldon's *Bloodline*.

**Ray Nickel**   American colonel and saboteur who flies over the opium fields in Laos with Pinkham and tells him about the drug trade; dies under suspicious circumstances in Maureen Howard's *Expensive Habits*.

**Dayton Nickles**   Mixed-blood best friend of Lee George on a Montana Indian reservation who later cares for the terminally ill Christine George Taylor in Michael Dorris's *A Yellow Raft in Blue Water*.

**Brenda Nicol**   Cousin who writes to Gary Gilmore in prison in Norman Mailer's The *Executioner's Song*.

**John (Johnny) Nicol**   Husband of Brenda Nicol in Norman Mailer's The *Executioner's Song*.

**Fray Nicolfis**   Nineteenth-century priest living in Walatowa whose diary Father Olguin reads in N. Scott Momaday's *House Made of Dawn*.

**Mario Nicolosi**   Author who is the neighbor and friend of Virgil Morgan in Scott Spencer's *Preservation Hall*.

**Fritz Jentand von Niemand**   Nazi physician who forces Sophie Zawistowska to send one of her two children to the Birkenau crematoriums in William Styron's *Sophie's Choice*.

**El Nifio Muerto (The Dead Child)**   American boy in Mexico who transmigrates into other characters, finally becoming Xotod, his lover and comrade in the Mayan jungle in William S. Burroughs's *The Wild Boys*.

**Nigel**   Slave who befriends Dana Franklin and marries Carrie in Octavia E. Butler's *Kindred*.

**Night Swan**   Retired Mexican flamenco dancer in Cubero with whom Tayo's Uncle Josiah has an affair; negotiates the buying of the spotted cattle from her cousin Ulibarri that become the object of Tayo's quest later in the novel; Tayo's first sexual partner in Leslie Marmon Silko's *Ceremony*.

**Araba Nightwing**   Trotskyite actress and underground leader of the Purple Group in Paul Theroux's *The Family Arsenal*.

**Sam Niles**   Divorced ex-Marine and claustrophobic who accidentally shoots Alexander Blaney; one of ten Los Angeles policemen-protagonists in Joseph Wambaugh's *The Choirboys*.

**Woodsy Niles**   Lover of Sally Buck; teaches Joe Buck to see himself as a cowboy in James Leo Herlihy's *Midnight Cowboy*.

**Edgar Carl (Ed) Nillson**   Oil speculator whose bribe causes the ruin of Senator Burden Day in Gore Vidal's *Washington, D.C.*

**Brita Nilsson**   Photographer living in New York City; inadvertently launches the reclusive novelist Bill Gray on a misguided attempt to rescue a hostage from the terrorist Abu Rashid in Lebanon; eventually moves from photographing writers to photographing terrorists in Don DeLillo's *Mao II*.

**Edna Nimienski**   Skinny peroxide blonde with whom Zeke Gurevich lives for three months in the Mojave Desert in William Herrick's *The Itinerant*.

**Nina**   Bard College graduate working as a salesperson at Lord & Taylor; former classmate and girlfriend of Peter Spangle; now having an affair with John Knapp; comes to realize she loves him in Ann Beattie's *Falling in Place*.

**Ronnie Nipple**   Neighbor of the Bloods; stops being a farmer and starts selling real estate; is the realtor for the Blood farm; his mother dies of blood poisoning after falling through a rotten floor in E. Annie Proulx's *Postcards*.

**Richard Nixon**   Vice president of the United States, buffoon, scamp, and would-be lover of Ethel Rosenberg in Robert Coover's *The Public Burning*.

**Mordecai Noah**   Editor of the *Evening Star* and the only Jew ever to be appointed sheriff of New York City in Gore Vidal's *Burr*.

**Jean-Marie Noblet**   Drinking companion of Jean Louis Lebris de Kérouac on a train trip to Brittany in Jack Kerouac's *Satori in Paris*.

**Nobuko**   Japanese actress who desires the spiritual freedom that Renate represents in Anaïs Nin's *Collages*.

**Domina Nocturna**   See Katje Borgesius.

**Doctor Nolan**   Woman psychiatrist who treats Esther Greenwood at Belsize, a private mental sanitarium in Sylvia Plath's *The Bell Jar*.

**Hezekiah (Uncle Hake) Nolan**   Slovenly brother of Jenny Anderson and fifty-two-year-old husband of Lora Bowen

Nolan; shot and killed by his nephew, Jan Anderson, in Fred Chappell's *The Inkling.*

**Ida Nolan**   Best friend of Louise Eborn; Louise suffers her fatal stroke at Ida's house; Ida's vision that the dead are always with the living closes Reynolds Price's *Love and Work.*

**Lora Bowen Nolan**   Nineteen-year-old housemaid who schemes first to marry Uncle Hake Nolan, then to usurp Jenny Anderson's position in the household, and finally to seduce Jan Anderson in Fred Chappell's *The Inkling.*

**Sheriff Nolan**   White authority with whom the Reverend Phillip Martin must negotiate in Ernest J. Gaines's *In My Father's Home.*

**William (Billy) Nolan**   Boyfriend of Christine Hargensen; supplies the bucket of pig's blood that is emptied on Carrie White in Stephen King's *Carrie.*

**Noonan**   Writer for *Country Daze;* gay man who is moving to San Francisco; Lucy's friend in Ann Beattie's *Love Always.*

**Mike Noonan**   Best-selling novelist who is grieving over the death of his wife, Jo; cannot recover from his grief and is incapable of writing; goes to his summer home to come to terms with his wife's death in Stephen King's *Bag of Bones.*

**Emil Nordquist**   Free-verse poet known as the Bard of the Prairie in John Updike's *Bech: A Book.*

**Hwi Noree**   Engineered by the Ixians for the sole purpose of wooing Leto II; falls in love with Leto II and devotes herself entirely to him in Frank Herbert's *God Emperor of Dune*

**Norm**   Father by Mira of Normie and Clark; divorces Mira to marry another woman in Marilyn French's *The Women's Room.*

**Norman**   Displaced caveman from Africa who worships peanuts in Stanley Elkin's *The Dick Gibson Show.*

**Bernard B. (Bernie) Norman (Normanovitz)**   Owner of Norman Pictures, later bought out by Jonas Cord, Jr.; develops the movie careers of Nevada Smith and Rina Marlowe in Harold Robbins's *The Carpetbaggers.*

**Mr. Norris**   Man persuaded in a bar to try trout fishing; awakened his first night camping by the sound of men attempting to leave a dead body outside his tent in Richard Brautigan's *Trout Fishing in America.*

**Theodore Theophilus (Ted) North**   Teacher who spends a summer in Newport, Rhode Island; while serving as a tutor, instructor, and reader, he is called upon to assist with several private problems; narrator of Thornton Wilder's *Theophilus North.*

**Eleanor Norton**   Schoolteacher whose obsessive spiritualism merges with others' superstition, religion, and grief following the mine disaster to create the Brunist sect; becomes Marcella Bruno's mother figure in Robert Coover's *The Origin of the Brunists.*

**Susan (Susie, Suze) Norton**   Lover of Ben Mears; helps Mears investigate the Marsten House and inadvertently becomes a vampire in Stephen King's *'Salem's Lot.*

**Wylie Norton**   Veterinarian and reverentially devoted husband of Eleanor Norton in Robert Coover's *The Origin of the Brunists.*

**Helga Noth**   German actress-wife of Howard Campbell and sister of Resi Noth in Kurt Vonnegut's *Mother Night.*

**Resi Noth**   Younger sister of Helga Noth and lover of Howard Campbell in Kurt Vonnegut's *Mother Night.*

**Father Tom Novak**   Young Catholic priest who directs the church's youth activities on the Montana Indian reservation where fifteen-year-old Rayona Taylor comes to live in Michael Dorris's *A Yellow Raft in Blue Water.*

**Sura Novi**   Native of Gaia whose inhabitants share a common planetary mind; assigned to Trantor, where she takes on the role of a barely literate local farmer; rescues and is befriended by Gendibal, who believes that her apparently unsophisticated mind will serve to alert him of unauthorized telepathic activity that might threaten the Second Foundation's plans in Isaac Asimov's *Foundation's Edge.*

**Olga Novotna**   Piano teacher to Paul Porterfield; she trains Paul but finally informs him that his musical talent is insufficient to achieve his goal of becoming a major pianist in David Leavitt's *The Page Turner.*

**Natalie Novotny**   Lesbian stewardess in Thomas Berger's *Who Is Teddy Villanova?*

**Daniel Nuñez**   Consumptive peasant leader of a guerrilla band in the Spanish Civil War; opposes both the military junta and the loyalists in William Herrick's *Hermanos!*

**Oliver (Ollie) Nuper**   Hypocritical racist and voyeur always on the edge of violence; tenant of Walter Boyle in John Gardner's *The Sunlight Dialogues.*

**B. Beaufield Nutbeem**   Handles national and foreign news, which he gets from listening to the radio, for newspaper *Gammy Bird;* came to Newfoundland from England; prides himself on finding and reporting on sexual abuse cases; has going-away party for himself during which men get drunk and sink his boat in E. Annie Proulx's *The Shipping News.*

**Nxumalo**   Sixteen-year-old boy; son of the chief of a South African tribe; a determined dreamer and restless with his home; travels to Zimbabwe in search of gold mines and begins a tradition that will carry on throughout the generations of his family in James A. Michener's *The Covenant.*

**Nydia**   Teenage neighbor of Harry Meyers and wife of Carlos; wants Meyers to tutor her in Jay Neugeboren's *Listen Ruben Fontanez.*

**Harold Nye**   Special agent of the Kansas Bureau of Investigation; appointed to serve under Alvin Dewey in investigating the Clutter murders in Truman Capote's *In Cold Blood.*

**Cora Nyhoff**   Sanitarium roommate of Rena Baker in Peter De Vries's *The Blood of the Lamb.*

**General Douglas D. Oakhart**   President of the Patriot League in Philip Roth's *The Great American Novel*.

**Owen Oarson**   Former Texas football star and former tractor salesman who tries unsuccessfully to become a Hollywood film producer; lover of Jill Peel; narrates part of Larry McMurtry's *Somebody's Darling*.

**Carroll Oberfield**   Prosperous, longtime owner of the Box O Ranch and cattle business in 1890s eastern Oregon; his methods of hay feeding sets the example for Lydia Sanderson and Tim Whiteaker in Molly Gloss's *The Jump-Off Creek*.

**J. J. O'Brien**   World War I veteran, entrepreneur, and influential alumnus who pays for Jack Curran to play football at Boniface College in Mark Steadman's *A Lion's Share*.

**Nate O'Brien**   Middle-aged, divorced, recovering alcoholic with a washed-up law career who is sent into the Pantanal region of Brazil to find World Tribes missionary Rachel Lane in John Grisham's *The Testament*.

**Obie O'Brien**   Flirtatious thirteen-year-old Girl Scout in Maureen Howard's *Natural History*.

**Ingrid Ochester**   Lover of Hugh Butterfield after he divorces his wife in Scott Spencer's *Endless Love*.

**O'Connor**   Irishman who carries Mexican artifacts in his pockets and lives the life of others in Anaïs Nin's *Seduction of the Minotaur*.

**Cecile (Ceci) O'Connor**   Waitress, estranged wife of Walter Wong, and lover of Paul Cattleman in Alison Lurie's *The Nowhere City*.

**Guido O'Connor**   Homosexual lover of Edward Henley in Shirley Ann Grau's *Evidence of Love*.

**Johnny O'Day**   Communist Party member and Indiana steelworker; instructs Ira Ringold in the philosophies of Communism and other leftist politics during World War II; after the publication of the exposé, *I Married a Communist*, feels betrayed by Ira and his bourgeois tendencies in Philip Roth's *I Married a Communist*.

**Pat O'Day**   FBI "Roving Investigator" who sends his child to the same preschool as Jack Ryan; is present when Mahmoud Haji Daryaei's men attempt to kidnap Ryan's daughter; rescues the children by killing the last two terrorists; arranges the trap that leads to Raman's capture; marries Andrea Price in Tom Clancy's *Executive Orders*.

**Tommy Odds**   Civil rights organizer who loses an arm to a sniper's bullets; rapes the white wife of his friend Truman Held in Alice Walker's *Meridian*.

**Ann O'Dell**   Refined, attractive ex-wife of Frank Bascombe; now married to wealthy Charley O'Dell in Deep River, Connecticut; her equilibrium is often disturbed by the connection to her ex-husband that their two children necessitate in Richard Ford's *Independence Day*.

**Blue Odell**   Cowboy, described by some as an Indian because he looks like his Salish grandmother, though his background is similar to that of his long-term partner, Tim Whiteaker, in 1890s eastern Oregon; feuds with Harley Osgood and Jack; shot by Osgood in Molly Gloss's *The Jump-Off Creek*.

**Charley O'Dell**   Fifty-seven-year-old wealthy owner of a one-man architectural design firm in Deep River, Connecticut; second husband of Ann O'Dell; inspires little good feeling either

538

from his two stepchildren or from their father in Richard Ford's *Independence Day*.

**Gaye Nell Odell**   Daughter of Mavis Odell; beauty queen and brown belt karateka in Harry Crews's *Karate Is a Thing of the Spirit*.

**Mary Odell**   See Mary Cheney Odell Curran.

**Mavis Odell**   Mother of Gaye Nell Odell in Harry Crews's *Karate Is a Thing of the Spirit*.

**Brian O'Donnell**   Art dealer who sells Jeremy Pauling's works; Mary Tell and her children find shelter in his boathouse in Anne Tyler's *Celestial Navigation*.

**Kevin Joseph O'Donnell**   Irish terrorist; founded Ulster Liberation Army; wants to liberate Ireland and make Britain and America pay for injustices to Irish; targets Jack Ryan's family in Tom Clancy's *Patriot Games*.

**Kermit (Boy) Oelsligle**   Orphan who accompanies his great-uncle Floyd Warner from California to Nebraska; abandoned to the care of two hippies, Joy and Stanley, in Wright Morris's *Fire Sermon*.

**Kevin O'Garvey**   Member of Parliament who supports the Irish Party; lawyer who defends Irish farmers' rights in Leon Uris's *Trinity*.

**Ellen (Ellie) Oglethorpe**   Solicitous nurse and second wife of Tom More in Walker Percy's *Love in the Ruins*.

**Aristides (Harry, Porky) O'Hara**   Slightly crippled shoemaker and member of the Church of the Covenant community; best friend of Roger Ashley in Thornton Wilder's *The Eighth Day*.

**Lance O'Hara**   Homosexual Hollywood star; his legendary good looks begin to fade, leaving him increasingly lonely and dependent on alcohol in John Rechy's *City of Night*.

**Samuel O'Hara**   Grandfather of Porky O'Hara and deacon of the Covenant Church; lets Roger Ashley know of John Ashley's interest in and assistance to the church in Thornton Wilder's *The Eighth Day*.

**Tom O'Hara**   Manager of one of Jake Hesse's shoe stores and lover of Orpha Chase in Jessamyn West's *The Life I Really Lived*.

**Bernard V. O'Hare**   Lieutenant who hunts down Howard Campbell in Kurt Vonnegut's *Mother Night*; friend and fellow prisoner of war who returns to Dresden with the author in *Slaughterhouse-Five*.

**Captain Bernard Eagle-I (Daffodil-II) O'Hare**   Pilot of President Wilbur Swain's helicopter in Kurt Vonnegut's *Slapstick*.

**Eddie O'Hare**   As a youth, is enamored by Marion Cole and has his first sexual experience with her; as an adult he continues to love Marion, even though he has no idea where she went after leaving her family in John Irving's *A Widow for One Year*.

**Mary O'Hare**   Nurse, wife of Bernard V. O'Hare, and recipient of the dedication of Kurt Vonnegut's *Slaughterhouse-Five*.

**Ohio**   See Robes Smith.

**Kenneth O'Keefe**   Fellow American student and best friend of Sebastian Dangerfield; obsessed with his inability to lose his virginity, he returns to America broke and in despair in J. P. Donleavy's *The Ginger Man*.

**Olaf**   Wireless officer on a cruise ship who competes with Allert Vanderveenan for Ariane's attention; relieved of duty and sedated when she disappears in John Hawkes's *Death, Sleep & the Traveler*.

**Old Doctor**   Master figure who absorbs newsreels and riot noises into himself and thereby stills them in William S. Burroughs's *The Ticket That Exploded*.

**Old Lodge Skins**   Cheyenne adoptive grandfather of Little Big Man in Thomas Berger's *Little Big Man*.

**Olga the Wise One**   Doctor and witch who buries the narrator to cure him of fever in Jerzy Kosinski's *The Painted Bird*.

**Father Olguin**   Walatowa priest who testifies at Abel's trial in N. Scott Momaday's *House Made of Dawn*.

**R. Daneel Olivaw**   Prototype humaniform robot assigned to work with and protect Elijah Baley; targeted for kidnapping by Dr. Kelden Amadiro, who wishes to study Daneel's design in Isaac Asimov's *The Robots of Dawn*.

**Earl Olive**   Replacement manager of the Centennial Club; dynamites the dam and the main lodge when the members turn against him in Thomas McGuane's *The Sporting Club*.

**Bump Oliver**   Dapper card-shark who cheats during a card game in William Kennedy's *Billy Phelan's Greatest Game*.

**Gideon Oliver**   Anthropologist known as "the skeleton detective" for his skill in analyzing human remains; while in France to lecture at a conference, he solves two recent murders and one more than forty years old in Aaron Elkins's *Old Bones*.

**Margaret Oliver**   Younger daughter of Thomas Oliver; tries to be her father's son by participating in his business affairs in Shirley Ann Grau's *The Condor Passes*.

**Stephanie Maria D'Alfonso Oliver**   Wife of Thomas Oliver; descended from a Sicilian family prominent in the New Orleans business world; dies young after bearing two children in Shirley Ann Grau's *The Condor Passes*.

**Thomas Henry (Old Man) Oliver**　Millionaire protagonist who rises from a background of poverty to build a successful family and financial empire in Shirley Ann Grau's *The Condor Passes*.

**Olivia**　Hippie hitchhiker and lover of Jeremy Pauling; narrates the eighth chapter of Anne Tyler's *Celestial Navigation*.

**Mary Kathleen (Mrs. Jack Graham) O'Looney**　Former lover of Walter F. Starbuck; bag lady who is in fact the powerful Mrs. Graham in Kurt Vonnegut's *Jailbird*.

**Gary Olson**　Sophomore and roommate of Bob Carlson's at Moo University, an aspiring creative writer and student of Timothy Monahan; uses his friends as subjects for stories in Jane Smiley's *Moo*.

**The Great Omar**　Stunt pilot who flies away from a Minneapolis fairgrounds with Adelaide Adare in Louise Erdrich's *The Beet Queen*.

**Brackett Omensetter**　Unnaturally natural newcomer to Gilean on the Ohio; his absolute intimacy with nature and lack of self-consciousness provide the narrative focus of William Gass's *Omensetter's Luck*.

**Evan Ondyk**　Psychotherapist and, briefly, lover of Kitty Dubin in Bernard Malamud's *Dubin's Lives*.

**Adele O'Neill**　Friend of Mira; beleaguered by multiple pregnancies and a philandering husband in Marilyn French's *The Women's Room*.

**Seamus O'Neill**　Best friend of Conor Larkin; reporter for the Irish press, member of the Irish Republican Brotherhood, and revolutionary for the Irish Catholics in Leon Uris's *Trinity*.

**Valentine O'Neill**　French-Irish fashion designer who becomes chief buyer and designer for Scruples, Billy Ikehorn Orsini's boutique in Judith Krantz's *Scruples*.

**Bernadette Ong**　Wife of John Ong and lover of Piet Hanema in John Updike's *Couples*.

**John Ong**　Korean nuclear physicist and husband of Bernadette Ong in John Updike's *Couples*.

**Ono**　Bandaged, sexless resident of the Golden Years Community in Jerzy Kosinski's *Cockpit*.

**Oogruk**　Asian whale hunter in 14,000 BPE; migrates across Bering Sea to become one of first Eskimos in Alaska in James Michener's *Alaska*.

**Opaku**　Large, eventually traitorous bodyguard of Colonel Elleloû in John Updike's *The Coup*.

**John Opie**　Thursday-night dinner guest of Joseph Johnson; an artist who paints Mary's portrait in Frances Sherwood's *Vindication*.

**Peter (Pete) Orcino**　Second husband of Tasmania Orcino in Jessamyn West's *A Matter of Time*.

**Tasmania (Tassie) Murphy Orcino**　Older sister of Blix Hollister; helps Blix die when her cancer becomes unbearable in Jessamyn West's *A Matter of Time*.

**Doctor (Doc) Orcutt**　Physician whose effort to cure Henry Pimber's lockjaw cannot match the magical healing powers of Brackett Omensetter's special poultice in William Gass's *Omensetter's Luck*.

**William (Bill) Orcutt III**　Architect and artist; designing new home for the Levovs; has an affair with Dawn Levov in Philip Roth's *American Pastoral*.

**Jack R. Ordway**　Lighthearted, self-proclaimed office drunk; fabricates stories about drunken weekends with his rich wife's friends in Richard Yates's *Revolutionary Road*.

**Manuel (Portagee) Oreza**　Coast Guard master chief who is living in retirement in Saipan when the Japanese seize control of the Marianas; improvises communications gear and serves as a "spotter" for American military and intelligence operations; and is reunited with Clark, whom he knew as John Kelly before Kelly's faked death (in *Without Remorse*) in Tom Clancy's *Debt of Honor*.

**Erny Orfing**　Traveling puppeteer; Goodparley's partner; later, tortures Goodparley because of his beliefs and allows Riddley to become his puppeteering partner in Russell Hoban's *Riddley Walker*.

**Oribasius**　Physician who befriends Julian as a youth and remains his lifelong companion in Gore Vidal's *Julian*.

**Oriki**　White-skinned daughter of Scarecrow in Calvin Hernton's *Scarecrow*.

**Father O'Riordan**　New curate after Joe Gannon leaves in Mary McGarry Morris's *Songs in Ordinary Time*.

**Ork**　Chief priest who believes he has been privileged to experience a visit from the divine presence in John Gardner's *Grendel*.

**Frankie Orloffski**　Sailor and skin diver from South Jersey; Al Bonham's partner in a charter boat business; finally voted captain of the *Naiad* in James Jones's *Go to the Widow-Maker*.

**Marian Ormsby**　See Marian Ormsby Forrester.

**Irv Ornstein**　Tanned and chatty fantasy baseball vacationer in Cooperstown, New York; serendipitously runs into Frank Bascombe, his long lost stepbrother, and supports him during an emergency; twice divorced but contemplates a third marriage to Erma in Richard Ford's *Independence Day*.

**Orr**　Air force pilot and inventive tentmate of Yossarian; intentionally ditches his plane and rows to Sweden and safety in an inflatable life raft in Joseph Heller's *Catch-22*.

**Morgan of Orris**   Morgan Sloat's twinner in an alternate world; pretender to the throne in the Territories; tries to destroy Jack Sawyer in Stephen King's and Peter Straub's *The Talisman*.

**Billy Ikehorn Orsini**   See Wilhelmina Hunnenwell Winthrop Ikehorn Orsini.

**Vito Orsini**   Italian film producer who marries Billy Ikehorn Orsini and scores a major success with his film *Mirrors* in Judith Krantz's *Scruples*.

**Wilhelmina Hunnenwell Winthrop Ikehorn (Billy, Honey) Orsini**   Owner of Scruples, a Beverly Hills boutique; hires Valentine O'Neill and Spider Elliott, who make the store a great success; marries film producer Vito Orsini after her first husband, businessman Ellis Ikehorn, dies in Judith Krantz's *Scruples*.

**Jesus Ortiz**   Young Hispanic assistant to Sol Nazerman; killed by the bullet intended for Nazerman during the robbery in Edward Lewis Wallant's *The Pawnbroker*.

**Don Enrique Ortiz De Leon**   Owner of ten acres that Bert Loomis and Sue Ames buy; his family's ruined hacienda is on the land; wishes to restore it but restoration is never completed in Harriett Doerr's *Consider This, Senora*.

**Fremont Osborn**   Uncle of Warren Howe and the inventor of the dustbowl in Wright Morris's *Cause for Wonder*.

**Oscar**   Adolescent falsely convicted of a rape committed by his friend George Levanter in Jerzy Kosinski's *Blind Date*.

**Oscar X**   Black American student at McCarthy College in Wisconsin; introduces Hakim Ellelou to the Muslim faith and encourages him to overthrow the white-devil in John Updike's *The Coup*.

**Harley Osgood**   Bounty hunter for timber wolf hides in 1890s eastern Oregon; recent third in a partnership with Danny Turnbow and Jack; squatter in a cabin owned by the dead or absent rancher Loeb; fuels a growing feud with Blue Odell and partner Tim Whiteaker; shoots Odell in Molly Gloss's *The Jump-Off Creek*.

**Iris Osgood**   Plump, pretty student of George Caldwell in John Updike's *The Centaur*.

**Henry O'Shay**   Itinerant showman who purports to display the mummified corpse of his faithless wife in Alice Walker's *Meridian*.

**Caesara O'Shea**   Famous, beautiful, vain, and charming actress who dates Zuckerman; she is having an affair with Fidel Castro in Philip Roth's *Zuckerman Unbound*.

**Durust Osman**   Very precise, gentle man; a lover of lemons and his sacred garden; owner of much land in Ceramos; has hatred for his son, Huseyin; treats his wife harshly in Mary Lee Settle's *Blood Tie*.

**Hatije Hanim Osman**   Wife of Durust Osman; described as fat and lethargic; has resentment for husband's ritualistic seclusion in his garden in Mary Lee Settle's *Blood Tie*.

**Huseyin Osman**   Son of wealthiest man in Ceramos, Durust Osman; falls in love with Lisa, the rich American, offering her lodging, yet robbing her of her freedom in Mary Lee Settle's *Blood Tie*.

**Osmond**   Cruel courtier and twinner of Sunlight Gardener in the alternate world of the Territories in Stephen King's and Peter Straub's *The Talisman*.

**Charles Ossing**   Businessman who hopes Kellog's program can help him with his own in T. Coraghessan Boyle's *The Road to Wellville*.

**Katrina Osterlaag**   See Rina Marlowe.

**Sean O'Sullivan**   Military governor of Rombaden, special assistant to General Hansen, commander of an occupation team in post–World War II Germany, and lover of Ernestine Falkenstein in Leon Uris's *Armageddon*.

**Otis**   Troubled teenager in William Faulkner's *The Reivers*.

**Otis**   Brother of Alfonso; regularly stops Alfonso from beating Jean in Gayl Jones's *Eva's Man*.

**John O'Toole**   Detective who helps to arrest Martha Horgan when she injures Joshua Barrett and takes Zachary hostage in Mary McGarry Morris's *A Dangerous Woman*.

**Sandy O'Toole**   Nurses and later becomes romantically involved with John Kelly after his recovery and during his campaign against Pam Madden's murderers; shelters and assists Doris; marries Kelly (as Clark) after Kelly's fake death in Tom Clancy's *Without Remorse*.

**Tommy O'Toole**   Cabin boy with whom Falcon has sex and for whom Cringle has sonlike compassion; is ordered to play flute so that slaves will dance and receive exercise aboard ship; loses mind after seeing Allmuseri god below deck in Charles Johnson's *Middle Passage*.

**Felix (N. J. Felix) Ottensteen**   Magazine writer and friend of Leslie Braverman in Wallace Markfield's *To an Early Grave*.

**Otto**   Husband to Sofia, father of Charles; German-American world-class chemist whose affair with Sofia resulted in marriage; relocated his family to Michigan in Julia Alvarez's *How the Garcia Girls Lost Their Accents*.

**Sefiorita Vastie Oubaleta**   Name assumed by Arista Prolo on a Spanish tour in Carlene Hatcher Polite's *Sister X and the Victims of Foul Play*.

**Blanche Overall**   Girlfriend of Orlando Pratt; Maude Coffin Pratt accuses her of incest in Paul Theroux's *Picture Palace*.

**Clay Overbury**   Ambitious protégé of Burden Day and husband of Enid Sanford in Gore Vidal's *Washington, D.C.*

**Enid Sanford Overbury**   See Enid Sanford.

**Merrill Overturf**   Diabetic who befriends Fred Trumper in Austria; dies while trying to locate a German tank at the bottom of the Danube River in John Irving's *The Water-Method Man.*

**Claire Ovington**   Lover of David Kepesh; brings him Shakespeare records and provides him with what sexual pleasure he is capable of in his new form in Philip Roth's *The Breast.*

**Melissa deKalb Owen**   Has an affair with David Wiley while he is married; calls his house and tells Gretchen; runs into David and Lexi Steiner on her honeymoon in Elizabeth Benedict's *Slow Dancing.*

**Antonia Owens**   Beautiful and mean-tempered daughter of Sally Owens and Michael (who dies when she is young); torments her quieter younger sister, Kylie, in Alice Hoffman's *Practical Magic.*

**Frances Owens**   One of a long line of Owens witches who, along with sister, Jet, raises orphaned nieces Gillian and Sally in an unconventional household in Alice Hoffman's *Practical Magic.*

**Gillian Owens**   Reckless and seductive younger sister of Sally; descendent of long line of Owens women known to be witches; has sequence of relationships with dangerous men until she meets and falls in love with Ben Frye in Alice Hoffman's *Practical Magic.*

**Jet Owens**   One of a long line of Owens witches who, along with sister, Frances, raises orphaned nieces Gillian and Sally in an unconventional household in Alice Hoffman's *Practical Magic.*

**Kylie Owens**   Tall, gangly daughter of Sally Owens and Michael (who dies when she is young); is teased by more popular sister, Antonia; last of a long line of Owens witches, she discovers magical abilities of her own in Alice Hoffman's *Practical Magic.*

**Sally Owens**   Conscientious older sister of Gillian; embarrassed to come from a long line of witches; tries to separate herself and her two daughters, Kylie and Antonia, from her aunts Jet and Frances by living a normal suburban life; falls in love with Garry Hallett in Alice Hoffman's *Practical Magic.*

**Rachel Owlglass**   Former lover of Benny Profane; helps pay for plastic surgery for her roommate, Esther Harvitz, in Thomas Pynchon's *V.*

**Gretchen Shurz Oxencroft**   Mother of Paul Hammer; gives him his fanatical crucifixion mission in John Cheever's *Bullet Park.*

**Oxie**   See Ted Pape.

**Oyp**   Ancient Egyptian tomb robber in a dream had by Alexander Main in *The Bailbondsman,* a novella in Stanley Elkin's *Searches and Seizures.*

**Eddy Pace**   Leader of a combo at Happy's Café in Gayl Jones's *Corregidora*.

**Ralph Packer**   Producer of underground films who moves to Greenwich Village in John Irving's *The Water-Method Man*.

**Jack Packerton**   Police captain and commander of West Valley Station in Los Angeles; unsatisfactory lover of Natalie Zimmerman in Joseph Wambaugh's *The Black Marble*.

**Paddy the Duke**   Seemingly arrogant, hostile presence in Frederick Exley's ward in the Avalon Valley Mental Hospital; isolates himself from the other patients and possesses a deeper understanding of alcoholism than Exley can in Frederick Exley's *A Fan's Notes*.

**Luis Pagan**   Spanish dancer who brings Ideal a daily cup of coffee; she seduces him in Carlene Hatcher Polite's *The Flagellants*.

**Ariah Page**   Long-suffering wife of James Page and mother of Richard Page; understands how Richard accidentally caused the death of Horace Abbott, but cannot explain to her husband in John Gardner's *October Light*.

**Clair (Miss Page) Page**   Prostitute and former high school teacher whose juju frees and protects Bill Kelsey in Hal Bennett's *Seventh Heaven*.

**James L. Page**   Seventy-three-year-old conservative Vermonter who threatens the life of his nonconformist sister, Sally Page Abbott, but eventually relents when he realizes how, by being too intimidating, he has caused the suicide of his son, Richard Page, in John Gardner's *October Light*.

**Richard Page**   Son of James Page; commits suicide because his father's demands make him feel inadequate in John Gardner's *October Light*.

**Arthur Paget**   The replacement of the Cavaliere; the new envoy to the Kingdom of the Two Sicilies in Susan Sontag's *The Volcano Lover*.

**Jawaharlal Madhar Pai**   Ambitious corporate lawyer hired to defend Erebus Entertainment against Oscar Crease's lawsuit who forfeits his job and his social position when he loses the suit in William Gaddis's *A Frolic of His Own*.

**Thomas "Tom" Paine**   Pamphleteer who inspires Americans to rebel against English tyranny; moves to Paris during the French Revolution; buried in America until his body is dug up and made off with by a couple of admirers; his early biographers attacked him for being an atheist in Frances Sherwood's *Vindication*.

**Doctor Palas**   Mexican physician stationed at Kulacan in Anaïs Nin's *Seduction of the Minotaur*.

**Michael (Mike) Palgrave**   See Morris Cohen.

**Carl Dean Palmers**   Student and follower of Eleanor Norton; falls in love with Elaine Collins in Robert Coover's *The Origin of the Brunists*.

**Mariana Paloma**   Virginal Mexican waitress who becomes the fiancée of Serge Duran in Joseph Wambaugh's *The New Centurions*.

**William (Pinky) Panck**   Soldier and follower of Johnny Church and Thankful Perkins; condemned to death for mutiny but spared by Cromwell's blanket pardon in Mary Lee Settle's *Prisons*.

**Pangle**   Simple-minded young man who is captivated by the fiddle playing of Stobrod Thewes, learns to play the banjo, and becomes Stobrod's companion in Charles Frazier's *Cold Mountain*.

**Dolly (Doll) Panik**    Semiautobiographical fictional character created by Margaret Flood in her novel *Child's Play*; nurse who has an affair with Tim Healy in Maureen Howard's *Expensive Habits*.

**Papa**    Father of Chantal and Pascal and husband of Honorine; plans to kill himself, Chantal, and his closest friend, Henri, by crashing the car he is driving into a stone barn; narrator of John Hawkes's *Travesty*.

**Ted (Oxie, Theodorik Paparikis) Pape**    Gimlet Street pimp and hustler who has become a bail bondsman and attempts to become a political force in Fred Chappell's *The Gaudy Place*.

**Nick Pappas**    Owner of Pappas's Sweet Shoppe; fiftyish; teaches James Bray magic tricks in Maureen Howard's *Natural History*.

**William (Will) Parchment**    Mate on the *Lillias Eden*, an old-timer and fairly good sailor, but a poor pilot; dies when the boat wrecks on Misteriosa Reef in Peter Matthiessen's *Far Tortuga*.

**Pard**    Friend of the narrator and of Trout Fishing in America; former machine-gunner and existentialist; lives with his girlfriend, the narrator, and the narrator's woman in the California bush in Richard Brautigan's *Trout Fishing in America*.

**Inspector Pardew**    Homicide detective who investigates the murders at Gerald's party; is obsessed with time; accuses Vachel of being the murderer in Robert Coover's *Gerald's Party*.

**Cargile Parham**    Physician and father of Sallie Parham in Jesse Hill Ford's *The Raider*.

**Sally Parham**    Daughter of Cargile Parham and wife and widow of Willy McCutcheon in Jesse Hill Ford's *The Raider*.

**Paris**    Lover of Helen; his spirit appears to her in Egypt in H. D.'s *Helen in Egypt*.

**Adeline (Addie) Parker**    Teenage granddaughter murdered by Clotilda Pilgrim; daughter of Ruby Parker and lover of Dunreith Smith in Cyrus Colter's *The Rivers of Eros*.

**Jennifer Parker**    Young assistant district attorney accused of obstruction of justice, which leads her on a struggle for her life and career in Sidney Sheldon's *Rage of Angels*.

**Larry Parker**    Opportunistic, risk-taking friend of Dick Pierce who rents his boat to Dick and casually involves him in a drug smuggling scheme in John Casey's *Spartina*.

**Miss Laura Parker**    High school teacher who persuades the family of Clay-Boy Spencer to allow him to try for a scholarship at the University of Richmond in Earl Hamner, Jr.'s *Spencer's Mountain*.

**Lester Parker**    Grandson of Clotilda Pilgrim; watches the decline of his grandmother and his sister, Addie Parker, in Cyrus Colter's *The Rivers of Eros*.

**Red Parker**    Heavy-drinking salesman and widower whose apartment Bob Slocum uses for extramarital affairs; fired by Slocum in Joseph Heller's *Something Happened*.

**Ruby Parker**    Daughter of Clotilda Pilgrim and Chester Jackson, wife of Zack Parker, and mother of Addie and Lester Parker; murdered by Zack in Cyrus Colter's *The Rivers of Eros*.

**Speedy Parker**    Old black man who bonds with Jack Parker and instructs him on how to procure the Talisman in Stephen King's and Peter Straub's *The Talisman*.

**Zack Parker**    Auto mechanic, philanderer, and murderer of his wife, Ruby Parker, in Cyrus Colter's *The Rivers of Eros*.

**Jerene Parks**    Adopted African-American child of Sam and Margaret Parks; disowned by parents when she reveals her homosexuality; roommate of Eliot Abrams; becomes friend of Philip Benjamin in David Leavitt's *The Lost Language of Cranes*.

**Margaret Parks**    Married to Sam; adoptive mother of Jerene; proper and feminine African American; disowns Jerene after she reveals her homosexuality in David Leavitt's *The Lost Language of Cranes*.

**Sam Parks**    Married to Margaret; adoptive father of Jerene; wealthy and conservative African American; disowns Jerene after she reveals her homosexuality in David Leavitt's *The Lost Language of Cranes*.

**Parkus**    Speedy Parker's twinner in the alternate world of the Territories; friend of Jack Sawyer's in Stephen King's and Peter Straub's *The Talisman*.

**Charles Stewart Parnell**    Rich Protestant landowner; Irish anarchist and supporter of Irish Catholic causes in Leon Uris's *Trinity*.

**Francois Parnientier**    See Bebe Chicago.

**Jimmy Parrish**    Former foreman at Guardian Farm, now uses a cane and spends all his evenings at the Lyon Café, spouting racetracks statistics and boring everyone in Alice Hoffman's *Here on Earth*.

**Al Parsons**    See Alexander Portnoy.

**Erleen Parsons**    Wife of Henry Parsons; submits to sexual assault by Willie Joe Worth so she can win her husband's release from jail in Jesse Hill Ford's *The Liberation of Lord Byron Jones*.

**Henry Parsons**    Husband of Erleen Parsons falsely accused of public drunkenness and resisting arrest; later, in despair and humiliation, kills his son in Jesse Hill Ford's *The Liberation of Lord Byron Jones*.

**Lyle Parsons**    First husband of Anney Boatwright and father of Reese; works at the Texaco station and Greenville County Racetrack to keep his pregnant wife from factory work; dies in a wreck; his death marks Anney's maturation from nineteen-year-old wife and mother of two to hardened adult in Dorothy Allison's *Bastard Out of Carolina*.

**Reese Parsons**    Sister of Bone and only legitimate child of Anney Boatwright Waddell; escapes her stepfather's abuse by accepting him as her father; works out her anger by wearing her mother's underwear while masturbating; enjoys the thrill of hitchhiking at age eight in Dorothy Allison's *Bastard Out of Carolina*.

**Partridge**    New York friend Quoyle meets in laundromat; acts as his mentor at *The Mockingbird Record* newspaper; moves to New Orleans after his wife lands job as truck driver; gives Quoyle name of man who hires him at *Gammy Bird* in E. Annie Proulx's *The Shipping News*.

**Pascal**    Son of Papa and Honorine and younger brother of Chantal; dies from undisclosed causes in John Hawkes's *Travesty*.

**Alexander Pascaleo**    Italian Catholic friend and roommate of Marshall Pearl at Harvard University; rides the railroads with Pearl and works with him in a St. Louis meatpacking plant in Mark Helprin's *Refiner's Fire*.

**Pat**    Woman friend of Jimmy Low; discusses jazz and recipes in the taped conversations of Jack Kerouac's *Visions of Cody*.

**Pat**    Black ex-college student in Copenhagen who wants money for an abortion in Cecil Brown's *The Life and Loves of Mr. Jiveass Nigger*.

**Lillian Patch**    Middle-class Harlem schoolteacher engaged to Max Reddick; frightened of the uncertainties of marriage to a writer in John A. Williams's *The Man Who Cried I Am*.

**Patricia (Pat)**    Schoolteacher and lover of John; with John, downstairs neighbor of Constance Marlow and Bob and finder of the Logan brothers' bowling trophies in Richard Brautigan's *Willard and His Bowling Trophies*.

**Bankey (Zack) Patterson**    Old black man who meets Forrest Mayfield just after Forrest has been rejected by his wife, Eva Kendal, in Reynolds Price's *The Surface of Earth*.

**Camack Patterson**    Memphis lawyer, cousin who introduces Eleanor Fite to Gratt Shafer, and best man at their wedding in Jesse Hill Ford's *Mountains of Gilead*.

**Jack Patterson**    English professor and regular guest on the late-night radio show hosted by Dick Gibson; tells of his infatuation with a child singing star in Stanley Elkin's *The Dick Gibson Show*.

**Pattie Mae**    Philo Skinner's assistant; a tyro dog handler in Joseph Wambaugh's *The Black Marble*.

**Paul**    Less-than-princely prince killed by a poisoned vodka Gibson meant for Snow White in Donald Barthelme's *Snow White*.

**Pauline**    Concert pianist and lover of George Levanter in Jerzy Kosinski's *Blind Date*.

**Amanda Pauling**    Spinster sister of Jeremy Pauling; narrates part of Anne Tyler's *Celestial Navigation*.

**Jeremy Pauling**    Artist and agoraphobic; common-law husband of Mary Tell and father of five of her six children in Anne Tyler's *Celestial Navigation*.

**Mary Pauling**    See Mary Tell.

**Wilma Pauling**    Mother of Jeremy Pauling and owner of a boardinghouse in Anne Tyler's *Celestial Navigation*.

**Becka Paulson**    Middle-aged wife of adulterer Joe Paulson; hears voices from a picture of Jesus; electrocutes herself and Joe in Stephen King's *The Tommyknockers*.

**Clive (Old Man) Paxton**    Father of Kathleen Paxton Hodge; so opposes her marriage to Taggert Hodge that he drives her into an institution; Taggert strangles him in revenge in John Gardner's *The Sunlight Dialogues*.

**Joe Paxton**    Black writer and resident of a 13th Street building managed by Norman Moonbloom in Edward Lewis Wallant's *The Tenants of Moonbloom*.

**Jerry (Boomaga) Payne**    Introvert-turned-extrovert boyfriend of Pookie Adams; narrator of John Nichols's *The Sterile Cuckoo*.

**Marcus (Marky) Payne**    Intransigent young black man awaiting trial for murder; quietly defies racial taboos by having an affair with the wife of Sidney Bonbon; eventually killed by Bonbon in Ernest J. Gaines's *Of Love and Dust*.

**Nicholas Payne**    Young man who travels west on his motorcycle; falls in love with Ann Fitzgerald and helps C. J. Clovis build bat towers; operated on for hemorrhoids in Thomas McGuane's *The Bushwhacked Piano*.

**Lucius Quintus Peabody**    See Volume I.

**Eddie Peace**    Small-time Hollywood actor with whom Marge Converse and Ray Hicks hide in Robert Stone's *Dog Soldiers*.

**Eva (Pearl) Peace**    Grandmother of Sula Peace and mother of Hannah and Plum Peace; owner of a boardinghouse in Toni Morrison's *Sula*.

**Hannah Peace**    Mother of Sula Peace and daughter of Eva Peace; dies from wounds suffered in a yard fire in Toni Morrison's *Sula*.

**Ralph (Plum) Peace**    Son of Eva Peace and brother of Hannah Peace; burned by his mother because of his excessive drug use in Toni Morrison's *Sula*.

**Sula Peace**   Daughter of Hannah Peace and granddaughter of Eva Peace; heroine engaged in the struggle for self-identity in Toni Morrison's *Sula*.

**Calvin Peachtree**   Black police detective in Thomas Berger's *Who Is Teddy Villanova?*

**Luther Peacock**   Deputy of Buddy Matlow; murdered by Joe Lon Mackey in Harry Crews's *A Feast of Snakes*.

**Maureen (Meringue Pie) Peal**   Neighbor to the MacTeers; set apart from the others for her "high-yellow" family's wealth and superior attitude; called "Meringue Pie" by Claudia and Frieda MacTeer in Toni Morrison's *The Bluest Eye*.

**Shelley Pearce**   Friend of screenwriter Gordon Walker; assistant to screenwriting agent Al Keochakian in Robert Stone's *Children of Light*.

**Jo-Jo Pearl**   Young, promising boxer trained by Felix and later killed in an intense fight; son of Leroy Pearl in Joyce Carol Oates's *You Must Remember This*.

**Leroy Pearl**   Bitter, angry, and alcoholic father of Jo-Jo in Joyce Carol Oates's *You Must Remember This*.

**Marshall Pearl**   Son of Katrina Perlé and Lev, but orphaned and adopted by the Livingstons; inherits visions from his mother; mortally wounded while fighting the Syrians at Daughters of Jacob Bridge in Israel in Mark Helprin's *Refiner's Fire*.

**Shannon Pearl**   Overweight, albino daughter of a Christian concert arranger and manager of a Christian bookstore; reveals a hate list of everyone who was ever mean to her and vows to mete out violent punishments to each; at a family picnic, she burns to death after spraying hot coals with lighter fluid in Dorothy Allison's *Bastard Out of Carolina*.

**James (Jamie) Pearson**   Former lover of Hattie Sherbrooke in Nicholas Delbanco's *Possession*.

**Reverend Pease**   Sick, confused old man Luther Corbett cares for in Mary McGarry Morris's *Songs in Ordinary Time*.

**Curtis G. Peavey**   Lawyer who plans to marry Roxy; accuses Chester Pomeroy of perversion in Thomas McGuane's *Panama*.

**Caleb Peck**   Musician and long-lost half brother of Daniel Peck; great-uncle of Duncan and Justine Peck; the object of the search in Anne Tyler's *Searching for Caleb*.

**Caroline Peck**   See Caroline Peck Mayhew.

**Daniel (Judge Peck) Peck**   Straight-backed and straitlaced grandfather of Justine and Duncan Peck; half brother of the missing Caleb Peck in Anne Tyler's *Searching for Caleb*.

**Duncan Peck**   Jack-of-all-trades given to wanderlust; grandson of Daniel Peck, husband of Justine Peck, and father of Meg Peck in Anne Tyler's *Searching for Caleb*.

**Jim Peck**   Hippie who intrudes on Joe Allston's property and becomes Allston's intellectual foe in Wallace Stegner's *All the Little Live Things*.

**Justine Peck**   Fortune-teller; granddaughter and fellow searcher of Daniel Peck, wife and cousin of Duncan Peck, and mother of Meg Peck in Anne Tyler's *Searching for Caleb*.

**Meg Peck**   See Margaret Rose Peck Milsom.

**General P. P. Peckem**   Rival of General Dreedle; scorned by ex-P.F.C. Wintergreen, who judges Peckem's prose pretentious and prolix in Joseph Heller's *Catch-22*.

**Lewis Peckham**   Another "lost soul" who has lived through Vietnam, tried to teach English and to run a cave he owns as a tourist attraction; he spends most of his time writing bad poetry and listening to Beethoven and Wagner in Walker Percy's *The Second Coming*.

**Missy Peckham**   Intrepid and resourceful pioneer in Alaska; common-law wife of Matthew Murphy; prospector, cook, nurse, judge's assistant, and finally passionate organizer and spokesperson for Alaska's advent to statehood in James Michener's *Alaska*.

**Frederich Pedersen**   Child musical prodigy; son of Karl and Mary Pedersen and brother of the adopted Jesse Harte in Joyce Carol Oates's *Wonderland*.

**Hilda Pedersen**   Child mathematics prodigy; daughter of Karl and Mary Pedersen and sister of the adopted Jesse Harte in Joyce Carol Oates's *Wonderland*.

**Jesse Pedersen**   See Jesse Harte.

**Jim Pederson**   Private in the Third Squad who pursues Cacciato; devout Christian known for his "moral stance"; dies in an ambush in Tim O'Brien's *Going After Cacciato*.

**Dr. Karl Pedersen**   Demonic diagnostic physician who adopts the boy Jesse Harte and attempts to mold him in his own image in Joyce Carol Oates's *Wonderland*.

**Marsha Pedersen**   Graduate English student who shares a flight and a motel room with Jane Clifford in Gail Godwin's *The Odd Woman*.

**Mary Pedersen**   Subservient wife of Dr. Karl Pedersen and mother of Frederich and Hilda Pedersen; attempts, along with her adopted son, Jesse Harte, to escape her husband's control in Joyce Carol Oates's *Wonderland*.

**Jill Peel**   Friend of Joe Percy and lover of Owen Oarson; former animation artist who becomes a Hollywood film director; narrates part of Larry McMurtry's *Somebody's Darling*; lover of Daniel Deck in *All My Friends Are Going to Be Strangers*.

**Raymond Peepgas**   Senior loan officer of bank that holds Charles Croker's loans; being sued for paternity by Finnish woman he had an affair with; tries but fails to take advantage of Croker's situation; marries Martha Croker in Tom Wolfe's *A Man In Full.*

**Francine Pefko**    Secretary and mistress of Dwayne Hoover in Kurt Vonnegut's *Breakfast of Champions.*

**Peg-leg**    Morgue attendant who helps C. Card steal the corpse of a murdered prostitute in Richard Brautigan's *Dreaming of Babylon.*

**Janov Pelorat**    Foundation historian who accompanies Golan Trevize; his interest in finding Earth serves as a cover for Trevize's true mission of locating the rival Second Foundation; paramour of Bliss in Isaac Asimov's *Foundation's Edge.*

**Miss Pemberton**    White prostitute, sex show manager, and former civil rights worker in Hal Bennett's *The Black Wine* and *Wait Until the Evening.*

**Thomas Pemberton**    Former 1960s activist; rector of St. Timothy's Episcopal Church; becomes friends with Rabbis Joshua Gruen and Sarah Blumenthal; called before council of bishops for improper views; decertified as a priest; recovers lost manuscript of secret ghetto archive; marries Sarah in E. L. Doctorow's *City of God.*

**Captain Pena**    Instrument of the Trujillo regime in the Dominican Republic; stands guard over the house arrest of the Mirabal family in Julia Alvarez's *In the Time of the Butterflies.*

**Harry Pena**    Virile fisherman in Kurt Vonnegut's *God Bless You, Mr. Rosewater.*

**Jill Pendleton**    Eighteen-year-old runaway drug addict who comes to live with Rabbit Angstrom as his lover and dies in a fire in John Updike's *Rabbit Redux.*

**Skip Pendleton**    Well-educated and well-connected commodities trader in New York; gives Alison Poole a sexually transmitted disease, but is later tricked into paying for an abortion she does not need; eventually breaks up her promising relationship with Dean Chasen in Jay McInerney's *Story of My Life.*

**Mrs. (Mrs. P.) Pendrake**    Unfaithful wife of the Reverend Silas Pendrake and adoptive mother of Jack Crabb in Thomas Berger's *Little Big Man.*

**Reverend Silas Pendrake**    Missouri preacher and adoptive father of Jack Crabb in Thomas Berger's *Little Big Man.*

**Warren Penfield**    Poet of Loon Lake whose work the book publishes posthumously; an inspiration and a catalyst to action for Joe Patterson in E. L. Doctorow's *Loon Lake.*

**Beverly Penn**    Ethereal and beautiful young daughter of wealthy publisher Isaac Penn; dying of consumption; marries burglar Peter Lake in Mark Helprin's *Winter's Tale.*

**Connie Penn**    Heterosexual high school classmate of Molly Bolt in Rita Mae Brown's *Rubyfruit Jungle.*

**Elton Penn**    Kentucky subsistence farmer and surrogate son of Jack Beechum; manages Beechum's land with the vision of responsible stewardship that Beechum's daughter, Clara Pettit, lacks in Wendell Berry's *The Memory of Old Jack.*

**Harry Penn**    Owner of *The Sun* and *The Whale* newspapers, son of wealthy publisher Isaac Penn; steadfastly maintains fairness and integrity of the papers in Mark Helprin's *Winter's Tale.*

**Isaac Penn**    Wealthy, powerful, and eccentric publisher of *The Sun* and *The Whale* newspapers; father of four children in Mark Helprin's *Winter's Tale.*

**Mary Penn**    Good-hearted wife of Elton Penn; her reliable country sensibility represents the values prized in Wendell Berry's *The Memory of Old Jack.*

**Sylphid Pennington**    Professional harpist, daughter of the actress Eve Frame and her second husband, actor Carlton Pennington; resents her mother's fourth husband, Ira Ringold; is repeatedly cruel to her mother and pits the mother against Ira in Philip Roth's *I Married a Communist.*

**Pennywise the Clown**    Shape that "IT," the monster haunting the residents of Derry, Maine, takes when it manifests itself; dressed as a clown, "IT" lures children and then kills them; the Losers Club is determined to defeat "IT" in Stephen King's *IT.*

**Will Pentacost**    Friend of Johnny Church and Thankful Perkins; whipped and chased naked through the streets of Burford the night Cromwell's men round up dissenters in Mary Lee Settle's *Prisons.*

**Lew Pentecost**    Rival comedian engaged in a staged feud with Harry Mercury in Peter De Vries's *Through the Fields of Clover.*

**Alvin Pepler**    Embittered former quiz show contestant and winner at "Smart Money"; testifies that a contestant, Hewlett Lincoln, was fed answers on the show; has been writing a book about his experiences for ten years and claims someone is doing a musical about his experiences; thinks Zuckerman's book, *Carnovsky,* is about him in Philip Roth's *Zuckerman Unbound.*

**Dr. Pepper**    Expert on drugs who adopts various disguises; visits Bucky Wunderlick in search of a mysterious drug in Don DeLillo's *Great Jones Street.*

**Ned (Lucky Ned) Pepper**    Leader of an outlaw gang that holds captive Mattie Ross, Rooster Cogburn, and LaBoeuf in Charles Portis's *True Grit.*

**Alfred Peracca**    Los Angeles judge in the second trial of Gregory Powell and Jimmy Smith; eventually relieved because of a heart condition in Joseph Wambaugh's *The Onion Field.*

**Percival**    See John.

**Senator Lloyd Percival**   U.S. senator with a secret collection of erotic art; investigated by Moll Robbins; is himself investigating PAC/ORD, a government intelligence operation in Don DeLillo's *Running Dog*.

**Bainbridge (Pooh) Percy**   Ellen Jamesian who blames T. S. Garp for Cushie Percy's death; after killing Garp and being institutionalized and discharged, she becomes a mother at age fifty-four and works with retarded children in John Irving's *The World According to Garp*.

**Christine Percy**   Senior on the swim team who tells Carlin Leander and Ivy Cooper that all the girls on the team are required to shave their private parts; she has fake ID the girls use to buy alcohol in Alice Hoffman's *The River King*.

**Cushman (Cushie, Cushion) Percy**   Sister of Stewart Percy, Jr., and Pooh, Randolph, and William Percy; T. S. Garp's first sexual partner; dies in childbirth in John Irving's *The World According to Garp*.

**Joe Percy**   Aging screenwriter and friend of Jill Peel; dies of a stroke; narrates part of Larry McMurtry's *Somebody's Darling*.

**Randolph (Dopey) Percy**   Brother of Stewart Percy, Jr., and Pooh, Cushman, and William Percy; dies of a heart attack in John Irving's *The World According to Garp*.

**Stewart (Fat Stew, Paunch, Stewie) Percy**   Father of Stewart Percy, Jr., and William, Randolph, Cushman, and Pooh Percy; history teacher at Steering School; dies of a heart attack in John Irving's *The World According to Garp*.

**Stewart (Stewie Two) Percy, Jr.**   Brother of Cushman, Pooh, Randolph, and William Percy; married and divorced in John Irving's *The World According to Garp*.

**William (Shrill Willy) Percy**   Brother of Stewart Percy, Jr., and Cushman, Pooh, and Randolph Percy; Yale graduate killed during the war in John Irving's *The World According to Garp*.

**Reeny (Reen) Jimson Perdew**   Friend and accomplice of Podjo Harris and Rufus Hutton in Shelby Foote's *September September*.

**R. G. Perdew**   Writer who passes himself off as Ezra Pound in Paul Theroux's *Picture Palace*.

**Ms. Pered**   Woman from the building management firm that leases Bryce Proctorr's apartment; birdlike, under a glorious pink-gold wig; chatters like a bird in Donald E. Westlake's *The Hook*.

**Doc Peret**   Medic who pursues Cacciato; pragmatist, theoretician, who believes deeply in science in Tim O'Brien's *Going After Cacciato*.

**Felix Perez**   Son of Manny, grandson of Lourdes, nephew of Pepe; Lourdes takes him in after his mother takes off with Manny in Maureen Howard's *Expensive Habits*.

**Fernando (Frankie) Pérez**   Cesar Castillo's best friend; is originally from Havana and is a good dancer; becomes a petty gangster; after a heart attack, becomes magnanimous; is wealthy and goes into partnership with Cesar on a nightclub in Oscar Hijuelos's *The Mambo Kings Play Songs of Love*.

**Juan Manuel (Manny) Perez**   Son of Lourdes; murders Bayard Strong in a botched robbery attempt of Golden Oldies; disappears after the murder in Maureen Howard's *Expensive Habits*.

**Lourdes Perez**   Daily maid of Margaret Flood; after Manny murders Bayard, she wears a black kerchief instead of her wig; takes in Manny's son, Felix, in Maureen Howard's *Expensive Habits*.

**Pepe Perez**   Son of Lourdes; gets in trouble for stealing a car; gets a job managing an Exxon station in Maureen Howard's *Expensive Habits*.

**Bernard (Bernie) Perk**   Pharmacist and regular guest on the late-night radio show hosted by Dick Gibson; tells of his attraction to a female customer with very large genitals in Stanley Elkin's *The Dick Gibson Show*.

**Adrien Perkheimer**   Jewish tourist photographer; to overcome clichés, he photographs Greece with no film in his camera in Wright Morris's *What a Way to Go*.

**Thankful Perkins**   Closest friend of Johnny Church; executed for advocating greater democracy and opposing Cromwell's Irish campaign, but remains pious and trusting throughout Mary Lee Settle's *Prisons*.

**Kathryn Perl**   Attorney who represents Virgil Morgan in Scott Spencer's *Preservation Hall*.

**Katrina Perlk**   Russian Jew arrested at Riga during World War II; wife of Lev; because she is forgotten by the crew of the *Lindos Transit*, on which she is a passenger, she dies after giving birth to Marshall Pearl in Mark Helprin's *Refiner's Fire*.

**Hermoine (Hannah) Perlmutter**   Resident of Emma Lazarus Retirement Home whose rejection by Otto Korner leads her to steal a treasured letter from him; she is wooed, won, lost, and regained by Benno Hamburger in Alan Isler's *The Prince of West End Avenue*.

**Morton (Morty) Perlmutter**   Cultural anthropologist and mentor of James Boswell in Stanley Elkin's *Boswell*.

**Farrell Permalee**   Brother of Harold Permalee and member of Ned Pepper's gang in Charles Portis's *True Grit*.

**Harold Permalee**   Brother of Farrell Permalee and member of Ned Pepper's gang in Charles Portis's *True Grit*.

**Dr. Roderick Perrault**   Renowned brain surgeon and mentor of Jesse Vogel in Joyce Carol Oates's *Wonderland*.

**Perry**    Houston hustler who befriends then betrays Joe Buck in James Leo Herlihy's *Midnight Cowboy*.

**Miss Perry**    Wealthy, elderly spinster who maintains a family friendship with Dick Pierce; she loans him money to finish building Spartina in John Casey's *Spartina*.

**Rae Perry**    Estranged from her family and desperately trying to make life with self-centered boyfriend Jessup work, discovers she is pregnant and seeks help and support from psychic Lila Grey in Alice Hoffman's *Fortune's Daughter*.

**Charles Henri Persaud**    Husband of Roxy; leaves her to have an affair with a Czech woman; nephew of Edgar Cosset, who is having an affair with Charles's sister-in-law; killed by lover's husband in Diane Johnson's *Le Divorce*.

**Roxy Persaud**    Stepsister of Isabel Walker; American living in Paris with French husband and daughter; husband leaves her, pregnant, for another woman; attempts suicide; bears a son after her husband is murdered in Diane Johnson's *Le Divorce*.

**Perseus**    Performer of heroic deeds who is now twenty years older, bored, and overweight; narrator of the *Perseid*, a novella in John Barth's *Chimera*.

**Mr. de Persia**    Miraculous restorer and repairman who escapes his enemies in a balloon, descends by parachute, and discovers the body of Addis Adair in William Goyen's *Come, The Restorer*.

**Armande Chamar Person**    Daughter of Madame Charles Chamar and wife of Hugh Person, who puts up with her capricious behavior and peculiar sexual proclivities; murdered by her husband as he dreams he is saving her from a fire in Vladimir Nabokov's *Transparent Things*.

**Dr. Henry Emery (Person Senior) Person**    Father of Hugh Person; dies trying on a pair of trousers in a clothing store in Switzerland while on a trip with his son in Vladimir Nabokov's *Transparent Things*.

**Hugh (Percy) Person**    Editor for a New York-based publishing house; makes a pilgrimage to Switzerland to find traces of his dead wife, Armande Chamar Person; trip discloses the story of his life and loves and his gradual transformation into someone dwelling in a realm of transparent things in Vladimir Nabokov's *Transparent Things*.

**Perta**    Birdy's fantasy mate and mother of his children in his dream state; female canary in William Wharton's *Birdy*.

**Pete**    Husband to Clara and stepfather of Charles and Susan; nurses Clara and longs for a closer relationship with his stepchildren in Ann Beattie's *Chilly Scenes of Winter*.

**Pete**    Operator of the gas station where Clyde Stout works; married to an ill-tempered woman in Jack Matthews's *Hanger Stout, Awake!*

**Pete (Jake)**    Owner and bartender at Pete's, favorite bar of J. Henry Waugh in Robert Coover's *The Universal Baseball Association, Inc., J. Henry Waugh, Prop.*

**M. A. (Medium Asshole) Pete**    Assistant to the procurement manager of Pure Pores Filters Company; goes on the Alaskan hunting expedition with Rusty Jethroe in Norman Mailer's *Why Are We in Vietnam?*

**Peter**    Lover of Ursula Vanderveenan and oldest friend of Allert Vanderveenan; psychiatrist who dies of a heart attack in his sauna in John Hawkes's *Death, Sleep & the Traveler*.

**Cleon (Oil King) Peters**    Itinerant preacher in William Goyen's *Come, The Restorer*.

**Harold (Brother Harold) Peters**    Member of the Order of St. Clement assigned to do cooking and menial labor at St. Clement's Hill Retreat House in J. F. Powers's *Morte D'Urban*.

**Harrison Peters**    Army colonel; marries Rhoda Henry after she divorces first husband; promoted to brigadier general in Herman Wouk's *War and Remembrance*.

**Mabel Peters**    See Mabel Peters Fry.

**Alton Christian Peterson**    See Alexander Portnoy.

**Harald Peterson**    Ambitious actor and playwright married to Kay Leiland Strong in Mary McCarthy's *The Group*.

**Melody Oriole-2 von Peterswald**    Granddaughter of Wilbur Swain in Kurt Vonnegut's *Slapstick*.

**Father Petrauskas**    Catholic priest; hides Joseph Barbanel's secret ghetto archive in E. L. Doctorow's *City of God*.

**Athanase Petrescu**    Romanian translator of American literature and escort of Henry Bech in Romania; wears sunglasses everywhere in John Updike's *Bech: A Book*.

**Andrew D. Petrie**    Charismatic politician and right-wing political theorist whose murder initiates the action of Joyce Carol Oates's *The Assassins*.

**Hugh (Hughie) Petrie**    Cartoonist brother of Andrew Petrie; his bungled suicide attempt renders him quadriplegic; narrates part of Joyce Carol Oates's *The Assassins*.

**Mark Petrie**    Friend of Ralphie and Daniel Glick; escapes 'Salem's Lot with Ben Mears after Petrie's parents are murdered by the owners of Marsten House in Stephen King's *'Salem's Lot*.

**Stephen Petrie**    Religious mystic and brother of Andrew Petrie in Joyce Carol Oates's *The Assassins*.

**Yvonne Radek Petrie**    Wife of slain politician Andrew Petrie; editing and completing her husband's manuscripts, she retreats into a life of intellect and emotional noninvolvement in Joyce Carol Oates's *The Assassins.*

**Petrov**    Bulgarian novelist turned playwright; friend of Vera Glavanakova in John Updike's *Bech: A Book.*

**Cameron Petrus**    Boring reporter for *Country Daze*; also draws the cartoon strip for *Country Daze* in Ann Beattie's *Love Always.*

**Pettecasockee**    Chickasaw Indian who follows Elias Mc-Cutcheon into the Civil War; son of Shokotee McNeilly and husband of Denise Chatillion in Jesse Hill Ford's *The Raider.*

**Regal Pettibone**    Son of Pourty Bloodworth; brother of Amos-Otis Thigpen, Noah Grandberry, and LaDonna Scales (who is also his lover); half brother of Jonathan Bass; friend of Nathaniel Turner Witherspoon in Leon Forrest's *The Blood-worth Orphans.*

**Stefanie Pettigrew**    Vivacious finishing school graduate who becomes William's son's fiancée in Cynthia Ozick's *Trust.*

**Clara Beechum Pettit**    Daughter of Jack and Ruth Beechum; marries a Louisville banker to escape the tobacco farming life of her father in Wendell Berry's *The Memory of Old Jack.*

**Gladston (Glad) Pettit**    Husband of Clara Beechum Pettit; Louisville banker completely estranged from the farming and community values of Port William, Kentucky, in Wendell Berry's *The Memory of Old Jack.*

**Red Pettus**    Bigoted bully who murders Toomer Smalls and is then killed by Toomer's dogs in Pat Conroy's *The Great Santini.*

**Sherman (Sherman Jones) Pew**    Mulatto son of Nigra Jones and Joy Little; rebels against his boss, Judge Fox Clane, by renting a house in a white neighborhood in Carson McCullers's *Clock Without Hands.*

**Pewter**    Fat, gray cat who lives next to the post office but has been adopted by Harry; assists Mrs. Murphy in unraveling the mystery of the murders and disappearances, then helps her drive an injured man's Porsche in Rita Mae Brown's *Cat on the Scent.*

**Mark Peyser**    Works with Lexi at the L.S. Immigrant Service Center in Elizabeth Benedict's *Slow Dancing.*

**Wallace Pfef**    Speculator who promotes the cultivation of the sugar beet crop in Argus, North Dakota; sometime lover of Karl Adare; godfather of Dot Adare in Louise Erdrich's *The Beet Queen.*

**Leopold ("Poldek") Pfefferberg**    Jewish high school teacher and Polish Army veteran who becomes Oskar Schindler's black-market connection; is rescued from labor camp by Oskar Schindler and immigrates to the U.S. after World War II in Thomas Keneally's *Schindler's List.*

**Joy Pfisterer**    Professor of equine management at Moo University, happiest when around horses; dating Dean Jellinek; dissatisfied with her relationship and suffers from depression, eventually entering therapy in Jane Smiley's *Moo.*

**Morgan "Morty" Pfitzer (Ziff)**    James Bray's friend, a young hellion; has affair with Lila Lee Bray in Maureen Howard's *Natural History.*

**Phantom**    Embodiment of Communism and archenemy of Sam Slick in Robert Coover's *The Public Burning.*

**Annie Phelan**    Wife of Francis Phelan and mother of Peg Quinn and Billy Phelan; raises the children on her own; offers to let Francis move back home in William Kennedy's *Ironweed.*

**Francis Phelan**    Husband of Annie Phelan and father of Peg Quinn and Billy Phelan; ex-baseball player who is homeless and alcoholic; works in a graveyard and sees and talks to dead people; left home when he dropped his thirteen-day-old son and killed him, but returns after twenty-two years away from his family in William Kennedy's *Ironweed.*

**Troy Phelan**    Aged playboy billionaire on the verge of death who leaves his fortune to his illegitimate daughter, Rachel Lane, and leaves the rest of his large family virtually nothing in John Grisham's *The Testament.*

**William Francis (Billy) Phelan**    Brassy bowler, pool player, and gambler in William Kennedy's *Billy Phelan's Greatest Game.*

**Phil**    First lover of Miriam Berg, who shares her with Douglas MacArthur Jackson; drunkard and failed poet in Marge Piercy's *Small Changes.*

**Phil**    Charming, astute publisher of Baron R. and employer of Hugh Person; according to R., Phil would like him to write books less like his own but more like those of other authors in Vladimir Nabokov's *Transparent Things.*

**Phillips**    Princeton-educated official at the U.S. Embassy in Romania; in charge of Henry Bech's schedule in John Updike's *Bech: A Book.*

**Phil Phillips**    Friend and colleague of George Caldwell in John Updike's *The Centaur.*

**Undine Phillips**    Landlady of Kennerly Kendal in Reynolds Price's *The Surface of Earth.*

**Ursula Phillips**    Grandmother who tells the narrator about his grandfather's career as a writer killed by a lecherous Hollywood producer in Tennessee Williams's *Moise and the World of Reason.*

**The Philosopher**    Russian university student who seeks privacy in public lavatories and commits suicide in one of them in Jerzy Kosinski's *Steps.*

**Phyllis** Loquacious friend of Clyde Stout and his mother; urges Clyde to be a better friend of his mother and to stop letting people take advantage of him; works at the Dairy Freeze in Jack Matthews's *Hanger Stout, Awake!*

**Father Piaggio** Reclusive priest subsidized by the Cavaliere to keep a diary of Vesuvius since 1779, never leaving his hermit's post in Susan Sontag's *The Volcano Lover.*

**Piano Girl** See Angela Williams Lavoisier Torch.

**George Pickett** Confederate general famous for his charge against the enemy on Cemetery Ridge during the Battle of Gettysburg in Michael Shaara's *The Killer Angels.*

**Luray Spivey Pickett** Café waitress and stepdaughter-in-law of Caleb Peck in Anne Tyler's *Searching for Caleb.*

**August "Gus" Pierce** Haddan School student from New York City; loyal friend to Carlin Leander; harassed by his schoolmates in Chalk House until Harry McKenna suffocates him in a toilet and his schoolmates dump his body in the Haddan River in Alice Hoffman's *The River King.*

**Bill Pierce** Steve Bell's law partner and friend; the poor boy who managed to become the bulwark of the Bell family's firm; husband of Heidi Pierce in Mary McGarry Morris's *A Dangerous Woman.*

**Charlie Pierce** Seventeen-year-old son of Dick and May Pierce; he and his younger brother, Tom, own a potential fortune in the first editions that make up the library given to them by Miss Perry in John Casey's *Spartina.*

**Dick Pierce** Stubborn, proud, quick-tempered fisherman determined to build a forty-five-foot boat, *Spartina;* his life is altered by an affair with Elsie Buttrick, the resultant pregnancy, and a punishing hurricane that threatens to destroy Dick's home and *Spartina* in John Casey's *Spartina.*

**Edward (Robert Jeffers, Andrew Miller, John Simms, Arthur Wills) Pierce** Mastermind of the great train robbery of 1855 in Michael Crichton's *The Great Train Robbery.*

**Heidi Pierce** Wife of Bill Pierce, childless, has a baby voice in Mary McGarry Morris's *A Dangerous Woman.*

**Jeffrey (Jeff) Pierce** Young writer who becomes a literary celebrity; loves Corrine Calloway, the wife of his friend and editor, Russell; heroin addiction consumes his life; admission to Russell of a onetime affair with Corrinne pushes the Calloways toward divorce; his death from AIDS-related causes brings the divorced couple toward reconciliation in Jay McInerney's *Brightness Falls.*

**May Pierce** Dick Pierce's wife and mother of his two sons; as stubborn in her own way as Dick, she weathers Dick's obsession with *Spartina* and his affair with Elsie Buttrick in John Casey's *Spartina.*

**Philo Pierce** Margaret Flood's first editor; raises dogs and children in Bucks County; edits a left-wing journal, owns a publishing house, writes essays on the flagging culture-at-large in Maureen Howard's *Expensive Habits.*

**Tom Pierce** Fifteen-year-old son of Dick and May Pierce; he and his older brother, Charlie, own a potential fortune in the first editions that make up the library given to them by Miss Perry in John Casey's *Spartina.*

**Walter Pierce** Bereaved father of Gus Pierce; teaches at high school during the week and performs as a magician at children's parties on the weekends in Alice Hoffman's *The River King.*

**Mort Piercy** Overweight, mentally unbalanced political radical who involves Jules Wendall in the Detroit riots of the late 1960s in Joyce Carol Oates's *them.*

**Reverend Andrew (Andy) Pike** Deceased predecessor of Jethro Furber to whom Furber silently and perpetually confides in William Gass's *Omensetter's Luck.*

**Jack Wilson Pike** Animal lover who accompanies David Bell and friends on a trip west to make a film in Don DeLillo's *Americana.*

**Paul Pike** Reporter; has a lantern jaw; claims to be doing a story on High Balsam in Gail Godwin's *Evensong.*

**Pilate** Milkman's aunt; grandmother of Hagar; haunted by her father's ghost; accidental victim of a homicide in Toni Morrison's *Song of Solomon.*

**Pilgrim** Four-year-old, dark-bay gelding, Morgan horse, purchased from Kentucky farm; subject of Tom Booker's technique and therapeutic equine insight; resident of the Booker farm; companion to Grace Maclean in Nicholas Evans's *The Horse Whisperer.*

**Billy Pilgrim** Soldier, prisoner of war, optometrist, and time traveler; husband of Valencia Pilgrim and mate of Montana Wildhack on Tralfamadore in Kurt Vonnegut's *Slaughterhouse-Five.*

**Clotilda (Clo) Pilgrim** Guilt-ridden, widowed seamstress who owns and manages a rooming house; mother of Ruby Parker by her brother-in-law, Chester Jackson; suffocates her granddaughter, Addie Parker, in Cyrus Colter's *The Rivers of Eros.*

**The Pilgrim** See Sarah Abbott Maulsby.

**Valencia Merble Pilgrim** Overweight wife of Billy Pilgrim; dies of carbon monoxide poisoning driving to her wounded husband in Kurt Vonnegut's *Slaughterhouse-Five.*

**Adam Pilitzky** Catholic lord after whom the town of Pilitz is named, employer of Jacob Eliezer, and adulterous husband of Theresa Pilitzky; eventually hangs himself in Isaac Bashevis Singer's *The Slave.*

**Theresa Pilitzky**    Promiscuous wife of Adam Pilitzky resisted by Jacob Eliezer in Isaac Bashevis Singer's *The Slave.*

**Fleur Pillager**    Sometimes itinerant Chippewa medicine woman who cares for the injured Karl Adare and disabled veteran Russell Kashpaw in Louise Erdrich's *The Beet Queen.*

**Pills**    Blacksmith who allows Greer, Cameron, and Magic Child to spend the night in his stables in Richard Brautigan's *The Hawkline Monster.*

**Charles Pilsudski**    Black playwright and friend of Osgood Wallop in Peter De Vries's *Mrs. Wallop.*

**Henry Pimber**    Landlord of Brackett Omensetter; seduced by the mysterious ease of his tenant and finally driven to suicide by Omensetter's neglect of worship in William Gass's *Omensetter's Luck.*

**Pindi**    Niaruna Indian, wife of Tukanu, lover of Lewis Moon, and mother of New Person in Peter Matthiessen's *At Play in the Fields of the Lord.*

**Pinhead**    Idiot nephew of George Bennett; comes to Pickerel Beach in the care of Miss Whitaker and is murdered by Mickey McCane in Doris Betts's *The River to Pickle Beach.*

**Celia del Pino**    Wife of Jorge, mother of Lourdes, Felicia, and Javier, grandmother of Pilar Puente; matriarch of the family; as an old woman, she believes she is the primary lookout for a possible invasion of her area of the island, Santa Teresa del Mar; upon her husband's death she vows to support the Castro regime and reports to the sugar cane fields for volunteer harvesting; communicates telepathically with her granddaughter; serves as her community's judge of the People's Court; after Lourdes and Pilar visit her in Cuba, she drowns herself in Cristina Garcia's *Dreaming in Cuban.*

**Ivanito del Pino**    Grandson of Celia, son of Felicia; is sent away to boarding school with his sisters; learns English by listening to American radio stations from Key West, Florida; wants to become a radio personality; at his Aunt Lourdes's urging, he defects to America in Cristina Garcia's *Dreaming in Cuban.*

**Javier del Pino**    Son of Jorge and Celia; his mother's favorite; moves to Prague, marries a Czech, and has a daughter; returns to be nurtured by his mother when his wife leaves him for a professor from Minsk; after sleeping for two months in his father's bed, he becomes an alcoholic and dies in Cristina Garcia's *Dreaming in Cuban.*

**Jorge del Pino**    Survived by his wife, Celia, and children, Lourdes, his favorite, Felicia, and Javier; once a revolutionary supporter of Fidel Castro but late in life becomes anti-communist; dies of stomach cancer in a New York hospital; after forty days in the grave each evening at twilight he visits Lourdes herself in Cristina Garcia's *Dreaming in Cuban.*

**Praeger de Pinto**    Farseeing managing editor of *The Sun* newspaper, elected to mayor of New York City; counselor and friend of newspaper owner Harry Penn and in love with Penn's daughter Jessica in Mark Helprin's *Winter's Tale.*

**Moishe Pipik**    Middle-aged Jewish-American man; bears strong physical resemblance to the famous novelist Philip Roth, and claims that this is in fact also his name; founds Anti-Semites Anonymous, a self-help group designed to weaken anti-Semitic sentiment; also founds Diasporism, a movement intended to return Israeli Jews to their pre-Holocaust European homes; poses as novelist Roth to gain publicity and funding for this project, thus drawing Roth's curiosity and anger in Philip Roth's *Operation Shylock: A Confession.*

**Jasper Pistareen**    Seedy writer for and editor of a semipornographic tabloid newspaper in Paul Theroux's *Waldo.*

**Miss Jane (Jane Brown, Ticey) Pittman**    Strong-willed black woman whose life from the Civil War to the civil rights movement is chronicled in Ernest J. Gaines's *The Autobiography of Miss Jane Pittman.*

**Joe (Chief) Pittman**    Husband of Miss Jane Pittman and horse breaker in Ernest J. Gaines's *The Autobiography of Miss Jane Pittman.*

**Pixie**    Daughter of Cassandra and granddaughter of Skipper and Gertrude; born seven and one half months after Cassandra and Fernandez's wedding; sent to live with Gertrude's cousin after Cassandra's death in John Hawkes's *Second Skin.*

**Augustus (Gus) Plebesly**    Timorous Los Angeles policeman who learns to live with fear in Joseph Wambaugh's *The New Centurions.*

**Angus Plow**    Food-hating passenger on the *Here They Come* who plans to expose food as evil in Gregory Corso's *The American Express.*

**John Plumber**    NBC commentator who, with coanchor Donner, is manipulated by former Vice President Kealty into launching a smear campaign against Jack Ryan based on partial leaks of CIA records; goes public with an admission of his and Donner's violations of journalistic integrity, effectively ending Kealty's campaign to oust Ryan in Tom Clancy's *Executive Orders.*

**Marilee Plummer**    Young black woman who accuses Marcus Steadman of raping her; later murdered; friend of Thalia in Joyce Carol Oates's *What I Lived For.*

**Christopher (Bumpy) Plumpton**    Married to Prudence, sister of Federick Exley's wife, Patience; retreats from his disapproving wife into a bachelor haven in their spacious Westchester home; instantly befriends Exley, who becomes a regular Sunday afternoon companion in Frederick Exley's *A Fan's Notes.*

**Freddy Plympton**    English landowner whose estate contains a private zoo where Brewster Ashenden encounters a female bear in heat in *The Making of Ashenden,* a novella in Stanley Elkin's *Searches and Seizures.*

**Frank Pointer**   Team doctor for the New York Mammoths in Mark Harris's *It Looked Like For Ever*.

**Edward W. A. (Ned) Pointsman**   English doctor involved in Pavlovian experiments at The White Visitation; engineers a scheme to study Tyrone Slothrop's responses to rocket technology in Thomas Pynchon's *Gravity's Rainbow*.

**Franz Pökler**   German engineer manipulated by Lieutenant Weissmann to cooperate in the building of rocket 00000 in Thomas Pynchon's *Gravity's Rainbow*.

**Poland**   Singing whore who lives above the Breedloves in Toni Morrison's *The Bluest Eye*.

**Carolyn Polhemus**   Assistant prosecuting attorney for Kindle County whose schemes, lies, and illicit affairs eventually lead to her violent death in Scott Turow's *Presumed Innocent*.

**Lazar Poliakov**   Resident of Emma Lazarus Retirement Home known as "the Red Dwarf" due to his diminutive stature and Communist beliefs; briefly suspected by Otto Korner for the death of Nahum Lipschitz in Alan Isler's *The Prince of West End Avenue*.

**Sam Polidor**   Scheming landlord of Russel Wren in Thomas Berger's *Who Is Teddy Villanova?*

**Bart Pollock**   General sales manager of Knox Business Machines; offers Frank Wheeler a promotion that undermines the Wheelers' plans to leave for Europe in Richard Yates's *Revolutionary Road*.

**Polyeidus**   Tutor of Bellerophon; equipped with limited faculties in the *Bellerophoniad*, a novella in John Barth's *Chimera*.

**Chester (Chet) Hunnicutt Pomeroy**   Formerly famous performer who tries to deal with life after fame; seeks to renew his relationship with Catherine Clay and invents the death of his living father in Thomas McGuane's *Panama*.

**Cody Pomeray**   Charismatic ex-car thief turned railroad brakeman; husband of Evelyn Pomeray and idealized friend and traveling companion of Jack Duluoz in Jack Kerouac's *Visions of Cody*; also appears in *Book of Dreams*, *Big Sur*, and *Desolation Angels*.

**Cody (The Barber) Pomeray, Sr.**   Improvident drifter; father of Cody Pomeray in Jack Kerouac's *Visions of Cody*.

**Cynthia Pomeroy**   Seventeen-year-old who exemplifies the wisdom of the body and is attractive to a variety of male imaginations; marries Arnold Soby at the conclusion of Wright Morris's *What a Way to Go*.

**Evelyn Pomeray**   Second wife of Cody Pomeray and mother of their three children; participates in the taped conversations of Jack Kerouac's *Visions of Cody*; also appears in *Book of Dreams*, *Big Sur*, and *Desolation Angels*.

**Jim Pomeroy**   Brother of Chet Pomeroy; dies on the day of the Boston subway fire in Thomas McGuane's *Panama*.

**Kate Pomeroy**   Wife of Rob Pomeroy; cannot forget her affair with Tommy Ryden; gives Milo Mustian his second sexual experience in Reynolds Price's *A Generous Man*.

**Rob (Rooster) Pomeroy**   Sheriff who heads the search for Rato Mustian in Reynolds Price's *A Generous Man*.

**Pomoroy**   Executive editor at a commercial book publishing house; commissions a book on the Jewish-American experience from Bruce Gold in Joseph Heller's *Good as Gold*.

**Annie (Girl Fried Egg) Pompa**   Front-office chief of the newspaper *West Condon Chronicle* in Robert Coover's *The Origin of the Brunists*.

**Poo Poo**   Nightmare figure that haunts Bradly in William S. Burroughs's *The Ticket That Exploded*.

**Alison Poole**   Aspiring young actress living in New York surrounded by a disaffected and hedonistic circle of friends; describes a privileged yet unhappy childhood and continues to resent her divorced parents; seeks sex and companionship from men; promising relationship with Dean Chasen is destroyed by infidelity and the underlying unhappiness of her life; narrator of Jay McInerney's *Story of My Life*.

**Isabelle Poole**   Twenty-three-year-old socialite who shoots Private First Class Litwak; married for six months to a major who is away serving in Italy in Maureen Howard's *Natural History*.

**Rebecca (Becca) Poole**   Sister of Alison Poole; an attractive, pleasure-seeking young woman who uses up men, their credit cards, and drugs as fast as she can get them, without concern for the wreckage she leaves behind in Jay McInerney's *Story of My Life*.

**Bub Poor**   Younger son of Captain Red Poor; disguises himself as Joino to delay Skipper from finding Cassandra in John Hawkes's *Second Skin*.

**Jomo Poor**   Elder son of Captain Red Poor; lost a hand in the fighting at Salerno and wears a hook in John Hawkes's *Second Skin*.

**Red (Captain Red) Poor**   Father of Bub and Jomo Poor; owner and captain of the *Peter Poor* in John Hawkes's *Second Skin*.

**Pop**   Husband of Emmy (Mary Elizabeth), stepfather of her recently deceased adult son, and stepgrandfather of her grandson; originally from Maine, works in a printer shop in Brooklyn; is moved by the letter of admonishment and loving advice his stepson leaves to his son in Joseph McElroy's *The Letter Left to Me*.

**Popkoff (Dr. P.)**   Pharmacologist employed by NESTER in Scott Spencer's *Last Night at the Brain Thieves' Ball*.

**Dmitry Arkadeyevich Popov**   Former KGB liaison with European terrorist groups who is hired to ensure that William

Henriksen's security firm gets the contract for the Olympics in Australia; discovers the existence of Rainbow; plans the IRA assault on John Clark's and Domingo Chavez's wives; escapes to America; realizes that John Brightling is planning to depopulate the earth; informs CIA, and is allowed to go free in Tom Clancy's *Rainbow Six*.

**Clarence Popp**   Hired hand and close friend of Otto Neumiller; helps Charles Neumiller (I) bury Otto in Larry Woiwode's *Beyond the Bedroom Wall*.

**Coach Herman Popper**   High school coach who is cruel and abusive to boys and to his wife in Larry McMurtry's *The Last Picture Show*.

**Ruth Popper**   Ignored and lonely wife of Coach Herman Popper; lover of Sonny Crawford in Larry McMurtry's *The Last Picture Show*.

**The Popsicle Queen**   See Mrs. Schnitzer.

**Mr. Porculey**   Attorney defending Billy Devore; a man in his seventies, apparently has suffered a stroke, with a drooping eyelid and a sagging cheek in Donald E. Westlake's *The Ax*.

**Rev. Eclair Porkchop**   Bishop of Soulville and head of the Church of the Holy Mouth in Ishmael Reed's *The Free-Lance Pallbearers*.

**Porky**   Fat heroin dealer who supplies drugs to Terry Wilson and Teddy and who enjoys degrading his addicts in Donald Goines's *Dopefiend*.

**Henry Porter**   Tenant of Macon Dead II, lover of First Corinthians Dead, and member of the racial revenge group called the Seven Days in Toni Morrison's *Song of Solomon*.

**Mitch Porter**   Unctuous steakhouse owner who pampers Lou Engel and J. Henry Waugh in Robert Coover's *The Universal Baseball Association, Inc., J. Henry Waugh, Prop.*

**Walter (Moon) Porter**   Pimp on the lam after killing a corrupt policeman; former member of a black high school athletic team and neighborhood gang gathering for a birthday testimonial honoring Chappie Davis in John A. Williams's *The Junior Bachelor Society*.

**Pamela Porterfield**   Mother of Paul Porterfield; comes to terms with her son's sexuality and her own divorce in David Leavitt's *The Page Turner*.

**Paul Porterfield**   Young man and aspiring pianist who accepts that his playing talent is insufficient to achieve greatness as a pianist and learns to live with himself, his mother, and his sexuality in David Leavitt's *The Page Turner*.

**Alexander (Alex, Alex P, Breakie, Al Parsons, Alton Christian Peterson) Portnoy**   Member of the American Civil Liberties Union, assistant commissioner of human opportunity for New York City, and special counsel to a United States congressional subcommittee; describes his emotional and sexual trials to his psychiatrist; narrator of Philip Roth's *Portnoy's Complaint*.

**Hannah Portnoy**   See Hannah Portnoy Feibish.

**Harold (Heshie) Portnoy**   Handsome, muscular cousin of Alex Portnoy; prevented by his father from marrying Alice Dembosky and killed in World War II in Philip Roth's *Portnoy's Complaint*.

**Jack (Jake) Portnoy**   Devoted employee of the Boston and Northeastern Life Insurance Company, husband of Sophie Portnoy, and father of Alex Portnoy; perpetually constipated in Philip Roth's *Portnoy's Complaint*.

**Sophie Ginsky (Red) Portnoy**   Overprotective mother of Alex Portnoy and wife of Jack Portnoy in Philip Roth's *Portnoy's Complaint*.

**Wanda Jane "Jinx" Possesski**   Young, vibrant Polish-American nurse with a history of being drawn into religious movements; becomes charter member of Moishe Pipik's group, Anti-Semitics Anonymous; in Israel, attempts to make peace between Pipik and the real Philip Roth; sleeps with Roth, after which she and Pipik disappear from Israel to a fate Roth can only imagine in Philip Roth's *Operation Shylock: A Confession*.

**Laura Post**   Unloved by parents; works as a nanny; believes she has been touched by the Holy Spirit; after being fired by Ann Foster, commits suicide in Mary Gordon's *Men and Angels*.

**Mrs. Post**   Faculty adviser in Theodora's Honors in Home Economics program in Bette Pesetsky's *Midnight Sweets*.

**Thelma Postgate**   See M. Evans.

**Anastasia Petrovna Potapov**   See Madame Charles Chamar.

**Charlie Potteiger**   Former farmer who sold out to developers; owns Potteiger's Store, where George Caldwell shops for food nearly every day in John Updike's *The Centaur*.

**Benny Potter**   Wisecracking student at Steering School; works for a New York magazine in John Irving's *The World According to Garp*.

**Richard (Ricky) Potter**   Young composer in Alison Lurie's *Real People*.

**Calvin Potts**   Black alcoholic; one of ten Los Angeles policemen-protagonists in Joseph Wambaugh's *The Choirboys*.

**James (Alexis) Potts**   College dropout, heroin addict, black separatist/nationalist, and friend of Dunreith Smith in Cyrus Colter's *The Rivers of Eros*.

**Gregory Ulas (Greg) Powell**   Habitual criminal convicted of and sentenced to die for the murder of Ian Campbell in Joseph Wambaugh's *The Onion Field*.

**James Powell**   Boat builder who constructs a skiff for Thomas Skelton in Thomas McGuane's *Ninety-Two in the Shade*.

**Lamar Powell**   Unprincipled, egotistical man who engages in affairs with women for their money or status; has an affair with Ashton Main; ambitious to hold the position of president of the Confederacy in John Jakes's *Love and War*.

**King Powers**   Head of large criminal organization in Boston and surrounding communities; loaned businessman Harvey Shepard a large amount of money as part of a land development deal and is demanding Shepard's entire business as payment; eventually arrested after being tricked into a fake gun deal by Spenser, a private detective hired by Shepard in Robert B. Parker's *Promised Land*.

**Samuel (Sam) Powers**   Suitor of Hattie Sherbrooke in Nicholas Delbanco's *Possession*.

**Innokenti Poznikov**   Arrogant, profit-hungry son of Marina and Ivan Poznikov; initiates brutal exploitation of Aleutian natives and slaughter of otter population in James Michener's *Alaska*.

**Marina Poznikova**   Ambitious and astute fur trader in Siberia; sponsors explorations in Aleutian Islands in eighteenth century to catch otter; married first to Ivan Poznikov then to Trofim Zhdanko; mother of Innokenti Poznikov in James Michener's *Alaska*.

**Jack Pozzi**   Ambitious, doggedly determined young poker hustler who in a last desperate attempt to achieve his dreams of fame and fortune, risks all that remains of his friend's inheritance in a poker game; demonstrates a capacity for great loyalty in his friendship with Jack Nashe, ultimately rediscovering a faith in human relationships in Paul Auster's *The Music of Chance*.

**Anastasia (Annie, Chalkline Annie, Virgin Jekyll and Miss Hyde) Pratt**   Schoolgirl who becomes Joe Buck's first lover behind the screen of the World movie theatre in James Leo Herlihy's *Midnight Cowboy*.

**Chester (Chet) Pratt**   Author of *Burn All Your Cities*, a successful novel made into a movie; becomes Pamela Hendricks's lover when he is hired as a speechwriter for Robert Kennedy in Richard Yates's *Disturbing the Peace*.

**Dean (Whaddayamean) Pratt**   Wimpiest of the ten Los Angeles policemen-protagonists of Joseph Wambaugh's *The Choirboys*.

**Jeannine (Jen) Pratt**   New classmate who befriends Conrad Jarrett in Judith Guest's *Ordinary People*.

**Mama and Papa Pratt**   Wealthy Cape Coders and benign despots; parents of Phoebe, Orlando, and Maude Coffin Pratt in Paul Theroux's *Picture Palace*.

**Maude Coffin Pratt**   Outspoken photographer, incestuous lover, and narrator of Paul Theroux's *Picture Palace*.

**Orlando (Ollie) Pratt**   Brother of Maude Coffin Pratt and lover of his younger sister, Phoebe Pratt, in Paul Theroux's *Picture Palace*.

**Paris Pratt**   Wealthy, divorced, and glamorous employer of Sebastian Fry; art connoisseur and collector; begins affair with Sebastian in Diane Johnson's *Loving Hands at Home*.

**Phoebe Pratt**   Younger sister of Maude Coffin Pratt and lover of their brother, Orlando Pratt, in Paul Theroux's *Picture Palace*.

**Preacher**   See James D. Smathers, Jr.

**Bobby Prell**   Orphaned West Virginian and corporal who returns from duty in the South Pacific nearly incapacitated by leg injuries; refuses to allow army doctors to amputate his leg and ends up selling war bonds in James Jones's *Whistle*.

**Marshall Preminger**   Professional lecturer, perpetual graduate student, and youngest owner in a Chicago condominium complex; commits suicide by leaping from a balcony in *The Condominium*, a novella in Stanley Elkin's *Searches and Seizures*.

**Philip (Phil) Preminger**   Father of Marshall Preminger; squanders his son's inheritance on a late-in-life romance in *The Condominium*, a novella in Stanley Elkin's *Searches and Seizures*.

**Alice Grumbauer Prentice**   Devoted but irresponsible mother of Robert Prentice; unflaggingly attempts to achieve artistic and social success through sculpting fanciful garden statuary in Richard Yates's *A Special Providence*.

**Captain Geoffrey (Pirate) Prentice**   British officer in the Special Operations Executive; capable of having other people's fantasies and famous for his Banana Breakfasts in Thomas Pynchon's *Gravity's Rainbow*.

**George Prentice**   Former husband of Alice Prentice and father of Robert Prentice; stolid but kind man who is mystified by Alice's artistic and social aspirations in Richard Yates's *A Special Providence*.

**Robert J. (Bob, Bobby) Prentice**   Awkward, introspective, self-effacing son of Alice and George Prentice; attains some measure of independence from his mother through infantry service in World War II in Richard Yates's *A Special Providence*.

**Susan Prentice**   Wife of Wayne Prentice; assistant director of UnicCare, charitable organization funded mostly by New York State and partly by tobacco companies; murdered by Bryce Proctorr in Donald E. Westlake's *The Hook*.

**Wayne Prentice**   Forty-four-year-old unsuccessful author; husband of Susan Prentice; writes seven books under his own name and four books under the pseudonym Tim Fleet; Bryce Proctorr decides to publish Prentice's next story under Proctorr's name, as long as Prentice murders Proctorr's wife, Lucie, and split Bryce's $1,100,000 advance in Donald E. Westlake's *The Hook*.

**Portia Prentiss**    Young black woman from a deprived background; student of Jane Clifford in Gail Godwin's *The Odd Woman*.

**Francis (Frank, Rector of Justin) Prescott**    Episcopal priest; founder and longtime headmaster of an exclusive boys' boarding school in Massachusetts; central character in Louis Auchincloss's *The Rector of Justin*.

**Harriet Winslow Prescott**    Wife of Francis Prescott; austere intellectual from an old Boston family in Louis Auchincloss's *The Rector of Justin*.

**Selina Rosheen Prescott**    Wife of Wylie Prescott; former rodeo star who, following her husband's death, becomes the richest woman in Texas in William Goyen's *Come, The Restorer*.

**Wylie Prescott**    Husband of Selina Rosheen Prescott; responsible for the destruction of the wilderness and for the growth of the polluted city of Rose, Texas, which he helped found in William Goyen's *Come, The Restorer*.

**Norman Pressman**    Husband of Sandy and father of Jennifer and Bucky; does not want to sell their house to an African-American family; owns a dry cleaning franchise he inherited from his father in Judy Blume's *Wifey*.

**Sandy Pressman**    Unhappy in her marriage, she has affairs with her brother-in-law Gordon, her best friend's husband, Vincent Mosley, and her old sweetheart, Shep Resnick; contracts gonorrhea, almost shoots herself, and then confesses all to her husband and stays with him in Judy Blume's *Wifey*.

**Drew Preston**    Blonde bombshell whom Dutch Schultz takes from Bo Weinberg, his former confederate; Billy Bathgate so admires her that he helps her to escape the mob in E. L. Doctorow's *Billy Bathgate*.

**Billy Pretty**    Man in his seventies who writes the Home News page for the *Gammy Bird*, devoted to such items as local gossip and recipes; is impotent; takes Quoyle out on his skiff and shows him landmarks of the sea in E. Annie Proulx's *The Shipping News*.

**Willard Pretty Boy**    Handsome young Native American man on a Montana reservation who is badly disfigured by an exploding land mine in World War II; his relationship with other characters is revealed only in the final section of Michael Dorris's *A Yellow Raft in Blue Water*.

**Mrs. Prevost**    Neighbor of Birdy; raises canaries in William Wharton's *Birdy*.

**Countess Cordula (Cordula Tobak) de Prey**    Cousin of Percy de Prey, friend of Ada Veen, and, at one time, mistress of Van Veen in Vladimir Nabokov's *Ada*.

**Count Percy de Prey**    Stout, foppish neighbor of the Veens of Ardis; his supposed affair with Ada Veen drives Van Veen to fits of jealousy and torment in Vladimir Nabokov's *Ada*.

**Laura (Mrs. de Shamble) Pribble**    Retired motion picture actress and, under an assumed name, brokerage client and briefly paramour of Joe Sandwich; finally marries Uncle Hamilton in Peter De Vries's *The Vale of Laughter*.

**Adah Price**    Brilliant, mute fourteen-year-old girl who moves from Bethlehem, Georgia, to the Kilanga Mission in the Belgian Congo with her family; daughter of Nathan and Orleana Price, twin sister of Leah Price, sister of Rachel and Ruth May Price; suffers from hemiplegia, but begins to speak when she moves back to Bethlehem; regains use of her right side after physical therapy; attends medical school and has a career researching viruses in Barbara Kingsolver's *The Poisonwood Bible*.

**Andrea Price**    Secret Service agent abruptly promoted to head of the Personal Protection Detail for President Jack Ryan; spearheads the initial response to the attempted kidnapping of Ryan's daughter; apprehends Iranian "sleeper" agent and fellow Secret Service officer Jeff Raman; marries Pat O'Day in Tom Clancy's *Executive Orders*.

**Dolores Price**    Raped when she was thirteen; mother Bernice dies in a car accident; drops out of college; ends up at Gracewood Institute, a mental hospital; recovers, marries Dante Davis, divorces him after her grandmother dies; meets Thayer Kitchen and marries him in Wally Lamb's *She's Come Undone*.

**Erline Price**    Young woman Glen Davis rapes and emotionally destroys after his release from prison in Larry Brown's *Father and Son*.

**Ian (Pricey) Price**    English mining associate of Oliver Ward; severely beaten in a mining dispute in Wallace Stegner's *Angle of Repose*.

**Leah Price**    Fourteen-year-old tomboy who moves in 1959 from Bethlehem, Georgia, to the Kilanga Mission in the Belgian Congo with her family; daughter of Nathan and Orleana Price, twin sister of Adah Price, sister of Rachel and Ruth May Price; marries Anatole and has four sons; dedicates her life to improving social conditions in Africa in Barbara Kingsolver's *The Poisonwood Bible*.

**Louanne Price**    Gets pregnant by Phillip Materson while he is engaged to Celia in Joan Chase's *During the Reign of the Queen of Persia*.

**Mrs. Price**    Wife of Richard Price in Frances Sherwood's *Vindication*.

**Nathan Price**    Domineering Baptist missionary husband of Orleanna Price, abusive father of Rachel, Leah, Adah, and Ruth May Price; World War II veteran consumed with guilt because the rest of his company died on the death march from Bataan; eventually deserted by his family; becomes an itinerate preacher in the jungle; dies in a fire set by outraged Africans in Barbara Kingsolver's *The Poisonwood Bible*.

**Orleanna Price**    Passive woman who moves with her family to the Kilanga Mission in the Belgian Congo in 1959; wife of

Baptist evangelist Nathan Price and mother of Rachel, Leah, Adah, and Ruth May Price; leaves her husband after their child Ruth May dies in Barbara Kingsolver's *The Poisonwood Bible.*

**Rachel Price**   Vain, attractive teenage girl who moves to the Kilanga Mission in the Belgian Congo with her family; daughter of Nathan and Orleana Price, sister of Leah, Adah, and Ruth May Price; becomes lover of Eeben Axelroot; marries Daniel DuPree; divorces and marries Remy Fairley, owner of the Equatorial Hotel in the French Congo; inherits and runs the hotel in Barbara Kingsolver's *The Poisonwood Bible.*

**Dr. Richard Price**   Husband of Mrs. Price; an acquaintance of Mary Wollstonecraft; a famous Dissenting minister, who is a friend of Jefferson, Franklin Condorcet, Samuel Johnson, and Priestley in Frances Sherwood's *Vindication.*

**Ruth May Price**   Sweet five-year-old girl who moves with her family to the Kilanga Mission in the Belgian Congo; daughter of Nathan and Orleana Price, sister of Leah, Adah, and Rachel Price; dies of a snakebite in Barbara Kingsolver's *The Poisonwood Bible.*

**Timothy Price**   Handsome, rich best friend of Patrick Bateman; works on Wall Street; quick-tempered; is totally unaware of Patrick's secret life in Bret Easton Ellis's *American Psycho.*

**Priest**   Old junky who sells Christmas seals in William S. Burroughs's *Nova Express* and *The Wild Boys;* gives his last fix to a cripple in pain in *Exterminator!*

**Alexander Priest**   Brother of Lucius Priest II in William Faulkner's *The Reivers.*

**Alison Lessep Priest**   Wife of Maury Priest I and mother of Lucius Priest II in William Faulkner's *The Reivers.*

**Lessep Priest**   Brother of Lucius Priest II in William Faulkner's *The Reivers.*

**Lucius (Boss) Priest (I)**   Father of Maury Priest I and bank president in William Faulkner's *The Reivers.*

**Lucius (Loosh) Priest (II)**   Grandson of Lucius Priest I in William Faulkner's *The Reivers.*

**Lucius Priest (III)**   Grandson of Lucius Priest II and narrator of William Faulkner's *The Reivers.*

**Maury Priest (I)**   Son of Lucius Priest I and father of Lucius Priest Il in William Faulkner's *The Reivers.*

**Maury Priest (II)**   Brother of Lucius Priest II in William Faulkner's *The Reivers.*

**Sarah Edmonds Priest**   Grandmother of Lucius Priest II in William Faulkner's *The Reivers.*

**Nina Gitana de la Primavera**   Captivating actress befriended by Renate and Bruce in Anaïs Nin's *Collages.*

**Prince O'Light**   Minister of Church Zealous who tries to save Savata in William Goyen's *The Fair Sister.*

**John Prince**   New York fashion designer who fires Valentine O'Neill when she begins producing her own designs in Judith Krantz's *Scruples.*

**Mort Prince**   Writer of clichéd existential novels about salvation through love in Walker Percy's *The Last Gentleman.*

**Doctor Prine**   Sadistic female psychiatrist in Thomas Berger's *Regiment of Women.*

**Julia Prine**   Friend of Frances Beecham; tall and slender; a people collector, the more offbeat, the better; intelligent with natural goodness in Mary McGarry Morris's *A Dangerous Woman.*

**Artie Pringle**   Boyhood friend of Billy Bumpers; lecture agent and leader of the Baredevils orgy group in Peter De Vries's *I Hear America Swinging.*

**Dash Pringle**   Daughter of Lucius Pringle and love interest of Marshall Pearl and Farrell in Mark Helprin's *Refiner's Fire.*

**Lucius Pringle**   Friend of Marshall Pearl; British colonist in Jamaica who tries, because he lost his father and three brothers to raids by Rastas, to destroy the Rasta camp, although he has only limited success in Mark Helprin's *Refiner's Fire.*

**Mary-Ann Pringle**   Girlfriend of Rusty Godowsky, object of Myra Breckinridge's desire, and eventual wife of Myron Breckinridge in Gore Vidal's *Myra Breckinridge.*

**Pik Prinsloo**   Seventy-one-year-old digger in the diamond mines of South Africa; unmarried and generally unsociable; his dream of finding a large diamond is realized in James A. Michener's *The Covenant.*

**Priscus**   Hellenist scholar and philosopher who becomes Julian's friend and mentor; narrates part of Gore Vidal's *Julian.*

**Muriel Pritchett**   Gregarious young dog trainer in Baltimore, Maryland; has one young son, Alexander; begins affair with Macon Leary; is left alone when Macon returns to his wife; fulfills a lifelong dream to travel to Paris at exactly the same time that Macon will be there, making for a convenient reconciliation in Anne Tyler's *The Accidental Tourist.*

**Andreas Procopirios**   Eldest son of Apelis and Nicoletta Procopirios in Nicholas Delbanco's *The Martlet's Tale.*

**Apelis Procopirios**   Middle, and favorite, son of Orsetta Procopirios in Nicholas Delbanco's *The Martlet's Tale.*

**Eleni Procopirios**   Wife of Manos Procopirios in Nicholas Delbanco's *The Martlet's Tale.*

**Manos Procopirios**   Youngest son of Orsetta Procopirios in Nicholas Delbanco's *The Martlet's Tale.*

**Nicoletta Procopirios**   Deceased wife of Apelis Procopirios and mother of Andreas and Sotiris Procopirios in Nicholas Delbanco's *The Martlet's Tale*.

**Orsetta Procopirios**   Eighty-year-old matriarch of the Procopirios family and holder of a hidden family treasure; mother of Manos, Apelis, and Triphon Procopirios; dying of peritonitis in Nicholas Delbanco's *The Martlet's Tale*.

**Sotiris (Sotis) Procopirios**   Son of Apelis Procopirios and grandson of Orsetta Procopirios, who entrusts him with the supposed location of a hidden family treasure in Nicholas Delbanco's *The Martlet's Tale*.

**Triphon Procopirios**   Eldest son of Orsetta Procopirios; now living in the United States in Nicholas Delbanco's *The Martlet's Tale*.

**Frank Proctor**   Economics expert and CIA agent in the Aegean; the locals indirectly blame him for the drowned students' deaths in Mary Lee Settle's *Blood Tie*.

**P. G. (Piggy) Proctor**   Nicole's agent and Jane's friend; sends Nicole tapes instead of letters or phone calls when she is in Vermont; takes care of Jane's wedding and funeral arrangements in Ann Beattie's *Love Always*.

**Barry Proctorr**   Nineteen-year-old son of Bryce Proctorr, and English literature major at Rutgers in Donald E. Westlake's *The Hook*.

**Betsy Proctorr**   Twenty-three-year-old daughter of Bryce Proctorr, a postgraduate architecture student at Brown in Donald E. Westlake's *The Hook*.

**Bryce Proctorr**   Forty-four-year-old author with a $1,100,000 advance and writer's block; decides to publish Wayne Prentice's story under his own name and split his advance on the condition that Wayne murders his wife, Lucie; goes insane and murders Wayne Prentice's wife, Susan, in Donald E. Westlake's *The Hook*.

**Ellen Proctorr**   First wife of Bryce Proctorr in Donald E. Westlake's *The Hook*.

**Lucie Proctorr**   Wife getting divorced from Bryce Proctorr in Donald E. Westlake's *The Hook*.

**Tom Proctorr**   Twenty-one-year-old son of Bryce Proctorr, studying engineering at MIT in Donald E. Westlake's *The Hook*.

**Benny Profane**   Former seaman called a yo-yo for riding back and forth on subway trains; involved with Josefina Mendoza, Rachel Owlglass, and the Whole Sick Crew; left on Malta by Herbert Stencil in Thomas Pynchon's *V.*

**Arista (Sister X) Prolo**   Exotic dancer who confronts sexism and racism in her pursuit of international artistic success as the First Lady of American Jazz Dance in Carlene Hatcher Polite's *Sister X and the Victims of Foul Play*.

**Victor Propp**   Respected writer who suffers from writer's block after the critical and popular success of his first novel twenty-five years before; becomes famous for the book he is always writing in Jay McInerney's *Brightness Falls*.

**Mr. Prospero**   Vice principal of the high school; catches Gretel Samuelson and Eugene Kessler selling term papers and suspends them in Alice Hoffman's *Local Girls*.

**Mary (Pokey) Prothero**   Heavy, cheerful daughter of a wealthy New York family; member of the Group in Mary McCarthy's *The Group*.

**Caleb Proudhammer**   Disgruntled Harlem youth who becomes a preacher after a series of misadventures that include being tortured on a southern prison farm; brother of Leo Proudhammer in James Baldwin's *Tell Me How Long the Train's Been Gone*.

**Leo Proudhammer**   Black actor from an impoverished Harlem family who struggles to establish himself in the white world of theater and movies; the effort leads to exhaustion and temporary heart failure; lover of Barbara King and Black Christopher; narrator of James Baldwin's *Tell Me How Long the Train's Been Gone*.

**Lois Provo**   Young woman who helps with the snake show at the fair and provides Milo Mustian with his first sexual experience in Reynolds Price's *A Generous Man*.

**Selma Provo**   Aunt of Lois Provo, later revealed as her unmarried mother in Reynolds Price's *A Generous Man*.

**Jane Provost**   See Jean Dean.

**Thomas Prowse**   Elderly accountant of Frances Beecham in Mary McGarry Morris's *A Dangerous Woman*.

**Wavey Prowse**   Second wife of Quoyle; mother of Herry, child with Down's syndrome; lost her philandering husband in boating accident; remains loyal to dead husband until she, like Quoyle, realizes that love does not have to hurt in E. Annie Proulx's *The Shipping News*.

**Prudence**   Pregnant wife of Sky; rents Fish and Katie Fisher's house in Sandra Scofield's *Beyond Deserving*.

**Bill Prufrock**   Half-breed Indian, writer for comedian Harry Mercury, and suitor and possible husband of Lee Mercury; his surname is said to mean Rolling Stone in Peter De Vries's *Through the Fields of Clover*.

**Cephus Prynne**   Chief Factor in Fort St. Sebastian; murdered by Gabriel Legge; found with letters of the English alphabet carved into his body in Bharati Mukherjee's *The Holder of the World*.

**Ms. Prynne**   Manager of an omega-shaped desert resort for errant clergy; recipient of the Reverend Thomas Marshfield's amorous letters and sermons and ultimately Marshfield's lover in John Updike's *A Month of Sundays*.

**Fabio Pucci**   Dolores Price's guidance counselor in high school; he convinces her to go to college after her mother's death; his partner, Gary, dies of AIDS in Wally Lamb's *She's Come Undone.*

**Murray (The Goose) Pucinski**   Killer for Legs Diamond; stalks Diamond and Speed Fogarty after being double-crossed in William Kennedy's *Legs.*

**Brigadier Ernest Pudding**   Senile figurehead at The White Visitation; dotes on his recollections of World War I trench warfare; involved in a sadomasochistic relationship with Katje Borgesius in Thomas Pynchon's *Gravity's Rainbow.*

**Lourdes Puente**   Daughter of Jorge and Celia del Pino, wife of Rufino, mother of Pilar; believes that a droopy eye enables her to see what others can't; raped by a soldier who carves on her stomach; owns the Yankee Doodle Bakery in Brooklyn; volunteers as an auxiliary policewoman; accompanies her daughter to Cuba, where she sponsors Ivanito del Pino's defection in Cristina Garcia's *Dreaming in Cuban.*

**Pilar Puente**   First and favorite grandchild of Celia del Pino; daughter of Lourdes and Rufino; is an accomplished painter; communicates telepathically with Celia; persuades her mother to accompany her to Cuba to meet her grandmother in Cristina Garcia's *Dreaming in Cuban.*

**Rufino Puente**   Husband of Lourdes and father of Pilar; buys a warehouse to make an art studio for his daughter and a workshop for himself; frequently has affairs so as to stay away from his wife in Cristina Garcia's *Dreaming in Cuban.*

**Dixie Lee Pugh**   Alcoholic, white blues singer from Louisiana; Dave Robicheaux's college roommate; served time in prison for manslaughter, where he met Sally Dio; works for Dio as lease agent in a front to monopolize key real estate in Montana in James Lee Burke's *Black Cherry Blues.*

**Harold Herman Pugh**   Murderer of Lois Fazenda in John Gregory Dunne's *True Confessions.*

**Bartolomeo (Tolo) Pumo**   One-eyed son of Efrosina Puma; becomes the servant of the Cavaliere in Susan Sontag's *The Volcano Lover.*

**Efrosina Pumo**   Famous sibyl in Susan Sontag's *The Volcano Lover.*

**The Pumpkin**   See Kay Campbell.

**Ed Punch**   Managing editor for *The Mockingbird Record* in New York; hires Quoyle during times his own children aren't home from college to work for him in E. Annie Proulx's *The Shipping News.*

**Eunice Punch**   Widowed mother of Mary Spofford; marries Dr. Emil Rappaport despite her daughter's efforts to match her with Frank Spofford in Peter De Vries's *Reuben, Reuben.*

**Cletus Purcel**   Onetime partner to Dave Robicheaux when both worked as homicide detectives for the New Orleans Police Department; leaves the force after accepting money to commit a murder; works as bodyguard and driver for Sally Dio in James Lee Burke's *Black Cherry Blues.*

**Frank Purcell**   Former Texas Ranger, currently security guard employed by Charlie McFarland; was instrumental in eliciting from Louie Bronk his confession of the murder of Tiny McFarland in Mary Willis Walker's *The Red Scream.*

**L. Westminster (Brother Dallas, Plucky) Purcell III**   Goofy-grinned, aristocratic ex-Duke halfback, drug dealer, abortion arranger, and fake priest; brings back The Corpse from the Vatican; shot to death while attempting to board the Icarus XC solar ballooon in Tom Robbins's *Another Roadside Attraction.*

**Purple Better One**   See Homer Mandrill.

**Nancy Putnam**   College girlfriend of Pookie Adams in John Nichols's *The Sterile Cuckoo.*

**Harry Pyecraft**   Motel owner whose Dew Drop Inn, scene of Gowan McGland's amours and suicide, becomes a literary tourist attraction in Peter De Vries's *Reuben, Reuben.*

**Noah Pym**   Tenacious Boston captain of whaling ship; one of the first Americans to sail through Aleutian Islands to Arctic Circle in James Michener's *Alaska.*

**Jack Python**   Popular television talk-show host and womanizer until he meets the love of his life, Jade Johnson; brother of television star Silver Anderson in Jackie Collins's *Hollywood Husbands.*

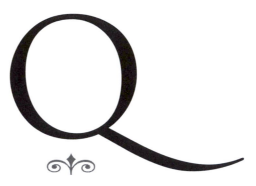

**Xi Qiaumo**  Former intelligence officer in Korea, now Chinese Central Committee member; expert in archeological research; member of The World Message Consortium and The Five in Carl Sagan's *Contact*.

**Catherine (Cat) Quarles**  Affectionate daughter of Eliza Quarles and mother of an illegitimate son in Alice Adams's *Listening to Billie*.

**Eliza Erskine Hamilton (Liza) Quarles**  Passionate woman who struggles to find success and independence; protagonist of Alice Adams's *Listening to Billie*.

**Evan Quarles**  Overweight, heavy-drinking older husband of Eliza Quarles; dies from an overdose of sleeping pills in Alice Adams's *Listening to Billie*.

**Sabina Quarles**  Lead actress in the television series *Manhattan*, a role that leads her from respected actress to Hollywood superstar in Danielle Steel's *Secrets*.

**Hazel Quarrier**  American missionary, wife of Martin Quarrier, and mother of Billy Quarrier; driven mad by the hardships of the South American jungle in Peter Matthiessen's *At Play in the Fields of the Lord*.

**Martin (Mart) Quarrier**  American missionary, husband of Hazel Quarrier, and father of Billy Quarrier; murdered by one of the Indians he attempts to convert in Peter Matthiessen's *At Play in the Fields of the Lord*.

**William (Billie) Martin Quarrier**  Son of Martin and Hazel Quarrier; accidental victim of his parents' misguided efforts as missionaries; dies of blackwater fever in Peter Matthiessen's *At Play in the Fields of the Lord*.

**Queen Charlotte**  Sister of Marie Antoinette; fancies herself a patron of enlightenment; has borne sixteen children; friends with Emma in Susan Sontag's *The Volcano Lover*.

**Queen Mother**  Mother of Jadav Singh in Bharati Mukherjee's *The Holder of the World*.

**Edward Quill**  Flamboyant friend of Dara and Jean; inherits money from Mrs. Aldridge; makes a one-woman play out of Mrs. Aldridge's autobiography, which Dara performs, unsuccessfully, in New York in Ann Beattie's *My Life, Starring Dara Falcon*.

**Virginia Quilty**  Beautiful pursuer of Randy Rivers, then Osgood Wallop, whom she marries in Peter De Vries's *Mrs. Wallop*.

**Emmett Quincy**  Member of Ned Pepper's outlaw gang that holds captive Mattie Ross, Rooster Cogburn, and LaBoeuf in Charles Portis's *True Grit*.

**B. A. Quinlan**  Unemotional head coach of the Dallas Cowboys, he would rather deal with ideas than with people in Peter Gent's *North Dallas Forty*.

**Longus Quinlan**  The Devores' marriage counselor; an African-American man in Donald E. Westlake's *The Ax*.

**James (Jim) Quinn**  Detroit businessman who owns a cabin on the grounds of the Centennial Club; longtime friend who always loses wax bullet duels with Vernor Stanton in Thomas McGuane's *The Sporting Club*.

**Peg Quinn**  Daughter of Francis and Annie Phelan; wife of George and mother of Daniel; a beautiful professional secretary; does not forgive Francis for leaving the family, but later accepts Francis back into their lives in William Kennedy's *Ironweed*.

**Sam Quinn**  Former stuntman; friend who supplies drugs to Gordon Walker in Robert Stone's *Children of Light.*

**Quint**  Amity fisherman hired to hunt the Great White Shark; killed during the hunt in Peter Benchley's *Jaws.*

**John Quint**  Articulate, self-confident soldier with whom Robert Prentice longs to establish a close buddy relationship; killed by a land mine while Prentice is hospitalized with pneumonia in Richard Yates's *A Special Providence.*

**Quoyle**  Mediocre newspaperman whose wife, Petal Bear, cheats on him before she dies in a car accident; moves with his aunt from New York to Newfoundland; finds his niche as reporter of the shipping news in the Newfoundland local newspaper, *Gammy Bird;* father of Bunny and Sunshine; marries Wavey Prowse in E. Annie Proulx's *The Shipping News.*

**Mr. R. (Baron R.)**   Demanding German writer whose books Hugh Person edits; confesses before he dies that his stepdaughter, Julia Moore, is the only woman he ever loved in Vladimir Nabokov's *Transparent Things*.

**Mrs. Rabbage**   Maid who works for the Turners in Alison Lurie's *Love and Friendship*.

**Jonathan "Jack" Rabbit**   Ninth-grade boy with a crush on Gretel Samuelson, who thinks he is terribly boring until he stops writing and calling her in Alice Hoffman's *Local Girls*.

**Lynne Rabinowitz**   Civil rights activist, wife of Truman Held, and mother of Camara in Alice Walker's *Meridian*.

**Rachel**   Slave who helps Leslie Collins care for a baby boy rejected by his mother in Harriette Simpson Arnow's *The Kentucky Trace*.

**Philip Rack**   Young married musician who gives piano lessons to Lucette Veen while reputedly carrying on a love affair with Ada Veen; Van Veen wants to challenge him to a duel, but changes his mind when he sees that Rack is dying in Vladimir Nabokov's *Ada*.

**Mrs. Rackover**   Housekeeper for the Levs who constantly rebukes Asher Lev in Chaim Potok's *My Name Is Asher Lev*.

**Nadine Rademacher**   Nude storyteller who leaves New York and travels to Texas with Glen Selvy in Don DeLillo's *Running Dog*.

**Male (Rad) Raditzer**   Sinister and unsought companion of Charlie Stark; falls overboard to his death in Peter Matthiessen's *Raditzer*.

**Rosemary Radley**   Television and film actress in London with a history of brief and impetuous affairs; alcoholic and psychotic with split personalities; angry at men in general; dramatic and unpredictable in her love affair with Fred in Alison Lurie's *Foreign Affairs*.

**Paul Rafferty**   Attorney for Alice Goodwin; friend of Dan and Theresa Collins, whom Alice and Howard first meet at a party; fails to get bail reduced sufficiently to allow Alice to return home as she awaits trial; urges Howard Goodwin not to sell the farm and Alice Goodwin not to testify in Jane Hamilton's *A Map of the World*.

**Ragnell**   Wife of Gawaine in Thomas Berger's *Arthur Rex*.

**Rahim**   Soul at the seventh aspect of Ralph Himebaugh in Robert Coover's *The Origin of the Brunists*.

**Raider (Big Raider)**   Jazz singer and boyfriend of Osella Barnes in Diane Johnson's *The Shadow Knows*.

**Faye (Faysie) Raider**   Roommate and lover of Molly Bolt at the University of Florida in Rita Mae Brown's *Rubyfruit Jungle*.

**Railroad Tommy**   Co-owner of the local barbershop and member of the racial revenge group called the Seven Days in Toni Morrison's *Song of Solomon*.

**Rain**   Female follower of Coransee in Octavia E. Butler's *Patternmaster*.

**John Rainbird**   Vietnam veteran who worked as a professional assassin for the Shop; he obsesses over tracking down Charlie and Andy McGee; kills Andy McGee and then is incinerated by Charlie in Stephen King's *Firestarter*.

**Rainbow**    Village resident who rapes a young Jewish woman and, finding himself trapped by a vaginal spasm, mutilates and kills her in Jerzy Kosinski's *The Painted Bird*.

**Colonel Rainsborough**    Officer in Cromwell's army who speaks out for greater democracy; reassigned to the North and mysteriously murdered, possibly by Cromwell's agents, in Mary Lee Settle's *Prisons*.

**Raisl**    Wife who has deserted Yakov Bok in Bernard Malamud's *The Fixer*.

**Carew Ralegh**    Sir Walter Ralegh's son in George Garrett's *Death of the Fox*.

**Elizabeth Throckmorton (Bess) Ralegh**    Wife of Sir Walter Ralegh in George Garrett's *Death of the Fox*.

**Sir Walter (Wat) Ralegh**    Poet, scholar, soldier, and courtier awaiting execution in George Garrett's *Death of the Fox*.

**Ralph**    Lover of Deirdre, who left Ben for him; younger, more handsome, and smarter than Ben in Bette Pesetsky's *Midnight Sweets*.

**Ralph**    Friend of Wendy Gahaghan; agrees to accept her and her unborn baby in Alison Lurie's *The War Between the Tates*.

**Jeff Raman**    Iranian "sleeper" agent who maintains his cover for years to become an American Secret Service agent on the Personal Protection Detail for President Jack Ryan; is discovered by Pat O'Day and arrested by Andrea Price in Tom Clancy's *Executive Orders*.

**White-Eye Ramford**    Blind New Orleans blues guitarist and street-musician; partner of Caleb Peck in Anne Tyler's *Searching for Caleb*.

**Ramirez**    Attentive hotel owner in Majorca in Gail Godwin's *The Perfectionists*.

**Marco Ramius**    Wily Soviet submarine captain; born a Lithuanian, the son of a high party official; he attempts to defect with a super-secret missile submarine in Tom Clancy's *The Hunt for Red October*.

**Ramos**    Psychiatrist for Janet Ross in Michael Crichton's *The Terminal Man*.

**Madame Ramoz**    Dictator's wife persuaded by George Levanter to influence the release of political prisoners in Jerzy Kosinski's *Blind Date*.

**Benjamin Turnbull Rand**    Dying chairman of the board of First American Financial Corporation and adviser to the president of the United States, befriends Chance and launches his political career in Jerzy Kosinski's *Being There*.

**Elizabeth Eve (EE) Rand**    Sexually frustrated wife of billionaire power broker Benjamin Turnbull Rand; falls in love with Chance in Jerzy Kosinski's *Being There*.

**Julie (Aunt Julie, Miss Julie) Rand**    Elderly aunt of Marcus Payne; has knowledge of Marshall Hebert's earlier criminal acts in Ernest J. Gaines's *Of Love and Dust*.

**Sam Rand**    Arkansas born infantryman who becomes a companion of John Quint and Robert Prentice in Richard Yates's *A Special Providence*.

**Evelyn Randall**    Attractive stepmother of Karen Randall; married to Joshua Randall, but having an affair with his brother, Peter Randall; drives Karen Randall to the hospital after her abortion in Jeffery Hudson's *A Case of Need*.

**Joshua (JD) Randall**    Karen Randall's father; husband of Evelyn Randall and brother of Peter Randall; wealthy, powerful, and cruel cardiac surgeon in Jeffery Hudson's *A Case of Need*.

**Karen Randall**    Troubled nineteen-year-old who goes to Arthur Lee asking for an abortion; mean and lying drug user; bleeds to death in the emergency room after a failed abortion, although she is not pregnant, in Jeffery Hudson's *A Case of Need*.

**Merrill Randall**    Elegant poet; Jack Duluoz walks out on Randall's poetry reading in Jack Kerouac's *Desolation Angels*.

**Peter Randall**    Brother of Joshua Randall; internist who performs abortions; very social and well liked; is having an affair with his brother's wife, Evelyn, in Jeffery Hudson's *A Case of Need*.

**Jim Randolph**    Married college instructor whom Maureen Wendall seduces and marries in Joyce Carol Oates's *them*.

**Varnum Random**    Poetry consultant for the Library of Congress and patient host of Raphael Urso and Jack Duluoz in Jack Kerouac's *Desolation Angels*.

**Ranec**    Talented, dark-skinned ivory carver who has been adopted by the Lion Camp; forces Ayla to choose between her two destinies: life with Ranec in the Lion Camp, or following Jondalar back to his own people in Jean Auel's *The Mammoth Hunters*.

**Aimes Rankin**    Cora's soft-spoken lover; a labor organizer who is killed at the munitions factory during a demonstration in Rita Mae Brown's *Six of One*.

**Peggy Rankin**    High school English teacher and occasional lover of Jacob Horner in John Barth's *The End of the Road*.

**Minnie Ransom**    Faith healer; dresses flamboyantly; loves jazz; in touch with ancient and spiritual worlds; works at the Southwest Community Infirmity; heals Velma Henry in Toni Cade Bambara's *The Salt Eaters*.

**Sammy Ransom**  Young black man and putative father of Mildred Sutton's illegitimate child in Reynolds Price's *A Long and Happy Life.*

**Emil Rappaport**  Widowed physician who treats and later marries Eunice Punck in Peter De Vries's *Reuben, Reuben.*

**Valeria Raresh**  Romanian psychiatrist and mother of Minna Raresh Corde; a strong-willed woman and political dissident; reveals her regard and appreciation of her son-in-law, Albert Corde, on her deathbed in Saul Bellow's *The Dean's December.*

**Rare Spectacled Bears**  Bears who escape the animal massacre in John Irving's *Setting Free the Bears.*

**Raschid**  See Keith Cain.

**Shelly Rasmussen**  Berkeley dropout and secretary to Lyman Ward in Wallace Stegner's *Angle of Repose.*

**Nurse (Big Nurse, Miss Ratshed, Mother Ratched) Ratched**  Domineering head nurse of a mental hospital ward; antagonist of Randle McMurphy in Ken Kesey's *One Flew Over the Cuckoo's Nest.*

**Shazar Lazarus Ratner**  Discoverer of Ratner's Star; kept alive in a biomembrane in Don DeLillo's *Ratner's Star.*

**Ludwig Rausch**  Married to Sally Cochran Rausch; founder of Rausch Cordage Company; local millionaire; Civil War veteran; involved in Ohio Republican politics at the state level in Helen Hooven Santmyer's *". . . And Ladies of the Club."*

**Sarah ("Sally") Cochran Rausch**  Graduate of Waynesboro Female College in 1868; charter member and later president of Waynesboro Woman's Club; married to Ludwig Rausch; mother of five in Helen Hooven Santmyer's *". . . And Ladies of the Club."*

**Angela Ravage**  Movie starlet and prize in an essay contest won by Tom Waltz in Peter De Vries's *Let Me Count the Ways.*

**Raven**  Model for Renate; owns a raven in Anaïs Nin's *Collages.*

**Blaine Raven**  Father of Genevieve Raven Reinhart and father-in-law of Carl Reinhart in Thomas Berger's *Reinhart in Love* and *Vital Parts.*

**Elijah Raven**  Best man at Bukka Doopeyduk's wedding; heretic Nazarene apprentice whose greeting is "Flim Flam Alakazam!" in Ishmael Reed's *The Free-Lance Pallbearers.*

**Genevieve Raven**  See Genevieve Raven Reinhart.

**Raven-heart**  Courageous Tlingit Indian slave who helps lead tribe in battles against Russian settlers in Sitka in James Michener's *Alaska.*

**Ravenstone**  See Jakob Gradus.

**Ravus**  See Jakob Gradus.

**Ezekial "Easy" Rawlins**  African-American World War II veteran and factory worker turned private investigator in postwar Los Angeles; self-educated, unmarried Houston native; haunted by World War II combat experiences; hired to locate missing person Daphne Monet, Rawlins inadvertently becomes involved in several homicides, is pursued by both police and underworld gangsters, and ultimately uncovers a complex web of duplicity and greed in Walter Mosley's *Devil in a Blue Dress.*

**Lacey Rawlins**  West Texas boy, friend of John Grady Cole, talented with horses; goes to Mexico with John Grady, but is more pragmatic than his friend, and returns home to Texas at the first available opportunity in Cormac McCarthy's *All the Pretty Horses.*

**Joan Rawshanks**  Movie star on location in San Francisco; appears in a reverie of Jack Duluoz in Jack Kerouac's *Visions of Cody.*

**Jamie Ray**  Homosexual minister and golfer at the retreat in John Updike's *A Month of Sundays.*

**Rayal**  Patternmaster, husband of Jansee, and father of Teray and Coransee in Octavia E. Butler's *Patternmaster.*

**Raymond**  Student who serves on the Cinema Committee with Hill Gallagher during the student rebellion in James Jones's *The Merry Month of May.*

**Mr. Raymonds**  Retired university professor; lecherous employer of Meridian Hill in Alice Walker's *Meridian.*

**Billy Reagan**  Hoodlum and brother of Tim Reagan; his quarrels with Legs Diamond result in the Hotsy Totsy Club shootout in William Kennedy's *Legs.*

**Tim Reagan**  Hoodlum and brother of Billy Reagan; killed by Legs Diamond in William Kennedy's *Legs.*

**Mercy Reardon**  Runs the pressers at Kolditis Cleaners; has an affair with Getso behind Birdy Dusser's back in Mary McGarry Morris's *A Dangerous Woman.*

**Reb**  Black North Carolinian and boyhood chum of George Washington in Cecil Brown's *The Life and Loves of Mr. Jiveass Nigger.*

**Reba**  See Rebecca Dead.

**The Rebbe**  Leader of Hasidic Jews who uses Arych Lev as an emissary and who assists Asher Lev in Chaim Potok's *My Name Is Asher Lev.*

**Red Bull**  Magical bull who chases all but one unicorn into the sea below King Haggard's castle in Peter S. Beagle's *The Last Unicorn.*

**The Red Girl**  Impresses Annie with her tree climbing, wild red hair, and lack of hygiene; operates as another replacement figure for Annie's mother as the object of her affections in Jamaica Kincaid's *Annie John*.

**Red John**  Drinker and womanizer said to be devil-possessed in Carlene Hatcher Polite's *The Flagellants*.

**Margrit (Maggie) Westoever Reddick**  Estranged spouse of Max Reddick to whom he returns in John A. Williams's *The Man Who Cried I Am*.

**Max (Mox) Reddick**  African-American journalist and novelist dying of cancer; receives from his murdered mentor and rival, Harry Ames, the story of a CIA contingency plan for removing the minority population of the United States into concentration camps in John A. Williams's *The Man Who Cried I Am*.

**James Redfield**  Truth-seeking unnamed narrator of James Redfield's *The Celestine Prophecy*, a high-paced adventure tale in which pursuit of an ancient Peruvian manuscript leads to a startling discovery for humankind.

**Martha Redford**  Judge in the Timothy Landry case who lectures patrolman Bumper Morgan after he perjures himself in Joseph Wambaugh's *The Blue Knight*.

**Mark Redinger**  Bohemian cousin of McFarland children; teaches tennis and works as a waiter; lives a life frowned upon by his uncle, Charlie McFarland; live-in boyfriend of his cousin Alison McFarland in Mary Willis Walker's *The Red Scream*.

**Stuart (Stu) Redman**  East Texan chosen by Mother Abagail to lead The Stand against Randall Flagg's forces in Stephen King's *The Stand*.

**Abigail (Parrish) Reed**  Wife of Leland and mother of Mary Alice; becomes murderously jealous when she discovers that her husband is having an affair with Elizabeth Channing; kills an innocent bystander, Sarah Doyle, with her car, plunges into Black Pond and is left to die by Henry Griswald in Thomas H. Cook's *The Chatham School Affair*.

**Leland Reed**  Young instructor of English literature at the Chatham School for Boys in the early 1920s; a World War I veteran who walks with a cane; married to the former Abigail Parrish with one daughter, Mary Alice; falls in love with Elizabeth Channing and builds a boat in which to sail away with her; may or may not have plotted to murder his wife; after his wife dies in a car accident and he is rejected by Channing, he takes the boat out and drowns himself in Thomas H. Cook's *The Chatham School Affair*.

**Marion Reed**  American student at the University of Minneapolis who studies Spanish under Salome Camila; dance teacher in Cuba and the United States; lifetime friend and sometimes lover of Salome Camila in Julia Alvarez's *In the Name of Salome*.

**Mary Alice Reed**  Eventually known as Alice Craddock, the young daughter of Leland and Abigail Reed; is driven insane when her mother and father each die tragically in 1927 in Chatham, Massachusetts; is adopted by Dr. Craddock and his wife, who both try unsuccessfully to help her put her past behind her in Thomas H. Cook's *The Chatham School Affair*.

**Mary Jane (The Monkey) Reed**  Semiliterate fashion model from West Virginia and lover of Alex Portnoy, who abandons her in an Athens hotel in Philip Roth's *Portnoy's Complaint*.

**Martha Reganhart**  Former wife of an artist; single-handedly supports two children with her work as a waitress; lives with Gabe Wallach for a time before she gives in to Sid Jaffe's proposal of marriage in Philip Roth's *Letting Go*.

**Reggie**  Attractive, French-looking young woman; heroin addict who as a child was sexually abused by her mother in Calvin Hernton's *Scarecrow*.

**Regina**  Young male homosexual and transvestite who caters to the sexual appetite of Harry Black until Black no longer has money to lavish on him in Hubert Selby, Jr.'s *Last Exit to Brooklyn*.

**Frank Reilly**  Coworker of Charlie Gordon; pities Gordon after the intelligence experiment fails in Daniel Keyes's *Flowers for Algernon*.

**Ignatius J. Reilly**  Thirty-year-old native New Orleanian; lives with his mother and routinely abuses her verbally; is finally forced to help his mother financially by getting a variety of dead-end jobs, his last being a hot dog street vendor in John Kennedy Toole's *A Confederacy of Dunces*.

**Mrs. Irene Reilly**  Aged mother of Ignatius J. Reilly; a native New Orleanian and widow with a drinking problem; finds comfort in newfound friendships with police officer Angelo Mancuso, his aunt, Santa Battaglia, and the man they want her to date, Claude Robichaux; stands up for herself by finally leaving her son to his own devices in John Kennedy Toole's *A Confederacy of Dunces*.

**Jack Reilly**  New York City Police detective assigned to investigate con games; separated from his wife, but cannot obtain a divorce for legal reasons; romantically involved with Karen Smith; has become friends with and tries to help Fred Fitch, a young man who is a frequent victim of con artists in Donald E. Westlake's *God Save The Mark*.

**Kathleen (Kate) Lynch Reilley**  Mother of Jack Curran and Susy Reilley and ex-wife of Johnny Curran in Mark Steadman's *A Lion's Share*.

**Susy Reilley**  Daughter of Kathleen Reilley and younger half sister of Jack Curran in Mark Steadman's *A Lion's Share*.

**Blaine Reinhart**  Rebellious but later conformist son of Carl and Genevieve Reinhart in Thomas Berger's *Vital Parts*.

**Carlo B. (Carl) Reinhart**  American soldier in Europe in World War II who later marries Genevieve Raven and fathers

Blaine and Winona Reinhart; recurrent protagonist of Thomas Berger's *Crazy in Berlin, Reinhart in Love,* and *Vital Parts.*

**Genevieve Raven (Gen) Reinhart**    Manipulative wife and later ex-wife of Carl Reinhart in Thomas Berger's *Reinhart in Love* and *Vital Parts.*

**George Reinhart**    Father of Carlo Reinhart in Thomas Berger's *Reinhart in Love.*

**Maw Reinhart**    Cantankerous mother of Carlo Reinhart in Thomas Berger's *Reinhart in Love.*

**Winona Reinhart**    Daughter of Carl and Genevieve Reinhart in Thomas Berger's *Vital Parts.*

**Maria-Teresa Reiter**    Fellow juror who tries to have an affair with Renne Sundheimer although he is married with a fourteen-year-old daughter in Mark Salzman's *The Soloist.*

**Remedios**    Old woman and healer (*curandera*) who can see the future and keeps Marta Rodríguez from moving north; later, helps Marta take a spell off her sister and helps her find her drowned son in Sandra Benítez's *A Place Where the Sea Remembers.*

**Joanne Remington**    Fiancée of Emmett Hunter; her affair with Phil Elliott helps get Elliott kicked out of football in Peter Gent's *North Dallas Forty.*

**Phil (CO) Renaldi**    Conscientious objector who works as an orderly in an army hospital and befriends Alfonso Columbato in William Wharton's *Birdy.*

**Renate**    Painter, part-time hostess at the Paradise Inn nightclub, and central character in Anaïs Nin's *Collages.*

**Dorothy (Dottie) Renfrew**    Aspiring social worker and lover of Dick Brown in Mary McCarthy's *The Group.*

**Beulah Beecham Renfro**    Wife of Ralph Renfro, mother of Jack Jordan Renfro and four other children, granddaughter of Granny Vaughn, and hostess of Granny's birthday reunion in Eudora Welty's *Losing Battles.*

**Ella Fay Renfro**    Sixteen-year-old sister of Jack Renfro; removes an heirloom wedding ring from the family Bible only to have it taken from her by Curly Stovall, who is attacked by Jack Renfro and subsequently has him arrested in Eudora Welty's *Losing Battles.*

**Gloria Short Renfro**    Orphan, wife of Jack Renfro, and former teacher at Banner School, who attended the state normal school for teachers in Eudora Welty's *Losing Battles.*

**Jack Jordan Renfro**    Oldest son of Beulah and Ralph Renfro and husband of Gloria Short Renfro; serves one-and-a-half years in Parchman State Penitentiary for aggravated battery and robbery, escapes to attend Granny Vaughn's birthday celebration,

and rescues Maud Eva Moody's car from the edge of Banner Top in Eudora Welty's *Losing Battles.*

**Lexie Renfro**    Unmarried sister of Ralph Renfro; cares for Julia Mortimer before her death in Eudora Welty's *Losing Battles.*

**Lady May Renfro**    Baby daughter of Jack and Gloria Renfro; born while her father is in prison in Eudora Welty's *Losing Battles.*

**Ralph Renfro**    Husband of Beulah Renfro and father of Jack Renfro and four other children; limps as the result of a dynamiting accident in Eudora Welty's *Losing Battles.*

**Red (Monsignor Renton) Renton**    Rector of the cathedral in the Roman Catholic diocese in J. F. Powers's *Morte D'Urban.*

**Shep Resnick**    Ex-boyfriend of Sandy Pressman; runs into Sandy years later at their country club and makes a pass at her even though he is married; resumes his affair with Sandy years later but refuses to leave his wife for her in Judy Blume's *Wifey.*

**Michael (Mike) S. Reusing (Rushing)**    Businessman who meets Francesca Bolt in an airport; his brief affair with her stimulates her short-lived effort at independence in Gail Godwin's *Glass People.*

**R. Giskard Reventlov**    Mechanoid robot with secret telepathic powers assigned with R. Daneel Olivaw to protect Elijah Baley; uses telepathic abilities to disable Gladia Delmarre's humaniform robot lover and to test Baley in order to assess suitability of Earth's inhabitants for space colonization in Isaac Asimov's *The Robots of Dawn.*

**Clara Walpole Revere**    Daughter of migrant farm workers, wife of Curt Revere, and lover of Lowry, by whom she has a son, Swan Revere; protagonist of Joyce Carol Oates's *A Garden of Earthly Delights.*

**Curt Revere**    Wealthy businessman who marries Clara Walpole in Joyce Carol Oates's *A Garden of Earthly Delights.*

**Steven (Swan) Revere**    Son of Clara Walpole by her lover, Lowry; kills his stepfather, Curt Revere, and himself in Joyce Carol Oates's *A Garden of Earthly Delights.*

**Revolver**    Gretel Samuelson's family's Labrador retriever; he attacks Mrs. Fisher's cat across the street and is chained up; Gretel feels sorry for him and lets him loose, so he runs away in Alice Hoffman's *Local Girls.*

**Lucius (Lucky) Rexford**    Fair, bright Chancellor of the University in John Barth's *Giles Goat-Boy.*

**John Reyes**    Doctor of Blix Hollister in Jessamyn West's *A Matter of Time.*

**Chester Reynolds**    Famous white anthropologist disguised as a Zuni kachina; kills Ernesto Cata and George Bowlegs in his effort to hide his fraudulent research; is killed by anonymous

Zunis for the sacrilege of impersonating a kachina in Tony Hillerman's *Dance Hall of the Dead.*

**Elizabeth Reynolds**   Daughter and older child of Margaret and Paul Reynolds in Anne Richardson Roiphe's *Up the Sandbox!*

**Ellen Reynolds**   Wife of Skip Reynolds in John Updike's *Bech: A Book.*

**John Reynolds**   Northern general who is offered command of the Union army but declines because he is not promised full control; dies at the beginning of the Battle of Gettysburg in Michael Shaara's *The Killer Angels.*

**Margaret Ferguson Reynolds**   Wife of Paul Reynolds and mother of Elizabeth and Peter Reynolds; housewife who fantasizes about what she could have been as she narrates Anne Richardson Roiphe's *Up the Sandbox!*

**Paul Reynolds**   Husband of Margaret Reynolds and father of Elizabeth and Peter Reynolds; history student who spends much time in the library researching revolutions in Anne Richardson Roiphe's *Up the Sandbox!*

**Peter Reynolds**   Son and younger child of Margaret and Paul Reynolds in Anne Richardson Roiphe's *Up the Sandbox!*

**Skip Reynolds**   Contact man for Henry Bech at the American embassy in Russia; former basketball player from Wisconsin; husband of Ellen Reynolds in John Updike's *Bech: A Book.*

**Rhea Rhadin**   Head receptionist at Silver Publishing Company in Rita Mae Brown's *Rubyfruit Jungle.*

**Captain Fahyi Rhallon**   Captain in the Iranian secret police; interrogates the American soldiers who are chasing Cacciato in Tim O'Brien's *Going after Cacciato.*

**Rheba**   White librarian in the art library where Jimson is employed; he rejects her advances in Carlene Hatcher Polite's *The Flagellants.*

**Lola Rhoades**   Cello-playing siren who invites Tom More to share her idyllic life in the Old South in Walker Percy's *Love in the Ruins.*

**Benton Rhodes**   Maine state trooper who, with partner Peter (Jingles) Gibbons, investigates mysterious explosion in Haven, Maine, in Stephen King's *The Tommyknockers.*

**Riau**   Friend of Toussaint; formerly a slave in the French colony Saint Domingue; ran away to join the maroons, a band of escaped slaves who live a migratory life in the mountains; has a child with a fellow maroon, Merbillay; leaves the revolution; protects Antoine Hebert from other slaves in the revolutionary camps in Madison Smartt Bell's *All Souls' Rising.*

**Ric (Armando) and Rac (Dolores)**   Spanish twins who exhibit demonic, uncontrollable behavior in Katherine Anne Porter's *Ship of Fools.*

**Graham Rice**   Coconspirator in Willie Hall's plan to lynch a white policeman; kills Thomas Wilkerson in John Edgar Wideman's *The Lynchers.*

**Richards**   Computer specialist who is an assistant to Gerhard at the Neuropsychiatric Research Unit in Michael Crichton's *The Terminal Man.*

**Richie**   Seven-year-old son of Rochelle; in foster care; visits with Rochelle in Sandra Scofield's *Beyond Deserving.*

**Mr. Richie**   Fourth-grade teacher of Gretel Samuelson and Jill Harrington; locked students in the coat closet if they talked out of turn in Alice Hoffman's *Local Girls.*

**Edward G. Ricks**   Unemployed paper company executive seeking work; murder victim shot by Burke Devore in Donald E. Westlake's *The Ax.*

**June "Junie" Ricks**   Eighteen-year-old daughter of the Rickses, she is having an affair with Lewis Ringer in Donald E. Westlake's *The Ax.*

**Mrs. Ricks**   Heavyset, middle-aged wife of Edward Ricks, she mistakes Burke Devore for her eighteen-year-old daughter's married lover and confronts him; murder victim of Burke Devore in Donald E. Westlake's *The Ax.*

**Beverly Ricord**   College sweetheart and lover of Shepherd Lewis in Ernest J. Gaines's *In My Father's House.*

**Albert Riddell**   Boyfriend of the sixteen-year-old Louise Attwater; on a date with him she meets her future husband, Todd Eborn, in Reynolds Price's *Love and Work.*

**Siegfried Rieber**   Anti-Semitic publisher of a women's trade journal who has a grotesque romance with Lizzi Spöckenkieker in Katherine Anne Porter's *Ship of Fools.*

**Tillie Ried**   Wife of Willie Ried and second cousin of Jacob Upshur; tongue-lasher of Tangierneck in Sarah E. Wright's *This Child's Gonna Live.*

**Willie Ried**   Husband of Tillie Ried; migrant worker in Sarah E. Wright's *This Child's Gonna Live.*

**Etta Rieff**   Wife of Morroe Rieff in Wallace Markfield's *To an Early Grave.*

**Morroe Rieff**   Speechwriter for a Jewish organization; gathers some friends of Leslie Braverman to attend Braverman's memorial service in Wallace Markfield's *To an Early Grave.*

**Brutus Rife**   Loves Celeste but married to another woman; wealthy and cruel; owns the munitions plant in town; father of Napoleon Bonaparte, Julius Caesar, Robert E. Lee, and Ulysses S. Grant; Celeste kills him in Rita Mae Brown's *Six of One.*

**Disraeli Rife**   Husband to Liz Rife who establishes a modern local newspaper to compete with the newspaper run by Nicole Smith in Rita Mae Brown's *Bingo*.

**Liz Rife**   Wife of Disraeli Rife, the richest man in Runnymede, and small-town socialite in Rita Mae Brown's *Bingo*.

**Rigolo**   Fifty-year-old bald man who owns the junkyard that Clyde Stout frequents in Jack Matthews's *Hanger Stout, Awake!*

**Evelyn Riker**   Woman friend of Philip Preminger in *The Condominium*, a novella in Stanley Elkin's *Searches and Seizures*.

**Joanne Riley**   Reformatory cellmate of Eva Medina Canada in Gayl Jones's *Eva's Man*.

**Brian Rimsky**   Boyhood friend of Jerome Neumiller and Charles Neumiller (II) in Larry Woiwode's *Beyond the Bedroom Wall*.

**Leo Rimsky**   Boyhood friend of Jerome Neumiller and Charles Neumiller (II) in Larry Woiwode's *Beyond the Bedroom Wall*.

**America Rincon**   Seventeen-year-old sister of Candido Rincon's former wife; now living with Candido; pregnant by him; from a small town in Mexico; raped by two strangers but tells Candido only that she was robbed; bears his daughter in T. Coraghessan Boyle's *The Tortilla Curtain*.

**Candido Rincon**   Mexican living illegally in the United States; first wife left him; her younger sister is pregnant by him; he survives in spite of disasters that occur whenever he has begun to amass enough funds to afford a true home for self and family in T. Coraghessan Boyle's *The Tortilla Curtain*.

**Lewis Ringer**   Suspect in the Rickses' murders; community college literature professor and lover of June Ricks; hangs himself in his garage in Donald E. Westlake's *The Ax*.

**Ira Ringold**   Larger-than-life radio actor also known as "Iron Rinn" or the "Iron Man"; brother of Murray Ringold; married silent film and radio actress Eve Frame in the late 1940s; was blacklisted from the popular radio show for Communist sympathizing; is ultimately disgraced by his wife, Eve, who in an attempt to exact revenge for Ira's infidelities, published an exposé, *I Married a Communist*, in Philip Roth's *I Married a Communist*.

**Murray Ringold**   Outspoken, leftist, World War II veteran; Nathan Zuckerman's high school teacher and lifelong friend; brother of Ira Ringold; married to Doris, who is killed in a mugging attempt; has one daughter, Lorraine, who dies of meningitis at age thirty; recounts the story of his brother's adventures as a Communist sympathizer and the man's ill-fated marriage to actress Eve Frame in Philip Roth's *I Married a Communist*.

**Sergeant Rink**   Police officer who solves the mystery of the murdered prostitute and the theft of her corpse in Richard Brautigan's *Dreaming of Babylon*.

**Johnny Rio**   Attractive Chicano homosexual from Texas who compulsively seeks impersonal sex with multiple partners in Los Angeles in John Rechy's *Numbers*.

**Rip**   Drug dealer to Clay whose valueless philosophy leads him to introduce Clay and Trent to murder and rape in Bret Easton Ellis's *Less Than Zero*.

**Bud Ripplemeyer**   Middle-aged Iowa banker who strives to maintain the solvency of local farms; crippled after being shot by an angry farmer; ex-husband of Karin Ripplemeyer, adoptive father of Du Thien, common-law husband of Jane Ripplemeyer/Jasmine Vijh and father of Jasmine's unborn child in Bharati Mukherjee's *Jasmine*.

**Du (Yogi) Ripplemeyer**   (See also Du Thien) Adopted son of Bud and Jane Ripplemeyer in Bharati Mukherjee's *Jasmine*.

**Jane Ripplemeyer**   (See also Jasmine Vijh) Alias adopted by Jasmine Vijh after she sees her husband's killer in New York and flees to Iowa; narrator and protagonist of Bharati Mukherjee's *Jasmine*.

**Karin Ripplemeyer**   Ex-wife of Bud Ripplemeyer; counselor who runs the county's Suicide Hot Line; devout Christian who will likely care for her crippled ex-husband after Jane Ripplemeyer/Jasmine Vijh leaves him at the end of Bharati Mukherjee's *Jasmine*.

**John Elmore Ritchie**   Black U.S. Army veteran of World War II; beaten and arrested by two white policemen; committs suicide by banging his head against the cell bars in Joyce Carol Oates's *Because It Is Bitter, and Because It Is My Heart*.

**Bob Ritter**   CIA deputy director, he plans covert operations against Colombian drug cartels with James Cutter and Moore; is manipulated by Cutter into giving him the information necessary to shut down the operation, but is enraged by the abandonment of American soldiers in hostile territory; assists Jack Ryan and John Clark in their efforts to rescue the light-infantry teams in Tom Clancy's *Clear and Present Danger*.

**Jamie Ritter**   Baby who survives the Andromeda Strain attack in Michael Crichton's *The Andromeda Strain*.

**Fran Rittersdorf**   Notebook keeper who is returning to Germany from Mexico, where she had gone to find a rich husband in Katherine Anne Porter's *Ship of Fools*.

**Maria Rivera**   Nestor Castillo's lover in Cuba; a mulatto who meets Nestor when he defends her against her abusive boyfriend; leaves Nestor to marry the man who was beating her in Oscar Hijuelos's *The Mambo Kings Play Songs of Love*.

**Buddy Rivers**   Teenage protagonist who is on his own after his father is hospitalized; remains suspended from school because there is no parent to sign for his return; rescues his fourteen-year-old girlfriend, Angela Figueroa, from a girls' shelter and hides out with her in his father's house in June Jordan's *His Own Where*.

**Clementine (Tish) Rivers**   Pregnant black teenager and lover of Fonny Hunt; narrator of James Baldwin's *If Beale Street Could Talk*.

**Ernestine (Sis) Rivers**   Settlement house worker and sister of Tish Rivers in James Baldwin's *If Beale Street Could Talk*.

**Joseph (Joe) Rivers**   Father of Tish Rivers in James Baldwin's *If Beale Street Could Talk*.

**Randall (Randy) Rivers**   Appleton, Indiana, novelist whose succès de scandale, *Don't Look Now, Medusa*, brings fame and distress in Peter De Vries's *Mrs. Wallop*.

**Reba (Miss Reba) Rivers**   See Volume I.

**Sharon Rivers**   Mother of Tish Rivers in James Baldwin's *If Beale Street Could Talk*.

**Stella Slobkin Rivers**   Mother of Randy Rivers and victim of literary matricide in Peter De Vries's *Mrs. Wallop*.

**Carlo Rizzi**   Abusive husband of Connie Corleone; killed in Michael Corleone's final purge in Mario Puzo's *The Godfather*.

**Enrico Salvatore (Ratso, Rico) Rizzo**   Swindler befriended by Joe Buck; dies on the bus to Florida with Joe in James Leo Herlihy's *Midnight Cowboy*.

**Tony Rizzoli**   Seals a ruthless pact with Constantin Demiris that gives him undreamed-of mastery over men and women for one all too brief moment in Sidney Sheldon's *Memories of Midnight*.

**Robair**   New Orleans Creole valet, butler, and friend first to Jonas Cord, then to Jonas Cord, Jr., in Harold Robbins's *The Carpetbaggers*.

**Dr. Robbins**   Eccentric (or perhaps just "too well") psychiatrist of Sissy Hankshaw Gitche and self-acknowledged author of Tom Robbins's *Even Cowgirls Get the Blues*.

**Moll Robbins**   Writer for *Running Dog*, researching an article on sex as big business in Don DeLillo's *Running Dog*.

**Robert**   Economics professor with whom Tarden lives and studies English; during a psychotic episode, tries to kill Tarden with a knife in Jerzy Kosinski's *Cockpit*.

**Roberts**   Detective who interrogates Stephen Rojack on suspicion of murder in Norman Mailer's *An American Dream*.

**Dave and Debbie Roberts**   Siblings who perform sex scenes in Boris Adrian's pornographic movie in Terry Southern's *Blue Movie*.

**Jeffrey Roberts**   WASPish southern advertising man and poet; friend and lover of Isadora Wing in Erica Jong's *How to Save Your Own Life*.

**Marion (Kiki) Roberts**   Mistress of Legs Diamond; with Diamond when he kidnaps Clem Streeter and Dickie Bartlett in William Kennedy's *Legs*.

**Robertson**   Head of the President's Science Advisory Committee who is the contact person between Project Wildfire and the president in Michael Crichton's *The Andromeda Strain*.

**Claude Robichaux**   Native New Orleanian who is mistakenly arrested by patrolman Angelo Mancuso during a melee caused by Ignatius J. Reilly; meets Mrs. Reilly as a guest in the home of Santa Battaglia and develops a relationship with the beleaguered woman in John Kennedy Toole's *A Confederacy of Dunces*.

**Alafair Robicheaux**   El Salvadoran refugee and adopted daughter of Dave Robicheaux; rescued by Robicheaux and wife, Annie, from a plane downed in the Gulf of Mexico; threatened by Sally Dio's men, she travels with her father to Montana during investigation in James Lee Burke's *Black Cherry Blues*.

**Annie Robicheaux**   Deceased wife of Dave Robicheaux murdered by two men in retribution during a previous investigation conducted by her husband; speaks to Robicheaux in his dreams and helps to guide his investigation of crimes linked to Sally Dio in James Lee Burke's *Black Cherry Blues*.

**Dave Robicheaux**   Retired New Orleans homicide detective; haunted by alcoholism and the loss of wife, Annie, during previous investigation; devoted to adopted daughter Alafair; conducts independent investigation into alleged drug-related homicide of waitress; leads him to Sally Dio in James Lee Burke's *Black Cherry Blues*.

**Jonathan Robillard**   Assistant pastor to the Reverend Phillip Martin in Ernest J. Gaines's *In My Father's House*.

**Raine Robinette**   Vacant actress who helps to corrupt the admiring Lucy Lamar in Walker Percy's *Lancelot*.

**Robinson**   Street criminal who accidentally kills Jesus Ortiz instead of Sol Nazerman during a robbery in Edward Lewis Wallant's *The Pawnbroker*.

**Brad Robinson**   Former college friend and eventual lover of Philip Benjamin; shy and private person in David Leavitt's *The Lost Language of Cranes*.

**Doris Robinson**   High school student whom Birdy reluctantly takes to the junior prom in William Wharton's *Birdy*.

**Henry Robinson**   Husband and killer of Dolores Brittain in Hal Bennett's *Wait Until the Evening*.

**Ira Robinson**   Employee of NESTER in Scott Spencer's *Last Night at the Brain Thieves' Ball*.

**Joan Robinson**   Ex-wife of Joey Robinson and mother of their three children; refined, elegant woman with a distant personality in John Updike's *Of the Farm*.

**Joey Robinson**   Thirty-five-year-old Harvard-educated son of Mary Robinson; returns to the family farm to mow the fields and introduce his new wife and stepson; narrator of John Updike's *Of the Farm.*

**Mary Robinson**   Mother of Joey Robinson; aging, yet strong-willed and determined woman whose love for her only son and her family farm causes her interpersonal problems in John Updike's *Of the Farm.*

**Peggy McCabe Robinson**   Second wife of Joey Robinson and mother of Richard McCabe; perceiving her new mother-in-law, Mary Robinson, as an enemy and rival, she exhibits jealousy and impatience in John Updike's *Of the Farm.*

**Taft Robinson**   Star running back and first black student enrolled by Logos College in Don DeLillo's *End Zone.*

**Harvey (Father Urban) Roche**   Priest whose attempt to remodel his fusty Order of St. Clement after the Jesuits ends in failure and humiliation; ultimately becomes the head of his province, but by then his be-a-winner spirit is dead in J. F. Powers's *Morte D'Urban.*

**Rochelle**   Maureen's younger sister; in jail for neglect because Rochelle's baby, Summer, drowned while in her care in Sandra Scofield's *Beyond Deserving.*

**Alain du Rocher**   Mysterious member of the du Rocher clan; long presumed murdered by the SS for his Resistance activities, in actuality he killed his cousin Guillaume and assumed Guillaume's identity in Aaron Elkins's *Old Bones.*

**Guillaume du Rocher**   Forbidding head of the du Rocher clan; murdered in self-defense by his cousin Alain in Aaron Elkins's *Old Bones.*

**Jules du Rocher**   Gluttonous, scheming love child of Mathilde and Alain du Rocher; eager to inherit a fortune without obstacles, he murders Alain du Rocher and Claude Fougeray in Aaron Elkins's *Old Bones.*

**Mathilde du Rocher**   Imperious wife of Rene du Rocher and mother of Jules; so fierce in her young love of Alain du Rocher that she convinces him to conceal the murder of his cousin Guillaume by assuming Guillaume's identity in Aaron Elkins's *Old Bones.*

**Rene du Rocher**   Mild-mannered husband of Mathilde du Rocher in Aaron Elkins's *Old Bones.*

**Rocketman**   See Lieutenant Tyrone Slothrop.

**Eigil Rødding**   Mysterious Danish count; brother of Astrid Wrendel-Kramp; appears to be carrying on the genetic experimentation begun by his dead father in Wallace Stegner's *The Spectator Bird.*

**Hettie Rodgers**   Attractive young woman whose desires for love and domestic bliss reflect the desires of generations of small-town Lawford women before her; girlfriend of Jack Hewitt, she betrays him with his close friend Wade Whitehouse in Russell Banks's *Affliction.*

**Marc Rodin**   Head of the French terrorist group Secret Army Organization (OAS) who hires the Jackal to assassinate Charles de Gaulle; directs the infiltration of the Presidential Security Corps; goes into hiding until the operation is over in Frederick Forsyth's *The Day of the Jackal.*

**Leandro Guzman (Palomino) Rodriguez**   Political activist in the Dominican Republic during the Trujillo regime; imprisoned for several years; husband of Maria Teresa Mirabal, who is killed by the regime, and father of Jacqueline in Julia Alvarez's *In the Time of the Butterflies.*

**Marta Rodríguez**   Sister of Chayo Marroquín; works as a chambermaid at an area hotel; puts a curse on her sister's unborn baby, but retracts it with the help of Remedios; gives birth to Richard, who drowns in the river; later, becomes employee and friend of Esperanza Clemente in Sandra Benítez's *A Place Where the Sea Remembers.*

**Elizabeth Roffe**   Only daughter of one of the wealthiest men in the world, who was recently killed in a mountain-climbing accident; married to Rhys Williams in Sidney Sheldon's *Bloodline.*

**Sam Roffe**   Head of Roffe and Sons, an international empire filled with desperate, cash-hungry family members; dies in a mysterious mountain-climbing accident; father of Elizabeth Roffe in Sidney Sheldon's *Bloodline.*

**Roger**   Ros's jealous husband; is killed by the police with croquet mallets in Robert Coover's *Gerald's Party.*

**Addie Rogers**   Member of Margaret's congregation; has painful arthritis; didn't approve of Margaret at first because she is the first woman rector of All Saints High Balsam in Gail Godwin's *Evensong.*

**Camille (Cam) Rogers**   More liberal sister of Honor Rogers; leaves home to live with a man in Marge Piercy's *The High Cost of Living.*

**Honor (Honorée) Rogers**   Overprotected seventeen-year-old whose main contacts with the outside world are Leslie McGivers and Bernie Guizot in Marge Piercy's *The High Cost of Living.*

**Joe Rogers**   Agent who works as a CIA aide in the expedition against the wild boys in William S. Burroughs's *The Wild Boys.*

**Mrs. (Mama) Rogers**   Overprotective mother of Honor Rogers in Marge Piercy's *The High Cost of Living.*

**Victoria (Victoria Maria San Felipe Sanchez) Rogers**   Puerto Rican prostitute allegedly raped by Fonny Hunt in James Baldwin's *If Beale Street Could Talk.*

**Josh Rogovin**    Techie; father of Ari; Shira's ex-husband who fights to take Ari away from his mother in Marge Piercy's *He, She and It.*

**Deborah Kelly Rojack**    Daughter of Barney Kelly; murdered by her husband, Stephen Rojack, in Norman Mailer's *An American Dream.*

**Stephen Richards (Raw-Jock) Rojack**    War hero, congressman, and college professor who murders his wife, Deborah Kelly Rojack; narrator of Norman Mailer's *An American Dream.*

**Rojos (Pizarro)**    Leader of the revolutionary movement in South America who lacks imagination; sends Ramón Cordes and his band to their deaths at the silver mine in William Herrick's *The Last to Die.*

**Dee Romano**    Laconic chief of police for West Condon in Robert Coover's *The Origin of the Brunists.*

**Natashya Romanov**    See Natashya Romanov Everett.

**Romarkin (Rom)**    Political refugee from Stalinist Russia; close friend of George Levanter in Jerzy Kosinski's *Blind Date.*

**Ronnie**    Bartender at the Village Tavern; friend of Roe Billins, Jerry Payne, and Harry Schoonover in John Nichols's *The Sterile Cuckoo.*

**Belle Rooney (Atkins)**    Wild and childlike wife of Orion Atkins; mother of Sharon Rose, Eula Stacy, and Fayrene Dee; dies after the birth of her third daughter in Wright Morris's *Plains Song for Female Voices.*

**Theodore Roosevelt**    New York City police commissioner in 1896; secretly enlists forensic psychologist Dr. Lazlo Kriezler's team to compile profile of serial killer in Caleb Carr's *The Alienist.*

**John Roper**    Brother of Simeon Roper, Puritan soldier, and follower of Johnny Church and Thankful Perkins; condemned to death for mutiny but spared in Cromwell's blanket pardon in Mary Lee Settle's *Prisons.*

**Simeon Roper**    Puritan soldier who, like his brother, John Roper, is condemned to death for mutiny but spared in Cromwell's blanket pardon in Mary Lee Settle's *Prisons.*

**Ros**    Actress and model in pornography; married to Roger and admired by everyone; is stabbed with an ice pick and killed in Robert Coover's *Gerald's Party.*

**Orlando "Romeo" Rosales**    Handsome, untalented nineteen-year-old waiter obsessed with popular movies and with his dream of becoming a movie star; boyfriend of Trinidad Gamboa; randomly chosen scapegoat who is shot, arrested, and forced to take the blame for the government's assassination of Senator Domingo Avila in Jessica Hagedorn's *Dogeaters.*

**Wanda (Marie) Rosario**    Lover of Beth Walker; sent to jail and loses custody of her children; with Walker, steals her children back and is forced to go underground in Marge Piercy's *Small Changes.*

**Rose**    Manager of the nightclub where Jake Jackson is robbed by a pickpocket in Richard Wright's *Lawd Today.*

**Dr. Burton L. Rose**    Third psychiatrist of John Wilder; solemn young doctor who compulsively eats mint candies in Richard Yates's *Disturbing the Peace.*

**Leonard (Lennie) Rose**    Jewish art student and Donna Stuart's first boyfriend at college; paints Donna and gives her paintings; introduces Jill Stuart to Mike Loesser in Marge Piercy's *Braided Lives.*

**Mr. Rose**    Father of Rose Rose; the leader of the migrant workers in the cider house; friend of Homer Wells; it is discovered that he has impregnated Rose Rose in John Irving's *The Cider House Rules.*

**Rose Rose**    Young African-American migrant worker who is impregnated by her father; she turns to Homer Wells for help, causing him to rethink his original rejection of the abortion procedures Dr. Wilbur Larch taught him in John Irving's *The Cider House Rules.*

**Rosella**    South European peasant who poses nude for Hugh's photography and works as a maid for Cyril in John Hawkes's *The Blood Oranges.*

**Ethel Greenglass Rosenberg**    Convicted traitor, atom spy, and love object of Richard Nixon in Robert Coover's *The Public Burning.*

**Joey Rosenberg**    Long-haired young beatnik and former champion athlete who reminds Jack Duluoz of Jesus Christ in Jack Kerouac's *Big Sur.*

**Julius Rosenberg**    Convicted traitor, atom spy, and husband of Ethel Rosenberg in Robert Coover's *The Public Burning.*

**Harris Rosenblatt**    Wealthy former college classmate of Bruce Gold and financial adviser to the White House in Joseph Heller's *Good as Gold.*

**Ethel Rosenblum**    Will Barrett's high school classmate, about whom he fantasizes during his fugue states; her being Jewish helps motivate one of his delusions in Walker Percy's *The Second Coming.*

**Lulu Rosencrantz**    Loyal gunman for Dutch Schultz in E. L. Doctorow's *Billy Bathgate.*

**Caroline Rosewater**    Socially pretentious and alcoholic wife of Fred Rosewater in Kurt Vonnegut's *God Bless You, Mr. Rosewater.*

**Eliot Rosewater**    Eccentric philanthropist, son of Lister Rosewater, husband of Sylvia Rosewater, and fan of Kilgore Trout;

central character in Kurt Vonnegut's *God Bless You, Mr. Rosewater*; hospital patient with Billy Pilgrim in *Slaughterhouse-Five*, and patron of Trout in *Breakfast of Champions*.

**Fred Rosewater**  Suicidal insurance salesman descended from the poor Rhode Island branch of the Rosewater family in Kurt Vonnegut's *God Bless You, Mr. Rosewater*.

**Lister Ames Rosewater**  Conservative U.S. senator and father of Eliot Rosewater in Kurt Vonnegut's *God Bless You, Mr. Rosewater*.

**Sylvia DuVrais Zetterling Rosewater**  Wife of Eliot Rosewater in Kurt Vonnegut's *God Bless You, Mr. Rosewater*.

**Rosey**  Best friend of Mariah Upshur; brings shame on Tangierneck and dies in childbirth in Sarah E. Wright's *This Child's Gonna Live*.

**Rosie**  Slovenly roommate of Sylvia and girlfriend of Frank in Jim Harrison's *A Good Day to Die*.

**Ardis (Bonita, Ardis Carter, Ardis Kármán, Marya Sharp, Mrs. Nigel Stock) Ross**  Self-centered mother of Elena Ross Howe in Joyce Carol Oates's *Do with Me What You Will*.

**Elena Ross**  See Elena Ross Howe.

**Frank Ross**  Father of Mattie Ross; killed by Tom Chaney in Charles Portis's *True Grit*.

**Janet (Jan) Ross**  Psychiatrist at the Neuropsychiatric Research Unit who counsels against giving Harold Benson the stage-three operation in Michael Crichton's *The Terminal Man*.

**Leo Ross**  Mentally disturbed father of Elena Howe in Joyce Carol Oates's *Do with Me What You Will*.

**Leonard Ross**  Inexperienced CIA field agent who works with Joseph Cutter to pursue Miles Kendig in Brian Garfield's *Hopscotch*.

**Malcolm Ross**  Influential and successful Seattle merchant; one of first capitalists to build empire on exploiting Alaskan resources; father of Lydia Ross in James Michener's *Alaska*.

**Mattie Ross**  Narrator who hires Rooster Cogburn to capture Tom Chaney, her father's murderer in Charles Portis's *True Grit*.

**Thomas (Tommy) Ross**  Boyfriend of Susan Snell; takes Carrie White to the prom as a favor to Susan Snell in Stephen King's *Carrie*.

**Rossie**  Son of Rachel, cousin of Anne, Katie, Celia, and Jenny in Joan Chase's *During the Reign of the Queen of Persia*.

**Porfiry Petrovich Rostnikov**  Inspector in the MVD, the police department of Moscow, assigned to the Bureau of Special Projects; recently demoted from procurator general's office due to repeated clashes with KGB; attempts to free his son, Josef, from military duty in Afghanistan and from prejudice against his Jewish wife, Sarah; is sent to Siberia to investigate the death of another police officer and uncovers a KGB plot in Stuart M. Kaminsky's *A Cold Red Sunrise*.

**Sarah Rostnikov**  Wife of Porfiry Petrovich Rostnikov, a police officer in Moscow; mother of Josef, a soldier serving in Afghanistan; suffers disabling headaches; learns that they result from a brain tumor and has surgery to remove it while her husband is on duty in Siberia in Stuart M. Kaminsky's *A Cold Red Sunrise*.

**Philip Roth**  Well-known Jewish-American novelist and literary figure who travels to Israel and repeatedly encounters another Philip Roth, who physically resembles him and is trading on his fame to promote Diasporism, the return of Israeli Jews to Europe; is drawn by these encounters into renewed speculation about his identity and sanity, and then into complex intelligence games being played by the Israelis and the Palestinians; eventually agrees to undertake a vaguely defined operation for the Mossad, the Israeli secret service; relates these events and repeatedly insists upon their veracity in Philip Roth's *Operation Shylock: A Confession*.

**Lady Jane Rotherhall**  Hostess for the Mensa meeting where Dane Tarrant meets her future husband, John Empson, in Gail Godwin's *The Perfectionists*.

**Arnold Rothstein**  Gangster who sponsors Legs Diamond's criminal beginnings in William Kennedy's *Legs*.

**Gloria Rowan**  Daughter of Thomas Rowan and lover of George Washington in Copenhagen in Cecil Brown's *The Life and Loves of Mr. Jiveass Nigger*.

**Thomas Rowan**  American political analyst in Copenhagen; has incestuous relations with his daughter, Gloria Rowan, in Cecil Brown's *The Life and Loves of Mr. Jiveass Nigger*.

**Roxy**  Stepmother of Chet Pomeroy; plans to marry Curtis Peavey in Thomas McGuane's *Panama*.

**Augustus Roy**  Descendant of Pennsylvania Quakers raised by his grandfather, Scranton Roy; husband of Zosie Shawano Roy, lover of Mary Shawano, and father of Rozina Roy, who disappears mysteriously in Louise Erdrich's *The Antelope Wife*.

**Brother Roy**  Preacher who has left his church but remains the one person who fully understands Glen Davis's angst in Larry Brown's *Father and Son*.

**Cally Roy**  Mostly Ojibwa girl, daughter of Rozina Roy and Richard Whiteheart Beads and twin sister of Deanna Whiteheart Beads; narrates much of the Shawano-Roy family story in Louise Erdrich's *The Antelope Wife*.

**Matilda Roy**  Nineteenth-century Ojibwa girl separated from her mother (Blue Pairie Woman) in a U.S. Cavalry raid, adopted by soldier Scranton Roy, and later adopted by a band of antelope in Louise Erdrich's *The Antelope Wife*.

**Rozina (Rozin) Roy**   Mixed-blood daughter of Augustus Roy and either Zosie or Mary Shawano; marries Richard Whiteheart Beads and Frank Shawano; mother of twins Deanna Whiteheart Beads and Cally Roy in Louise Erdrich's *The Antelope Wife*.

**Scranton Roy**   U.S. Cavalry soldier who raids a peaceful Ojibwa village in nineteenth-century Dakota, adopts a baby girl from that village, and breastfeeds both this daughter (Matilda Roy) and his son in Louise Erdrich's *The Antelope Wife*.

**Zosie Shawano Roy**   Ojibwa woman who marries Augustus Roy; twin sister of Mary Shawano and co-mother of Rozina Roy in Louise Erdrich's *The Antelope Wife*.

**Nellie Royster**   Elderly domestic and friend of Mrs. Greco; slain and set afire by Bobby Bryant in Hal Bennett's *Seventh Heaven*.

**Lillian Rubenstein-Kraft**   Nat's lover and the university provost's ex-wife; loves Nat and stays with him after his wife dies in David Leavitt's *Equal Affections*.

**Daniela Rubin**   Member of the French Resistance during World War II; she and Jacqueline Levy-Monot travel together to escape occupied France; help smuggle Jewish children to safety; endure a Nazi concentration camp together; Daniela dies on the death march to Magdenberg in Marge Piercy's *Gone to Soldiers*.

**Tessie Rubin**   Jewish widow and Holocaust survivor; mistress of Sol Nazerman in Edward Lewis Wallant's *The Pawnbroker*.

**Ruby**   Troubled young man with severe emotional problems; works as a waterboy at the laundromat for a short time but can never hold a job; marries Ruth Grey in Jane Hamilton's *Book of Ruth*.

**Ruby**   Bootlegger's daughter and prostitute visited by Albert Riddell in Reynolds Price's *Love and Work*.

**Delores del Ruby**   Lesbian forewoman of the Rubber Rose Ranch in Tom Robbins's *Even Cowgirls Get the Blues*.

**Robert Rudleigh**   Tourist fisherman who, with his wife, hires Thomas Skelton as a guide in Thomas McGuane's *Ninety-Two in the Shade*.

**Dr. Jeffery Rudner**   Psychoanalyst, lover of Isadora Wing, and tennis partner of Bennett Wing in Erica Jong's *How to Save Your Own Life*.

**Carlos Rueda**   Argentine playwright and musician; married to Cecelia; father of Teresa; has gift of envisioning what has happened to those disappeared by the regime in Argentina; tells their stories to relatives; tells his wife's story; eventually they are reunited in Lawrence Thornton's *Imagining Argentina*.

**Cecelia Rueda**   Wife of Carlos; mother of Teresa; journalist taken and tortured by the regime in Argentina; eventually reunited with her husband in Lawrence Thornton's *Imagining Argentina*.

**Teresa Ruedos**   Daughter of Carlos and Cecelia Rueda; imprisoned, tortured, and killed in Lawrence Thornton's *Imagining Argentina*.

**Cardinal Ruffo**   Once a friend of the Cavaliere, he is put to death for making a treaty with the rebels that accepted a capitulation with terms in Susan Sontag's *The Volcano Lover*.

**Henry (Roscoe) Rules**   Meanest of the ten Los Angeles policemen-protagonists of Joseph Wambaugh's *The Choirboys*.

**Ironwood (Landlord) Rumble**   Foundling and blind musician in Leon Forrest's *The Bloodworth Orphans*.

**Bertram Rumfoord**   Harvard professor and military historian researching the Dresden raid in Kurt Vonnegut's *Slaughterhouse-Five*.

**Bobby Rupp**   Boyfriend of Nancy Clutter; briefly a suspect in the murder case because of her father's disapproval of the romance in Truman Capote's *In Cold Blood*.

**Michael S. Rushing**   See Michael S. Reusing.

**Eliza Rushmore**   Literary agent of Isadora Wing in Erica Jong's *How to Save Your Own Life*.

**Maria Ruskin**   Mistress of Sherman McCoy; married to a seventy-two-year-old wealthy financier; she is at the wheel of Sherman's car when hit-and-run accident occurs in Tom Wolfe's *The Bonfire of the Vanities*.

**Professor Rolfe Alan Ruskin**   Husband of the much younger Sarah Ruskin; card-carrying nuclear physicist, Nobel laureate, and scientific consultant to the Spanish Republic in William Herrick's *Hermanos!*

**Sarah Ruskin**   Fellow Communist Party worker and lover of Jake Starr and wife of Rolfe Ruskin; aids British volunteers on their way to the Spanish Civil War in William Herrick's *Hermanos!*

**Russell**   Small-time thief and drug addict; robs an illegal Mafia card game with Frankie and is turned in to the authorities for drug peddling by Jackie Cogan in George V. Higgins's *Cogan's Trade*.

**Buck Russell**   Posse member who favors sexual experiences with black women; lover of Della Brame in Reynolds Price's *A Generous Man*.

**James (Father Jim) Russell**   Priest; as a child, lived in Old Halvorsen Place in Larry Woiwode's *Beyond the Bedroom Wall*.

**Ruta**    Maid to Deborah Kelly Rojack and spy for Barney Kelly; seduced by Stephen Rojack after he murders Deborah in Norman Mailer's *An American Dream.*

**George Herman (Babe) Ruth**    Star outfielder for the New York Yankees who is the lover of Mason Tidewater, according to Tidewater's memoirs in Jay Neugeboren's *Sam's Legacy.*

**Damon Rutherford**    Imaginary wonderboy rookie pitcher for the Pioneers; killed by a bean ball in Robert Coover's *The Universal Baseball Association, Inc., J. Henry Waugh, Prop.*

**Diana Rutherford**    Twenty-year-old undergraduate student; occasional nursemaid and lover of Nathan Zuckerman; becomes fed up with Zuckerman's obsession with his critics and his continued state of inactivity in Philip Roth's *The Anatomy Lesson.*

**Willy Rutter**    Thug and bully in Paul Theroux's *The Family Arsenal.*

**Swami Rutuola**    Indian faith healer who succeeds in curing Tony Nailles of the sadness that confines him to bed for a month in John Cheever's *Bullet Park.*

**John Ruxton**    Fort doctor; married Martha when she was fourteen and he was thirty-nine; has had several children with his bibi (Indian mistress) in Bharati Mukherjee's *The Holder of the World.*

**Martha Ruxton**    Wife of the fort doctor, married him when she was fourteen and he was thirty-nine; chubby, pink, freckled, and blond in Bharati Mukherjee's *The Holder of the World.*

**Caroline Muller Ryan**    Wealthy doctor; wife of Jack Ryan; targeted by Ulster Liberation Army terrorists in Tom Clancy's *Patriot Games.*

**Elizabeth (Liz) O'Brien Ryan**    Friend and confidante of Isabel Moore in Mary Gordon's *Final Payments.*

**Emmet Ryan**    Police lieutenant, and father of Jack Ryan, who, with his partner Tom Douglas, tracks John Kelly's slayings of drug dealers; finally apprehends Kelly and allows him one hour to set things in order, which Kelly uses to fake his death in Tom Clancy's *Without Remorse.*

**Jack (John Patrick) Ryan**    Hero of Tom Clancy's central novels who returns to government service as national security adviser to President Durling; learns the "rules" of post–cold war geopolitics as Japan, China, and India join forces to cripple America and seize land in Siberia; devises strategies to counter the military and economic threats; is appointed vice president, only to become president when Sato kamikazes an airliner into a presidential address to a joint session of Congress in Tom Clancy's *Debt of Honor.* Also appears in *Executive Orders, Clear and Present Danger, The Cardinal of the Kremlin, Patriot Games,* and *The Hunt for Red October.*

**John Ryan**    Husband of Liz Ryan and unscrupulous seducer of her friend Isabel Moore in Mary Gordon's *Final Payments.*

**Mr. Ryan**    Mr. Arnold's roommate in the home; a former contractor, he plays a pivotal role in Will Barrett's plan to form his own utopian community in Walker Percy's *The Second Coming.*

**Rydag**    Adopted son of Taluta and Nezzie; he is a mix of two races and represents the future of the two existing civilizations in Jean Auel's *The Mammoth Hunters.*

**Hawkins Ryden**    Uncle of the mysterious Tommy Ryden; rides with the posse on the chance of finding something belonging to Tommy that will repay him for having taken care of Tommy and his mother in Reynolds Price's *A Generous Man.*

**Miss Jack Ryden**    Mother of Tommy Ryden in Reynolds Price's *A Generous Man.*

**Tommy Ryden**    Father of Lois Provo and lover of Kate Pomeroy; supposedly killed in World War II in Reynolds Price's *A Generous Man.*

**Ekaterina Alexandrovna (Kate) Ryleyeva**    Russian translator and escort of Henry Bech; translates science fiction into Ukrainian; helps Bech spend the rubles given to him as Russian royalties in John Updike's *Bech: A Book.*

**Coke Rymer**    Blond youth who helps Mina Morgan destroy Peter Leland but is destined to be her victim in an even more hideous destruction in Fred Chappell's *Dagon.*

**Cecile Sabat**   Great aunt of Wiley Wright and grandmother of Helene Wright; her death causes Helene's emotionally wrenching visit to her Louisiana birthplace in Toni Morrison's *Sula*.

**Rochelle Sabat**   Daughter of Cecile Sabat and mother of Helene Wright; estranged from her daughter because of her life as a madam in a Louisiana bordello in Toni Morrison's *Sula*.

**Sabatini**   Bookie who allows Samuel Paul Berman to develop a large gambling debt in Jay Neugeboren's *Sam's Legacy*.

**Hassan i Sabbah**   Prophet whose teachings represent a threat to control addicts in William S. Burroughs's *The Ticket That Exploded* and *Nova Express*.

**Mickey (Morris) Sabbath**   Retired puppeteer; first wife, Nikki Kantarakis, disappeared; second wife, Roseanne Cavanaugh, supports him; adulterous lover of Drenka Balich; haunted by thoughts of his older brother killed during World War II; after Drenka dies and Roseanne asks him to leave, decides to kill himself but does not in Philip Roth's *Sabbath's Theater*.

**Nikki Kantarakis Sabbath**   Actress and first wife of Mickey Sabbath; disappears and is never located in Philip Roth's *Sabbath's Theater*.

**Roseanne Cavanaugh Sabbath**   Second wife of Mickey Sabbath; supports him; high school art teacher; recovering alcoholic; asks Mickey to leave her when he mocks her recovery in Philip Roth's *Sabbath's Theater*.

**Barbara Sabich**   Wife of prosecuting attorney Rusty Sabich who never recovers from her husband's infidelity, in Scott Turow's *Presumed Innocent*.

**Rusty Sabich**   Chief deputy prosecuting attorney for Kindle County with all-consuming attraction to Carolyn Polhemus, who is not his wife; when Polhemus is murdered, he is put on trial; husband of Barbara Sabich in Scott Turow's *Presumed Innocent*.

**Sabrina (Bu, Sabu)**   Daughter of George Cain and Nichole in George Cain's *Blueschild Baby*.

**Sally Sachs**   Painter and lover of Ricky Potter in Alison Lurie's *Real People*.

**Joe Sagessa**   Police sergeant assigned to drive Alfonso Columbato and Birdy while they catch stray dogs in William Wharton's *Birdy*.

**Lena St. Clair**   Daughter of Ying-Ying St. Clair; half Caucasian and half Chinese; works for her husband's architect firm; splits all household expenses with husband in Amy Tan's *The Joy Luck Club*.

**Ying-Ying St. Clair**   Mother of Lena St. Clair; is abandoned by her first husband and aborts their baby boy; enters a second, loveless marriage to an American man she meets in China; gives birth to a baby boy with no brain in Amy Tan's *The Joy Luck Club*.

**Waldo St. Cloud**   Narrator and protagonist of Osgood Wallop's *The Duchess of Obloquy* in Peter De Vries's *Mrs. Wallop*.

**Albert St. Dennis**   Aging British poet and visiting Distinguished Professor of Poetry at Woodslee University in Joyce Carol Oates's *Unholy Loves*.

**Oliver St. Ives**   Middle-aged actor who discusses his plans with Sally about starring in a film featuring a gay superhero in Michael Cunningham's *The Hours*.

**Angela Grace St. John**   Wife of a Los Angeles doctor; has an affair with Abel in N. Scott Momaday's *House Made of Dawn*.

**Saloman Saint-Jupe**   Works for the Worthingtons; makes the financial arrangements with the families for the boys; on Tuesday evenings, dresses like a woman and goes by the name Madame Sara in Herbert Gold's *Slave Trade*.

**Sal**   Friend and partner in crime of the youthful Vinnie; later friend and drinking companion of Mike Kelly in Hubert Selby, Jr.'s *Last Exit to Brooklyn*.

**Art Salerno**   Employee and best friend of Stan Waltz; husband of Lena Salerno in Peter De Vries's *Let Me Count the Ways*.

**Lena Salerno**   Wife of Art Salerno and quasi-mistress of Stan Waltz in Peter De Vries's *Let Me Count the Ways*.

**John (Angel of Death, The Grim Reaper) Sallow**   Professional wrestler who defeats James Boswell and precipitates a crisis of the will and a lengthy reappraisal of Boswell's personal values in Stanley Elkin's *Boswell*.

**Sally**   Public television producer; lives in New York City with her lover, Clarissa Vaughan, in Michael Cunningham's *The Hours*.

**Sally**   Commune-mate of Beth Walker; rears an illegitimate child with the help of the women's commune in Marge Piercy's *Small Changes*.

**Sally Ann**   Teenage daughter of Vic; wears jeans with sewn-on patches that have risqué sayings on them; wants to have sex with Gerald in Robert Coover's *Gerald's Party*.

**Hilary Saltwood**   Son of an English sea captain; rebels in his decision to become a missionary; fervent and sincere in his beliefs; lives with the Hottentots of South Africa to fulfill his mission in James A. Michener's *The Covenant*.

**Philip Saltwood**   Vacations in South Africa in the late 1970s; descendant of Saltwood family of England; diamond prospector; falls in love with Susanna VanDoor in James A. Michener's *The Covenant*.

**Ben Saltz**   Jewish scientist and husband of Irene Saltz; they are involved in partner swapping with Carol and Eddie Constantine in John Updike's *Couples*.

**Irene Saltz**   Community social activist and wife of Ben Saltz in John Updike's *Couples*.

**Sam**   Registrar who refuses to allow Will Harris to register to vote in Junius Edwards's *If We Must Die*.

**Sam**   First of two fetuses spontaneously aborted by Anne Sorenson; narrates part of Frederick Busch's *Manual Labor*.

**Sam**   White civil rights activist who researches the life of Tunis G. Campbell on the Georgia Sea Islands in Nicholas Delbanco's *News*.

**Sam the Lion**   Owner of the picture show, pool hall, and café in Thalia; onetime lover of Lois Farrow; dies of a stroke in Larry McMurtry's *The Last Picture Show*.

**Harry Sam**   Polish dictator of Harry Sam and former used-car salesman who disappears into the john for thirty years after catching a ravaging illness in Ishmael Reed's *The Free-Lance Pallbearers*.

**The Saminone**   Black-talking inner voice—the voice of the Sam or Sambo in one—signifying in mysterious hallucinatory appearances to Max Reddick in John A. Williams's *The Man Who Cried I Am*.

**Artur (Slim-Jim, Uncle Sammler) Sammler**   Elegant septuagenarian and Anglophile; survivor of a mass grave in Nazi-occupied Poland; concerned observer and critic of twentieth-century America's sexual emancipation, crime in the streets, technological mania, cultural leveling, and moral decline; protagonist and central intelligence of Saul Bellow's *Mr. Sammler's Planet*.

**Shula (Shula-Slawa) Sammler**   Daughter of Artur Sammler, ex-wife of Eisen, and a scavenger and collector who devotes herself to unconnected intellectual pursuits and to her father's nonexistent project on H. G. Wells in Saul Bellow's *Mr. Sammler's Planet*.

**Sammy the Butcher**   Member of the Nova Mob in William S. Burroughs's *Nova Express* and *The Ticket That Exploded*.

**Kid Sampson**   Pilot sliced in two by a propeller in a freak accident, after which McWatt commits suicide in Joseph Heller's *Catch-22*.

**Margo Sampson**   Successful architect and divorcée who lives in Boulder, Colorado; has two teenage children, Stuart and Michelle; falls in love with a friend's ex-husband, Andrew Broder; decides to take a chance at merging families with Broder and his daughter in Judy Blume's *Smart Women*.

**Michelle Sampson**   Sixteen-year-old daughter of Margo Sampson; has an affair with one of her mother's old lovers just for the experience in Judy Blume's *Smart Women*.

**Stuart Sampson**   Seventeen-year-old son of Margo Sampson in Judy Blume's *Smart Women*.

**Robert Samson**   White owner of the plantation on which Miss Jane Pittman lives during the civil rights movement; father of Tee Bob Samson and the mulatto Timmy in Ernest J. Gaines's *The Autobiography of Miss Jane Pittman*.

**Robert (Tee Bob) Samson, Jr.**   Privileged white son of Robert Samson and half brother by the same father of the mulatto Timmy; commits suicide after being rejected by Mary Agnes LeFabre in Ernest J. Gaines's *The Autobiography of Miss Jane Pittman*.

**Lev Samsonov**   Russian dissident doctor and scientist exiled to Siberia; married for two years to Ludmilla Samsonov; does not know she is a KGB agent using him as cover to reach the West; father of Karla, who dies in a fall; believes her death is part of a government conspiracy to silence him; insists on an investigation, which leads to several deaths in Stuart M. Kaminsky's *A Cold Red Sunrise*.

**Ludmilla Samsonov**   Wife of Lev Samsonov, famous Russian doctor and dissident; in reality is a KGB agent both monitoring Samsonov and using him to reach the West; threatened in this mission by the investigation into the accidental death of Samsonov's daughter; arranges the murder of the initial investigator to prevent this in Stuart M. Kaminsky's *A Cold Red Sunrise*.

**Samuel**   Cantankerous, misanthropic judge of Israel who anoints the shepherd youth David as King of Israel after Saul falls out of favor with God in Joseph Heller's *God Knows*.

**Reverend Samuel**   Married to Corrine; takes in children given to him by Celie's stepfather because he and his wife can have no children; goes on mission to Africa; marries Nettie after his wife's death in Alice Walker's *The Color Purple*.

**Brenda Samuels**   Prostitute who gives Thomas Spellacy information that helps him solve the murder of Lois Fazenda in John Gregory Dunne's *True Confessions*.

**Frances "Franny" Samuelson**   Mother of Gretel and Jason, best friend of Margot; after her husband leaves she gets terminal cancer in Alice Hoffman's *Local Girls*.

**Gretel Samuelson**   Daughter of Frances; becomes Sonny Garnet's lover, but dumps him when she discovers he is a drug dealer; is hired as associate editor for a magazine that Eugene Kessler publishes in Alice Hoffman's *Local Girls*.

**Jason Samuelson**   Brother of Gretel, son of Frances; gets a job at the Food Star market; dates Terry LoPacca; pawns items from his mother's house; dies of a heroin overdose in Alice Hoffman's *Local Girls*.

**Sam Samuelson**   Husband of Frances, father of Jason and Gretel; leaves his family and marries a woman named Thea in Alice Hoffman's *Local Girls*.

**Thea Samuelson**   Marries the father of Jason and Gretel after he divorces their mother, Frances; ten years younger than Frances in Alice Hoffman's *Local Girls*.

**Marilyn Sanburne**   Mayor's wife in the town of Crozet; leader of the project to excavate and ultimately restore the servants' quarters at Monticello in Rita Mae Brown's *Murder at Monticello*.

**Cecelia Sanchez**   New assistant professor of Spanish at Moo University, originally from Costa Rica; good-looking; has brief affair with Tim Monahan and longer one with Chairman X in Jane Smiley's *Moo*.

**Manuel (Kid Sanchez) Sanchez**   Ex-boxer who works for Everett Henshaw during apricot season; idolized by Tasmania Orcino in Jessamyn West's *A Matter of Time*.

**Raphael Nicholas (Nicky) Sanchez**   Homosexual set designer for Boris Adrian's pornographic movie in Terry Southern's *Blue Movie*.

**Max Sand**   See Nevada Smith.

**Tony Sanders**   Screenwriter for Boris Adrian's pornographic movie in Terry Southern's *Blue Movie*.

**George Sanderson**   Professor of history and thesis adviser who takes a special interest in Leslie McGivers; having an open marriage, he takes Honor Rogers as his lover in Marge Piercy's *The High Cost of Living*.

**Lydia Bennett Sanderson**   Pioneer woman who narrates part of the novel through journal entries and letters; widow of Lars Sanderson; turns down Tim Whiteaker's proposal of marriage in Molly Gloss's *The Jump-Off Creek*.

**Naomi (Mary Joy) Sandifer**   Mother of Ralph Sandifer and wife of Buddy Sandifer; author of lurid, erotic adventures in Thomas Berger's *Sneaky People*.

**Ralph Virgil (Ralphie) Sandifer**   Fifteen-year-old midwestern hero of Thomas Berger's *Sneaky People*.

**Virgil (Buddy) Sandifer**   Unctuous used car salesman, unfaithful husband of Naomi Sandifer, and father of Ralph Sandifer in Thomas Berger's *Sneaky People*.

**Hiram Sandlin**   Brilliant headmaster of experimental Fair Haven School until he dies of a massive heart attack in Gail Godwin's *Evensong*.

**Sandra**   See Mayo.

**Joey Sands**   Beautiful male prostitute and heroin addict who flees Manila and joins a rebel guerrilla group after accidentally witnessing the government's assassination of Senator Domingo Avila in Jessica Hagedorn's *Dogeaters*.

**Judith Sands**   Reclusive novelist sought out by Doctor Mann; permits Renate to read her hidden manuscript; contributor to Renate's planned magazine in Anaïs Nin's *Collages*.

**Felix (The Great Sandusky) Sandusky**   Strongman and early teacher who advises James Boswell to deny his impulse for ego aggrandizement in Stanley Elkin's *Boswell*.

**Betty Sandwich**   See Betty MacNaughton.

**Hamilton (Ham) Sandwich**   Infant son of Joe and Naughty Sandwich; named for Uncle Hamilton in the hope of an inheritance in Peter De Vries's *The Vale of Laughter*.

**Joe Sandwich**   Inept stockbroker and perpetual life of the party; dies in a spectacular bicycle mishap; narrates part of Peter De Vries's *The Vale of Laughter.*

**Blaise Delacroix Sanford**   Fierce, ambitious publisher of the prestigious *Washington Tribune;* uses his power and wealth to manipulate others in Gore Vidal's *Washington, D.C.*

**Enid Sanford**   Volatile wife of Clay Overbury; sent to an asylum by her father, Blaise Sanford; killed in a car crash in Gore Vidal's *Washington, D.C.*

**Frederika Sanford**   Harshly critical mother of Peter Sanford, wife of Blaise Sanford in Gore Vidal's *Washington, D.C.*

**Peter Sanford**   Sharp-tongued editor of *The American Idea;* son of Blaise and Frederika Sanford in Gore Vidal's *Washington, D.C.*

**Lola San-Marquand**   Artistic director of the Actors' Means Workshop and wife of Saul San-Marquand in James Baldwin's *Tell Me How Long the Train's Been Gone.*

**Saul San-Marquand**   Artistic director of the Actors' Means Workshop and husband of Lola San-Marquand in James Baldwin's *Tell Me How Long the Train's Been Gone.*

**Sansori**   Japanese ornithologist who relates the tale of how a dodo bird helped a medieval emperor defeat his enemies in Stanley Elkin's *The Dick Gibson Show.*

**Danny Santini**   Father of Gil Santini; stays with Harry Meyers to protect Meyers from possible attack by Jackson's brother in Jay Neugeboren's *Listen Ruben Fontanez.*

**Gil Santini**   Murdered five-year-old son of Danny Santini in Jay Neugeboren's *Listen Ruben Fontanez.*

**Santos**   Freed slave seemingly oblivious to pain; brings Rutherford to Papa Zeringue, to whom he owes money; finally strong-arms Papa when he realizes Papa owned the *Republic,* a slave trader that carried Allmuseri tribe members, of whom he is a descendant in Charles Johnson's *Middle Passage.*

**Jesus (Chuy) Santos**   Resourceful but shady local villager with beautiful singing voice who starts taxi service in village of Ibarra in Harriet Doerr's *Stones for Ibarra.*

**Lydia Santos**   Cesar Castillo's last mistress; she is a Puerto Rican factory worker, thirty years his junior with two young children; Cesar's jealousy alarms her so much that she leaves him in Oscar Hijuelos's *The Mambo Kings Play Songs of Love.*

**Dr. Abe Sapirstein**   Devil worshipper and physician to Rosemary Woodhouse during her pregnancy with Satan's son in Ira Levin's *Rosemary's Baby.*

**Charlie (Chaim) Sapistein**   Real estate agent, father figure to Daniel Ginsberg, and lover of Anita Mendelsohn after Murray Mendelsohn's death; dreams of becoming a rabbi despite being unable to read because of dyslexia in Jay Neugeboren's *An Orphan's Tale.*

**Sarah**   Betrothed of Coalhouse Walker, Jr.; killed while trying to talk with Vice President James Sherman in E. L. Doctorow's *Ragtime.*

**Aunt Sarah**   Slave mother of Nigel; befriends Dana Franklin in Octavia E. Butler's *Kindred.*

**Alexis Saranditis**   Father of Dania Saranditis and friend of Mehemet Effendi in Nicholas Delbanco's *The Martlet's Tale.*

**Dania Saranditis**   Daughter of Alexis Saranditis and lover of Mehemet Effendi and Sotiris Procopirios in Nicholas Delbanco's *The Martlet's Tale.*

**Sarge**   Balfour salesman who teaches Allie the mechanics of sex without love in Walker Percy's *The Second Coming.*

**Frank Sargent**   Mining associate of Oliver Ward; loves Susan Ward in Wallace Stegner's *Angle of Repose.*

**Aunt Saro Jane**   Folk seer and former slave in Sarah E. Wright's *This Child's Gonna Live.*

**Lady Margaret Sarpie**   Member of an aristocratic New Orleans family and sometime literary critic for a local newspaper; lives largely in a world of artifice and fantasy; criticizes others' novels while spending years slowly writing her own insipid romance in Ellen Gilchrist's *Victory Over Japan.*

**Col. John Sartoris**   See Volume I.

**Torajiro Sato**   Japanese airline pilot whose father was killed in World War II; sees his brother's ship destroyed by American torpedoes and identifies his son's body after his son's fighter explodes an American bomb while landing; avenges their deaths by flying his 747 into the U.S. Capitol building during the president's address to a joint session of Congress, killing the president and the majority of the American government and narrowly missing Jack Ryan in Tom Clancy's *Debt of Honor.*

**Satterfield**   Curator of a museum of maritime trade in Massachusetts in Bharati Mukherjee's *The Holder of the World.*

**Ellie Sattler**   Twenty-four-year-old paleobotanist; colleague of Alan Grant; guest of John Hammond at Isla Nublar, a remote Costa Rican island resort; displays courage and resourcefulness when confronted by genetically engineered dinosaurs in Michael Crichton's *Jurassic Park.*

**Saul**   David's predecessor as God's favorite; warrior King of Israel who grows jealous of David's success in battle and David's popularity with the people; paranoid ruler who is prone to depression and spells of madness, and who makes numerous attempts to have David killed in Joseph Heller's *God Knows.*

**Danny Saunders**   Brilliant friend of Reuven Matter; leaves his Hasidic faith to become a psychologist in Chaim Potok's *The Chosen;* marries Rachel Gordon after treating her catatonic cousin Michael in *The Promise.*

**Reb Isaac Saunders**   Anti-Zionist Hasidic rabbi who passes on his deep faith to his son, Danny, by rearing him in silence in Chaim Potok's *The Chosen* and *The Promise.*

**Leonard Saunders**   Coconspirator in Willie Hall's plan to lynch a white policeman in John Edgar Wideman's *The Lynchers.*

**Levi Saunders**   Sickly younger son of Reb Saunders; becomes Reb's designated successor as rabbi when Danny Saunders becomes a psychologist in Chaim Potok's *The Chosen;* gradually grows into the role of rabbi in *The Promise.*

**Michelle Saunders**   Young reporter for *The Clarion* who writes better and more serious stories as she becomes better able to understand the people in Runnymede in Rita Mae Brown's *Bingo.*

**Alan Savage**   Son of professor Byron Savage; successful scholar; intelligent, suave, and a little cynical; later becomes Iris's fiancé in Joyce Carol Oates's *Because It Is Bitter, and Because It Is My Heart.*

**Byron Savage**   Iris's Courtney's professor at college and later her father-in-law; good-tempered husband of Gwendolyn Savage and father of Alan Savage in Joyce Carol Oates's *Because It Is Bitter, and Because It Is My Heart.*

**Gwendolyn Savage**   Wife of Byron Savage and mother of Alan Savage; eagerly sets up her son and Iris in Joyce Carol Oates's *Because It Is Bitter, and Because It Is My Heart.*

**Joan Savage**   Rock star Harlan managed; ex-husband is James Savage; never forgives Harlan for sleeping with her ex-husband; stabs Harlan with a knife in Gayl Jones's *The Healing.*

**Naughton James Savage**   Joan Savage's ex-husband; scientist originally from Maine; sleeps with Harlan; doesn't like Joan's music in Gayl Jones's *The Healing.*

**Tony Savanola**   Catholic neighbor of the Luries; although he does not hate Jews, he bows to Eddie Kulanski's pressure and helps torment David Lurie in Chaim Potok's *In the Beginning.*

**Savata**   Sister of Ruby Drew; becomes a bishop in the Light of the World Holiness Church, but finally resists her sister's efforts to save her in William Goyen's *The Fair Sister.*

**Jack Sawyer**   Twelve-year-old boy who travels through the real world and an alternative world of the Territories seeking a talisman with healing powers to cure his cancer-stricken mother in Stephen King's and Peter Straub's *The Talisman.*

**Lily Cavanaugh Sawyer**   Mother of Jack Sawyer; faded B-movie actress suffering from cancer in Stephen King's and Peter Straub's *The Talisman.*

**Doctor (Adolphus Asher Ghoulens, King of Anti Evil, Raymond) Sax**   See Volume I.

**Klara Sax**   Famous American artist and former housewife; in the early 1990s supervised a massive project to paint American bombers abandoned in the desert; was married to Albert Bronzini; had an affair with Nick Shay, a former student of Bronzini's; estranged from her daughter, Teresa; takes various lovers and husbands, but remains essentially alone in Don DeLillo's *Underworld.*

**Madeleine Saxon**   See Mary-Jane Saxon Kirkland.

**Rosie Sayers**   Fourteen-year-old African-American girl; after she is bitten by a fox, she is given to her mother's boyfriend, Alvin Crooms, to be a maid, but is rescued by Mary McNutt; is shot and killed by Paris Trout in Pete Dexter's *Paris Trout.*

**LaDonna Scales**   Daughter of Pourty Bloodworth; sister of Amos-Otis Thigpen, Noah Grandberry, and Regal Pettibone (who is also her lover); half sister of Jonathan Bass in Leon Forrest's *The Bloodworth Orphans.*

**Jimmy Scalisi**   Bank robber and skilled craftsman with a pistol who works with Eddie Coyle in George V. Higgins's *The Friends of Eddie Coyle.*

**Red Scalotta**   Millionaire bookmaker and sexual pervert in Joseph Wambaugh's *The Blue Knight.*

**Scanlon**   Last of the patients influenced by Randle McMurphy left at the mental hospital after McMurphy dies and Chief Bromden escapes in Ken Kesey's *One Flew Over the Cuckoo's Nest.*

**Mary Scanlon**   Single friend of Elsie Buttrick who moves in with Elsie to help her raise her child in John Casey's *Spartina.*

**Scarecrow**   Successful black writer and expatriate; confusion over racial and sexual roles leads to his murdering four people and his own death; protagonist of Calvin Hernton's *Scarecrow.*

**Vitellio Scarpia**   Baron who is an exceptionally cruel man put in charge of suppressing republican opposition in Naples by the queen; experiences sexual pleasure by debasing and humiliating the object of his desire; murdered by a diva after he has tortured her lover in Susan Sontag's *The Volcano Lover.*

**Peter Scatterpatter**   Translator of the anonymous *A Manual for Sons* in Donald Barthelme's *The Dead Father.*

**Miller (Mill) Schabb**   Partner in the mob-run Regents Sportsmen's Club, Inc.; with Croce Torre, attempts to kill The Greek Almas in George V. Higgins's *The Digger's Game.*

**Beatrice (Bea) Schachter**   Experienced teacher who befriends Sylvia Barrett and helps her make it through her first year at Calvin Coolidge High School; respected and loved by students in Bel Kaufman's *Up the Down Staircase.*

**Mona Schaedel** Mother of Sandy and Myra; a widow who has just begun to date again in Judy Blume's *Wifey*.

**Raymond (Ray) Schaefer** Guileless American professor and cousin of Sophie Butts; smitten with Claire Fougeray in Aaron Elkins's *Old Bones*.

**Anna Schaeffer** Agent for Asher Lev; bolsters Lev and sells Lev's paintings to the Manhattan Museum of Art in Chaim Potok's *My Name Is Asher Lev*.

**Moira Schaffner** Secretary at the Love Clinic and naively romantic girlfriend of Tom More in Walker Percy's *Love in the Ruins*.

**Scheherazade (Sherry)** Sister of Dunyazade; must invent a way to prevent the king from raping and killing a virgin every night in the *Dunyazadiad,* a novella in John Barth's *Chimera*.

**Lieutenant Scheisskopf** Humorless and absurdly ambitious officer obsessed with uniformity and winning parades; eventually promoted to general in Joseph Heller's *Catch-22*.

**André Schevitz** Zuckerman's agent; married to Mary; helpful in all aspects of Zuckerman's life but wants Zuckerman to live more lavishly than he does in Philip Roth's *Zuckerman Unbound*.

**Jack Schiff** Curmudgeonly and defensive physically disabled professor of political geography; left by wife on eve of hosting party for graduate students in the novella, *Her Sense of Timing,* in Stanley Elkin's *Van Gogh's Room at Arles*.

**Dr. Schiff** Woman psychiatrist who treats Hilary Wiggen; enamored of Henry Wiggen in Mark Harris's *It Looked Like For Ever*.

**Lawrence (Larry) Schiller** Journalist who investigates Gary Gilmore's life in Norman Mailer's *The Executioner's Song*.

**Father Schimmelpfennig** Catholic priest, spiritual adviser to the Neumiller family in Hyatt, North Dakota, and special friend of Martin Neumiller in Larry Woiwode's *Beyond the Bedroom Wall*.

**Oskar Schindler** German businessman from Moravia who operated enamelware factory in Cracow during World War II; used business as way to protect Jewish workers from starving and being sent to death camps in Thomas Keneally's *Schindler's List*.

**Schmendrick** Magician who frees the unicorn from Mommy Fortuna's Midnight Carnival and helps her find other unicorns in Peter S. Beagle's *The Last Unicorn*.

**Mr. Schmidt** Adoptive father of Adrian Bonner; withheld his food, tortured or killed any animal he showed affection for, beat him in front of his school friends, and worked him until he dropped in Gail Godwin's *Evensong*.

**Mrs. Schmidt** Adoptive mother of Adrian; withheld his food, tortured or killed any animal he showed affection for, beat him in front of his schoolfriends, and worked him until he dropped in Gail Godwin's *Evensong*.

**Nectar Schmidt** College roommate of Geneva Spofford; paramour, then second wife of Jack Dumbrowski in Peter De Vries's *Reuben, Reuben*.

**Fran Otto Schmitt** Woman who escorts her husband's body home to Germany in Katherine Anne Porter's *Ship of Fools*.

**Schmuel** Father-in-law of Yakov Bok in Bernard Malamud's *The Fixer*.

**Millie Schnell** Widow of Dutch Schnell in Mark Harris's *It Looked Like For Ever*.

**Brandon Schnitzer** Younger brother of Susie Schnitzer; shares their father's values, not Susie's in Harriette Simpson Arnow's *The Weedkiller's Daughter*.

**Herman (Bismarck) Schnitzer** Radically right-wing father of Susie Schnitzer; racial bigot on a weed-killing campaign; fears having his Detroit suburb overrun by weeds and blacks in Harriette Simpson Arnow's *The Weedkiller's Daughter*.

**Mrs. (The Popsicle Queen) Schnitzer** Mother of Susie Schnitzer; conforms to her husband's WASPish country-club lifestyle in Harriette Simpson Arnow's *The Weedkiller's Daughter*.

**Susan Marie (Susie) Schnitzer** Intelligent, self-aware fifteen-year-old heroine of Harriette Simpson Arnow's *The Weedkiller's Daughter*.

**Sammy Schoelkopf** Son of the next-farm neighbors of Mary Robinson; occasionally mows the fields for her in John Updike's *Of the Farm*.

**Marvin Schoenbrun** Tenant of the 70th Street building managed by Norman Moonbloom in Edward Lewis Wallant's *The Tenants of Moonbloom*.

**Buddy Schonbeck** Boyhood friend of Jerome Neumiller and Charles Neumiller (II) in Larry Woiwode's *Beyond the Bedroom Wall*.

**Harry (Schoons) Schoonover** College roommate and drinking buddy of Jerry Payne; owner of the Screaming Bitch, an automobile in John Nichols's *The Sterile Cuckoo*.

**Dr. Schott** President of Wicomico State Teachers College in John Barth's *The End of the Road*.

**Emil Schransky** German-Russian captain of New England merchant ship; brutal exploiter of both sea animal and native populations in Alaskan coastal waters in James Michener's *Alaska*.

**Kenneth (Kenny, Dr. Yankem) Schreuer**   Dentist, tennis and radio soap-opera enthusiast, and former student of George Caldwell in John Updike's *The Centaur*.

**O. Schrutt**   Former Nazi stormtrooper; dope-taking night watchman who beats the zoo animals; put in a cage in John Irving's *Setting Free the Bears*.

**Marshall Schulman**   Los Angeles deputy district attorney who prosecutes Gregory Powell and Jimmy Smith in Joseph Wambaugh's *The Onion Field*.

**Dutch Schultz**   1930s mob leader, once known as Arthur Flegenheimer, who tries unsuccessfully to maintain his failing influence and brings Billy Bathgate into the rackets in E. L. Doctorow's *Billy Bathgate*.

**Schumann**   Ship's doctor who falls in love with his drug-addicted patient La Condesa as he is returning, a dying man, to Germany in Katherine Anne Porter's *Ship of Fools*.

**Kurt von Schuschnigg**   Chancellor of Austria coerced by Hitler into agreeing to the German Anschluss in 1938 in John Irving's *Setting Free the Bears*.

**Charles (Charlie, Old Patroon) Schuyler**   Law clerk in Aaron Burr's office commissioned to write Burr's memoirs; narrator of Gore Vidal's *Burr*.

**Dr. Abigail Schwartz**   Psychoanalyst of Isadora Wing in Erica Jong's *How to Save Your Own Life*.

**Scooter (Mister Man)**   Young black narrator of Albert Murray's *Train Whistle Guitar*.

**Carlos Scotobal**   Bank clerk and police informer in Merida, Mexico, in Nicholas Delbanco's *News*.

**Scott**   Professor and member of the Centennial Club in Thomas McGuane's *The Sporting Club*.

**Scott**   See Hud.

**Abra Scott**   Ambitious graduate student before the war; follows her lover Oscar Kahan into the OSS during World War II; marries Daniel Balaban after the war and travels to Japan in Marge Piercy's *Gone to Soldiers*.

**David (David Darling) Scott**   American painter traveling with Jenny Brown, with whom he has a hopeless affair, in Katherine Anne Porter's *Ship of Fools*.

**General Hector Scott**   Retired military officer and lover of Aurora Greenway in Larry McMurtry's *Terms of Endearment*.

**Ida Scott**   Promising black jazz singer from Harlem; sister of Rufus Scott and lover of Vivaldo Moore in James Baldwin's *Another Country*.

**Kendra Scott**   Young Colorado schoolteacher who moves to Desolation, Alaska, to teach in small school; has intuitive connection to natives; marries Rick Venn, grandson of Tom Venn, in James *Michener's Alaska*.

**Rufus Scott**   Down-and-out black jazz musician who commits suicide in a frenzy of despair; brother of Ida Scott, friend of Vivaldo Moore and Cass Silenski; one-time lover of Eric Jones; lover and abuser of Leona in James Baldwin's *Another Country*.

**Baby Lazar Scruggs**   Exotic dancer whom Arista Prolo cannot outdance; overprotected by her mother in Carlene Hatcher Polite's *Sister X and the Victims of Foul Play*.

**Matthew (Matt) Scudder**   Middle-aged former New York City cop; recovering alcoholic, earns a sparse living as an unlicensed private detective in Lawrence Block's *A Dance at the Slaughterhouse and other detective novels*.

**Ian Scuffling**   See Lieutenant Tyrone Slothrop.

**Dominic (Scuz) Scuzzi**   Los Angeles police sergeant in charge of the vice squad in Joseph Wambaugh's *The Choirboys*.

**Harry Seagraves**   Paris Trout's lawyer; unhappily married to Lucy Seagraves; well known and respected in his community; has an affair with Hanna Trout; is shot and killed by Paris Trout in Pete Dexter's *Paris Trout*.

**Fletcher Lynd (Fletch, Fletcher Gull) Seagull**   Young seagull from Jonathan Livingston Seagull's flock who, after perfecting his flying, returns to the flock to teach the young gulls in Richard Bach's *Jonathan Livingston Seagull*.

**Jonathan Livingston (Jon, Jonathan Gull) Seagull**   Seagull who refuses to accept ordinary life and seeks a more meaningful existence by striving to perfect his flying skills, which he does after transcending life in Richard Bach's *Jonathan Livingston Seagull*.

**Vurl Seaman**   College boyfriend of Blix Hollister in Jessamyn West's *A Matter of Time*.

**Sean**   Brother of Nell, husband of Marie; a drama teacher at Louise Wiley's school in Elizabeth Benedict's *Slow Dancing*.

**Dr. Kennard Sear**   Tiresias figure who heads the college infirmary in John Barth's *Giles Goat-Boy*.

**Ivor (Istvan Szegedyi) Sedge**   Hungarian refugee, painter, and former lover of Violet Clay in Gail Godwin's *Violet Clay*.

**Ethan Segal**   Lover of Jack Laws and friend of Pammy Wynant; shares an office with her in Don DeLillo's *Players*.

**Cruz Segovia**   Los Angeles police sergeant and best friend of Bumper Morgan; killed by a robber in Joseph Wambaugh's *The Blue Knight*.

**Joey Seldon**    Blind man who sells popcorn and candy; regains his sight but doesn't let others know until he shoots a bank robber who turns out to be Robert Haddad in Mary McGarry Morris's *Songs in Ordinary Time.*

**Bertha Selig**    Sister with whom Sol Nazerman lives in Edward Lewis Wallant's *The Pawnbroker.*

**Beatrice Fetner (Bebe) Sellars**    Wife of Jack Sellars; amateur philosopher who is much in love with her husband after many years of marriage in Doris Betts's *The River to Pickle Beach.*

**Jack S. Sellars**    Husband of Bebe Sellars; nature lover who read and studied while a maintenance man at Duke University; has successfully lived down the childhood trauma of his father's murder in Doris Betts's *The River to Pickle Beach.*

**Selma**    Cousin of Libby, Rachel, Grace, Elinor, and May; her father, Del, burned her hand on a lantern globe when he was drunk in Joan Chase's *During the Reign of the Queen of Persia.*

**The Swede Selvig**    Informant for Billy Bray; educated man with a screw loose; married to a rich woman in Maureen Howard's *Natural History.*

**Glen Selvy**    Buyer of erotic art for Senator Lloyd Percival, undercover agent of Radial Matrix, and lover of Moll Robbins and Nadine Rademacher; murdered in Don DeLillo's *Running Dog.*

**The Senator**    Successful politician of Kelly's parents' age; divorced with children; sexually active with younger women; admired by Kelly in Joyce Carol Oates's *Black Water.*

**Ouida Senza**    Brazilian boarder in the house of Anton and Theodora Wait; heavy and dark; believes in many religions; is afraid of the Immigration and Naturalization Service; dates Mr. Griggs; holds a Brazilian party at the Waits' house in Diane Johnson's *Lying Low.*

**Serena**    Mysterious prostitute and lover of George Levanter; murders a chauffeur with a metal rat-tail comb in Jerzy Kosinski's *Blind Date.*

**Mikhail Eduardovich Sergetov**    Nonvoting Politburo member responsible for energy production and distribution who briefs Politburo on long-term effects of terrorist destruction of a major Soviet oil refinery; unwillingly assists in laying plans for war against NATO; becomes secretary-general of the USSR in a coup to prevent nuclear war in Tom Clancy's *Red Storm Rising.*

**David Serrano**    Former babysitter for McFarland family; discovered Tiny McFarland's body; was originally accused of the murder, but later exonerated; found murdered in warehouse in Austin in Mary Willis Walker's *The Red Scream.*

**Sethe**    Escaped slave of Sweet Home Plantation in Kentucky; now resides in Ohio; mother of two girls and two boys; kills daughter and tries to kill other children to avoid the family's return to the plantation; friend and lover of Paul D in Toni Morrison's *Beloved.*

**Erect Severehead**    Television news analyst who reports on the assassination of Trick E. Dixon in Philip Roth's *Our Gang.*

**Kalik Shabazz**    Tailor who is a Muslim convert saving his money for a trip to Mecca; formerly the operator of an all-night barbecue and shrimp shack in Carlene Hatcher Polite's *Sister X and the Victims of Foul Play.*

**Lewis Shackleford**    Friend and business partner to George Carver, Sr., whose betrayal induces the family to begin anew in Memphis in Peter Taylor's *A Summons to Memphis.*

**Booker Shad**    Jazz musician encouraged by Jimson and Charlie Parker; disintegrates through the use of drugs in Carlene Hatcher Polite's *The Flagellants.*

**Hazel Shade**    Beloved daughter of John and Sybil Shade; commits suicide after a blind date, Pete Dean, walks out on her in the last of many frustrations in her short life in Vladimir Nabokov's *Pale Fire.*

**John Francis (S) Shade**    Author of the poem *Pale Fire,* professor of English, and expert on Alexander Pope; mistakenly murdered by an escaped lunatic who intended to shoot Judge Goldsworth, Shade's neighbor; Charles Kinbote interprets the murder in a more personal light in Vladimir Nabokov's *Pale Fire.*

**Sybil (Mrs. S) Shade**    Wife of John Shade portrayed lovingly in his poem *Pale Fire;* in contrast, Charles Kinbote's commentaries jealously depict her as a harpy in Vladimir Nabokov's *Pale Fire.*

**Shadrack**    Shell-shocked war veteran who befriends Sula and leads the annual Suicide Day Parade in Toni Morrison's *Sula.*

**Adam Shafer**    Head of the Department of Anthropology at Vanderbilt University, husband of Octavia Shafer, and father of Gratt Shafer; comes to Somerton to explore the forty mounds there in Jesse Hill Ford's *Mountains of Gilead.*

**Adam Gideon Shafer**    Infant son of Gratt and Patsy Jo Shafer; named for his grandfathers in Jesse Hill Ford's *Mountains of Gilead.*

**Gratt Shafer**    Graduate of Vanderbilt University in 1939, son of Adam and Octavia Shafer, and father of Adam Gideon Shafer; has a lengthy affair with Patsy Jo McCutcheon before marrying Eleanor Fite and marries Patsy Jo after Eleanor's death in Jesse Hill Ford's *Mountains of Gilead.*

**Octavia Ashmore (Madam) Shafer**    Wife of Adam Shafer and mother of Gratt Shafer in Jesse Hill Ford's *Mountains of Gilead.*

**Patricia Josephine (Patsy Jo) McCutcheon Shafer**   Daughter of Thomas McCutcheon, lover and later wife of Gratt Shafer, and mother of Adam Gideon Shafer in Jesse Hill Ford's *Mountains of Gilead*.

**Mrs. de Shamble**   See Laura Pribble.

**Sonny Shanks**   Rodeo star and lover of Eleanor Guthrie; dies in an automobile accident in Larry McMurtry's *Moving On*.

**Shaper**   Blind harpist who creates a history of noble causes to justify the aggression of the Scyldings in John Gardner's *Grendel*.

**Dr. Ben Shapiro**   Army friend and best man of Walter F. Starbuck in Kurt Vonnegut's *Jailbird*.

**Shar**   See Sherton.

**Sharon**   Pregnant woman slain in her Beverly Hills home in a Charles Manson–style massacre in Jerzy Kosinski's *Blind Date*.

**Marya Sharp**   See Ardis Ross.

**Shaun**   Assistant to Ruth Gower, builds exquisite table models of Ruth's sets and oversees their life-size construction for the stage; gets AIDS and decides to move back to Ireland to spend time with his brother in Gail Godwin's *Evensong*.

**Darby Shaw**   Young, female law student who accidentally becomes involved in a high-profile murder case of two Supreme Court justices through a legal brief she writes; she works to bring the perpetrators to justice in John Grisham's *The Pelican Brief*.

**Jimmy Shaw**   Retired pugilist who operates the Queen's Head, the pub where Edward Pierce meets Edgar Trent in Michael Crichton's *The Great Train Robbery*.

**Matt Shaw**   Owner and editor of the Hickory, Massachusetts, *Blade;* pays Ben Marvel $15 for the "Edgewise" column, minus deductions for quoted matter in Peter De Vries's *Through the Fields of Clover*.

**Rick Shaw**   Albermarle County sheriff who tries to unravel the motives behind the seemingly random violence; a thorough investigator, he is always a step behind Harry's cat in identifying the motive and murderer in Rita Mae Brown's *Cat on the Scent*.

**Cecille Shawano**   Mostly Ojibwa kung fu teacher in Minneapolis who is known for her tendency to embellish the truth; younger sister of Frank Shawano and Klaus Shawano in Louise Erdrich's *The Antelope Wife*.

**Frank Shawano**   Mostly Ojibwa baker in Minneapolis who spends his life trying to reproduce the magical blitzkuchen; brother of Klaus Shawano; lover and later husband of Rozina Roy in Louise Erdrich's *The Antelope Wife*.

**Klaus Shawano**   Mostly Ojibwa man from Minneapolis who kidnaps and is obsessively in love with the "antelope woman"

Sweetheart Calico; brother of Frank Shawano in Louise Erdrich's *The Antelope Wife*.

**Mary Shawano**   Ojibwa woman who is lover to her sister's husband, Augustus Roy; twin sister of Zosie Shawano Roy and co-mother of Rozina Roy in Louise Erdrich's *The Antelope Wife*.

**David Shawcross**   Friend and publisher of Abe Cady in Leon Uris's *QB VII*.

**Shawn**   Rock star who joins the Indians and becomes a brother of Corey in Marge Piercy's *Dance the Eagle to Sleep*.

**Roger Shawn**   Army lieutenant looking for the downed Scoop VII satellite in Michael Crichton's *The Andromeda Strain*.

**Marian Shay**   Wife of Nick Shay, a waste management executive in Phoenix, Arizona; works as a member of various civic committees; has affair with Nick's younger associate, Brian Glassic; uses illegal drugs in Don DeLillo's *Underworld*.

**Matty Shay**   Younger brother of Nick Shay; former government weapons scientist who joins a research institute dedicated to promoting health and economic welfare in the Third World; serves in Vietnam; becomes fascinated by the reports of a serial murderer called the Texas Highway Killer in Don DeLillo's *Underworld*.

**Nick Shay**   Middle-aged, upper-level executive in a waste-management firm in Phoenix, Arizona; believes his father was killed by the mob; believes also that a baseball he owns is the legendary, long-lost home run ball hit by Bobby Thomson to win the pennant for the '51 Giants; has an affair with Klara Sax; accidentally kills a man; suspects that his wife is having an affair with his associate, Brian Glassic, in Don DeLillo's *Underworld*.

**Sheba**   Gentle, often stoned fourth wife of Colonel Elleloû; accompanies him to the Balak only to be kidnapped by his enemies in John Updike's *The Coup*.

**Bobby Sheen**   Playboy from Wichita Falls who seduces Jacy Farrow in Larry McMurtry's *The Last Picture Show*.

**Mrs. Margaret Shelburne**   Arranges for Christianna Wheeler to see the Dionne quintuplets and to meet with Mrs. Dionne, a meeting Christianna declines after having traveled from Kentucky to Canada for this purpose in Bobbie Ann Mason's *Feather Crowns*.

**Anne-Maria Sherbrooke Sheldon**   Daughter of Daniel Sherbrooke and wife of Willard Sheldon; Mormon missionary in Guatemala whose letters are read by Maggie Sherbrooke in Nicholas Delbanco's *Sherbrookes;* mentioned in *Possession*.

**Willard Sheldon**   Husband of Anne-Maria Sherbrooke; Mormon missionary in Guatemala in Nicholas Delbanco's *Sherbrookes*.

**Mary Wollstonecraft Godwin Shelley**    Daughter of Mary Wollstonecraft and William Godwin; wife-to-be of Percy Shelley in Frances Sherwood's *Vindication*.

**Percy Shelley**    Mary's husband-to-be; a famous poet; still married to Harriet when he courts Mary in Frances Sherwood's *Vindication*.

**Harvey Shepard**    Land developer and businessman in Hyannis, Massachusetts; married to college sweetheart, Pam, who has recently left him, with three children; in debt to loan shark named King Powers; hires Spenser, a private detective, to locate Pam and eventually to rescue him from Powers in Robert B. Parker's *Promised Land*.

**Pam Shepard**    Wife of Harvey Shepard and mother of three in Hyannis, Massachusetts; flees the home and is taken in by a group of militant feminists led by Rose Alexander; takes part in a bank robbery to gain funds for a feminist revolution, during which a guard is killed; she is saved from jail and returned to her family by private detective Spenser in Robert B. Parker's *Promised Land*.

**Lenny Shepherd**    New York cowboy-style disk jockey who picks up Doreen in Sylvia Plath's *The Bell Jar*.

**Anne-Maria Sherbrooke**    See Anne-Maria Sherbrooke Sheldon.

**Daniel (Peacock) Sherbrooke**    Grandfather of Judah Sherbrooke and builder of the Sherbrooke mansion in Nicholas Delbanco's *Sherbrookes*.

**Harriet (Hattie) Sherbrooke**    Spinster sister of Judah Sherbrooke in Nicholas Delbanco's *Possession* and *Sherbrookes*.

**Ian Daniel Sherbrooke**    Son of Judah and Maggie Sherbrooke and an actor in Nicholas Delbanco's *Sherbrookes*.

**Judah (Jude) Porteous Sherbrooke**    Owner of Sherbrooke estate, husband of Maggie Sherbrooke, and father of Ian and Seth Sherbrooke in Nicholas Delbanco's *Possession* and *Sherbrookes*.

**Lisbeth McPherson Sherbrooke**    First wife of Judah Sherbrooke; killed in an accident in Nicholas Delbanco's *Possession*.

**Margaret (Maggie, Meg, Megan) Cutler Sherbrooke**    Wife of Judah Sherbrooke and mother of Ian and Seth Sherbrooke in Nicholas Delbanco's *Possession* and *Sherbrookes*.

**Seth Sherbrooke**    Son of Judah and Maggie Sherbrooke who dies of crib death in Nicholas Delbanco's *Possession* and *Sherbrookes*.

**Sherton (Shar)**    Race car driver and rebellious lover of Karen Herz; commits suicide by racing his car into a retaining wall in Joyce Carol Oates's *With Shuddering Fall*.

**Barbara Sherwood**    Court stenographer who lives briefly with Arthur Axelrod before her death in Scott Spencer's *Endless Love*.

**Sam Shields**    Father of Marie Shields Griswold; brings charges of manslaughter against Joseph Chase in Jessamyn West's *The Life I Really Lived*.

**Donald Shimoda**    Mysterious, laconic, and Christlike biplane pilot; guides Richard Bach to spiritual enlightenment in Bach's *Illusions: The Adventures of a Reluctant Messiah*.

**Stephen Shipler**    A lover of Lexi Steiner; works for a Washington law firm, offers Lexi a job in Elizabeth Benedict's *Slow Dancing*.

**Mr. Shipley**    Georgia cotton farmer who employs Grange and Margaret Copeland; rumored to be the father of Margaret's illegitimate son Star in Alice Walker's *The Third Life of Grange Copeland*.

**Lettiece Shipman**    Methodist female African slave; a heavy drinker who often acquires her liquor from Thomas Keene, with whom she has an affair and calls her master; is jealous of Fanny Cooper because of her engagement to Thomas in Hugh Nissenson's *The Tree of Life*.

**Shira Shipman**    Young Jewish woman and mid-level artificial-intelligence expert who returns to her childhood home following the end of her marriage and the loss of her son; falls in love with robot, Yod, in Marge Piercy's *He, She and It*.

**Shirley**    Best friend of Michelle; disillusioned with school and teachers; smokes pot and hangs out on the streets in Alexis Deveaux's *Spirits in the Street*.

**Bo Shmo**    Dynamic and charismatic cowboy who gained fame by playing Buttermilk Sky backward; tries to kill the Loop Garoo Kid for being too abstract in Ishmael Reed's *Yellow Back Radio Broke Down*.

**Jan Sholto**    Active telepath and mother of two children by Doro in Octavia E. Butler's *Mind of My Mind*.

**Gloria Short**    See Gloria Short Renfro.

**Jack Short**    Married chemistry teacher of Haddan School who has an on-again, off-again romance with the painting teacher Lynn Vining in Alice Hoffman's *The River King*.

**Gid Shorter**    Younger son of Hattie Mayfield in Reynolds Price's *The Surface of Earth*.

**Hatt Shorter**    See Hattie Mayfield.

**James Shorter**    Dead husband of Hattie Mayfield in Reynolds Price's *The Surface of Earth*.

**Whitby Shorter**    Older son of Hattie Mayfield in Reynolds Price's *The Surface of Earth*.

**Shosha (Shoshele)**    Oldest daughter of Bashele and Zelig; as an adult, she remains childlike both physically and intellectually, and her innocence captivates Aaron Greidinger, whom she loves and marries in Isaac Bashevis Singer's *Shosha*.

**Chief Showcase**   Patarealist Crow Indian whose people were destroyed by coming out into the open instead of staying hidden; tries to get the white man by introducing him to smoking so he will die of lung cancer in Ishmael Reed's *Yellow Back Radio Broke-Down*.

**Edwin Shuck**   American embassy operative who tries to include Jack Flowers in a blackmail scheme in Paul Theroux's *Saint Jack*.

**Shumla**   Seventeenth-century Turkish war hero who is the subject of the consul's wife's latest biography and with whom she falls in love in Anaïs Nin's *Collages*.

**James T. Shuster**   Police homicide detective in Thomas Berger's *Killing Time*.

**Aunt Sidney (Sid)**   Sister of May Grey and aunt of Matt and Ruth Grey; never-married choir director of schoolchildren; becomes Ruth's pen pal and best friend and gives her emotional support and money from time to time in Jane Hamilton's *The Book of Ruth*.

**Jer Sidone**   Drummer who shares an apartment with Stanley Katz in Edward Lewis Wallant's *The Tenants of Moonbloom*.

**Duvey Siegal**   Young Jewish-American man from Detroit, he is killed in action during World War II; brother of Ruthie Siegal; inappropriately attracted to his young cousin Naomi Levy-Monot in Marge Piercy's *Gone to Soldiers*.

**Mother (Ma) Sigafoos**   Formulator and purveyor of Mother Sigafoos's Bloody Mary Mix and other Land's Sakes Brands products in Peter De Vries's *I Hear America Swinging*.

**Fay Silberman**   Widow who meets Gabe Wallach's father on a European tour and later becomes engaged to him in Philip Roth's *Letting Go*.

**Clarissa (Cass) Silenski**   Friend and patron of Vivaldo Moore and Rufus Scott; wife of Richard Silenski and lover of Eric Jones in James Baldwin's *Another Country*.

**Richard Silenski**   New York schoolteacher and novelist; husband of Cass Silenski in James Baldwin's *Another Country*.

**Silent One**   Speechless inmate of the child center; befriends the narrator and together they derail a trainload of peasants coming home from market in Jerzy Kosinski's *The Painted Bird*.

**Cutlass da Silva**   A pirate who is killed for sacking a Mecca-bound pilgrim ship in Bharati Mukherjee's *The Holder of the World*.

**Eli Silver**   Dedicated pediatrician whose son dies in an automobile accident while Silver attends to his wife's minor injuries;

arranges the adoption by Phil and Annie Sorenson of Elizabeth Bean's baby in Frederick Busch's *Rounds*.

**Fred Silver**   Bryce Proctorr's lawyer in Donald E. Westlake's *The Hook*.

**Gwen Silver**   Wife of Eli Silver; leaves him following their son's death in an automobile accident, but returns to try to salvage the marriage in Frederick Busch's *Rounds*.

**Judith Silver**   Attorney; fourth wife of Gordon Stone; cares for him when he is dying of lung cancer; marries David Green after deaths of Gordon and Crystal Sinclair in Marge Piercy's *Storm Tide*.

**Susan Silverman**   High school guidance counselor in suburban Boston; divorced, dedicated to work; romantically involved with Spenser, a Boston private detective in Robert B. Parker's *Promised Land* and all other Spenser novels.

**Shirley Silverstein**   See Maggie MacGregor.

**Peter Sim**   Childhood friend and schoolmate of Nicholas Delbanco in Nicholas Delbanco's *In the Middle Distance*.

**Harvey Simkin**   Wealthy and clever New York lawyer of Moses Herzog in Saul Bellow's *Herzog*.

**Della Simmons**   Young black woman, former playmate of Rachel Hutchins, and now servant to the Hutchins family; deeply in love with Rob Mayfield, she remains his mistress even during his engagement to Rachel in Reynolds Price's *The Surface of Earth*.

**Henry Simmons**   English valet who is engaged to Edweena Wills; becomes a close friend of and confidant to Theophilus North in Thornton Wilder's *Theophilus North*.

**Jennifer Simmons**   Attractive ex-student of professor Jack Schiff; technician for home assistance firm the professor hires in the novella *Her Sense of Timing*, in Stanley Elkin's *Van Gogh's Room at Arles*.

**Elvira K. Tewksbury Simms**   Mother of Jed Tewksbury and remarried widow of Buck Tewksbury; encourages Jed to seek his fortune away from Dugton, Alabama, in Robert Penn Warren's *A Place to Come To*.

**Jake Simms**   Bumbling bank robber and kidnapper of Charlotte Emory; father of Mindy Callender's unborn child in Anne Tyler's *Earthly Possessions*.

**Simon**   Passenger on the *Here They Come* who exchanges fairy tales for Dad Deform's religious statues in Gregory Corso's *The American Express*.

**Erin (Chippo) Simon**   Friend of both the Reverend Phillip Martin and Martin's former lover, Johanna Sims, in Ernest J. Gaines's *In My Father's House*.

**Tom Simon** Employee of NESTER in Scott Spencer's *Last Night at the Brain Thieves' Ball*.

**Charity Prudence Eversole Simons** Married woman from Philadelphia who has given birth to the son of a man other than her husband and wishes to abandon the child, whom Leslie Collins finally adopts in Harriette Simpson Arnow's *The Kentucky Trace*.

**Carolyn Simpson** High school classmate and lover of Molly Bolt in Rita Mae Brown's *Rubyfruit Jungle*.

**Samantha (Sam) Simpson** Friend of Mira; forced by an improvident husband to become financially independent in Marilyn French's *The Women's Room*.

**Stephen (Steve) Simpson** College roommate of Oliver Barrett IV; helps Barrett following the death of Barrett's wife Jenny in Erich Segal's *Oliver's Story*.

**Etienne Sims** See Robert X.

**Johanna Sims** Deserted mother of the Reverend Phillip Martin's unacknowledged, illegitimate children including Robert X in Ernest J. Gaines's *In My Father's House*.

**Pearl Sims** Piano teacher of Renay Davis from sixth through twelfth grade in Ann Allen Shockley's *Loving Her*.

**Crystal Sinclair** Mother of Laramie; appears vulnerable but actually scheming, manipulative, and wanton; tries to use sexuality to ensnare David Greene; dies driving to confront David about his relationship with Judith Stone after having been given drinks by John Mosley Lynch in Marge Piercy's *Storm Tide*.

**Laramie Sinclair** Son of Crystal Sinclair; frightened; lonely; clings emotionally to David Greene, the only person who has ever been truly kind and attentive to him; dies in autombile accident that also kills his mother, the driver, in Marge Piercy's *Storm Tide*.

**Anna Maude Singe** Benjamin Dill's lawyer and lover; best friend and lawyer of Felicity; helps Ben find Felicity's murderer in Ross Thomas's *Briarpatch*.

**Fred Singer** Television commentator who attends many of the gatherings of expatriate Americans at the home of the Gallaghers during the student riots in Paris in James Jones's *The Merry Month of May*.

**Sidney (Sid) Singer** Lawyer who is David Dehn's partner; helps Dehn build a temple and establish the Beechwood Jewish community in Jerome Weidman's *The Temple*.

**Jadav Singh** Raja, King of Devgad, a Hindu-ruled disfigurement on the Muslim map of South India, and a deeply embedded thorn in the flesh of Emperor Aurangzeb; has unswerving hatred for all Sunni Muslims; saves Hannah from an angry mob and becomes her lover in Bharati Mukherjee's *The Holder of the World*.

**Pearl Singh** Daughter of Hannah Eastman Fitch Legge and Jadav Singh; born in 1701 somewhere in the South Atlantic on Hannah's voyage home in Bharati Mukherjee's *The Holder of the World*.

**Sukhwinder Singh** Uncompromising Sikh nationalist who kills Prakash Vijh with a bomb and whose unexpected appearance in New York City as a hotdog vendor impels Jasmine Vijh's flight to Iowa in Bharati Mukherjee's *Jasmine*.

**Pa Ansumana Sisay** Honorary father of Aruna Sisay, honorary grandfather of Boone Westfall, and esteemed village elder in Richard Dooling's *White Man's Grave*.

**Aruna Sisay** Former Peace Corps volunteer who embraces the Mendes culture; assists Boone Westfall in navigating the culture and politics of the Sierra Leone tribes in order for Westfall to find his lost friend, while attempting to minimize the damage inflicted upon the native population by the arrogant white man in Richard Dooling's *White Man's Grave*.

**Murray Jay Siskind** Visiting professor in the popular culture department at the College-on-the-Hill in Blacksmith, a small village in the northern Midwest; is particularly interested in starting a department of Elvis studies, much like Jack Gladney's Department of Hitler Studies; becomes infatuated with Babette Gladney in Don DeLillo's *White Noise*.

**Sissie** Prostitute whose murder Willie Hall plans in John Edgar Wideman's *The Lynchers*.

**Sister Josie** Young black nun with gold teeth; attends Catalina Kate on the wandering island in John Hawkes's *Second Skin*.

**Sister Louise** Administrator of Sacred Heart Hospital in Edward Lewis Wallant's *The Children at the Gate*.

**Sister X** See Arista Prolo.

**Sittina (Queen of Shendy)** Artistic, prolific third wife of Colonel Elleloû; the only one of his wives to go with him into exile in John Updike's *The Coup*.

**Miriam Skates** Artistic rival of Moise whose jealousy over Moise's recognition by a college art professor leads her to embarrass Moise publicly in Tennessee Williams's *Moise and the World of Reason*.

**Arthur Gallup (Galloper) Skeel** Young man who aids Theophilus North in ridding his sister, Elspeth Skeel, of her terrible headaches in Thornton Wilder's *Theophilus North*.

**Elspeth Skeel** Sister of Arthur Skeel; has excruciating headaches that seem incurable until Theophilus North uses his so-called electric hands in Thornton Wilder's *Theophilus North*.

**Skeeter** See Hubert H. Farnsworth.

**Skelton**  Father of Thomas Skelton; pretends to be an invalid but is discovered to be out on the town late each night in Thomas McGuane's *Ninety-Two in the Shade.*

**Goldsboro Skelton**  Grandfather of Thomas Skelton; shady businessman who lends his grandson money for a boat in Thomas McGuane's *Ninety-Two in the Shade.*

**Thomas Skelton**  Key West fishing guide killed by his business competitor, Nichol Dance, in Thomas McGuane's *Ninety-Two in the Shade.*

**Hugh Skeys**  Husband of Fanny Blood in the wine business, heavy-waisted and thick-jowled; takes Fanny to Portugal in Frances Sherwood's *Vindication.*

**Fred Skinner**  Husband of Susy Skinner and colleague of Paul Cattleman in Alison Lurie's *The Nowhere City.*

**Philo (Richard) Skinner**  Chain-smoking dog handler and dognapper in Joseph Wambaugh's *The Black Marble.*

**Susy Skinner**  Wife of Fred Skinner and friend of Katherine Cattleman in Alison Lurie's *The Nowhere City.*

**Skipper**  Young black man, recently paroled, who is a hostile student of Eric Eisner in the New York literacy program in Phillip Lopate's *Confessions of Summer.*

**Skipper (Edward, Papa Cue Ball, Skip)**  Father of Cassandra and the baby born to Catalina Kate, grandfather of Pixie, husband of Gertrude, and father-in-law of Fernandez; served four years on the USS *Starfish*; fifty-nine-year-old narrator of John Hawkes's *Second Skin.*

**Lars Skjellerup**  Norwegian reindeer rancher; stakes early successful gold-mining claim in Nome; helps maintain order during chaotic Nome gold rush; becomes Presbyterian Reverend in Barrow in James Michener's *Alaska.*

**Vladimir Skrapinov**  Soviet ambassador to the United States who believes Chance can speak Russian in Jerzy Kosinski's *Being There.*

**Egbert Skully**  Persistent Dublin landlord whom Sebastian Dangerfield manages to elude in J. P. Donleavy's *The Ginger Man.*

**Sky**  Husband of Prudence; rents Fish and Katie Fisher's house, has a baby face that takes a long time to age and then gets soft all at once in Sandra Scofield's *Beyond Deserving.*

**Slab**  Artist who compulsively paints pictures of cheese Danishes; member of the Whole Sick Crew in Thomas Pynchon's *V.*

**Hugh Slade**  Married veterinarian with whom Isabel Moore has an abortive affair in Mary Gordon's *Final Payments.*

**Willard Slade**  Gifted artist; first love and inspiration of Alice Prentice in Richard Yates's *A Special Providence.*

**Baxter Slate**  Intellectual and suicide; one of ten Los Angeles policemen-protagonists of Joseph Wambaugh's *The Choirboys.*

**Ormand Slaughter**  Retarded hired man who is the object of Orpha Chase's first infatuation in Jessamyn West's *The Life I Really Lived.*

**Sledge (Doctor)**  Illegitimate and crippled infant son of Mildred Sutton; named after the doctor who delivered him because no one will admit to being his father in Reynolds Price's *A Long and Happy Life.*

**Sam (Uncle Sam, The Yankee Peddler) Slick**  Quintessential American spirit in Robert Coover's *The Public Burning.*

**Neil Sligh**  Potential blackmailer of Alma Marvel; suitor of Lee Mercury in Peter De Vries's *Through the Fields of Clover.*

**Ed Slipper**  Fourth-oldest prisoner in America and a trustee in the prison where Leo Feldman is incarcerated in Stanley Elkin's *A Bad Man.*

**Linda Sliski**  Roommate of Wendy Gahaghan in Alison Lurie's *The War Between the Tates.*

**Bijelo Slivinca**  Father and leader of the Slivinca family, all of whom work for the Ustashi terrorists; plans Gottlob Wutt's death; killed by Wutt in John Irving's *Setting Free the Bears.*

**Todor Slivinca**  Son of Bijelo Slivinca; teaches Vratno Javotnik to ride a motorcycle; survives Gottlob Wutt's grenade attack and kills Javotnik after the war in John Irving's *Setting Free the Bears.*

**Morgan Sloat**  Jack Sawyer's deceased father's business partner, father of Richard, and Jack's antagonist in Stephen King's and Peter Straub's *The Talisman.*

**Richard Sloat**  Morgan Sloat's son and Jack Sawyer's friend; accompanies Jack in his quest to find the talisman in Stephen King's and Peter Straub's *The Talisman.*

**Bob (Bobby) Slocum**  New York market research executive whose ambitions consist of being awarded Andy Kagle's job as head of sales and the opportunity to give a speech at the company convention in Puerto Rico; narrator of Joseph Heller's *Something Happened.*

**Derek Slocum**  Brain-damaged third child and second son of Bob Slocum in Joseph Heller's *Something Happened.*

**Mrs. Slocum**  Bored and lonely wife of Bob Slocum; drinks and flirts to excess in Joseph Heller's *Something Happened.*

**Betty (Bettyle) Slonim**  American actress who performs in Yiddish theaters, melancholy mistress of Sam Dreiman, and, briefly, lover of Aaron Greidinger; commits suicide in Isaac Bashevis Singer's *Shosha.*

**Jillsy Sloper**   Charwoman at a publishing house; admires T. S. Garp's *The World According to Bensenhaver*, which Garp dedicates to her in John Irving's *The World According to Garp*.

**Leslie Slote**   Foreign service officer; attempts to help Natalie Jastrow escape from Europe; attempts to convince politicians of Nazi attrocities against Jews but is not believed or deliberately ignored; joins the OSS; parachutes into France on D-Day; later killed while helping French resistance in Herman Wouk's *War and Remembrance*.

**Lieutenant Tyrone (Ian Scuffling, Rocketman) Slothrop**   American officer assigned to the Political Warfare Executive, which studies him while he studies the V-2 rocket; lover of Katje Borgesius, Greta Erdmann, and Geli Tripping; subject of Pavlovian experiments as a child in Thomas Pynchon's *Gravity's Rainbow*.

**Doctor Slovotkin**   Sadistic prison physician; hanged by rioting women convicts in John Hawkes's *The Passion Artist*.

**Billy Small**   Black alcoholic and robber; partner of Gregory Powell in Joseph Wambaugh's *The Onion Field*.

**Big Red (L. J. Griggs) Smalley**   Traveling evangelist and faith healer in George Garrett's *Do, Lord, Remember Me*.

**Arrabelle Smalls**   Black housekeeper for the Meecham family and mother of Toomer Smalls in Pat Conroy's *The Great Santini*.

**Toomer Smalls**   Black merchant of flowers, herbs, and honey; son of Arrabelle Smalls; killed by Red Pettus in Pat Conroy's *The Great Santini*.

**James D. (Jimmy, Preach, Preacher) Smathers, Jr.**   Red-haired friend and alter ego of James Christopher; dies as the result of a severe beating by Jack Davis in Fred Chappell's *It Is Time, Lord*.

**Louis B. Smilesburger**   Cover name used by an elderly, crippled man working for the Mossad, the Israeli intelligence agency; initially approaches Philip Roth, the famous Jewish-American novelist, undercover, offering financial support for Diasporism, the return of Israeli Jews to Europe; later convinces Roth to leave the details of the operation out of *Operation Shylock,* his novel/memoir in Philip Roth's *Operation Shylock: A Confession*.

**Smiley**   Leader of a gang of black men hired by Miss Ann and Mr. Cleveland to steal the corpse of a murdered prostitute in Richard Brautigan's *Dreaming of Babylon*.

**Annabel Smith**   Lover of Mortimer Dille; he leaves Theodora Waite for her in Bette Pesetsky's *Midnight Sweets*.

**Anna Castagne Bolling Smith**   Prosaic mother of Binx Bolling and of his six half brothers and sisters in Walker Percy's *The Moviegoer*.

**Benny Smith**   Brother of Mama Lavorn and handyman for L. B. Jones; serves as a professional mourner at funerals in Jesse Hill Ford's *The Liberation of Lord Byron Jones*.

**Chester (Chessy) Smith**   Dates, and later marries, Julia; poor carpenter; he and Julia adopt Nichole in Rita Mae Brown's *Six of One*; has an affair with Trudy Archer in *Loose Lips*.

**Clarence Smith**   Married to Fern; father of Cletus and Wayne; tenant farmer; neighbor and friend of Lloyd Wilson; driven to despair by Fern's infidelity with Wilson and loss of cross-claim against Wilson in wife's divorce case against him; shoots Wilson and later commits suicide in William Maxwell's *So Long, See You Tomorrow*.

**Clark (Clarkie) Smith**   Insurance executive married to Janet Belle Smith in Alison Lurie's *Real People*.

**Cletus Smith**   Son of Clarence and Fern; lives with great-aunt Jenny after Fern leaves Clarence; becomes friend of narrator; stops seeing narrator after Clarence is accused of murder; encounters narrator in high school corridor after move to Chicago; does not speak to him in William Maxwell's *So Long, See You Tomorrow*.

**Clinch Smith**   Excommunicated Scientologist and rejected lover who goes berserk and kills Scientologists in William S. Burroughs's *Exterminator!*

**Dunreith (Smitty) Smith**   Troublemaker and married lover of Addie Parker in Cyrus Colter's *The Rivers of Eros*.

**Emmet Smith**   Uncle to Samantha Hughes, he has had trouble adjusting to life after his tour in Vietnam but begins to recover when he visits the Vietnam War memorial in Bobbie Ann Mason's *In Country*.

**Fern Smith**   Married to Clarence, mother of Cletus and Wayne; falls in love with neighbor Lloyd Wilson; divorces Clarence; moves to Chicago with children after Wilson's murder and Clarence's suicide in William Maxwell's *So Long, See You Tomorrow*.

**Gabrielle Smith**   Young socialite who hides her true identity to make it on her own as an actress on the hit television series *Manhattan* in Danielle Steel's *Secrets*.

**George Smith**   Closet pederast who annoys Sol Nazerman with long-winded monologues on literature and philosophy in Edward Lewis Wallant's *The Pawnbroker*.

**Ginny Cook Smith**   Sister of Caroline Cook and Rose Cook Lewis, who raise her after their mother dies; wife of Tyler (Ty) Smith; sexually abused and emotionally manipulated daughter of Larry Cook; together with Rose, recipient of shares in Larry Cook's 1,000 acres; takes care of Rose when she is diagnosed with breast cancer; lover of Jess Clark; narrator of the novel who leaves her husband and becomes a waitress in Jane Smiley's *A Thousand Acres*.

**Harold (little-Smith) Smith**   Securities broker married to Marcia Smith in John Updike's *Couples*.

**Herbert (Herb) Smith**   Father of Johnny Smith; argues with his wife, Vera, over her newfound religious convictions in Stephen King's *The Dead Zone*.

**Irene Smith**   Mother of Samantha Hughes, she has worked hard to move on after her husband died in Vietnam but who may be running away from her past in Bobbie Ann Mason's *In Country*.

**Janet Belle Smith**   Short story writer, mother of three children, wife of Clark Smith, and lover of Nick Donato in Alison Lurie's *Real People*.

**Jimmy Lee (Jimmy Youngblood) Smith**   Mulatto drug addict and partner of Gregory Powell; convicted of and sentenced to die for the murder of Ian Campbell in Joseph Wambaugh's *The Onion Field*.

**John (Johnny) Smith**   Psychically acute man whose brain is permanently damaged—thus creating the dead zone—following an automobile accident in Stephen King's *The Dead Zone*.

**Josephine Holtzapple Smith**   Chester's mother; doesn't like his wife, Juts Smith, and has never invited her over; says that she won't accept an adopted child, but eventually does; was in love with Hansford Hunsenmeir while they were both married, but he left her in Rita Mae Brown's *Loose Lips*.

**Julia Ellen (Juts) Hunsenmeir Smith**   Younger sister of Louise (Wheezie) Hunsenmeir Trumbell; daughter of Cora Hunsenmeir; wife of Chester (Chessy) Smith and mother of Nichole (Nickel) Smith; opens a beauty salon with her sister; catches her husband cheating and mourns for two years in Rita Mae Brown's *Loose Lips*. Marries Ed Tutweiler Walters in *Bingo*; fights with her sister in *Six of One*.

**Karen Smith**   Young professional woman living in New York City; romantically involved with Jack Reilly, a police officer separated from his wife; befriends and tries to help Fred Fitch, a friend of Jack's who has become the target of an elaborate con game; briefly considers leaving Jack for Fred, but ultimately decides she prefers the romantic fantasy Jack offers in Donald E. Westlake's *God Save The Mark*.

**K. D. Smith**   Is actually named Coffee (after his great-grandfather), but nicknamed Kentucky Derby, or K. D. for short; is a resident of the all-black town of Ruby, Oklahoma; is the nephew of Deek (Deacon) and Steward Morgan and the son of the deceased Ruby Morgan; marries Arnette Fleetwood; has an affair with Gigi, one of the Convent women; is one of the group of men who raid the Convent in Toni Morrison's *Paradise*.

**Lonnie Smith**   Fatally ill and fervently Roman Catholic half brother of Binx Bolling in Walker Percy's *The Moviegoer*.

**Marcia Burnham (little-Smith) Smith**   Wife of Harold Smith; they swap partners with Janet and Frank Appleby in John Updike's *Couples*.

**Matt Smith**   New publisher of *Country Daze*; self-centered and Maureen's lover in Ann Beattie's *Love Always*.

**Miguel Moreno (Brown, Brownie, Miguelito) Smith**   Engineer aboard the *Lillias Eden* who leaves the boat to join the Jamaicans who threaten its safety in Peter Matthiessen's *Far Tortuga*.

**Mr. Smith**   Joseph Johnson's lover in Frances Sherwood's *Vindication*.

**Nevada (Max Sand) Smith**   Half-blood Kiowa Indian who avenges the brutal deaths of his parents and becomes an outlaw; works for Jonas Cord, Sr.; teaches Jonas Cord, Jr., to ride horses and serves as a father figure for him; becomes a film star in movie westerns and the husband of Rina Marlowe in Harold Robbins's *The Carpetbaggers*.

**Nichole (Nickel) Smith**   Adopted daughter of Julia Ellen and Chester in Rita Mae Brown's *Loose Lips*; thirty-five-years-old bisexual; buys Cora's old home and moves back to Runnymeade in *Six of One*. Also appears in *Bingo*.

**Pamela Smith**   Former girlfriend of Charles whose dynamic but erratic life is a counterpoint to Charles's predictable life in Ann Beattie's *Chilly Scenes of Winter*.

**Perry Edward Smith**   Psychotic criminal, man of ungovernable anger, and murderer of the Clutter family in Truman Capote's *In Cold Blood*.

**Ray Smith**   Los Angeles defense attorney; first to defend Jimmy Smith in Joseph Wambaugh's *The Onion Field*.

**Rebel Smith**   Okie cherry orchard boss and friend of Pretty Boy Floyd; the narrator works for her as a child in Richard Brautigan's *Trout Fishing in America*.

**Father Rinaldo Smith**   Addled but dedicated priest and Tom More's confessor in Walker Percy's *Love in the Ruins*.

**Robert Smith**   North Carolina Mutual Life Insurance salesman who commits suicide by jumping from the top of Mercy Hospital in Toni Morrison's *Song of Solomon*.

**Robes (Ohio) Smith**   Admirer of Abeba Torch; considered shiftless by Angela Lavoisier in Ellease Southerland's *Let the Lion Eat Straw*.

**Ruth Smith**   American consul in Copenhagen and lover of George Washington; commits suicide in Cecil Brown's *The Life and Loves of Mr. Jiveass Nigger*.

**Father Simon Smith**   Friend of Tom More; has withdrawn from his responsibilities as parish priest and mans an isolated fire-watch tower in the Louisiana wilderness, assisted only by a mental deficient named Milton Guidry; holds rights to property Bob Comeaux wants for a Qualitarian Life Center in Walker Percy's *The Thanatos Syndrome*.

**Smith Smith**  Hero of C. Card's latest daydream; most famous private investigator of Babylon and beloved of Nana-dirat in Richard Brautigan's *Dreaming of Babylon*.

**Tony Smith**  Art professor from South Orange, New Jersey, whose patronage of the emotionally distraught Moise is Moise's salvation in Tennessee Williams's *Moise and the World of Reason*.

**Tyler (Ty) Smith**  Only son of farmer who leaves him 160 acres; husband of Ginny Cook Smith; brother-in-law of Pete and Rose Cook Lewis; son-in-law of Larry Cook; builds new hog farm facility after Larry bequeaths property; accused of conspiring with Caroline and Larry Cook; loses his acreage and moves to Texas in Jane Smiley's *A Thousand Acres*.

**Vera Helen Smith**  Religiously fanatical mother of Johnny Smith; believes that her son's psychic gifts should be used to further God's plan in Stephen King's *The Dead Zone*.

**Ware Smith**  Health-food devotee who lives in the mountains with Kate and fathers their child in Gail Godwin's *Glass People*.

**Wayne Smith**  Younger son of Clarence and Fern in William Maxwell's *So Long, See You Tomorrow*.

**Word (Frederico, Smitty) Smith**  Sportswriter and author of a history of the suppressed or imagined Patriot League in Philip Roth's *The Great American Novel*.

**Smithson**  Medical officer for the Arizona highway patrol in Michael Crichton's *The Andromeda Strain*.

**Smokey**  Drug addict wife of Porky; handles her husband's drug money in Donald Goines's *Dopefiend*.

**Freddy Smoot**  Youth who explores the young Eva Medina Canada sexually with a dirty popsicle stick in Gayl Jones's *Eva's Man*.

**Smoothbore**  See Sylvania Berlew.

**Snake**  See Kenneth Dumpson.

**Snake**  Drug addict and pimp who is killed during a robbery in Donald Goines's *Dopefiend*.

**Snapper**  Handsome homosexual who emasculates male patrons of porno theaters while performing fellatio on them in Jerzy Kosinski's *Cockpit*.

**Corporal Snark**  Snobbish mess officer who mashes soap into sweet potatoes to prove soldiers have no taste in Joseph Heller's *Catch-22*.

**Ralph Fielding Snell**  Prissy "Man of Letters" whose Foreword and Epilogue frame Jack Crabb's oral autobiography in Thomas Berger's *Little Big Man*.

**Susan (Sue, Suze) Snell**  Sympathetic classmate of Carrie White and author of *My Name is Susan Snell* in Stephen King's *Carrie*.

**Flem Snopes**  See Volume I.

**Snowden**  Air force gunner wounded by flak on a bombing mission over Avignon; dies in Yossarian's arms after Yossarian treats him for the wrong wound in Joseph Heller's *Catch-22*.

**Rachel Sojourner**  Sister-in-law of Beulah Renfro and possibly the mother of Gloria Short Renfro in Eudora Welty's *Losing Battles*.

**Henry Soames**  Overweight owner of a diner and surrogate father of Callie Wells's son in John Gardner's *Nickel Mountain*.

**Iggy Soames**  Son of an artist; friend and confidant of Susie Schnitzer in Harriette Simpson Arnow's *The Weedkiller's Daughter*.

**Pearly Soames**  Violent, dictatorial leader of Short Tails crime gang, obsessed with color and with pursuing nemesis Peter Lake in Mark Helprin's *Winter's Tale*.

**Sobaka**  Head of the Soviet Writers' Union who becomes a nonperson in John Updike's *Bech: A Book*.

**Egon Sobotnik**  Czechoslovakian prisoner at the Jadwiga concentration camp; provides a surgical record book that is used against Adam Kelno in a libel trial in Leon Uris's *QB VII*.

**Arnold Soby**  Middle-aged pursuer of Cynthia Pomeroy; college professor in search of the wisdom of the body in Wright Morris's *What a Way to Go*.

**Robert Hopper Softly**  Physically stunted director of Logicon Project, an attempt to develop a cosmic language based on mathematical principles in Don DeLillo's *Ratner's Star*.

**Gladia Solaria**  See Gladia Delmarre.

**Alice (Mamaw) Sole**  Mother of Lillian Meecham and grandmother of Ben, Mary Anne, Karen, and Matt Meecham in Pat Conroy's *The Great Santini*.

**Roy Soleil**  Dockmaster wounded with a fishing gaff by Nichol Dance in Thomas McGuane's *Ninety-Two in the Shade*.

**Virgil (Turk) Sollozzo**  Narcotics importer who is responsible for the shooting of Don Corleone in Mario Puzo's *The Godfather*.

**Solomon**  Slow-witted son of David and Bathsheba who irritates his father with his literal-mindedness and whose mother seeks to advance him to his father's throne in Joseph Heller's *God Knows*.

**Solomon**  African slave who, according to myth, literally flies away from the Virginia plantation where he is enslaved, leaving his wife and twenty-one children behind; his descendants are the erroneously named Dead family in Toni Morrison's *Song of Solomon.*

**Howard Solomon**   Cocaine-addicted head producer of famed Orpheus Studios in Hollywood; husband of Poppy Solomon in Jackie Collins's *Hollywood Husbands.*

**Poppy Solomon**   Hollywood hostess wife of producer Howard Solomon in Jackie Collins's *Hollywood Husbands.*

**Caitlin Somers**   Spends summers with her father, Lamb, and school year with her mother, Phoebe; returns to the Vineyard to marry Joseph Brudegher; has child, Masie, with him; leaves Masie with her father and goes to Venice; commits suicide in her sailboat in Judy Blume's *Summer Sisters.*

**Lambert Mayhew (Lamb) Somers**   Raised by his paternal grandparents after his parents die in a car crash; marries Phoebe and has two children, Caitlin and Sharkey; lives in Cambridge part of the year and in the summer on Martha's Vineyard; second marriage to Trisha, who tries to act motherly toward his children in Judy Blume's *Summer Sisters.*

**Mr. Somerset**   Aging resident of Wilma Pauling's boarding house in Anne Tyler's *Celestial Navigation.*

**Sonny**   Black petty officer on the USS *Starfish* and loyal friend and companion of Skipper in John Hawkes's *Second Skin.*

**Catchick Sookian**   The lightest-skinned trader at Fort St. Sebastian; an Armenian in Bharati Mukherjee's *The Holder of the World.*

**Sordino**   See Edmond Behr-Bleibtreau.

**Anne (Annie) Sorenson**   Artist who, with her husband, Phil Sorenson, renovates a house in Maine and comes to terms with the loss of two children by spontaneous abortions; narrates part of Frederick Busch's *Manual Labor;* she and Phil adopt Elizabeth Bean's baby in *Rounds.*

**George (Big George, Rub-a-dub) Sorensen**   Mental patient obsessed with cleanliness who captains the fishing boat in Ken Kesey's *One Flew Over the Cuckoo's Nest.*

**Michael (Mike) Sorenson**   Baby born to Elizabeth Bean and adopted by Annie and Phil Sorenson; kidnapped by Horace L'Ordinet, his natural father, but later returned to the Sorensons; found to have sickle-cell anemia as passed on genetically from L'Ordinet in Frederick Busch's *Rounds.*

**Philip (Phil) Sorenson**   Poet, home handyman, husband of Anne Sorenson, and father of the dead fetus, Sam; narrates part of Frederick Busch's *Manual Labor;* with Anne, adopts a son in *Rounds.*

**Connie (Consolata) Sosa**   Oldest and only white resident of the Convent, a house inhabited by women from sullied pasts, located on the outskirts of the all-black town of Ruby, Oklahoma; is visually impaired, but can see with a psychic third-eyesight; is a healer who can bring dying people back to life; once had an affair with Deek (Deacon) Morgan; murdered by one of the Morgan brothers in a raid on the Convent in Toni Morrison's *Paradise.*

**Sourian**   Runs a filthy fruit stand across the street from the Brays' home in Maureen Howard's *Natural History.*

**Joey de Sousa**   Catherine Bray's friend and next-door neighbor; postman in Maureen Howard's *Natural History.*

**Eleanor (Ellie) Sowerby**   Cousin of Roy Bassart and close friend of Lucy Nelson in Philip Roth's *When She Was Good.*

**Julian Sowerby**   Womanizing uncle of Roy Bassart; earns Lucy Nelson Bassart's unyielding animosity by his opposition to the continuation of her marriage to Roy in Philip Roth's *When She Was Good.*

**Major de Spain**   See Volume I.

**Manfred de Spain**   See Volume I.

**Peter Spangle**   Lover of Cynthia Forrest; classmate and former boyfriend of Nina; goes to Spain to retrieve his brother; returns to United States and visits Nina; eventually returns to Cynthia in Ann Beattie's *Falling in Place.*

**Dewey Spangler**   Syndicated newspaper and magazine columnist and old acquaintance of Albert Corde; accidentally runs into Corde in Romania and, under the guise of getting together with an old friend, surreptitiously interviews the dean and publishes a patronizing and self-congratulatory column about their visits in Saul Bellow's *The Dean's December.*

**Kitty Sparks**   Mother of Jane Clifford, wife of Ray Sparks, and mother of Emily, Jack, and Ronnie Sparks in Gail Godwin's *The Odd Woman.*

**Ray Sparks**   Contractor, husband of Kitty Sparks, and stepfather of Jane Clifford in Gail Godwin's *The Odd Woman.*

**Sparrow**   Sidekick of Larry, the leader of a group of killers and thieves who benefit from Michael Banks's theft of a horse, Hard Rock, whom they expect to win one race in John Hawkes's *The Lime Twig.*

**Col. Harold J. Sparrow**   See Frank Wirtanen.

**Tyler Spaulding**   Julia Prine's friend; a dour-faced young woman; the new director of Harmony House in Mary McGarry Morris's *A Dangerous Woman.*

**Bill Spear**   See Willie Spearmint.

**Willie (Bill Spear) Spearmint**   Black writer trying to write his first book and lover of Irene Bell; destroys the manuscript of Harry Lesser's unfinished novel in Bernard Malamud's *The Tenants.*

**Patty Speed**   Ruthless black queen of the numbers game and secret lover of city councilman Randolph Banks in Julian Mayfield's *The Grand Parade*.

**Thomas Garrison (T. G.) Speidel**   Cynical journalist who forms an early friendship with Roger Ashley in Chicago; becomes a significant part of Roger's education in Thornton Wilder's *The Eighth Day*.

**Desmond (Des) Spellacy**   Brother of Thomas Spellacy; monsignor in the Los Angeles diocese whose career is ruined because of his business dealings with corrupt businessmen including Jack Amsterdam and Dan T. Campion in John Gregory Dunne's *True Confessions*.

**Mary Margaret Maher Spellacy**   Wife of Thomas Spellacy; confined to a mental hospital in John Gregory Dunne's *True Confessions*.

**Thomas (Tom) Spellacy**   Brother of Desmond Spellacy; Los Angeles policeman who sets up the arrest of Jack Amsterdam for the murder of Lois Fazenda; narrates parts of John Gregory Dunne's *True Confessions*.

**Didi Spence**   Friend of Alison Poole who is from a wealthy family and spends her large allowance primarily on drugs; she dates rich men mainly to get money to support her drug habit; enters treatment but is unable and unwilling to leave behind her previous lifestyle in Jay McInerney's *Story of My Life*.

**Clay-Boy Spencer**   Oldest son of Clay and Livia Spencer; becomes the first in his family and the first resident of New Dominion, Virginia, to go to college in Earl Hamner, Jr.'s *Spencer's Mountain*.

**Clayton (Clay) Spencer**   Virginia mill worker and father of eleven children; sacrifices his dream of building his own home atop Spencer's Mountain so his oldest son will have the opportunity to go to college in Earl Hamner, Jr.'s *Spencer's Mountain*.

**Elizabeth (Eliza) Spencer**   Mother of Clay Spencer and matriarch of the Spencer clan; forced to learn to cope with life without her husband, Zebulon Spencer, who is killed when a tree falls on him in Earl Hamner, Jr.'s *Spencer's Mountain*.

**Kenti Spencer**   Daughter of Marzala and Nathan; imaginative child; unaware of seriousness of situation when her brother Sundiata (Sonny) disappears in Toni Cade Bambara's *These Bones Are Not My Child*.

**Kofi Spencer**   Son of Marzala and Nathan; jealous of attention given to his older brother Sundiata (Sonny); after brother's disappearance wants to run away; when brother returns, helps him readjust to former life and resentment dissipates in Toni Cade Bambara's *These Bones Are Not My Child*.

**Marzala Rawls Spencer**   Wife of Nathan; mother of Sundiata, Kofi, and Kenti; when Sundiata (Sonny) disappears during Atlanta's missing and murdered children's case, becomes obsessed with finding him; reunites with estranged husband; when Sonny is found, increases her efforts to help victimized African Americans in Toni Cade Bambara's *These Bones Are Not My Child*.

**Nathan Spencer**   Husband of Marzala; father of Sundiata, Kofi, and Kenti; separated from wife; Vietnam veteran; conducts independent investigations into disappearance of Sundiata (Sonny) with aid from friends who are also veterans; joins independent groups searching for perpetrators; eventually reunites with Marzala in Toni Cade Bambara's *These Bones Are Not My Child*.

**Olivia (Livia, Livy) Spencer**   Mother of eleven children in depression-era Virginia and mainstay of the Spencer family in Earl Hamner, Jr.'s *Spencer's Mountain*.

**Sharon Spencer**   Tutor of Regan MacNeil; becomes horrified as she watches Regan become possessed by a demon in William Peter Blatty's *The Exorcist*.

**Sundiata (Sonny) Spencer**   Twelve-year-old son of Marzala and Nathan; musically talented; kidnapped by ring of child pornographers; escapes when car he is in with captors is hit by a train; reunited with his family but fearful and withdrawn; eventually returns to normal in Toni Cade Bambara's *These Bones Are Not My Child*.

**Virgil Spencer**   Brother of Clay Spencer and uncle of Clay-Boy Spencer, who lives with Virgil while going to college in Richmond in Earl Hamner, Jr.'s *Spencer's Mountain*.

**Zebulon Spencer**   Father of Clay Spencer and patriarch of the Spencer clan; predicts his grandson Clay-Boy will follow a new, unknown path for killing a white deer in Earl Hamner, Jr.'s *Spencer's Mountain*.

**Spengler**   Centennial Club member who writes a history of the club for its anniversary in Thomas McGuane's *The Sporting Club*.

**Spenser**   Private detective working in Boston; former heavyweight boxer and police officer; romantically involved with Susan Silverman; lives according to traditional notions of honor and masculinity; highly literate; talented cook; is hired by Harvey Shepard to locate Shepard's missing wife and eventually rescues both Shepards from disaster in Robert B. Parker's *Promised Land*.

**Jane Spenser**   Lucy's sister; lives in California with her daughter, Nicole Nelson; marries a young tennis instructor; dies in a motorcycle accident in Ann Beattie's *Love Always*.

**Lucy Spenser**   Hildon's lover and oldest friend; Jane's sister; writes a love advice column under the name Cindi Coeur; uses cocaine and enjoys living in Vermont; becomes guardian of her niece after her sister dies in Ann Beattie's *Love Always*.

**McClintic Sphere**   Black jazz musician and lover of Paola Maijstral; provides the advice, "keep cool, but care" in Thomas Pynchon's *V.*

**Sol Spiegel**   Specialist in salvage and fallout survival equipment; accompanies Warren Howe to Schloss Riva in Wright Morris's *Cause for Wonder.*

**Dr. Maximilian (Max) Spielman**   Mathematical psycho-proctologist and first tutor of George Giles; wishes to protect Giles from the disappointments of human existence by concealing from him that he is a boy and not a goat in John Barth's *Giles Goat-Boy.*

**Dr. O. (Doc) Spielvogel**   Psychiatrist who treats Alex Portnoy and labels his condition Portnoy's Complaint in Philip Roth's *Portnoy's Complaint.*

**Dr. Henry J. Spivack**   Sarcastic, garrulous Bellevue mental patient encountered by John Wilder in Richard Yates's *Disturbing the Peace.*

**Doctor (Doc) Spivey**   Psychiatrist pliably under the domination of Big Nurse in Ken Kesey's *One Flew Over the Cuckoo's Nest.*

**Jake Spivey**   Childhood friend of Benjamin Dill, he has become a billionaire; suspected in having a hand in the murder of Felicity in Ross Thomas's *Briarpatch.*

**Lizzi Spöckenkieker**   Spinster who has a comical affair with Siegfried Rieber in Katherine Anne Porter's *Ship of Fools.*

**Frank Spofford**   Retired chicken farmer and aspiring author who reads assiduously, hoping to qualify as a derivative writer; father of George Spofford and grandfather of Geneva Spofford; narrates part of Peter De Vries's *Reuben, Reuben.*

**Geneva Spofford**   Daughter of George and Mary Spofford and granddaughter of Frank Spofford; educated at Wycliffe College for Women, jilted by Tad Springer, impregnated by Gowan McGland; miscarries, then marries Alvin Mopworth in Peter De Vries's *Reuben, Reuben.*

**George Spofford**   Son of Frank Spofford, husband of Mary Spofford, and father of Geneva Spofford; runs the family poultry business in Peter De Vries's *Reuben, Reuben.*

**Mary Punck (Mare) Spofford**   Wife of George Spofford and mother of Geneva Spofford; fabricates an affair with Gowan McGland to preserve her daughter's reputation in Peter De Vries's *Reuben, Reuben.*

**Jake Spoon**   Former member of McRae's and Call's Texas Ranger unit; gambler, womanizer, doesn't like to work hard; life ruled by chances; suggests the cattle drive to Montana; takes Lorena Wood with him, promising to get her to San Francisco; accidentally joins up with a gang of horse thieves and is captured and hanged by McRae and Call in Larry McMurtry's *Lonesome Dove.*

**Whacker Spradlin**   Town drunk of Port William, Kentucky, in Wendell Berry's *A Place on Earth.*

**Isaac Sprague**   Fabian is apprenticed to him; Fabian sends him pictures and Sprague sends his comments; recommends Fabian to magazines for work; visits Fabian in person before he dies to admire his work in Howard Norman's *The Bird Artist.*

**Jane Sprague**   Pregnant and mildly retarded wife of Jim Sprague; lives in the 70th Street building managed by Norman Moonbloom in Edward Lewis Wallant's *The Tenants of Moonbloom.*

**Jim Sprague**   Slightly retarded husband of Jane Sprague; lives in a tenement managed by Norman Moonbloom in Edward Lewis Wallant's *The Tenants of Moonbloom.*

**Marva Sprat**   Wife of Jack Sprat; fantasizes love affairs with major-league baseball players in Mark Harris's *It Looked Like For Ever.*

**Newton (Jack) Sprat**   Husband of Marva Sprat and manager of the California baseball team in Mark Harris's *It Looked Like For Ever.*

**Roberta (Bobsy) Springer**   Mother of Tad Springer and paramour of Gowan McGland in Peter De Vries's *Reuben, Reuben.*

**Thaddeus (Tad) Springer**   Son of Bobsy Springer; courts then jilts Geneva Spofford in Peter De Vries's *Reuben, Reuben.*

**Josh Spritzer**   Orthodontist and father of one of Ann August's friends in California; dates Adele Diamond, but stops calling her; is known as a playboy in Mona Simpson's *Anywhere but Here.*

**Sprog**   Main character in Fred Trumper's translation of *Akthelt and Gunnel;* castrated and exiled for attempting to make love with Akthelt's wife in John Irving's *The Water-Method Man.*

**William Japheth Sproul III**   Theology student who becomes an ardent follower of Nathan Vickery in Joyce Carol Oates's *Son of the Morning.*

**Josiah Squibb**   Cook for whom Rutherford works aboard the *Republic;* becomes ship surgeon after the surgeon is killed; nurses Rutherford when he is sick; kills and fillets Cringle, upon Cringle's request, and feeds Cringle's remains to those aboard; is rescued along with Rutherford and Baleka by the *Juno* in Charles Johnson's *Middle Passage.*

**Joshua (Josh) Stafford**   Driven lawyer in a large practice who is the legal adviser of billionaire Troy Phelan and must handle his holographic will in John Grisham's *The Testament.*

**Dr. Heinrich Stahlmann**   Scholar at the University of Chicago under whom Jed Tewksbury studies classical literature in Robert Penn Warren's *A Place to Come To.*

**Major Staley**   Commander of Air Force ROTC at Logos College and expert on modern warfare in Don DeLillo's *End Zone.*

**The Stalker**  Obsessed man who stalks Yolanda ("Yo") Garcia for several years; tricks Yo into seeing him in a final confrontation in Julia Alvarez's *Yo!*

**Dave Stallworth**  Basketball player for the New York Knicks whose determination to come back after a heart attack is admired by Samuel Paul Berman in Jay Neugeboren's *Sam's Legacy*.

**Henry (Old Henry) Stamper**  Independent and stubborn patriarch of a family of nonunion loggers; father of Hank and Lee Stamper in Ken Kesey's *Sometimes a Great Notion*.

**Henry (Hank, Hankus) Stamper, Jr.**  Strong and self-reliant leader of a family of nonunion Oregon loggers; son of Henry Stamper and in conflict with his half brother, Lee Stamper, in Ken Kesey's *Sometimes a Great Notion*.

**Joe Benjamin (Joby, Joe Ben, Josephus) Stamper**  Good-natured cousin of Hank and Lee Stamper; drowns when caught under a log in Ken Kesey's *Sometimes a Great Notion*.

**Leland (Lee) Stamper**  Younger half brother of Hank Stamper; returns to Oregon from Yale University seeking revenge on Hank in Ken Kesey's *Sometimes a Great Notion*.

**Vivian (Viv) Stamper**  Wife of Hank Stamper caught in the middle of his conflict with his half brother, Lee, in Ken Kesey's *Sometimes a Great Notion*.

**Baron Egon Bodo von Stams**  Attaché at the Austrian embassy in Washington; he and Theophilus North become great friends, and he enlists North to help him win the attention of Persis Tennyson in Thornton Wilder's *Theophilus North*.

**Dr. Stanhope**  White liberal physician who testifies at the trial of Ida Carlisle in Hal Bennett's *A Wilderness of Vines*.

**Walter F. Stankiewicz**  See Walter F. Starbuck.

**Stanley**  Black chauffeur and attendant of Thomas Oliver; narrates part of Shirley Ann Grau's *The Condor Passes*.

**Stanley**  Hippie; with Joy, his girlfriend, travels with Floyd Warner and Kermit Oelsligle and apparently causes the fire that destroys a house in Wright Morris's *Fire Sermon*.

**Stanley**  Retired janitor and leader of an underground movement for male liberation in Thomas Berger's *Regiment of Women*.

**Tolitha Wingo Stanopoulos**  Daring wife of Amos Wingo, she deserts both her husband and son in the middle of the depression; her individualism helps save her grandchildren in Pat Conroy's *The Prince of Tides*.

**Joel Stansky**  Editor at the *Village Voice* with whom Salley Gardens is sexually intimate on a periodic basis in Susan Cheever's *Looking for Work*.

**Vernor Stanton**  Insanely competitive member of the Centennial Club who has a dueling gallery in his basement; incites a battle between club members and friends of Earl Olive in Thomas McGuane's *The Sporting Club*.

**Neva Stapleton**  See Neva Blanche Stapleton Manning.

**Star**  Illegitimate son of Margaret Copeland and, allegedly, her white employer, Mr. Shipley; poisoned by his mother in infancy in Alice Walker's *The Third Life of Grange Copeland*.

**Ruth Starbuck**  Translator and former refugee; wife of Walter F. Starbuck in Kurt Vonnegut's *Jailbird*.

**Walter F. (Walter F. Stankiewicz) Starbuck**  Protégé of Alexander McCone; later diplomat, presidential adviser, convict, and corporate officer; protagonist and narrator of Kurt Vonnegut's *Jailbird*.

**Charles P. (Char, Charlie) Stark**  Navy enlisted man of good family and artistic ambitions; forced by his association with Male Raditzer to face his own frailty in Peter Matthiessen's *Raditzer*.

**Charlotte Sylvester (Shar) Stark**  Wife betrayed by Charlie Stark in Peter Matthiessen's *Raditzer*.

**Clarice Starling**  FBI trainee drawn into a complex psychological game with Hannibal Lecter, an imprisoned cannibalistic serial killer and former psychiatrist, to track down another serial killer in Thomas Harris's *The Silence of the Lambs*. Starling also is a central character in Harris's *Hannibal* (1999).

**Andrew Starr**  Man whose wife and daughter are murdered by Joseph Detweiler in Thomas Berger's *Killing Time*.

**Jacob (Jacobito, Jacques, Jake, Jakey, Capitin Jacobito Estrella, Comrade Comic Star) Starr**  American revolutionary fighting for the loyalist cause in the Spanish Civil War; union organizer, Latin-American expert, protégé of Carl Vlanoc, lover of Sarah Ruskin, and friend of Greg Ballard; tormented romantic who becomes a cold-blooded killer in William Herrick's *Hermanos!*

**Marcus Steadman**  Local black leader and activist in Joyce Carol Oates's *What I Lived For*.

**Johann (Hans) Steckfuss**  Dubious Swiss doctor supervising cybernetic experiments in Thomas Berger's *Vital Parts*.

**Pepper Steep**  Modern dance instructor and regular guest on the late-night talk show hosted by Dick Gibson in Stanley Elkin's *The Dick Gibson Show*.

**Carl Stein**  Colleague of Paul Galambos in Scott Spencer's *Last Night at the Brain Thieves' Ball*.

**James I. (Bugger, Jim) Stein**  Jewish attorney and National Guard captain who serves as commanding officer of C-for-

Charlie Company until relieved of his post by Colonel Gordon Tall in James Jones's *The Thin Red Line*.

**Andrew Steinborn**   Ghostwriter and novelist; dates Lillian Worth, a nurse and poet; is hired to novelize *Passionate Intensity* in Ann Beattie's *Love Always*.

**Lexi Steiner**   Attorney for the Los Angeles Immigrant Service Center; takes a job teaching at UCLA; loves David Wiley and Nell; gets pregnant with David's child in Elizabeth Benedict's *Slow Dancing*.

**Mark Steiner**   Bryce Proctorr's accountant in Donald E. Westlake's *The Hook*.

**Mr. Steiner**   Father of Lexi Steiner; retired art gallery owner living in Cuernavaca in Elizabeth Benedict's *Slow Dancing*.

**Mrs. Steiner**   Mother of Lexi Steiner; retired art gallery owner living in Cuernavaca in Elizabeth Benedict's *Slow Dancing*.

**Stella**   Wheelchair-bound muscular dystrophy victim and lover of Samuel Paul Berman in Jay Neugeboren's *Sam's Legacy*.

**Herbert Stencil**   Son of Sidney Stencil; has been searching since 1945 for the mysterious V., who is mentioned in Stencil's father's diary; involved with the Whole Sick Crew; takes Benny Profane to Malta in Thomas Pynchon's *V.*

**Sidney Stencil**   Father of Herbert Stencil; works for the British Foreign Office; stationed in Florence in 1899, encounters Hugh and Evan Godolphin and Victoria Wren; stationed on Malta in 1919, encounters Father Fairing and Veronica Maganese in Thomas Pynchon's *V.*

**Jack Stephano**   Private detective; hires bounty hunters to pursue Patrick Lanigan in order to retrieve the millions of dollars stolen from his clients; FBI arrests him and threatens to close his business; cooperates with FBI and tells them how Patrick was found and what was done to him in John Grisham's *The Partner*.

**Mitchell Stephens**   Negligence lawyer who is always angry; father of Zoe, a drug addict who has AIDS and frequently calls him to ask for money; represents the Burnells and the Walkers in a negligence lawsuit against the city and state; is thwarted in the suit by Nichole Burnell, who lies in her deposition in Russell Banks's *The Sweet Hereafter*.

**Angela (Helen Brown) Sterling**   World's highest paid movie actress, who commits suicide after performing explicit sex acts in Boris Adrian's pornographic movie in Terry Southern's *Blue Movie*.

**Alejandro Stern**   Criminal defense lawyer for accused murderer Rusty Sabich, who goes to any and all lengths to prove his client's innocence in Scott Turow's *Presumed Innocent*.

**Irving Stern**   Middle-aged socialist critic in John Updike's *Bech: A Book*.

**Itzhak Stern**   Jewish accountant employed in textile factory who works with Oskar Schindler to place Jewish workers in Schindler's factory; at Oskar's request, he writes report on treatment of Jews in Plaszow for a Zionist rescue mission in Budapest that uses it to help publicize war atrocities in Germany; sent to Plaszow labor camp, but rescued by Oskar Schindler and survives the war in Thomas Keneally's *Schindler's List*.

**Artie Sternlicht**   Columbia University student and political activist; friend of Susan Isaacson Lewin in E. L. Doctorow's *The Book of Daniel*.

**Bergen Stettner**   Wealthy straw man for Iranian investors in money laundering operation in Lawrence Block's *A Dance at the Slaughterhouse*.

**Anita Stevens**   Nurse and girlfriend of Emmet Smith; her on-again, off-again relationship with him is a symptom of his inability to adjust to life after his tour in Vietnam in Bobbie Ann Mason's *In Country*.

**Coach (Steve) Stevens**   Baseball coach at Lopin High School and friend of Carl Brown in Betty Smith's *Joy in the Morning*.

**Colonel Stevens**   Fatherly administrator of Kilrainey Army Hospital in James Jones's *Whistle*.

**George Kingfish Stevens**   Radio character jailed for robbing Amos's place; freed from jail by Minnie Yellings in Ishmael Reed's *The Last Days of Louisiana Red*.

**Gladys Stevens**   Woman whose voice is used in the voice-reminder system at Project Wildfire in Michael Crichton's *The Andromeda Strain*.

**Domenic Stevick**   Older brother of Mr. Stevick (Lyle); Roman Catholic priest; half brother of Felix Stevick in Joyce Carol Oates's *You Must Remember This*.

**Enid Stevick**   Youngest daughter of Mr. Stevick (Lyle); timid, intense, and neurotic; secret lover of her uncle Felix Stevicks in Joyce Carol Oates's *You Must Remember This*.

**Felix Stevick**   World War II veteran, professional boxer, and later rich businessman; cynical, playful, and oversexual; adored by women; half brother of Mr. Stevick (Lyle), uncle and lover of Enid in Joyce Carol Oates's *You Must Remember This*.

**Geraldine Stevick**   Oldest daughter of Mr. Stevick (Lyle); ordinary young mother of several children in Joyce Carol Oates's *You Must Remember This*.

**Hannah Stevick**   Daughter from peasant family; housewife married to Mr. Stevick (Lyle); mother of four children in Joyce Carol Oates's *You Must Remember This*.

**Karl Stevick** Father of Mr. Stevick (Lyle); successful politician who divorced Lyle's mother to marry a younger "show girl"; cynical, amused, and proud; rich, famous, and powerful in Port Oriskany until his suicide in Joyce Carol Oates's *You Must Remember This.*

**Lizzie Stevick** Second daughter of Mr. Stevick (Lyle); beautiful woman with a bad name; trained as a club singer in Joyce Carol Oates's *You Must Remember This.*

**Lyle Stevick** Second son of Karl Stevick, father of Enid and half brother of Felix; owner of a small furniture store; cynical, humorous, and often feels disadvantaged; later obsessed about bomb shelters, fearing nuclear wars in Joyce Carol Oates's *You Must Remember This.*

**Warren Stevick** Son of Mr. Stevick (Lyle); wounded and disfigured Korean War veteran; law school student; intense, sensitive, and idealistic; manipulated lover of Miriam in Joyce Carol Oates's *You Must Remember This.*

**James (Jamie) Stewart** Wealthy owner of Virginia farm; mourns the absence of his wife, Carry; has become a recluse, unable to care for himself; worries that daughter, Lisa, will squander his money in Mary Lee Settle's *Blood Tie.*

**Lisa Stewart** Daughter of James Stewart; nicknamed "queen of the cats" by Basil; falls for Huseyin, who uses her in Mary Lee Settle's *Blood Tie.*

**Annabelle Stiffarm** Native American teenager, ally of Foxy Cree, both of whom harass Rayona Taylor when she moves onto their Montana reservation in Michael Dorris's *A Yellow Raft in Blue Water.*

**Edith Stilling** Widowed neighbor of Terry Bluvard; accepts the relationship between Bluvard and Renay Davis in Ann Allen Shockley's *Loving Her.*

**Kevin Stillman** High school bully and friend of Conrad Jarrett in Judith Guest's *Ordinary People.*

**Greg Stillson** Unscrupulous insurance and real estate agent, congressman, and presidential candidate whose plans for starting a nuclear war Johnny Smith discovers; assassinated by Smith in Stephen King's *The Dead Zone.*

**Johnny Cash Stillwater** Introverted widowed father of two daughters, one of whom commits suicide while the other is abused by boyfriends; proposes to Alice Greer after returning to his Cherokee country; grandfather of Turtle in Barbara Kingsolver's *Pigs in Heaven.*

**Turtle Stillwater** Orphaned, abused Cherokee girl left in Taylor's car and adopted by Taylor Greer; invited to Oprah Winfrey's show for saving Lucky Buster's life; granddaughter of Johnny Cash Stillwater in Barbara Kingsolver's *Pigs in Heaven.*

**Stinger** Bourne Island cane cutter who befriends Saul Amron in Paule Marshall's *The Chosen Place, the Timeless People.*

**Stingo (Cracker, the Reverend Wilbur Entwistle, Stinky)** Southern aspiring writer who chronicles his relationship with Sophie Zawistowska and Nathan Landau in Brooklyn in 1947; narrator of William Styron's *Sophie's Choice.*

**Mrs. Nigel Stock** See Ardis Ross.

**Freddy Stockwell** Father of Emily Turner in Alison Lurie's *Love and Friendship.*

**Patricia Stockwell** Mother of Emily Turner in Alison Lurie's *Love and Friendship.*

**Anastasia (Stacey) Stoker** Nurse in the New Tammany Psyche Clinic, wife of Maurice Stoker, daughter of Virginia R. Hector, and nymphomaniacal lover of George Giles; she and Giles couple in the belly of a computer in John Barth's *Giles Goat-Boy.*

**Giles Stoker** See Stoker Giles.

**Maurice Stoker** Brother of Lucky Rexford and ruler of the dark Power Plant in John Barth's *Giles Goat-Boy.*

**Boney Stokes** Nosy and self-righteous store owner; opposes the Stampers in Ken Kesey's *Sometimes a Great Notion.*

**Melba Stokes** Christian Scientist and employer of Tisha Dees in Arthenia J. Bates's *The Deity Nodded.*

**Robin Stokes** Thirty-something African-American businesswoman who lives in Scottsdale, Arizona; uses astrology to guide her life; has knack for picking the wrong men; an only child of ailing parents for whom she feels responsible; overcomes her man-crazy nature at her father's death in Terry McMillan's *Waiting to Exhale.*

**Brian Stollerman** First husband of Isadora Wing; she divorces him when he becomes schizophrenic in Erica Jong's *Fear of Flying.*

**Dora Stolnitz** First lover of Aaron Greidinger; Communist Party member who becomes disenchanted by its policies under Stalin in Isaac Bashevis Singer's *Shosha.*

**Andrew Stone** Self-made millionaire; father of Angel Stone and her half brother and husband, Michael Tarleton; spends years trying to gain control of Angel's company in M. F. Beal's *Angel Dance.*

**Angel Stone** American feminist author and heiress to her grandmother's company of organized drug smugglers; estranged wife of Michael Tarleton and partner of Julia; hires Kat Alcazar as her companion, secretary, and bodyguard in M. F. Beal's *Angel Dance.*

**Arabella Stone** See Milo Hamilton.

**Dr. Edgar Stone**    Self-important English master whose refusal to take a salary cut is a partial cause of Dorset Academy's demise in Richard Yates's *A Good School*.

**Edith Stone**    Pretty, dreamy, teenage daughter of Dr. Edgar Stone; a romantic image to the boys of Dorset Academy, she experiences sexual initiation with student council president Larry Gaines in Richard Yates's *A Good School*.

**Gordon Stone**    Retired sociology professor and writer; married to Judith Silver, his fourth wife, has five children by previous wives; dying of lung cancer; gives tacit approval to Judith's love affair with David Greene partly to encourage Greene's candidacy for town selectman; dies in Marge Piercy's *Storm Tide*.

**Jeremy Stone**    Stanford University bacteriology professor who developed the idea of Project Wildfire and who is the leader of a group of scientists in Michael Crichton's *The Andromeda Strain*.

**Miriam Berg Stone**    Independent woman who trades a Ph.D. and a promising career in computers for a husband and children; begins to regain self-confidence, self-esteem, and independence by the end of Marge Piercy's *Small Changes*.

**Neil Stone**    Husband of Miriam Berg in Marge Piercy's *Small Changes*.

**Rachel Stone**    Millionaire mother of Andrew Stone and grandmother of Angel Stone; leaves her millions to Angel in M.F. Beal's *Angel Dance*.

**Willie Stone**    Friend of Bill Flower, with whom he splits winning lottery ticket; almost completely silent and waiflike; former optometrist, his vision of the world ominously foreshadows the ways in which John Nashe and Jack Pozzi will remain indebted to him in Paul Auster's *The Music of Chance*.

**Hiram Stonebraker**    United States major general who coordinates the Berlin airlift in Leon Uris's *Armageddon*.

**Carol Stoner**    Wife of Sonny, mother of Lester; sick in bed with cancer, dies in Mary McGarry Morris's *Songs in Ordinary Time*.

**Lester (Les) Stoner**    Son of Sonny Stoner, boyfriend of Alice Fermoyle; valedictorian of his class in Mary McGarry Morris's *Songs in Ordinary Time*.

**Sonny Stoner**    Town sheriff, has a grating air of weary solicitude in Mary McGarry Morris's *A Dangerous Woman;* has an affair with Eunice Bonifante in *Songs in Ordinary Time*.

**Captain Bruno Storm**    See Raymond Mainwaring.

**Brigit Stott**    Novelist and academic who teaches at Woodslee University; involved in a turbulent love affair with music professor Alexis Kessler in Joyce Carol Oates's *Unholy Loves*.

**Colonel Stotz**    Early investigator of the murder of Breckenridge Lansing; as a private citizen he solves the mystery in Thornton Wilder's *The Eighth Day*.

**Clyde (Hanger) Stout**    Kind teenager who works as a mechanic at Pete's gas station, where he practices free-hanging; after being drafted into the army, he wins the free-hanging competition, but does not receive the prize money; narrator of Jack Matthews's *Hanger Stout, Awake!*

**Marshal Excell Prentiss (Curly) Stovall**    Storekeeper in Banner, Mississippi, who takes an heirloom wedding ring and Jack Renfro's horse and truck in payment for Renfro's debts in Eudora Welty's *Losing Battles*.

**Marian Strademyer**    Secretary for George Lockwood I at Lockwood & Co.; mistress of Penrose Lockwood in John O'Hara's *The Lockwood Concern*.

**Richard Throckett Straker**    Partner of Barlow; buys the Marsten House as a home for the vampire Barlow in Stephen King's *'Salem's Lot*.

**John (Johnny Stranger, Mother Strange) Strange**    Texan and mess sergeant; returns from duty in the South Pacific with metal fragments in his hand to discover that his wife loves another man and that his plans to start a new life as a restaurateur will never become reality in James Jones's *Whistle*.

**Linda Sue Strange**    Wife of Johnny Strange; while Johnny is stationed in the South Pacific, she becomes involved with a more adventurous married lover and abandons her plans to open a restaurant with her husband in James Jones's *Whistle*.

**Victor (Don Victor) Strasser**    Father-in-law of Grace Strasser-Mendana and father of four warring sons; takes over Boca Grande from his wife's family and dies at age ninety-five in Joan Didion's *A Book of Common Prayer*.

**Antonio Strasser-Mendana**    Youngest son of Victor Strasser, husband of Isabel Strasser-Mendana, and brother of Edgar, Luis, and Little Victor Strasser-Mendana; succeeds Little Victor to power in Boca Grande in Joan Didion's *A Book of Common Prayer*.

**Bianca Strasser-Mendana**    Wife of Little Victor Strasser-Mendana in Joan Didion's *A Book of Common Prayer*.

**Edgar Strasser-Mendana**    Oldest son of Victor Strasser, husband of Grace Strasser-Mendana, and father of Gerardo Strasser-Mendana; upon his death, leaves Grace 59.8 percent of the arable land in Boca Grande in Joan Didion's *A Book of Common Prayer*.

**Elena Strasser-Mendana**    Widow of Luis Strasser-Mendana; attracted to her nephew, Gerardo Strasser-Mendana, in Joan Didion's *A Book of Common Prayer*.

**Gerardo Strasser-Mendana**   Son of Grace Strasser-Mendana and lover of Charlotte Douglas; makes a failed power grab in Boca Grande in Joan Didion's *A Book of Common Prayer.*

**Grace Tabor Strasser-Mendana**   Widow of Edgar Strasser-Mendana and daughter-in-law of Victor Strasser; narrator of Joan Didion's *A Book of Common Prayer.*

**Isabel Strasser-Mendana**   Wife of Antonio Strasser-Mendana in Joan Didion's *A Book of Common Prayer.*

**Luis Strasser-Mendana**   Second son of Victor Strasser; killed after being president of Boca Grande for fifteen months in Joan Didion's *A Book of Common Prayer.*

**Victor (Little Victor) Strasser-Mendana**   Third son of Victor Strasser and lover of Charlotte Douglas; succeeds to power in Boca Grande after the death of his brother Luis in Joan Didion's *A Book of Common Prayer.*

**Ray Stratton**   College roommate of Oliver Barrett IV in Erich Segal's *Love Story.*

**Doctor Strauss**   Neurosurgeon who teams with Nemur to perform the intelligence operation on Charlie Gordon in Daniel Keyes's *Flowers for Algernon.*

**Streamline**   Unemployed friend of Jake Jackson; named for his slick, straight black hair in Richard Wright's *Lawd Today.*

**Scotty Streck**   Bowler beaten in a match by Billy Phelan; dies of a heart attack in William Kennedy's *Billy Phelan's Greatest Game.*

**Clem Streeter**   Trucker tortured by Legs Diamond in William Kennedy's *Legs.*

**Michael (Mike) Strelchuk**   Miner whose heroism following a mine explosion is unavailing; he and his companions are among the dead in Robert Coover's *The Origin of the Brunists.*

**Henry Stringer**   State's attorney; an elegant man out of Yale Law School who gardens and breeds collies; tough, unsmiling, smart fellow who hates to lose in Maureen Howard's *Natural History.*

**Phillipos Stritsas**   Lover of Chrysanthi and look-alike of Sotiris Procopirios in Nicholas Delbanco's *The Martlet's Tale.*

**Aloysius James Strohe**   Brewer; grandfather of Ellen Strohe in Larry Woiwode's *What I'm Going to Do, I Think.*

**Ellen Sidone Anne Strohe**   Newly married wife of Chris Van Eenanam and a central character in Larry Woiwode's *What I'm Going to Do, I Think.*

**Grandma Strohe**   Wife of A. J. Strohe and grandmother of Ellen Strobe in Larry Woiwode's *What I'm Going to Do, I Think.*

**Bayard Bidwell (Baby) Strong**   Sixteen-year-old son of Margaret Flood; lives with his father, Pinkham; commutes between mother and father on the New York subways; cleans up his parents' messes; stabbed to death by Mannie in Maureen Howard's *Expensive Habits.*

**Charley Strong**   Outstanding student of Francis Prescott; World War I hero wounded in action; lives in Paris with Prescott's daughter, Cordelia Turnbull, after the war; author of a manuscript collected by Brian Aspinwall in Louis Auchincloss's *The Rector of Justin.*

**Kay Leiland Strong**   Vassar graduate who works in merchandising at Macy's, marries and is divorced from Harald Peterson; falls to her death from the twentieth floor of a building; police rule her death an accident, but other members of the Group believe it to be suicide in Mary McCarthy's *The Group.*

**Pinkham (Pinky) Strong**   Father of Margaret Flood's son; weds Margaret after Bayard is born; becomes disillusioned with his life after Ray Nickel is murdered; leaves Margaret; owns and lives in Golden Oldies, a secondhand clothing store; quits drinking and returns to Margaret after Bayard's murder in Maureen Howard's *Expensive Habits.*

**Loren Stroop**   Weathered midwestern farmer who has developed a plan for a new kind of planting machine; suffers a stroke and eventually dies from winter exposure; his plans for the planting machine are discovered by a Moo University student and a professor, promising the financial salvation of the university in Jane Smiley's *Moo.*

**Ferguson (Fergie) Stroup**   Bachelor-priest at sixty-eight; called Stroup the Swoop because he trains his students in the grand, sweeping gestures of the high Anglo-Catholic mass; professionally biased toward his own gender in Gail Godwin's *Evensong.*

**Daniel Strunk**   Loner once married to a Cherokee Indian who was killed in an Indian massacre; helps Leslie Collins make saltpeter in Harriette Simpson Arnow's *The Kentucky Trace.*

**Donna Stuart**   Jill Stuart's promiscuous cousin, she rooms with her in college; is raped by a boy in town, gets pregnant, and has an illegal abortion; moves out of Jill's room their senior year; marries Peter Crecy; works as the weather girl for a station in New York; dies of blood loss from a second abortion in Marge Piercy's *Braided Lives.*

**J. E. B. (Jeb) Stuart**   Colorful and untrustworthy Southern general who fails to keep Robert E. Lee informed of the movements of the Union army preceding the Battle of Gettysburg in Michael Shaara's *The Killer Angels.*

**Jill Stuart**   Poor girl from Detroit; wears hand-me-downs and shoplifts; argues violently with her mother; goes away to college at the University of Michigan; loses her virginity to Mike Loesser; gets pregnant and self-aborts; moves to New York after graduation from college and becomes engaged to Howie, whom she does not marry in Marge Piercy's *Braided Lives.*

**Malcolm Stuart**   Jill's father; works for the city servicing trolleys; is a Celt; can have a violent temper in Marge Piercy's *Braided Lives*.

**Pearl Stuart**   Jill's mother; has been married three times; is Jewish; reads palms and tea leaves; sarcastic and manipulative; she and Jill become friends in middle age in Marge Piercy's *Braided Lives*.

**Robert Stuart**   Handsome cad and possible murderer; charms amateur sleuth Blanche White in Barbara Neely's *Blanche Among the Talented Tenth*.

**Sir Lewis Stukely**   Sir Walter Ralegh's kinsman and betrayer in George Garrett's *Death of the Fox*.

**Stupid Ludmila**   Half-crazed woman living in the forest with her dog; her father allowed her to be raped by "a herd of drunken peasants" because she refused to marry the son of the village psalmist; killed by village women angry because Ludmila entices their husbands in Jerzy Kozinski's *The Painted Bird*.

**The Subliminal Kid**   Technical sergeant specializing in putting out Rewrite Bulletins at the subliminal level in William S. Burroughs's *The Ticket That Exploded;* defector from the Nova Mob working in collaboration with the Nova Police in *The Soft Machine*.

**Sugarman**   Candy butcher on the Grand Central railroad; lives in the 13th Street building managed by Norman Moonbloom in Edward Lewis Wallant's *The Tenants of Moonbloom*.

**Baby Suggs (Grandma Baby)**   Mother-in-law of Sethe; a caller; bought by her son and sent to Ohio; contemplates colors at the end of her life in Toni Morrison's *Beloved*.

**Devi Sukhavati**   Trained physician and India's leading molecular biologist; both stylish and decisive; member of The World Message Consortium and The Five in Carl Sagan's *Contact*.

**Sula**   See Sula Peace.

**Suliana**   Mute female who is abused by Patternists in Octavia E. Butler's *Patternmaster*.

**Sullivan**   Female sculptor who accompanies David Bell and friends on a trip west to make a documentary film in Don DeLillo's *Americana*.

**Sullivan (Sully)**   Seagull who is Jonathan Livingston Seagull's first flight instructor after Jonathan transcends earthly life in Richard Bach's *Jonathan Livingston Seagull*.

**Miss Sullivan**   Tough Girl Scout leader in Maureen Howard's *Natural History*.

**Paco Sullivan**   American soldier, one of ninety-three men to survive an attack at Fire Base Harriet in Vietnam; badly injured; recuperates in hospitals; works as a dishwasher in a small diner owned by a World War II veteran; spied upon by a young neighbor, Cathy; leaves after reading Cathy's diary in Larry Heinemann's *Paco's Story*.

**Gina Summers**   Prostitute specializing in sadomasochism; one of her clients is Los Angeles policeman Baxter Slate in Joseph Wambaugh's *The Choirboys*.

**Sun**   Underworld drug dealer in George Cain's *Blueschild Baby*.

**Reinhardt (Renne) Sundheimer**   Thirty-six-year-old virgin; was a child prodigy on the cello, but his career is ruined after he develops sensitive hearing; becomes a music teacher of Kyung-hee Kim; is on a murder trial jury and hangs the jury; is attracted to Maria Teresa Reiter, a fellow jurist, and tries to have sex with her; narrates Mark Salzman's *The Soloist*.

**Adam Sunraider**   Son of unnamed white woman and unknown father; raised as black by black Baptist preacher Alonzo Hickman under the name Bliss; runs away from Hickman and poses as a filmmaker before becoming a U.S. senator; racist; shot by young black man while he is speaking in the Senate in Ralph Ellison's *Juneteenth*.

**Sunshine**   Indian second wife of Little Big Man and mother of their son, Morning Star, in Thomas Berger's *Little Big Man*.

**Sunshine**   Younger daughter of Quoyle and Petal Bear; found with her older sister, Bunny, sliding naked on a floor covered with dish detergent at the home of a man who bought them from her mother; is reunited with her father, after which they move to Newfoundland in E. Annie Proulx's *The Shipping News*.

**Buffy Surface**   Former girlfriend of Brewster Ashenden in *The Making of Ashenden*, a novella in Stanley Elkin's *Searches and Seizures*.

**Susan**   Sixteen-year-old who becomes pregnant after sleeping with Lee Mellon; becomes a North Beach character in Richard Brautigan's *A Confederate General from Big Sur*.

**Susanne**   Homeless young white woman in a drug commune on the Zuni reservation; she assists Joe Leaphorn in tracking George Bowlegs and protects Leaphorn from Chester Reynolds in Tony Hillerman's *Dance Hall of the Dead*.

**Mary Sutton**   Mother of Mildred Sutton in Reynolds Price's *A Long and Happy Life*.

**Mike Sutton**   Owner of a hardware store; takes care of Margot Molinaro's house when it is hit by a strange geomagnetic storm, an odd infestation of spiders, and a hailstorm; marries Margot; opens a chain of hardware stores across South Florida; has a son named Frankie in Alice Hoffman's *Local Girls*.

**Mildred Sutton**   Young black woman and childhood friend of Rosacoke Mustian; dies in childbirth in Reynolds Price's *A Long and Happy Life*.

**Colonel Sutton-Smith**    Retired English colonel who invents the Do Easy method for doing things in William S. Burroughs's *Exterminator!*

**Suzie**    Indian prostitute under the protection of Comandante Guzmàn in Peter Matthiessen's *At Play in the Fields of the Lord.*

**Per Svenberg**    Expert cinematographer who, though he fails to win an Oscar, becomes famous for his work on Vito Orsini's *Mirrors* in Judith Krantz's *Scruples.*

**Eliza Mellon (Betty Brown) Swain**    Wilbur Swain's Neanderthaloid twin sister; bitter over her brother's success; killed by an avalanche on Mars in Kurt Vonnegut's *Slapstick.*

**Letitia Swain**    Mother of Eliza and Wilbur; supported the tests that claimed Wilbur was smarter and allows her twins to be separated so that at least one of them can do well in life in Kurt Vonnegut's *Slapstick.*

**Wilbur Rockefeller Daffodil-11 (Bobby Brown) Swain**    Giant Neanderthaloid who becomes a doctor and president of the United States; twin brother of Eliza Mellon Swain; narrator of Kurt Vonnegut's *Slapstick.*

**Daniel Swan**    Friend of Ann August's in California with whom she bakes cakes for school projects; keeps caramels in his pockets; stays friends with Ann and Adele Diamond in adulthood in Mona Simpson's *Anywhere but Here.*

**Esco Swanger**    Member of Monroe's Cold Mountain Church who helps Ada Monroe after her father's death; husband of Sally Swanger in Charles Frazier's *Cold Mountain.*

**Sally Swanger**    Cold Mountain woman who helps Ada Monroe after the death of Ada's father; wife of Esco Swanger in Charles Frazier's *Cold Mountain.*

**Jessica Swanlake**    Lover of Roger Mexico in Thomas Pynchon's *Gravity's Rainbow.*

**Carol Severin Swanson**    Narrator who in his midlife crisis reminisces about his sexual conquests; retreats to the Huron Mountains of Michigan to renew his spirit and to see a wolf in the daylight in Jim Harrison's *Wolf.*

**Mister Swanson**    Member of the review board for the post office where Jake Jackson is employed in Richard Wright's *Lawd Today.*

**Sam Swartwout**    Collector of the Port of New York and longtime friend of Aaron Burr in Gore Vidal's *Burr.*

**Romana Swartz**    Poet, nudist, and lover of Dave Wain; witnesses Jack Duluoz's alcoholic breakdown during a retreat at Big Sur in Jack Kerouac's *Big Sur.*

**Mark Sway**    Eleven-year-old boy; target of the Mafia; hires Reggie Love as his lawyer; secures money and FBI protection; leads the FBI to the body of murder victim in John Grisham's *The Client.*

**Ricky Sway**    Emotionally sensitive younger brother of Mark Sway; experiences psychological trauma and goes into a catatonic state after witnessing the capture of his brother, Mark, by Jerome Clifford and Clifford's suicide in John Grisham's *The Client.*

**Sweeney**    Head of the Provos, a terrorist group in Paul Theroux's *The Family Arsenal.*

**Dan Sweeney**    Friend of Conor Larkin, gunrunner, and head of the Irish Republican Brotherhood in Leon Uris's *Trinity.*

**Berenice Sweet**    Older sister of Hard Candy Sweet, student at the University of Georgia, and Miss Rattlesnake of 1975; murdered by Joe Lon Mackey in Harry Crews's *A Feast of Snakes.*

**Chuck Sweet**    Classmate of Marybeth Howe from Bettendorf, Iowa; is studying art; ex-athlete; sleeps with Marybeth and wants to help her escape from the police in Diane Johnson's *Lying Low.*

**Hard Candy Sweet**    Cheerleader at Mystic High School and girlfriend of Willard Miller in Harry Crews's *A Feast of Snakes.*

**Robert (Bob, Sweetie) Sweet**    High school classmate and later employer of Carl Reinhart; owner of a rejuvenation clinic in Thomas Berger's *Vital Parts.*

**Sweetheart Calico**    Native American plains woman and descendant of the antelope people who is kidnapped and taken to Minneapolis by Klaus Shawano in Louise Erdrich's *The Antelope Wife.*

**Sweetman**    See Orin Wilkerson.

**Lila Swenson**    Sioux woman who befriends Samantha De Vere after De Vere is raped by three men in Gail Godwin's *Violet Clay.*

**George Swiebel**    Former actor turned contractor in Chicago, best friend of Charlie Citrine, streetwise mingler with many types, and host of the poker party that leads to Citrine's troubles with Rinaldo Cantabile in Saul Bellow's *Humboldt's Gift.*

**Swoop**    See Swoop Ferguson.

**Stephanie Sykes**    Nicole Nelson's character's name on the soap opera *Passionate Intensity* in Ann Beattie's *Love Always.*

**Sylvia**    File clerk who leaves her job to go west with her lover, Tim, and the unnamed narrator; has an affair with the narrator and returns to Valdosta, Georgia, in Jim Harrison's *A Good Day to Die.*

**Sylvie**    Black servant whose service in the Kendal household spans three generations in Reynolds Price's *The Surface of Earth.*

**Istvan Szegedyi**    See Ivor Sedge.

**Pablo Tabor**   Slim, speed-taking man in the Coast Guard; runs away to Palmas, where he becomes a violent gunrunner; meets Father Egan at the Tecan ruins and escapes the revolution with Frank Holliwell in the mission boat; is killed by Holliwell in Robert Stone's *A Flag for Sunrise.*

**Tadziewski (Tad)**   Lover of Valerie in Marilyn French's *The Women's Room.*

**Tahneh**   Female Telikohn tribal leader who befriends Alanna Verrick in Octavia E. Butler's *Survivor.*

**David Talbot**   Seventy-four-year-old Englishman and member of the Talamasca, a secret organization dedicated to the worldwide study of occult, paranormal, and metaphysical phenomena; the only human friend of the vampire Lestat; is accosted by Lestat and turned into a powerful vampire against his will in Anne Rice's *The Tale of the Body Thief.*

**Gordon (Shorty) Tall**   Lieutenant colonel and battalion commander who relieves James Stein of his command and replaces him with George Band, whom he also removes from that post in James Jones's *The Thin Red Line.*

**Talut**   Tall, strong, red-bearded headman of the Lion Camp; husband of Nezzie and adoptive father of Rydag, Talut is fair and open-minded as he welcomes Ayla and Jondalar into his camp in Jean Auel's *The Mammoth Hunters.*

**Mr. Tamworth**   Black-bearded secretary of Baron R.; begins collecting material to write the definitive biography of his employer in Vladimir Nabokov's *Transparent Things.*

**Francis Tanaguchi**   Japanese-American practical joker; one of ten Los Angeles policemen-protagonists in Joseph Wambaugh's *The Choirboys.*

**Tangee**   Black hoodlum and friend of Jesus Ortiz in Edward Lewis Wallant's *The Pawnbroker.*

**Tania**   Painter who always includes an image of Ros in her paintings; married to Howard; is drowned in Gerald's bathtub in Robert Coover's *Gerald's Party.*

**Tanks**   Moving-van driver; joins Frank Bascombe watching crime scene investigation at the hotel where they both happen to be staying; divorced; ponders the idea of selling his home in Alhambra, California, and moving to Haddam, New Jersey, in Richard Ford's *Independence Day.*

**Flight Lieutenant Tanner**   Fellow patient with Ben Flesh in a tropical disease ward in a North Dakota hospital; suffers from leukopenia in Stanley Elkin's *The Franchiser.*

**Tante Lou**   Elderly aunt of schoolteacher Grant Wiggins and close friend of Miss Emma in Ernest J. Gaines's *A Lesson Before Dying.*

**Tanya**   Teacher who is the girlfriend of Thomas Wilkerson in John Edgar Wideman's *The Lynchers.*

**Louis Tappe**   Health inspector and scientist who marries, cares for, and observes the neurotic Sita Kozka in Louise Erdrich's *The Beet Queen.*

**Albert Taylor (A. T.) Tappman**   Mild-mannered air force chaplain and Anabaptist; befriends Yossarian in Joseph Heller's *Catch-22.*

**Tar Baby**   Mixed-race recluse who boards at the home of Eva Peace in Toni Morrison's *Sula.*

**Tarden**    Pseudonym by which the anonymous Ruthenian exile, ex-intelligence agent, and narrator is made known to the reader of Jerzy Kosinski's *Cockpit*.

**Michael B. Tarleton**    Illegitimate half-black son of Andrew Stone; married to Angel Stone, whom he does not know is his half sister; murdered while investigating drug-smuggling activities in the company Angel has inherited in M. F. Beal's *Angel Dance*.

**William D. Tarleton**    Adoptive father of Michael Tarleton in M. F. Beal's *Angel Dance*.

**Tarn**    Head of the Romanian Writers' Union in John Updike's *Bech: A Book*.

**Dane Tarrant**    See Dane Tarrant Empson.

**Mama Bekwa Tataba**    Small, feisty Congolese woman who lives with the Price family and earns a small stipend as housekeeper; leaves the Price household when she can no longer tolerate Nathan's condescension and ignorance in Barbara Kingsolver's *The Poisonwood Bible*.

**Brian Tate**    Professor of political science, husband of Erica Tate, father of Muffy and Jeffo Tate, and lover of Wendy Gahaghan in Alison Lurie's *The War Between the Tates*.

**Erica Parker Tate**    Wife of Brian Tate, mother of Muffy and Jeffo Tate, and the object of Sanford Finkelstein's devotion in Alison Lurie's *The War Between the Tates*.

**Jeffrey (Jeffo) Tate**    Teenage son of Erica and Brian Tate in Alison Lurie's *The War Between the Tates*.

**Matilda (Muffy) Tate**    Teenage daughter of Erica and Brian Tate in Alison Lurie's *The War Between the Tates*.

**Tateh (Baron Aslikenazy)**    Husband of Mameh and father of The Little Girl; moviemaker who marries Mother in E. L. Doctorow's *Ragtime*.

**Phillip Tattaglia**    Sicilian gangster and head of the Tattaglia family, rivals of the Corleones in Mario Puzo's *The Godfather*.

**Sarah (Sally) Taubman (Tompkins)**    Curvaceous illegitimate daughter from Lower East Side of New York; burlesque dancer until she meets and marries middle-class Richard Heissenhuber; has daughter, Jane; dies suddenly of bee sting in Susan Isaacs's *Almost Paradise*.

**Beatrice (Bea) Taussig**    American scientist working on the Tea Clipper antiballistic missile project; sexually obsessed with Candi Long, Al Gregory's lover; is uncovered by her own irrational anger when her sexual advances on Long are rejected in Tom Clancy's *The Cardinal of the Kremlin*.

**Manolo Tavarez**    Law student and political activist in the Dominican Republic; imprisoned for several years and later killed; husband of Minerva Mirabal and father of Minou and Manolito in Julia Alvarez's *In the Time of the Butterflies*.

**Taweeda**    Old Niaruna Indian woman in Kori's band and love object of Tukanu in Peter Matthiessen's *At Play in the Fields of the Lord*.

**Angela Taylor**    Girlfriend of Willie Hall in John Edgar Wideman's *The Lynchers*.

**Charlotte Taylor**    Works in insurance office; marries Frank at age thirty-nine; mother of Felicitas; widowed six months after her birth; one of the women who belongs to Father Cyprian's circle in Mary Gordon's *The Company of Women*.

**Christine George Taylor**    Native American woman who grows up on a Montana reservation in the shadow of her handsome and beloved younger brother, Lee George, and is now terminally ill; daughter of Ida George and mother of Rayona Taylor in Michael Dorris's *A Yellow Raft in Blue Water*.

**Cletus (Old Man Taylor) Taylor**    Abusive father of Molly Taylor, father-in-law of Eddie White, and grandfather of Jimmy and Joe White; dies from having drunk lye in Larry McMurtry's *Leaving Cheyenne*.

**Danny Taylor**    Childhood friend of Ethan Allen Hawley and town drunk, he drinks himself to death after signing over the rights to his land to Hawley for $1,000, with which he was presumably to enter a rehabilitation center in John Steinbeck's *The Winter of Our Discontent*.

**Douglas Taylor**    Idealistic reform mayor of Gainesboro; assassinated by white supremacist Hank Dean after leading a group of black children into a public school in Julian Mayfield's *The Grand Parade*.

**Elgin Taylor**    Recently discharged African-American military man who has a passionate love affair with and then marries Christine George; father of Rayona Taylor in Michael Dorris's *A Yellow Raft in Blue Water*.

**Felicitas Taylor**    Daughter of Frank and Charlotte Taylor; has an affair with Robert Cavendish; at his request, sleeps with another man; becomes pregnant, not knowing if Cavendish or the other man is the father; bears daughter, Linda; reunites with her mother, mother's friends, and Father Cyprian in Mary Gordon's *The Company of Women*.

**Frank Taylor**    Seminary student; leaves at age twenty-four without taking priestly orders; marries Charlotte at age thirty-nine; fathers Felicitas, dies when she is six months old in Mary Gordon's *The Company of Women*.

**Franklin Pierce Taylor**    Wealthy natural father of Paul Hammer in John Cheever's *Bullet Park*.

**George Taylor**    Advertising agency boss of John Wilder; wealthy, handsome, married, and a compulsive womanizer in Richard Yates's *Disturbing the Peace*.

**Molly Taylor**   See Molly Taylor White.

**Rayona Taylor**   Mixed-blood African-American and Native American teenage girl who moves from Seattle to a Montana Indian reservation when her mother becomes ill; daughter of Christine George Taylor and Elgin Taylor in Michael Dorris's *A Yellow Raft in Blue Water.*

**Sonny Taylor**   Sixteen-year-old neighbor of Francie Coffin and member of the Ebony Earls gang; provides the alibi that is instrumental in Junior Coffin's release from jail in Louise Meriwether's *Daddy Was a Number Runner.*

**Zachary Taylor**   Hollywood's sexiest leading man, he finds love on the set of the hit television series *Manhattan* in Danielle Steel's *Secrets.*

**Zachary Barrington Taylor**   Ardent bisexual, the lover of both Jeff and Bernice Coates; officer in the OSS during World War II, he survives the war as well as two marriages of convenience; at end of the war, assists Bernice in obtaining the legal documents to assume a man's identity so she can continue her career as a pilot in Marge Piercy's *Gone to Soldiers.*

**Tayo**   Half-breed World War II veteran who suffers with battle fatigue; goes through Indian healing ceremony; protagonist in Leslie Marmon Silko's *Ceremony.*

**Vaslav Tchitcherine**   Soviet intelligence officer, lover of Geli Tripping, and half brother of Oberst Enzian, whom Vaslav is determined to find and kill in Thomas Pynchon's *Gravity's Rainbow.*

**Teacher**   See Bruce Thomas.

**Teague**   Vicious leader of the Home Guard band around Cold Mountain, he kills real and suspected outliers and their family members in Charles Frazier's *Cold Mountain.*

**Clovis Techy**   Older woman Waldo has an affair with and murders in Paul Theroux's *Waldo.*

**Ted**   Colleague of Thomas Eborn; writes a sensitive poem on the death of Eborn's mother in Reynolds Price's *Love and Work.*

**Teddy**   Drug addict and boyfriend of Terry Wilson in Donald Goines's *Dopefiend.*

**Teddy (Teddybear)**   Owner and bartender of the Snag Saloon in Ken Kesey's *Sometimes a Great Notion.*

**Teets**   Black man who has slept with his sister in Paul Theroux's *Picture Palace.*

**Tekla**   Peasant chambermaid for Aaron Greidinger; her earthy sensuality not only lures him into bed but also proves to him, he says, the existence of God in Isaac Bashevis Singer's *Shosha.*

**Darcy Tell**   Daughter of Mary Tell and common-law stepdaughter of Jeremy Pauling in Anne Tyler's *Celestial Navigation.*

**Mary Tell**   Common-law wife of Jeremy Pauling; mother of Darcy Tell and five children by Pauling; narrates part of Anne Tyler's *Celestial Navigation.*

**Rex Temple**   Aging Pulitzer Prize–winning novelist who has not produced a novel in twenty years; heavy drinker and friend of Scarecrow in Calvin Hernton's *Scarecrow.*

**Francie Templeton**   Wife of Joe Templeton in Joan Didion's *Run River.*

**Joe Templeton**   Father of Lily Knight McClellan's aborted baby; schemes for land that was once in the McClellan family in Joan Didion's *Run River.*

**Archer Tennyson**   Husband of Persis Tennyson; commits suicide under highly suspect circumstances in Thornton Wilder's *Theophilus North.*

**Persis Tennyson**   Granddaughter of Dr. James Bosworth and widow of Archer Tennyson; becomes friends with Theophilus North, who clears her husband's name in Thornton Wilder's *Theophilus North.*

**Ter**   Son of Susie Schnitzer's godfather; cousin whom Susie harbors in her room after he robs a bank and is wounded in Harriette Simpson Arnow's *The Weedkiller's Daughter.*

**Teray**   Brother of Coransee and son of Rayal and Jansee, who challenges his brother for the Pattern in Octavia E. Butler's *Patternmaster.*

**George Terrence**   Married to Hazel, a former roommate of Connie Birch; thought to be one candidate for his true father by John Jaimison in Dawn Powell's *The Golden Spur.*

**Terri**   Student who serves on the Cinema Committee with Hill Gallagher during the student rebellion in James Jones's *The Merry Month of May.*

**Alma Caldwell Terrio**   Sister of George Caldwell and aunt of Peter Caldwell; lives in Troy, New York, in John Updike's *The Centaur.*

**William Denis Terwilliger, Jr.**   See Billy Twillig. Adventurer who owns a gold mine in Ghost Town and uses the gold dust to gamble in Anaïs Nin's *Collages.*

**Tessio**   Gangster who betrays the Corleone family in Mario Puzo's *The Godfather.*

**Mark Tesslar**   Polish Jewish doctor who testifies against Adam Kelno in Leon Uris's *QB VII.*

**Agnes Andresen (Little Aggie) Tewksbury**   First wife of Jed Tewksbury; dies in a Chicago hospital in Robert Penn Warren's *A Place to Come To.*

**Buck Tewksbury**   Father of Jed Tewksbury and husband of Elvira K. Tewksbury; killed when his mule-drawn wagon runs over him in a freak accident in Robert Penn Warren's *A Place to Come To.*

**Elvira K. Tewksbury**   See Elvira K. Tewksbury Simms.

**Jediah (Jed, Old Broke-Nose) Tewksbury**   Native of Dugton, Claxford County, Alabama, who tries to escape his past only to return to it after receiving a Ph.D. from the University of Chicago, becoming an internationally known Dante scholar, and being absorbed into the society life in Nashville; narrator of Robert Penn Warren's *A Place to Come To.*

**Captain Texeira**   Aging sailor devoted to his boat (the *Lydia P.*) and Miss Perry; his advice to Dick Pierce before the hurricane strikes helps to save *Spartina* in John Casey's *Spartina.*

**Anna Agati (Utch, Utchka) Thalhammer**   Wife of the unnamed narrator and mother of Bart and Jack; has an affair with Severin Winter when she and her husband and the Winters swap mates in John Irving's *The 158-Pound Marriage.*

**Beata Thangbee**   Spiritualist who interprets dreams and picks numbers for gamblers; pointed out to Ideal as an example of an evil thing in Carlene Hatcher Polite's *The Flagellants.*

**Min (Minnie) Tharrington**   Lover of Rob Mayfield before, during, and after his marriage to Rachel Hutchins in Reynolds Price's *The Surface of Earth.*

**Fairy Thatcher**   Friend and contemporary of Celeste Chalfonte; plays bridge with Celeste, Fannie Jump Creighton, and Ramelle Bowman; Marxist; runs away to Germany and dies in a concentration camp in Rita Mae Brown's *Six of One.*

**Harry K. Thaw**   Profligate son of a millionaire and husband of Evelyn Nesbit; shoots Stanford White, his wife's lover; judged insane and sentenced to the State Hospital in E. L. Doctorow's *Ragtime.*

**Pierre Thaxter**   Friend of Charlie Citrine and fellow editor on *The Ark,* a proposed prestigious journal for intellectuals; mismanages funds and is kidnapped in Argentina in Saul Bellow's *Humboldt's Gift.*

**Lonzo Thayer**   State trooper who gambles with Kenny Doyle in Mary McGarry Morris's *Songs in Ordinary Time.*

**Theodora**   Lebanese intelligence agent who gives Tarden the coded documents that lead to his enlistment with the Service in Jerzy Kosinski's *Cockpit.*

**Theodore (Thedo)**   Bartender at Happy's Café in Gayl Jones's *Corregidora.*

**Theseus**   Greek hero and foster father who protects and advises Helen in H. D.'s *Helen in Egypt.*

**Thetis**   Greek goddess and mother of Achilles; speaks to Helen in H. D.'s *Helen in Egypt.*

**Ruby Thewes**   Native of the Cold Mountain region who fends for herself from infancy and comes to Black Cove to help Ada Monroe learn how to manage the farm; skillful survivor mystically in tune with the natural world; neglected daughter of Stobrod Thewes in Charles Frazier's *Cold Mountain.*

**Stobrod Thewes**   Fiddle player who enlists in the Confederate army and then deserts and returns home to Cold Mountain; ne'er-do-well and scofflaw; negligent father of Ruby Thewes in Charles Frazier's *Cold Mountain.*

**Jax Thibodeaux**   Taylor's easygoing boyfriend, a bohemian keyboard player in Barbara Kingsolver's *Pigs in Heaven.*

**Thiele**   Arrogant, authoritarian captain of the German NM *Vera* in Katherine Anne Porter's *Ship of Fools.*

**Amos-Otis Thigpen**   Son of Pourty Bloodworth; brother of Regal Pettibone, LaDonna Scales, and Noah Grandberry; half brother of Jonathan Bass in Leon Forrest's *The Bloodworth Orphans.*

**Thomas**   Motherless son and possible murderer of The Dead Father in Donald Barthelme's *The Dead Father.*

**Bob Thomas**   Dean of students of Haddan School, considered the real man in charge of Haddan in Alice Hoffman's *The River King.*

**Bruce (Teacher) Thomas**   Peer of Raymond Douglas noted for his wit and talent in providing information in Herbert Simmons's *Man Walking on Eggshells.*

**Ed Thomas**   Friend who, on his deathbed, helps convince James Page that life is good if one submits to its seasons and cycles and that in the end, nothing is irrelevant in John Gardner's *October Light.*

**Sister M. Thomas**   See Jennie Denton.

**Mack Thomas**   Former pimp, fighter, and gambler; performs in the Hippodrome and is a favorite stud horse of the customers in Cyrus Colter's *The Hippodrome.*

**Mutt Philmore Thomas**   Husband of Ursa Corregidora; throws the pregnant Ursa down a flight of stairs, causing her to undergo a hysterectomy in Gayl Jones's *Corregidora.*

**William (Will) Thomas**   Eccentric pianist and music instructor who becomes the lover of Emily Turner in Alison Lurie's *Love and Friendship.*

**Bo Thompson**   Obnoxious friend of Clyde Stout; works at Pete's gas station with Clyde in Jack Matthews's *Hanger Stout, Awake!*

**Ruthie Thompson**  Girlfriend of Rossie; jolly and easygoing; at sixteen drops out of high school pregnant in Joan Chase's *During the Reign of the Queen of Persia*.

**Wilhelmina Thoms**  Longtime loyal secretary at the Coaltown mines who makes Breckenridge Lansing appear to be more effective at his job than he is by doing the work herself in Thornton Wilder's *The Eighth Day*.

**Billy Thorne**  Firebrand leftist writer and husband of Diana Day in Gore Vidal's *Washington, D.C.*

**Freddy Thorne**  Dentist and husband of Georgene Thorne; arranges an abortion for Foxy Whitman in John Updike's *Couples*.

**Georgene Thorne**  Wife of Freddy Thorne and lover of Piet Hanema in John Updike's *Couples*.

**John "Jack" Thorne**  Fifty-five-year-old retired professor of applied engineering; colleague of Richard Levine/Ian Malcolm; uses his technological wizardry to outfox vicious dinosaurs in Michael Crichton's *The Lost World*.

**Lucas Thorpe**  Tall, yellow-haired boy who survives the ambush that nearly killed Thomas Fitch, and who distinguishes himself by his enthusiasm for vengeance, tries to run to Marlborough for reinforcements and is killed by the Nipmuc in Bharati Mukherjee's *The Holder of the World*.

**Katharine Thrale**  Woman in her late thirties who befriended Margaret when she was a teenager; taught her Greek and showed her how to make incense out of rosemary and sage in Gail Godwin's *Evensong*.

**Three Little Prigs**  Harvard alumni hired onto the English faculty at Polycarp College; objects of harassment by Tom Waltz in Peter De Vries's *Let Me Count the Ways*.

**Mary Throckmorton**  Cousin of Bess Ralegh and a guest at Sir Walter Ralegh's last dinner in George Garrett's *Death of the Fox*.

**Winifred (Winnie) Throop**  Aunt and chaperone of Cynthia Pomeroy; confidante of Arnold Soby in Wright Morris's *What a Way to Go*.

**Richard Thurman**  Small-time producer of televised boxing matches and husband of rich murder victim, Amanda; suspected of arranging robbery in which his wife was killed; target of Matt Scudder's investigation in Lawrence Block's *A Dance at the Slaughterhouse*.

**Mrs. Andrew Thwaites**  Mean-spirited widow who donates to the Order of St. Clement, the sanitarium that becomes the St. Clement's Hill Retreat House; mother of Sally Thwaites Hopwood in J. F. Powers's *Morte D'Urban*.

**Ticey**  See Miss Jane Pittman.

**Mason Tidewater**  Light-skinned black who pitched for the Brooklyn Royal Dodgers and is a janitor in a charity rummage shop; author of his baseball memoir in Jay Neugeboren's *Sam's Legacy*.

**Sara Tidwell**  Also known as "Sara Laughs"; independent black woman in the town of Castle Rock; the victim of a brutal gang-rape and murder at the turn of the century, a long-buried secret that threatens to tear apart the present-day Castle Rock in Stephen King's *Bag of Bones*.

**Tien**  Daughter of Alanna Verrick and Diut in Octavia E. Butler's *Survivor*.

**Tierney**  Homicide detective and lover of Betty Bayson; capriciously murdered in Thomas Berger's *Killing Time*.

**Kathleen Tigler**  See Kathleen Fleisher.

**Gustave Nicholas (Nick) Tilbeck**  Former lover of Allegra Vand and father of her only child in Cynthia Ozick's *Trust*.

**Miss Tilbeck**  Daughter of Nick Tilbeck and Allegra Vand; unravels the secrets of her origin and eventually meets her biological father; narrator of Cynthia Ozick's *Trust*.

**Glen Tiles**  Police chief of Haddan in Alice Hoffman's *The River King*.

**Clara Tillinghast**  Research editor of a prominent New York magazine's Department of Factual Verification and Jamie Conway's controlling boss in Jay McInerney's *Bright Lights, Big City*.

**Michael Tillman**  Professor of economics in Cedar Bend, Iowa; lover of Jellie Braden; son of alcoholic garage owner who taught him about machinery; high school basketball star until injured; rides a motorcycle; goes to India to find Jellie Braden in Robert James Waller's *Slow Waltz in Cedar Bend*.

**Tim**  Marries Terry LoPacca, works in the accounting department at the LoPaccas' bakery; a fanatical Beatles fan in Alice Hoffman's *Local Girls*.

**Tim (Timmy)**  Vietnam War veteran who is killed when he, his lover Sylvia, and the unnamed narrator blow up an earthen dam in Jim Harrison's *A Good Day to Die*.

**Pedda Timanna**  Trader at Fort St. Sebastian; a merchant-adventurer, not a beholden middleman like Kashi Chetty or Catchick Sookian in Bharati Mukherjee's *The Holder of the World*.

**Timmy**  Mulatto half brother of Tee Bob Samson; banished by Robert Samson, his white father in Ernest J. Gaines's *The Autobiography of Miss Jane Pittman*.

**Timur**  Brother of the mute Kemal; falls in love with Lale, the drowned student; lives in seclusion in a cave, a fugitive protected and kept alive by Kemal; becomes the prey of the Gendarmes in Mary Lee Settle's *Blood Tie*.

**Tinch (Stench)**    Stuttering, foul-breathed English teacher at Steering School; freezes to death in John Irving's *The World According to Garp*.

**Ora Lee Tingle**    Prostitute and police groupie in Joseph Wambaugh's *The Choirboys*.

**Rebecca Tinker**    Daughter of Theodora Waite and Rudolf Tinker, twin of Robert, sister of Sheryl, half sister of John and Bonita; goes to school in Vermont in Bette Pesetsky's *Midnight Sweets*.

**Robert Tinker**    Son of Theodora and Rudolf, twin of Rebecca, brother of Sheryl, half brother of John and Bonita; goes to school in southern Connecticut in Bette Pesetsky's *Midnight Sweets*.

**Rudolf Tinker**    Husband separated from Theodora Waite, father of Sheryl, Rebecca, and Robert, stepfather of John and Bonita; expert on the grotesque, writes *The Grotesque in Norse Myths* and dedicates it to a woman Theodora has never heard of; leaves Theodora for Marilyn in Bette Pesetsky's *Midnight Sweets*.

**Sheryl Tinker**    Daughter of Theodora and Rudolf, sister of Rebecca and Robert, half sister of John and Bonita; goes to school in northern Connecticut in Bette Pesetsky's *Midnight Sweets*.

**Tiny**    Chief guard in cellblock F and organizer of the great cat massacre in John Cheever's *Falconer*.

**Lonnie Tishman**    Dates Adele Diamond and sleeps on her sofa bed every night; builder who never makes money; Adele breaks up with him because he yells at her daughter in Mona Simpson's *Anywhere but Here*.

**Colonel Tishnar**    Former member of the British Intelligence Service whom Renate meets at Paradise Inn in Anaïs Nin's *Collages*.

**Sasha Tkach**    Police officer in Moscow; devoted to wife, Maya, and young daughter, Pulcharia; loyal to his supervisor and mentor, Porfiry Petrovich Rostnikov, despite Rostnikov's frequent clashes with authority; briefly slips into brutality when his wife and daughter are threatened by muggers during assignment, and considers quitting when the muggers are freed for diplomatic reasons in Stuart M. Kaminsky's *A Cold Red Sunrise*.

**Cordula Tobak**    See Countess Cordula de Prey.

**Holmer Toibb**    Mrs. Bliss's original recreational therapist; murdered one year after she stops seeing him; his murder prompts her to see another therapeusist, who turns out to be Milt Yellin in Stanley Elkin's *Mrs. Ted Bliss*.

**Robert M. (Bob) Toland**    NSA intelligence analyst and naval reservist; helps plan strikes against Soviet forces in Iceland in Tom Clancy's *Red Storm Rising*.

**Avery Tolar**    Easygoing senior partner deeply involved with Mafia work of the firm; enables Abby McDeere to gather incriminating evidence against the firm through his own weakness for women and liquor in John Grisham's *The Firm*.

**Abigail Howland Mason Tolliver**    Granddaughter of William Howland; becomes the final keeper of the Howland land and fortune; principal narrator of Shirley Ann Grau's *The Keepers of the House*.

**John Tolliver**    Husband of Abigail Mason Tolliver; lawyer and politician who loses his bid for governor when his wife's grandfather's marriage to a black woman is revealed in Shirley Ann Grau's *The Keepers of the House*.

**Tom**    Paid companion of Harry in Jerzy Kosinski's *Cockpit*.

**Tom**    Dean of the seminary and husband of Evangeline in Gail Godwin's *Evensong*.

**Tom**    Attacker who joins Jeff and Luke in attempting to castrate Will Harris in Junius Edwards's *If We Must Die*.

**Tom**    Monsignor, cousin of Nora; suffers from gallstones and an ulcer in Mary McGarry Morris's *Songs in Ordinary Time*.

**Tomek**    Ruthenian child whom Tarden taunts during an airplane flight in Jerzy Kosinski's *Cockpit*.

**Tommyknockers**    Supernatural forces that cause citizens of Hazen, Maine, to communicate telepathically, lose teeth, and harness power in mysterious ways in Stephen King's *The Tommyknockers*.

**Reverend Tonkle**    Tabernacle evangelist who converts Greta Wanderhope in Peter De Vries's *The Blood of the Lamb*.

**Tony**    Imaginary friend of Daniel Torrance; reveals to Torrance the dangers of the Overlook Hotel in Stephen King's *The Shining*.

**Tony**    Best friend of Mary Agnes in Mary McGarry Morris's *Songs in Ordinary Time*.

**Dawn Melody Topp**    See Dawn Melody Batelle.

**Sheila Anne (Topper) Topp**    Ex-convict and lesbian friend of Carole Batelle; raises Dawn Batelle as her own daughter until Carole takes the child away in M. F. Beal's *Amazon One*.

**Topper**    See Sheila Anne Topp.

**Harriet Toppingham**    Fashion editor of *Fashion and Interiors* who hires Spider Elliott as a fashion photographer, but fires him when he discovers that she is a lesbian in Judith Krantz's *Scruples*.

**Abeba Williams Lavoisier (African Flower, Piano Girl) Torch**    Wife of Daniel Torch and mother of nine sons and six daughters; dies of cancer when the youngest are still small in Ellease Southerland's *Let the Lion Eat Straw*.

**Askia-Touré Torch**   Second oldest son of Abeba and Daniel Torch in Ellease Southerland's *Let the Lion Eat Straw*.

**Daniel A. (Reverend Brother) Torch**   Husband of Abeba Torch and father of their fifteen children; struggles with bouts of madness in Ellease Southerland's *Let the Lion Eat Straw*.

**Daniel-Jr. Torch**   Oldest son of Abeba and Daniel Torch in Ellease Southerland's *Let the Lion Eat Straw*.

**Kora Torch**   Oldest daughter of Abeba and Daniel Torch in Ellease Southerland's *Let the Lion Eat Straw*.

**Daniel (Danny) Torrance**   Five-year-old son of John and Winnifred Torrance; sensitive to supernatural phenomena; communicates psychically with Dick Hallorann in Stephen King's *The Shining*.

**John Daniel (Jack) Torrance**   Husband of Winnifred Torrance and father of Daniel Torrance; former alcoholic who accepts a job as winter caretaker at the Overlook Hotel; under the influence of ghosts, he tries to murder his wife and son in Stephen King's *The Shining*.

**Winnifred (Wendy) Torrance**   Wife of John Torrance and mother of Daniel Torrance in Stephen King's *The Shining*.

**Croce (Richey Torrey) Torre**   Mafia member who runs Regents Sportsmen's Club, Inc., with The Greek Almas and Miller Schabb; plans gambling junkets to Mafia establishments; killed when he attempts to eliminate The Greek Almas in George V. Higgins's *The Digger's Game*.

**Lucinda de la Torre**   Young woman from the Dominican Republic who attends boarding school and college in the United States; lives in the Dominican Republic as an adult; cousin to Yo in Julia Alvarez's *Yo!*

**Leon Tortshiner**   Survivor of concentration camps in Poland and Russia and husband of Masha Bloch Tortshiner; refuses to divorce her, until she becomes pregnant with Herman Broder's child in Isaac Bashevis Singer's *Enemies, A Love Story*.

**Masha Bloch Tortshiner**   Polish concentration camp survivor, wife of Leon Tortshiner, mistress and, after her divorce from Tortshiner, third wife of Herman Broder; commits suicide after the death of her mother and Broder's desertion in Isaac Bashevis Singer's *Enemies, A Love Story*.

**John Big Bluff (Priest of the Sun) Tosamah**   American Indian spiritual leader living in Los Angeles in N. Scott Momaday's *House Made of Dawn*.

**Joey Tosh**   Thirty-eight-year-old detective on the Haddan police force who has a weekend job as a security guard at the Middleton mall; has been best friends with his partner, Abe Gray, since second grade; accepts a bribe to lay off the investigation of Gus Pierce's murder and becomes estranged from Abe in Alice Hoffman's *The River King*.

**Israbestis Tott**   Senile historian and town ancient whose fragmented recollections of the main events of the novel open William Gass's *Omensetter's Luck*.

**Sean Touhey**   Handsome actor who observes Rocco Klein and Larry Mazilli to study for a role as a police officer; offers Rocco a part in his new movie, but reneges after he gets drunk with Rocco one evening in Richard Price's *Clockers*.

**Toussaint**   Principal hero of the slave revolution in the French colony Saint Domingue; taken, together with his family, to France; becomes a prisoner in Fort de Joux in Madison Smartt Bell's *All Souls' Rising*.

**Ward Townes**   Prosecutor in the Trout murder trial; is the same age as Seagraves in Pete Dexter's *Paris Trout*.

**Gregory Townley**   Husband of Elizabeth Adams; dentist in Julius Lester's *And All Our Wounds Forgiven*.

**Mickey Townsend**   Local horse trainer and former suitor of Mary Lou Valiant; a shrewd gambler, Mickey becomes the prime suspect in two murders after it is discovered that both victims owed him thousands of dollars in poker debts in Rita Mae Brown's *Murder, She Meowed*.

**Rosanna Townsend**   Mistress of a brothel at 41 Thomas Street in New York City in Gore Vidal's *Burr*.

**Richie Tozier**   Joker and prankster of The Losers Club who provides amusement, wry wit, and often immense sensitivity to the other members of the club in Stephen King's *IT*.

**Traceleen**   African-American maid and nanny for the affluent Weiss family; confidante of Crystal Weiss; wise but nonjudgmental observer of the shenanigans of wealthy southern society folk in Ellen Gilchrist's *Victory Over Japan*.

**Kenneth Trachtenberg**   Thirty five-year-old assistant professor of Russian literature at a college in the Midwest; raised in France by American parents, relocates to the United States to avoid the shadow of his father, Rudi, an accomplished ladies' man; narrator of Saul Bellow's *More Die of Heartbreak*.

**Tralala**   Adolescent initiated without feeling into sexual activity at age fifteen; undergoes rapid moral disintegration and becomes a figure of scorn on the part of her associates—"johns," fellow thieves, and prostitutes in Hubert Selby, Jr.'s *Last Exit to Brooklyn*.

**Kutunda Traore**   Last lover of Colonel Ellelô; formerly an itinerant beggar, she uses her position as concubine to become Ellelô's adviser, then betrays him to become the consort of his successor and a governmental minister in her own right in John Updike's *The Coup*.

**Mark (Markie) Trattman**   Compulsive womanizer who runs an illegal card game for the mob; robs his own card game but is killed by Jackie Cogan for a robbery committed by Frankie and Russell in George V. Higgins's *Cogan's Trade*.

**Emory Travis**   Middle-aged homosexual friend of Sebastian Michael and Tony Lewis; unsuccessfully propositions Johnny Rio in John Rechy's *Numbers.*

**Joseph Travis**   Wheelwright, small farmer, and last owner of Nat Turner; killed in the slave insurrection of August 21, 1831, in William Styron's *The Confessions of Nat Turner.*

**Grady Traynor**   Overprotective ex-husband of Molly Cates; father of Jo Beth Traynor; works as Texas State trooper, assigned to protect Molly after she receives threatening letters from an unknown source that later turns out to be Alison McFarland in Mary Willis Walker's *The Red Scream.*

**Jo Beth Traynor**   Serene and calm daughter of Molly Cates; mature beyond her years; worries about her mother's safety; hopes her mother and father will reunite in marriage in Mary Willis Walker's *The Red Scream.*

**Dewey Treadwell**   Los Angeles police lieutenant and sycophantic underling of Hector Moss in Joseph Wambaugh's *The Choirboys.*

**Mary Treadwell**   American divorcée who attempts to remain disengaged from the lives of the ship's passengers in Katherine Anne Porter's *Ship of Fools.*

**Miss Lucille (Little Sister Lucille) Treasure**   Old woman proud of her virginity and contemptuous of her fallen sister in Alice Walker's *Meridian.*

**Miss Margaret Treasure**   Septuagenarian spinster; convinced she is pregnant following her first sexual experience in Alice Walker's *Meridian.*

**Cass Trehune**   Wealthy woman Joe Buck hopes will be his first New York client in James Leo Herlihy's *Midnight Cowboy.*

**Tremlow**   Wireless operator of the USS *Starfish;* leads a mutiny and physically assaults Skipper in John Hawkes's *Second Skin.*

**Bette Tremont**   Mother of John Jr. and Joan and wife of John Sr.; dominating personality who finds fault and complaint in most everything; suffers a heart attack in William Wharton's *Dad.*

**Billy Tremont**   Son of John Jr.; has dropped out of the University of California at Santa Cruz; accompanies his father on a cross-country car trip; aspires to move back to France with his girlfriend and be a writer in William Wharton's *Dad.*

**John (Jack, Jacky, Johnny) Tremont Jr.**   Son of John Sr. and painter; returns to the United States from France when his mother suffers a heart attack; helps increase his father's independence and nurses him through lapses of senility; learns the complex nature of his mother and father in William Wharton's *Dad.*

**John (Jack) Tremont Sr.**   Struggles with senility after his wife suffers a heart attack; father of Jack Tremont, Jr., in William Wharton's *Dad.*

**Trent**   Friend of Clay who uncritically enjoys a life that includes hard drugs, free sex, rape, and video games; fails to criticize even murder, though he does criticize Clay's reticence in Bret Easton Ellis's *Less Than Zero.*

**Edgar Trent**   President of Huddleston & Bradford, a banking firm whose gold Edward Pierce steals in Michael Crichton's *The Great Train Robbery.*

**Elizabeth Trent**   Daughter of Edgar Trent; romanced by Edward Pierce, who wishes to gain information from her in Michael Crichton's *The Great Train Robbery.*

**Donna Trenton**   Young wife and mother trapped in her stalled Pinto with her son for three days in the middle of the summer; driven out by dehydration and the slow death of her son, Donna is forced to confront the rabid dog that holds them at bay in Stephen King's *Cujo.*

**Tad Trenton**   Four-year-old son of Donna and Vic Trenton and victim of dehydration; originally afraid of the monster in his closet, Tad clings to Vic's "Monster Words" as a way to combat his fears, even as his imagined monsters become real in the form of a rabid dog in Stephen King's *Cujo.*

**Vic Trenton**   Estranged husband of Donna Trenton, father of Tad; the "Monster Words" he wrote for Tad serve as a talisman in Stephen King's *Cujo.*

**Manny Tressler**   Retired real estate lawyer who lives in the Towers; represents Mrs. Bliss when she appears in court; helps her learn how to use a checkbook and calculator after her husband, Ted, passes away Stanley Elkin's *Mrs. Ted Bliss.*

**Golan Trevize**   Foundation councilman whose suspicion that the rival Second Foundation survives to control the Seldon Plan results in his exile from Terminus and in his assignment to find the Second Foundation; selected by Gaia to determine the best future for humanity because of his innate insight in Isaac Asimov's *Foundation's Edge.*

**Thomas Tringham**   Youngest employee at Fort St. Sebastian; when the English East India Company is blamed for inciting a riot, supposed justice is dispensed by cutting off Thomas's nose in a public ceremony in Bharati Mukherjee's *The Holder of the World.*

**Maria (Primi) Trinidad**   Immigrant from the Dominican Republic to the United States, where she works as a maid for the Garcia family; mother of Sarita in Julia Alvarez's *Yo!*

**Trip**   Vice president for research of a wholly black-owned company; reasserts acquaintance with the unnamed male narrator and main character in an effort to show his connectedness to a black social identity he has long abandoned in Darryl Pinckney's *High Cotton.*

**Moses Tripp**   Man who is stabbed by Eva Medina Canada when he makes sexual advances toward her in Gayl Jones's *Eva's Man.*

**Bobby Trippe**    Popular but weak-willed suburbanite who is sodomized by vicious mountain men in James Dickey's *Deliverance*.

**Geli Tripping**    Young German witch; lover of Vaslav Tchitcherine and Tyrone Slothrop in Thomas Pynchon's *Gravity's Rainbow*.

**Father Trissotin**    Priest who counsels Hippolyte in Susan Sontag's *The Benefactor*.

**Tristram**    Lover of La Belle Isold and husband of Isold of the White Hands in Thomas Berger's *Arthur Rex*.

**Vaso Trivanovich**    Olympic wrestler who becomes a Chetnik freedom fighter and flees Tito's Yugoslavia to live in Vienna; teaches Severin Winter to wrestle in John Irving's *The 158-Pound Marriage*.

**Rita Tropf–Ulmwehrt**    Photographer; takes photographs of Egon and Gisela for a magazine article before running off with Egon to visit Helmuth in Walter Abish's *How German Is It*.

**Carrie Trout**    Mother, by her half brother, William Body, of Abraham Dolphin in Leon Forrest's *The Bloodworth Orphans*.

**Hanna Nile Trout**    Paris Trout's wife of two years; married Paris hoping he would change, but instead is abused by him; has an affair with Harry Seagraves; attempts to divorce her husband in Pete Dexter's *Paris Trout*.

**Kilgore Trout**    Prolific science fiction writer in Kurt Vonnegut's *God Bless You, Mr. Rosewater* and *Breakfast of Champions;* mentioned in *Slaughterhouse-Five* and the pseudonym of Dr. Robert Fender in *Jailbird*.

**Leo Trout**    Ornithologist on Bermuda and father of Kilgore Trout in Kurt Vonnegut's *Breakfast of Champions*.

**Paris Trout**    Fifty nine-year-old white store owner and the only person in Cotton Point, Georgia, who will loan money to African Americans; admits to shooting Rosie Sayers, but feels no remorse; abuses his wife and thinks she is poisoning him; murders his mother, Harry Seagraves, and Carl Bonner and commits suicide in Pete Dexter's *Paris Trout*.

**Trout Fishing in America**    Embodiment and voice of the American spirit; occasionally appears in human form and at other times as an activity, a hotel, a slogan, or a costume; writes letters to Pard and an ardent admirer; friend of the narrator of Richard Brautigan's *Trout Fishing in America*.

**Trout Fishing in America Shorty**    Legless, middle-aged wino and occasional resident of San Francisco; the narrator imagines shipping him to Nelson Algren in a large crate in Richard Brautigan's *Trout Fishing in America*.

**Elux Troxl**    Agent for a Honduran cartel attempting to hire Billy Twillig to help manipulate the money curve in Don DeLillo's *Ratner's Star*.

**Christine Truax**    Teenage daughter of Valerie; her rape motivates Valerie's militant feminism in Marilyn French's *The Women's Room*.

**Harriet Truckenmiller**    Wife of Kenny Truckenmiller; owns and operates Nanette's Beauty Salon in John Irving's *The World According to Garp*.

**Kenny Truckenmiller**    Husband of Harriet Truckenmiller; wife- and child-beater who assassinates Jenny Fields in John Irving's *The World According to Garp*.

**Trudi**    Friend of Ruthie Siegal's, who marries Ruthie's ex-boyfriend Leib in Marge Piercy's *Gone to Soldiers*.

**Pallas Truelove**    Youngest woman in the Convent, a group of mostly black women with sullied pasts who live on the outskirts of the all-black town of Ruby, Oklahoma; is run off a highway, raped, and left to drown by two truck drivers; rescued by group of Native Americans; refuses to acknowledge that she is pregnant, but eventually comes to terms with it in Toni Morrison's *Paradise*.

**Rafael Leonidas (El Jefe) Trujillo**    Dictator of the Dominican Republic; responsible for the imprisonment and execution of Minerva, Patria, and Maria Teresa Mirabal in Julia Alvarez's *In the Time of the Butterflies*.

**Louise (Wheezie) Hunsenmeir Trumbell**    Older sister of Julia (Juts) Hunsenmeir Smith; daughter of Cora Hunsenmeir; wife of Paul (Pearlie) Trumbell; mother of Mary and Maizie, very religious, plays the piano, fights with her sister her whole life in Rita Mae Brown's *Six of One, Bingo*, and *Loose Lips*.

**Maizie Trumbell**    Youngest daughter of Louise Hunsenmeir Trumbell in Rita Mae Brown's *Six of One* and *Loose Lips*.

**Mary Trumbell**    Oldest daughter of Louise Hunsenmeir Trumbell in Rita Mae Brown's *Six of One* and *Loose Lips*.

**Paul (Pearlie) Trumbell**    Husband to Louise and father of Mary and Maizie; works at the munitions factory; likes to collect figures of naked women and paint their nipples red with nail polish in Rita Mae Brown's *Six of One* and *Loose Lips*.

**Colm Trumper**    Son of Fred Trumper and Sue Kunft Trumper in John Irving's *The Water-Method Man*.

**Fred (Boggle, Bogus, Thump-Thump) Trumper**    Graduate student at the University of Iowa who translates *Akthelt and Gunnel;* husband of Sue Kunft Trumper and father of Colin Trumper; after being divorced, marries Tulpen; tries the water-method cure for his urinary tract infection; narrator of parts of John Irving's *The Water-Method Man*.

**Sue Kunft Trumper**    See Sue Kunft Trumper Bennett.

**Angela Whittling Trust**    Aged owner of the Tri-City Tycoons; lover of many baseball greats, including Luke Gofannon, and tempter of Roland Agni in Philip Roth's *The Great American Novel*.

**Dan Tucker**    Cincinnati lawyer and longtime friend of Alexander Main in *The Bailbondsman*, a novella in Stanley Elkin's *Searches and Seizures*.

**Henry Tucker**    Drug smuggler and pimp who uses bodies of Vietnam casualties to smuggle high-quality Asian heroin into the United States; becomes a major supplier for East Coast drug dealers including the Mafia; has Pam Madden and others brutally murdered to discourage disobedience among his prostitutes; is killed by John Kelly in Tom Clancy's *Without Remorse*.

**Tee Tucker**    Harry's Welsh Corgi dog who locates a long-dead infant and manages to lead people to it; together with his two cat pals, he drives a Porsche to safety when the owner is shot in the head; provides the "brawn" to Mrs. Murphy's "brains" in Rita Mae Brown's *Cat on the Scent*.

**Alistair Tudsbury**    Globe-trotting British journalist and radio reporter; father of Pamela Tudsbury; killed on the way to interview General Montgomery at El Alamein when his jeep hits a land mine in Herman Wouk's *War and Remembrance*.

**Pamela Tudsbury**    Daughter of Alistair; assists him with his written and broadcast journalism, but after his death finds she does not have his ability; becomes a military aide-de-camp to a British military officer; marries Victor Henry after his divorce in Herman Wouk's *War and Remembrance*.

**Tukanu (Farter)**    Niaruna Indian warrior with a talent for exuberant farting in Peter Matthiessen's *At Play in the Fields of the Lord*.

**Beck Tull**    Inept tool salesman who marries Pearl Cody because her maiden-lady delicacy fascinates him; after fathering three children with her, he leaves; his defection mars each of his children in Anne Tyler's *Dinner at the Homesick Restaurant*.

**Cody Tull**    Oldest son of Pearl and Beck Tull; a handsome loner who constantly competes with his younger brother Ezra; a showy overachiever who garners final success but little emotional warmth as he matures in Anne Tyler's *Dinner at the Homesick Restaurant*.

**Ezra Tull**    Second son of Pearl and Beck Tull; a dreamy, affable, handsome, but soft boy who attracts people of all ages; his favorite possession is his pearwood recorder and his life's ambition is to provide people with "comfort food" in Anne Tyler's *Dinner at the Homesick Restaurant*.

**Jenny Tull**    Daughter of Pearl and Beck Tull, eight years old when Beck leaves the family; becomes a pediatrician; marries three times; her last marriage is to a man with many children in Anne Tyler's *Dinner at the Homesick Restaurant*.

**Lucas Tull**    Son of Cody and Ruth Tull; a sensitive boy who resembles both his grandfather Beck and uncle Ezra more than his father; as the principal representative of the third generation, he loves his grandmother, Pearl Beck, in Anne Tyler's *Dinner at the Homesick Restaurant*.

**Pearl Cody Tull**    Unsuccessful as woman, mother, and matriarch; her husband leaves her with three children under the age of fourteen; emotionally cold, she becomes an abusive mother who binds her children to her in Anne Tyler's *Dinner at the Homesick Restaurant*.

**Ruth Spivey Tull**    Ezra's fiancée, whom his brother, Cody, steals and marries; feisty and countrified, Ruth finds it hard to adjust to life with Cody, but her defection to Cody breaks Ezra's heart in Anne Tyler's *Dinner at the Homesick Restaurant*.

**Tulpen**    English-born film editor who eventually marries Fred Trumper in John Irving's *The Water-Method Man*.

**Margaret Mary Bernadette (Peggy) Tumulty**    Faithful secretary and ultimately lover of Russel Wren in Thomas Berger's *Who Is Teddy Villanova?*

**Blind Tupper**    Newsagent at the newsstand in Billy Bray's office building in Maureen Howard's *Natural History*.

**Danny Turnbow**    Neighbor of Lydia Sanderson; kills and poisons animals with strychnine to attract and kill wolves; leaves business partnership with Harley Osgood and Jack when he learns that the wolf bounty is rescinded in Molly Gloss's *The Jump-Off Creek*.

**Cordelia (Cordie) Turnbull**    Embittered, twice-married daughter of Francis Prescott; carries on an affair with her father's former student Charley Strong in Louis Auchincloss's *The Rector of Justin*.

**Turner**    Black wide receiver on a college football team; takes boxing lessons from Phil Sorenson; roommate of I. R. Demby in Frederick Busch's *Rounds*.

**Emily Stockwell (Emmy) Turner**    Wife of Holman Turner and lover of Will Thomas in Alison Lurie's *Love and Friendship*.

**Fred Turner**    Young assistant professor of English from Vinnie's university, doing research in London; refined, self-conscious, and strikingly handsome; husband of Roo March and lover of Rosemary Radley in Alison Lurie's *Foreign Affairs*.

**Holman Turner**    English instructor at Convers College and husband of Emily Turner in Alison Lurie's *Love and Friendship*.

**Hyacinth Turner**    New Orleans spiritualist who attempts to get Clotilda Pilgrim to face the past in Cyrus Colter's *The Rivers of Eros*.

**Lou-Ann Turner**    House slave and mother of Nat Turner; dies when her son is fifteen in William Styron's *The Confessions of Nat Turner*.

**Nathaniel (Nat) Turner**    Literate slave and preacher who leads an insurrection of other slaves against their Virginia owners on August 21, 1831; hanged in William Styron's *The Confessions of Nat Turner*.

**Samuel Turner**   Owner of Turner's Mills, he teaches Nat Turner carpentry and promises him his freedom, but then sells him to pay the mill's debts in William Styron's *The Confessions of Nat Turner*.

**Seneca Turtle**   One of the Convent women, a group of mostly black women with sullied pasts who live on the outskirts of the all-black town of Ruby, Oklahoma; leaves her husband, Eddie, after he is imprisoned for killing a child in a hit-and-run accident in Toni Morrison's *Paradise*.

**L. Clark Tuttle**   Pesky young American interviewer who writes an article for the *London Observer* titled "Bech's Best Not Good Enough" in John Updike's *Bech: A Book*.

**Billy (William Denis Terwilliger, Jr.) Twillig**   Young mathematical genius and first winner of the Nobel Prize for mathematics; recruited for Field Experiment Number One, an attempt to decode mysterious signals from outer space in Don DeLillo's *Ratner's Star*.

**Two-Headed Ravana**   Impaled for the murder of Cephus Prynne, well-known local cutthroat who has never before attacked a white man; earned his name for the goiter on his neck in Bharati Mukherjee's *The Holder of the World*.

**Charles Tye**   Forty-two-year-old medical director of the local health clinic; marries Gus Eubanks, his second wife; his first wife left him and their daughter, Jennifer, three years before; a recovering alcoholic in Gail Godwin's *Evensong*.

**Haywood Tye**   Young cousin of Charles, whom he hopes to send to medical school in Gail Godwin's *Evensong*.

**Jennifer (Jenn) Tye**   Daughter of Charles Tye; feels she is responsible for every person in the world; becomes Gus's partner in Eubanks and Tye Construction in Gail Godwin's *Evensong*.

**Tyke**   Pet cat mourned by Jack Duluoz in Jack Kerouac's *Big Sur*.

**Tyrone**   Saxophonist and lover of Marie Canada; has sex with the young Eva Medina Canada in Gayl Jones's *Eva's Man*.

**Ugly One**   One of the wives of Boronai in Peter Matthiessen's *At Play in the Fields of the Lord*.

**The Ugly Spirit**   See Mr. Bradly Mr. Martin.

**Camille MacNamara Ulichni**   Granddaughter of Ellen and Vincent MacNamara; successful lawyer; married, but has a Jewish lover; at odds with her agoraphobic mother, Magdalene, in Mary Gordon's *The Other Side*.

**Stuart Ullman**   Employee of the Overlook Hotel who interviews John Torrance for the position of winter caretaker in Stephen King's *The Shining*.

**Uncle**   Drug dealer and pimp who shelters orphaned boys in his Manila hovel and trains them to be pickpockets and prostitutes; attempts to betray Joey Sands to the government after Joey witnesses the government's assassination of an opposition leader in Jessica Hagedorn's *Dogeaters*.

**Uncle Clyde**   Husband of Aunt Bessie; Dandy Benson boards at their Maryland farm during summers in his boyhood in Ed Bullins's *The Reluctant Rapist*.

**Larry Underwood**   Rock star in love with Nadine Cross; second lead in Stephen King's *The Stand*.

**Unferth**   Brother-killer and Scylding hero who seeks an honorable death from Grendel but is refused in John Gardner's *Grendel*.

**Smokey Updike**   Proprietor of Oatley Tap bar, where Jack Sawyer finds temporary work on his journey west in Stephen King's and Peter Straub's *The Talisman*.

**Bard Tom Upshur**   Husband of Margaret Upshur and father of Percy Upshur; once owned Tangierneck in Sarah E. Wright's *This Child's Gonna Live*.

**Bardetta Tometta Upshur**   Daughter of Mariah Upshur and Dr. Albert Grene in Sarah E. Wright's *This Child's Gonna Live*.

**Bertha Ann (Mamma Bertha) Upshur**   Sister of Aunt Cora Lou, wife of Percy Upshur, and mother of Jacob, Levi, Thomas, and Emerson Upshur in Sarah E. Wright's *This Child's Gonna Live*.

**Emerson Upshur**   Son of Bertha Ann and Percy Upshur; singer in Sarah E. Wright's *This Child's Gonna Live*.

**Gesus (Little Gee, Gezee) Upshur**   Youngest son of Mariah and Jacob Upshur in Sarah E. Wright's *This Child's Gonna Live*.

**Horace (Rabbit) Upshur**   Middle son of Mariah and Jacob Upshur in Sarah E. Wright's *This Child's Gonna Live*.

**Jacob (Sparrow) Upshur**   Husband of Mariah Upshur and father of William, Horace, and Gesus Upshur; singer in Sarah E. Wright's *This Child's Gonna Live*.

**Levi (Lark) Upshur**   Son of Bertha Ann and Percy Upshur and brother of Jacob, Thomas, and Emerson Upshur; singer in Sarah E. Wright's *This Child's Gonna Live*.

**Margaret (Mom Margaret) Upshur**   Wife of Bard Tom Upshur and grandmother of Percy Upshur in Sarah E. Wright's *This Child's Gonna Live*.

**Mariah Harmon (Rah) Upshur**   Wife of Jacob Upshur and mother of Gesus, William, Horace, and Bardetta Tometta Upshur; twenty-three-year-old protagonist of Sarah E. Wright's *This Child's Gonna Live*.

**Percy (Pop Percy) Upshur**   Husband of Bertha Ann Upshur, father of Jacob, Levi, Thomas, and Emerson Upshur, and lover of Bannie Upshire Dudley; once owned Tangierneck in Sarah E. Wright's *This Child's Gonna Live*.

**Thomas (Tom) Upshur**   Son of Bertha Ann and Percy Upshur; singer in Sarah E. Wright's *This Child's Gonna Live*.

**William (Skeeter) Upshur**   Oldest son of Jacob and Mariah Upshur in Sarah E. Wright's *This Child's Gonna Live*.

**Uranian Willy (The Heavy Metal Kid, Willy the Fink, Willy the Rat)**   Nova Police agent in William S. Burroughs's *Nova Express*; member of the Nova Mob who goes over to The Other Side, offering a plan of total exposure of the mob's operations in *The Soft Machine*.

**Father Urban**   See Harvey Roche.

**Gregoria (Mama, Manina) Urena**   Estranged wife of Nicholas Urena; mother of Ramona and Salome Urena in Julia Alvarez's *In the Name of Salome*.

**Nicolas (Nisidas, Papa) Urena**   Poet, judge, and political activist in the Dominican Republic in the late 1800s; estranged husband of Gregoria Urena; father of Ramona and Salome Urena in Julia Alvarez's *In the Name of Salome*.

**Pedro (Pibin) Henriquez Urena**   Dominican Republic citizen; doctoral student at the University of Minnesota, later a professor at Harvard; brother of Salome Camila in Julia Alvarez's *In the Name of Salome*.

**Ramona (Mon) Urena**   Dominican Republic citizen; protective aunt of Salome Camila Henriquez Urena; sister of Salome Urena in Julia Alvarez's *In the Name of Salome*.

**Salome (Herminia) Urena**   National poet of the Dominican Republic in the late 1800s; opens and runs a school for girls; succumbs to tuberculosis complicated by pregnancy; wife of Francisco Henriquez and mother of Salome Camila in Julia Alvarez's *In the Name of Salome*.

**Salome Camila Henriquez Urena**   Daughter of a famous poet and a former president of the Dominican Republic; born in Haiti where her family was in exile; writer and professor at Vassar; moves to Cuba during Castro's revolution; daughter of Salome Urena in Julia Alvarez's *In the Name of Salome*.

**Stan Uris**   Member of The Losers Club; Stan helped in the members' childhood attempt to kill "IT," but cannot cope as an adult with returning to Derry to fight "IT" another time in Stephen King's *IT*.

**Tally Urquhart**   Oldest living relative of "the queen of the county," Tally is discovered to be harboring the missing plane in her fall barn in Rita Mae Brown's *Cat on the Scent*.

**Raphael (Raff) Urso**   Poet, former sexual rival of Jack Duluoz, and author of the tribute "To Jack Duluoz, Buddha-fish" in Jack Kerouac's *Desolation Angels*; also appears in *Book of Dreams*. See also Yuri Gligoric.

**Uru (Brother Uru)**   Leader of the Bantu revolt in Walker Percy's *Love in the Ruins*.

**U2 Polyglot**   College dean who writes "The Egyptian Dung Beetle in Kafka's *Metamorphosis*," pushes a light ball of excrement by the tip of his nose, and removes the hoodoo from Bukka Doopeyduk in Ishmael Reed's *The Free-Lance Pallbearers*.

**Uyuyu (Yoyo)**   Tiro Indian who is converted first to Catholicism and then to Protestantism; ultimately murders Protestant missionary Martin Quarrier in Peter Matthiessen's *At Play in the Fields of the Lord*.

**V. (The Bad Priest, The lady V., Veronica Manganese, Vera Meroving, Victoria Wren)**   Mysterious woman for whom Herbert Stencil searches; continuously replaces parts of her body with inanimate materials; as Victoria Wren, has an affair with a spy in Egypt and encounters Hugh and Evan Godolphin and Sidney Stencil in Florence in 1899; as "the lady V.," has an affair with Mélanie l'Heuremaudit in Paris in 1913; as Veronica Manganese, becomes involved with Italian politics on Malta with Sidney Stencil, Father Fairing, and Evan Godolphin in 1919; as Vera Meroving, attends Foppl's "Siege Party" in South-West Africa in 1922 with Lieutenant Weissmann and Kurt Mondaugen; as the Bad Priest, presumably dies on Malta in the 1940s in Thomas Pynchon's *V.*

**Vachel**   Dwarf attending the party; accused by Inspector Pardew of murdering Ros in Robert Coover's *Gerald's Party*.

**Vadim (McNab) Vadimovich**   Famous author of books in Russian and English; coy about revealing his name in the autobiography he narrates, which comprises Vladimir Nabokov's *Look at the Harlequins!*

**Vahine (Heinie, Myrn, Myrna)**   Singer of Chinese and Hawaiian ancestry; sexual partner of Charlie Stark in Peter Matthiessen's *Raditzer*.

**B. Valentine**   Florist with whom J. Henry Waugh discusses funeral flowers in Robert Coover's *The Universal Baseball Association, Inc., J. Henry Waugh, Prop.*

**Stephano Valentine**   Lover of Junior Everett; helps Everett perpetuate a colossal scam that nets millions of dollars but also leads to their deaths in Peter Gent's *Texas Celebrity Turkey Trot*.

**Whitney Cable Valentine**   Highly paid mediocre actress and ex-wife of Mannon Cable in Jackie Collins's *Hollywood Husbands*.

**Peter Valerian**   Approachable and earnest leading world expert in the consideration of and search for intelligent extraterrestrial life, with whom Eleanor Arroway studied at Cal Tech; consistently enthusiastic supporter of Arroway's research in Carl Sagan's *Contact*.

**Valerie**   Lobotomized fellow patient with Esther Greenwood at a private mental hospital in Sylvia Plath's *The Bell Jar*.

**Valerie**   Resident in orthopedics specializing in joint injuries and lover of Tarden, until in hiding while supposedly out of town, he watches and listens as she makes love with another man in Jerzy Kosinski's *Cockpit*.

**Valerie**   Daughter of May; cousin of Anne, Katie, Celia, Jenny, and Rossie in Joan Chase's *During the Reign of the Queen of Persia*.

**Valerie (Val)**   Harvard graduate student and social activist slain by police during an act of militant feminism in Marilyn French's *The Women's Room*.

**Valerio**   Valet of the Cavaliere in Susan Sontag's *The Volcano Lover*.

**Adelia (Addie) Valiant**   Daughter of Mary Lou and younger sister of Charles (Chark); girlfriend of cocaine addict Nigel Danforth; a suspect in Linda Forloines's mysterious disappearance in Rita Mae Brown's *Murder, She Meowed*.

**Charles (Chark) Valiant**   Son of Mary Lou and older brother of Addie; becomes a prime suspect in the killing of Nigel Danforth, Addie's current flame, in Rita Mae Brown's *Murder, She Meowed*.

**Alex Valnikov**   Brother of A. M. Valnikov; butcher, grocer, and caterer in Joseph Wambaugh's *The Black Marble*.

**Andrei Mikhailovich (A. M., Andrushka, Val) Valnikov**
Alcoholic Los Angeles burglary detective; protagonist of Joseph Wambaugh's *The Black Marble*.

**Letitia Van Allen**    Masochistic talent agent and lover of Rusty Godowsky in Gore Vidal's *Myra Breckinridge*.

**Martin (Matty Van) Van Buren**    Lawyer and politician believed to be the illegitimate son of Aaron Burr in Gore Vidal's *Burr*.

**Allegra Vand**    Pretentious heir of a family trust, money from which supports her flamboyant lifestyle and the activities of others in Cynthia Ozick's *Trust*.

**Enoch Vand**    Formerly radical husband of Allegra Vand in Cynthia Ozick's *Trust*.

**Pieter Van Damm**    Violinist, eunuch, and prisoner at the Jadwiga concentration camp; testifies against Adam Kelno in Leon Uris's *QB VII*.

**Marie Van der Hoevel**    Dissatisfied wife of Schuyler; she has a brief affair with Larry Parker in John Casey's *Spartina*.

**Schuyler Van der Hoevel**    Slick young filmmaker and occasional drug dealer, whose footage of Dick Pierce at work becomes part of a documentary in John Casey's *Spartina*.

**Mrs. Walter J. Vander Meer**    Wealthy widow who briefly acts as patroness to Alice Prentice in Richard Yates's *A Special Providence*.

**Horst Vanderhoof**    Los Angeles park violinist; plays Russian music for A. M. Valnikov and Natalie Zimmerman in Joseph Wambaugh's *The Black Marble*.

**Allert (Alan) Vanderveenan**    Husband of Ursula and shipboard lover of Ariane; middle-aged Dutchman who may have once been a psychiatric patient; unwillingly takes a cruise at Ursula's insistence and is later tried and acquitted of responsibility for Ariane's disappearance; narrator of John Hawkes's *Death, Sleep & the Traveler*.

**Ursula Vanderveenan**    Sensual wife of Allert Vanderveenan and lover of Peter; leaves Allert after his trial in John Hawkes's *Death, Sleep & the Traveler*.

**Hendrik VanDoorn**    Courageous Dutchman; a wandering grazier moving slowly eastward across South Africa trying to make ends meet; devoted and married to Johanna VanDoorn; father of many children in James A. Michener's *The Covenant*.

**Joanna VanDoorn**    Dutch woman; naive sixteen-year-old who marries Hendrik VanDoorn against her parents' wishes; uneducated; has many children; keeps Hendrik at the center of her life in James A. Michener's *The Covenant*.

**John Van Dorn**    Project manager of coolant division at Grand Mer nuclear facility; owner of Belle Ame private school; supplies molar sodium 24 (NA 24) from the reactor cooling system for Comeaux's "Blue Boy" project; seduces Tom More's wife, Ellen; runs a pornography ring through the school in Walker Percy's *The Thanatos Syndrome*.

**Carlotta Van Dusen**    Celeste's sister; runs the Catholic school; does not get along with Celeste in Rita Mae Brown's *Six of One*.

**Vanna Vane**    Cesar Castillo's lover; blonde Miss Mambo 1954; becomes pregnant with Cesar's baby and has an abortion in Oscar Hijuelos's *The Mambo Kings Play Songs of Love*.

**Christofer (Chris) Van Eenanam**    Husband of Ellen Strohe; graduate student and a central character in Larry Woiwode's *What I'm Going to Do, I Think*.

**Ellen Sidone Anne Strobe Van Eenanam**    See Ellen Sidone Anne Strobe.

**Spencer Van Moot**    Complainer and scrounger; one of ten policemen-protagonists in Joseph Wambaugh's *The Choirboys*.

**Clair Van Orphen**    Once-famous novelist now in reduced circumstances; employer of Connie Birch; career revitalized when she is told to modernize her stories; helps John Jaimison look for his possible father in Dawn Powell's *The Golden Spur*.

**JR Vansant**    Eleven-year-old tycoon from Long Island whose short-lived financial career drives the action in William Gaddis's *JR*.

**Tom Van Sant**    Friend of Jean Warner and Dara Falcon's lover; investor in Snell's Greenhouse, competition to the Warner's greenhouse; leaves Dara to have a son with another woman in Ann Beattie's *My Life, Starring Dara Falcon*.

**Helen Van Vleck**    See Helen Van Vleck Barber.

**Varda**    Creator of collages who lives on a converted ferry boat in Sausalito in Anaïs Nin's *Collages*.

**Varnak**    Chukchi hunter in 29,000 BPE; migrates east from Siberia to Alaska; one of the first members of Athapascan tribe in James Michener's *Alaska*.

**Joseph (Joe) Varney**    Marine colonel and rival of Bull Meecham in Pat Conroy's *The Great Santini*.

**Alaric Vas**    Mother of Fabian Vas; commits adultery with Botho August, the lighthouse keeper, when her husband is away; convinces her son to marry Cora Holly; dies in a suspicious boat accident in Howard Norman's *The Bird Artist*.

**Fabian Vas**    Bird artist and murderer of Botho August; marries Cora Holly, five minutes later is arrested; he later marries Margaret Handle, his first and only love in Howard Norman's *The Bird Artist*.

**Orkney Vas**    Carpenter, boat builder, and harvester of wild birds; leaves to hunt so he can make money for his son's arranged marriage; runs off after Fabian kills Botho August and plays the scapegoat for the crime; presumed guilty of the murder his son committed in Howard Norman's *The Bird Artist*.

**Scratch Vatic**    Perpetually hungry passenger on the *Here They Come* in Gregory Corso's *The American Express*.

**Klementi Vladimirovich Vatutin**    KGB counterintelligence officer who discovers that Misha Filitov is spying for the Americans; discovers and nearly stops the defection of Nikolay Borissovich Gerasimov in Tom Clancy's *The Cardinal of the Kremlin*.

**Clarissa Vaughan**    Intelligent editor organizing a party for her beloved friend Richard Brown, who calls her "Mrs. Dalloway"; lives with her lover, Sally, in 1990s New York; meets Laura Brown, Richard's mother, after he commits suicide in Michael Cunningham's *The Hours*.

**Julia Vaughan**    Nineteen-year-old daughter of Clarissa Vaughan; friend of Mary Krull in Michael Cunningham's *The Hours*.

**Lawrence P. Vaughan**    Power- and money-hungry mayor of Amity; his refusal to close the beaches results in two deaths in Peter Benchley's *Jaws*.

**Thurzah Elvira Jordan (Granny) Vaughn**    Widowed grandmother of Beulah Beecham Renfro and her six Beecham brothers; rears them when their parents drown; celebrates her ninetieth birthday at a family reunion in Eudora Welty's *Losing Battles*.

**Chandler Vaught**    Genial automobile tycoon and patriarch of the family that befriends Will Barrett in Walker Percy's *The Last Gentleman*.

**Jamison MacKenzie (Jamie, Jimmy) Vaught**    Son of Chandler Vaught; science prodigy who is baptized before he dies in Walker Percy's *The Last Gentleman*.

**Katherine Gibbs (Kitty) Vaught**    Daughter of Chandler Vaught; Will Barrett's uncertain love in Walker Percy's *The Last Gentleman*.

**Mrs. Vaught**    Wife of Chandler Vaught; detects conspiracies to destroy the South and America in Walker Percy's *The Last Gentleman*.

**Rita (Ree) Vaught**    Meddlesome former wife of Sutter Vaught; her altruism conceals her own selfishness in Walker Percy's *The Last Gentleman*.

**Sutter Vaught**    Son of Chandler Vaught; libertine and suicidal coroner who refuses to be Will Barrett's mentor in Walker Percy's *The Last Gentleman*.

**Valentine (Sister Johnette Mary Vianney, Val) Vaught**    Daughter of Chandler Vaught; becomes a fierce but compassionate nun in Walker Percy's *The Last Gentleman*.

**Solomon Veasey**    Preacher who impregnates and almost murders a young woman; accidental companion to Inman during part of Inman's westward journey in Charles Frazier's *Cold Mountain*.

**Adelaida (Ada, Adochka) Veen**    Daughter of Demon Veen and Marina Veen, half sister of Lucette Veen, sister and lover of Van Veen, and wife of Andrey Vinelander; the subject of Van's chronicle in Vladimir Nabokov's *Ada*.

**Aqua Durmanov Veen**    Twin of Marina Veen, wife of Demon Veen, and supposed mother of Van Veen; commits suicide after a life of anguish and madness in Vladimir Nabokov's *Ada*.

**Ivan (Van) Veen**    Famous doctor, professor, and expert on Terra and theories of time; son of Demon Veen and Marina Veen, brother of Ada Veen, and half brother of Lucette Veen; celebrates his long love affair with Ada in his chronicle, Vladimir Nabokov's *Ada*.

**Lucinda (Lucette) Veen**    Daughter of Marina and Daniel Veen and half sister of Ada and Van Veen; commits suicide when Van, with whom she is hopelessly in love, rejects her once too often in Vladimir Nabokov's *Ada*.

**Marina Durmanov Veen**    Famous actress in her day; twin sister of Aqua Veen, wife of Daniel Veen, mistress of Demon Veen, and mother of Van, Ada, and Lucette Veen; substitutes Van for her sister's dead child in Vladimir Nabokov's *Ada*.

**Walter D. (Dan, Daniel, Red, Durak Walter) Veen**    Husband of Marina Veen and father of Lucette Veen; unaware that Ada is his cousin Demon Veen's daughter, he brings her up as his own in Vladimir Nabokov's *Ada*.

**Walter D. (Dementiy, Demon, Raven, Dark Walter) Veen**    Rich and notorious rake; husband of Aqua Veen, lover of Marina Veen, and father by Marina of Van and Ada in Vladimir Nabokov's *Ada*.

**Dhiren Velayudum**    Revolutionary Indian separatist and poet; lover of Jellie Braden; father of their daughter, Jaya; killed in an ambush in Robert James Waller's *Slow Waltz in Cedar Bend*.

**Jaya Velayudum**    Daughter of Dhiren and Jellie Braden; living in India although mother returned to United States after death of Dhiren in Robert James Waller's *Slow Waltz in Cedar Bend*.

**Mrs. Edward Venable**    Newport socialite and hostess for Bodo Stains; has many elaborate social gatherings at her cottage in Thornton Wilder's *Theophilus North*.

**Jean Sweet Venable**    Journalist gathering information for an article on Robert Softly's Logicon Project in Don DeLillo's *Ratner's Star*.

**Arthur Vendler**    Delicatessen owner who provides promotional dinners to radio talk show guests in Stanley Elkin's *The Dick Gibson Show.*

**Tom Venn**    Brought to Alaska by father and Missy Peckham; grows from shopkeeper to manager of first Alaskan cannery for wealthy Seattle merchant Malcolm Ross; marries boss's daughter Lydia; has son Malcolm; works to represent Seattle capitalists' interests in preventing Alaska from becoming a state in James Michener's *Alaska.*

**Vera**    Stripper at the Frolic Club, wife of Carl, and lover of E. L. Fletcher in Jerry Bumpus's *Anaconda.*

**Lee (LuAnne) Verger**    Wife of Lionel, mother of David and Laura, lover of Gordon Walker; drug-addicted schizophrenic actress in Robert Stone's *Children of Light.*

**Verily**    Housekeeper of Judge Fox Clane; quits after fifteen years when the judge refuses to pay Social Security in Carson McCullers's *Clock Without Hands.*

**Johannes Verne**    Son of Zachery Verne, orphaned at six when his grandfather kills his father; grows up alone in California desert and early Los Angeles, guided by Miss Nesselrode, local Indians, and a mysterious protector; falls in love with Meghan Laurel and lives to avenge his father in Louis L'Amour's *The Lonesome Gods.*

**Zachery Verne**    Highly literate and terminally ill former sailor; father of Johannes Verne; works odd jobs around country; respected gunman and friend of desert Indians; killed by Spanish father-in-law when he returns to California with his son in Louis L'Amour's *The Lonesome Gods.*

**Veronika**    Belgian woman who marries a wealthy industrialist as part of a sexual pact with Tarden; when she becomes unruly, Tarden has her raped by derelicts and finally kills her by exposing her to the radiation from a fighter plane's radar system while he sits in its cockpit in Jerzy Kosinski's *Cockpit.*

**Gulian C. Verplanck**    Defeated anti-Tammany candidate in New York; a writer-lawyer in Gore Vidal's *Burr.*

**Alanna (Lanna) Verrick**    Afro-Asian orphan adopted by Jules and Neila Verrick; narrates part of Octavia E. Butler's *Survivor.*

**Jules Verrick**    Adoptive father of Alanna Verrick and leader of the Verrick Colony of Missionaries in Octavia E. Butler's *Survivor.*

**Neila Verrick**    Wife of Jules Verrick and adoptive mother of Alanna Verrick in Octavia E. Butler's *Survivor.*

**Comtesse Lilianne de Vertdulac**    Poor French countess who provides room and board for Billy Winthrop in Paris, teaches him French, and improves her fashion sense in Judith Krantz's *Scruples.*

**Sister Johnette Mary Vianney**    See Valentine Vaught.

**Vic**    Sally Ann's alcoholic father; best friend of Gerald; is wounded by the police, and later shot and killed (out of pity) by Gerald in Robert Coover's *Gerald's Party.*

**Ashton Vickery**    Callous, unreflective uncle of Nathan Vickery in Joyce Carol Oates's *Son of the Morning.*

**Elsa Vickery**    Rural teenager who is brutally raped and gives birth to religious seeker Nathan Vickery in Joyce Carol Oates's *Son of the Morning.*

**Nathanael William (Nathan) Vickery**    Monomaniacal, tormented religious leader whose search for God brings him to the brink of madness in Joyce Carol Oates's *Son of the Morning.*

**Opal Sayer Vickery**    Protective grandmother of Nathan Vickery in Joyce Carol Oates's *Son of the Morning.*

**Thaddeus Aaron Vickery**    Physician and grandfather of Nathan Vickery; his pragmatic, atheistic outlook puts him at odds with his religious grandson in Joyce Carol Oates's *Son of the Morning.*

**Norman Victman**    Shopping-center idea man whose advancement is deliberately sabotaged by Leo Feldman in Stanley Elkin's *A Bad Man.*

**Victoria Regina (Vickie)**    Madeline Whitfield's champion miniature schnauzer; stolen and mutilated by Philo Skinner in Joseph Wambaugh's *The Black Marble.*

**Vidal**    Brother of Abel; dies during Abel's childhood in N. Scott Momaday's *House Made of Dawn.*

**Lucky Videndi**    See Lucia Angelina Elena Videndi Grant.

**Elsabeth Vigee-Lebrun**    Famous woman artist who paints Emma Hart in Susan Sontag's *The Volcano Lover.*

**Jean Claude Vigneron**    Urologist who prescribes the water-method technique for Fred Trumper's urinary tract problems in John Irving's *The Water-Method Man.*

**Jasmine (Jyoti) Vijh**    (See also Jane Ripplemeyer.) Young Indian woman, born Jyoti Vijh, who comes to the United States illegally after her husband's murder; in America, is raped and kills rapist; becomes nanny for a young, upscale couple in New York, then an Iowa housewife who leaves her crippled common-law husband Bud Ripplemeyer when she is pregnant with their child; adoptive mother of Vietnamese boy Du Thien; narrator and protagonist of Bharati Mukherjee's *Jasmine.*

**Prakash Vijh**    Husband of Jasmine (Jyoti) Vijh; considers Indian traditions outdated; apprentice electronics repairman who prepares to attend an American technical institute but is killed by a terrorist bomb while still in India in Bharati Mukherjee's *Jasmine.*

**Marina Vilar**    Terrorist plotting to bomb the New York Stock Exchange in Don DeLillo's *Players.*

**Rafael Vilar**　Terrorist arrested for killing a man on the floor of the New York Stock Exchange in Don DeLillo's *Players*.

**Harold Vilitzer**　Crooked politician and former ward boss in Saul Bellow's *More Die of Heartbreak* who used his powers as executor of his sister's estate to cheat his niece and nephew out of their inheritance; under federal surveillance and estranged from his family, he suffers a heart attack and dies after being confronted by nephew Benn Crader.

**Teddy Villanova**　Nonexistent character and red herring in Thomas Berger's *Who Is Teddy Villanova?*

**Felicia del Pino Villaverde**　Daughter of Celia and Jorge del Pino, mother of Luz, Milagro, and Ivanito Villaverde, and estranged wife of Hugo; contracts syphilis from her husband and tries to kill him; attempts to kill herself and her son; as a punishment, her children are sent to boarding school; Felicia is sent to guerrilla camp to embrace the government's regime in Cristina Garcia's *Dreaming in Cuban*.

**Hugo Villaverde**　Abusive and estranged husband of Felicia and father of Luz, Milagro, and Ivanito Villaverde; a merchant marine who occasionally visits Cuba and his family; gives his wife syphilis; leaves his family in 1966 when Felicia attempts to kill him; returns to Cuba and tries to reconcile with his daughters in Cristina Garcia's *Dreaming in Cuban*.

**Luz Villaverde**　Twin sister of Milagro; believes her mother destroyed her father; considers herself and her sister of be protected from their mother by the double helix of being a twin; wants to be a veterinarian and move to Africa; secretly visits her father and hides his gifts away from her mother in Cristina Garcia's *Dreaming in Cuban*.

**Milagro Villaverde**　Plans to go to Africa with her twin sister; feels sympathy for her mother until her sister reminds her of Felicia's problems; secretly visits her father and hides his gifts away from her mother in Cristina Garcia's *Dreaming in Cuban*.

**George (Steenie) Villiers**　Duke of Buckingham and favorite of King James I in George Garrett's *Death of the Fox*.

**Jane Villiers de l'Isle-Adam**　Wicked witch who attempts to poison Snow White but accidentally poisons Paul in Donald Barthelme's *Snow White*.

**Vincent (Vincennti, Vinnie)**　Youngster arrested at age twelve for stealing a hearse; follows a career of theft and debauchery; associates with male transvestites and homosexuals; at age forty, marries and produces children but is no more fulfilled by this part of his life than by his earlier years in Hubert Selby, Jr.'s *Last Exit to Brooklyn*.

**Andrey Andreevich Vinelander**　Arizona rancher of Russian heritage and Orthodox faith who marries Ada Veen in Vladimir Nabokov's *Ada*.

**Lynn Vining**　Painting teacher at Haddan School who has an on-again, off-again romance with Jack Short, the married chemistry teacher in Alice Hoffman's *The River King*.

**Vinogradus**　See Jakob Gradus.

**Mildred Vinton**　Bookstore clerk and member of the Pauling household; narrates part of Anne Tyler's *Celestial Navigation*.

**Virginia**　Widow of Arthur; finds out Arthur had no service record and received no benefits in Bette Pesetsky's *Midnight Sweets*.

**Maria Viskova**　Polish Jewish doctor and Communist; colleague of Adam Kelno in the Jadwiga concentration camp in Leon Uris's *QB VII*.

**Apollonia Vitelli**　Young Sicilian woman and first wife of Michael Corleone; killed by a bomb meant for her husband in Mario Puzo's *The Godfather*.

**Vivian (Vee)**　Mistress of Karl Larkin believed to be mute in Octavia E. Butler's *Mind of My Mind*.

**Vivian (Vive)**　Singer at Happy's Café; Ursa Corregidora catches Vivian in bed with Ursa's husband, Tadpole McCormick, in Gayl Jones's *Corregidora*.

**Carl (Comrade Truth, Untruth, General Carlos Verdad) Vlanoc**　Representative of Joseph Stalin in the Western Hemisphere; supervisor of Jake Starr in William Herrick's *Hermanos!*.

**Helene Cady Vogel**　Daughter of Benjamin Cady and wife of Jesse Vogel in Joyce Carol Oates's *Wonderland*.

**Jesse Vogel**　See Jesse Harte.

**Serenus Vogel**　See Kelcey.

**Shelley Vogel**　Runaway daughter of Jesse and Helene Vogel in Joyce Carol Oates's *Wonderland*.

**Ben Voler**　Mira's fellow graduate student and lover in Marilyn French's *The Women's Room*.

**Brock Vond**　FBI agent who worked on incarcerating and reforming political rebels during the 1960s; seduces Frenesi Gates, a political radical, from her husband, Zoyd Wheeler; attempts to round up his old drug-smuggling enemies who have converged on Vineland, California, in Thomas Pynchon's *Vineland*.

**Kurt Vonnegut, Jr.**　Editor of the "Confessions of Howard Campbell Jr." in Kurt Vonnegut's *Mother Night*; appears briefly in *Slaughterhouse-Five* and *Breakfast of Champions*.

**Hinckle Von Vampton**　Grand Master of the Knights Templar who has acquired powers from the Arabians; starts a magazine, *The Benign Monster*, for which he creates a "Negro Viewpoint" and a "Talking" android in Ishmael Reed's *Mumbo Jumbo*.

**Hugo Von Vorst**   Nonagenarian actor and possible villain in the legends of Jane Clifford's family in Gail Godwin's *The Odd Woman.*

**Adolph Vorakers**   With William and Elizabeth, a beneficiary of the Vorakers' fortune who is executor of the will and refuses to disperse funds until pending lawsuits are settled in William Gaddis's *Carpenter's Gothic.*

**William Vorakers**   With Elizabeth and Adolph, a beneficiary of the Vorakers' fortune who urges Elizabeth to leave her husband, Paul, and who dies mysteriously in a plane crash in William Gaddis's *Carpenter's Gothic.*

**Arkady Voronov**   Creole son of Russian priest Vasili Voronov and Aleut Cidaq (Sofia Kuchovskaya); leader of Sitka settlement in final attack from Tlingit tribe; marries Praskovia Kostilevskaya; one of the last Russians to leave the territory in James Michener's *Alaska.*

**Vasili Voronov**   Devoted and compassionate Russian Orthodox priest sent to head church in Aleutian Islands; marries native Aleut, Cidaq (Sofia Kuchovskaya), has son, Arkady; leaves family to become Metropolitan of Russian Church in St. Petersburg in James Michener's *Alaska.*

**Adolph Voss**   Nazi colonel; physician who heads the medical experimental section at the Jadwiga concentration camp in Leon Uris's *QB VII.*

**Konrad Vost**   Widower of Claire, father of Mirabelle, and son of Eva Laubenstein and Konrad Vost the Father; taught to respect and love women as a prisoner of rioting women convicts, one of whom is his mother, in John Hawkes's *The Passion Artist.*

**Konrad Vost the Father**   Father of Konrad Vost; drenched in flammable liquid and set afire by his wife, Eva Laubenstein, in John Hawkes's *The Passion Artist.*

**Denton Voyles**   Director of the FBI in John Grisham's *The Pelican Brief.*

**Helen Vrobel**   Wardrobe lady for Boris Adrian's pornographic movie in Terry Southern's *Blue Movie.*

**Charles (Charles II) Xavier Vseslav the Beloved**   Last king of Zembla and son of Queen Blenda in Vladimir Nabokov's *Pale Fire.* See Dr. Charles Kinbote.

**Vyella (Vy)**   Self-made preacher and friend of Mariah Upshur in Sarah E. Wright's *This Child's Gonna Live.*

**Wadal**   Ragged leader of itinerant beggars; former owner of Kutunda, who denies knowing Colonel Elleloû at the end of John Updike's *The Coup.*

**Anney Boatwright Parsons Waddell**   Mother of Bone Boatwright and Reese Parsons; sacrifices her eldest child's innocence to her physically and sexually abusive husband, Glen Waddell; leaves her family and moves away with Glen, supposedly to protect Bone from further violence, in Dorothy Allison's *Bastard Out of Carolina.*

**Glen Waddell**   Husband of Anney Boatwright; sees Anney's family and children as threats to his marriage; turns violent toward Bone; eventually forces the final separation between mother and daughter by raping and beating Bone in Dorothy Allison's *Bastard Out of Carolina.*

**Johnston (Roy Earle) Wade**   Crazed insurance magnate and acquaintance of Lee Mellon in Richard Brautigan's *A Confederate General from Big Sur.*

**Walter Wade**   Arbiter of style in Binx Bolling's fraternity; fiancé of Kate Cutrer in Walker Percy's *The Moviegoer.*

**Byrum (Big Byrom) Powery Wader**   Experienced fisherman and turder; dies when the *Lillias Eden* wrecks on Misteriosa Reef in Peter Matthiessen's *Far Tortuga.*

**Jack Wagner**   Casual friend of Bryce Proctorr, a magazine journalist and aspiring playwright; came to New York from Missouri, graduated from Antioch, has a wife, Cindy, and two sons; a bookish man with dark-framed glasses and a Vandyke beard in Donald E. Westlake's *The Hook.*

**Jarry Wagner**   Buddhist, poet, and friend who introduces Jack Duluoz to mountain climbing in Jack Kerouac's *Desolation Angels;* mentioned in *Big Sur.*

**Peter Wagner**   Philosophical and suicidal character in the comic-fantastic paperback *The Smugglers of Lost Souls' Rock,* the interior novel within John Gardner's *October Light.*

**Dave Wain**   Poet, friend, and traveling companion of Jack Duluoz and lover of Romana Swartz in Jack Kerouac's *Big Sur.*

**Anton (Teddy) Wait**   Twice-divorced brother of Theodora and one of the owners of the house in which Marybeth Howe and Ouida Senza rent rooms; famous nature photographer; fascinated by Marybeth in Diane Johnson's *Lying Low.*

**Theodora (Theo) Wait**   Sister of Anton and one of the owners of the house in which Marybeth Howe and Ouida Senza rent rooms; ballet teacher in her sixties; involved in environmental and social issues; is taken hostage by prisoners and dies in an explosion in Diane Johnson's *Lying Low.*

**Abner Palmer Waite**   Father of Theodora Waite, husband of Pauline; deserts them in Bette Pesetsky's *Midnight Sweets.*

**Mrs. Waite**   Theodora's mother; beautiful, dies at twenty-eight in Bette Pesetsky's *Midnight Sweets.*

**Theodora Waite**   Becomes a burglar after Abner Waite deserts her and their daughter, Pauline; wins money for college in a baking contest; starts business, The Cookie Lady, and expands it into franchises; marries Rudolf Tinker in Bette Pesetsky's *Midnight Sweets.*

**Wald Waldemar**   Horse player and only surviving blood relative of Von Humboldt Fleisher; Charlie Citrine gives Uncle Waldemar half his share of the money from the Caldofredo script in Saul Bellow's *Humboldt's Gift.*

**Waldo**   Juvenile delinquent and aspiring writer who goes to jail, then college, and shoots his older lover in Paul Theroux's *Waldo.*

**Alexandra Walker (de Morigny)**   Middle of three orphaned sisters adopted and raised in lavish wealth; becomes a countess by marrying a powerful man whose pride is in his pedigree; sister of Megan and Hilary in Danielle Steel's *Kaleidoscope*.

**Brooder Walker**   Riddley's father; crushed by a metal machine at thirty-three; was a "connexion man" in Russell Hoban's *Riddley Walker*.

**Coalhouse Walker, Jr.**   Educated black ragtime pianist whose Model T is trashed by Willie Conklin and others; organizes a gang to blow up the Emerald Isle fire station and occupies the Morgan Library; shot when he surrenders to the New York police in E. L. Doctorow's *Ragtime*.

**Elias Walker**   Father of Rebecca Easton; arrived in Brookfield, Massachusetts, in 1658; by 1665, bought 300 acres of land from Charles Muster's three sons in Bharati Mukherjee's *The Holder of the World*.

**Elizabeth Ann (Beth, Bethie, Cindy, Cynthia) Walker**   Woman who leaves her traditional marriage and finds independence and her true identity as a lesbian in Marge Piercy's *Small Changes*.

**Evelyn Walker**   Twenty-year-old wife of Mike Walker, mother of three sons; lonely neighbor of Tim Whiteaker and Blue Odell; sends notes to Lydia Sanderson and considers her a friend in Molly Gloss's *The Jump-Off Creek*.

**Gordon Walker**   Divorced, fortyish screenwriter and actor; substance abuser and lover of Lee (LuAnne) Verger in Robert Stone's *Children of Light*.

**Hilary Walker**   Oldest of three orphaned sisters cut off from every loving source; bitter woman who turns her hurt and rage into a successful career at the expense of any personal life; sister of Megan and Alexandra in Danielle Steel's *Kaleidoscope*.

**Isabel Walker**   Young American film school dropout staying with her stepsister and niece in Paris; initially finds France and the French difficult; has an affair with stepsister's husband's uncle; becomes accustomed to French life and concludes she is no longer an American but "a person without a country" in Diane Johnson's *Le Divorce*.

**James (Jim) Hayes Walker**   Husband of Beth Walker in Marge Piercy's *Small Changes*.

**Jenny Walker**   Wife of Wilkie Walker; secretary, research assistant, and unnamed coauthor of his books; distressed when he distances himself from her, she falls in love with Lee Weiss and maintains relationship both with husband and Lee in Alison Lurie's *The Last Resort*.

**Mrs. Loraine Walker**   Secretary to Ivar Harstad, provost, at Moo University; has most of the university faculty, staff, and administration in fear of her; has long-standing mate, Martha Lake; uncovers the Arlen Martin/Dr. Lionel Gift plans for a Costa Rican gold mine in Jane Smiley's *Moo*.

**Megan Walker (Ramsey)**   Youngest of three orphaned sisters adopted by family of comfortable means; becomes a doctor in the rural South; sister of Alexandra and Hilary Walker in Danielle Steel's *Kaleidoscope*.

**Mike Walker**   Owner of the Walker Ranch; husband of Evelyn Walker, father of three boys; trades with Lydia Bennett Sanderson for milk; disapproves of Lydia's independence but allows his wife to form a friendship with her in Molly Gloss's *The Jump-Off Creek*.

**Riddley Walker**   Puppeteer of Punch and Pooty with Orfing in Russell Hoban's *Riddley Walker*.

**Risa Walker**   Wife of Wendell Walker and mother of Sean, who is killed in bus accident; is having an affair with Billy Ansel; believes she predicted the accident; wants to sue over her son's death; divorces her husband in Russell Banks's *The Sweet Hereafter*.

**Sam Walker**   American soldier for the Allied forces during World War II; brilliant actor; unfaithful husband and neglectful father; husband of Solange Bertrand in Danielle Steel's *Kaleidoscope*.

**Shurley (Shurl) Walker**   Proprietor of a successful bar and former member of a black high school athletic team and neighborhood gang gathering for a birthday testimonial honoring Chappie Davis in John A. Williams's *The Junior Bachelor Society*.

**Tump Walker**   Coach of the Mystic High School Rattlers in Harry Crews's *A Feast of Snakes*.

**Wendell Walker**   Husband of Risa Walker and father of Sean, who is killed in bus accident; owns the town's hotel and is experiencing financial difficulties; wants to sue over his son's death to relieve some of his money problems in Russell Banks's *The Sweet Hereafter*.

**Wilkie Walker**   Naturalist and best-selling writer; cantankerous environmentalist; married to Jenny; wants to drown himself because he thinks he has colon cancer; suicide attempts fail; discovers he does not have cancer in Alison Lurie's *The Last Resort*.

**Leesy Walkes**   Elderly widow and great-aunt of Vere Walkes in Paule Marshall's *The Chosen Place, the Timeless People*.

**Vere (Vereson) Walkes**   Grand-nephew of Leesy Walkes; befriends Allen Fuso in Paule Marshall's *The Chosen Place, the Timeless People*.

**Hugh Wall**   Welsh former union organizer who lives on the income of his wife, an advertising copywriter; they rent a room to Eric Eisner in their Holland Park, London, home in Phillip Lopate's *Confessions of Summer*.

**Gabriel (Gabe) Wallach**   Live-in lover of Martha Reganhart and friend of Paul and Libby Herz, with whose separate and combined fortunes he is constantly involved in Philip Roth's *Letting Go*.

**Herb Wallagher**   Former professional football player confined to a wheelchair by a waterskiing accident; marries Clarice, his black physiotherapist; widely seen as inspirational figure, but when interviewed by sportswriter Frank Bascombe proves to be embittered, violent, and subject to wild mood swings in Richard Ford's *The Sportswriter*.

**Emelyn Walley**   Black radical and murderer in Nicholas Delbanco's *News*.

**Wallner**   Hot-rodding member of Gottlob Wut's German Motorcycle Unit Balkan 4; succeeds Wut as leader of the group, although he is later relieved of command in John Irving's *Setting Free the Bears*.

**Emma Wallop**   Widow, retired nurse, erstwhile landlady of Randy Rivers, and putative model for his fictional Mrs. Lusk; actual model for Osgood Wallop's Mrs. St. Cloud in *The Duchess of Obloquy*, the film that she finances; narrates part of Peter De Vries's *Mrs. Wallop*.

**Osgood Wallop**   Son of Emma Wallop; author of the novella *The Duchess of Obloquy* in Peter De Vries's *Mrs. Wallop*.

**Ralph Wallop**   Homosexual son of Cora Frawley; theatrical designer in Peter De Vries's *Mrs. Wallop*.

**Carleton Walpole**   Migrant farm worker and father of Clara Walpole in Joyce Carol Oates's *A Garden of Earthly Delights*.

**Clara Walpole**   See Clara Walpole Revere.

**Horace Walpole**   A frail elderly friend of the Cavaliere in Susan Sontag's *The Volcano Lover*.

**Walter**   Mistreated German shepherd guard dog; nearly castrates dognapper Philo Skinner in Joseph Wambaugh's *The Black Marble*.

**Ed Tutweiler Walters**   An emotionally and economically stable widower who is attractive to two sisters, Julia Ellen Hunsenmeir Smith and Louise Trumbull, who compete for his affection in Rita Mae Brown's *Bingo*.

**Rover Walters**   Black half brother of Forrest Mayfield from his mother's affair with Robinson Mayfield in Reynolds Price's *The Surface of Earth*.

**Taifa Walters**   Teenage niece and adopted daughter of amateur sleuth Blanche White; spends summer vacation at Amber Cove, an exclusive all-black resort in Maine; offers Blanche insights about intraracial prejudice within the black community in Barbara Neely's *Blanche Among the Talented Tenth*.

**Elsie Wishnotski Waltz**   Wife of Stan Waltz, mother of Tom Waltz, and saved evangelical Christian; successfully manages a furniture moving business when her husband is incapacitated in Peter De Vries's *Let Me Count the Ways*.

**Stanley (Stan) Waltz**   Agnostic owner of a moving and storage business, husband of Elsie Waltz, father of Tom Waltz, and victim of a twelve-year hangover; framing narrator and one of two protagonists of Peter De Vries's *Let Me Count the Ways*.

**Thomas (Tom) Waltz**   Son of Stan and Elsie Waltz and psychological product of his parents' antithetical religious views; member of the English faculty and eventually acting president of Polycarp College; taken acutely ill at the shrine of Lourdes; central narrator and co-protagonist of Peter De Vries's *Let Me Count the Ways*.

**Sarkin Aung Wan**   Refugee from the Vietnam War and girlfriend of Paul Berlin, whom she urges to deny his obligations in Tim O'Brien's *Going after Cacciato*.

**Wanda (Kickapoo)**   Adopted daughter of Orpha Chase; marries her mother's lover, Gregory McGovern, in Jessamyn West's *The Life I Really Lived*.

**Wanda**   Flashy girlfriend of Jimmy Scalisi; has some scruples and a big mouth in George V. Higgins's *The Friends of Eddie Coyle*.

**Ben Wanderhope**   Dutch immigrant father of Don Wanderhope; delivers ice, then hauls garbage; fluctuates between faith and reason and is finally confined to an asylum in Peter De Vries's *The Blood of the Lamb*.

**Carol Wanderhope**   Daughter of Don and Greta Wanderhope; dies of leukemia at age twelve in Peter De Vries's *The Blood of the Lamb*.

**Don Wanderhope**   Son of Ben Wanderhope, husband of Greta Wanderhope, and father of Carol Wanderhope; reared in the Dutch Reformed faith; briefly confined to a tuberculosis sanitarium; succeeds his father in the garbage business and later becomes successful in advertising; narrator of Peter De Vries's *The Blood of the Lamb*.

**Greta Wigbaldy Wanderhope**   Youthful lover, then alcoholic wife of Don Wanderhope; a suicide in Peter De Vries's *The Blood of the Lamb*.

**Louie Wanderhope**   Elder brother of Don Wanderhope; studies medicine at the University of Chicago and dies at age twenty in Peter De Vries's *The Blood of the Lamb*.

**Dr. Joseph Wanless**   Original creator of the Lot Six experiment; later suffers a stroke and regrets his involvement in tampering with the brains of his volunteers; he does his best to convince Captain Hollister to let Charlie McGee and her family live a normal life in Stephen King's *Firestarter*.

**Betsey MacCaffrey Wapshot** See Volume I.

**Coverly Wapshot** See Volume I.

**Ezekiel Wapshot** See Volume I.

**Honora Wapshot** See Volume I.

**Leander Wapshot** See Volume I.

**Melissa Scaddon Wapshot** See Volume I.

**Moses Wapshot** See Volume I.

**Sarah Coverly Wapshot** See Volume I.

**Ted Warburton** Television executive and colleague of David Bell; writes anonymous memos from fictional characters in Don DeLillo's *Americana*.

**Lyman Ward** Retired history professor who researches and writes about his grandparents, Oliver and Susan Ward; narrator of Wallace Stegner's *Angle of Repose*.

**Oliver Ward** Mining engineer who is the husband of Susan Ward and the grandfather of Lyman Ward; pursues various jobs across the West and in Mexico, including a large irrigation project in Idaho, in Wallace Stegner's *Angle of Repose*.

**Oliver Burling (Ollie) Ward** Son of Susan and Oliver Ward in Wallace Stegner's *Angle of Repose*.

**Susan Burling (Sue) Ward** Artist and writer who portrays the West while seeking to return to the more cultivated East; wife of Oliver Ward and grandmother of Lyman Ward in Wallace Stegner's *Angle of Repose*.

**Sarah McClellan Warfield** Twice-married sister of Everett and Martha McClellan; abandons the family farm and moves to Philadelphia in Joan Didion's *Run River*.

**Adam Warner** Attorney and presidential candidate in love with Jennifer Parker in Sidney Sheldon's *Rage of Angels*.

**Barbara Warner** Mother of Frank, Bob, Drake, and Sandra Warner; widow who likes an uneventful life; becomes engaged to Dowell Churnin in Ann Beattie's *My Life, Starring Dara Falcon*.

**Bob Warner** Husband of Jean Warner and brother of Frank, Drake, and Sandra Warner; works at the family greenhouse; feels his time is monopolized by his mother in Ann Beattie's *My Life, Starring Dara Falcon*.

**Drake Warner** Brother of Bob, Frank, and Sandra Warner and single father of Louise; never spends time with the Warner family; marries Bonnie Collingwood in secret in Ann Beattie's *My Life, Starring Dara Falcon*.

**Floyd Warner** Aged man on an archetypal journey involving conflict between young and old; abandons his great-nephew Kermit Oelsligle to the care of two hippies in Wright Morris's *Fire Sermon*.

**Frank Warner** Brother of Bob, Drake, and Sandra Warner and brother-in-law of Jean; married to Janey; has three young children; sleeps with Dara Falcon; works at the family greenhouse; has an alcohol problem and drives his car into an embankment one night in Ann Beattie's *My Life, Starring Dara Falcon*.

**Janey Warner** Married to Frank Warner, has three young children; blames Dara Falcon for the breakup of Jean and Bob Warner's marriage in Ann Beattie's *My Life, Starring Dara Falcon*.

**Jean Warner** Only child whose parents died in a plane accident when she was six; grew up under the care of her aunt; married to Bob Warner, whom she leaves; friend of Dara Falcon, whom she idolizes; later marries John; narrator of Ann Beattie's *My Life, Starring Dara Falcon*.

**Louise Warner** Young daughter of Drake Warner; is being raised by her grandmother and is very shy; must go to therapy for an eating disorder in Ann Beattie's *My Life, Starring Dara Falcon*.

**Marie Warner** Young daughter of Sandra Warner; reads aloud; loves her Uncle Bob in Ann Beattie's *My Life, Starring Dara Falcon*.

**Sandra Warner** Sister of Bob, Frank, and Drake Warner and single mother of Marie; is uptight and unpleasant; becomes engaged to Jasper Cismont in Ann Beattie's *My Life, Starring Dara Falcon*.

**Mrs. Warren** Teaches Celia and once taught Libby; keeps Celia after school day after day in Joan Chase's *During the Reign of the Queen of Persia*.

**Bill Warwick** Struggling actor who finds his big break on the hit television series *Manhattan*, despite the scandal of having an estranged, drug-addicted wife in Danielle Steel's *Secrets*.

**Donald Washburn II** Character who appears in many guises and under many pseudonyms in Thomas Berger's *Who Is Teddy Villanova?*

**Benji Washington** Son of a black undertaker in Colleton, the first African American to attend Colleton High School; his expertise as a football player makes that integration a success in Pat Conroy's *The Prince of Tides*.

**Booker T. Washington** Educator and unsuccessful negotiator between the New York police and Coalhouse Walker, Jr., in E. L. Doctorow's *Ragtime*.

**George (Byron, Efan, Julius Makewell, Anthony Miller, Paul Winthrop) Washington** Young black American and part-time gigolo stranded in Copenhagen; protagonist of Cecil Brown's *The Life and Loves of Mr. Jiveass Nigger*.

**Henry Washington**    Called Mr. Henry by Claudia and Frieda; boarder who lives briefly with the MacTeer family after leaving his girlfriend; gives the girls pennies and calls them Greta Garbo and Ginger Rogers; socializes with the town's prostitutes; gets thrown out of the MacTeers' for attempting to touch Frieda in Toni Morrison's *The Bluest Eye*.

**Louisa Wasserman**    See Louisa Calloway.

**Michael Wasserman**    Husband of Louisa Calloway; writer of an ongoing psychology dissertation and compulsive reader of detective novels in Alice Adams's *Families and Survivors*.

**Eddie Watanabe**    Parole officer of David Axelrod in Scott Spencer's *Endless Love*.

**Harmonia H. (H. H.) Waters**    Elderly female writer in Alison Lurie's *Real People*.

**Johnny Waters**    Drug-taking movie actor who seduces Maria Wyeth in Joan Didion's *Play It As It Lays*.

**Christine (Chrissie) Watkins**    First victim of the Great White Shark in Peter Benchley's *Jaws*.

**C-J Watkins**    Uncle of Abeba Torch, he poses as her friend but sexually molests her over the period of a year in Ellease Southerland's *Let the Lion Eat Straw*.

**Watney**    English rock musician who visits Bucky Wunderlick hoping to get from him a mysterious drug in Don DeLillo's *Great Jones Street*.

**Caroline Watson**    Fictional turn-of-the-century American painter based on real painters, such as Mary Cassatt; leaves Philadelphia for Paris; returns to her father's house with an illegitimate son, Stephan Watson; leaves him and returns to Paris; after Stephan's death she lives with his widow, Jane, who inherits Caroline's estate in Mary Catherine Gordon's *Men and Angels*.

**Jane Watson**    Daughter-in-law of artist Caroline Watson; medieval scholar; she shares Caroline's letters and journals with Anne Foster in Mary Catherine Gordon's *Men and Angels*.

**Katherine Epps Watson**    Wife of Thad Watson; dies giving birth to Eva Kendal's mother in Reynolds Price's *The Surface of Earth*.

**Matthew (Mat) Watson**    Town blacksmith who employs Brackett Omensetter in William Gass's *Omensetter's Luck*.

**Stephan Watson**    Illegitimate son of Caroline Watson; married to Jane; alcoholic; commits suicide in Mary Gordon's *Men and Angels*.

**Thad Watson**    Grandfather of Eva Kendal; killed himself when Eva's grandmother died giving birth to Eva's mother in Reynolds Price's *The Surface of Earth*.

**Tom Watson**    Denver pool shark who befriends young Cody Poineray in Jack Kerouac's *Visions of Cody*.

**Luther Watt**    Friend of Mabry Jenkins; twice wins the all-around rodeo championship in Peter Gent's *Texas Celebrity Turkey Trot*.

**Ernst Watzek-Trummer**    Austrian egg man; portrays the Austrian eagle by donning chicken feathers and parading through Vienna; moves to Kaprun with the Marters; keeper of the 1939 Grand Prix racing motorcycle in John Irving's *Setting Free the Bears*.

**J. Henry Waugh**    Actuarial, neurotic inventor of the dice-driven, imaginary Universal Baseball League in Robert Coover's *The Universal Baseball Association, Inc., J. Henry Waugh, Prop.*

**Wayne**    Has had three wives; father of Will with second wife, Jody; lives in Florida with third wife; arrested after wife's pill bottle and boxes of cocaine are found in rental car of woman with whom he had a two-week fling in Ann Beattie's *Picturing Will*.

**Mead Weaks**    Short, slight, breathless chairman of a college English department; unable to relate to his son, Mead Weaks II; ineffective in relating to people in Frederick Busch's *Rounds*.

**Mead Weaks II**    Son of the chairman of a college English department; mentally unstable drug user; leads authorities to rescue Mike Sorenson after Horace L'Ordinet kidnaps the baby in Frederick Busch's *Rounds*.

**Wealtheow**    Hostage queen to Hrothgar and comforter of warriors decimated by Grendel, who respects her as a source of grace in a problematic universe in John Gardner's *Grendel*.

**Roland Weary**    Prisoner of war who dies of gangrene in Kurt Vonnegut's *Slaughterhouse-Five*.

**Father Weatherbee**    Authentic priest whom Will Barrett meets in the convalescent home where Leslie Cupp has placed him; determines that the old man can lead him to God in Walker Percy's *The Second Coming*.

**Charles Webb**    White man who befriends Cecil Braithwaite in Europe in John Edgar Wideman's *Hurry Home*.

**Cromwell (Ace) Webster**    Incompetent commanding officer of an American battalion in the Spanish Civil War in William Herrick's *Hermanos!*

**Major Wedburn**    Former lover of Cassie Bender and Connie Birch; leaves his fortune to Connie Birch, not knowing she is dead; money goes to her son, Jonathan Jaimison, in Dawn Powell's *The Golden Spur*.

**Lorna Weech**    Widow of Ron Weech and lover of his slayer, Valentine Hood, in Paul Theroux's *The Family Arsenal*.

**Ron Weech**    Cruel thug and thief murdered by Valentine Hood in Paul Theroux's *The Family Arsenal*.

**Caroline Weed**    See Caroline Weed Hubble.

**Frederick Murdoch (Freddie) Weed**    Shipyard owner and father of Caroline Weed in Leon Uris's *Trinity*.

**Bunny Weeks**    Homosexual restaurateur in Kurt Vonnegut's *God Bless You, Mr. Rosewater*.

**Gabriel Weeks**    Professor of art history, husband of Ann Weeks, and lover of Jane Clifford in Gail Godwin's *The Odd Woman*.

**Virgil Weeks**    Watchman of the cabin used by Chris Van Eenanam and Ellen Strohe on their honeymoon in Larry Woiwode's *What I'm Going to Do, I Think*.

**Robin and Ethel Weems**    Researchers in sex physiology and friends of Joe and Naughty Sandwich in Peter De Vries's *The Vale of Laughter*.

**Florence Wegenlied**    Sister of Carrie Bolt and mother of Jennifer Denman in Rita Mae Brown's *Rubyfruit Jungle*.

**Dr. Weidman**    Physician to the Luries; his misdiagnosis of David Lurie's deviated septum leaves David vulnerable to a variety of childhood diseases in Chaim Potok's *In the Beginning*.

**Ben Weilman**    Old friend of Martha Horgan's family; lets Martha stay with him after her aunt kicks her out in Mary McGarry Morris's *A Dangerous Woman*.

**Barnet (Barn) Weiner**    Poet and critic; friend of Leslie Braverman in Wallace Markfield's *To an Early Grave*.

**Mr. Weiner**    Smiling, paunchy, balding Jewish man who buys Gram's farm; purring and sleek, smokes cigars in Joan Chase's *During the Reign of the Queen of Persia*.

**Lester Weinstock**    Public relations agent for Arvey Film Studio who is assigned to Dolly Moon following her success in Vito Orsini's *Mirrors;* falls in love with Moon, even though she is eight months pregnant by another man, in Judith Krantz's *Scruples*.

**David (Dave) Weintraub**    Expatriate American who introduces Samantha Everton to the Gallaghers in James Jones's *The Merry Month of May*.

**Abraham Weiss**    Bronx district attorney running for reelection; vigorously prosecutes the case against Sherman McCoy in order to insure reelection in Tom Wolfe's *The Bonfire of the Vanities*.

**Crystal Weiss**    Southern belle, wife of Manny Weiss and mother of King and Crystal Anne; kindhearted, heavy-drinking dilettante who dabbles in poetry and civic works; stays in an unhappy marriage for the money in Ellen Gilchrist's *Victory Over Japan*.

**Lee Weiss**    Former psychotherapist; now owner of women-only guest house in Key West; falls in love with Jenny Walker in Alison Lurie's *The Last Resort*.

**Lenny Weiss**    Compulsively responsible, single, middle-aged brother in a wealthy, Jewish New Orleans family; tries to maintain and protect the family's beach house in Ellen Gilchrist's *Victory Over Japan*.

**Manny Weiss**    Husband of Crystal Weiss, stepfather of King and father of Crystal Anne; wealthy Jewish lawyer from a powerful New Orleans family; tries to maintain control over his wife and keep up the appearance of social propriety in Ellen Gilchrist's *Victory Over Japan*.

**Maxie Weiss**    Press agent for Glory Green in Alison Lurie's *The Nowhere City*.

**Major S. O. Weiss**    Military psychiatrist who tries to bring Birdy out of catatonic state in William Wharton's *Birdy*.

**Hugh Weisskopf**    Director of the Emma Lazarus Retirement Home; his main concerns are that the home appears decorous and he himself appears elegant and suave in Alan Isler's *The Prince of West End Avenue*.

**Lieutenant (Captain Dominus Blicero, Major Weissmann) Weissmann**    Debauched German officer encountered by Kurt Mondaugen at Foppl's Siege Party in Thomas Pynchon's *V.;* former lover of Oberst Enzian and, while engaged in building rocket 00000, the sexual manipulator of Katje Borgesius and Gottfried, finally firing the latter inside the completed rocket, in *Gravity's Rainbow*.

**Farmer Weitling**    Germanic Mennonite who hears voices and is killing the children of Tecan; is befriended by Father Egan, who thinks he can change him in Robert Stone's *A Flag for Sunrise*.

**Terrence (Genial) Weld**    Thief considered by Inspector Lee to be responsible for the suicide of John Harrison in William S. Burroughs's *The Ticket That Exploded*.

**Tom Weld**    Neighbor of Joe Allston; develops a hillside into a subdivision in Wallace Stegner's *All the Little Live Things*.

**Marion Wellington**    Episcopalian aristocrat instructor of comparative religion at Polycarp College, and fiancée, then wife, of Tom Waltz in Peter De Vries's *Let Me Count the Ways*.

**Calliope (Callie) Wells**    Abandoned sixteen-year-old who weds Henry Soames for the sake of her illegitimate son, Jimmy, in John Gardner's *Nickel Mountain*.

**Floyd Wells**    Cellmate of Richard Hickock in the Kansas State Penitentiary; tells Hickock about the Clutter family; informs police after the murders and becomes the most important witness in the murder trial in Truman Capote's *In Cold Blood*.

**Homer Wells** Grows up in the St. Cloud's Orphanage and learns medicine and gynecology from Dr. Wilbur Larch before heading out into the world; amiable and thoughtful protagonist of John Irving's *The Cider House Rules*.

**Will Wells** Black hired hand on Jack Beechum's farm; they work together until a destructive rage leads Wells into a fist fight with Beechum in Wendell Berry's *The Memory of Old Jack*.

**Edward Welsh** Ill-tempered first sergeant who hates Private Witt and is instrumental in Witt's transfer out of C-for-Charlie Company in James Jones's *The Thin Red Line*.

**Welshinger** St. Paul vice officer who regularly doctors evidence and brutalizes citizens for sex and money; murders dime-a-dance girls Ruby Fahey and Charlene Martenson; dictates Mr. White's confession; commits suicide after learning that Detective Wesley Horner plans to expose him as the murderer in Robert Clark's *Mr. White's Confession*.

**Howard Wendall** Policeman who rapes and then marries the young Loretta Botsford; killed in a factory accident in Joyce Carol Oates's *them*.

**Jules Wendall** Son of Loretta Wendall; young, idealistic pursuer of the American dream; becomes involved in the Detroit riots of the late 1960s in Joyce Carol Oates's *them*.

**Loretta Botsford Wendall** Poor Detroit woman, mother of Jules and Maureen Wendall, wife of Howard Wendall and later of Pat Furlong; her life between 1936 and the late 1960s is chronicled in Joyce Carol Oates's *them*.

**Mama Wendall** Domineering mother-in-law of Loretta Wendall in Joyce Carol Oates's *them*.

**Maureen (Reeny) Wendall** Daughter of Loretta Wendall; becomes involved in prostitution and is badly beaten by her stepfather, Pat Furlong; seduces Jim Randolph away from his wife and marries him in Joyce Carol Oates's *them*.

**Dr. Kerstine Wentworth** Anthropologist sailing on the *Castel Felice*; becomes the companion of Dr. Norman Yas in Calvin Hernton's *Scarecrow*.

**William (Bill) Wentworth** Superintendent at the Casino who befriends Theophilus North by permitting him to give private tennis lessons to youngsters in Thornton Wilder's *Theophilus North*.

**Arnold Wermy** Cliché-spouting president of Rugg College in Paul Theroux's *Waldo*.

**Wolfgang Werner** Los Angeles policeman from Stuttgart and one object of Francis Tanaguchi's practical jokes in Joseph Wambaugh's *The Choirboys*.

**WESCAC** West Campus Automatic Computer and true father of George Giles in John Barth's *Giles Goat-Boy*.

**Horner Wesley** Widowed St. Paul police lieutenant assigned to investigate the murders of dime-a-dance hall employees Ruby Fahey and Charlene Martenson; realizes his fellow officer, Welshinger, got the confession from White, and is the real murderer; is unable to exonerate White in Robert Clark's *Mr. White's Confession*.

**Boone Westfall** Michael Killigan's best friend, he travels to Sierra Leone to locate him; adopted by the Mende villagers and renamed Gutawa Sisay in Richard Dooling's *White Man's Grave*.

**Clarence Weston, Sr.** Corporation chairman aided and exploited by George Levanter in Jerzy Kosinski's *Blind Date*.

**Mrs. Wetwilliam** Mayflower Society luminary and regional chairman of the Daughters of the American Revolution; social rival of Alma Marvel in Peter De Vries's *Through the Fields of Clover*.

**Alice Greenwood (Alice Jackson) Weylin** Freeborn black ancestor of Dana Franklin; enslaved by Rufus Weylin in Octavia E. Butler's *Kindred*.

**Margaret Weylin** Mother of Rufus Weylin and wife of Tom Weylin in Octavia E. Butler's *Kindred*.

**Rufus (Rufe) Weylin** White ancestor of Dana Franklin in Octavia E. Butler's *Kindred*.

**Tom Weylin** Father of Rufus Weylin and husband of Margaret Weylin in Octavia E. Butler's *Kindred*.

**Herbert (Spermwhale, Spermy) Whalen** Veteran Los Angeles policeman; one of ten protagonists in Joseph Wambaugh's *The Choirboys*.

**Richard Wharfinger** Seventeenth-century playwright and author of *The Courier's Tragedy*, which in one variant mentions the mysterious Tristero in Thomas Pynchon's *The Crying of Lot 49*.

**Mr. What's-his-name** Alliteration-prone United States vice president who succeeds Trick E. Dixon in Philip Roth's *Our Gang*.

**Mabel Wheady** Young black prostitute who loves Jesus Ortiz and tries to discourage him from associating with hoodlums in Edward Lewis Wallant's *The Pawnbroker*.

**Alma S. Wheeler** Sister of Wad and Boone Wheeler; lives on the family tobacco farm in Hopewell, Kentucky; assists in the birth and care of James and Christianna Wheeler's quintuplets in 1900; is married to Thomas Hunt, a traveling salesman, in Bobbie Ann Mason's *Feather Crowns*.

**Amanda "Mandy" Wheeler** Wife of Wad Wheeler; lonely and isolated; assists with the birth and care of James and Christianna Wheeler's quintuplets in 1900; caught having sex with their brother-in-law, Thomas Hunt; commits suicide in Bobbie Ann Mason's *Feather Crowns*.

**April Wheeler**   Failed actress and wife of Frank Wheeler; her dreams of moving to Paris with her family are thwarted, and she dies attempting to abort her third child in Richard Yates's *Revolutionary Road*.

**Boone Wheeler**   Unmarried brother of Wad and Alma Wheeler; lives on the family's tobacco farm in Hopewell, Kentucky; uses his asthma as an excuse to avoid work; adds the gruesome memorabilia of James and Christianna Wheeler's quintuplets to his scrapbook in Bobbie Ann Mason's *Feather Crowns*.

**Christianna "Christie" Wheeler**   Wife of James Wheeler, with whom she starts a tobacco farm; in 1900 gives birth to quintuplets, all of whom die within a month's time; tours with her husband and the mummified remains of the quintuplets through the South, a tour that begins as an educational lecture and turns into a carnival sideshow; she and her husband give the remains of the quintuplets to the Institute of Man in Washington, D.C., in Bobbie Ann Mason's *Feather Crowns*.

**Earl Wheeler**   Father of Frank Wheeler; experiences lifelong disappointment because a promised promotion never occurs in Richard Yates's *Revolutionary Road*.

**Franklin H. (Frank) Wheeler**   Husband of April Wheeler; outwardly supports her plans to move to Paris, but inwardly is afraid to abandon his job at Knox Business Machines in Richard Yates's *Revolutionary Road*.

**James Wheeler**   Husband of Christianna Wheeler; moves his wife and their three children, Clint, Jewel, and Nannie, to Hopewell, Kentucky; borrows money from his Uncle Wad Wheeler to buy land to start a tobacco farm; in 1900 his wife gives birth to quintuplets, all of whom die within a month's time; in the fall of 1900, tours with his wife and the mummified remains of the quintuplets through the South; he and his wife give the remains of the quintuplets to the Institute of Man in Washington, D.C., in Bobbie Ann Mason's *Feather Crowns*.

**Luke Wheeler**   Temporary farmhand at Pretty Pass and probable second husband of Ma Sigafoos in Peter De Vries's *I Hear America Swinging*.

**Prarie Wheeler**   Daughter of Zoyd Wheeler and Frenesi Gates; she is placed in the care of DL Chastain while hiding out from Brock Vond, who wishes to control her the way he controls her mother; with DL she learns how her parents' attempts at political activism in the 1960s were foiled in Thomas Pynchon's *Vineland*.

**Wad Wheeler**   Head of the Wheeler family; brother of Alma and Boone; husband of Amanda; lends his nephew, James Wheeler, money to start a tobacco farm in Hopewell; when James and Christianna Wheeler's quintuplets are born in 1900,

he charges ten cents' admission to view the babies; after the quintuplets die, encourages James and Christianna to tour with the mummified remains of their children so that they may sooner repay the debt they owe him in Bobbie Ann Mason's *Feather Crowns*.

**Zoyd Wheeler**   Old hippie who maintains an illusion of insanity in order to collect checks from the government; he is the ex-husband of Frenesi Gates and the father of Prarie Wheeler; tries his best to raise his daughter while avoiding capture by Brock Vond for rampant drug use in Thomas Pynchon's *Vineland*.

**Judge Whimplewopper**   Midget with a long, detachable nose that is the subject of a series of features in the *National Enquirer* in Ishmael Reed's *The Free-Lance Pallbearers*.

**Mortimer (Mort) Whipple**   Mayor of West Condon in Robert Coover's *The Origin of the Brunists*.

**Whispering Dan**   Former tobacco auctioneer who is saved and called to prophesy after his radical laryngectomy; broadcasts his nightly warnings of the Coming End via an implanted valve between his esophagus and trachea and a microphone pressed to his heart in Gail Godwin's *Evensong*.

**Kenneth Whistler**   Union organizer and spellbinding speaker in Kurt Vonnegut's *Jailbird*.

**Miss Whitaker**   Nurse of the idiot Pinhead; murdered by Mickey McCane in Doris Betts's *The River to Pickle Beach*.

**Corporal Whitcomb**   Atheist and assistant to Chaplain Tappman; sends fill-in-the-blank form letters of condolence in Joseph Heller's *Catch-22*.

**Donald (Don) Whitcomb**   Reclusive Steering School teacher mistakenly thought to be Helen Holm's lover following T. S. Garp's death; writes Garp's biography in John Irving's *The World According to Garp*.

**Elihue Micah (Soaphead Church) Whitcomb**   Spiritualist and psychic reader consulted by Pecola Breedlove in her search for blue eyes in Toni Morrison's *The Bluest Eye*.

**Blanche White**   African-American domestic worker turned accidental sleuth; single, adoptive parent to niece Taifa and nephew Malik; accompanies kids to Amber Cove, an exclusive all-black resort in Maine; uncovers secrets surrounding two seemingly unconnected deaths in Barbara Neely's *Blanche among the Talented Tenth*.

**Carietta (Carrie) White**   High school student who uses her telekinetic powers for vengeance against classmates who tormented her in Stephen King's *Carrie*.

**Eddie White**   Husband of Molly Taylor White; dies after falling from an oil derrick in Larry McMurtry's *Leaving Cheyenne*.

**Francis White**  Officer in Cromwell's army and Cromwell's emissary to the dissenting soldiers; pleads with Cromwell to keep his word, but is considered cowardly by Johnny Church in Mary Lee Settle's *Prisons*.

**Gary Cooper White**  Drifter from Florida who, after being picked up by Theresa Dunn, kills her in Judith Rossner's *Looking for Mr. Goodbar*.

**Herbert W. White**  Amateur photographer and grocery warehouse clerk framed for the murders of two dime-a-dance hall girls; suffers from a memory impairment; coerced into confession by Officer Welshinger, the real murderer, and sentenced to twenty five years solitary confinement, released in 1967 at age sixty-three with all memory recovered in Robert Clark's *Mr. White's Confession*.

**Joe White**  See Joe.

**Judith Stoloff (Jude) White**  Mother of Isadora Wing; former artist who cannot tolerate anything ordinary in Erica Jong's *Fear of Flying*.

**Margaret White**  Religious fanatic who believes that the powers of her daughter, Carrie White, are evil in Stephen King's *Carrie*.

**Miriam (Miri) White**  Sister of Patsy White Carpenter and sister-in-law of Jim Carpenter; saved from drug addiction by her sister in Larry McMurtry's *Moving On*.

**Molly Taylor White**  Daughter of Cletus Taylor, wife of Eddie White, lover of Gideon Fry and Johnny McCloud, and mother of Jimmy and Joe; narrates part of Larry McMurtry's *Leaving Cheyenne*.

**Roger White II**  African-American attorney in large, mostly white Atlanta law firm; known as Too White; serves as a conduit between city's black mayor and white power structure and Charles Croker in Tom Wolfe's *A Man In Full*.

**Snow White**  Disillusioned housewife and proponent of the women's movement; lives with seven dwarfs while waiting for Paul, her prince, to arrive in Donald Barthelme's *Snow White*.

**Stanford (Stanny) White**  Famous architect who seduces Evelyn Nesbit; killed by Nesbit's husband, Harry K. Thaw, in E. L. Doctorow's *Ragtime*.

**Tim Whiteaker**  Partner with Blue Odell, with whom he establishes cattle business and the 1,300-acre Half Moon ranch in 1890s in eastern Oregon; proposes to Lydia Bennett Sanderson; reluctant participant in a feud with Harley Osgood and Jack in Molly Gloss's *The Jump-Off Creek*.

**Chief White Halfoat**  Half-blood Creek Indian from Oklahoma, where his family moved from place to place, pursued as human divining rods by geologists in search of oil in Joseph Heller's *Catch-22*.

**Les Whitehall**  Lucy's ex-love, a college professor, who left her for a student; asks her for a job recommendation in Ann Beattie's *Love Always*.

**Margaret Whitehead**  Young girl who befriends Nat Turner when he works for her mother; only white person Turner kills in the insurrection in William Styron's *The Confessions of Nat Turner*.

**Glenn Whitehouse**  Abusive, angry, alcoholic man whose vicious, uncontrollable temper destroys the lives of his wife and children; ultimately, the cycle of abuse completes itself when his own son murders him; husband of Sally Whitehouse, father of Rolfe and Wade Whitehouse in Russell Banks's *Affliction*.

**Jill Whitehouse**  Intelligent yet troubled child scarred by the divorce of her parents, the superficiality of her materialistic mother, and the alcoholism of her abusive father in Russell Banks's *Affliction*.

**Lillian Whitehouse**  Shallow, materialistic woman who manipulates her family in a ruthless pursuit of the comforts of middle-class life; perpetually scarred by the death of her father and the abuse of her former husband; twice married to and twice divorced from Wade Whitehouse; mother of Jill Whitehouse in Russell Banks's *Affliction*.

**Rolfe Whitehouse**  High school history teacher who escapes small-town Lawford life and a legacy of familial abuse; narrates the final days of his brother's life in an attempt to reconcile himself to his own identity and personal history; brother of Wade Whitehouse, son of Glenn and Sally Whitehouse in Russell Banks's *Affliction*.

**Sally Whitehouse**  Tragic victim of years of domestic abuse who vainly attempts to protect her children, only to find herself an unwitting participant in the vicious manipulations of her violent husband; eventually freezes to death, abandoned and alone in her own home; mother of Rolfe and Wade Whitehouse, wife of Glenn Whitehouse in Russell Banks's *Affliction*.

**Wade Whitehouse**  Bitter man whose hopes for a nuclear family and a comfortable life as the local sheriff in small town, Lawford, are destroyed by the legacy of familial abuse perpetrated by his father; devoted yet tormented parent and husband; murders his father and friend; disappears; brother of Rolfe Whitehouse, son of Glenn and Sally Whitehouse in Russell Banks's *Affliction*.

**Madeline Dills Whitfield**  Pasadena divorcée; owner of the victim of a dognapping in Joseph Wambaugh's *The Black Marble*.

**Elizabeth Fox (Foxy) Whitman**  Pregnant wife of Ken Whitman; lover and later wife of Piet Hanema in John Updike's *Couples*.

**Ken Whitman**  Research biologist married to Foxy Whitman in John Updike's *Couples*.

**Jean Lavette Whittier**  Independent woman who manages the Seldon bank in 1930s San Francisco; Dan Lavette is her first husband, John Whittier is her second; mother of Tom and Barbara Lavette in Howard Fast's *Second Generation*.

**Nora Jane Whittington**   Plucky, naive young woman from Virginia; ventures to San Francisco for a boyfriend who turns out to be unfaithful; begins a relationship with a bookstore owner after trying to rob him and starts to develop some independence in Ellen Gilchrist's *Victory Over Japan*.

**Miss Whittle**   Chief matron of the Alcanthia County home for light-skinned orphan girls in Burnside, Virginia, in Hal Bennett's *A Wilderness of Vines*.

**Ishmael Whittman**   Incompetent white officer promoted along a separate and unequal track intersecting the career of his black nemesis, Abraham Blackman, during combat in World War II, Korea, and Vietnam in John A. Williams's *Captain Blackman*.

**The Whole Sick Crew**   Name given to a group that includes the artist Slab, record executive Gouverneur (Roony) Winsome, his wife, Mafia, Fu, and Charisma in Thomas Pynchon's *V.*

**Ada Wickersham**   Hotel operator in Manantiales; last person known to have befriended John Ashley; helps Ashley escape to Chile in Thornton Wilder's *The Eighth Day*.

**Hilary Margaret Wiggen**   Youngest daughter of Henry Wiggen; expresses her frustrations in screaming fits in Mark Harris's *It Looked Like For Ever*.

**Grant Wiggins**   African-American rural Louisiana native and university-educated teacher; questions his effectiveness in teaching poor black children; reluctantly agrees to help Jefferson, a condemned young man facing execution, to confront his impending death with dignity and humanity in Ernest J. Gaines's *A Lesson Before Dying*.

**Richard (Bubbles) Wiggins**   Prosperous blue-collar worker in a local factory and former member of a black high school athletic team and neighborhood gang gathering for a birthday testimonial honoring Chappie Davis in John A. Williams's *The Junior Bachelor Society*.

**Theo G. (Tio) Wiggins**   Wealthy black father of Martha Kinship and grandfather of Teddy and Lucinda Kinship in Shelby Foote's *September September*.

**Wiggins sisters**   Three sisters called Big, Little, and Evelyn; mountain girls with rough manners but good intentions who sing in Colonel Happy Tucker's medicine show; Colonel Happy doesn't pay them and tries to force his sexual advances upon them; they become friends with Christianna Wheeler in Bobbie Ann Mason's *Feather Crowns*.

**George Wilcox**   Frail, elderly Canadian widower provoked into killing his former brother-in-law in L. W. Wright's *The Suspect*.

**The Wild Child (Wile Chile)**   Feral adolescent girl whom Meridian Hill tries to befriend; struck and killed by a speeding car in Alice Walker's *Meridian*.

**Wilder**   Toddler son of Babette Gladney and an ex-husband; cries for hours on end for no reason; babbles on occasion but speaks very little for a child his age; is a grounding force for Babette, his stepfather Jack Gladney, and Gladney's colleague Murray Jay Siskind in Don DeLillo's *White Noise*.

**Janice Brady Wilder**   Long-suffering wife of John Wilder; divorces him and marries their friend Paul Borg in Richard Yates's *Disturbing the Peace*.

**John C. Wilder**   Heavy-drinking advertising-space salesman whose plans to make a movie of his experiences in Bellevue Mental Hospital lead to further emotional collapses in Richard Yates's *Disturbing the Peace*.

**Marjorie Wilder**   Mother of John Wilder; wants John to assume control of her highly successful candy company, but he rejects the prospect in Richard Yates's *Disturbing the Peace*.

**Tom (Tommy) Wilder**   Lonely, withdrawn son of John and Janice Wilder; characteristically replies "I don't know, I don't care" to his father's inquiries in Richard Yates's *Disturbing the Peace*.

**Bert Wilderman**   Free-hanging opponent of Clyde Stout in Jack Matthews's *Hanger Stout, Awake!*

**Montana Wildhack**   B-movie starlet and Billy Pilgrim's mate on Tralfamadore in Kurt Vonnegut's *Slaughterhouse-Five*.

**David Wiley**   Father of Louise, ex-husband of Gretchen; quits his job as a reporter and takes a job as a newspaper editor in Los Angeles so that Louise can live with him part of the year and so that he will be closer to Lexi Steiner; asks Lexi to marry him in Elizabeth Benedict's *Slow Dancing*.

**Louise Wiley**   Fourteen-year-old daughter of David Wiley; her list of likes and dislikes is long and unequivocal; has a crush on an eighteen-year-old boy named Bliss in Elizabeth Benedict's *Slow Dancing*.

**Orin (Sweetman) Wilkerson**   Drunken, philandering father of Thomas Wilkerson; jailed for murder in John Edgar Wideman's *The Lynchers*.

**Thomas Wilkerson**   Teacher involved in Willie Hall's plan to lynch a white policeman; killed by fellow conspirator Graham Rice in John Edgar Wideman's *The Lynchers*.

**John Wilkes**   Phoenix gardener who assumes the role of a successful young millionaire businessman and agrees to back Renate's planned magazine in Anaïs Nin's *Collages*.

**Will**   Slave cruelly treated by his owner; brutally kills many whites in the insurrection in William Styron's *The Confessions of Nat Turner*.

**Will**　First husband of Nina Eberhardt; nice, normal, straight-laced lawyer; struggles to understand Nina's ambivalence about relationships and marriage in Sue Miller's *Family Pictures*.

**Will**　Five-and-a-half-year-old son of Wayne and Jody; lives with mother and visits father and father's new wife in Florida; when father is arrested, thinks police have come to tell him his mother is dead in Ann Beattie's *Picturing Will*.

**Willard**　Three-foot-high papier-mâché bird placed by John and Patricia among the Logan brothers' stolen bowling trophies in Richard Brautigan's *Willard and His Bowling Trophies*.

**Buddy Willard**　Yale medical student and steady boyfriend of Esther Greenwood; their romance ends with his stay at a tuberculosis sanitorium and her suicide attempt in Sylvia Plath's *The Bell Jar*.

**Mr. Willard**　Father of Buddy Willard; takes Esther Greenwood to visit his son at a sanitorium for tuberculosis patients in Sylvia Plath's *The Bell Jar*.

**Mrs. (Nelly) Willard**　Overbearing mother of Buddy Willard in Sylvia Plath's *The Bell Jar*.

**Colin Willes**　Thriller writer, socialite, and ladies' man with whom Salley Gardens has a protracted affair in Susan Cheever's *Looking for Work*.

**William**　Attorney for his former wife, Allegra Vand, and guardian of her inheritance in Cynthia Ozick's *Trust*.

**Williams**　Black handyman and janitor at the Isaacson building in E. L. Doctorow's *The Book of Daniel*.

**Bessie Williams**　Black singer at Mildred Sutton's funeral in Reynolds Price's *A Long and Happy Life*.

**Edward (Eddie) Williams**　Black student at Calvin Coolidge High School who sees every event as racially discriminatory in Bel Kaufman's *Up the Down Staircase*.

**Jack Williams**　Marshal of Billy, Oregon, and saloon owner; friend of Magic Child in Richard Brautigan's *The Hawkline Monster*.

**Jo Bob Williams**　Aggressive offensive lineman for the Dallas Cowboys who spends much of his time making life miserable for Phil Elliott and various rookies in Peter Gent's *North Dallas Forty*.

**Nathan (Slim) Williams**　Postal worker and friend of Jake Jackson; suffers from tuberculosis in Richard Wright's *Lawd Today*.

**Rhys Williams**　Originally from a poor coal-mining family in Wales; becomes the head of family owned and operated worldwide conglomerate Roffe and Sons by marrying the president of it; husband of Elizabeth Roffe in Sidney Sheldon's *Bloodline*.

**William (Clean Willy) Williams**　Accomplice of Edward Pierce in Michael Crichton's *The Great Train Robbery*.

**William Carlos Williams**　Seventy-two-year-old physician and poet; Jack Duluoz visits Williams in New Jersey, accompanied by Irwin Garden, Simon Darlovsky, and Raphael Urso in Jack Kerouac's *Desolation Angels*.

**Willie**　Crew member on Thomas Hudson's boat during submarine hunting in Ernest Hemingway's *Islands in the Stream*.

**Gerald (Gerry) Willis**　Son of Kitty Willis Dubin by her first marriage; rejects his adoptive father's name after deserting the army and fleeing to Stockholm in Bernard Malamud's *Dubin's Lives*.

**Martin Willis**　Arizona highway patrol officer who kills five people and then commits suicide after being exposed to the Andromeda Strain in Michael Crichton's *The Andromeda Strain*.

**Walter Willis**　Customer in a hair salon in John Edgar Wideman's *Hurry Home*.

**Daniel Cable Wills**　Boston attorney and father of Daniel Compton Wills and Andrew Collier; serves as control to OSS agent General Aubrey Gammage in World War II; frees the formula for synthetic rubber from the Nazis for use by the Allies in George V. Higgins's *Dreamland*.

**Daniel Compton (Comp) Wills**　Boston attorney, son of Daniel Cable Wills, and half brother of Andrew Collier; denies blood kinship with Collier and seduces Collier's wife; narrator of George V. Higgins's *Dreamland*.

**Edweena (Toinette) Wills**　Fiancée of Henry Simmons in Thornton Wilder's *Theophilus North*.

**Willy the Fink, Willy the Rat**　See Uranian Willy.

**Clarence Arthur Wilmot**　Presbyterian minister and patriarch of the Wilmot family; resigns his ministry to become a door-to-door encyclopedia salesman; husband of Stella Wilmot; father of Jared, Esther, and Theodore (Teddy) Wilmot; dies in 1920 of tuberculosis, a broken man; central figure of the first part of John Updike's saga of the Wilmot family, *In the Beauty of the Lilies*.

**Emily Sifford Wilmot**　Wife of Teddy Wilmot; daughter-in-law of Stella Wilmot; mother of Essie and Danny Wilmot; physically unattractive and lame but intelligent, loving, and able woman who makes a good home for her husband and children in John Updike's *In the Beauty of the Lilies*.

**Esther "Essie" Wilmot**　Daughter of Teddy and Emily Wilmot; sister of Danny Wilmot; granddaughter of Clarence and Stella Wilmot; mother of Clark; rises to the pinnacle of success and fame as the Hollywood actress "Alma DeMott"; fails as a wife and mother; central figure in the third part of John Updike's saga of the Wilmot family, *In the Beauty of the Lilies*.

**Stella Wilmot**　Wife of Clarence Wilmot and mother of Jared, Esther, and Theodore Wilmot; strong but subservient woman who tries unsuccessfully to understand her husband's loss of faith and subsequent physical and spiritual decline in John Updike's *In the Beauty of the Lilies*.

**Theodore "Teddy" Wilmot**    Third and last child of Clarence and Stella Wilmot; husband of Emily Jeanette Sifford Wilmot; father of Essie and Danny Wilmot; traumatized as a young boy by his father's spiritual and physical collapse; a mailman; central figure in the second part of John Updike's saga of the Wilmot family, *In the Beauty of the Lilies*.

**Anthony (Tony) Wilson**    Abusive husband of Sarah Grimes Wilson in Richard Yates's *Easter Parade*.

**Clyde Wilson**    Husband of Evalin McCabe Wilson in Diane Johnson's *The Shadow Knows*.

**Evalin McCabe (Ev) Wilson**    Maid and babysitter for N. Hexam; Hexam believes that Wilson was murdered in Diane Johnson's *The Shadow Knows*.

**Geoffrey Wilson**    Father of Tony Wilson; falsely claims to be a London war refugee; inherits a dilapidated mansion and becomes the object of Esther Grimes's flirting in Richard Yates's *Easter Parade*.

**George Wilson**    Arthur Lee's lawyer; African American; helps Berry investigate the murder charges in Jeffery Hudson's *A Case of Need*.

**Lloyd Wilson**    Husband of Marie; father of four daughters and two sons; tenant farmer; neighbor and friend of Clarence and Fern Smith; falls in love with Fern; murdered by Clarence Smith in William Maxwell's *So Long, See You Tomorrow*.

**Marie Wilson**    Wife of Lloyd; mother of four daughters and two sons; knows of husband's infidelity with Fern Smith; moves to town with daughters; wins legal separation and monetary settlement but refuses to divorce husband in William Maxwell's *So Long, See You Tomorrow*.

**Peter Wilson**    Second son of Tony and Sarah Grimes Wilson; acts as guardian to his aunt, Emily Grimes, in her last days in Richard Yates's *Easter Parade*.

**Samuel (Gunner) Wilson**    Jet pilot who does nighttime reconnaissance of Piedmont, Arizona, in Michael Crichton's *The Andromeda Strain*.

**Sarah Grimes Wilson**    Older sister of Emily Grimes and wife of Tony Wilson; becomes alcoholic in middle age, endures abuse by her husband, and dies after a fall in Richard Yates's *Easter Parade*.

**Terry Wilson**    Girlfriend of Teddy, who leads her into the world of drugs and prostitution; institutionalized after Minnie's suicide in Donald Goines's *Dopefiend*.

**Martin (Mart) Winch**    Middle-aged first sergeant who returns from duty in the South Pacific with a heart ailment to find that his wife is promiscuous; becomes involved with Carol Firebaugh; continues to help three of his men—John Strange, Marion Landers, and Bobby Prell—after their return to the United States in James Jones's *Whistle*.

**Bennett Wing**    Chinese psychoanalyst and second husband of Isadora Wing in Erica Jong's *Fear of Flying* and *How to Save Your Own Life*.

**Isadora Zelda White Stollerman Wing**    Jewish poet who searches for herself through affairs and two marriages in Erica Jong's *Fear of Flying* and *How to Save Your Own Life*.

**Brother Wingfare**    Evangelical preacher whose religious activity contrasts with the nonreligious righteousness of Old Jack Beechum in Wendell Berry's *The Memory of Old Jack*.

**Amos Wingo**    Head of the Wingo clan in Colleton, North Carolina; a religious fanatic with a sincerely Christian outlook; the defection of his wife warps his son, Henry, in Pat Conroy's *The Prince of Tides*.

**Henry Wingo**    Brutal husband and father who strives for easy success but always fails, ruining his family in the process, in Pat Conroy's *The Prince of Tides*.

**Lila Trent Wingo**    Ambitiously selfish wife of Henry Wingo, her desire to improve the social status of her family demands silence on every issue, no matter how pivotal to the psychological health of her children, in Pat Conroy's *The Prince of Tides*.

**Luke Wingo**    Elder son of Henry and Lila; a keen individualist with a love so strong for his younger siblings and Colleton Island that it ends his life in Pat Conroy's *The Prince of Tides*.

**Sallie Pierson Wingo**    Tom's wife and the mother of his three daughters; she is an overachieving physician from a textile worker background; she struggles to save her marriage in Pat Conroy's *The Prince of Tides*.

**Savannah Wingo**    Tom's twin by birth; a natural, but psychotic, genius who writes brilliant poetry based on the beauties and horrors of her early life in Pat Conroy's *The Prince of Tides*.

**Tom Wingo**    Second, sensitive son of Henry and Lila; a coach and teacher whose loyalty to family ruins his chance to achieve "ideal" love in Pat Conroy's *The Prince of Tides*.

**Suzanne Winograd**    Professional tennis player who behaves childishly in Mark Harris's *It Looked Like For Ever*.

**Euston Peters Winslow-Davis**    Horribly deformed dwarf who is wealthy enough to travel continuously; friend of Hellos and witness to Scarecrow's murder of her in Calvin Hernton's *Scarecrow*.

**Mafia Winsome**    Novelist who has developed a theory known as Heroic Love; a member of the Whole Sick Crew in Thomas Pynchon's *V.*

**Winston**   Partner of Carmen, old friend of Katie and the Fishers, everybody's confidant; interested in geneology; drives a school bus in Seattle and goes to Salt Lake City to trace his lineage in Sandra Scofield's *Beyond Deserving*.

**George Winston**   Wealthy financier and founder of the Columbus Group; sells his business to Raizo Yamata; returns to the business when the finance markets crash, only to discover that Yamata has used his company to cause the crash; assists in brokering the deal with financiers and European banks that restores stability to the market in Tom Clancy's *Debt of Honor*.

**Dorabella Winter**   Younger daughter of Edith and Severin Winter, sister of Fiordiligi Winter, and friend and playmate of Jack and Bart; badly cut by shattering glass in John Irving's *The 158-Pound Marriage*.

**Edith Fuller Winter**   Wife of Severin Winter, mother of Dorabella and Fiordiligi Winter, close friend of Utch Thalhammer and the unnamed narrator; has an affair with the narrator when the couples swap mates; attempts to seduce and humble George James Bender in John Irving's *The 158-Pound Marriage*.

**Fiordiligi Winter**   Older daughter of Edith and Severin Winter, sister of Dorabella Winter, and playmate and friend of Jack and Bart; badly cut by shattering glass in John Irving's *The 158-Pound Marriage*.

**Kurt Winter**   Husband of Katrina Marek and father of Severin Winter; famous painter who does nude, erotic paintings of Katrina in John Irving's *The 158-Pound Marriage*.

**Miss Winter**   Music teacher who befriends Meridian Hill in Alice Walker's *Meridian*.

**Severin Winter**   Son of Kurt and Katrina Marek and nephew of Vaso Trivanovich and Zivan Knezevich, who teach him to wrestle; husband of Edith Fuller Winter and father of Dorabella and Fiordiligi Winter; university German teacher and wrestling coach who has an affair with Audrey Cannon in John Irving's *The 158-Pound Marriage*.

**Ex-P.F.C. Wintergreen**   Mail clerk whose control over communications gives him virtual command of the Twenty-seventh Air Force Headquarters; a snide little punk who enjoys working at cross purposes in Joseph Heller's *Catch-22*.

**Thor Wintergreen**   Idealistic descendant of the European elite and member of Berbelang's Third World group; outsmarted and killed by Biff Musclewhite in Ishmael Reed's *Mumbo Jumbo*.

**Amos (Amos Jordan) Winthrop**   Father of Monica Winthrop and rival of Jonas Cord, Sr.; atones for his feud with the elder Cord by saving the life of Jonas Cord, Jr., after a plane crash in Harold Robbins's *The Carpetbaggers*.

**Billy (Honey) Winthrop**   See Wilhelmina Hunnenwell Winthrop Ikehorn Orsini.

**Monica Winthrop**   Daughter of Amos Winthrop, ex-wife of Jonas Cord, Jr., and mother of Jo-Ann in Harold Robbins's *The Carpetbaggers*.

**Frank (Blue Fairy Godmother, Col. Harold J. Sparrow) Wirtanen**   United States Army major and spymaster of Howard Campbell in Kurt Vonnegut's *Mother Night*.

**The Witchfinder**   From the Bambara Chiefdom, the most powerful witchfinder in Sierra Leone; brought to Boone Westfall's village to identify the witches and locate evil medicines hidden by local villagers; blackmails Boone Westfall into murdering an innocent young woman in Richard Dooling's *White Man's Grave*.

**Nathaniel Turner (Spoons) Witherspoon**   Custodian at Dolphin's Lounge and keen observer of the lives of his many friends; confidant and eulogizer of Regal Pettibone in Leon Forrest's *The Bloodworth Orphans*.

**Private Witt**   Boxer from Kentucky whose antagonistic behavior toward James Stein and Edward Welsh causes him to be transferred to the Cannon Company in James Jones's *The Thin Red Line*.

**Pia Wittkin**   Best friend of Isadora Wing in high school and college in Erica Jong's *Fear of Flying*.

**Wolf**   Werewolflike creature who befriends Jack in the Territories and accompanies him on much of his westward journey in the real world; saves Jack's life as he loses his own in Stephen King's and Peter Straub's *The Talisman*.

**Charlotte Wolf**   Noncirculating librarian at Calvin Coolidge High School who says students are not to be sent to the school library for any reason whatsoever and no books are to be removed from library shelves until the card catalog is brought up to date in Bel Kaufman's *Up the Down Staircase*.

**John (Jack) Wolf**   New York City book editor and publisher who discovers Jenny Fields and later, T. S. Garp; uses his cleaning woman, Jillsy Sloper, as a barometer of a book's probable success; makes Garp famous by capitalizing on various family tragedies as advertising techniques in John Irving's *The World According to Garp*.

**Wolf-Boy**   Character from Dalton Harron's lost manuscript who appears in Harron's recurrent dreams in Susan Sontag's *Death Kit*.

**Dr. Wolfe**   Physician who first diagnoses Ben Flesh's multiple sclerosis in Stanley Elkin's *The Franchiser*.

**Rodger Wolfherald**   Passenger who burns the *Here They Come* in Gregory Corso's *The American Express*.

**Wolfie (Fat Morty)**   American mercenary, Jew, and confederate of Lewis Moon; bombs and strafes the Niaruna village on orders from Comandante Guzmán in Peter Matthiessen's *At Play in the Fields of the Lord*.

**Fred Wolfpits**   Homosexual collector of Orientalia and college classmate of Waldo in Paul Theroux's *Waldo*.

**Charles Wollstonecraft**   Son of Edward and Mrs. Wollstonecraft, brother of Mary, Ned, Everina, and Eliza Wollstonecraft; joins the navy in Frances Sherwood's *Vindication*.

**Edward Wollstonecraft**   Husband of Mrs. Wollstonecraft, father of Mary, Ned, Everina, Eliza, and Charles Wollstonecraft; becomes a mean drunk; abuses his family and hangs all five of his hunting dogs in Frances Sherwood's *Vindication*.

**Edward Wollstonecraft, Sr.**   Father of Edward Wollstonecraft, grandfather of Mary, Ned, Everina, Eliza, and Charles Wollstonecraft; owns three blocks of houses in Spitalfields, London, in Frances Sherwood's *Vindication*.

**Eliza Wollstonecraft**   Daughter of Edward and Mrs. Wollstonecraft, sister of Mary, Ned, Everina, and Charles Wollstonecraft; opens a school for girls along with Mary and Everina Wollstonecraft and Fanny Blood; becomes a governess in Scotland after the school fails; runs a school with Everina in Dublin until Eliza dies in 1830 in Frances Sherwood's *Vindication*.

**Everina Wollstonecraft**   Daughter of Edward and Mrs. Wollstonecraft, sister of Mary, Ned, Eliza, and Charles Wollstonecraft; opens a school for girls along with Mary and Eliza Wollstonecraft and Fanny Blood; becomes a governess in Scotland again after the school fails; runs a school with Eliza in Dublin until Eliza dies in 1830 in Frances Sherwood's *Vindication*.

**Fanny Wollstonecraft**   Daughter of Mary Wollstonecraft and Gilbert Imlay, half sister of Mary Godwin Shelley; a melancholy young woman; commits suicide in Frances Sherwood's *Vindication*.

**Mary Wollstonecraft**   Daughter of Edward and Mrs. Wollstonecraft, sister of Ned, Everina, Eliza, and Charles Wollstonecraft; physically and emotionally abused by both parents and sexually abused by Annie, the maid; opens a school for girls along with Everina and Eliza Wollstonecraft and Fanny Blood; after the school closes, accepts a job as governess in Ireland; has affair with Richard Kingsborough, her employer's son, until she is fired; moves back to London and becomes a writer; her book *A Vindication of the Rights of Woman* comes out in 1792; has a breakdown and ends up in Bedlam until Joseph Johnson rescues her; goes to Paris to write about the French Revolution; meets the American Gilbert Imlay; has his child, Fanny; after Gilbert leaves her for an actress, Mary moves back to England and attempts suicide; marries William Godwin; dies at thirty-seven after giving birth to Mary Godwin Shelley in Frances Sherwood's *Vindication*.

**Mrs. Wollstonecraft**   Wife of Edward Wollstonecraft, mother of Mary, Ned, Everina, Eliza, and Charles Wollstonecraft; illiterate; unaffectionate toward her children, submissive toward her husband in Frances Sherwood's *Vindication*.

**Ned Wollstonecraft**   Son of Edward and Mrs. Wollstonecraft, brother of Mary, Everina, Eliza, and Charles Wollstonecraft, steals all the inheritance from his grandfather that was to be divided equally among his siblings; has the personality of a petty despot; is a successful solicitor in Frances Sherwood's *Vindication*.

**Womwom**   Soul at the seventh aspect of Wylie Norton in Robert Coover's *The Origin of the Brunists*.

**Walter Wong**   Fuller Brush salesman and husband of Ceci O'Connor in Alison Lurie's *The Nowhere City*.

**Jing-Mei (June) Woo**   Daughter of Suyuan Woo; copywriter for advertising firm; takes deceased mother's place at the mahjongg table; travels to China to meet her twin half sisters her mother left behind; narrator of Amy Tan's *The Joy Luck Club*.

**Suyuan Woo**   Mother of Jing-Mei Woo; left twin girls behind in China; immigrates to America in 1949; cleans houses; dies of a cerebral aneurysm in Amy Tan's *The Joy Luck Club*.

**John Wood**   Elderly farmer and participant in the Indian massacre who pleads guilty and is hanged in Jessamyn West's *The Massacre at Fall Creek*.

**John (Johnny) Wood, Jr.**   Participant in the Indian massacre who is given a last-minute reprieve at the gallows in Jessamyn West's *The Massacre at Fall Creek*.

**Reba Reese Wood**   Second wife of John Wood and sister of George Benson in Jessamyn West's *The Massacre at Fall Creek*.

**Susannah Wood**   Starlet paramour of Carter Lang; beaten up by an actor in Joan Didion's *Play It As It Lays*.

**Luther (Woodie) Woodcock**   Light-skinned black medic from Abraham Blackman's Charlie Company in Vietnam; infiltrated along with other such white soldiers by Blackman into strategic positions to thwart racist command decisions in the American military in John A. Williams's *Captain Blackman*.

**Andrew John Woodhouse**   Infant son of Satan and Rosemary Woodhouse; born with yellow eyes, orange hair, and budding horns, claws, and tail in Ira Levin's *Rosemary's Baby*.

**Guy Woodhouse**   Actor; husband of Rosemary Woodhouse; to further his career, conspires with devil worshippers in the seduction of his wife by Satan in Ira Levin's *Rosemary's Baby*.

**Rosemary Woodhouse**   Young New Yorker and wife of Guy Woodhouse; chosen without her knowledge to be the mother of Satan's firstborn son in Ira Levin's *Rosemary's Baby*.

**Bernard Woodruff**   Susan Lowenstein's adolescent son whom her husband forces to play the violin; miserable and alienated, Bernard learns about football and life from Coach Tom Wingo in Pat Conroy's *The Prince of Tides*.

**Herbert Woodruff**   Susan Lowenstein's violin-playing husband; a world-famous virtuoso, he is an unfaithful husband and a too-demanding father in Pat Conroy's *The Prince of Tides*.

**Harry Woods**    Twenty-one-year-old dishwasher obsessed with Stephanie Sykes; lives at the hotel where he works; Nicole visits him to lose her virginity in Ann Beattie's *Love Always.*

**Lorena Woods**    Prostitute; dreams of going to San Francisco; stops working when Jake Spoon promises to take her there; they follow the cattle drive, but she is abducted, raped, and held captive by Indians; rescued by Gus McCrae in Larry McMurtry's *Lonesome Dove.*

**Woody**    Priest and golf player at the retreat in John Updike's *A Month of Sundays.*

**David (Dave, Davidele, Davy) Woolf**    Nephew of Bernie Norman; takes over management of Norman's movie studio after it is bought by Jonas Cord, Jr.; dies at Anzio in World War II in Harold Robbins's *The Carpetbaggers.*

**Leonard Woolf**    Protective, concerned husband of Virginia Woolf who has taken her to the suburb of Richmond to recuperate in Michael Cunningham's *The Hours.*

**Virginia Woolf**    Brilliant twentieth-century novelist in the process of composing *Mrs. Dalloway;* wife of Leonard Woolf; suffers from depression, excruciating headaches, and bouts of auditory hallucinations; commits suicide by drowning in 1941 in Michael Cunningham's *The Hours.*

**Eddie Wormsley**    Gentle friend of Dick Pierce; Dick and his family live with Eddie after their home is severely damaged by a hurricane in John Casey's *Spartina.*

**Willie Joe Worth**    Former alcoholic, police officer in Somerton, and lover of Emma Jones; to keep his name from being revealed in divorce proceedings against her, Worth murders L. B. Jones and mutilates his body in Jesse Hill Ford's *The Liberation of Lord Byron Jones.*

**Worthington (Mr. W.)**    Supervisor of Paul Galambos; promises to let Galambos do sex experiments in Scott Spencer's *Last Night at the Brain Thieves' Ball.*

**Daria Erskine Paulus Worthington**    Introspective wife of Smith Worthington and half sister of Eliza Quarles; treated in a sanitarium after her fourth miscarriage in Alice Adams's *Listening to Billie.*

**Francis Worthington**    Brother of January Worthington and relative of Luci Worthington; is a bishop in Haiti; trains the young slave boys to be gentlemen in Herbert Gold's *Slave Trade.*

**January (Jan) Worthington**    Brother of Francis Worthington and relative of Luci Worthington; wealthy head of the slavery ring in Herbert Gold's *Slave Trade.*

**Luci Worthington**    Relative of January and Francis Worthington; meets Sid in San Francisco and follows him to Paris; works with Mahmoud Fils-Aimé in Herbert Gold's *Slave Trade.*

**Smith Worthington**    Hardworking international businessman married to Daria Worthington in Alice Adams's *Listening to Billie.*

**Wally Worthington**    Fiancé of Candy Kendall; Wally's family runs the cider house and gives Homer his first job when he leaves St. Cloud's Orphanage in John Irving's *The Cider House Rules.*

**Ben Wosznik**    Brunist songwriter and spiritual whip in Robert Coover's *The Origin of the Brunists.*

**Woytek**    Childhood friend George Levanter encourages to defect to the West; with his lover Gibby and others, slain in a Charles Manson–style massacre in Jerzy Kosinski's *Blind Date.*

**Russel (Russ) Wren**    Erudite detective whose imagination fuels his bizarre adventures; narrator of Thomas Berger's *Who Is Teddy Villanova?*

**Astrid Wrendel-Kramp**    Mysterious Danish countess, the offspring of her father's incestuous affair, with whom the Allstons lodge on the journey to Denmark; becomes the Allstons' guide, taking them to meet Karen Blixen and her own mysterious family in Wallace Stegner's *The Spectator Bird.*

**Helene Sabat Wright**    Mother of Nel Wright and daughter of Rochelle Sabat in Toni Morrison's *Sula.*

**Heritage (Kam, Kamikazee) Wright**    Activist with a penchant for spray painting the sides of buildings; survives the explosion, goes on the run, and murders Bill Armiston for betraying the group in M. F. Beal's *Amazon One.*

**Lucille Wright**    Inquisitive friend of Helen Clarke; accompanies Helen to the Blackwood home for tea; relates the story of the Blackwood family poisonings in Shirley Jackson's *We Have Always Lived in the Castle.*

**Nel Wright**    Best friend of Sula Peace; daughter of Helene Wright and wife of Jude in Toni Morrison's *Sula.*

**Robert Wright**    Philadelphia publisher who agrees to publish Charles Schuyler's memoirs of Aaron Burr by a ghostwriter in Gore Vidal's *Burr.*

**Wiley Wright**    Husband of Helene Wright in Toni Morrison's *Sula.*

**Willie (Father) Wright**    Religious fanatic; one of ten Los Angeles policemen-protagonists in Joseph Wambaugh's *The Choirboys.*

**Maurice Xavier Wu**    Anthropologist with a special interest in caves; unearths evidence for a prehistoric temporary reversal of the evolutionary process (reverse evolution) in Don DeLillo's *Ratner's Star.*

**Bullet Wulff**    Meets Loyal Blood in the emergency room; fossil hunter who asks Loyal to work with him; he and Loyal work together for three years in the summers; in the winters, has a laundromat in Las Vegas in E. Annie Proulx's *Postcards.*

**Bucky Wunderlick**    Popular rock singer who suddenly quits his band, escapes to a small New York apartment, and gets involved in elaborate intrigue over a mysterious drug; narrator of Don DeLillo's *Great Jones Street.*

**Jerry Wung**    Chinese-American tenant in the Mott Street building managed by Norman Moonbloom in Edward Lewis Wallant's *The Tenants of Moonbloom.*

**Gottlob Wut**    Leader of the German Motorcycle Unit Balkan 4; killed by his men in an outhouse in John Irving's *Setting Free the Bears.*

**Sarah Wyatt**    Friend of Walter F. Starbuck and wife of Leland Clewes in Kurt Vonnegut's *Jailbird.*

**Norine Wyckoff**    Elderly woman who enlists the aid of Theophilus North in ridding her house of its ghosts in Thornton Wilder's *Theophilus North.*

**Sarah Wydman**    English lady and lover of Abe Cady; speaks for the English Jewish community in Leon Uris's *QB VII.*

**Francine Wyeth**    Mother of Maria Wyeth and wife of Harry Wyeth; runs her car off a highway in Nevada and is eaten by coyotes in Joan Didion's *Play It As It Lays.*

**Harry Wyeth**    Gambler father of Maria Wyeth in Joan Didion's *Play It As It Lays.*

**Maria (Mrs. Lang) Wyeth**    Depressed movie actress who is committed to a sanitarium after abetting the suicide of BZ; wife of Carter Lang and mother of Kate Lang in Joan Didion's *Play It As It Lays.*

**Lyle Wynant**    Wall Street businessman who, as a government informer, becomes involved in a plot to bomb the New York Stock Exchange in Don DeLillo's *Players.*

**Pammy Wynant**    Employee of Grief Management Council in the World Trade Center; wife of Lyle Wynant and friend of Ethan Segal and Jack Laws in Don DeLillo's *Players.*

# X, Y, Z

**Belfast X**  Black Irish London junkie who sells a virgin-wool sports jacket to Black Will during one of Black Will's junkets in Carlene Hatcher Polite's *Sister X and the Victims of Foul Play*.

**Chairman (Jake) X**  Eccentric chair of the Horticulture Department at Moo University, last of the great 1960s revolutionists; in a twenty-year relationship with "Lady X" (Beth), whom he later marries; has an affair with Cecelia Sanchez; incites a riot against the proposed gold mine in Jane Smiley's *Moo*.

**Robert X (Etienne Sims)**  Illegitimate son of Johanna Sims and the Reverend Phillip Martin; mysteriously and inopportunely appears to identify himself and to confront his father in Ernest J. Gaines's *In My Father's House*.

**Father Xantes**  Roman Catholic missionary who competes with his Protestant counterparts for the souls of the South American Indians in Peter Matthiessen's *At Play in the Fields of the Lord*.

**Xolod**  Mayan boy into whom the narrator is transformed in William S. Burroughs's *The Soft Machine;* lover and comrade of El Nifio Muerto in the Mayan jungle in *The Wild Boys*.

**Yamaiuchi**  Marion Peabody Barrett's smiling butler; a Jehovah's Witness, he refuses to take orders from Will Barrett in Walker Percy's *The Second Coming*.

**Jimmy Yamamoto**  Japanese-American trumpet player; best friend of Teddy Maki; must fight for the Japanese in the Philippines during World War II even though he considers himself an American; his rebellious nature leads him to a tragic end in Richard Wiley's *Soldiers in Hiding*.

**Kazuko Yamamoto**  Japanese wife of Jimmy Yamamoto; nationalistic and in support of the war; pregnant when her husband is killed in World War II; marries Teddy Maki after the war is over in Richard Wiley's *Soldiers in Hiding*.

**Raizo Yamata**  Japanese industrialist who plans to cause an economic crisis in America, driving dollar values down and yen values up; is eventually arrested and extradited to America for trial in Tom Clancy's *Debt of Honor*.

**Robert (Bob) Yamm**  Midget pinch hitter for the Kakoola Reapers; commanded under threat of death not to swing his bat in Philip Roth's *The Great American Novel*.

**Nick Yanov**  Field sergeant of the Wilshire Police Station in Joseph Wambaugh's *The Choirboys*.

**Yardley**  Cynical and senior drinking buddy of Jack Flowers in Singapore in Paul Theroux's *Saint Jack*.

**Dr. Norman Yas**  Sixty-one-year-old beatnik psychiatrist; self-proclaimed existential psychotherapist with a novel approach to schizophrenia; traveler aboard the *Castel Felice* in Calvin Hernton's *Scarecrow*.

**Mikhail Yasov**  Russian field chief who attempts to hire his former opponent, Miles Kendig (a retired CIA agent), but who later leads the Russian pursuit of Kendig, who has threatened to publish a book that will expose Russian government secrets, in Brian Garfield's *Hopscotch*.

**Yates**  Quiet drinking buddy of Jack Flowers in Singapore in Paul Theroux's *Saint Jack*.

**Jackson (William [Bill, Willie] Carter) Yeager**  Former writer and member of the editorial staff of Black Christian Publishing Company; killed his wife's lover, decapitated his wife, and joined the Hippodrome's cast in Cyrus Colter's *The Hippodrome*.

**Fanny Yellin**   "Crazy" wife of Gabe Yellin, a wealthy archconservative businessman; Fanny is overmedicated and stays in her bedroom when she is not psychiatrically hospitalized; speaks out against the greediness and power-mongering of her husband and his family in Ellen Gilchrist's *Victory Over Japan.*

**Milton (Junior, Milt) Yellin**   Former business associate of Ted Bliss; later, recreational therapeusist and friend of Dorothy; marries Ellen Bliss in Stanley Elkin's *Mrs. Ted Bliss.*

**Ed Yellings**   Black American itinerant who succeeds in the gumbo business and who is murdered by agents of the Louisiana Red Corporation because he is close to discovering a cure for heroin addiction in Ishmael Reed's *The Last Days of Louisiana Red.*

**Minnie (Minnie the Moocher, Queen of the Moochers) Yellings**   Youngest daughter of Ed Yellings; brought up by Nanny Lisa on Louisiana Red stories, which depict black men as brutish louts; burns her father's gumbo business; frees Andy Brown and Kingfish Stevens from jail; is shot by Chorus; PaPa LaBas goes to the underworld to plead for her in Ishmael Reed's *The Last Days of Louisiana Red.*

**Street Yellings**   Son of Ed Yellings; prisoner who has his consciousness raised while in jail; upon escaping, is granted asylum in an emerging African nation, but Max Kasavubu returns him to the United States, where he and his brother, Wolf Yellings, kill each other in a quarrel over which of them will run their father's gumbo business in Ishmael Reed's *The Last Days of Louisiana Red.*

**Wolf Yellings**   Wise son of Ed Yellings; runs the gumbo business following his father's murder, but is killed in a shootout with his brother, Street Yellings, in Ishmael Reed's *The Last Days of Louisiana Red.*

**Yellow Kidney**   Respected Pikuni warrior who is captured and mutilated because of the bragging of Fast Horse during a horse raid on a Crow camp; found by the Spotted Horse People (Cheyenne), who care for him; mistakenly murdered by a white man in retribution for the acts of Owl Child's band in James Welch's *Fools Crow.*

**Sir Henry Yelverton**   Attorney general of England in George Garrett's *Death of the Fox.*

**Johnny Yen (Yenshe)**   Switch artist who performs by changing sexes in William S. Burroughs's *Nova Express, The Soft Machine,* and *The Ticket That Exploded.*

**Sam Yerger**   Hemingway-like writer and longtime friend of Emily Bolling in Walker Percy's *The Moviegoer.*

**Yin-Li**   Chinese urologist who corresponds with Jack Flood; a graduate of the University of Minnesota; keeps the books of a bicycle factory in Maureen Howard's *Expensive Habits.*

**Yod**   Robot with human emotions, created to be an ideal man, Shira falls in love with him in Marge Piercy's *He, She and It.*

**Waverly Yong**   Daughter of Lindo Jong; child national chess champion; once divorced and now engaged; mother of Shoshana; tax attorney in Amy Tan's *The Joy Luck Club.*

**Yossarian (Yo-Yo)**   Air force captain in World War II, bombardier, and malingerer traumatized by the death of Snowden and the absurdity and malignity of Catch-22 in Joseph Heller's *Catch-22.*

**Guy Young**   Handsome homosexual actor; has a brief sexual encounter with Johnny Rio in John Rechy's *Numbers.*

**Kemal Young**   Mute Turkish boy who miraculously speaks near the end of the novel after his brother Timur's horrific murder; sits apart from the crowds and absorbs myriad details about the gendarmes in Mary Lee Settle's *Blood Tie.*

**Jimmy Youngblood**   See Jimmy Lee Smith.

**Younger Bear**   Cheyenne friend of Little Big Man; becomes a Contrary in Thomas Berger's *Little Big Man.*

**Younger Brother**   See Mother's Younger Brother.

**Mark Youngerman**   Basketball player at Olinger High School and student of George Caldwell in John Updike's *The Centaur.*

**Margie Young-Hunt**   Attractive tarot card reader; lover and confidante of several New Baytown men who tries unsuccessfully to compromise Ethan Allen Hawley's newfound status by seducing him in John Steinbeck's *The Winter of Our Discontent.*

**Perry Yturbide**   Ex-convict and friend of Cody Pomeray and Billie Dabney; his excessive affection for young girls frightens Jack Duluoz in Jack Kerouac's *Big Sur.*

**Yves**   French male prostitute with whom Eric Jones falls in love in James Baldwin's *Another Country.*

**Yvette**   French prostitute who is hired as a body double for Arabella in Boris Adrian's pornographic movie in Terry Southern's *Blue Movie.*

**Robin Zacharias**   Air force pilot, downed over Vietnam and questioned by Nikolay Yevgeniyevich Grishanov; reveals attack plans against the USSR; is eventually released due to secret negotiations with the Soviets in Tom Clancy's *Without Remorse.*

**Zachary**   Child Martha Horgan takes hostage after he witnesses what happens between her and Joshua Barrett in Mary McGarry Morris's *A Dangerous Woman.*

**Elfrida Zaehner**   Sister of Albert Corde and mother of Mason Zaehner; haughty and indifferent, with a string of ex-husbands; tries to advise Albert on the proceedings of a university student's murder and the maneuverings of their unscrupulous cousin lawyer Max Detillion in Saul Bellow's *The Dean's December.*

**Mason Zaehner** Young nephew of Albert Corde; a brash college student activist with a strong liberal streak; accuses Corde of wrongly interacting in the investigation of a fellow university student's murder in which he becomes entangled, eventually fleeing the country before he is implicated further in Saul Bellow's *The Dean's December*.

**Zagayek** Adulterous husband of a paralytic wife who has an incestuous bond with his daughter; his lasciviousness, sadism, and greed oppress the village peasants; tavern owner and bailiff who arranges Jacob Eliezer's freedom in Isaac Bashevis Singer's *The Slave*.

**Moishe (Reb Moishe) Zakolkower** Civic leader of Josefov, Poland, and one of three men who ransom Jacob Eliezer out of slavery in Isaac Bashevis Singer's *The Slave*.

**Alan Zapalac** Exobiology instructor at Logos College in Don DeLillo's *End Zone*.

**Vera Chipmunk-5 Zappa** Farmer, slave owner, and friend of Wilbur Swain in Kurt Vonnegut's *Slapstick*.

**Eva Maria Zawistowska** Eight-year-old daughter of Sophie Zawistowska; dies in a Birkenau crematorium in William Styron's *Sophie's Choice*.

**Jan Zawistowska** Ten-year-old son of Sophie Zawistowska confined in the children's camp at Auschwitz; his fate remains unknown in William Styron's *Sophie's Choice*.

**Zofia Maria Biegańska (Irma Griese, Sophie, Zosia) Zawistowska** Polish Catholic survivor of Auschwitz, lover of Nathan Landau, and central character in Stingo's tale in William Styron's *Sophie's Choice*.

**Zeb-un-nissa** Gabriel Legge's black bibi (mistress); on the birth of their first son, puts on her finest silks and visits Gabriel's home in Bharati Mukherjee's *The Holder of the World*.

**Zed** See Sanford Finkelstein.

**Zelig** Father of Shosha; leaves his wife, Bashele, for another woman in Isaac Bashevis Singer's *Shosha*.

**Philippe "Papa" Zeringue** Creole gangster kingpin to whom Rutherford Calhoun is indebted; blackmails Rutherford to either pay up or marry Isadora Bailey; finally relinquishes Rutherford from debt and gives up Isadora when he realizes Rutherford has the log from the *Republic*, which names him as owner of an illegal slave ship in Charles Johnson's *Middle Passage*.

**Trofim Zhdanko** Stalwart and loyal Ukrainian cossack; pardoned by Tsar Peter Romanoff for murdering tyrannical governor; sent by tsar to explore easternmost region of Russian empire; marries Marina Poznikova in James Michener's *Alaska*.

**George Ziad** Palestinian intellectual and activist engaged in various forms of anti-Zionist resistance; abandons life as American professor to live in the midst of the conflict, bringing along his reluctant wife, Anna, and son, Michael; while a graduate student in Chicago befriends young Philip Roth, who later becomes a famous Jewish-American novelist; reinitiates contact with Roth in Israel; offers Roth various forms of support and encouragement for Diasporism project in Philip Roth's *Operation Shylock*.

**Horace Zifferblatt** Militant clockwatcher and J. Henry Waugh's manager in Robert Coover's *The Universal Baseball Association, Inc., J. Henry Waugh, Prop.*

**Amanda Ziller** Vegetarian wife of John Paul Ziller, mother of Baby Thor, and lover of many men and women including Plucky Purcell; admirer of butterflies, mysticism, and motorcycles; eye-opener of Marx Marvelous and heroine in Tom Robbins's *Another Roadside Attraction*.

**John Paul Ziller** Husband of Amanda Ziller, co-owner of Captain Kendrick's Hot Dog Wildlife Preserve, drummer, artist, and magician; wears a loincloth on his body and a bone through his nose; dies with Mon Cul and The Corpse on the Icarus XC solar balloon in Tom Robbins's *Another Roadside Attraction*.

**Louis M. Zimmerman** Lecherous principal of Olinger High School; disliked by George Caldwell and others; rumored to have fathered Corinna Appleton's son, Skippy Appleton, in John Updike's *The Centaur*.

**Natalie Kelso (Natasha) Zimmerman** Los Angeles burglary detective; A. M. Valnikov's partner and eventually his fiancée in Joseph Wambaugh's *The Black Marble*.

**Danielle Zimmern** Instructor of French and divorced wife of Leonard Zimmern in Alison Lurie's *The War Between the Tates*.

**Leonard D. Zimmern (Lennie, L. D.)** Professor of English; father of Roo in Alison Lurie's *Foreign Affairs*. In *The War Between the Tates* he is the former husband of Danielle Zimmern; also appears in *Real People*.

**Ruth (Roo) Zimmern** Daughter of Danielle and Leonard Zimmern in Alison Lurie's *The War Between the Tates*.

**Chase Zorn** Adopted Peruvian son of Radford Zorn; arrested at fifteen for stealing cars and wine; sent to Fair Haven after spending time at the Menninger Clinic; drops out of high school when his father has a stroke and takes over his business in Gail Godwin's *Evensong*.

**Radford Zorn** Father of Chase; a theme-park mogul, unable or unwilling to provide Chase with a home; has a stroke and Chase comes home to take care of him in Gail Godwin's *Evensong*.

**Carol Goff Zuckerman** Wife of Henry Zuckerman; mother of son Leslie, fourteen, and daughters Ruth, thirteen, and Ellen, eleven; a smart, pretty woman who is devoted to her family; becomes aware of Henry's infidelities and must deal with his midlife crisis in Philip Roth's *The Counterlife*.

**Henry Zuckerman**   Forty-something dentist and family man; has had a number of mistresses; becomes obsessed with his ability to perform sexually after a medical procedure; tries to come to terms with the divergent paths that he and his brother, Nathan, have traveled in Philip Roth's *The Counterlife*. Also appears in *Zuckerman Unbound*.

**Laura Zuckerman**   Nathan Zuckerman's wife, from whom he is separated; virtuous lawyer who supports people hiding in Canada from the draft in Philip Roth's *Zuckerman Unbound*.

**Nathan Zuckerman**   Forty-something Jewish-American novelist living in New York City; is tormented by the negative reactions of his family and critics to his most recent novel, *Carnovsky;* suffers from mysterious chronic pain in his neck and shoulders; looks for comfort in women, drugs, and alcohol; decides to abandon writing and his "harem" of nursemaid lovers and become a doctor; is a continuing character in Philip Roth's *The Ghost Writer, Zuckerman Unbound, The Anatomy Lesson, The Counterlife,* and *I Married a Communist,* among others.

**Selma Zuckerman**   Faithful and patient mother of Nathan and Henry Zuckerman and wife of Victor Zuckerman; lives in Miami; practices with her son, Nathan, answers to reporters' questions; husband has a stroke and is in a nursing home in Philip Roth's *Zuckerman Unbound*.

**Victor Zuckerman**   Nathan Zuckerman's father; former chiropodist; falls into a coma in Miami before *Carnovsky* is published; his last word is "bastard" in Philip Roth's *Zuckerman Unbound*.

**Harry Zwingli**   Police detective in Thomas Berger's *Who Is Teddy Villanova?*

**Herbie Zylstra**   Brother of Lorna Sue; friend of Thomas Chippering; takes blame for criminal acts by Lorna Sue; sent to reform school; continues throughout to protect Lorna Sue from herself and consequences of madness; reveals truth to Thomas in Tim O'Brien's *Tomcat in Love*.

**Lorna Sue Zylstra**   Sister of Herbie; obsessed by family and brother; marries Thomas Chippering; often regresses to childhood state; responsible for acts of arson and vandalism blamed on brother; revealed to be psychotic in Tim O'Brien's *Tomcat in Love*.

# Volume II
# Title Index

# VOLUME II
# AUTHOR INDEX

Douglas (Doug) Manley
James (Roe) Monroe
The Stalker
Lucinda de la Torre
Maria (Primi) Trinidad

## HARRIETTE SIMPSON ARNOW
### (See also Volume I)

*The Kentucky Trace* (1974)
William David Collins
William David Leslie Collins II
Sadie Hawkins
Isaac Huffacre
Jethro
Little Brother Leaping Fish
Rachel
Charity Prudence Eversole Simons
Daniel Strunk

*The Weedkiller's Daughter* (1969)
Robert Thomas Hedrick IV
Ben Holmes
Mollie Catharine (Katy) McWhorter
Gertie Kendrick Nevels
Brandon Schnitzer
Herman (Bismarck) Schnitzer
Mrs. (The Popsicle Queen) Schnitzer
Susan Marie (Susie) Schnitzer
Iggy Soames
Ter

## ISAAC ASIMOV

*Foundation's Edge* (1982)
Bliss
Harla Branno
Munn Li Compor
Delora Delarmi
Stor Gendibal
Sura Novi
Janov Pelorat
Golan Trevize

*The Robots of Dawn* (1983)
Vasilia Aliena
Kelden Amadiro
Elijah (Lije) Baley
Gladia Delmarre
Han Fastolfe
Vasilia Fastolfe
Giskard
Gladia
R. Daneel Olivaw

R. Giskard Reventlov
Gladia Solaria

## LOUIS AUCHINCLOSS
### (See also Volume I)

*The Rector of Justin* (1964)
Brian Aspinwall
Eliza Dean
David (Davey) Griscam
Jules Griscam
Horace Havistock
Reverend Duncan Moore
Francis (Frank, Rector of Justin)
  Prescott
Harriet Winslow Prescott
Charley Strong
Cordelia (Cordie) Turnbull

## JEAN AUEL

*The Clan of the Cave Bear* (1980)
Ayla
Broud
Brun
Creb
Iza

*The Mammoth Hunters* (1985)
Ayla
Jondalar
Mamut
Nezzie
Ranec
Rydag
Talut

*The Plains of Passage* (1990)
Attaroa
Ayla
Jondalar

*The Valley of Horses* (1982)
Ayla
Jondular

## PAUL AUSTER

*The Music of Chance* (1990)
Bill Flower
Calvin Murks
John Nashe
Jack Pozzi
Willie Stone

## RICHARD BACH

*Illusions: The Adventures of a Reluctant Messiah* (1977)
Richard Bach
Donald Shimoda

*Jonathan Livingston Seagull* (1970)
Chiang (Elder Gull, The Elder)
Fletcher Lynd (Fletch, Fletcher Gull)
  Seagull
Jonathan Livingston (Jon, Jonathan
  Gull) Seagull
Sullivan (Sully)

## JAMES BALDWIN
### (See also Volume I)

*Another Country* (1962)
Steve Ellis
Jane
Eric Jones
Leona (Anne)
Daniel Vivaldo (Viv) Moore
Ida Scott
Rufus Scott
Clarissa (Cass) Silenski
Richard Silenski
Yves

*If Beale Street Could Talk* (1974)
Daniel
Arnold Hayward
Adrienne Hunt
Alonzo (Fonny) Hunt
Frank Hunt
Mrs. Hunt
Sheila Hunt
Clementine (Tish) Rivers
Ernestine (Sis) Rivers
Joseph (Joe) Rivers
Sharon Rivers
Victoria (Victoria Maria San Felipe
  Sanchez) Rogers

*Tell Me How Long the Train's Been Gone* (1968)
Christopher (Black Christopher) Hall
Jerry
Barbara King
Caleb Proudhammer
Leo Proudhammer
Lola San-Marquand
Saul San-Marquand

## M. F. BEAL

### Amazon One (1975)
William (Bill) Armiston
Carole (C. B.) Batelle
Dawn Melody (Dawn Melody Topp)
   Batelle
Jersey Carmody
Kamikazee
Marina (Rina) Karsh
Atlas Androgyne (Atlas Atlantis)
   Maartens
Sheila Anne (Topper) Topp
Heritage (Kam, Kamikazee) Wright

### Angel Dance (1977)
Maria Katerina Lorca Guerrera (Kat)
   Alcazar
Julia
Lenore
Vincente Pesola (Vince) Muzguiz
Andrew Stone
Angel Stone
Rachel Stone
Michael B. Tarleton
William D. Tarleton

## ANN BEATTIE

### Chilly Scenes of Winter (1976)
Charles
Clara
Laura
Sam McGuire
Pete
Pamela Smith

### Falling in Place (1980)
Cynthia Forrest
Brandt Knapp
John Knapp
John Joel Knapp
Louise Knapp
Mary Knapp
Nina
Peter Spangle

### Love Always (1985)
Edward Bartlett
Cindi Coeur
Hildon
Maureen Hildon
Nicole Nelson
Noonan
Cameron Petrus

P. G. (Piggy) Proctor
Matt Smith
Jane Spenser
Lucy Spenser
Andrew Steinborn
Stephanie Sykes
Les Whitehall
Harry Woods

### My Life, Starring Dara Falcon 1997)
Grace Aldridge
Liam Cagertown
Dowell Churnin
Dara Falcon
Franny Feldstone
Edward Quill
Tom Van Sant
Barbara Warner
Bob Warner
Drake Warner
Frank Warner
Janey Warner
Jean Warner
Louise Warner
Marie Warner
Sandra Warner

### Picturing Will (1989)
Mel Anthis
Jody
Wayne
Will

## LOUIS BEGLEY

### The Man Who Was Late (1992)
Ben
Paul Decaze
Veronique Decaze
Jack

## MADISON SMARTT BELL

### All Souls' Rising (1995)
Claudine Arnaud
Michel Arnaud
Pere Bonne-chance
Choufleur
Isabelle Cigny
Antoine Hébert
Captain Maillart
Risu
Toussaint

## SAUL BELLOW
## (See also Volume I)

### The Dean's December (1982)
Albert Corde
Minna Raresh Corde
Valeria Raresh
Dewey Spangler
Elfrida Zaehner
Mason Zaehner

### Herzog (1964)
Lucas (Luke) Asphalter
Ramona Donsell
Valentine (Val) Gersbach
June (Junie) Herzog
Madeleine Pontritter (Mady) Herzog
Moses El Kanah (Butterfingers, Fish-
   bones, Fuckyknuckles, Ikey-Fishbones,
   Ikey-Moe, Mose, Moshe) Herzog
Sandor Himmelstein
Harvey Simkin

### Humboldt's Gift (1975)
Rinaldo (Ronald) Cantabile
Charles (Charlie) Citrine
Kathleen (Kathleen Tigler) Fleisher
Von Humboldt Fleisher
Renata Flonzaley
Menasha Klinger
Renata (Fat-Tits, Renata Flonzaley,
   Miss Universe) Koffritz
Louie Lutz
Naomi Lutz
George Swiebel
Pierre Thaxter
Kathleen Tigler
Wald Waldemar

### More Die of Heartbreak (1987)
Benn Crader
William Layamon
Kenneth Trachtenberg
Harold Vilitzer

### Mr. Sammler's Planet (1970)
Margotte Arkin
Walter Bruch
Eisen
Lionel Feffer
Angela Gruner
Dr. Arnold (Elya) Gruner
Dr. V. Govinda Lal
Artur (Slim-Jim, Uncle Sammler)
   Sammler
Shula (Shula-Slawa) Sammler

## PETER BENCHLEY

### *Jaws* (1974)
Ellen Brody
Martin Brody
Great White Shark
Matthew (Matt) Hooper
Harry Meadows
Quint
Lawrence P. Vaughan
Christine (Chrissie) Watkins

## ELIZABETH BENEDICT

### *Slow Dancing* (1985)
Bosworth ("Boz")
Molly Compton
Michael Cooper
Curtis
Easterbrook
Emma
Roger Gaston
Gretchen
Richard Healy
Ingstrom
Paul Jacobson
Eric Lord
Marie
Nell
Melissa deKalb Owen
Mark Peyser
Sean
Stephen Shipler
Lexi Steiner
Mr. Steiner
Mrs. Steiner
David Wiley
Louise Wiley

## SANDRA BENÍTEZ

### *A Place Where the Sea Remembers* (1994)
Lina Beltrán
Rafael Beltrán
Beto Burgos
César Burgos
Esperanza Clemente
Justo Flores
Fulgencio Llanos
Candelario Marroquín
Rosario (Chayo) Marroquín
Remedios
Marta Rodríguez

## HAL BENNETT

### *The Black Wine* (1968)
Dolly Anderson
Viola Anderson
Lizzie Bartley
Robert Bartley
Ida (Cordelia) Carlisle
Maybelline (Mae) Cobb
Norman Eisenberg
Judith Finkel
Clair Hunter
David Hunter
Henry Hunter
Jerry Kaplan
Eloise (Hunter) McLindon
Miss Pemberton

### *Lord of Dark Places* (1970)
Miss Lavinia Barton
Odessa Barton
Tony Brenzo
Mary Cheap
Lamont Cranston Jones
Mavis (China Doll) Lee
Joe Market
Madame Eudora Market
Odessa Barton Market
Ramona Market
Roosevelt Market
Titus Market

### *Seventh Heaven* (1976)
Viola Anderson
Herman Baskerville
Maria Befies
Bobby Bryant
Reverend Winston Cobb
Dicey
Mrs. Greco
Bill Kelsey
Serena Kelsey
Zachary Kelsey
Aunt Keziah
Clair (Miss Page) Page
Nellie Royster

### *Wait Until the Evening* (1974)
Cora Brittain
Dolores Brittain
Kevin Brittain
Minnie Brittain
Paul Brittain
Percy Brittain
Shadrach (Grandpa, Mr. Brittain) Brittain

Ida (Cordelia) Carlisle
Maybelline (Mae) Cobb
Reverend Winston Cobb
The Idiot
Eric (Cop) Magee
Janet Magee
Joe Market
Titus Market
Miss Pemberton
Henry Robinson

### *A Wilderness of Vines* (1966)
Luann Asher
Birchie Bartley
Calvin LeRoy Bartley
Lizzie Bartley
Robert Bartley
Blessed Belshazzar
Darlene Mosby Carlisle
Ida (Cordelia) Carlisle
Maybelline (Mae) Cobb
Reverend Winston Cobb
Charlie Hooker
Janus Manning
Janus Eugene (Gene) Manning II
Neva Blanche Stapleton Manning
Otha Manning
Dr. Stanhope
Miss Whittle

## THOMAS BERGER
## (See also Volume I)

### *Arthur Rex* (1978)
Agravaine
Arthur
Gawaine
Guinevere
Isold of the White Hands
La Belle Isold
Lady of the Lake
Launcelot
Margawse
Merlin
Mordred
Morgan la Fey
Ragnell
Tristram

### *Killing Time* (1967)
Arthur Bayson
Betty Starr Bayson
Harry C. Clegg
Joseph (Joe) Detweiler
Henry Webster Melrose

James T. Shuster
Andrew Starr
Tierney

### *Little Big Man* (1964)

Caroline (Calamity Jane) Crabb
Jack (Little Big Man) Crabb
Olga Crabb
George Armstrong Custer
James Butler (Duck Bill, Wild Bill)
  Hickok
Hump
Little Horse
Morning Star
Old Lodge Skins
Mrs. (Mrs. P.) Pendrake
Reverend Silas Pendrake
Ralph Fielding Snell
Sunshine
Buffalo Wallow Woman
Younger Bear

### *Regiment of Women* (1973)

Lieutenant Aster
Georgie Cornell
Harriet (Harry the Rapist)
Charlie Harrison
Doctor Prine
Stanley

### *Reinhart in Love* (1962)

Beatrice (Bea, Bee) Fedder
Niles Fedder
Lorenz T. Goodykuntz
Claude Humbold
Splendor Gallant Mainwaring
Gloria Monday
Blaine Raven
Genevieve Raven (Gen) Reinhart
George Reinhart
Maw Reinhart

### *Sneaky People* (1975)

Horse Hauser
Clarence Honeywell
Leo Kirsch
Laverne Linda Hogan Lorraine
Naomi (Mary Joy) Sandifer
Ralph Virgil (Ralphie) Sandifer
Virgil (Buddy) Sandifer

### *Vital Parts* (1970)

Raymond (Captain Bruno Storm)
  Mainwaring
Splendor Gallant Mainwaring
Gloria Monday

Dr. Barker Munsing
Eunice Munsing
Blaine Raven
Blaine Reinhart
Carlo B. (Carl) Reinhart
Genevieve Raven (Gen) Reinhart
Winona Reinhart
Johann (Hans) Steckfuss
Captain Bruno Storm
Robert (Bob, Sweetie) Sweet

### *Who Is Teddy Villanova?* (1977)

Gus Bakewell
Alice Ellish
Carl Knox
Natalie Novotny
Calvin Peachtree
Sam Polidor
Margaret Mary Bernadette (Peggy)
  Tumulty
Teddy Villanova
Donald Washburn II
Russel (Russ) Wren
Harry Zwingli

# WENDELL BERRY
# (See also Volume I)

### *The Memory of Old Jack* (1974)

Joe Banion
Nettie Banion
Jack (Old Jack) Beechum
Lightening Berlew
Sylvania (Smoothbore) Berlew
Milton Burgess
Andy Catlett
Bess Feltner Catlett
Henry Catlett
Wheeler Catlett
Burley (Uncle Burley) Coulter
David (Dave) Coulter
Hannah Coulter
Jarrat Coulter
Mathew Burley (Mattie) Coulter
Nathan Coulter
Jonah (J., Jayber, Jaybird) Crow
Ben Feltner
Margaret (Little Margaret) Feltner
Margaret Finley Feltner
Mat Feltner
Nancy Beechum Feltner
Mrs. (Suzy) Hendrick
Frank Lathrop
Jasper Lathrop

Ruth Lightwood
Sims McGrother
Clay McInnis
Rose McInnis
Elton Penn
Mary Penn
Clara Beechum Pettit
Gladston (Glad) Pettit
Will Wells
Brother Wingfare

### *Nathan Coulter* (1960)

Jack (Old Jack) Beechum
Margaret Finley Feltner
Mat Feltner

### *A Place on Earth* (1967)

Joe Banion
Nettie Banion
Jack (Old Jack) Beechum
Big Ellis
Milton Burgess
Andy Catlett
Bess Feltner Catlett
Henry Catlett
Wheeler Catlett
Burley (Uncle Burley) Coulter
Hannah Coulter
Jarrat Coulter
Nathan Coulter
Tom Coulter
Annie Crop
Gideon Crop
Ida Crop
Jonah (J., Jayber, Jaybird) Crow
Bess Feltner
Hannah Feltner
Margaret (Little Margaret) Feltner
Margaret Finley Feltner
Mat Feltner
Virgil Feltner
Ernest (Shamble) Finley
Stanley Gibbs
Mrs. (Suzy) Hendrick
Frank Lathrop
Jasper Lathrop
Roger Merchant
Whacker Spradlin

# DORIS BETTS

### *The River to Pickle Beach* (1972)

George Bennett
Pauline (Polly) Buncombe
Willis Buncombe

Foley Dickinson
Earl Fetner
Grace Fetner
Mary Ruth Packard Fetner
Randy Fetner
Treva (Tweet) Fetner
Troy Fetner
Mickey McCane
Pinhead
Beatrice Fetner (Bebe) Sellars
Jack S. Sellars
Miss Whitaker

## WILLIAM PETER BLATTY

*The Exorcist* (1971)
Burke Dennings
Captain (Nowonmai, Satan) Howdy
Damien Karras
William F. Kinderman
Chris MacNeil
Regan Teresa (Rags) MacNeil
Lankester Merrin
Sharon Spencer

## LAWRENCE BLOCK

*A Dance at the Slaughterhouse* (1992)
Mick Ballou
Elaine Mardell
Matthew (Matt) Scudder
Bergen Stettner
Richard Thurman

## JUDY BLUME

*Smart Women* (1983)
Andrew Broder
Francine "B. B." Brady Broder
Sara Broder
Clare Carleton-Robbins
Margo Sampson
Michelle Sampson
Stuart Sampson

*Summer Sisters* (1998)
Joseph Brudegher
Tawny Leonard
Victoria (Vix) Leonard
Caitlin Somers
Lambert Mayhew (Lamb) Somers

*Wifey* (1978)
Gordon Lefferts
Myra Lefferts

Lisbeth Mosley
Vincent Mosley
Norman Pressman
Sandy (Sondra) Pressman
Shep Resnick
Mona Schaedel

## T. CORAGHESSAN BOYLE

*The Road to Wellville* (1993)
John Harvey Kellog
Will Lightbody
Charles Ossing

*The Tortilla Curtain* (1995)
Delaney Mossbacher
Kyra Mossbacher
America Rincon
Candido Rincon

## RICHARD BRAUTIGAN

*The Abortion* (1971)
Mrs. Charles Fine Adams
Harlow Blade, Jr.
Foster
Doctor Garcia
Vida Kramar
Mr. Librarian (Candyman)

*A Confederate General from Big Sur* (1964)
Cynthia
Roy Earle
Elaine
Elizabeth
Jesse
Augustus Mellon
Lee Mellon
Susan
Johnston (Roy Earle) Wade

*Dreaming of Babylon* (1977)
Miss Ann (Our Lady of the Limitless Bladder)
C. (Eye, Stew Meat) Card
Mr. Cleveland
Dr. Abdul Forsythe
Dr. Francis
Sam Herschberger
Nana-dirat
Peg-leg
Sergeant Rink
Smiley
Smith Smith

*The Hawkline Monster* (1974)
Cameron
Greer
Susan Hawkline
Jane Hawkline
Professor Hawkline
Hawkline Monster
Marvin Cora Jones
Magic Child
Mr. Morgan
Pills
Jack Williams

*Trout Fishing in America* (1967)
Art
Maria Callas
Alonso Hagan
Charles Hayman
The Mayor of the Twentieth Century
Mr. Norris
Pard
Rebel Smith
Trout Fishing in America
Trout Fishing in America Shorty

*Willard and His Bowling Trophies* (1975)
Bob
John
Logan brothers
Patricia (Pat)
Willard

## CECIL BROWN

*The Life and Loves of Mr. Jiveass Nigger* (1969)
Pat
Ned Green
Bob (Satan) Jacobs
Jero
Melvin (Doc) Jerrell
Reb
Gloria Rowan
Thomas Rowan
Ruth Smith
George (Byron, Efan, Julius Makewell, Anthony Miller, Paul Winthrop) Washington

## LARRY BROWN

*Father and Son* (1996)
Dorris Baker
Sue Baker
Frankie Barlow

Bobby Blanchard
Mary Blanchard
Jewell Coleman
David
Emma Lee Davis
Glen Davis
Randolph (Puppy) Davis
Theron Davis
Virgil Davis
Ed Hall
Judy Hall
Erline Price
Brother Roy

## RITA MAE BROWN

### Bingo (1988)

Charles Falkenroth
Jackson Frost
Regina Frost
Peter Gerald Grayson
Disraeli Rife
Liz Rife
Michelle Saunders
Julia Ellen (Juts) Hunsenmeir Smith
Nichole (Nickel) Smith
Louise Trumbell
Ed Tutweiler Walters

### Cat on the Scent (1999)

Blair Bainbridge
Cynthia Cooper
Mary Minor (Harry) Haristeen
Miranda Hogendobber
Mrs. Murphy
Pewter
Rick Shaw
Tee Tucker
Tally Urquhart

### Loose Lips (1999)

Trudy Archer
(Extra) Billy Bitters
Ramelle Bowman
Celeste Chalfonte
Cora Zepp Hunsenmeir
Hansford Hunsenmeir
Chester (Chessy) Smith
Josephine Holtzapple Smith
Julia Ellen (Juts) Hunsenmeir Smith
Nichole (Nickel) Smith
Louise (Wheezie) Hunsenmeir Trumbell
Maizie Trumbell
Mary Trumbell
Paul (Pearlie) Trumbell

### Murder, She Meowed (1996)

Nigel Danforth
Linda Forloines
Will Forloines
Coty Lamont
Mickey Townsend
Adelia (Addie) Valiant
Charles (Chark) Valiant

### Murder at Monticello (1994)

Mary Minor Haristeen
Pharamond Haristeen
Miranda Hogendobber
Marilyn Sanburne

### Rubyfruit Jungle (1973)

Alice Bellantoni
Polina Bellantoni
Leota B. Bisland
Carl Bolt
Carrie Bolt
Molly (Moll) Bolt
Calvin
Ep Denman
Jennifer (Jenna) Denman
Leroy Denman
Ted Denman
Brockhurst (Broc, Broccoli) Detwiler
Paul Digita
Holly
Connie Penn
Faye (Faysie) Raider
Rhea Rhadin
Carolyn Simpson
Florence Wegenlied

### Six of One (1978)

(Extra) Billy Bitters
Ramelle Bowman
Celeste Chalfonte
Curtis Chalfonte
Spottiswood (Spotty) Chalfonte
Fannie Jump Creighton
Cora Hunsenmeir
Aimes Rankin
Brutus Rife
Chester (Chessy) Smith
Julia Ellen (Juts) Hunsenmeir Smith
Nichole (Nickel) Smith
Fairy Thatcher
Louise (Wheezie) Hunsenmeir Trumbell
Maizie Trumbell
Mary Trumbell
Paul (Pearlie) Trumbell
Carlotta Van Dusen

## ED BULLINS

### The Reluctant Rapist (1973)

Aunt Bess (Bessie)
Steven (Chuckie, Dandy, Steve, Stevie)
  Benson
Jack Bowen
Marie Ann Bowen
Uncle Clyde
Ricardo S. (Rick) Evans
Lenard (Len)
Lou Ellen

## JERRY BUMPUS

### Anaconda (1967)

Carl
Claire
Adaline Fletcher
E. L. Fletcher
Jimmy
Alonzo (Lon) McCaferty
Vera

## JAMES LEE BURKE

### Black Cherry Blues (1989)

Sally Dio
Darlene American Horse
Dixie Lee Pugh
Cletus Purcel
Alafair Robicheaux
Annie Robicheaux
Dave Robicheaux

## WILLIAM S. BURROUGHS
## (See also Volume I)

### Exterminator! (1973)

A. J. (Merchant of Sex) (See Volume I)
B. J.
Dr. (Doc) Benway (See Volume I)
Audrey Carsons
Ali Juan (God of Street Boys) Chapulte-
  pec
Clancy
Jerry (the Lemon Kid)
Johnny
William (Bill, Billy, Lee the Agent, El
  Hombre Invisible, Klinker, Inspector
  J. Lee, William Seward) Lee (See Vol-
  ume I)
Homer (Purple Better One) Mandrill
Tio Mate

*Patternmaster* (1976)
Amber
Coransee
Lady Darah
Iray
Jansee
Joachim
Michael
Rain
Rayal
Suliana
Teray

*Survivor* (1978)
Choh
Dint
Gehl
Gehnahteh
Nathan James
Natahk
Tahneh
Tien
Alanna (Lanna) Verrick
Jules Verrick
Neila Verrick

## GEORGE CAIN

*Blueschild Baby* (1970)
James (J. B.) Black
George (Georgie, Daddy George, Junior) Cain
Keith (Raschid) Cain
Mom Cain
Pop (Grandad) Cain
Ralph (Ralphie) Cotton
Jose
Nandy
Nichole
Raschid
Sabrina (Bu, Sabu)
Sun

## TRUMAN CAPOTE
## (See also Volume I)

*In Cold Blood* (1965)
Roy Church
Bonnie Fox Clutter
Herbert William Clutter
Kenyon Clutter
Nancy Clutter
Alvin Adams (Al) Dewey
Clarence Duntz
Richard Eugene (Dick) Hickock

Susan Kidwell
Harold Nye
Bobby Rupp
Perry Edward Smith
Floyd Wells

## CALEB CARR

*The Alienist* (1994)
John Beecham
Sara Howard
Lazlo Kriezler
John Schuyler Moore
Theodore Roosevelt

## JOHN CASEY

*Spartina* (1989)
Elsie Buttrick
Joxer Goode
Larry Parker
Miss Perry
Charlie Pierce
Dick Pierce
May Pierce
Tom Pierce
Mary Scanlon
Captain Texeira
Marie Van der Hoevel
Schuyler Van der Hoevel
Eddie Wormsley

## FRED CHAPPELL

*Brighten the Corner Where You Are* (1989)
Virgil Campbell
Lewis Dorson
Burrell Farnum
Janie Forbes
Jubal Henry
Jess Kirkman
Joe Robert Kirkman

*Dagon* (1968)
Bella
Dagon
Enid
Annie Leland
Peter Leland
Sheila Leland
Ed Morgan
Mina Morgan
Coke Rymer

*The Gaudy Place* (1972)
Arkie
Clemmie
Andrew T. Harper
Katherine (Katy) Harper
Linn Harper
Zebulon Johns (Zeb) Mackie
James Parker (Arkie) McClellan
Oxie
Ted (Oxieodorik Paparikis) Pape

*The Inkling* (1965)
Jan Anderson
Jenny Nolan Anderson
Timmie Anderson
Lora Bowen
Ronny (Root) Hughes
Hezekiah (Uncle Hake) Nolan
Lora Bowen Nolan

*It Is Time, Lord* (1963)
Virgil Campbell
Cory Christopher
David (Davy) Christopher
James (Jimmy) Christopher
Julia Christopher
Sylvia Christopher
Jack Davis
Judy Davis
Mavis
Preacher
James D. (Jimmy, Preach, Preacher) Smathers, Jr.

## JOAN CHASE

*During the Reign of the Queen of Persia* (1983)
Anne
Rolfe Barker
Hank Browning
Rachel Buck
Tom Buck
Burl
Celia
Corley
Dan
Del
Della
Della's mother
Elinor
Florence
Grace "Grady"
Hat
Jenny

Jimmy
Katie
Jacob "Grandad" "Jake" Krauss
Lil "Gram" "Queenie" Krauss
Libby
Phillip Materson
May
Molly
Rosalie Morgan
Neil
Louanne Price
Rossie
Selma
Ruthie Thompson
Valerie
Mrs. Warren
Mr. Weiner

## JOHN CHEEVER
## (See also Volume I)

*Bullet Park* (1969)
Marietta Drum Hammer
Paul Hammer
Eliot Nailles
Nellie Nailles
Tony Nailles
Gretchen Shurz Oxencroft
Swami Rutuola
Franklin Pierce Taylor

*Falconer* (1978)
Chicken Number Two
Deputy Warden Chisholm
Cuckold
Eben Farragut
Ezekiel (Zeke) Farragut
Marcia Farragut
Jody
Cardinal Thaddeus Morgan
Tiny

*The Wapshot Scandal* (1964)
Mr. Applegate
Dr. Lemuel (Bracciani) Cameron
Emile Cramner
Griza
Norman Johnson
Gertrude (Dirty Gertie) Lockhart
Betsey MacCaffery Wapshot (See Volume I)
Coverly Wapshot (See Volume I)
Ezekiel Wapshot (See Volume I)
Honora Wapshot (See Volume I)
Leander Wapshot (See Volume I)

Melissa Scaddon Wapshot (See Volume I)
Moses Wapshot (See Volume I)
Sarah Coverly Wapshot (See Volume I)

## SUSAN CHEEVER

*The Cage* (1982)
Cecile Bristol
Julia Bristol
William Bristol

*Looking for Work* (1979)
Mike Abrams
Max Angelo
Jason Gardens
Salley Gardens
Joel Stansky
Colin Willes

## SANDRA CISNEROS

*The House on Mango Street* (1989)
Esperanza Codero

## TOM CLANCY

*The Cardinal of the Kremlin*
(1988)
Archer
Gennady Iosifovich Bondarenko
Mikhail Semyonovich (Misha) Filitov
Mary Pat Foley
Nikolay Borissovich Gerasimov
Al Gregory
Andrey Il'ych Narmonov
Jack (John Patrick) Ryan
Beatrice (Bea) Taussig
Klementi Vladimirovich Vatutin

*Clear and Present Danger* (1989)
Domingo (Ding) Chavez
John Clark
Felix Cortez
James Cutter
Daniel Murray
Bob Ritter
Jack (John Patrick) Ryan

*Debt of Honor* (1994)
John Clark
Roger Durling
Robert (Robby) Jackson
Manuel (Portagee) Oreza

Jack (John Patrick) Ryan
Torajiro Sato
George Winston
Raizo Yamata

*Executive Orders* (1996)
Mahmoud Haji Daryaei
Pat O'Day
John Plumber
Andrea Price
Jeff Raman
Jack (John Patrick) Ryan

*The Hunt for Red October* (1984)
James Greer
Marco Ramius
Jack (John Patrick) Ryan

*Patriot Games* (1987)
James Greer
Sean Miller
Kevin Joseph O'Donnell
Caroline Muller Ryan
Jack (John Patrick) Ryan

*Rainbow Six* (1998)
Carol Brightling
John Brightling
Domingo (Ding) Chavez
John Clark
William Henriksen
John Killgore
Dmitry Arkadeyevich Popov

*Red Storm Rising* (1986)
Pavel Leonidovich (Pasha) Alekseyev
(General) Andreyev
Mike Edwards
Daniel X. McCafferty
Edward Morris
Mikhail Eduardovich Sergetov
Robert M. (Bob) Toland

*Without Remorse* (1993)
Mark Charon
James Greer
Nikolay Yevgeniyevich (Kolya) Grishanov
Walter (Wally) Hicks
John Kelly
Pamela (Pam) Madden
Sandy O'Toole
Emmet Ryan
Henry Tucker
Robin Zacharias

## ROBERT CLARK

*Mr. White's Confession* (1998)
Margaret (Maggie)
Welshinger
Horner Wesley
Herbert W. White

## JACKIE COLLINS

*Hollywood Husbands* (1986)
Heaven Anderson
Silver Anderson
Clarissa Browning
Mannon Cable
Melanie-Shanna Cable
Jade Johnson
Zachary Klinger
Wes Money
Jack Python
Howard Solomon
Poppy Solomon
Whitney Cable Valentine

## CYRUS COLTER

*The Hippodrome* (1973)
Bea
Cleo
Darlene
Donald
Iris
Alberto (Albert [Bert, Bertie]
  Kalandyk) Mogadiscio
Mack Thomas
Jackson (William [Bill, Willie] Carter)
  Yeager

*The Rivers of Eros* (1972)
Alexis
Ambrose Hammer
Chester (Ches) Jackson
Pearl (Pearlie) Jackson
Adeline (Addie) Parker
Lester Parker
Ruby Parker
Zack Parker
Clotilda (Clo) Pilgrim
James (Alexis) Potts
Dunreith (Smitty) Smith
Hyacinth Turner

## EVAN CONNELL
## (See also Volume I)

*Mr. Bridge* (1969)
Madge Arlen

Grace Barron
Virgil Barron
Carolyn (Corky) Bridge
Douglas Bridge
India Bridge
Ruth Bridge
Walter Bridge
Harriett
Alice Jones
Julia

## PAT CONROY

*The Great Santini* (1976)
Virgil (Virge) Hedgepath
Benjamin (Ben) Meecham
Karen Meecham
Lillian Meecham
Mary Anne Meecham
Matthew (Matt) Meecham
W. P. (Bull) Meecham
Red Pettus
Arrabelle Smalls
Toomer Smalls
Alice (Mamaw) Sole
Joseph (Joe) Varney

*The Prince of Tides* (1986)
Patrick Flaherty
Sarah Jenkins
Gunther Kraus
Susan Lowenstein
Otis Miller
Isabel Newbury
Reese Newbury
Todd Newbury
Tolitha Wingo Stanopoulos
Benji Washington
Amos Wingo
Henry Wingo
Lila Trent Wingo
Luke Wingo
Sallie Pierson Wingo
Savannah Wingo
Tom Wingo
Bernard Woodruff
Herbert Woodruff

## THOMAS H. COOK

*The Chatham School Affair* (1996)
Elizabeth Rockbridge Channing
Alice Craddock
Sarah Doyle

Arthur Griswald
Henry Griswald
Mildred Griswald
Abigail Reed
Leland Reed
Mary Alice Reed

## ROBERT COOVER

*Gerald's Party* (1986)
Alison
Gerald (Gerry)
Gerald's wife
Howard
Inspector Pardew
Roger
Ros
Sally Ann
Tania
Vachel
Vic

*The Origin of the Brunists* (1966)
Father Battista Baglione
Abner Baxter
Frances (Black Piggy, Franny) Baxter
Nathan (Black Hand, Nat) Baxter
Paul (Black Peter, Paulie) Baxter
Sarah Baxter
Angela (Angie) Bonali
Charlie Bonali
Etta Bonali
Vince Bonali
Happy Bottom
Antonio Bruno
Emilia Bruno
Giovanni Bruno
Marcella Bruno
Joe Castiglione
Theodore (Ted) Cavanaugh
Tommy (Kit, Kitten) Cavanaugh
Hiram Clegg
Clara Collins
Elaine Collins
Ely Collins
Wanda Cravens
Barney Davis
Domiron
Wesley Edwards
Elan
Jim Elliott
Wally Fisher
Ralph Himebaugh
Lou Jones
Karmin

Ko-li
Colin Meredith
Justin (Tiger) Miller
Eleanor Norton
Wylie Norton
Carl Dean Palmers
Annie (Girl Fried Egg) Pompa
Rahim
Dee Romano
Michael (Mike) Strelchuk
Mortimer (Mort) Whipple
Womwom
Ben Wosznik

### The Public Burning (1977)
Dwight David Eisenhower
Richard Nixon
Phantom
Ethel Greenglass Rosenberg
Julius Rosenberg
Sam (Uncle Sam Yankee Peddler)
  Slick

### The Universal Baseball Association, Inc., J. Henry Waugh, Prop. (1968)
Jock Casey
Benny Diskin
Lou Engel
Hettie Irden
Molly
Pete (Jake)
Mitch Porter
Damon Rutherford
B. Valentine
J. Henry Waugh
Horace Zifferblatt

## GREGORY CORSO

### The American Express (1961)
D
Daphne
Dad Deform
Horatio (Sgarlotto) Frump
Carrol Grilhiggen
Harry
Hinderov
Angus Plow
Simon
Scratch Vatic
Rodger Wolfherald

## HARRY CREWS

### Car (1972)
Homer Edge

Joe
Easton (Easy) Mack
Herman Mack
Junell Mack
Mister Mack
Margaret (Margo)

### A Feast of Snakes (1976)
Duffy Deeter
Susan Gender
George
Lottie Mae
Lummy
Beatriz Dargan (Beeder) Mackey
Big Joe Mackey
Joe Lon Mackey
Shep Martin
Buddy Matlow
Willard Miller
Luther Peacock
Berenice Sweet
Hard Candy Sweet
Tump Walker

### Karate Is a Thing of the Spirit (1971)
Belt (Alonzo Fiber)
George
John Kaimon
Lazarus
Marvin
Jefferson Davis Munroe
Gaye Nell Odell
Mavis Odell

## MICHAEL CRICHTON

### The Andromeda Strain (1969)
Karen Anson
Alan Benedict
Charles (Barton) Burton
Edgar Comroe
Lewis Crane
Mark William Hall
Peter Jackson
Jaggers
Christian Kirke
Peter Leavitt
Arthur Manchek
Arthur Morris
Jamie Ritter
Robertson
Roger Shawn
Smithson
Gladys Stevens
Jeremy Stone

Martin Willis
Samuel (Gunner) Wilson

### The Great Train Robbery (1975)
Robert Agar
Sir John Alderston
Barlow
Richard Burgess
Teddy Burke
Bill Chokee
Laurence Chubb, Jr.
Henry Fowler
Edward Harranby
Jeremy Johnson, Sr.
Susan Lang
McPherson
Miss (Brigid Lawson, Lady Charlotte
  Simms) Miriam
Alice Nelson
Edward (Robert Jeffersndrew Miller,
  John Simms, Arthur Wills) Pierce
Jimmy Shaw
Edgar Trent
Elizabeth Trent
William (Clean Willy) Williams

### Jurassic Park (1990)
Alan Grant
John Hammond
Ian Malcolm
Ellie Sattler

### The Lost World (1995)
R. B. "Arby" Benton
Kelly Curtis
Sarah Harding
Richard Levine
Ian Malcolm
John "Jack" Thorne

### The Terminal Man (1972)
John Anders
Craig Beckerman
Harold Franklin (Harry) Benson
Angela (Doris Blankfurt) Black
John Ellis
Farley
Gerhard
Manon
Roger A. (Rog) McPherson
Robert Morris
Ramos
Richards
Janet (Jan) Ross

## MICHAEL CUNNINGHAM

*The Hours* (1998)
Angelica Bell
Julian Bell
Quentin Bell
Vanessa Bell
Nelly Boxall
Dan Brown
Laura Brown
Richard (Richie) Brown
Walter Hardy
Kitty
Mary Krull
Louis
Oliver St. Ives
Sally
Clarissa Vaughan
Julia Vaughan
Leonard Woolf
Virginia Woolf

## H. D.
## (See also Volume I)

*Helen in Egypt* (1961)
Achilles
Helen (Helena, Helen of Troy)
Paris
Theseus
Thetis

## NICHOLAS DELBANCO

*Fathering* (1973)
Chloe Duboise
Andrew (Jake) Hepburn III
Alain Hugues
Chantal Hugues
Alexander Mueller
Elizabeth Mueller
Hans Mueller
Marian Mueller
Robert Mueller
Susan Mueller

*In the Middle Distance* (1971)
Astrid
Jean Burling
Tunis G. Campbell
Andrea Delbanco
Barbara Delbanco
Evelyn (Eve) Delbanco

Michael Delbanco
Nicholas (Nicky) Delbanco
Nat Kott
Peter Sim

*The Martlet's Tale* (1966)
Anna-Maria Charaiambos
Chrysanthi (Chrýsomou)
Mehmet Effendi
Sotiris (Sotis) Procopirios
Andreas Procopirios
Apelis Procopirios
Eleni Procopirios
Manos Procopirios
Nicoletta Procopirios
Orsetta Procopirios
Triphon Procopirios
Alexis Saranditis
Dania Saranditis
Phillipos Stritsas

*News* (1970)
Adelina
Allan
Tunis G. Campbell
Elaine Dade
Gifford (Gip)
Harrison (Hal, Harry)
Karen
Sam
Carlos Scotobal
Emelyn Walley

*Possession* (1977)
Samson Finney
James (Jamie) Pearson
Samuel (Sam) Powers
Anne-Maria Sherbrooke Sheldon
Harriet (Hattie) Sherbrooke
Judah (Jude) Porteous Sherbrooke
Lisbeth McPherson Sherbrooke
Margaret (Maggie, Meg, Megan) Cutler
    Sherbrooke
Seth Sherbrooke

*Sherbrookes* (1978)
Hal Boudreau
Sarah (Sally) Conover
Samson Finney
Andrew Kincannon
Anne-Maria Sherbrooke Sheldon
Willard Sheldon
Daniel (Peacock) Sherbrooke
Harriet (Hattie) Sherbrooke
Ian Daniel Sherbrooke
Judah (Jude) Porteous Sherbrooke

Margaret (Maggie, Meg, Megan) Cutler
    Sherbrooke
Seth Sherbrooke

*Small Rain* (1975)
Elise Crawford
Reuben Crawford
Harald von Einzeedle
James von Einzeedle
Maija von Einzeedle
Thomas von Einzeedle
Anthony (Jeeves) Hope-Harding
Janet Hope-Harding

## DON DELILLO

*Americana* (1971)
Clinton Harkavy Bell
David Bell
Bobby Brand
Clevenger
Carol Deming
Weede Denney
Binky Lister
Jack Wilson Pike
Sullivan
Ted Warburton

*End Zone* (1972)
Anatole Bloomberg
Myna Corbett
Emmett Creed
Gary Harkness
Taft Robinson
Major Staley
Alan Zapalac

*Great Jones Street* (1973)
Azarian
Bohack
Edward B. (Ed, Eddie) Fenig
Globke
Opel Hampson
Hanes
Dr. Pepper
Watney
Bucky Wunderlick

*Mao II* (1991)
Charles Everson
Bill Gray
George Haddad
Karen Janney
Scott Martineau
Brita Nilsson

J. Pierpont Morgan
Mother
Mother's Younger Brother (Younger
  Brother)
Evelyn Nesbit
Sarah
Tateh (Baron Aslikenazy)
Harry K. Thaw
Coalhouse Walker, Jr.
Booker T. Washington
Stanford (Stanny) White

## HARRIET DOERR

*Consider This, Senora* (1993)
Francisco Alvarado
Susan Ames
Tim Ames
Frances Bowles
Ursula Bowles
Don Enrique Ortiz De Leon
Altagracia Gomez
Bert Loomis

*Stones for Ibarra* (1984)
Remedios Acosta
Richard Everton
Sara Everton
Luis Fuentes
(Cura) Juan Gomez
Maria (de) Lourdes
Jesus (Chuy) Santos

## J. P. DONLEAVY

*The Ginger Man* (1965)
Christine
Percy Clocklan
Marion Dangerfield
Sebastian Dangerfield
Lilly Frost
MacDoon
Tony Malarkey
Mary
Kenneth O'Keefe
Egbert Skully

## RICHARD DOOLING

*White Man's Grave* (1994)
Moussa Kamara
Michael Killigan
Randall Killigan
Sam Lewis

Kabba Lundo
Idrissa Moiwo
Jenisa Moiwo
Aruna Sisay
Pa Ansumana Sisay
Boone Wesffall
The Witchfinder

## MICHAEL DORRIS

*A Yellow Raft in Blue Water* (1987)
Babe
Clara
Foxy (Kennedy) Cree
Pauline George Cree
Ellen DeMarco
Evelyn Dial
Sky (Norman) Dial
Ida George
Lee George
Father Hurlburt
Dayton Nickles
Father Tom Novak
Willard Pretty Boy
Annabelle Stiffarm
Christine George Taylor
Elgin Taylor
Rayona Taylor

## JOHN GREGORY DUNNE

*True Confessions* (1977)
Jack Amsterdam
Dan T. Campion
Frank Crotty
Hugh Danaher
Lois Fazenda
Fuqua
Corinne Morris
Harold Herman Pugh
Brenda Samuels
Desmond (Des) Spellacy
Mary Margaret Maher Spellacy
Thomas (Tom) Spellacy

## JUNIUS EDWARDS

*If We Must Die* (1963)
Flip
Will Harris
Jeff
Luke
Sam
Tom

## STANLEY ELKIN

*A Bad Man* (1967)
Bisch
Leonard Dedman
Billy Feldman
Isidore Feldman
Leo Feldman
Lilly Feldman
Warden Fisher
Dr. Freedman
Silvia Lane
Ed Slipper
Norman Victman

*Boswell* (1964)
James Boswell
Margaret Boswell
Leon Herlitz
Nate Lace
Principessa Margaret dei Medici
Morton (Morty) Perlmutter
John (Angel of Death, Grim Reaper)
  Sallow
Felix (The Great Sandusky) Sandusky

*The Dick Gibson Show* (1971)
Edmond (Sordino) Behr-Bleibtreau
Lieutenant Collins
Louis Credenza
Miriam Desebour
Dick (Tex Ellery, Ted Elmer, Ted Elson,
  Ellery Loyola, Marshall Maine, etc.)
  Gibson
Henry Harper
Miriam Desebour Kranz
Norman
Jack Patterson
Bernard (Bernie) Perk
Sansori
Sordino
Pepper Steep
Arthur Vendler

*The Franchiser* (1976)
Julius Finsberg
Patty Finsberg
Finsberg children
Benjamin (Ben) Flesh
Roger Foster
Dick (Tex Ellery, Ted Elmer, Ted Elson,
  Ellery Loyola, Marshall Maine, etc.)
  Gibson
Flight Lieutenant Tanner
Dr. Wolfe

Tom Booker
Joan Dyer
Robert Graves
Liz Hammond
Harry Logan
Annie Graves Maclean
Grace Maclean
Pilgrim

## FREDERICK EXLEY

*A Fan's Notes* (1968)
Mr. Blue
The Counselor
Earl Exley
Frederick (Fred, Freddy) Exley
Patience Exley
Frank Gifford
Paddy the Duke
Christopher (Bumpy) Plumpton

## HOWARD FAST
## (See also Volume I)

*Second Generation* (1978)
Bernie Cohen
Marcel Duboise
Sam Goldberg
Barbara Lavette
Dan Lavette
Eloise Clawson Lavette
Joe Lavette
Tom Lavette
Adam Levy
Clair Levy
Jake Levy
Joshua Levy
Sally Levy
May Ling
Jean Lavette Whittier
Feng Wo

## WILLIAM FAULKNER
## (See also Volume I)

*The Reivers* (1962)
Bobo Beauchamp
James Thucydides (Tennie's Jim, Thucydus) Beauchamp (See Volume I)
Lucas Quintus Carothers McCaslin Beauchamp (See Volume I)
Tennie Beauchamp (See Volume I)
Lucius Binford (See Volume I)

Calvin (Uncle Cal) Bookwright (See Volume I)
Sam Caldwell
Uncle Willy Christian
Jason Lycurgus Compson (II) (See Volume I)
Miss Corrie
Carothers (Roth) Edmonds (See Volume I)
Carothers McCaslin (Old Cass) Edmonds (See Volume I)
Zachary Taylor (Zack) Edmonds (See Volume I)
Walter Ewell (See Volume I)
Sam Fathers (See Volume I)
Louis Grenier
Hope (Hub) Hampton (I) (See Volume I)
Hope (Little Hub) Hampton (II) (See Volume I)
Boon Hogganbeck (See Volume I)
Everbe Corinthia (Miss Corrie) Hogganbeck
Lucius Priest Hogganbeck (See Volume I)
Ikkemotubbe (Doom) (See Volume I)
Issetibbeha (See Volume I)
Colonel Linscomb
Butch Lovemaiden
Ludus
Luster (See Volume I)
Isaac (Ike) McCaslin (See Volume I)
Lucius Quintus Carothers (Old Carothers) McCaslin (See Volume I)
Ned McCaslin
Theophilus (Uncle Buck) McCaslin (See Volume I)
McWillie
Minnie (See Volume I)
Otis
Lucius Quintus Peabody (See Volume I)
Alexander Priest
Alison Lessep Priest
Lessep Priest
Lucius (Boss) Priest (I)
Lucius (Loosh) Priest (II)
Lucius Priest (III)
Maury Priest (I)
Maury Priest (II)
Sarah Edmonds Priest
Reba (Miss Reba) Rivers (See Volume I)
Bayard Sartoris (II)
Col. John Sartoris
Flem Snopes (See Volume I)

Major de Spain (See Volume I)
Manfred de Spain (See Volume I)
Lemuel Stevens
Uncle Willy

## SHELBY FOOTE
## (See also Volume I)

*September September* (1977)
Pod Jo (Pod J) Harris
Rufus (Rufe) Hutton
Eben Kinship
Lucinda (Sister Baby) Kinship
Martha Wiggins Kinship
Theo (Ted, Teddy) Kinship
Reeny (Reen) Jimson Perdew
Theo G. (Tio) Wiggins

## JESSE HILL FORD

*The Liberation of Lord Byron Jones* (1965)
Jimmy Bivens
Stanley Bumpas
Toonker Burkette
Johnnie Price Burkhalter
Oman Hedgepath
Emma Lee Lessenbery Jones
George Gordon Lord Byron (L. B.) Jones
Mama Lavorn
T. K. Morehouse
William (Sonny Boy) Mosby
Nella Liseth Mundine
Steve Mundine
Ike (Mr. Ike) Murphy
Erleen Parsons
Henry Parsons
Benny Smith
Willie Joe Worth

*Mountains of Gilead* (1961)
Toonker Burkette
Eleanor Fite
Gabe French, Sr.
Gabriel (Gabe) French
Mattie French
George Gordon Lord Byron (L. B.) Jones
Bo Jack Markham
Thomas Gideon (Tom) McCutcheon
Rev. Bartholomew Luther Meeks
Camack Patterson
Adam Shafer

Adam Gideon Shafer
Gratt Shafer
Octavia Ashmore (Madam) Shafer
Patricia Josephine (Patsy Jo) Mc-
    Cutcheon Shafer

*The Raider* (1975)
Edward Ashe
Ellen Poe Ashe
Betsy
Dutt Callister
Fancy Callister
Denise Chatillion
Jasper Coon
Col. Ennis Dalton
Gabriel (Gabe) French
Sim Homby
Timothy (Snail) Laird
Leola
Elias McCutcheon
Isaac McCutcheon
Jake McCutcheon
Thomas Gideon (Tom) McCutcheon
Willy McCutcheon
Shokotee McNeilly
Jane Nail
Sally Parham
Cargile Parham
Pettecasockee

## RICHARD FORD

*Independence Day* (1995)
Clarissa Bascombe
Frank Bascombe
Paul Bascombe
Myrlene Beavers
Karl Bemish
Sally Caldwell
Charlane
Ted Houlihan
Carter Knott
Vonda Lusk
Joe Markham
Phyllis Markham
Betty McLeod
Larry McLeod
Ann O'Dell
Charley O'Dell
Irv Ornstein
Tanks

*The Sportswriter* (1986)
Victory Wanda (Vicki) Arcenault
Frank Bascombe

X Dykstra-Bascombe
Walter Luckett
Herb Wallagher

## LEON FORREST

*The Bloodworth Orphans* (1977)
Jonathan Staunch Bass
Arlington Bloodworth III
Arlington Bloodworth, Sr.
Pourty Ford Worthy Bloodworth y
    Bloodworth
William S. (Willie) Body (Bloodworth)
Bella-Lenore Boltwood
Carl-Rae Bowman
Industrious Bowman
Abraham Ulysses (Abe) Dolphin
Rachel Rebecca Carpenter (Sister
    Rache) Flowers
W. W. W. (C. C. C., W. A. D., W. F.)
    Ford
Noah Ridgerook Grandberry
Lavinia Masterson
Regal Pettibone
Ironwood (Landlord) Rumble
LaDonna Scales
Amos-Otis Thigpen
Carrie Trout
Nathaniel Turner (Spoons) Wither-
    spoon

## FREDERICK FORSYTH

*The Day of the Jackal* (1971)
Jacqueline Dumas
Paul (the Armourer) Goossens
The Jackal ("le Chacal")
Claude Lebel
Marc Rodin

## CHARLES FRAZIER

*Cold Mountain* (1997)
Inman
Junior
Monroe
Ada Monroe
Pangle
Esco Swanger
Sally Swanger
Teague
Ruby Thewes
Stobrod Thewes
Solomon Veasey

## MARILYN FRENCH

*The Women's Room* (1977)
Ava (Delilah Lee)
Clarissa
Kyla Forrester
Isolde (Iso)
Martha Jackson
Lily
Mira (née Ward)
Norm
Adele O'Neill
Samantha (Sam) Simpson
Tadziewski (Tad)
Christine Truax
Valerie (Val)
Ben Voler

## WILLIAM GADDIS
## (See also Volume I)

*Carpenter's Gothic* (1985)
Elizabeth Booth
Paul Booth
Edie Grimes
Mr. McCandles
Adolph Vorakers
William Vorakers

*A Frolic of His Own* (1994)
Harold Basie
Oscar Crease
Trish Helmsley
Christina Lutz
Harry Lutz
Jawaharlal Madhar Pai

*JR* (1975)
Stella Bast Angel (Engels)
Edward Bast
Mr. Beaton
Governor John (Blackjack) Cates
Dave Davidoff
Thomas Eigen
Jack Gibbs
Amy Moncrieff Joubert
JR Vansant

## ERNEST J. GAINES

*The Autobiography of Miss Jane
Pittman* (1971)
Jimmy Aaron
Big Laura
Corporal Brown

Jane Brown
Albert Cluveau
Edward Stephen (Ned, Ned Brown)
  Douglass
Mary Agnes LeFabre
Joe (Chief) Pittman
Miss Jane (Jane Brown, Ticey) Pitiman
Robert (Tee Bob) Samson, Jr.
Robert Samson
Ticey
Timmy

*In My Father's House* (1978)
Octave Bacheron
Billy
Angelina (Nanane) Bouie
Albert Chenal
Chippo
Elijah Green
Shepherd (Shep) Lewis
Alma Martin
Reverend Phillip J. Martin
Anthony McVay
Howard Mills
Sheriff Nolan
Beverly Ricord
Jonathan Robillard
Erin (Chippo) Simon
Johanna Sims
Robert X (Etienne Sims)

*A Lesson Before Dying* (1993)
Jefferson
Tante Lou
Miss Emma
Grant Wiggins

*Of Love and Dust* (1967)
Louise Bonbon
Sidney Bonbon
Pauline Guerin
Marshall Hebert
Frank James (Jim, Geam) Kelly
Marcus (Marky) Payne
Julie (Aunt Julie, Miss Julie) Rand

## CRISTINA GARCIA

*Dreaming in Cuban* (1992)
Herminia Delgado
Celia del Pino
Ivanito del Pino
Javier del Pino
Jorge del Pino
Lourdes Puente
Pilar Puente

Rufino Puente
Milagro Villaverde
Felicia del Pino Villaverde
Hugo Villaverde
Luz Villaverde

## JOHN GARDNER

*Grendel* (1971)
Dragon
Grendel (Cowface)
Hrothgar
Hrothulf
Hygmod
Ork
Shaper
Unferth
Wealtheow

*Nickel Mountain* (1973)
Simon Bale
Doc Cathey
Norma Denitz
Willard Freund
Goat Lady (Mother)
Jimmy
Fred (Old Man) Judkins
George Loomis
Henry Soames
Calliope (Callie) Wells

*October Light* (1976)
Horace Abbott
Sally Page Abbott
John F. Alkahest
Johann Fist
Dickey Hicks
Uwis Hicks
Virginia Page (Ginny) Hicks
Jane
Ariah Page
James L. Page
Richard Page
Ed Thomas
Peter Wagner

*The Sunlight Dialogues* (1972)
Walter (Walter Arlis Benson) Boyle
Esther Clumly
Fred Clumly
Freeman
Arthur Taggert (Old Man) Hodge, Sr.
Benjamin (Ben) Hodge, Sr.
Kathleen Paxton Hodge
Luke Hodge

Mildred Jewel (Millie) Hodge
Taggert Faeley (The Sunlight Man, Tag)
  Hodge
William B. (Will) Hodge, Sr.
R. V. Kleppmann
Oliver (Ollie) Nuper
Clive (Old Man) Paxton

## BRIAN GARFIELD

*Hopscotch* (1975)
Joseph Cutter
Carla Fleming
Glenn Follett
Miles Kendig
Myerson
Leonard Ross
Mikhail Yasov

## GEORGE GARRETT

*Death of the Fox* (1971)
Sir Francis Bacon
Gregory Brandon
Elizabeth I
James I (James VI of Scotland)
Carew Ralegh
Elizabeth Throckmorton (Bess) Ralegh
Sir Walter (Wat) Ralegh
Sir Lewis Stukely
Mary Throckmorton
George (Steenie) Villiers
Sir Henry Yelverton

*Do, Lord, Remember Me* (1965)
Elijah J. (Hookworm) Cartwright
L. J. Griggs
Judith
Howie Loomis
Miami
Moses (Moze)
Big Red (L. J. Griggs) Smalley

## WILLIAM GASS

*Omensetter's Luck* (1966)
Reverend Jethro (Furb) Furber
Clifford Huffley
Brackett Omensetter
Doctor (Doc) Orcutt
Reverend Andrew (Andy) Pike
Henry Pimber
Israbestis Tott
Matthew (Mat) Watson

Milo (Arabella Stone) Hamilton
Stewart Landshorough
Lewis Lanier
Minerva (Minnie Mouse) Means
Ivor (Istvan Szegedyi) Sedge
Lila Swenson

## DONALD GOINES

*Dopefiend* (1971)
Billy Banks
Bessy Mae
Minnie
Porky
Smokey
Snake
Teddy
Terry Wilson

## HERBERT GOLD

*Slave Trade* (1979)
Father Brice
Mahmoud Fils-Aimé
Sid Kasdan
Lucien
Saloman Saint-Jupe
Francis Worthington
January (Jan) Worthington
Luci Worthington

## MARY GORDON

*The Company of Women* (1980)
Robert Cavendish
Father Cyprian
Charlotte Taylor
Felicitas Taylor
Frank Taylor

*Final Payments* (1978)
Margaret Casey
Eleanor Lavery
David Lowe
Isabel Moore
Joseph Moore
Father Mulcahy
Elizabeth (Liz) O'Brien Ryan
John Ryan
Hugh Slade

*Men and Angels* (1985)
Anne Foster
Michael Foster
Laura Post

Caroline Watson
Jane Watson
Stephan Watson

*The Other Side* (1989)
Dan MacNamara
Ellen Costelloe MacNamara
Vincent MacNamara
Camille MacNamara Ulichni

## WILLIAM GOYEN
## (See also Volume I)

*Come, The Restorer* (1974)
Ace Adair
Addis Adair
Jewel Adair
Mr. de Persia
Cleon (Oil King) Peters
Selina Rosheen Prescott
Wylie Prescott

*The Fair Sister* (1963)
Ruby Drew
Cubsy Hall
Canaan Johnson
Orondo McCabe
Prince O'Light
Savata

## SHIRLEY ANN GRAU
## (See also Volume I)

*The Condor Passes* (1971)
Anna Oliver Caillet
Anthony Caillet
Robert Caillet
Maurice Lamotta
Mama (Ma)
Margaret Oliver
Stephanie Maria D'Alfonso Oliver
Thomas Henry (Old Man) Oliver
Stanley

*Evidence of Love* (1977)
Harold Evans
Abigail Morton Henley
Edward Milton Henley
Eleanor Halsey Henley
Lucy Roundtree Evans Henley
Stephen Henley
Thomas Henley
Guido O'Connor

*The House on Coliseum Street* (1961)
Fred Aleman

Aurelie Caillet
Doris
Michael Kern
Anthony Mitchell
Joan Claire Mitchell

*The Keepers of the House* (1964)
Oliver Brandon
Edward Delatte
Margaret Carmichael Howland
Robert Carmichael Howland
William Howland
Abigail Howland Mason
Gregory Edward Mason
Abigail Howland Mason Tolliver
John Tolliver

## HANNAH GREEN

*I Never Promised You a Rose Garden*
(1964)
Anterrabae
Deborah (Deb) Blau
Esther Blau
Jacob Blau
Susan (Suzy) Blau
Carla
Doctor Fried
Lactamaeon

## JOHN GRISHAM

*The Client* (1993)
Jerome Clifford
Roy Foltrigg
Reggie Love
Barry (The Blade) Muldanno
Mark Sway
Ricky Sway

*The Firm* (1991)
DeVasher
Oliver Lambert
Nathan Locke
Abby McDeere
Mitchell McDeere
Ray McDeere
Avery Tolar

*The Partner* (1997)
Benny Aricia
Charles Bogan
Hamilton Jaynes
Patrick Lanigan
Trudy Lanigan

Sandy McDermott
Eva Miranda
Jack Stephano

*The Pelican Brief* (1992)
Thomas Callahan
Fletcher Coal
Gray Grantham
Darby Shaw
Denton Voyles

*The Testament* (1999)
Rachel Lane
Nate O'Brien
Troy Phelan
Joshua (Josh) Stafford

## JUDITH GUEST

*Ordinary People* (1976)
Karen Susan Aldrich
Tyrone C. Berger
Ray Hanley
Beth Jarrett
Calvin (Cal) Jarrett
Conrad Keith (Con) Jarrett
Jordan (Buck, Bucky) Jarrett
Joe (Joey, Laze) Lazenby
Jeannine (Jen) Pratt
Kevin Stillman

## DAVID GUTERSON

*Snow Falling on Cedars* (1995)
Ishmael Chambers
Nels Gudmundsson
Carl Heine
Alvin Hooks
Hatsue Imada
Kabuo Miyamoto

## JESSICA HAGEDORN

*Dogeaters* (1991)
Rosario "Baby" Alacran
Severo Alacran
Daisy Avila
Domingo Avila
Oswaldo "Pepe" Carreon
Trinidad Gamboa
Pucha Gonzaga
Rio Gonzaga
Nicasio Ledesma
Orlando "Romeo" Rosales

Joey Sands
Uncle

## JANE HAMILTON

*The Book of Ruth* (1988)
Miss Finch
Elmer Grey
Matt Grey
May Grey
Ruth Grey
Ruby
Aunt Sidney (Sid)

*A Map of the World* (1994)
Audrey Collins
Dan Collins
Lizzy Collins
Theresa Collins
Alice Gardner Goodwin
Claire Goodwin
Emma Goodwin
Howard Goodwin
Nellie Goodwin
Aunt Kate
Robbie MacKessy
Paul Rafferty

## EARL HAMNER, JR.

*Spencer's Mountain* (1961)
Colonel Coleman
Clyde Goodson
Miss Laura Parker
Clay-Boy Spencer
Clayton (Clay) Spencer
Elizabeth (Eliza) Spencer
Olivia (Livia, Livy) Spencer
Virgil Spencer
Zebulon Spencer

## MARK HARRIS
## (See also Volume I)

*It Looked Like For Ever* (1979)
Suicide Alexander
Barbara
Bertilia (Bert)
Beansy Binz
Ben Crowder
Jerry Divine
Sidney Jerome (Sid) Goldman
Holly
Ev McTaggart

Patricia Moors
Frank Pointer
Dr. Schiff
Herman H (Dutch) Schnell
Millie Schnell
Marva Sprat
Newton (Jack) Sprat
Berwyn Phillips (Red) Traphagen
Henry Whittier (Author, Hank)
   Wiggen
Hilary Margaret Wiggen
Holly Webster Wiggen (See Volume I)
Suzanne Winograd

## THOMAS HARRIS

*The Silence of the Lambs* (1988)
Jack Crawford
Hannibal Lecter (Hannibal the Canni-
   bal)
Clarice Starling

## JIM HARRISON

*A Good Day to Die* (1973)
Frank
Chief Joseph
Rosie
Sylvia
Tim (Timmy)

*Wolf* (1971)
Barbara
Laurie
Carol Severin Swanson

## JOHN HAWKES
## (See also Volume I)

*The Blood Oranges* (1971)
Catherine
Cyril
Dolores
Eveline
Fiona
Hugh
Meredith
Rosella

*Death, Sleep & the Traveler* (1974)
Ariane
Olaf
Peter
Allert (Alan) Vanderveenan
Ursula Vanderveenan

*The Lime Twig* (1961)
Margaret Banks
Michael Banks
T. Cowles
William Hencher
Larry
Jimmy Needles
Sparrow

*The Passion Artist* (1979)
Claire
Gagnon
Hania
Hermann Herzenbrecher
Anna Kossowski
Kristel
Eva Laubenstein
Mirabelle
Doctor Slovotkin
Konrad Vost
Konrad Vost the Father

*Second Skin* (1964)
Big Bertha
Uncle Billy
Cassandra (Candy)
Fernandez
Gertrude
Harry
Sister Josie
Kate (Catalina Kate)
Miranda
Pixie
Bub Poor
Jomo Poor
Red (Captain Red) Poor
Skipper (Edward, Papa Cue Ball, Skip)
Sonny
Tremlow

*Travesty* (1976)
Chantal
Henri
Honorine
Papa
Pascal

## LARRY HEINEMANN

*Paco's Story* (1986)
Cathy
Gallagher
The Ghosts
Jesse
The Medic

Ernest Monroe
Paco Sullivan

## JOSEPH HELLER

*Catch-22* (1961)
Captain (Aarfy) Aardvaark
Appleby
Captain Black
Colonel Cargill
Colonel Cathcart
Clevinger
Major de Coverley
Nurse Cramer
Doc Daneeka
Dobbs
General Dreedle
Sue Ann Duckett
Dunbar
Dori Duz
Captain Flume
Captain Havermeyer
Hungry Joe
Huple
Washington Irving
Lieutenant Colonel Korn
Luciana
Major Major Major Major
McWatt
Milo Minderbinder
Colonel Moodus
Lieutenant Mudd
Lieutenant Nately
Orr
General P. P. Peckem
Kid Sampson
Lieutenant Scheisskopf
Corporal Snark
Snowden
Albert Taylor (A. T.) Tappman
Corporal Whitcomb
Chief White Halfoat
Ex-P.F.C. Wintergreen
Yossarian (Yo-Yo)

*God Knows* (1984)
Bathsheba
David
Joab
Samuel
Saul
Solomon

*Good as Gold* (1979)
Andrea Biddle Conover

Pugh Biddle Conover
Belle Gold
Bruce Gold
Gussie Gold
Julius Gold
Sid Gold
Lionel (Bulldog) Greenspan
Maxwell (Skip) Lieberman
Ralph Newsome
Pomoroy
Harris Rosenblatt

*Something Happened* (1974)
Arthur (Art) Baron
Johnny Brown
Jack Green
Andy Kagle
Virginia (Virgin) Markowitz
Martha
Red Parker
Bob (Bobby) Slocum
Derek Slocum
Mrs. Slocum

## MARK HELPRIN

*Refiner's Fire* (1977)
Nancy May Baker
Big Tub
Farrell
Lev (Arich Ben Barak)
Lydia Levy
Paul Levy
Livingston (Lischinsky)
Alexander Pascaleo
Marshall Pearl
Katrina Perlk
Dash Pringle
Lucius Pringle

*Winter's Tale* (1983)
Craig Binky
Christiana Friebourg
Virginia Gamely
Asbury Gunwillow
Peter Lake
Hardesty Marratta
Cecil Mature (Wooley)
Jackson Mead
Reverend Mootfowl
Beverly Penn
Harry Penn
Isaac Penn
Praeger de Pinto
Pearly Soames

## ERNEST HEMINGWAY
(See also Volume I)

*The Garden of Eden* (1986)
Catherine Bourne
David Bourne
Marita

*Islands in the Stream* (1970)
Boise (Boy)
Roger Davis
Eddy
Henry
Honest Lil (Lillian)
Andrew Hudson
David (Dave, Davy, Mr. David) Hudson
Thomas (Mr. Tom, Tomfis) Hudson
Tom (Schatz) Hudson
Lillian
Willie

*True At First Light* (1999)
Charo
Gin Crazed
Debba
Ernie
Miss Mary
Ngui
The Informer

## FRANK HERBERT

*God Emperor of Dune* (1981)
Leto Atreides II
Moneo Atreides
Siona Atreides
Duncan Idaho
Hwi Noree

## JAMES LEO HERLIHY
(See also Volume I)

*Midnight Cowboy* (1965)
Juanita Collins Harmeyer (Mother
  Goddam) Barefoot
Tombaby (Princess) Barefoot
Joe (Cowboy, Tex) Buck
Sally Buck
Townsend Pederson (Towny) Locke
Woodsy Niles
Perry
Anastasia (Annie, Chalkline Annie, Vir-
  gin Jekyll and Miss Hyde) Pratt
Enrico Salvatore (Ratso, Rico) Rizzo
Cass Trehune

## CALVIN HERNTON

*Scarecrow* (1974)
Joseppi Banascalco
Cederberge
Martin Handson
Orville Handson
Putsy Handson
Hellos
Juanita
Kaisa
Wantman Krane
Maria
Reverend Kenneth McIntoch
Oriki
Reggie
Scarecrow
Rex Temple
Dr. Kerstine Wentworth
Euston Peters Winslow-Davis
Dr. Norman Yas

## WILLIAM HERRICK

*Hermanos!* (1969)
Gregory (Greg) Ballard
Mack Berg
Archie Cohen
Charles Evans (Charlie) Flagg
Joe (José) Garms
Rolfe Keepsake
Daniel Nuñez
Professor Rolfe Alan Ruskin
Sarah Ruskin
Jacob (Jacobito, Jacques, Jake, Jakey,
  Capitin Jacobito Estrella, Comrade
  Comic Star) Starr
Carl (Comrade Truth, Untruth, Gen-
  eral Carlos Verdad) Vlanoc
Cromwell (Ace) Webster

*The Itinerant* (1967)
Dr. Abe Abramson
Matthew (Matt) Cahn
Ida (Ida Bitch) Delson
Rachel Mary Conyngham Farrell
Simon Xavier Farrell
Charles Evans (Charlie) Flagg
Pacifici Bartola Ahmed Gurevich
Samuel Ezekiel (Jakie, Red, Zeke)
  Gurevich
Miriam
Edna Nimienski

*The Last to Die* (1971)
Buteo

Ramón (Cortés) Cordes
Delgado
Marguerite
Max
Rojos (Pizarro)

## GEORGE V. HIGGINS

*Cogan's Trade* (1974)
John (Johnny, Squirrel) Amato
Barry Caprio
Steve Caprio
Jack (Jackie) Cogan
Frankie
Kenny Gill
Mitch
Russell
Mark (Markie) Trattman

*The Digger's Game* (1973)
The Greek Almas
Jerry (Digger) Doherty
Paul Doherty
Harrington
Miller (Mill) Schabb
Croce (Richey Torrey) Torre

*Dreamland* (1977)
Andrew Collier
General Aubrey T. Gammage
Ellen Shipp Hadley
Henry Morgan
Daniel Cable Wills
Daniel Compton (Comp) Wills

*The Friends of Eddie Coyle* (1972)
Jackie Brown
Eddie (Eddie Fingers, Paulie) Coyle
Dillon
Dave (Foles) Foley
Jimmy Scalisi
Wanda

## OSCAR HIJUELOS

*The Mambo Kings Play Songs of Love*
(1989)
Desi Arnaz
Cesar Castillo
Eugenio Castillo
Marfa Castillo
Nestor Castillo
Pablo Castillo
Pedro Castillo
Delores Fuentes

Julian Garcia
Luisa Garcia
Fernando (Frankie) Perez
Maria Rivera
Lydia Santos
Vanna Vane

## TONY HILLERMAN

### *Dance Hall of the Dead* (1973)
George Bowlegs
Ernesto Cata
Ted Isaacs
Joe Leaphorn
Chester Reynolds
Susanne

## RUSSELL HOBAN

### *Riddley Walker* (1980)
Lorna Elswint
Abel Goodparley
Granser
Drop John
Lissener
Erny Orfing
Brooder Walker
Riddley Walker

## ALICE HOFFMAN

### *Fortune's Daughter* (1985)
Jason Grey
Lila Grey
Richard Grey
Jessup
Rae Perry

### *Here on Earth* (1997)
Chris
Coop
Annabeth Cooper
Belinda Cooper
Mr. Cooper
Richard Cooper
Judith Dale
Ken Helm
Hollis
Bill "the Judge" Justice
Louise Justice
Susanna "Susie" Justice
Lori
Ed Milton
Alan Murray

Gwen Murray
Hank Murray
Henry Murray
Julie Murray
Marcheline "March" Murray
Jimmy Parrish

### *Local Girls* (1999)
Mrs. Brandon
Mr. Castle
Mrs. Castle
Mrs. Dennison
Desmond Garnet
Sonny Garnet
Grandma Frieda
Jill Harrington
Mrs. Harrington
Eugene Kessler
Natalie LeFrance
Jack Lerner
Eddie LoPacca
Terry LoPacca
Margot Molinaro
Mrs. Molinaro
Tony Molinaro
Mr. Prospero
Jonathan "Jack" Rabbit
Revolver
Mr. Richie
Frances "Franny" Samuelson
Gretel Samuelson
Jason Samuelson
Sam Samuelson
Thea Samuelson
Mike Sutton
Tim

### *Practical Magic* (1995)
Ben Frye
Gary Hallett
Antonia Owens
Frances Owens
Gillian Owens
Jet Owens
Kylie Owens
Sally Owens

### *The River King* (2000)
Peggy Anthony
Maureen Brown
Eileen Byers
Pete Byers
Sean Byers
Betsy Chase
Ivy Cooper

Helen Davis
Amy Ellison
Melissa Endicott
Charlotte Evans
Nathaniel Gibb
Abel "Abe" Gray
Ernest Gray
Florence Gray
Frank Gray
Margaret Gray
Wright Gray
Dennis Hardy
Eric Herman
Pie Hobson
Annie Jordan Howe
Dr. George Howe
Lois Jeremy
Heidi Lansing
Carlin Leander
David Linden
Harry McKenna
Christine Percy
August "Gus" Pierce
Walter Pierce
Jack Short
Bob Thomas
Glen Tiles
Joey Tosh
Lynn Vining

## MAUREEN HOWARD

### *Expensive Habits* (1986)
Harry Bidwell
Mrs. Bidwell
Bernice Blau
Hannah Brandt
Mrs. Casey
George Darby
Mary Darby
Ginger Flood
Jack (Johnny, John Sarsfield) Flood
Lily Flood
Margaret (Maggie) Flood
Rose Flood
Max Gideon
Mrs. Grogan
Jane Healy
Tim Healy
Dotty Schwartz Klotz
Red Klotz
Emily Licht
Mrs. Lynch
Ned Lynch

T. S. Garp
Walt Garp
Ernie Holm
Helen Holm
Ellen James
Michael Milton
Roberta (Captain Energy, Robert) Muldoon
Stewart (Stewie Two) Percy, Jr.
Bainbridge (Pooh) Percy
Cushman (Cushie, Cushion) Percy
Randolph (Dopey) Percy
Stewart (Fat Stew, Paunch, Stewie) Percy
William (Shrill Willy) Percy
Benny Potter
Jillsy Sloper
Tinch (Stench)
Harriet Truckenmiller
Kenny Truckenmiller
Donald (Don) Whitcomb
John (Jack) Wolf

## SUSAN ISAACS

*Almost Paradise* (1989)
James Cobleigh
Nicholas Cobleigh
Jane Cobleigh (Heissenhuber)
Winifred Cobleigh (Tuttle)
Rhodes Heissenhuber
Richard Heissenhuber
Dorothy Heissenhuber (Rhodes)
Sarah (Sally) Taubman (Tompkins)

## ALAN ISLER

*The Prince of West End Avenue* (1994)
Freddy Blum
Ralph Comyns
Magda Damrosch
Mandy Dattner
Tosca Dawidowicz
Benno Hamburger
Meta Korner
Otto Korner
Alice (Contessa) Krebs
Gerhardt Kunstler
Nahum Lipschitz
Hermoine (Hannah) Perlmutter
Lazar Poliakov
Hugh Weisskopf

## SHIRLEY JACKSON
## (See also Volume I)

*We Have Always Lived in the Castle* (1962)
Charles Blackwood
Constance Blackwood
Julian Blackwood
Mary Katherine (Merricat) Blackwood
Helen Clarke
Jim Clarke
Jim Donell
Lucille Wright

## JOHN JAKES

*Love and War* (1984)
Elkanah Bent
Billy Hazard
Brett Hazard
George Hazard
Ashton Main
Charles Main
Cooper Main
Orry Main
Lamar Powell

## GISH JEN

*Mona in the Promised Land* (1996)
Helen Chang
Mona Chang
Barbara Gugelstein
Alfred Knickerbocker
Seth Mandel

*Typical American* (1991)
Helen Chang
Ralph Chang
Theresa Chang
Grover Ding

## CHARLES JOHNSON

*Middle Passage* (1990)
Isadora Bailey
Baleka
Jackson Calhoun
Riley Calhoun
Rutherford Calhoun
Reverend Peleg Chandler
Peter Cringle
Ebenezer Falcon
Tommy O'Toole
Santos

Josiah Squibb
Philippe "Papa" Zeringue

## DIANE JOHNSON

*Le Divorce* (1997)
Edgar Cosset
Charles Henri Persaud
Roxy Persaud
Isabel Walker

*Loving Hands at Home* (1968)
Garth Fry
Joan Fry
Karen Fry
Mahonri Fry
Patty Fry
Sebastian Fry
Paris Pratt

*Lying Low* (1979)
Alistair Burnham
Julie Burnham
Mr. Griggs
Marybeth Howe (Lynn Lord)
Ouida Senza
Chuck Sweet
Anton (Teddy) Wait
Theodora (Theo) Wait

*The Shadow Knows* (1974)
Osella Barnes
Inspector Dyce
A. J. Harper
Bess Harvill
Gavin Hexam
N. Hexam
Mr. and Mrs. Hoaglund
Andrew Mason
Raider (Big Raider)
Clyde Wilson
Evalin McCabe (Ev) Wilson

## GAYL JONES

*Corregidora* (1975)
Austin Bradley
Corregidora
Correy (Mama) Corregidora
Dorita (Great Gram) Corregidora
Gram (Grandmama) Corregidora
Ursa (U. C., Ursa Corre, Urs, Ursie) Corregidora
Mr. Deak
Mr. Floyd

Mose Grundy
Harold
Jeffy (Jeff)
Jimmy (Jim)
Catherine (Cat, Catty) Lawson
Lurene
Martin
May Alice
Tadpole (Crawdad, Tad, Taddy)
   McCormick
Max Monroe
Eddy Pace
Theodore (Thedo)
Mutt Philmore Thomas
Vivian (Vive)

*Eva's Man* (1976)
Alfonso (Fonso)
Miss Billie
Eva Medina (Eve, Sweet) Canada
John Canada
Marie Canada
Davis (Davy) Carter
Charlotte
Davis
Elvira
Eva
James (Hawk) Hunn
Jean
Emil Kerouac
Mr. Valentino (Val) Logan
Medina
Elvira Moody
Otis
Joanne Riley
Freddy Smoot
Moses Tripp
Tyrone

*The Healing* (1998)
Harlan Truth Eagleton
Josef Ehelich von Fremd
Norvelle Goodling
Grandmother Jaboti
Nicholas Jess Love
Joan Savage
Naughton James Savage

## JAMES JONES
## (See also Volume I)

*Go to the Widow-Maker* (1967)
Carol Abernathy
Hunt Abernathy
Al Bonham

Letta Bonham
Cathie Chandler Finer
Sam Finer
Lucia Angelina Elena Videndi (Lucky)
   Grant
Ron Grant
Jim Grointon
Lisa Halder
René Halder
Doug Ismaileh
Frankie Orloffski
Lucky Videndi

*The Merry Month of May* (1971)
Anne-Marie
Bernard
Edith de Chambrolet
Daniel
Samantha-Marie (Sam) Everton
Florence
Harry Gallagher
Hill Gallagher
Louisa Dunn Hill Gallagher
McKenna Hartley Gallagher
Eleanor Hartley
Jonathan James (Jack) Hartley III
Ferenc Hofmann-Beck
Martine
Raymond
Fred Singer
Terri
David (Dave) Weintraub

*The Thin Red Line* (1962)
George R. (Brass Band, Tall George)
   Band
John Bell
Don Doll
Corporal Fife
James I. (Bugger, Jim) Stein
Gordon (Shorty) Tall
Edward Welsh
Private Witt

*Whistle* (1978)
Colonel Baker
Carol Ann Firebaugh
Frances Highsmith
Major Hogan
Marion Landers
Bobby Prell
Colonel Stevens
John (Johnny Stranger, Mother
   Strange) Strange
Linda Sue Strange
Martin (Mart) Winch

## ERICA JONG

*Fear of Flying* (1973)
Charles (Charlie) Fielding
Adrian Goodlove
Brian Stollerman
Judith Stoloff (Jude) White
Bennett Wing
Isadora Zelda White Stollerman Wing
Pia Wittkin

*How to Save Your Own Life* (1977)
Josh Ace
Michael Cosman
Britt Goldstein
Rosanna Howard
Gretchen Kendall
Hope Lowell
Jeannie Morton
Jeffrey Roberts
Dr. Jeffery Rudner
Eliza Rushmore
Dr. Abigail Schwartz
Bennett Wing
Isadora Zelda White Stollerman Wing

## JUNE JORDAN

*His Own Where* (1971)
Angela Figueroa
Buddy Rivers

## STUART M. KAMINSKY

*A Cold Red Sunrise* (1988)
Dimitri Galich
Emil Karpo
Krasnikov
Sergei Mirasnikov
Porfiry Petrovich Rostnikov
Sarah Rostnikov
Lev Samsonov
Ludmilla Samsonov
Sasha Tkach

## BEL KAUFMAN

*Up the Down Staircase* (1965)
Sylvia (Syl) Barrett
Paul Barringer
Samuel Bester
Alice Blake
Maxwell E. Clarke
Frances Egan
Joseph (Joe) Ferone

Valerie
Veronika

*The Painted Bird* (1965)
Anton (the Quail)
Anulka
Black One
Ewka
Garbos
Gavrila
Jealous
Labina
Lekh
Stupid Ludmila
Makar
Marta
The Mitka (the Cuckoo Master)
Olga the Wise One
Rainbow
Silent One

*Steps* (1968)
The Philosopher

## JUDITH KRANTZ

*Scruples* (1978)
Curt Arvey
Aunt Cornelia (Cornie)
Peter (Spider) Elliott
Comte Edouard de la Cote de Grace
Fiorio (Fifi) Hill
Joshua Isaiah (Josh) Hillman
Ellis Ikehorn
Maggie (Shirley Silverstein) MacGregor
Dolly Moon
Valentine O'Neill
Vito Orsini
Wilhelmina Hunnenwell Winthrop
   Ikehorn (Billy, Honey) Orsini
John Prince
Per Svenberg
Harriet Toppingham
Comtesse Lilianne de Vertdulac
Lester Weinstock

## WALLY LAMB

*She's Come Undone* (1992)
Dante Davis
Grandma Holland
Roberta Jaskiewicz
Thayer Kitchen
Dolores Price
Fabio Pucci

## LOUIS L'AMOUR

*The Lonesome Gods* (1983)
Jacob Finney
(Don) Isidro
Meghan Laurel
(Miss) Nesselrode
Johannes Verne
Zachery Verne

## DAVID LEAVITT

*Equal Affections* (1989)
Walter Bayles
April Cooper
Danny Cooper
Louise Cooper
Nat Cooper
Eleanor Friedman
Lillian Rubenstein-Kraft

*The Lost Language of Cranes* (1986)
Eliot Abrams
Owen Benjamin
Philip Benjamin
Rose Benjamin
Jerene Parks
Margaret Parks
Sam Parks
Brad Robinson

*The Page Turner* (1998)
Richard Kennington
Joseph Mansourian
Olga Novotna
Pamela Porterfield
Paul Porterfield

## JULIUS LESTER

*And All Our Wounds Forgiven* (1994)
Elizabeth Adams
Robert Card
Andrea Williams Marshall
John Calvin Marshall
Gregory Townley

## IRA LEVIN

*Rosemary's Baby* (1967)
Minnie Castevet
Roman Castevet
Terry Gionoffrio
Dr. Hill
Edward (Hutch) Hutchins

Steven Marcato
Dr. Abe Sapirstein
Andrew John Woodhouse
Guy Woodhouse
Rosemary Woodhouse

## PHILLIP LOPATE

*Confessions of Summer* (1979)
Jack (Jackie, Jacques) Bogardes
Cora
Marie Curtin
Eric Eisner
Bruno Fisher
Teddy Forster
Horace Hinton
Charles (Charlie) Kroegel
Skipper
Hugh Wall

## ALISON LURIE

*Foreign Affairs* (1984)
Edwin Francis
Ruth (Roo) March
Virginia (Vinnie) Miner
Charles (Chuck) Mumpson
Rosemary Radley
Fred Turner
Leonard D.  (L.D.) Zimmern

*The Last Resort* (1998)
Dorrie Jackson
Myra Jackson
Perry Jackson
Jenny Walker
Wilkie Walker
Less Weiss

*Love and Friendship* (1962)
Julian Fenn
Miranda Fenn
Allen Ingram
William Wigglesworth (Billy) Lumkin
Mrs. Rabbage
Freddy Stockwell
Patricia Stockwell
William (Will) Thomas
Emily Stockwell (Emmy) Turner
Holman Turner

*The Nowhere City* (1965)
Katherine Cattleman
Paul Cattleman
Ceci

Dr. Isidore (Iz) Einsam
Glory Green
Cecile (Ceci) O'Connor
Fred Skinner
Susy Skinner
Maxie Weiss
Walter Wong

*Real People* (1969)
Charlie Ryan Baxter
Theodore (Teddy) Berg
Nick Donato
Kenneth Foster
Gerald (Gerry) Grass
Caroline Kent
Richard (Ricky) Potter
Sally Sachs
Clark (Clarkie) Smith
Janet Belle Smith
Harmonia H. (H. H.) Waters
Leonard D. Zimmern

*The War Between the Tates* (1974)
Sanford (Sandy, Zed) Finkelstein
Wendy (Wendee) Gahaghan
Dr. Bernard M. (Bernie) Kotelchuk
Ralph
Linda Sliski
Brian Tate
Erica Parker Tate
Jeffrey (Jeffo) Tate
Matilda (Muffy) Tate
Zed
Danielle Zimmern
Leonard D. (Lennie) Zimmern
Ruth (Roo) Zimmern

## NORMAN MAILER
## (See also Volume I)

*An American Dream* (1965)
Cherry
Eddie (Uncle Ganooch) Ganucci
Barney Oswald Kelly
Deborah Caughlin Mangaravidi Kelly
Lieutenant Leznicki
Shago Martin
Cherry Melainie
Roberts
Deborah Kelly Rojack
Stephen Richards (RawJock) Rojack
Ruta

*The Executioner's Song* (1979)
April Baker

Nicole Kathryne Baker (Nicole
  Kathryne Gilmore, Nucoa Butterball)
  Barrett
Mont Court
Vern Damico
Bessie Gilmore
Gary Mark Gilmore
Mikal Gilmore
Brenda Nicol
John (Johnny) Nicol
Lawrence (Larry) Schiller

*Why Are We in Vietnam?* (1967)
Ollie Totem Head Water Beaver
M. A. (Medium Asshole) Bill
D. J. (Jellicoe Jethroe, Ranald Jethroe)
Luke (Paragon) Fellinka
Gottfried (Son of Gutsy, Texas) Hyde,
  Jr.
Gottfried (Gotsie, Gutsy) Hyde, Sr.
Alice Hallie Lee (Death-row Jethroe)
  Jethroe
Rusty (David Rutherford Jethroe, Jelli-
  coe Jethroe, Sir Jet-Throne) Jethroe
M. A. (Medium Asshole) Pete

## BERNARD MALAMUD
## (See also Volume I)

*Dubin's Lives* (1979)
Fanny Bick
Gerald Dubin
Kitty Willis Dubin
Maud Dubin
William B. Dubin
Roger Foster
Evan Ondyk
Gerald (Gerry) Willis

*The Fixer* (1966)
B. A. Bibokov
Yakov Shepsovitch (Yakov Ivanovitch
  Dologushev) Bok
Marfa Vladimirovna Golov
Zhenia (Zhenechka) Golov
Gregor Gronfein
Vladislav Grigorievitch Grubeshov
Nikolai Maximovitch Lebedev
Zinaida Nikolaevna (Zina) Lebedev
Raisl
Schmuel

*A New Life* (1961)
Leo Duffy
Dr. Gerald Gilley

Pauline Gilley
Seymour (Sam, Sy) Levin

*The Tenants* (1971)
Irene Bell
Sam Clemence
Harry Lesser
Irving Levenspiel
Willie (Bill Spear) Spearmint

## WALLACE MARKFIELD

*To an Early Grave* (1964)
Inez Braverman
Leslie Braverman
Holly Levine
Felix (N. J. Felix) Ottensteen
Etta Rieff
Morroe Rieff
Barnet (Barn) Weiner

## MARGARET MARON

*Bootlegger's Daughter* (1992)
Deborah Knott

## PAULE MARSHALL
## (See also Volume I)

*The Chosen Place, the Timeless People*
(1969)
Harriet Shippen Amron
Saul Amron
Cuffee Ned
Delbert (Delly)
Ferguson (Fergy)
Allen Fuso
Lyle Hutson
Merle Kinbona
Stinger
Leesy Walkes
Vere (Vereson) Walkes

*Daughters* (1992)
Justin Beaufils
Celestine Bellegarde
Lowell Carruthers
Robeson Daniels
Vincereta ("Viney") Daniels
Astral Forde
Estelle Mackenzie
Primus Mackenzie
Ursa Mackenzie

## BOBBIE ANN MASON

*Feather Crowns* (1993)
Mrs. Blankenship
Brother Coronett
Clary "Mittens" Dowdy
Dr. Foote
Thomas Hunt
Dr. Graham Johnson
Mr. W. Greenberry McCain
Mr. Mullins
Mrs. Margaret Shelburne
Alma S. Wheeler
Amanda "Mandy" Wheeler
Boone Wheeler
Christianna "Christie" Wheeler
James Wheeler
Wad Wheeler
Wiggins sisters

*In Country* (1985)
Dawn Goodwin
Tom Hudson
Dwayne Hughes
Mamaw Hughes
Samantha Hughes
Lonnie Malone
Emmet Smith
Irene Smith
Anita Stevens

*Spence and Lila* (1988)
Bill Belton
Catherine Culpepper
Lee Culpepper
Lila Culpepper
Nancy Culpepper
Spence Culpepper

## JACK MATTHEWS

*Hanger Stout, Awake!* (1967)
Penny Barker
Jim Boynton
Dan Comisky
Pete
Phyllis
Rigolo
Clyde (Hanger) Stout
Bo Thompson
Bert Wilderman

## PETER MATTHIESSEN

*At Play in the Fields of the Lord* (1965)
Aeore (Child-Star, Riri'an)

Azusa
Boronai
Dick
Padre Fuentes
El Comandante Rulino Guzmán
Fausto Guzmán
Señora Dolores Estella Carmen Maria
  Cruz y Peralta Guzmán
Andy Huben
Leslie (Les) Huben
Kori
Mercedes
Alvin (Joe Redcloud) Moon
Irma (Big Irma) Moon
Meriwether Lewis (Kisu-Mu) Moon
New Person
Pindi
Hazel Quarrier
Martin (Mart) Quarrier
William (Billie) Martin Quarrier
Suzie
Taweeda
Tukanu (Farter)
Ugly One
Uyuyu (Yoyo)
Wolfie (Fat Morty)
Father Xantes

*Far Tortuga* (1975)
Captain Andrew Avers
Captain Raib Avers
Jim Eden (Buddy) Avers
Junior (Speedy, Speedy-Boy) Bodden
Athens Ebanks
Captain Desmond Eden
Vemon Dilbert (Blue Nose) Evers
Wodie Greaves
William (Will) Parchment
Miguel Moreno (Brown, Brownie,
  Miguelito) Smith
Byrum (Big Byrom) Powery Wader

*Raditzer* (1961)
Carter Adams
Robert Ariyoshi
Carl
Jack Gioncarlo
Heinie
Hoak
Male (Rad) Raditzer
Charles P. (Char, Charlie) Stark
Charlotte Sylvester (Shar) Stark
Vahine (Heinie, Myrn, Myrna)

## WILLIAM MAXWELL
## (See also Volume I)

*So Long, See You Tomorrow* (1980)
Jenny Evans
I
Clarence Smith
Cletus Smith
Fern Smith
Wayne Smith
Lloyd Wilson
Marie Wilson

## JULIAN MAYFIELD
## (See also Volume I)

*The Grand Parade* (1961)
Alonzo (Lonnie) Banks
Randolph (Randy) Banks
Chick Bolton
Clarke Bryant
Jonah Dean (J. D.) Carson
Angus Cleveland
Hank Dean
Mary McCullogh
Patty Speed
Douglas Taylor

## CORMAC McCARTHY

*All the Pretty Horses* (1993)
Alejandra
Duena Alfonsa
Jimmy Blevins
John Grady Cole
Don Hector
Lacey Rawlins

## MARY McCARTHY

*The Group* (1963)
Elizabeth (Polly) Andrews
Dick Brown
Hartshorn Priss Crockett
Helena Davidson
Elinor (Lakey) Eastlake
Elizabeth (Libby) MacAusland
Harald Peterson
Mary (Pokey) Prothero
Dorothy (Dottie) Renfrew
Kay Leiland Strong

## CARSON McCULLERS
### (See also Volume I)

*Clock Without Hands* (1961)
John Jester Clane
Johnny Clane
Judge Fox Clane
Grown Boy
Dr. Kenneth Hale Hayden
Nigra Jones
Joy (Mrs. Ossie Little) Little
Ossie Little
J. T. Malone
Martha Malone
Sherman (Sherman Jones) Pew
Verily

## JOSEPH McELROY

*The Letter Left to Me* (1988)
Emmy (Mary Elizabeth)
Father
Mother

## THOMAS McGUANE

*The Bushwhacked Piano* (1971)
Cletus James (C. J.) Clovis
Wayne Codd
Ann Fitzgerald
Duke and Edna (La) Fitzgerald
Nicholas Payne

*Ninety-Two in the Shade* (1973)
Faron Carter
Miranda Cole
Nichol Dance
Myron Moorhen
James Powell
Robert Rudleigh
Skelton
Goldsboro Skelton
Thomas Skelton
Roy Soleil

*Panama* (1977)
Catherine Clay
Jesse James
Curtis G. Peavey
Chester (Chet) Hunnicutt Pomeroy
Jim Pomeroy
Roxy

*The Sporting Club* (1969)
Mary Beth Duncan

Fortescue
Janey
Earl Olive
James (Jim) Quinn
Scott
Spengler
Vernor Stanton

## JAY McINERNEY

*Bright Lights, Big City* (1984)
Tad Allagash
Megan Avery
Amanda Conway
Jamie Conway
Clara Tillinghast

*Brightness Falls* (1992)
Corrine Calloway
Russell (Crash) Calloway
Trina Cox
Washington Lee
Bernard (Bernie) Melman
Jeffrey (Jeff) Pierce
Victor Propp

*Story of My Life* (1988)
Dean Chasen
Francesca Greene
Jeannie
Skip Pendleton
Alison Poole
Rebecca (Becca) Poole
Didi Spence

## TERRY McMILLAN

*Waiting to Exhale* (1992)
Bernadine Harris
Savannah Jackson
Gloria Matthews
Robin Stokes

## LARRY McMURTRY

*All My Friends Are Going to Be Strangers* (1972)
Daniel (Danny) Deck
Lorena Deck
Sally Bynum Deck
Emma Greenway Horton
Melanie, Teddy, and Tommy Horton
Thomas (Flap) Horton
Jill Peel

*Horseman, Pass By* (1961)
Homer Lisle (Granddad) Bannon
Jewel Bannon
Lonnie Bannon
Halmea
Hud (Huddie)
Jesse Logan
Scott

*The Last Picture Show* (1966)
Abilene
Billy
Frank Crawford
Sonny Crawford
Charlene Duggs
Gene Farrow
Jacy Farrow
Lois Farrow
Lester Marlow
Duane Moore
Genevieve Morgan
Coach Herman Popper
Ruth Popper
Sam the Lion
Bobby Sheen

*Leaving Cheyenne* (1963)
Adam Fry
Gideon (Gid) Fry
Mabel Peters Fry
Jimmy
Joe
Jonathan (Johnny) McCloud
Mabel Peters
Cletus (Old Man Taylor) Taylor
Eddie White
Joe White
Molly Taylor White

*Lonesome Dove* (1985)
Clara Allen
Woodrow F. Call
Newton Dobbs
Elmira Johnson
July Johnson
Augustus McCrae
Jake Spoon
Lorena Woods

*Moving On* (1970)
David (Davey) Carpenter
James (Jim) Carpenter
Patsy White Carpenter
Clara Clark
Eleanor Guthrie
Emma Greenway Horton

Craig Lister
Colin "Mack" Mackey
Claire Mayo
Ann McNulty
Kevin Moss
Wesley Mount
John O'Toole
Bill Pierce
Heidi Pierce
Julia Prine
Thomas Prowse
Mercy Reardon
Tyler Spaulding
Sonny Stoner
Ben Weilman
Zachary

### Songs in Ordinary Time (1995)
Mary Agnes
Miss Arkaday
Eunice Bonifante
Linda Braller
Mr. Briscoe
Bobby Busco
Carl Carper
Hildie Carper
Peter Carper
Grondine Carson
Henry Clay
Earlie Corbett
Luther Corbett
Kenny Doyle
Omar Duvall
Alice Fermoyle
Benjamin (Benjy) Fermoyle
Bridget Fermoyle
Marie Fermoyle
Norm Fermoyle
Sam Fermoyle
Jack Flaherty
Joe Gannon
Coach Graber
Rosemary Grady
Jarden Greene
Astrid Haddad
Robert Haddad
Jimmy Heinze
Billy Hendricks
Eddy Hendricks
Bernard (Bernie) Hinds
Cleveland Hinds
Nora Hinds
Kenny
Jessie Klubock

Louis (Louie) Klubock
Mr. Klubock
Helen Fermoyle LaChance
Renie LaChance
Mr. Lee
Bernadette Mansaw
Sister Martin
Claire Mayo
May Mayo
Howard Menka
Jozia Menka
Janice Miller
Mr. Miller
Mrs. Miller
Weeb Miller
Kyle Mooney
Travis (Blue) Mooney
George Morgan
Laura Morgan
Marilyn Morgan
Tommy Mullins
Father O'Riordan
Reverend Pease
Joey Seldon
Carol Stoner
Lester (Les) Stoner
Sonny Stoner
Lonzo Thayer
Tom
Tony

## WRIGHT MORRIS
## (See also Volume I)

### Cause for Wonder (1963)
Katherine Morley (Kitty) Brownell
Brian (Art) Caffrey
Etienne Dulac
Seymour Gatz
Charles Ames Homey
Warren P. Howe
Fremont Osborn
Grace Osborn
Sol Spiegel

### Fire Sermon (1971)
Joy
Kermit (Boy) Oelsligle
Stanley
Floyd Warner

### The Fork River Space Project (1977)
P. O. Bergdahl
O. P. Dahlberg
Kelcey (Serenus Vogel)

Alice Kelcey
Harry Lorbeer

### Plains Song for Female Voices (1991)
Cora Atkins
Emerson Atkins
Fayrene Dee Atkins
Orion Atkins
Sharon Rose Atkins
(Beulah) Madge Atkins (Kibbee)
Blanche Kibbee
Caroline Kibbee
Ned Kibbee
Belle Rooney (Atkins)

### What a Way to Go (1962)
Signor (Cee-Pee) Condotti-Pignata
Dr. Luther Hodler
Konrad Holzapfel
Mathilde Kollwitz
Adrien Perkheimer
Cynthia Pomeroy
Arnold Soby
Winifred (Winnie) Throop

## TONI MORRISON

### Beloved (1988)
Beloved
Denver
Amy Denver
Paul D. Garner
Sethe
Baby Suggs (Grandma Baby)

### The Bluest Eye (1970)
Aunt Jimmy
Bay Boy
Blue Jack
Cholly Breedlove
Pauline Williams (Polly) Breedlove
Pecola Breedlove
Sammy Breedlove
Woodrow Cain
China
Geraldine
Junior
Claudia MacTeer
Frieda MacTeer
Mama MacTeer
Mr. MacTeer
Miss Marie (Maginot Line)
Maureen (Meringue Pie) Peal
Poland
Henry Washington

Elihue Micah (Soaphead Church)
  Whitcomb

*Paradise* (1997)
Mavis Albright
Lone DuPres
Gigi (Grace)
Deek (Deacon) Morgan
Soane Morgan
Steward Morgan
K. D. Smith
Connie (Consolata) Sosa
Pallas Truelove
Seneca Turtle

*Song of Solomon* (1977)
Guitar Bains
Crowell Byrd
Heddy Byrd
Sing Byrd
Susan Byrd
Circe
Reverend Cooper
First Corinthians Dead
Hagar Dead
Mary Magdalene (Lena) Dead
Macon (Jake) Dead I
Macon Dead II
Macon (Milk, Milkman) Dead III
Pilate Dead
Rebecca (Reba) Dead
Ruth Foster (Miss Rufie) Dead
Empire State
Freddie
Hospital Tommy
Jake
Pilate
Henry Porter
Railroad Tommy
Robert Smith
Solomon

*Sula* (1973)
Chicken Little
Dewey
Albert (Ajax) Jacks
Jude
Eva (Pearl) Peace
Hannah Peace
Ralph (Plum) Peace
Sula Peace
Cecile Sabat
Rochelle Sabat
Shadrack
Tar Baby

Helene Sabat Wright
Nel Wright
Wiley Wright

## WALTER MOSLEY

*Devil in a Blue Dress* (1990)
Dewitt Albright
Raymond "Mouse" Alexander
Daphne Monet
Ezekial "Easy" Rawlins

## BHARATI MUKHERJEE

*The Holder of the World* (1993)
Mr. Abraham
Dubash (Oliver, Ortencio) Ali
Andrew
Mughal Emperor Aurangzeb
Throat-Cut de Azvedo
Jay Basu
Nawab Haider Beg
Bhagmati
Blake
Antonio Careri
Chase
Kashi Chetty
Attila Csycsyry
Ephraim Curtis
Devon
Edward Easton
Rebecca Easton
Morad Farah
Robert Fitch
Susannah Fitch
Thomas Fitch
Gavin
Giles
Samuel Higginbottham
Sarah Higginbottham
Hubert
Yellow-Beard Huyghen
Padma S. Iyer
Venn Iyer
Bugs Kilken
Felicity "Fleece" Legge
Gabriel Legge
Hannah Easton Fitch Legge
Morgan Legge
Henry Manning
Hester Manning
Beigh Masters
Marquis de Mussy
  Charles Jonathan Samuel Muster

Cephus Prynne
Queen Mother
John Ruxton
Martha Ruxton
Satterfield
Cutlass da Silva
Jadav Singh
Pearl Singh
Catchick Sookian
Lucas Thorpe
Pedda Timanna
Thomas Tringham
Two-Headed Ravana
Elias Walker
Zeb-un-nissa

*Jasmine* (1989)
Taylor Hayes
Darrel Lutz
Bud Ripplemeyer
Du (Yogi) Ripplemeyer
Jane Ripplemeyer
Karin Ripplemeyer
Sukhwinder Singh
Du Thien
Jasmine (Jyoti) Vijh
Prakash Vijh

## ALBERT MURRAY

*Train Whistle Guitar* (1974)
Miss Tee (Auntee) Boykin
Luzana (Old Luze) Cholly
Little Buddy Marshall
Scooter (Mister Man)

## VLADIMIR NABOKOV
## (See also Volume I)

*Ada* (1969)
Mlle Ida (Mlle L., Guillaume de Mon-
  parnasse) Larivière
Count Percy de Prey
Countess Cordula (Cordula Tobak) de
  Prey
Philip Rack
Adelaide (Ada, Adadochka) Veen
Aqua Durmanov Veen
Ivan (Van) Veen
Lucinda (Lucette) Veen
Marina Durmanov Veen
Walter D. (Dan, Daniel, Red, Durak
  Walter) Veen

Walter D. (Dementiy, Demond, Raven, Dark Walter) Veen
Andrey Andreevich Vinelander

*Look at the Harlequins!* (1974)
Gerard (Gerry) Adamson
Louise Adamson
Annette
Bel
Iris Black
Ivor Black
Anna Ivanovna (Annette) Blagovo
Dolly von Borg
Baroness Bredow (née Tolstoy)
Isabel (Bel)
Ninel Ilinishna (Ninella, Nonna) Langley
McNab
Vadim (McNab) Vadimovich

*Pale Fire* (1962)
Queen Blenda
Conmal (Duke of Aros)
Jean (Jane Provost) Dean
Mr. Degré
Disa, Duchess of Payn (Queen Disa)
Judge Hugh Warren Goldsworth
Jakob (Jacques d'Argus, James de Gray, Mr. Degré, Jack Degree, Jacques de Grey, G, Jack Grey, Ravenstone, Ravus, Vinogradus) Gradus
Dr. Charles (K.) Kinbote
Jane Provost
Hazel Shade
John Francis (S) Shade
Sybil (Mrs. S) Shade
Charles (Charles II) Xavier Vseslav the Beloved

*Transparent Things* (1972)
Madame Charles (Anastasia Petrovna Potapov) Chamar
Julia Moore
Armande Chamar Person
Dr. Henry Emery (Person Senior) Person
Hugh (Percy) Person
Phil
Mr. R. (Baron R.)
Mr. Tamworth

## BARBARA NEELY

*Blanche Among the Talented Tenth* (1994)
Robert Stuart

Taifa Walters
Blanche White

## JAY NEUGEBOREN

*An Orphan's Tale* (1976)
Eliezer Fogel
Daniel (Charles Fogelstein, Danny) Ginsberg
Sol (Uncle Sol) Kantor
Anita Mendelsohn
Ephraim Mendelsohn
Hannah Mendelsohn
Murray (Moses, Moshe) Mendelsohn
Max Mittleman
Charlie (Chaim) Sapistein

*Listen Ruben Fontanez* (1968)
Manuel (Manny) Alvarez
Carlos
Ruben Fontanez
Jackson
Marty
Harry (Mad-Man) Meyers
Sarah Meyers
Nydia
Danny Santini
Gil Santini

*Sam's Legacy* (1974)
Benjamin Samson (Ben) Berman
Samuel Paul (Sam) Berman
Gabriel C. (Dutch) Cohen
Flo
Amos (Brick) Johnson
George Herman (Babe) Ruth
Sabatini
Dave Stallworth
Stella
Mason Tidewater

## FAE MYENNE NG

*Bone* (1993)
Dulcie Fu
Leon Leong
Nina Leong
Ona Leong
Leila Louie
Mason Louie

## JOHN NICHOLS

*The Sterile Cuckoo* (1965)
Grandfather Adams

Marian and Bob Adams
Pookie (Pooks) Adams
Roe Billins
Joe Grubner
Jerry (Boomaga) Payne
Nancy Putnam
Ronnie
Harry (Schoons) Schoonover

## ANAÏS NIN
## (See also Volume I)

*Collages* (1964)
Betty
Bill
Bruce
Emile
Harry
Henri
John
Ken
Count Laundromat
Leontine
Lisa
Doctor Mann
Max
Nobuko
Nina Gitana de la Primavera
Raven
Renate
Judith Sands
Shumla
William Dennis Terwilliger, Jr.
Colonel Tishnar
John Wilkes
Varda

*Seduction of the Minotaur* (1961)
Adele
Lillian Beye (See Volume I)
Diana
Djuna (See Volume I)
Edward
Fred
Mr. Hansen
Hatcher
Doctor Hernandez
Jay (See Volume I)
Larry (See Volume I)
The Lie Detector (See Volume I)
Lietta
Lillian
Michael Lomax
Maria

Miguelito
O'Connor
Doctor Palas

## HUGH NISSENSON

**The Tree of Life** (1985)
John Chapman
Fanny Cooper
Thomas Keene
Lettiece Shipman

## HOWARD NORMAN

**The Bird Artist** (1994)
Botho August
Paulette Bath
Lambert Charibon
Romeo Gilette
Enoch Handle
Margaret Handle
Cora Holley
Mitchell Kelb
Isaac Sprague
Alaric Vas
Fabian Vas
Orkney Vas

**The Northern Lights** (1987)
Pelly Bay
Charlotte
Anatole (Anthony) Krainik
Mina Krainik
Noah Krainik
Levon Makowisite

## JOYCE CAROL OATES

**The Assassins** (1975)
Andrew D. Petrie
Hugh (Hughie) Petrie
Stephen Petrie
Yvonne Radek Petrie

**Because It Is Bitter, and Because It Is
My Heart** (1990)
Duke Courtney
Iris Courtney
Leslie Courtney
Persia Courtney
Nancy Dorsey
Jinx (Verlyn Rayburn) Fairchild
Minnie Fairchild
Sugar Baby Fairchild
Eddy Furlong

"Little Red" (Patrick Wesley) Garlock
Vernon Garlock
Vesta Garlock
John Elmore Ritchie
Alan Savage
Byron Savage
Gwendolyn Savage

**Black Water** (1992)
Kelly Kelleher
The Senator

**Childwold** (1976)
Arlene Bartlett
Evangeline Ann (Laney) Bartlett
Vale Bartlett
Fitz John Kasch

**Cybele** (1979)
Risa Allen
Cathleen Diehl
Cynthia Locke
Edwin Locke

**Do with Me What You Will** (1973)
Ardis Carter
Meredith (Mered) Dawe
Elena Ross (Elena Kármán) Howe
Marvin Howe
Jack Morrissey
Ardis (Bonita, Ardis Carter, Ardis Kár-
    mán, Marya Sharp, Mrs. Nigel Stock)
    Ross
Elena Ross
Leo Ross
Marya Sharp
Mrs. Nigel Stock

**Expensive People** (1967)
Elwood Everett
Natashya Romanov (Nada, Tashya)
    Everett
Richard (Dickie) Everett

**A Garden of Earthly Delights** (1967)
Lowry
Clara Walpole Revere
Curt Revere
Steven (Swan) Revere
Carleton Walpole

**My Heart Laid Bare** (1998)
Abraham Licht
Darian Licht
Elisha Licht
Esther Licht
Harwood Licht

Millicent Licht
Thurston Licht

**Son of the Morning** (1978)
Esther Leonie Beloff
Reverend Marian Miles Beloff
William Japheth Sproul III
Ashton Vickery
Elsa Vickery
Nathanael William (Nathan) Vickery
Opal Sayer Vickery
Thaddeus Aaron Vickery

**them** (1969)
Patrick (Pat) Furlong
Bernard Geffen
Nadine Greene
Mort Piercy
Jim Randolph
Howard Wendall
Jules Wendall
Loretta Bostford Wendall
Mama Wendall
Maureen (Reeny) Wendall

**Unholy Loves** (1979)
Alexis Kessler
Albert St. Dennis
Brigit Stott

**What I Lived For** (1992)
Thalia Braunbeck-Corcoran
Jerome (Corky) Corcoran
Sean Corcoran
Theresa Corcoran
Timothy Patrick Corcoran
Charlotte Drummond
Ross Drummond
Christina Kavanaugh
Harry Kavanaugh
Marilee Plummer
Marcus Steadman

**With Shuddering Fall** (1964)
Karen Herz
Mr. Herz
Max
Sherton (Shar)

**Wonderland** (1971)
Dr. Benjamin Cady
Reva Denk
Jesse (Jesse Pedersen, Jesse Vogel) Harte
Dr. Talbot Waller (Trick) Monk
Dr. Karl Pedersen
Frederich Pedersen
Hilda Pedersen

Mary Pedersen
Dr. Roderick Perrault
Helene Cady Vogel
Shelley Vogel

*You Must Remember This* (1987)
Miriam Brancher
Vince Mattiuzzio
Jo-Jo Pearl
Leroy Pearl
Domenic Stevick
Enid Stevick
Felix Stevick
Geraldine Stevick
Hannah Stevick
Karl Stevick
Lizzie Stevick
Lyle Stevick
Warren Stevick

## TIM O'BRIEN

*Going After Cacciato* (1978)
Paul Berlin
Cacciato
Hamijolli Chand
Lieutenant Corson
Stink Harris
Li Van Hgoc
Oscar Johnson
Eddie Lazzutti
Lieutenant Sidney Martin
Jim Pederson
Doc Peret
Captain Fahyi Rhallon
Sarkin Aung Wan

*Tomcat in Love* (1998)
Thomas Chippering
Donna Kooshof
Herbie Zylstra
Lorna Sue Zylstra

## JOHN O'HARA
## (See also Volume I)

*The Lockwood Concern* (1965)
Preston Hibbard
Morris Homestead
Ernestine (Tina) Lockwood
George Bingham (Bing) Lockwood, Jr.
Abraham Lockwood
Adelaide Hoffner Lockwood
Agnes Wynne Lockwood
George Bingham Lockwood
Geraldine Lockwood

Moses Lockwood
Penrose Lockwood
Wilma Lockwood
Arthur McHenry (See Volume I)
Marian Strademyer

## TILLIE OLSEN

*Yonnondio* (1974)
Elias (Old Man) Caldwell
Anna Holbrook
Jim Holbrook
Mazie (Big-eyes) Holbrook
Sheen McEvoy

## CYNTHIA OZICK

*The Cannibal Galaxy* (1983)
Joseph Brill
Naphtali Brill
Albert Charles Garson
Iris Garson
Ephram Gorchak
Beulah Lilt
Hester Lilt

*The Messiah of Stockholm* (1987)
Lars Andemening
Adela Ecklund
Heidi Ecklund
Olle Ecklund

*Trust* (1966)
Stefanie Pettigrew
Gustave Nicholas (Nick) Tilbeck
Miss Tilbeck
Allegra Vand
Enoch Vand
William

## ROBERT B. PARKER

*Promised Land* (1976)
Rose Alexander
Hawk
King Powers
Harvey Shepard
Pam Shepard
Susan Silverman
Spenser

## WALKER PERCY

*Lancelot* (1977)
Anna
Elgin Buell

Troy Dana
Janos Jacoby
Lancelot Andrewes (Lance) Lamar
Lily Lamar
Lucy Lamar
Lucy Cobb Lamar
Mary Margaret Reilly (Margot) Lamar
Maury Lamar
Robert Merlin
Percival
Raine Robinette

*The Last Gentleman* (1966)
Forney Aiken
Ed Barrett
Willston Bibb (Billy, Will) Barrett
Father Boomer
Gamow
Mort Prince
Chandler Vaught
Jamison MacKenzie (Jamie, Jimmy)
   Vaught
Katherine Gibbs (Kitty) Vaught
Mrs. Vaught
Rita (Ree) Vaught
Sutter Vaught
Valentine (Sister Johnette Mary Vian-
   ney, Val) Vaught

*Love in the Ruins* (1971)
Buddy Brown
Alistair Fuchs-Forbes
Max Gottlieb
Hester
Art Immelmann
Ives
Thomas (Doc, Tom, Tommy) More, Jr.
Doris More
Samantha More
Ellen (Ellie) Oglethorpe
Lola Rhoades
Moira Schaffner
Father Rinaldo Smith
Uru (Brother Uru)

*The Moviegoer* (1961)
Dr. Bolling
Emily Bolling
John Bickerson (Binx, Jack) Bolling
Emily Bolling Cutrer
Jules Cutrer
Kate Cutrer
Harold Graebner
Sharon Kincaid
T. Royce Kincaid

Laramie Sinclair
Gordon Stone

## DARRYL PINCKNEY

*High Cotton* (1992)
Bargetta
Djuna Barnes
Betty
Buzzy
Uncle Castor
Aunt Clara
Sister Egba
Grandfather Eustace
Jeanette
Maurice
Trip

## DAVID PLANTE

*The Family* (1978)
Albert B. Francoeur
André J. Francoeur
Aricie Melanie Atalie Lajoie (Reena)
  Francoeur
Arsace Louis Pylade (Jim) Francoeur
Daniel R. Francoeur
Edmond R. Francoeur
Julien E. Francouer
Philip P. Francoeur
Richard A. Francoeur

## SYLVIA PLATH

*The Bell Jar* (1963)
Betsy
Constantin
Dodo Conway
Doreen
Joan Gilling
Doctor Gordon
Esther (Elly Higginbottom) Greenwood
Mrs. Greenwood
Philomena Guinea
Hilda (The Dove)
Irwin
Jay Cee
Marco
Doctor Nolan
Lenny Shepherd
Valerie
Buddy Willard
Mr. Willard
Mrs. (Nelly) Willard

## CARLENE HATCHER POLITE

*The Flagellants* (1967)
Black Cat
Mr. Coffee
Mrs. Fitzpatrick
Frog
Ideal
Inez
Jimson (Jim)
Johnny Lowell
Luis Pagan
Red John
Rheba
Booker Shad
Beata Thangbee

*Sister X and the Victims of Foul Play*
(1975)
Abyssinia (Sister 'ssinia)
Lila Chand Bibi
Willis B. Black
Hubby
Sefiorita Vastie Oubaleta
Arista (Sister X, Glynda, Girl of the
  Glen) Prolo
Baby Lazar Scruggs
Kalik Shabazz
Black Will (Willis B. Black)
Belfast X

## KATHERINE ANNE PORTER
## (See also Volume I)

*Ship of Fools* (1962)
Karl Baumgartner
Jenny (Jane, Jenny Angel, Johanna
  Engel) Brown
La Condesa
William (Wilhelm) Denny
Echegaray
Wilhelm Freytag
Karl Glocken
Wilibald Graf
Arne Hansen
Hutten
Kifthe Hutten
Johann
Julius Lowenthal
Heinrich Lutz
Ric (Armando) and Rac (Dolores)
Siegfried Rieber
Fran Rittersdorf
Fran Otto Schmitt
Schumann

David (David Darling) Scott
Lizzi Spöckenkieker
Thiele
Mary Treadwell

## CHARLES PORTIS

*True Grit* (1968)
Tom Chaney
Reuben (Rooster) Cogburn
Daggett
Mrs. Floyd
Moon Garrett
LaBoeuf
Ned (Lucky Ned) Pepper
Farrell Permalee
Harold Permalee
Emmett Quincy
Frank Ross
Mattie Ross

## CHAIM POTOK

*The Chosen* (1967)
Davey Cantor
Rav Gershenson
David Malter
Reuven (Bobby) Malter
Manya
Danny Saunders
Levi Saunders
Reb Isaac Saunders

*In the Beginning* (1975)
Miriam Bader
Shmuel Bader
Mrs. Horowitz
Eddie Kulanski
Alex Lurie
David (Davey) Lurie
Max Lurie
Meyer Lurie
Ruth Lurie
Sarah Lurie
Saul (Rav Shaul) Lurie
Tony Savanola
Dr. Weidman

*My Name Is Asher Lev* (1972)
Rav Yosef Cutler
Jacob Kahn
Tanya Kahn
Reb Yudel Krinsky
Aryeh Lev
Asher Lev

Rivkeh Lev
Yitzchok Lev
Mrs. Rackover
The Rebbe
Anna Schaeffer

### The Promise (1969)
Rav Gershenson
Abraham Gordon
Joseph Gordon
Michael Gordon
Rachel Gordon
Sarah Gordon
Rav Jacob Kalman
David Malter
Reuven (Bobby) Malter
Manya
Danny Saunders
Levi Saunders
Reb Isaac Saunders

## DAWN POWELL

### The Golden Spur (1962)
Cassie Bender
Costance Birch
Alvine Harshawe
Jonathan Jaimison, Jr.
Dr. Kellsey
George Terrence
Clair Van Orphen
Major Wedburn

## J. F. POWERS

### Morte D'Urban (1962)
Wilfrid (Wilf) Bestudik
Billy Cosgrove
Sally Thwaites Hopwood
John (Jack) Kelleher
Harold (Brother Harold) Peters
Red (Monsignor Renton) Renton
Harvey (Father Urban) Roche
Mrs. Andrew Thwaites

## REYNOLDS PRICE

### A Generous Man (1966)
Della Brame
Yancy Breedlove
Puss Ellis
Dr. Joel Fuller
Macey Gupton

Marise Gupton
Jake Hasty
Baby Lou (Baby Sister) Mustian
Horatio (Rato) Mustian, Jr.
Jasper (Papa) Mustian
Milo Mustian
Pauline Mustian
Rosacoke Mustian
Sissie Abbott Mustian
Kate Pomeroy
Rob (Rooster) Pomeroy
Lois Provo
Selma Provo
Buck Russell
Hawkins Ryden
Miss Jack Ryden
Tommy Ryden

### A Long and Happy Life (1962)
Landon Allgood
Isaac Alston
Marina (Miss Marina) Alston
Willie Duke Aycock
Wesley Beavers
Estelle
Arnold Gupton
Frederick Gupton
Macey Gupton
Marise Gupton
Manson Hargrove
Mae
Aunt Mannie Mayfield
Baby Lou (Baby Sister) Mustian
Horatio (Rato) Mustian, Jr.
Jasper (Papa) Mustian
Milo Mustian
Pauline Mustian
Rosacoke Mustian
Sissie Abbott Mustian
Sammy Ransom
Sledge (Doctor)
Mary Sutton
Mildred Sutton
Bessie Williams

### Love and Work (1968)
Alix
Bo Browder
Cal
Jane Eborn
Jim Eborn
Louise Attwater (Lou) Eborn
Thomas (Tom) Eborn
Todd Eborn

Norman Gaul
Sybil Hedden
Ida Nolan
Albert Riddell
Ruby
Ted

### The Surface of Earth (1975)
Thorne Bradley
Margaret Jane (Polly) Drewry
Elvira Jane
Veenie Goodwin
Walter S. Grainger
Rachel Hutchins
Raven Hutchins
Bedford Kendal
Charlotte Watson Kendal
Eva Kendal
Kennerly Kendal
Rena Kendal
Mag
Alice Matthews
Anna Goodwin Mayfield
Forrest Mayfield
Hattie (Hatt Shorter) Mayfield
Raven Hutchins (Hutch) Mayfield
Robinson Mayfield
Robinson (Rob) Mayfield
Bankey (Zack) Patterson
Undine Phillips
Gid Shorter
Hatt Shorter
James Shorter
Whitby Shorter
Della Simmons
Sylvie
Min (Minnie) Tharrington
Rover Walters
Katherine Epps Watson
Thad Watson

## RICHARD PRICE

### Clockers (1992)
Darryl Adams
Ronald (Strike) Dunham
Victor Dunham
Tyrone Jeeter
Patty Klein
Rocco Klein
Rodney Little
Larry Mazilli
Sean Touhey

## E. ANNIE PROULX

### The Shipping News (1993)
Petal Bear
Beety Buggit
Dennis Buggit
Jack Buggit
Bunny
Tert Card
Agnis Hamm
B. Beaufield Nutbeem
Partridge
Billy Pretty
Wavey Prowse
Ed Punch
Quoyle
Sunshine

### Postcards (1992)
Jewell Blood
Loyal Blood
Marvin (Dub) Blood
Mernelle Blood
Minkton (Mink) Blood
Beatrice (Billy) Handy
Robert (Ray) MacWay
Ronnie Nipple
Bullet Wulff

## MARIO PUZO

### The Godfather (1969)
Kay Adams
Luca Brasi
Peter Clemenza
Constanzia (Connie) Corleone
Michael Corleone
Santino (Sonny) Corleone
Vito (Don Corleone, The Godfather) Corleone
Johnny Fontane
Thomas (Tom) Hagen
Mark McCluskey
Carlo Rizzi
Virgil (Turk) Sollozzo
Phillip Tattaglia
Tessio
Apollonia Vitelli

## THOMAS PYNCHON

### The Crying of Lot 49 (1966)
Emory Bortz
Clayton (Bloody) Chiclitz
Genghis Cohen
Randolph Driblette
Mike Fallopian
Dr. Hilarius
Pierce Inverarity
Stanley Koteks
Oedipa (Oed) Maas
Wendell (Mucho) Maas
Metzger (Baby Igor)
John Nefastis
Richard Wharfinger

### Gravity's Rainbow (1973)
Seaman Bodine
Katje (Domina Nocturna) Borgesius
Emil (Satire) Bummer
Clayton (Bloody) Chiclitz
Oberst Enzian
Margherita (Greta, Gretel) Erdmann
Gerhardt (Der Springer) von Göll
Gottfried
Professor Doctor Laszlo Jamf
Major Duane Marvy
Roger Mexico
Kurt Mondaugen
Edward W. A. (Ned) Pointsman
Franz Pökler
Captain Geoffrey (Pirate) Prentice
Brigadier Ernest Pudding
Lieutenant Tyrone (Ian Scuffling, Rocketman) Slothrop
Jessica Swanlake
Vaslav Tchitcherine
Geli Tripping
Lieutenant (Captain Dominus Blicero, Major Weissmann) Weissman

### V (1963)
Pig Bodine
Clayton (Bloody) Chiclitz
Dudley Eigenvalue, D.D.S.
Father Fairing
Foppl
Evan Godolphin
Hugh Godolphin
Esther Harvitz
Mélanie (La Jarretière) L'Heuremaudit
Fausto Maijstral
Paola (Ruby) Maijstral
Signor Rafael Mantissa
Josephine (Fina) Mendoza
Kurt Mondaugen
Rachel Owlglass
Benny Profane
Slab
McClintic Sphere
Herbert Stencil
Sidney Stencil
V. (The Bad Priest, The lady V., Veronica Manganese, Vera Meroving, Victoria Wren)
Lieutenant (Captain Dominus Blicero, Major Weissmann) Weissman
The Whole Sick Crew
Mafia Winsome

### Vineland (1990)
Darryl Louise (DL) Chastain
Frenesi Gates
Brock Vond
Prarie Wheeler
Zoyd Wheeler

## JOHN RECHY

### City of Night (1963)
Miss Ange
Miss Destiny
Ed King
Lance O'Hara

### Numbers (1967)
Tony Lewis
Sebastian Michaels
Johnny Rio
Emory Travis
Guy Young

## JAMES REDFIELD

### The Celestine Prophecy (1993)
James Redfield

## ISHMAEL REED

### The Free-Lance Pallbearers (1967)
Cipher X
Bukka (Make-um-shit) Doopeyduk
M/Neighbor
Fannie Mae
Rev. Eclair Porkchop
Elijah Raven
Harry Sam
U2 Polyglot
Judge Whimplewopper

### The Last Days of Louisiana Red (1974)
Amos
Big Sally
Andy Brown

Chorus
Max Kasavubu
PaPa (Papa) LaBas
Nanny Lisa
George Kingfish Stevens
Ed Yellings
Minnie (Minnie the Moocher, Queen
    of the Moochers) Yellings
Street Yellings
Wolf Yellings

*Mumbo Jumbo* (1972)
Berbelang
Charlotte
Abdul Hamid
Black Herman
Woodrow Wilson Jefferson
PaPa (Papa) LaBas
Biff Musclewhite
Hinckle Von Vampton
Thor Wintergreen

*Yellow Back Radio Broke-Down*
(1969)
Drag Gibson
John Wesley Hardin
Innocent (Pope)
Zozo Labrique
Loop Garoo Kid
Skinny McCullough
Mustache Sal
Bo Shmo
Chief Showcase

## ANNE RICE

*Interview with the Vampire* (1976)
Armand
Claudia
Babette Freniere
Lestat
Louis
Madeleine

*The Tale of the Body Thief* (1992)
Lestat
Raglan James
Louis
David Talbot

## HAROLD ROBBINS

*The Carpetbaggers* (1961)
Jonas Cord, Jr.
Jonas Cord, Sr.

Jennie (Judy Belden, Sister M. Thomas)
    Denton
Jo-Ann
Geraldine Marlowe
Harrison (Harry) Marlowe
Rina (Katrina Osterlaag) Marlowe
Ronald (Laddie) Marlowe
Bernard B. (Bernie) Norman (Nor-
    manovitz)
Robair
Nevada (Max Sand) Smith
Amos (Amos Jordan) Winthrop
Monica Winthrop
David (Dave, Davidele, Davy) Woolf

## TOM ROBBINS

*Another Roadside Attraction* (1971)
Baby Thor
The Corpse
Father Gutstadt
Jesus Christ
Nearly Normal Jimmy
Marx Marvelous
Mon Cul
L. Westminster (Brother Dallas,
    Plucky) Purcell III
Amanda Ziller
John Paul Ziller

*Even Cowgirls Get the Blues* (1976)
Chink
Countess
Dr. Felix Dreyfus
Julian Gitche
Sissy Hankshaw Gitche
Bonanza (Sally Elizabeth Jones) Jelly-
    bean
Dr. Robbins
Delores del Ruby
Madame Zoe

## ANNE RICHARDSON ROIPHE

*Up the Sandbox!* (1970)
Dr. Beineke
Fidel Castro
Dora Grossbart
John
Dr. Maria Lopez
Elizabeth Reynolds
Margaret Ferguson Reynolds
Paul Reynolds
Peter Reynolds

## JUDITH ROSSNER

*Looking for Mr. Goodbar* (1975)
Ali (Eli)
Katherine (Kitty) Dunn
Theresa (Terry, Tessie, Theresita) Dunn
Thomas Dunn
Martin Engle
Brooks Hendell
Brigid Dunn Kelly
Tony Lopanto
James Morrisey
Gary Cooper White

## PHILIP ROTH
(See also Volume I)

*American Pastoral* (1997)
Dawn Levov
Jerry Levov
Meredith (Merry) Levov
Seymour "Swede" Levov
William (Bill) Orcutt III

*The Anatomy Lesson* (1983)
Milton Appel
Gloria Galanter
Jaga
Jenny
Diana Rutherford
Nathan Zuckerman

*The Breast* (1972)
David Alan (Dave) Kepesh
Dr. Klinger
Claire Ovington

*The Counterlife* (1986)
Maria
Carol Goff Zuckerman
Henry Zuckerman
Nathan Zuckerman

*The Ghost Writer* (1979)
Amy (Anne Frank) Bellette
Emanuel Isidore (E. I., Manny) Lonoff
Hope (Hopie) Lonoff
Nathan Zuckerman

*The Great American Novel* (1973)
Roland (Rollie) Agni
Ulysses S. (Mistah Baseball) Fairsmith
Gilbert (Gil) Gamesh
Luke (Luke the Loner) Gofannon
Michael (Mike, Mike the Mouth) Mas-
    terson

## ERICH SEGAL

*Love Story* (1970)
Jennifer Cavilleri (Jenny) Barrett
Oliver (Old Stonyface) Barrett III
Oliver (Ollie) Barrett IV
Philip (Phil) Cavilleri
Ray Stratton

*Oliver's Story* (1977)
Oliver (Old Stonyface) Barrett III
Oliver (Ollie) Barrett IV
Marcie Binnendale
Philip (Phil) Cavilleri
Marcie Binnendale Nash
Stephen (Steve) Simpson

## HUBERT SELBY, JR.

*Last Exit to Brooklyn* (1964)
Harry Black
George (Georgette) Hanson
Mike Kelly
Regina
Sal
Tralala
Vincent (Vincennti, Vinnie)

## MARY LEE SETTLE
## (See also Volume I)

*Blood Tie* (1978)
Turget Bay
Captain of the Gendarmes
Ariadne Hanim
Melek Hanim
Minci Hanim (Monkey)
Horst
Basil de Montfort
Durust Osman
Hatije Hanim Osman
Huseyin Osman
Frank Proctor
Jamie Stewart
Lisa Stewart
Timur
Kemal Young

*Prisons* (1973)
Baxter
John (Johnny) Candoe
Charity
Corporal Jonathan (Johnny) Church
Oliver (Ironsides) Cromwell
Cornet Henry (Harry) Denne

William (Little Will) Dogood
Sir Thomas (Black Tom) Fairfax
Nell Lacy
Peregrine Lacy
Sir Valentine Lacy
Lazarus
Robbie Lokyar
Gideon MacKarkle
Laodocious Martin
William (Pinky) Panck
Will Pentacost
Thankful Perkins
Colonel Rainsborough
John Roper
Simeon Roper
Francis White

## MICHAEL SHAARA

*The Killer Angels* (1974)
Lewis (Lew, Lo) Armistead
John Buford
Joshua Lawrence Chamberlain
Richard (Dick, Baldy) Ewell
Arthur Lyon Fremantle
Richard Brooke (Dick) Garnett
Winfield Scott Hancock
Ambrose Powell Hill
Robert Edward Lee
James (Old Pete Dutchman) Longstreet
George Gordon Meade
George Pickett
John Reynolds
J. E. B. (Jeb) Stuart

## SIDNEY SHELDON

*Bloodline* (1977)
Alec Nichols
Vivian Nichols
Elizabeth Roffe
Sam Roffe
Rhys Williams

*Master of the Game* (1982)
Alexandra Blackwell
David Blackwell
Eve Blackwell
Kate Blackwell
Tony Blackwell
Jamie McGregor

*Memories of Midnight* (1990)
Constantin Demiris

Melina Demiris
Catherine Douglas
Tony Rizzoli

*Rage of Angels* (1980)
Kenneth Bailey
Robert DiSilva
Michael Moretti
Jennifer Parker
Adam Warner

## FRANCES SHERWOOD

*Vindication* (1993)
Agnes
Mr. Andrews
Annie
Mary Frances Bishop
Mr. Bishop
Catherine Blake
William Blake
Fanny Blood
Rebecca "Jelly" Christie
Thomas Christie
Cook
Mrs. Dawson
Dr. George Fordyce
Henry Fuseli
Sophia Fuseli
William Godwin
Gilbert Imlay
Joseph Johnson
Lady Kingsborough
Richard Kingsborough
William Kingsborough
Lars
Marguerite
Mrs. Mason
Mrs. McCamb
John Opie
Thomas "Tom" Paine
Dr. Richard Price
Mrs. Price
Mary Wollstonecraft Godwin Shelley
Percy Shelley
Hugh Skeys
Mr. Smith
Charles Wollstonecraft
Edward Wollstonecraft
Edward Wollstonecraft, Sr.
Eliza Wollstonecraft
Everina Wollstonecraft
Fanny Wollstonecraft
Mary Wollstonecraft

Mrs. Wollstonecraft
Ned Wollstonecraft

## CAROL SHIELDS

### *The Stone Diaries* (1993)
Alice Flett
Barker Flett
Clarentine Flett
Magnus Flett
Cuyler Goodwill
Daisy Goodwill
Mercy Goodwill

## ANN ALLEN SHOCKLEY

### *Loving Her* (1974)
Terrence (Terry) Bluvard
Fran Brown
Denise Davis
Jerome Lee Davis
Renay Davis
Jean Gail
Mr. Herald
Vance Kenton
Phil Millard
Pearl Sims
Edith Stilling

## LESLIE MARMON SILKO

### *Ceremony* (1977)
Betonie
Josiah
Ts'eh Montao
Night Swan
Tayo

## HERBERT SIMMONS
## (See also Volume I)

### *Man Walking on Eggshells* (1962)
Argustus (Mr. Andy) Anderson
Wilbur Anderson
Banny Douglas
Helen Douglas
Hosea Douglas
Mae Douglas
Raymond Charles Douglas
Carl (Lobo) Logan
Codene McClusky
Bruce (Teacher) Thomas

## MONA SIMPSON

### *Anywhere but Here* (1987)
Art
Ann August
Adele Diamond
Ted Diamond
Hishan (John)
Bert Keller
Nan Keller
Peter Keller
Lillian
Benny (Ben) Measey
Carol Measey
Hal Measey
Jimmy Measey
Josh Spritzer
Daniel Swan
Lonnie Tishman

## ISAAC BASHEVIS SINGER
## (See also Volume I)

### *Enemies, A Love Story* (1972)
Shifrah Puah Bloch
Herman Broder
Tamara Luria Broder
Yadwiga Pracz Broder
Rabbi Milton Lampert
Leon Tortshiner
Masha Bloch Tortshiner

### *Shosha* (1978)
Bashele
Celia Chentshiner
Haiml Chentshiner
Sam Dreiman
Morris Feitelzolm
Aaron (Arele, Tsutsik) Greidinger
Shosha (Shoshele)
Betty (Bettyle) Slonim
Dora Stolnitz
Tekla
Zelig

### *The Slave* (1962)
Jan Bzik
Benjamin Eliezer
Jacob (Reb Jacob) Eliezer
Gershon
Zelda Leah
Adam Pilitzky
Theresa Pilitzky
Zagayek
Moishe (Reb Moishe) Zakolkower

## JANE SMILEY

### *The Age of Grief* (1987)
Dana McManus Hurst
David McManus Hurst
Leah Hurst
Lizzie Hurst
Stephanie Hurst

### *Moo* (1995)
Margaret Bell
Earl Butz
Bob Carlson
John Vernon Cates
Diane
Elaine Dobbs-Jellinek
Keri Donaldson
Dr. Lionel Gift
Ivar Harstad
Nils Harstad
Marly Hellmich
Mary Jackson
Dean Jellinek
Sherri Johnson
Dr. Bo Jones
Helen Levy
Arlen Martin
Timothy Monahan
Gary Olson
Joy Pfisterer
Cecelia Sanchez
Loren Stroop
Mrs. Loraine Walker
Chairman (Jake) X

### *A Thousand Acres* (1991)
Marvin (Marv) Carson
Howard Clark
Jess Clark
Loren Clark
Caroline Cook
Laurence (Larry, Daddy) Cook
Ken LaSalle
Linda Lewis
Peter (Pete) Lewis
Rose Cook Lewis
Mary Livingston
Ginny Cook Smith
Tyler (Ty) Smith

## BETTY SMITH
## (See also Volume I)

### *Joy in the Morning* (1963)
Annie McGairy Brown

Carl (Carlton Braun) Brown
Anthony Byrd
James W. (Jim) Darwent
Margo Hansmon
Henry
Aggie Lopin
Goldie Lopin
Annie McGairy
Victor (Prof) Newcool
Coach (Steve) Stevens

## LEE SMITH

*Something in the Wind* (1971)
Bentley T. Hooks
Charles Windham Hughes
Brooke Kincaid
Carter Kincaid
Carolyn Kincaid

## SUSAN SONTAG

*The Benefactor* (1963)
Frau Anders
Professor Bulgaraux
Hippolyte
Jean-Jacques
Lucrezia
Maestro
Monique
Father Trissotin

*Death Kit* (1967)
Jim Allen
Dalton (Diddy) Harron
Joan Harron
Paul Harron
Angelo (Joe) Incardona
Myra Incardona
Mary
Hester Nayburn
Jessie Nayburn
Wolf-Boy

*The Volcano Lover* (1992)
William Beckford
Mrs. Cadogan
Admiral Caracciolo
Catherine
Il Cavaliere (Sir William Hamilton)
Charles
Domenico Cirillo
Eleonora de Fonseca Pimentel
Fanny
Fatima
Goethe

Emma Hart (Emma Hamilton)
Jack
Athanasius Kircher
Arthur Paget
Father Piaggio
Bartolomeo (Tolo) Pumo
Efrosina Pumo
Queen Charlotte
Cardinal Ruffo
Vitellio Scarpia
The Hero (Lord Nelson)
The King
Valerio
Elsabeth Vigee-Lebrun
Horace Walpole

## ELLEASE SOUTHERLAND

*Let the Lion Eat Straw* (1979)
Jackson (Crazy Jack) Gold
Mamma Habblesham
Angela Williams Lavoisier
Arthur Lavoisier
Robes (Ohio) Smith
Abeba Williams Lavoisier (African
   Flower, Piano Girl) Torch
Askia-Touré Torch
Daniel A. (Reverend Brother) Torch
Daniel-Jr. Torch
Kora Torch
C-J Watkins

## TERRY SOUTHERN
## (See also Volume I)

*Blue Movie* (1970)
Boris (B., King B.) Adrian
Arabella
Pamela Dickensen
Feral
C. D. Harrison
Les (Rat Prick) Harrison
Tina Marie (Teeny Marie) Holt
Morton L. (Morty) Kanovitz
Cardinal von Kopf
Sidney H. (Sid) Krassman
Abe (Lynx) Letterman
Nathan (Lips) Malone
Dave and Debbie Roberts
Raphael Nicholas (Nicky) Sanchez
Tony Sanders
Angela (Helen Brown) Sterling
Helen Vrobel
Yvette

## NICHOLAS SPARKS

*The Notebook* (1996)
Noah Calhoun
Lon Hammond
Allie Nelson

## SCOTT SPENCER

*Endless Love* (1979)
Arthur Axelrod
David (Dave) Axelrod
Rose Axelrod
Ann Butterfield
Hugh Butterfield
Jade Butterfield
Keith Butterfield
Sam (Sammy) Butterfield
Ecrest
Susan Henry
Stu Neihardt
Ingrid Ochester
Barbara Sherwood
Eddie Watanabe

*Last Night at the Brain Thieves' Ball*
(1973)
Acoraci
Leon Anderson
Paul Lloyd Galambos
Miss Mitchell
Popkoff (Dr. P.)
Ira Robinson
Tom Simon
Carl Stein
Worthington (Mr. W.)

*Preservation Hall* (1976)
Melissa Cavanaugh
Thomas (Tom, Tommy) Douglas
Gary Fish
Bob Halpin
Gerald Healey
Earl Morgan
Lillian Belsito Douglas (Lil) Morgan
Tracy Keating Morgan
Virgil (Fatboy, Vernon) Morgan
Munt
Mario Nicolosi
Kathryn Perl

## MARK STEADMAN

*A Lion's Share* (1975)
George Bogger
Mackey Brood

Brodie
Ralph C. (Rafie) Gawber
Valentine (Val) Hood
Mayo (May, Sandra)
Murf
Araba Nightwing
Willy Rutter
Sweeney
Lorna Weech
Ron Weech

*Picture Palace* (1978)
Frank Fusco
Woodrow (Woody) Leathers
Blanche Overall
R. G. Perdew
Mama and Papa Pratt
Maude Coffin Pratt
Orlando (Ollie) Pratt
Phoebe Pratt
Teets

*Saint Jack* (1973)
Jack Flowers (Fiori)
Desmond Frogget
Gladys
Gopi
Gunstone
Chop Hing Kheng Fatt (Big Hing)
William Leigh
Edwin Shuck
Yardley
Yates

*Waldo* (1967)
Sybil Czap
Edwin
Emma
Grammy
Mona
Jasper Pistareen
Clovis Techy
Waldo
Arnold Wermy
Fred Wolfpits

## ROSS THOMAS

*Briarpatch* (1985)
Gene Colder
Benjamin (Ben) Dill
Anna Maude Singe
Jake Spivey

## LAWRENCE THORNTON

*Imagining Argentina* (1987)
Martin Benn
Carlos Rueda
Cecelia Rueda
Teresa Ruedos

## JOHN KENNEDY TOOLE

*A Confederacy of Dunces* (1980)
Santa Battaglia
Darlene
Burma Jones
Lana Lee
Mr. Gus Levy
Angelo Mancuso
Myrna Minkoff
Ignatius J. Reilly
Mrs. Irene Reilly
Claude Robichaux

## SCOTT TUROW

*Presumed Innocent* (1987)
Lip Lipranzer
Carolyn Polhemus
Barbara Sabich
Rusty Sabich
Alejandro Stern

## ANNE TYLER

*The Accidental Tourist* (1985)
Julian Edge
Rose Leary Edge
Charles Leary
Macon Leary
Porter Leary
Sarah Leary
Muriel Pritchett

*Breathing Lessons* (1988)
Serena Gill
Daisy Moran
Fiona Moran
Ira Moran
Jesse Moran
Maggie Moran

*Celestial Navigation* (1974)
Brian O'Donnell
Olivia
Amanda Pauling
Jeremy Pauling

Wilma Pauling
Mr. Somerset
Darcy Tell
Mary Tell
Mildred Vinton

*The Clock Winder* (1972)
Elizabeth (Liz, Gillespie Emerson)
   Abbott
John Abbott
Julia Abbott
Mr. Cunningham
Andrew Emerson
Margaret Emerson
Matthew Emerson
Pamela Emerson
Peter Emerson
Timothy Emerson

*Dinner at the Homesick Restaurant*
(1982)
Beck Tull
Cody Tull
Ezra Tull
Jenny Tull
Lucas Tull
Pearl Cody Tull
Ruth Spivey Tull

*Earthly Possessions* (1977)
Lacey Debney Ames
Murray Ames
Mindy Callender
Alberta Emory
Amos Emory
Catherine (Selinda) Emory
Charlotte Ames Emory
Jiggs Emory
Julian Emory
Linus Emory
Saul Emory
Oliver (O. J.) Jamison
Jake Simms

*Morgan's Passing* (1980)
Brindle Gower
Louisa Gower
Morgan Gower
Emily Meredith
Leon Meredith

*Saint Maybe* (1991)
Bee Bedloe
Danny Bedloe
Daphne Bedloe
Doug Bedloe

Ian Bedloe
Claudia Bedloe-Daley
Cicely Brown
Agatha Dean
Lucy Dean
Thomas Dean
Rita DiCarlo
Reverent Emmett

*Searching for Caleb* (1976)
Sulie Boudrault
Alonzo Divich
Eli Everjohn
Caroline Peck Mayhew
Sam Mayhew
Margaret Rose Peck (Meg, Meggie)
  Milsom
Caleb Peck
Caroline Peck
Daniel (Judge Peck) Peck
Duncan Peck
Justine Peck
Luray Spivey Pickett
White-Eye Ramford

# JOHN UPDIKE
## (See also Volume I)

*Beck: A Book* (1970)
Hannah Bech
Henry Bech
Mildred Belloussovsky-Dommergues
Bobochka
Eustace Chubb
Hannah Ann Collins
Mrs. Beatrice Latchett (Bea) Cook
Char Ecktin
Ruth Eisenbraun
John Kingsgrant Forbes
Vera Glavanakova
Josh Glazer
Jòrgen Josiah (Goldy) Goldschmidt
Eva Hassel
Miss Haynsworth
Jason Honeygale
Anatole Husac
Tory Ingersoll
Torquemada Langguth
Norma Latchett
Mr. Linnehan
Merissa Merrill
Wendell Morrison
Myshkin
Emil Nordquist

Athanase Petrescu
Petrov
Phillips
Ellen Reynolds
Skip Reynolds
Ekaterina Alexandrovna (Kate)
  Ryleyeva
Sobaka
Irving Stern
Tarn
L. Clark Tuttle

*The Centaur* (1963)
Corinna Appleton
Harry (Doc) Appleton
Hester Appleton
Skippy Appleton
Catherine Kramer (Cassie, Chariclo)
  Caldwell
George W. (Chiron, Sticks) Caldwell
Peter Caldwell
Becky Davis
Johnny Dedman
Ray (Deify) Deifendorf
Penny Fogleman
Heller
Mim Herzog
Al Hummel
Vera Hummel
Kegerise
Pop Kramer
Minor Kretz
Judith (Judy) Lengel
Reverend March
Iris Osgood
Phil Phillips
Charlie Potteiger
Kenneth (Kenny, Dr. Yankem)
  Schreuer
Alma Caldwell Terrio
Mark Youngerman
Louis M. Zimmerman

*The Coup* (1978)
Candace (Candy, The One Who Is Al-
  ways Wrapped, The Muffled One)
  Cunningham
Dorfû
King Edumu IV, Lord of Wanjiji
Colonel Hakim Félix (Bini, Happy)
  Elleloû
Michaelis Ezana
Angelica Gibbs
Donald X. Gibbs
Kadongolimi

Mr. Klipspringer
Barry Little
Esmerelda Miller
Mtesa
Sidi Mukhtar
Opaku
Oscar X
Sheba
Sittina (Queen of Shendy)
Kutunda Traore
Wadal

*Couples* (1968)
Frank Appleby
Janet Appleby
Carol Constantine
Eddie Constantine
Matt Gallagher
Terry Gallagher
Bea Guerin
Roger Guerin
Angela Hanema
Nancy Hanema
Piet Hanema
Ruth Hanema
Leon Jazinski
Bernadette Ong
John Ong
Ben Saltz
Irene Saltz
Harold (little-Smith) Smith
Marcia Burnham (little-Smith) Smith
Freddy Thorne
Georgene Thorne
Elizabeth Fox (Foxy) Whitman
Ken Whitman

*In the Beauty of the Lilies* (1996)
Clark Lazlo
Clarence Arthur Wilmot
Emily Sifford Wilmot
Esther "Essie" Wilmot
Stella Wilmot
Theodore "Teddy" Wilmot

*Marry Me* (1976)
Jerry Conant
Ruth Conant
Richard (Dick) Mathias
Sally Mathias

*A Month of Sundays* (1975)
Amos
Thaddeus (Ned) Bork
Doctor Reverend Wesley Augustus
  Chillingworth

Alicia Crick
Fred
Frances (Frankie) Harlow
Gerald (Gerry) Harlow
Jane Chillingworth Marshfield
Martin Marshfield
Reverend Thomas (Tom) Marshfield
Stephen Marshfield
Ms. Prynne
Jamie Ray
Woody

*Of the Farm* (1965)
Doc Graaf
Dean McCabe
Richard McCabe
Joan Robinson
Joey Robinson
Mary Robinson
Peggy McCabe Robinson
Sammy Schoelkopf

*Rabbit at Rest* (1990)
Harry "Rabbit" Angstrom
Janice (Jan) Springer Angstrom
Judy Angstrom
Teresa "Pru" Lubell Angstrom
Nelson Angstrom

*Rabbit Is Rich* (1981)
Harry "Rabbit" Angstrom
Janice (Jan) Springer Angstrom
Nelson Angstrom

*Rabbit Redux* (1971)
Earl Angstrom
Harry "Rabbit" Angstrom
Janice Springer (Jan) Angstrom
Mary Angstrom
Miriam (Mim) Angstrom
Nelson Frederick Angstrom
Hubert H. (Skeeter) Farnsworth
Billy Fosnacht
Peggy Fosnacht
Beatrice (Babe) Greene
Jill Pendleton
Frederick (Fred) Springer
Rebecca Springer
Charlie Stavros

# LEON URIS
## (See also Volume I)

*Armageddon* (1964)
Shenandoah Blessing
Lotte Böhm

Nelson Goodfellow (Big Nellie) Bradbury
Scott Davidson
Ernestine (Erna) Falkenstein
Hildegaard (Hilde Diehl) Falkenstein
Ulrich Falkenstein
Andrew Jackson (Chip) Hansen
Neal Hazzard
Heinrich Hirsch
Marion (Sister Mary) Hodgkiss
Igor Karlovy
Sean O'Sullivan
Hiram Stonebraker

*QB VII* (1970)
Thomas Bannister
Abraham (Abe) Cady
Ben Cady
Terrence (Terry) Campbell
Anthony Gilray
Robert Highsmith
Adam Kelno
Angela Brown Kelno
Stephan Kelno
David Shawcross
Egon Sobotnik
Mark Tesslar
Pieter Van Damm
Maria Viskova
Adolph Voss
Sarah Wydman

*Trinity* (1976)
Atty Fitzpatrick
Caroline Weed Hubble
Jeremy Hubble
Roger Hubble
Andrew Ingram
Brigid Larkin
Conor Larkin
Dary Larkin
Liam Larkin
Oliver Cromwell MacIvor
Shelley MacLeod
Kevin O'Garvey
Seamus O'Neill
Charles Stewart Parnell
Dan Sweeney
Frederick Murdoch (Freddie) Weed

# GORE VIDAL

*Burr* (1973)
Dr. Dominie Bogart
William Cullen Bryant

Col. Aaron Burr
Theodosia Burr
Mary Eliza Chase
Nelson Chase
William de la Touche Clancey
Mr. Craft
Matthew L. (Matt) Davis
Professor George Orson Fuller
Reginald Gower
Alexander Hamilton
Thomas Jefferson
Helen Jewett
Eliza Bowen Jumel
William Leggett
Mordecai Noah
Charles (Charlie, Old Patroon)
    Schuyler
Sam Swartwout
Rosanna Townsend
Martin (Matty Van) Van Buren
Gulian C. Verplanck
Robert Wright

*Julian* (1964)
Julian Augustus
Constantius Augustus (Constans)
Callistus
Eusebia
Gallus
Helena
Libanius
Maximus
Oribasius
Priscus

*Myra Breckinridge* (1968)
Myra (Myron) Breckinridge
Rusty (Ace Mann) Godowsky
Buck (Ted Percey) Loner
Dr. Randolph Spenser Montag
Mary-Ann Pringle
Letitia Van Allen

*Washington, D.C.* (1967)
Diana Day
James Burden Day
Kitty Day
Harold Griffiths
Edgar Carl (Ed) Nillson
Clay Overbury
Blaise Delacroix Sanford
Enid Sanford
Frederika Sanford
Peter Sanford
Billy Thorne

# KURT VONNEGUT
## (See also Volume I)

### Breakfast of Champions (1973)
Fred T. Barry
Col. Looseleaf Harper
Wayne Hoobler
Celia Hoover
Dwayne Hoover
George (Bunny) Hoover
Rabo Karabekian
Kazak (See Volume I)
Harry LeSabre
Bonnie MacMahon
Francine Pefko
Eliot Rosewater
Kilgore Trout
Leo Trout
Kurt Vonnegut, Jr.

### Cat's Cradle (1963)
Bokonon
Julian Castle
Philip Castle
Hazel (Mom) Crosby
H. Lowe Crosby
Angela (Mrs. Harrison C. Conners) Hoenikker
Dr. Felix Hoenikker
Franklin (Frank) Hoenikker
Newton (Little Newt) Hoenikker
John (Jonah)
Lionel Boyd (Bokonon) Johnson
Dr. Schlichter von Koenigswald
Earl McCabe
Claire Minton
Horlick Minton
Miguel (Papa) Monzano
Mona Aamons Monzano

### God Bless You, Mr. Rosewater (1965)
Amanita Buntline
Diana Moon Glampers
Norman Mushari
Harry Pena
Caroline Rosewater
Eliot Rosewater
Fred Rosewater
Lister Ames Rosewater
Sylvia DuVrais Zetterling Rosewater
Kilgore Trout
Bunny Weeks

### Jailbird (1979)
Leland Clewes
Dr. Robert (Frank X. Barlow, Kilgore Trout) Fender

Alexander Hamilton McCone
Daniel McCone
Mary Kathleen (Mrs. Jack Graham) O'Looney
Dr. Ben Shapiro
Ruth Starbuck
Walter F. (Walter F. Stankiewicz) Starbuck
Kenneth Whistler
Sarah Wyatt

### Mother Night (1962)
Howard W. Campbell, Jr.
George Kraft
Helga Noth
Resi Noth
Bernard V. O'Hare
Kurt Vonnegut, Jr.
Frank (Blue Fairy Godmother, Col. Harold J. Sparrow) Wirtanen

### Slapstick (1976)
Cordelia Swain Cordiner
Fu Manchu
Dr. Stewart Rawlings Mott
Captain Bernard Eagle-1 (Daffodil-II) O'Hare
Melody Oriole-2 von Peterswald
Eliza Mellon (Betty Brown) Swain
Letitia Vanderbilt Rockefeller Swain
Wilbur Rockefeller Daffodil-II (Bobby Brown) Swain
Vera Chipmunk-5 Zappa

### Slaughterhouse-Five (1969)
Howard W. Campbell, Jr.
Edgar Derby
Paul Lazzaro
Resi North
Bernard V. O'Hare
Mary O'Hare
Billy Pilgrim
Valencia Merble Pilgrim
Eliot Rosewater
Bertram Rumfoord
Kilgore Trout
Kurt Vonnegut, Jr.
Roland Weary
Montana Wildhack

# ALICE WALKER

### The Color Purple (1982)
Albert
Shug Avery
Sophia Butler

Celie
Corrine
Nettie
Reverend Samuel

### Meridian (1976)
Camara (Princess)
Anne-Marion Coles
George Daxter
Eddie
Eddie Jr. (Rundi)
Feather Mae
Truman (True) Held
Gertrude Hill
Meridian Hill
Walter Longknife
Louvinie
Rims Mott
Tommy Odds
Henry O'Shay
Lynne Rabinowitz
Mr. Raymonds
Miss Lucille (Little Sister Lucille) Treasure
Miss Margaret Treasure
The Wild Child (Wile Chile)
Miss Winter

### The Third Life of Grange Copeland (1970)
Brownfield (Brown) Copeland
Daphne (Daffy) Copeland
Grange Copeland
Josie Copeland
Margaret Copeland
Mem R. Copeland
Ornette Copeland
Ruth Copeland
Judge Harry
Mr. Shipley
Star

# MARY WILLIS WALKER

### The Red Scream (1994)
Louie Bronk
Molly Cates
Sister Addine Dodgen
Tanya Klein
Alison McFarland
Andrea Wendell McFarland
Charlie McFarland
Georgia McFarland
Stuart McFarland
Frank Purcell

Mariana Paloma
Augustus (Gus) Plebesly

### The Onion Field (1973)

Arthur Alarcon
Mark Brandler
Pierce R. (P. R.) Brooks
Sheldon Brown
Raymond Byrne
Adah Campbell
Chrissie Campbell
Ian James Campbell
Dino Fulgoni
Julius Griffin
Phil Halpin
Helen (Moms) Hettinger
Karl Hettinger
Charles Hollopeter
Irving Kanarek
Thomas Le Sage
Charles Maple
John Moore
Alfred Peracca
Gregory Ulas (Greg) Powell
Marshall Schulman
Billy Small
Ray Smith
Jimmy Lee (Jimmy Youngblood) Smith

## ROBERT PENN WARREN

### A Place to Come To (1977)

Maria McInnis Beaufort
Michael X. (Butty) Butler
James Lawford Carrington
Rozelle Hardcastle Butler (Beauty
   Queen of Dugton High, Miss Pritty-
   Pants, Rose) Carrington
Dauphine Finkel
Rebecca Carrington (Dee-Dee, Mrs.
   David McInnis) Jones-Talbot
David McInnis
Elvira K. Tewksbury Simms
Dr. Heinrich Stahlmann
Agnes Andresen (Little Aggie) Tewksbury
Buck Tewksbury
Jediah (Jed, Old Broke-Nose) Tewksbury

## JEROME WEIDMAN

### The Temple (1975)

Monroe Blumenfeld

Morris (Michael [Mike] Palgrave)
   Cohen
Rachel Cohen
Anthony X. (Tony) D'Alessandro
David (Dave) Dehn
Bella Biaggi Delm
Hella (Helen Drake) Drachenfels
Don Fortgang
Rabbi Goldfarb
Fanny Mintz
Sidney (Sid) Singer

## JAMES WELCH

### Fools Crow (1986)

Fast Horse
Feather Woman
Fools Crow
Heavy Shield Woman
Yellow Kidney

## EUDORA WELTY
## (See also Volume I)

### Losing Battles (1970)

Brother Bethune
Aycock Comfort
Maud Eva Moody
Oscar Moody
Julia Mortimer
Beulah Beecham Renfro
Ella Fay Renfro
Gloria Short Renfro
Jack Jordan Renfro
Lady May Renfro
Lexie Renfro
Ralph Renfro
Rachel Sojourner
Marshal Excell Prentiss (Curly) Stovall
Thurzah Elvira Jordan (Granny) Vaughn

### The Optimist's Daughter (1972)

Major Rupert Bullock
Tennyson Bullock
Tish Bullock
Adele Courtland
Nate Courtland
Mr. Dalzell
Laurel McKelva (Polly) Hand
Philip Hand
Mrs. Martello
Becky Thurston McKelva
Clinton (Clint, Judge Mac) McKelva

Wanda Fay Chisom McKelva
Missouri

## JESSAMYN WEST
## (See also Volume I)

### The Life I Really Lived (1979)

Joseph Raymond (Joe, Joey) Chase
Orpha (Mrs. Dudley, Mrs. Hesse, Tum-
   bleweed) Chase
Alonzo T. (Lon, Lonnie) Dudley
Burt Griswold
Marie Shields Griswold
Jacob (Jake) Hesse
Crit Matthews
Ebon Matthews
Gregory (Greg) McGovern
Ralph Navarro
Tom O'Hara
Sam Shields
Ormand Slaughter
Wanda (Kickapoo)

### The Massacre at Fall Creek (1975)

Luther (Lute) Bemis
Ora (Ory) Bemis
George Benson
Black Antler
Benjamin (Ben) Cape
Caleb (Cale) Cape
Hannah (Hannay) Cape
Lizzie Cape
Jud Clasby
Norah (Norry) Culligan
Oscar Achilles (O. A., Ossie) Dilk
Folded Leaf
Charles (Charlie) Fort
John Wood
John (Johnny) Wood, Jr.
Reba Reese Wood

### A Matter of Time (1966)

John Everett Henshaw
Blix Murphy Hollister
Milt Hollister
Basil (Blackie) Murphy
Le Cid (Cid) Murphy
Marmion Murphy
Maude Hobhouse Murphy
Orland Murphy
Peter (Pete) Orcino
Tasmania (Tassie) Murphy Orcino
John Reyes

Manuel (Kid Sanchez) Sanchez
Vurl Seaman

## DONALD E. WESTLAKE

### The Ax (1997)
Kane Bagley Asche
Garrett Roger Blackstone
Detective Burton
Betsy Devore
Bill "Billy" Devore
Burke Devore
Margaret Devore
Everett Boyd Dunes
Herbert Coleman Everly
Hauck Curtis Exman
Upton "Ralph" Fallon
James Halstead
Mr. Porculey
Longus Quinlan
Edward G. Ricks
June "Junie" Ricks
Mrs. Ricks
Lewis Ringer

### God Save The Mark (1967)
Gertie Divine
Fred Fitch
Jack Reilly
Karen Smith

### The Hook (2000)
Jimmy Branley
Isabelle de Fuentes
Detective Grasso
Fred Gustav
Molly Gustav
Willard Hartman
Janet Higgins
Mrs. Hildebrand
George Jenkins
Jill
Arthur Johnson
Joe Katz
Joshua Katz
Sam Katz
Shelly Katz
Larry
Lawyer Bob
Detective Maurice
Jerry Mossman
Ms. Pered
Susan Prentice
Wayne Prentice
Barry Proctorr

Betsy Proctorr
Bryce Proctorr
Ellen Proctorr
Lucie Proctorr
Tom Proctorr
Marcia Rierdon
Fred Silver
Mark Steiner
Jack Wagner

## WILLIAM WHARTON

### Birdy (1978)
Alfonso
Birdie
Birdy
Alfonso (Al) Columbato
Mr. Lincoln
Corporal Lumbowski
Perta
Mrs. Prevost
Phil (CO) Renaldi
Doris Robinson
Joe Sagessa
Major S. O. Weiss

### Dad (1981)
Dr. Delibro
Joan Lazio
Bette Tremont
Billy Tremont
John (Jack, Jacky, Johnny) Tremont, Jr.
John (Jack) Tremont, Sr.

## JOHN EDGAR WIDEMAN

### Hurry Home (1970)
Albert
Cecil Otis Braithwaite
Esther Brown Braithwaite
Simon Braithwaite
Carlos
Charles Webb
Walter Willis

### The Lynchers (1973)
Anthony
Willie (Littleman) Hall
Graham Rice
Leonard Saunders
Sissie
Tanya
Angela Taylor
Orin (Sweetman) Wilkerson
Thomas Wilkerson

## THORNTON WILDER
(See also Volume I)

### The Eighth Day (1967)
Archbishop of Chicago
Constance (Constance Ashley-Nishimura) Ashley
John Barrington Ashley
Lily Scolastica Ashley
Marie-Louise Scolastique Dubois Ashley
Roger Berwyn (Trent Frazier) Ashley
Sophia Ashley
Peter Bogardus
Wellington (Don Velantén Bristé) Bristow
Olga Sergeievna Doubkov
Dr. Gillies
Beata Kellerman-Ashley
Anne Lansing
Breckenridge (Breck) Lansing
Eustacia Sims (Eustachie, Stacey) Lansing
Félicité Marjolaine Dupuy Lansing
Fisher Lansing
George Sims Lansing
Aristides (Harry, Porky) O'Hara
Samuel O'Hara
Thomas Garrison (T. G.) Speidel
Colonel Stotz
Wilhelmina Thoms
Ada Wickersham

### Theophilus North (1973)
Alice
Diana Bell
Dr. Bosco
Dr. James McHenry Bosworth
Sarah Bosworth
Mrs. Amelia Cranston
Flora (Mrs. Edward Darley) Deland
Josiah Dexter
Mr. Diefendorf
Charles Fenwick
Eloise Fenwick
George Francis Granberry
Myra Granberry
Elbert Hughes
Hilary Jones
Mrs. Doris Keefe
Benjamino (Benjy, Mino) Matera
Theodore Theophilus (Ted) North
Henry Simmons
Arthur Gallup (Galloper) Skeel
Elspeth Skeel
Baron Egon Bodo von Stams

Archer Tennyson
Persis Tennyson
Mrs. Edward Venable
William (Bill) Wentworth
Edweena (Toinette) Wills
Norine Wyckoff

## RICHARD WILEY

*Soldiers in Hiding* (1986)
Milo Maki
Teddy Maki
Jimmy Yamamoto
Kazuko Yamamoto

## JOHN A. WILLIAMS

*Captain Blackman* (1972)
Captain Abraham Blackman
Ishmael Whittman
Luther (Woodie) Woodcock

*The Junior Bachelor Society* (1976)
Charles (Chappie) Davis
Kenneth (Snake) Dumpson
Cudjo Evers
Swoop Ferguson
D'Artagnan (Dart) Foxx
Clarence (Clarie) Henderson
Ezzard (Chops, Ezz) Jackson
Walter (Moon) Porter
Shurley (Shurl) Walker
Richard (Bubbles) Wiggins

*The Man Who Cried I Am* (1967)
Charlotte Ames
Harry Ames
Moses Lincoln Boatwright
Michelle Bouilloux
Reverend Paul Durrell
Alfonse Edwards
Jaja Enzkwu
Minister Q
Lillian Patch
Margrit (Maggie) Westoever Reddick
Max (Mox) Reddick
The Saminone

## TENNESSEE WILLIAMS
## (See also Volume I)

*Moise and the World of Reason* (1975)
Big Lot
Charlie
Invicta

Lance
Moise
Ursula Phillips
Miriam Skates
Tony Smith

## LARRY WOIWODE

*Beyond the Bedroom Wall* (1975)
Donny Ennis
Conrad Jones
Edward (Ed) Jones
Electra Jones
Elling Jones
Jerome Jones
Lionell Jones
Marie Krull
Selmer Krull
Alpha Jones Neumiller
Augustina Neumiller
Becky Neumiller
Charles John Christopher Neumiller (I)
Charles (Chuck, Chuckie) Neumiller (II)
Cheri Neumiller
Davey Neumiller
Elaine Neumiller
Emil Neumiller
Fred Neumiller
Jay Neumiller
Jerome Neumiller
Katherine Neumiller
Laura Neumiller
Lucy Neumiller
Marie Neumiller
Martin Neumiller
Otto Neumiller
Rose Marie Neumiller
Susan Neumiller
Timothy (Tim) Neumiller
Tom Neumiller
Vince Neumiller
Clarence Popp
Brian Rimsky
Leo Rimsky
James (Father Jim) Russell
Father Schimmelpfennig
Buddy Schonbeck

*What I'm Going to Do, I Think* (1969)
Anna Clausen
Orin Clausen
Nelson Hartis
Aloysius James Strohe
Ellen Sidone Anne Strohe

Grandma Strohe
Christofer (Chris) Van Eenanam
Virgil Weeks

## TOM WOLFE

*The Bonfire of the Vanities* (1987)
Reginald Bacon
Peter Fallow
Thomas Killian
Lawrence Kramer
Sherman McCoy
Maria Ruskin
Abraham Weiss

*A Man In Full* (1998)
Elizabeth Armholtz
Inman Armholtz
Charles Croker
Martha Croker
Serena Croker
Fareek Fanon
Conrad Hensely
Raymond Peepgas
Roger White II

## HERMAN WOUK
## (See also Volume I)

*War and Remembrance* (1978)
Carter Aster
Byron Henry
Janice Henry
Louis Henry
Madeline Henry
Natalie Jastrow Henry
Rhoda Henry
Victor "Pug" Henry
Warren Henry
Aaron Jastrow
Berel Jastrow
Harrison Peters
Leslie Slote
Alistair Tudsbury
Pamela Tudsbury

## L. W. WRIGHT

*The Suspect* (1985)
Karl Allberg
Carlyle Burke
Cassandra Mitchell
George Wilcox

## RICHARD WRIGHT
## (See also Volume I)

### *Lawd Today* (1963)
Blanche
Blue Juice
Doc Higgins
Howard
Jake Jackson
Lil Jackson
Albert (Al) Johnson
Robert (Bob) Madison
Rose
Streamline
Mister Swanson
Nathan (Slim) Williams

## SARAH E. WRIGHT

### *This Child's Gonna Live* (1969)
Lettie Cartwright
Aunt Cora Lou
Haim Crawford
Bannie Upshire Dudley
Dr. Albert Grene
Effie (Mamma Effie) Harmon
Pop Harmon
Frannie Jefferson
Ol Jefferson
Lil Bits
Mamie
Miss Naomi
Tillie Ried
Willie Ried
Rosey
Aunt Saro Jane
Bard Tom Upshur
Bardetta Tometta Upshur
Bertha Ann (Mamma Bertha) Upshur
Emerson Upshur
Gesus (Little Gee, Gezee) Upshur

Horace (Rabbit) Upshur
Jacob (Sparrow) Upshur
Levi (Lark) Upshur
Margaret (Mom Margaret) Upshur
Mariah Harmon (Rah) Upshur
Percy (Pop Percy) Upshur
Thomas (Tom) Upshur
William (Skeeter) Upshur
Vyella (Vy)

## RICHARD YATES

### *Disturbing the Peace* (1975)
Dr. Jules Blomburg
Paul R. Borg
Dr. Myron T. Brink
Dr. Chadwick
Charlie
Bill Costello
Nathan Epstein
Pamela (Pam) Hendricks
Carl Munchin
Chester (Chet) Pratt
Dr. Burton L. Rose
Dr. Henry J. Spivack
George Taylor
Janice Brady Wilder
John C. Wilder
Marjorie Wilder
Tom (Tommy) Wilder

### *Easter Parade* (1976)
Donald Clellon
Andrew Crawford
Howard Dunninger
Lars Ericson
John (Jack) Flanders
Emily (Emmy) Grimes
Esther (Pookie) Grimes
Walter Grimes
Anthony (Tony) Wilson

Geoffrey Wilson
Peter Wilson
Sarah Grimes Wilson

### *A Good School* (1978)
Alice Draper
Jack Draper
Robert (Bob, Pop) Driscoll
Terry Flynn
Lawrence Mason (Larry) Gaines
William (Bill) Grove
W. Alcott (Old Bottle-ass) Knoedler
Jean-Paul (Frenchy) La Prade
Dr. Edgar Stone
Edith Stone

### *Revolutionary Road* (1961)
Milly Campbell
Sheppard Sears (Shep) Campbell
Mrs. Helen Givings
Howard Givings
John Givings
Maureen Grube
Jack R. Ordway
Bart Pollock
April Wheeler
Earl Wheeler
Franklin H. (Frank) Wheeler

### *A Special Providence* (1969)
Eva Grumbauer Forbes
Owen Forbes
Maude Larkin
Sterling Nelson
Alice Grumbauer Prentice
George Prentice
Robert J. (Bob, Bobby) Prentice
John Quint
Sam Rand
Willard Slade
Mrs. Walter J. Vander Meer

# CONTRIBUTORS

Katherine Anne Ackley
Scott W. Allen
Suzanne A. Allen
Lisa L. Antley
Leonard R. N. Ashley
Robert D. Attenweiler
Ken Autrey
Max L. Autrey
James R. Bailey
Elizabeth B. Baker
Jan Bakker
Rae Galbraith Ballard
Sandra Ballard
Sarah Barnhill
Vanu "Bill" W. Barrett
Anne I. Barton
Gay Barton
Judith S. Baughman
Ronald Baughman
Harry McBrayer Bayne
Gloria J. Bell
Elaine Bender
Kristin Berkey-Abbott
Edith Blicksilver
Edward B. Borden
William K. Bottorff
Maureen Boyd
Muriel Wright Brailey
Marlena E. Bremseth
Stephen C. Brennan
Jean M. Bright
J. M. Brook
Mary Hughes Brookhart
Charles D. Brower
Donald M. Brown

Wylie Brown
Matthew Joseph Bruccoli
Beth L. Brunk
J. A. Bryant, Jr.
Paul T. Bryant
Martin Bucco
Ron Buchanan
Linda K. Bundtzen
David G. Byrd
John Calabro
Joseph Caldwell
Roseanne V. Camacho
John Canfield
Delores Carlito
Thomas Carmichael
Diane Carr
David J. Carroll
Jean W. Cash
Leonard Casper
William H. Castles, Jr.
Ronald Cella
Jim C. Chin
Mona Choucair
Henry A. Christian
Gary M. Ciuba
Samuel Coale
Carol Bebee Collins
R. G. Collins
Daniel T. Cornell
Karen F. Costello-McFeat
Carol Cumming
Tom Dabbs
Christopher C. Dahl
Thomas E. Dasher
Joan F. Dean

S. Renee Dechert
Laurie Bernhardt Demarest
Marc Demarest
Carolyn C. Denard
James E. Devlin
R. H. W. Dillard
Joanne Dobson
Sharon D. Downey
Paul A. Doyle
Margaret Dunn
Joyce Dyer
Wilton Eckley
Catherine A. Eckman
Peter G. Epps
Barbara J. Everson
Ann Dahlstrom Farmer
Carol Farrington
Kathy A. Fedorko
Rebecca E. Feind
Dianne S. Fergusson
Benjamin Franklin Fisher
Mathew D. Fisher
Joseph M. Flora
Erwin H. Ford II
Edward Halsey Foster
Elaine Dunphy Foster
Abigail Franklin
Rebecca Jane Franklin
Benjamin Franklin V
June M. Frazer
Timothy C. Frazer
Joan Frederick
Robert S. Frederickson
Michael J. Freeman
Linda Garner

Helen S. Garson
Lisa L. Gay
Robert F. Geary Jr.
Boyd W. Geer
Gary Geer
Marcia Kinder Geer
Kelly S. Gerald
Sinda Gregory
Donald J. Greiner
Johnanna L. Grimes
James A. Grimshaw, Jr.
Virginia B. Guilford
Susan Elizabeth Gunter
Judith Giblin Haig
Robert L. Haig
Lee Emling Harding
Herbert Hartsook
Melissa Walker Heidari
Australia Henderson
Suzann Hick
Sharon K. Higby
William Higgins
Dorothy Combs Hill
James W. Hipp
E. Jens Holley
Susan Luck Hooks
Steven P. Horowitz
Brooke Horvath
Helen R. Houston
Lillie P. Howard
Glenda A. Hudson
Theodore R. Hudson
Heather L. Hughes
Rebecca E. Hurst
Vernon Hyles
Laura Ingram
Betty J. Irwin
Dennis Isbell
Michael Jasper
David K. Jeffrey
Greg Johnson
Thomas L. Johnson
Allan Johnston
Kirkland C. Jones
Norma R. Jones
James L. de Jongh
Richard A. Kallan
Steven G. Kellman
Alison M. Kelly
Mary Lou Kete
Sue Lashe Kimball
Jackie Kinder
Harriet L. King
Seema Kurrup

Janet Sanders Land
Ellen B. Lane
Jim E. Lapeyre
Doris Lucas Laryea
Helen T. Lasseter
Norman Lavers
Leota S. Lawrence
Richard Layman
Suzanne Leahy
Frank H. Leavell
Dan Lee
Dawn Lee Terry Leonard
Peggy J. Lindsey
May Harn Liu
Leslie P. Lochamy
Charlene Loope
Barbara Lootens
Susan T. Lord
Robert E. Lougy
Charles F. Loveless
Dennis Loyd
Mark T. Lucas
Gary D. MacDonald
Jane Compton Mallison
Daniel Marder
Seth D. Martin
Amanda Gwyn Mason
Wanda L. Mattress
John R. May
Jo Mayer
Len McCall
Charlotte S. McClure
Joseph R. McElrath, Jr.
Warren McInnis
Nellie Y. McKay
Mary H. McNulty
Mary Cease Megra
Gary B. Meyer
Joseph Milicia
Paul W. Miller
Joseph R. Millichap
Eva Mills
Carey S. Minderhout
Judith B. Mobley
Rayburn S. Moore
Steven Moore
Gregory L. Morris
Stephanie Morris
Patrick D. Morrow
Lynn M. Morton
Charmaine A. Mosby
Michael Mullen
Robert M. Myers
Charles C. Nash

Peter Nazareth
Christine Nelson
Emmanuel S. Nelson
Jennifer Castillo Norman
Jennifer Norton
Douglas A. Noverr
Lance Olsen
Steven E. Olson
Kevin Hunter Orr
Jacqueline E. Orsagh
Julie M. Overton
Clark W. Owens
Donna Padgett
Jeffrey D. Parker
Robert L. Phillips, Jr.
Edward J. Piacentino
Roxane V. Pickens
M. Gilbert Porter
Robert E. Preissle
Barbara J. Price
Diane Dufva Quantic
Elizabeth Lee Rametta
Jennifer L. Randisi
J. R. Raper
Michael W. Raymond
Peter J. Reed
Edward C. Reilly
Josephine Rentz
Katheryn L. Rios
Barbara Rippey
Carmen S. Rivera
William Roba
William M. Robins
Donna Brumback Romein
Kimberly Roppolo
Walter W. Ross
Stephen J. Rubin
Judith Ruderman
Edward J. Ruggero
Christine A. Rydel
Robert M. Ryley
Elaine B. Safer
Arthur M. Saltzman
Leslie Sanders
Michael J. Sasso
Linda Schlafer
Richard J. Schrader
Mitzi Schrag
Richard R. Schramm
Elizabeth Schultz
Lucille M. Schultz
Katherine C. Schwartz
Marilyn J. Seguin
Dean Shackelford

David Shelter
Allan Shepherd
Thelma J. Shinn
Carl R. Shirley
Paula W. Shirley
Alan Shucard
Michael K. Simmons
Jean Sims
Thomas R. Smith
Virginia Whatley Smith
Kathryn Snell
Andew B. Spencer
Teresa Steppe
Cynthia L. Storm
Robert D. Sturr
Suzanne T. Stutman
Jack R. Sublette
Jon Christian Suggs
Guy Szuberla

Stephen L. Tanner
David M. Taylor
Estelle W. Taylor
Richard C. Taylor
Heidi Thompson
Eleanor Q. Tignor
Lindsey S. Tucker
Richard Tuerk
Susan Hayes Tully
Nancy Lewis Tuten
Gordon Van Ness III
Ronald Walcott
Joseph S. Walker
Richard Walser
Mary Ellen Williams Walsh
Virginia Weathers
Robert W. Weathersby II
Carolyn E. Wedin
William Wehmeyer

Sylvia H. Weinberg
Jennifer Welsh
Holly Westcott
Warren Westcott
Mary Ellen R. Westmoreland
John Whalen-Bridge
Heather L. Williams
Kathleen Murat Williams
Crystal Williamson
J. Randal Woodland
Hammett Worthington-Smith
Mary E. Wright
Joseph J. Wydeven
Delbert E. Wylder
Deborah L. Yerkes
Pamela A. Zager
Anne R. Zahlan